Jacques Waardenburg
Islam

Religion and Reason

Volume 40

Walter de Gruyter · Berlin · New York
2002

Jacques Waardenburg

Islam

Historical, Social, and Political Perspectives

Walter de Gruyter · Berlin · New York
2002

∞ Printed on acid-free paper which falls within the guidelines of the ANSI
to ensure permanence and durability.

Library of Congress Cataloging-in-Publication Data

Waardenburg, Jean Jacques.
    Islam : historical, social, and political perspectives / Jacques
Waardenburg.
      p.   cm. − (Religion and reason ; 40)
    Includes bibliographical references and index.
    ISBN 3 11 017178 3
    1. Islam.   2. Islam and state.   3. Islam and politics.   4. Islam
− 20th century.   I. Title.   II. Series.
BP161.2 .W24   2002
297 − dc21
                                                 2002022212

Die Deutsche Bibliothek − CIP-Einheitsaufnahme

Waardenburg, Jean Jacques:
Islam : historical, social, and political perspectives / Jacques Waarden-
burg. − Berlin ; New York : de Gruyter, 2002
   (Religion and reason ; Vol. 40)
   ISBN 3-11-017178-3

Printed in Germany
Cover design: Christopher Schneider, Berlin
Disk conversion: Readymade, Berlin

Preface

A first starting point for the following essays is the idea that the practice of Islam is an ordinary human phenomenon like the practice of other religions. A second starting point is that Muslims are ordinary human beings like the others.

To Muslim readers who would object that Islam is not that ordinary, I would say that any culture and any religion is extraordinary both to those consciously adhering to it and to those who are fascinated by it. The ways, however, in which people deal with a culture and a religion and what they make of them are human activities.

To Western readers who are somewhat shocked that Islam is different from what they are accustomed to, I would say that we should stop constructing Islam from a purely Western point of view that makes it something extraordinary for Westerners. Admitting that Muslims are different does not imply that Muslims are completely different, and saying that Islam is different does not imply that it is radically foreign.

Especially during the last two centuries, Muslims and Islam have become part of the common Western experience, just as the West has become part of the Muslim experience. The colonial period brought Muslims and Westerners in new relationships with each other, but in their imperial views the then dominating Europeans had a distorted perception. Consequently, the relationships were imbalanced and Islam remained "foreign". It seems to me, however, that in the course of the last half century this foreignness has largely been reduced to specific items, such as the position of women or the concept of the state and its laws. In many respects indeed, Muslims and Islam have in fact become part of ordinary Western life, not least because so many Muslim immigrants have settled in the West. Westerners and Muslims alike can now see Islam as a particular variety of the broader spectrum of human experience.

This book presents historical, social, and political perspectives on Islam, that is to say different ways of approaching and viewing it, from the angle of different scholarly disciplines. One link between such perspectives is the question of meaning in general and in particular that of meaning in religions.

I have always been interested in what things mean to people, especially where such meanings, in the feeling of the people concerned, take on a religious quality. The main problem then is where to find these meanings and how to describe them. This problem runs like a thread through the essays of the book, testifying to the fact that I approach Islam from the field of the science of religion, *science des religions, Religionswissenschaft*.

This approach is somewhat unconventional.

The essays start by inquiring about changes in belief that took place before and during the rise of Islam and about the role of reasoned argumentation in the Qur'ān (Chapters 1 and 2). I describe Islam primarily as a sign and signification system that is open to various interpretations and applications and that may or may not have specifically religious references in particular cases. The problem is how to study the corresponding religious meanings (Chapters 3 and 4). Examples are given of various interpretations of Islam, both on a personal, intellectual level and on a social, practical level, including Islamic readings of human rights (Chapters 5 through 8).

I consciously stress the articulations made of Islam in social reality, paying attention to its strong but not immutable religious traditions and its increasing function as a civil religion in Muslim majority states (Chapters 9 and 10). Arabia and its puritan Wahhābī movement provides a nice example of this (Chapters 11 and 12). Another example is the Islamic reform and revival movements (Chapters 13 and 14). In the second half of the twentieth century, the call (*da'wa*) of such movements and new Islamic ideologies led to an immense variety of new orientations all over the Muslim world (Chapters 15 and 16). The book ends by placing contemporary Islam in the present-day political context. Attention here focuses on Islamic states based on *Sharī'a*, Islamic protest movements, and differing articulations of Islam in different countries (Chapters 17 through 19).

Following up a suggestion made by the publishers, I added an introduction giving my own scholarly itinerary and the wider context of Islamic studies during the last decades. The revolutionary impact of Edward Said's accusation that "Orientalism" has been a form of Western domination and Eurocentrism is recognized, but would need a separate treatment. I also confined myself largely to Islamic studies as pursued in Europe. Their development in North America and in Muslim countries since the mid-twentieth century would also need separate treatment by qualified analysts.

For some fifty years, I have been interested in subjects as diverse as Islam and perceptions of Islam, Orientalism and Islamic studies in a broader sense, relations between the Muslim and the Western worlds including their religions, Muslim minorities in the West and non-Muslim minorities in Muslim countries, and last but not least in questions of method and theory in the study of religions in general and Islam in particular. I have always been fascinated by the ways in which scholars, believers, artists, and intellectuals have perceived their own and other people's religions.

Although I had sometimes thought it would be useful to bring together some of my older and newer essays, published and unpublished, and reworking them for publication, this plan could take a more definite shape only during the year 2000–1. Walter de Gruyter Publishers' interest in such a publication and a year of academic retreat at the German *Wissenschaftskolleg* in Berlin allowed to realize the idea. I could withdraw and experience a relative solitude while reconsidering my intellectual offspring of the last forty years. We decided first of all to concentrate on publications concerning Islam. The results are a one-man production and of my own responsibility.

Thanks to the *Fellowdienste* of the *Wissenschaftskolleg* and in particular the strenuous efforts of Mitch Cohen to put my *hollandish* English into present-day American English shape, the present book can see the light. I do hope that it arouses interest in the way I treat Islam. I am neither a professional social scientist nor an expert philologist, but someone specialized in the scholarly study of religions in general and Islam in particular.

For the transliteration of Arabic terms I used the current simplified English system. Only in the first two chapters did I add diacritical signs, since a number of Arabic terms are used here. I did not delete diacritical signs when quoting the titles of books and articles using such signs.

The footnotes and incidental bibliographies give the necessary references for each chapter. At the end of the book, however, some more recent publications are mentioned for further reading on the topics of the Introduction and the following sections of the book. Most of these references are in English.

My own particular treatment of the subjects and the problems they involve underscores that these problems deserve further research. Ideally, this would take place in interdisciplinary cooperation among scholars with different perspectives and different backgrounds, including Muslim ones. Much research work is waiting.

I do hope that the book will be useful especially for students as well as for a broader public interested in Islam and Muslims. Islam is one of the—ordinary and extra-ordinary—ways people give shape to their lives. Much is to be learned about it still. I venture to hope that intellectuals, scholars, and students with a Muslim background will also read the book with profit.

Finally, I think back with gratitude to all those from whom I received education and encouragement to pursue my studies, my parents above all. I am grateful to family and friends who gave their trust and assured the human background of my searching ventures. Last but not least, I appreciate the criticism and opposition of those who, whether with outspoken or silent reprobation, forced me to greater precision in research and rational clarity in expression.

Wissenschaftskolleg Berlin   August 2, 2001

The manuscript of this book was submitted before the events of 11 September 2001 took place in New York and Washington, D.C. Muslims as well as scholars of Islam and other people reject the idea that Islam as such could allow this attack or allow terrorist activities in general. Yet, the latter have happened with an appeal being made to Islam and a call to *jihād*. The subject has been discussed extensively both in Western and Muslim media. In responding to the challenge, I see a fundamental tension between the use of power and the claims of justice. There are innocent victims both of terrorism and of a war against terrorism, in Western and in Muslim countries.

In the nearly three months since the fateful day people have asked what has motivated this action at this moment. Some have raised the question of its foreseeable and unforeseeable effects. Others ponder about not only Muslim but also Western responsibilities. My own questioning concerns the future. How are we now to view relationships between Muslim and non-Muslim individuals and groups?

Once an international war has been declared on terrorism, how can it be avoided that people everywhere become terrorized precisely by the fear of terrorist attacks or of being viewed as potential terrorists? For half a century efforts have been made to improve communication between Muslims and Westerners. How can we now escape from distrust and anxieties? Which norms or kind of ethics should we follow to improve communication, cooperation, dialogue? My concern is to obtain reliable knowledge of Islam as a religion, civilization and way of life, but also to make life more livable and improve human relationships. In contrast to those who are obliged to take ad hoc decisions in difficult situations, my quest is that of a broader vision. I have published a book in French on the relations between Islam and the West.[1] And I am preparing a volume, *Muslims and Others*, as a sequence to the present one.

Lausanne   December 3, 2001

---

[1] Jacques WAARDENBURG, *Islam et Occident face à face: Regards de l'Histoire des Religions* (Islam and the West Face to Face: A Perspective from the History of Religions), Geneva: Labor et Fides, 1998.

Content

Section 1: The Beginnings

Chapter 1
Changes in Belief and the Rise of Islam 23

Section 3: Structures and Interpretations of Islam

Section 4: Muslim Presentations of Islam and of Human Rights

Section 9: The International Scene and Islam

Introduction

and a Form of Acknowledgments

From a scholarly point of view, "Islam" is a tricky word. People use it to mean different things. As a consequence, whenever it is used we have to inquire what is meant. In its strict sense, the Arabic term *islām* indicates a religious act and attitude, that of "surrender". Then it became the name of a religion that Muhammad, as a prophet, brought to the Arabs and that was held to have a universal validity. It is in this sense that I propose to use it in the context of examining Islam as a religion.

However, in scholarly as well as wider usage, also in Arabic, Islam took much broader empirical meanings, such as the civilization in which Islam is the dominant religion, or a community that upholds Islam as its religion. It took on meanings more spiritual, too, such as that of the one eternal monotheistic religion proper to humankind since the days of Adam, that is to say since the outset. Whenever it was neglected or abused through idolatry, prophets appeared who preached again this universal and "natural" religion of humankind. It also meant the prescriptions of the *Sharī'a* (law) that humankind should follow, the doctrines of the *'aqīda* (creed) humankind should adopt, and the spirituality of the *ma'rifa* (insight) into divine realities, through which humankind would attain true religious experience and knowledge. Acceptance of Islam, as Muslims see it, is the prerequisite for eternal bliss.

1. 1950–2000: Memories in Context

Let me say something about what Islam meant in the Netherlands some sixty years ago. When I grew up, in the last colonial days, the notion of Islam was linked to missions, colonial administration, and scholarship. Islam's direct links to the missions were weak indeed, since the government practically did not allow Christian missionaries to work in Muslim regions. The links with the colonial administration were clearer, to the degree that the average Dutchman was more or less familiar with the colonies. The inhabitants of the East Indies had their own way of life and religion; most of them were Muslims. In the nineteenth century there had been uprisings with calls to *jihād* and appeals to Islam. As a consequence, if it wanted to have calm and order in the colonies, the colonial power had to know more about Islam and its prescripts. Christiaan Snouck Hurgronje (1857–1936) was considered the authority on this matter.

The third association that at least intellectuals would have with the notion of Islam was that as a subject of scholarship. This was primarily the domain of some learned and privileged minds, "Orientalists" more or less removed from the world, who devoted themselves in particular to the study of the Qur'ān and Islamic texts from medieval times, published or unpublished. People referred here to Arent Jan Wensinck (1882–1939), a scholar striking through his knowledge, helpfulness, and exemplary modesty. More concretely, Islam implied the anthropological study of Muslim peoples and societies of Indonesia, including their languages, history, and archeology. Some people would then associate the study of Islam with the training that future colonial administrators received at the Universities of Leiden and—at the time less liberal—Utrecht. World War Two closed us off from the world for five years (1940–45). Then, after three confused years of negotiations and military campaigns, Indonesia became independent (1948). Islam's meaning and relevance in the Dutch context changed completely, as it must have changed in the British, French, and other colonial contexts when Muslim colonies became sovereign states. In 1948, I enrolled at the University of Amsterdam.

Indonesia's independence had important implications for the Dutch scene. The earlier missionary elan of many Dutch Catholics and Protestants started to make way for support for Indonesian Christians who constituted a relatively small minority in the country. The colonial administrators returned to the Netherlands with an expertise that was not very useful.

The existing chairs for Arabic combined with Islamic Studies at the universities were maintained, but there were not many new students, since the field offered little opportunities for the future. The field of studies of contemporary Muslim societies widened now from Indonesia to include countries in the Middle East, Africa, and South Asia. The University of Amsterdam founded an Institute for the Study of the Modern Middle East, with attention paid to the social sciences, too.

A new, internationally oriented Institute of Social Studies was created in The Hague in 1952. The language used there was English. It concentrated on development problems, with students and staff from developing countries as well as from the West. Islam and Muslim societies figured in the program. Some students from Indonesia who knew Dutch received scholarships at Dutch universities.

Since the late 1940s, the notion of Islam started to evoke a wide world of peoples and countries that had obtained or were in the process of obtaining independence. It suggested a world accessible to those who were somewhat familiar with Islam and wanted to experience Muslim societies, if possible with a job. Islam suggested something fascinating to be studied and to be encountered; it suggested an adventurous future, a chance to develop oneself. No longer did the study of Islam aim to administer Muslim peoples; rather, it expressed a new kind of sympathy for people who had fought or still fought for their independence and had to find their way on the world scene. Last but not the least, after the experiences of World War Two and independence movements, we had some concern for the future of the world at large. Government and economic interests supported such initiatives.

Internationally, Islam started to attract new kinds of public interest. The creation of Pakistan (1947) was a case in point. The creation of the state of Israel (1948) led to a new interest in the regional context. People who had returned from Indonesia or the Middle East gave talks about their "experience" with Islam. Moreover, the Arab world and Iran became relevant to Dutch business.

Muslims themselves started to appear on the scene. In 1947, the Holland Mission of the Rabwa branch of the Ahmadiyya movement started to work in The Hague and opened the new Mubarak Mosque there in 1955. Among the Moluccans and some other Indonesians who found shelter in the country, there were a few hundred Muslims who could build a mosque in 1956.

After my studies of law, theology, and science of religion in Amsterdam (1948–54) and of Arabic in Leiden (1954–55), I went to Paris in January 1956. I prepared my doctoral dissertation on the image some Orientalists had formed of Islam. The opportunity to repeatedly visit Louis Massignon (1887–1962), who had become an emeritus professor two years earlier, turned out to be most fortunate for my inquiry and scholarly research.

Another remarkable scholar of Islam in Paris at the time was Henry Corbin (d. 1977). Where Massignon saw the boundaries of Islam transcended by mystical souls, Corbin saw them overcome by gnostic minds on a more esoteric level.

In the Paris I discovered in the years 1956–59, Islam was on many lips. During the Algerian war (1954–62), Islam was seen here primarily as a social and political entity, and this gave rise to intense political debates. This facilitated my contacts and discussions with Frenchmen and Muslims in Paris. These people's various political and other involvements made the concept of Islam much more intense and diversified than I had known it in the Netherlands, where discussions about Islam had a more distant, academic character.

In their courses on Arabic and Islam, the professors rarely spoke of contemporary Islam. Also, there was hardly anyone who offered a course on Islam as a "religion" from the perspective of the science of religions, since it fell outside the official "laicistic" order of French society. The only exception was the *Cinquième Section* of the *Ecole Pratique des Hautes Etudes*, which had been created explicitly for the scholarly study of religions. French sociologists of religion during those years paid hardly any attention to Islam. One exception was Jacques Berque (d. 1995), but he was not an ordinary sociologist.

After submitting my dissertation at the University of Amsterdam (1961), I had the chance to pursue post-doctoral work at the Institute of Islamic Studies of McGill University, Montreal for a year (1962–63).

The Institute, founded by the Canadian scholar W. Cantwell Smith, was a novelty in Islamic studies. Its staff and its graduate students included both Westerners and Muslims, with courses and seminars in common. It had an excellent library, with immediate access to the stacks. My main duties were to carry out my own research project and participate in the Institute's seminars, with a little teaching besides. In a way, this year at McGill brought me back on the track of Islamic studies, something that would have been much more difficult in the Netherlands at the time.

In his *Modern Islam in India* (1943), Smith had shown the extent to which the newer Muslim interpretations and presentations of Islam in nineteenth and twentieth-century India had been conditioned by the political and economic context of the time and served the interests of particular groups. A few years later, at the Institute, he would start addressing the study of Islam as a religion in a more direct way. This resulted in his *Islam in Modern History* (1957).

In his book *The Meaning and End of Religion*, which appeared in 1964, Smith conceptualizes Islam as a "cumulative" religious tradition in which people (Muslims) think about general problems to which they give answers in Islamic terms, developing prescriptions with reference to scripture (Qur'ān) and early tradition (*Sunna*) as sources of the cumulative tradition. The impulse to look for solutions to given problems by referring to this cumulative tradition rests on what he indicates by the category of "faith". Consequently, to study a religion like Islam adequately, we have to view it in terms of a continuing interchange between the data of its cumulative tradition and the faith of given people in given contexts. In fact, Smith wants to drop the concept of "religion" altogether, contending that it obstructs an adequate understanding of the concerns of the people involved.

In this view, "Islam" is ultimately an ideological force that moves people and makes them see meaning in life and significance in history and current reality.

Looking back, the initiative of the McGill Institute of Islamic Studies was unique. It created an experimental situation among researchers of different backgrounds. Since the early 1950s it has offered an opportunity to Muslim students to pursue Islamic studies on a graduate level in the West and in this way contributed to preparing a certain small Muslim elite for positions of broader responsibility.

My third experience, after Paris and Montreal, was a stay of four years (1964–68) at the Near Eastern Center of the University of California at Los Angeles. The founder and director at the time was Gustav E. von Grunebaum (d. 1972). UCLA and McGill are among the few North American universities that offer PhD programs in Islamic studies.

Von Grunebaum had studied in Austria and represented a Central European Orientalist tradition.

For von Grunebaum, Islam essentially was a culture and civilization that had reached its peak in the high Middle Ages. A specialist in medieval Arabic literature, he had not only conducted historical studies but also presented an analysis of the components of this civilization, including its political structure, social organization, and religion.

A next point of interest was to compare medieval Islamic civilization with the contemporaneous Byzantine and Latin ones, to look at their mutual relations and distinct features. In fact, von Grunebaum's ambition was to study medieval Islamic civilization both from a historical and from what he called a cultural-anthropological perspective. By combining the two perspectives, he wanted to develop a more abstract theory of culture (*Kulturlehre*).

For contemporary Islam, von Grunebaum's key concept was that of Westernization. When he spoke of "modern" Islam, this was in fact an Islam based on a Western, probably largely American model. He thought this model had to be followed because Western technology, economics, and social behavior would impose themselves on the Muslim world, followed by Western ideas, ideals, and norms. For von Grunebaum, the West was exemplified in the USA, although he remained attached to European culture. He thought that imposing Western economic and political hegemony was initially a Western interest, but that in the end it would also be in the interest of the Muslim world itself. One could read in his texts a kind of cultural self-assurance that combined a European superiority syndrome with American political pragmatism. During the 1960s, he also became interested in forms of Islamic piety.

I sometimes had the impression that, for von Grunebaum, Islam constituted the counterpoint to the West as he projected or constructed it and with which he identified. He could sometimes call Islam anti-humanistic and anti-modern, and he stressed the differences between Islam and "the West". It is fascinating to speculate on the American need for expertise on Islam and the way in which von Grunebaum's view of Islam corresponded with and answered this need at the time.

When I had the opportunity to see some other centers of Islamic studies in the USA, I could admire the "stars" brought together in the

New World during the 1960s and 1970s: Franz Rosenthal at Yale, Joseph Schacht at Columbia, Bernard Lewis at Princeton, Wilfred Cantwell Smith, Annemarie Schimmel and Muhsin Mahdi at Harvard, George Makdisi at the University of Pennsylvania, Majid Khadduri at Johns Hopkins, Fazlur Rahman in Chicago, and Clifford Geertz at the Princeton Institute for Advanced Study.

Special mention is due to the efforts Charles Adams at McGill and Richard Martin in Tucson, Arizona made to better integrate Islamic studies and the scholarly study of religions at the time. From the 1970s on, Islamic studies in North America increasingly took its own course. It no longer followed European models.

When I returned to the Netherlands in 1968 to work on Islam and the Phenomenology of Religion at the University of Utrecht, I found that interest in Islam was changing compared with the mid-1950s. Research on Islam was increasing; some scholars from abroad were appointed. At the University of Leiden, Arabic and Islam now had two distinct chairs.

With the events in the Middle East, especially the June 1967 war, interest in the region increased and positions were taken. On the one hand, there was a strong pro-Israel lobby corresponding with the prevailing mood of the Dutch at the time. On the other hand, a Palestine Committee was founded that defended the rights of the Palestinians, who had started to organize themselves in those years. In the years to come, the Committee would severely criticize the Israeli administration of the Arab territories occupied in 1967 and in particular the Israeli settlement and military policies in these territories. Dutch economic interests in the region increased. As a result of the October 1973 war, the Arab oil-producing countries' oil boycot targeted in particular the Netherlands and the USA because of their pro-Israel policies.

A new perspective on Muslims and Islam opened itself, however, with the arrival in the 1960s of tens of thousands of Turkish and Moroccan workers to work in the expanding Dutch industry. Although many of them went back after a few years with their savings, quite a number remained. With the admission of their families, Muslim communities established themselves. At the beginning there was a certain curiosity and even helpfulness on the part of the population. At the beginning of the 1980s, the government started a policy of integrating immigrants into Dutch society.

During my years abroad, my interest in global problems had grown. I remember comparing the position of an Islamicist with that of a nuclear scientist. Both scholars have to deal with a substance that, if it exploded, could have catastrophic consequences. This may have been a fantasy of mine in a gloomy mood, but there was some truth in it. Few people in the mid-1960s realized the explosive potentials of an Islam applied ideologically and politically.

With these rising interests in Islam in the Netherlands, I slowly became more involved in matters here that had to do with Islam. In the early 1970s, I was one of a group of younger scholars who started the Dutch association "Middle East and Islam" (MOI), comparable in purpose to the "Middle East Studies Association" (MESA) in North America and the "British Society for Middle Eastern Studies" (BRISMES) in Britain. In 1974, we started a working group in Utrecht on the situation of Muslim immigrants. Around the same time, Henri van Praag and Yehuda Ashkenazy started to organize meetings to promote knowledge among Christians, Jews, and Muslims about each others' religions.

In 1982, I chaired a committee that had to report to a government department on existing religious facilities for Muslims and Hindus in the country. Although our recommendations were not followed, I became more involved with the problems of Muslim immigrants. During those years we also worked with some colleagues on a kind of handbook concerning Islam (*Islam: Norm, ideal and reality*) that appeared in 1984 and saw its fifth revised and enlarged edition in the year 2000. I was asked to do work for Dutch security, but I declined.

In 1987, I moved to the University of Lausanne, appointed at the chair of science of religions. My main interest, however, remained Islam, and I started to pay attention to problems of dialogue between Christians and Muslims. After reaching the legal age of retirement in 1995, I still had the opportunity to organize or participate in some research conferences and workshops with participants from various parts of the world, including Muslim countries.

I became aware that Islamic studies were changing and that the name itself had come under attack. Besides the study of the "classical" civilization and religion of Islam, including Qur'ān and *hadīth*, nineteenth- and twentieth-century developments—including processes, structures, and relationships—had become a focus of attention. In addition to the independent and secluded scholars wrestling their way through difficult texts, there have now been several generations of more socially oriented researchers who work together or at least in interaction with each other. Many of them have a social science background, often anthropologists who did fieldwork in a Muslim society. They meet each other around topics like the individual and society around the Mediterranean, Islam and Muslims in Europe, civil society in the Middle East, or the public sphere in Muslim societies. They constitute mobile networks with much scholarly and other interaction. These networks have their own sponsors and managers and can result in interesting publications.

I was struck lately, for instance, by the creation of the international Institute for the Study of Islam in the Modern World, better known as ISIM in Leiden, with Dutch government funding but having an independent status. It not only stimulates research on contemporary developments in Muslim societies but also participates in international research projects with periodic meetings of researchers also in Muslim countries. Last but not least, it has provided funding to some Dutch universities to create professorships in the field. And that means something in the Netherlands. If only we had had this fifty years ago, my Islamic studies would have been different. Yet, I would not like to have missed the ideal of the independent scholar, the intellectual with a free mind who has to find his or her own way.

2. 1950–2000: The International Scene

The growing attention given to Islam in a country like the Netherlands simply reflects some major events on the international scene that attested a growing role of Islam in the turbulences of social and political life in Muslim countries. I often think how relatively quiet the Muslim context was at the time of classical Islamic studies with Orientalists who could look at the Muslim world in past and present from a relative height, without being really disturbed by it—at least judging by their work. Let me remind the reader of some events that, in a very direct way, would give rise to new conceptualizations and new ways of studying Islam as part of social and political forces.

One person who gave to Islam a new kind of international dimension at the time was Faisal ibn ʿAbd al-ʿAzīz (Ibn Saʿūd), King of Saudi Arabia (1964–75). He was the founder of several international Islamic organizations based in Saudi Arabia, including the "Organization of Islamic Conference" (OIC), founded in 1969 after the attack on the Jerusalem mosque by an Australian visitor. He also gave Saudi Arabia a prominent role in promoting and sustaining the cause of Islam in various ways in a number of African and Asian countries, as well as in Europe and North America.

In the second half of 1978, Iran experienced its revolutionary movement against the Shah. After the latter's departure in January 1979, this turned into an "Islamic" revolution under Khomeinī and the Shīʿī clergy of the country. The establishment of the Islamic Republic of Iran took the West by surprise; this fact alone shows how little insight there was into grass-roots events in Muslim societies, not only in Western political circles but also among students of Islam and Muslim societies in general.

One of the consequences of the Iranian revolution was that "Islamic movements" focused on further islamizing Muslim societies. Such movements had already existed for a long time, but the successful Iranian paradigm now gave them new impetus. These movements organized themselves at the grass-roots and worked from below, as the Muslim Brethren and other movements had done, sometimes using violence, as in

the assassination of Sadat in Egypt in 1981. Their pressure on governments to give more heed to *Sharī'a* prescriptions in national legislation
did not fail in its purpose. In a number of countries, more or less liberal
and even secular governments started to orient themselves more toward
Islam, certainly in their discourse but often also in practice, by furthering
the construction of mosques, elaborating Islamic teaching, and furthering
the application of *Sharī'a* prescriptions, at least in civil law.

I just want to draw attention to the fact that, precisely at this time, in
1978, Edward Said published his *Orientalism*, a book that would have
considerable influence in Muslim societies. A Christian himself, Said
accused generations of Islamic scholars of having constructed in the West
a public image of Islam that directly or indirectly served Western political
purposes of dominating Muslim societies. Notwithstanding its interest in
Islam, Orientalism was accused of being profoundly ethnocentric and
subversive of Muslim interests. Said's revolt against Orientalism was an
intellectual protest against current Western domination of the Muslim
world.

An important movement on the intellectual level has been the "Islamization of knowledge" campaign spearheaded by Ismail al-Faruqi and
Seyyed Hossein Nasr. In contrast to Western learning based on neutrality
in metaphysical and religious matters, its proponents advocate basing
Muslim education, teaching, and research on solid Islamic premises,
parallel to the principles of Christian—Catholic as well as Protestant—
universities. Even apart from this movement, teaching Islam on various
levels has increased tremendously, not only in Muslim countries but also
in the West, including for *da'wa* (missionary) purposes. Supplementing
older venerable Islamic institutions of learning like the Azhar in Cairo,
new faculties of *Sharī'a* and Islamic theology have been founded, and new
institutions have been created for the purpose in Saudi Arabia and Iran.
Moreover, several international Islamic universities were created in the
1980s, for instance in Islamabad, Kuala Lumpur, and Khartoum. Muslim
students from a great variety of countries can study Islam here in a
Muslim spirit—different from Islamic studies as pursued at Western
universities.

Another revealing development was the reversal of religious policy in
the former Muslim republics of the USSR. Whereas in Soviet times
"scientific atheism" was the guiding doctrine, after independence the
Central Asian and Caucasian Muslim republics again gave Islam a place
in public life.

Explicitly armed "Islamist" movements in countries like Egypt (*al-
Jihād*), Algeria (FIS; GIA), and lately Afghanistan (*tālibān*) exercising
violence against innocent people have aroused strong reactions. Yet Islam
as such should not be identified with terrorist activities. The classical
teachings of Islam as of other religions place strict limits on any use of

violence even against those considered as enemies. Ascribing violence to Islam as an intrinsic part of this religion has always been an element creating revulsion for Islam in the West.

On a global scale, the simple proclamation of inherent and unavoidable tensions, if not necessarily between Christianity and Islam, then at least between the West and Islam and of the West among Muslims, has contributed to creating a kind of fear of Islam in the West. On a microscale, a similar perception plays a role in the assessment that Israel is threatened by political enemies motivated by Islam, rather than by ordinary social and political motivations and interests in a struggle for justice.

A final reason why "Islam" has been disturbing for the Western consciousness is the sheer presence of Muslim immigrants to Europe and North America, long considered a bastion of Christianity.

3. 1950–2000: Islamic Studies

Over the last fifty years there has been tremendous progress in our knowledge of Islam, its texts and history, of Muslim societies past and present, and of Muslim creations in thought and literature. One has only to look at publishers' catalogues to realize the richness of the field at the present compared with some decades ago. It instills some modesty as well.

Apart from a massive increase in factual knowledge, there have been significant developments in method and theory, interdisciplinary research, and the acceptance of new paradigms. The concept of Islam in scholarship has been critically assessed and subsequently revised. Attempts have been made to emancipate the field from overly Western value orientations. Cooperation with scholars coming from different cultures is improving, and more attention is being paid to what is or was significant to the people we study. We confine ourselves here to giving at least a first orientation about progress in empirical research carried out in the nine fields that are the subject of the present book. For further literature, the reader is directed to the "Selected Literature" sections at the end of each chapter and to the English-language books mentioned under "Further Reading" at the end of this book.

3.1. The Beginnings

When I was a student in the early 1950s, given the Muslim sources that were available, the question of the origins of Islam was thought to be largely solved. The transition from *jāhilīya* (ignorance) to Islam through Muhammad's message and work was thought to have been radical. Jewish and Christian influences on early Muslim texts and rituals were identified, while space was given to Muhammad's originality. Qur'anic passages, as analyzed by Theodor Nöldeke and his collaborators, were put in a kind of chronological order corresponding with what were considered the principal stages of Muhammad's life and work.

The biography of Muhammad had been reconstituted with the help of a critical reading of the early *hadīth* and *sīra* literature (early biographies of Muhammad), which contained data about the prophet's life. This picture of the prophet, however, was revised through research in the following years. In his studies on Muhammad in Mecca and Medina (1953 and 1956), William Montgomery Watt focused on the social, economic, and political reality in which Muhammad's and the early adherents' history must be placed, beyond the prophet's personal life story. This starting point led to Maxime Rodinson's "secular" biography of Muhammad, which was published in the mid-1960s and became popular. Joseph Chelhod (1958, 1964) and Joseph Henninger (1959) insisted on the continuing importance of ancient structures of Arab society and views of life. Textual allusions to alternative prophets in Arabia led to further anthropological questions, which Dale Eickelman treated in his study about Musaylima (1968). Patricia Crone and Michael Cook applied a radical historical criticism in the 1970s. Using available non-Islamic, mainly Christian sources of the time, they questioned the Muslim historiography of early Islam as such, considering it a construction of later times. In this critical view, Islam was not founded by one single person, and the person of Muhammad was not really historically accessible. In brief, this approach advocates that scholarship should be much more critical toward early Islamic writings on Muhammad and Islam. Robert G. Hoyland published in 1997 in English translation documentary evidence of seventh-century sources speaking about Islam as it was perceived at the time by non-Muslims as well as Muslims.

About the same time, further research on the Qur'ān also led to new questions. Toshihiko Izutsu's semantic analysis of the relationships between Qur'anic concepts and between them and similar concepts in pre-Islamic poetry revealed fundamental patterns of meaning. The Meccan texts, which have a more universal intent than the Medinan ones, were especially interesting. Text-critical research, however, posed some intriguing questions. John Wansbrough applied to the Qur'ān the method of form criticism that Rudolf Bultmann had applied to the New Testament. He concluded that some passages of the Qur'ān must date from later periods. The presence of Syriac terms in the Qur'ān had already drawn the attention of earlier generations of scholars, and Arthur Jeffery had published an inventory of this "foreign" vocabulary in 1938. In the 1970s, Günter Lüling submitted the hypothesis that there had been an originally Christian corpus behind certain Meccan passages. In 2000, Christoph Luxenberg (pseudonym) published Christian Syriac and Qur'anic Arabic text sequences whose parallels could not be ascribed to mere accident. The earlier discovery of old manuscript fragments of the Qur'ān in a mosque in Sanaa (Yemen) has added to a new interest in the history of the Qur'anic text, in particular in the passages of the Meccan period. Angelika Neuwirth published a larger study on the Meccan *sūras*.

The early *hadīth* literature has also attracted new interest and been further questioned. William Graham showed the high authority that the *hadīth qudsī* traditions—considered as immediate revelations—enjoyed in early Islam. Historical critical research had shown that the *hadīth* literature indicates what was held to be significant in the Muslim community in its first two centuries. Critical research by Gauthier Juynboll and others in the 1980s showed complex constructions that underlie reports on a number of *isnāds* and the authority attributed to certain traditionists.

3.2. Islam as a Religion

In the last decades, some important studies appeared on the history of Islamic religion. W. Madelung unraveled the history of the first caliphs residing in Medina. Praise is due to Joseph van Ess for his presentation of the development of Islamic thought in the first two centuries. Henri Laoust had already shown the interdependence of theological and juridical thought and their connections with social and political realities in the many orientations and schools that Islam has known in the course of its history. Familiar with the work of Ibn Taymīya, Laoust had earlier already revealed the latter's influence on present-day Islamic reform movements.

Annemarie Schimmel published widely on the more esthetic, poetical expressions of Islamic mysticism in general, while concentrating on South Asian Islam. W. Chittick and others concentrated on more systematized expressions, in particular those of Ibn al-ʿArabī.

The in-depth study of Islamic medieval religious texts, both of piety and of religious thought, has opened up a spiritual universe that is not yet part of the general culture of the European and North American public. But interest in it is increasing through publications by scholars with a Muslim background who are sensitive to what may be called the "life values" of Islam. In this context, mention should be made of various studies published by Seyyed Hossein Nasr, including the two volumes of texts of "Islamic Spirituality" that he edited.

The study of Islam as a religion is not exhausted, however, by the study of its classical "religious sciences" as taught at the Muslim institutions of learning. Already in the Qur'ān, the presence of *āyāt*, signs or symbols of God, is one of the main themes. So there is reason to study the religious aspects of Islam in accordance precisely with Muslim perceptions of significant things as signs or symbols that can be decoded with the help of the Qur'ān.

In cultural anthropology, Clifford Geertz has already been particularly attentive to the symbolic aspects of life in Muslim communities. This should be extended to a more general level. For the study of Islam as a religion, we may try to reconstruct the "meaningful connections" that particular individuals or groups project onto reality to make this reality meaningful. Research on present-day Islamic movements, for instance, has to pay attention not only to their political aspects and their socioeconomic background but also to the meanings of their religious symbols and ideological symbolizations for the people concerned.

The question how individual Muslims and Muslim groups have interpreted life and the world and how we can at least partially reconstruct those interpretations is a pivotal question in the study of Islam as a religion.

3.3. Structures and Interpretations of Islam

The question whether Islam as such has one or more particular structures and what the nature of such a structure is has been repeatedly discussed. One answer has been to contrast rational and irrational elaborations of Islam. H.A.R. Gibb and others have seen a fundamental tension between the rational systematizations carried out by the jurists and theologians and the more immediate experiences of the mystics. This contrast has also led to tensions between different kinds of religious leadership: 'ulamā' claiming authority on the basis of their knowledge of Scripture and the "religious sciences" ('ulūm al-dīn), and Sūfī sheykhs claiming authority on the basis of personal spiritual insight.

Another contrast proposed is that between official and popular Islam. The first comprises the religious prescriptions and doctrines supposed to be valid for all Muslims. It is Islam as defined and articulated by the scholars possessing knowledge of Scripture, tradition, and the law. The second consists of the ways and forms in which Islam is in fact lived by people in local contexts. It is an empirical living reality within the tradition of local communities. If official Islam claims to be universally valid, popular Islam by definition is diversified and may contain elements of protest that official Islam tries to avoid. Scholars of Islam in the more classical, "Orientalist" sense of the word tended to concentrate on "official" Islam on the basis of texts. The study of local empirical forms of Islam is carried out in fieldwork by anthropologists, who have also done theoretical work about particular structures of Muslim societies.

Self-interpretations of Islam have become a special subject of study. What are the rules that are followed in Muslim interpretations of particular texts, prescriptions, and doctrines? A similar question pertains to Islam itself. Are there certain rules for interpreting Islam taken as a system or entity in itself and studied in the Islamic religious sciences? To what extent are more free articulations and "constructions" of Islam possible?

As soon as "Islam" is considered to be something definitely fixed, particular interpretations of it are held to be authoritative. From a scholarly point of view, however, we leave open the question what Islam itself could be, paying attention to the diverse interpretations and presentations Muslims have given to it.

3.4. Muslim Presentations of Islam and of Human Rights

Not only interpretations of Islam in the Muslim community, but also sympathetic presentations of Islam by Muslims have become a subject of research. I mentioned W. C. Smith's study on "modern" Islam in India, which examined the ways in which Indian Muslims presented their Islam as "modern" in writings meant for Western readers. Any presentation of Islam to outsiders is of course linked to its articulation in the Muslim community itself, that is to say the Muslims' own understanding and interpretation.

In the end, these discussions touch the question of the identity of a Muslim and a Muslim community. The question becomes acute in situations of encounter—and specifically in tensions and conflicts—with non-Muslims when social boundaries and spiritual borders are at stake. But also within the Muslim community, the question has been raised in order to delineate and distinguish sectarians from true Muslims. Both questions have important ethical aspects. The discussions on human rights are illuminating in this respect.

In the course of the late 1970s and early 1980s, several Islamic declarations of human rights were formulated, implying an Islamic stand toward the Universal Declaration of Human Rights accepted by the United Nations in 1948. The Islamic declarations have attracted attention and have become the subject of several studies. Some authors consider the Islamic declaration an alternative to the Universal Declaration, others rather as a specification of the Universal Declaration that is valid specifically for Muslims.

It seems to me that we are dealing here primarily with questions of ethics and law, whereby the discussions about human rights, also among Muslims, reveal different ethico-religious positions. Unfortunately, not many studies have been made of Muslim ethics until now, but the human rights issue has pushed interest into this direction. Within the Muslim community, complaints about injustice, tyranny, corruption, discrimination, etc. can be made in terms of religious law (*Sharī'a*) and state law, but also in terms of human rights declarations, Islamic or otherwise. The case of Muslim women's movements in Muslim countries has been strengthened, for instance, by the appeal to human rights.

In the West, Islam has sometimes been accused of being opposed to human rights, and the sometimes sad human rights situation in certain

Muslim countries is cited as an argument. Human conditions in Muslim countries as well as the interpretations and applications—as well as the political use—that Muslims and others make of declarations of human rights have become a subject of study and commitment, for example by the Sudanese scholar Abdullahi Ahmed An-Na'im.

3.5. Social Reality and Islam

The social sciences have given a powerful impetus to Islamic studies by focusing on the empirical reality of Muslim societies. After previous travellers' accounts and expeditions organized to explore unknown Muslim regions, field research started in the nineteenth century, within the political context of the time. Snouck Hurgronje's descriptions of Mecca in 1884–5 and of Acheh by the end of the century are cases in point. French, British, and Russian researchers did the same in Muslim regions occupied by their countries. After World War One, anthropological fieldwork became more impartial, and this increased greatly after World War Two. Research took place both on an empirical and on a theoretical level.

The expression "sociological" studies was less linked to empirical fieldwork. One could speak for instance of a "sociological" approach to early Islam in historical studies by W. Montgomery Watt, or of a "sociological" approach to Islam as such and to the Muslim *umma* in particular in the work of Louis Massignon, Louis Gardet, and Jacques Berque. For C.A.O. van Nieuwenhuijze, a sociological approach implied theoretical considerations that distinguished it from a philological-historical one.

The important point, however, that all social sciences approaches have in common is that they do not treat Islam as a reified or idealized reality, but as practices and beliefs embedded in social reality.

This opens the way to research on the interdependence between social structures, Muslim movements, and references to Islam.

Already in colonial times if not earlier, Islam as a living social reality was often seen in terms of religious traditions that stand in the way of modernization and development. With the development projects launched in most Muslim countries in the 1950s, a key question was whether or not Islam as such stood in the way of the needed economic and social development. The USSR with its policies of "de-Islamization" was quite successful in the economic development of its Muslim regions in Central Asia. In Muslim countries, the question was more subtle: how to change traditions that stand in the way of development but that are legitimated religiously? One way was to ask Muslim *fuqahā'* (scholars of Islamic law) to reconsider traditional rules. Another way was for the state to bypass religion and to impose the necessary changes, by force if needed, as being in the national economic interest. A better knowledge of existing Muslim traditions and practices, such as provided by the social sciences, could help to weaken or circumvent them in development plans. The political leaders had no special regard for religious obstacles to the country's development. This held also true for the *Sūfī turuq*.

The social sciences and in particular political science research have shown the struggle for survival on the part of religious institutions, *Sūfī* brotherhoods, and Islamic movements in countries where the state assumed increasing control. They studied the role played by Islam in situations of tension and conflict and the use made of Islam on all sides, if only to mobilize people for particular causes. This had already happened in the nationalist movements of independence, but it ebbed away in the fervor of nationalist and left-wing ideologies. However, with the increasing relevance of Islam in public discourse and political action since the early 1970s, appealing to Islam turned out to be a useful political instrument. Islam could indeed be used to legitimate ideas and actions of parties that were in fact opposed to each other. Politically speaking, this implied a "battle for Islam", to win the people for one's own particular interpretation and application of it.

3.6. The Case of Arabia

Islam has always known a kind of puritan reform movements calling for the strict application of Qur'ān and Sunna and of the *Sharī'a* in general. These movements constitute a tradition in themselves, closely linked to the Hanbalī school of law, whose spiritual fathers include Ahmad ibn Hanbal (d. 855) as well as Ibn Taymīya (1263–1328), whom I have already mentioned.

This line came to power in Najd, Arabia, in an alliance concluded in 1744 between the Hanbalī scholar Muhammad ibn 'Abd al-Wahhāb and the leadership of the tribe Sa'ūd in Najd. The Sa'ūds succeeded in establishing a "Wahhābī" empire in Arabia, first at the beginning of the nineteenth century and then again in the twentieth century. Arabia, which had always seemed somewhat mysterious to the West, with Mecca and Medina inaccessible for non-Muslims, now attracted new attention, first with its Wahhābī zealots, then because of its particular claims to be an Islamic state with no place for non-Muslims, and of course because of its large oil reserves.

3.7. Islamic Reform and Modernization

The various modernization and reform movements that arose in Muslim societies since the nineteenth century were met with hope and enthusiasm by those who felt the pressure of age-old social, cultural, and religious traditions existing at the time. They had an impact on the organization of the new national states after independence and their forms of "official" Islam. These movements were also of considerable interest to the West, since they signaled a willingness to change the rather traditional and static forms that Islam had taken.

From the 1930s onward, scholars of Islam started to study with interest and sympathy some leading figures in these modernization and reform movements, such as Muhammad ʿAbduh and Muhammad Rashīd Ridā in Egypt and Sayyid Ahmad Khān in India. Similar movements elsewhere (Turkey, Iran, North Africa, Indonesia, Tsarist Russia) also drew attention. The reform movements indeed gave new interpretations of Islam as a religion by going back to the sources of Islam (Qur'ān and *Sunna*), giving due weight to reason. They answered the increasing challenges by the West with an effort to be modern themselves, within the confines admitted by Islam. In addition to these reform movements and their efforts to overcome the traditional Islam, for instance through better education, there were of course other movements, too. On the one hand, there were those who may be called more or less "secular" modernists, for whom Islam played a role primarily in the private sphere and who aligned with the West. On the other hand, there were those who considered Islam a social order to be imposed on society by means of Islamic organizations like the Muslim Brotherhood. These favored social and political action keeping a distance to the West. It was only later, in the 1970s, that greater numbers of ideological and activist *daʿwa* movements would arise, striving for a thorough Islamization or re-Islamization of Muslim societies.

3.8. Islamic Ideology

No less than in other religions, ideologies have always been present in Islam. The twentieth century in particular saw the rise of powerful Islamic ideologies able to mobilize great numbers of Muslims, including on an international scale. Examples are the Muslim Brotherhood, which arose in Egypt in 1928, and the *Jamāʿat-i Islāmī*, which arose in British India before World War Two and developed further in Pakistan. These and similar Islamic movements cannot be called "otherworldly"; they have concrete social and political aims.

In fact, Islamic ideology is not restricted to Islamic movements. In many Muslim quarters, Islam itself has been ideologized, expressed, articulated, and lived in terms of ideas that mobilize people. In this way, Islam can be made not only a way of life but also an ideal reality. In extreme cases, it is made an absolute on earth, with devotees ready to sacrifice themselves to the cause of Islam. Westerners of some fifty years ago, accustomed to a more or less subdued Islam, probably would have been surprised if they had seen the discipline and vitality with which Muslims can act nowadays when Islam is at stake.

A useful distinction is that between Islamic ideologies legitimating a given state of affairs, for instance proclaimed Islamic states, and ideologies protesting against a given state of affairs in the name of Islam. In the latter case, Islamic ideology has a militant or even revolutionary potential.

Both practically and theoretically, Islamic ideologies tend to consider power as something fundamentally given that is needed to reach one's goal. *Sūfī* quarters, however, would be less naïve and more hesitant about power. In Muslim societies there is indeed a certain ambiguity about the use of power for the sake of imposing Islam or *Sharī'a*, on the one hand, and, on the other, the reverse: the use of Islam for the sake of increasing power.

The effectiveness of Islamic ideologies is not only a matter of power, however. On a deeper level, it is the particular call (*da'wa*) addressed to the people that brings about transformation and commitment. In present-day societies, however, a *da'wa* tends to take particular ideological forms that can be spread further through the media.

3.9. The Political Scene and Islam

In Muslim discourse, the idea of an Islamic state has a particular significance as the establishment of an Islamic order and the realization of justice according to the *Sharī'a*. In the national movements for the establishment of independent Muslim countries, there was usually a wing that wanted an Islamic state. The same desire for an Islamic state arises in Muslim societies among those who are in political, economic, or social need.

By the end of the Ottoman Caliphate in 1924, there was practically no "Islamic" state left. Then, in 1932, Saudi Arabia was united as an Islamic kingdom. Before the end of the 1970s, Iran and Pakistan had become Islamic states based on *Sharī'a*. Libya, Bangladesh, Sudan, and the *tālibān* in Afghanistan made similar claims. In most cases, the Islamic state was proclaimed from above, by the head of state supported by the military. Only in Iran did it result from a popular revolution that was later transformed into a religious one, with Khomeinī as ultimate leader.

The appeal to Islam, however, has not only legitimated power or its seizure; it also has legitimated political protest against misuse of power, justifying tyrannocide as in the case of Sadat (d. 1981). In this case, Islam serves as a vehicle of moral, ideological, and political protest.

The political scene in the various Muslim countries differs widely and we should resist the temptation to impose overly general schemes to explain political events in which references to Islam are made. On a global scale, too, it is impossible to generalize developments in the Muslim part of the world or relationships that exist or may develop. And an appeal to Islam can always be made as a defense against foreign power and domination.

Selected Literature

CRONE, Patricia, and Michael COOK, *Hagarism: The Making of the Islamic World*, Cambridge: Cambridge University Press, 1977.

ESS, Joseph van, *Theologie und Gesellschaft im 2. und 3. Jahrhundert Hidschra: Eine Geschichte des religiösen Denkens im frühen Islam*, 6 Vols., Berlin and New York: Walter de Gruyter, 1991–7.

GRUNEBAUM, Gustave Edmund von, *Modern Islam: The Search for Cultural Identity*, Berkeley: University of California Press, 1962 (pocket ed. New York: Vintage Books, 1964).

LAOUST, Henri, *Les schismes dans l'islam: Introduction à une étude de la religion musulmane*, Paris: Payot, 1965.

LÜLING, Günter, *Über den Ur-Qur'ān: Ansätze zur Rekonstruktion vorislamischer christlicher Strophenlieder im Qur'ān*, Erlangen: H. Lüling, 1974.

LUXENBERG, Christoph, *Die syro-aramäische Lesart des Koran: Ein Beitrag zur Entschlüsselung der Koransprache*, Berlin: Das Arabische Buch, 2000.

RODINSON, Maxime, *Mohammed*, New York: Pantheon Books, 1971 (French original 1961).

WANSBROUGH, John S., *Quranic Studies: Sources and Methods of Scriptural Interpretation*, London: Oxford University Press, 1975.

—, *The Sectarian Milieu: Content and Composition of Islamic Salvific History*, London: Oxford University Press, 1978.

WATT, William Montgomery, *Muhammad at Mecca*, Oxford: Clarendon Press, 1953.

—, *Muhammad at Medina*, Oxford: Clarendon Press, 1956.

Section 1

The Beginnings

Chapter 1
Changes in Belief and the Rise of Islam

Quite a few studies of religion in ancient Arabia, in particular Central Arabia including the Hejaz, concentrate on the religious situation before Islam and aim to discover the continuities and differences between the ancient religion of the Arabs and Islam. Our problem here is slightly different, namely: what changes in the relationships between groups of spiritual beings—including both deities and spirits—of the ancient religion may have taken place already before the rise of Islam? To what extent do these changes foreshadow the new kind of classification of spiritual beings that would be proclaimed in the Qur'ān and become accepted and current in Islam?

In these changes of relationship between spiritual beings there is not only a conflict between gods (in which Allāh wins), but also a conflict between the high god (Allāh) and those spiritual beings called *jinn*[1] (where Allāh is not the unqualified winner). Our subject here is especially the latter conflict and we shall focus on the significance that Allāh and the lower intermediary spiritual beings had before, during, and also after the process of Islamization in Arabia.

The conflict between Allāh, the other deities, and the *jinn* must have represented a struggle between various groups and parties in Arabia, in which Muhammad's claim to prophethood and the movement resulting from it played a decisive role. On the one hand, this religious and ideological development can hardly be understood without references to an earthly history at whose end the early Muslim community emerged as victor. On the other hand, this historical ending itself cannot be understood adequately without taking into account the changes that occurred

---

[1]   "*Djinn*, according to the Muslim conception bodies (*adjsām*) composed of vapour or flame, intelligent, imperceptible to our senses, capable of appearing under different forms and of carrying out heavy labours (al-Baydāwī, *Tafsīr*, S. 72:1; al-Damīrī, Ḥayawān, s.v. *djinn*)": D.B. MACDONALD et al., Art. "Djinn", pp. 546–7. The word is a plural indicating a collective; the singular is *jinnī*, fem. *jinnīya*. The form *jānn* is also used as the equivalent of the form *jinn*, sometimes also used for the singular. Cf. HENNINGER, "Geisterglaube bei den vorislamischen Arabern", pp. 309–11; WENSINCK, "The Etymology of the Arabic Djinn (Spirits)"; ZBINDEN, *Die Djinn des Islam und der altorientalische Geisterglaube*, pp. 79–80.

in the world of spiritual beings, changes that gave a religious and ideological significance to the earthly course of events. The changes in the
function, classification, and meaning of spiritual beings took place at the
same time as major economic, social, and political changes occurred in
the societies whose members gave their loyalty to these beings in one way
or another.

1. Spiritual Beings before Islam

Religious developments among the nomadic Bedouin were different from
those in the settled areas, oases, and towns, among which Mecca deserves
special attention here.

1.1. The Bedouin

Among the Bedouin, according to J. Henninger[2], belief in *jinn* may have
been present since ancient times, although it was probably more developed among the settled people than the nomads, as has been the case
more recently. More typical of the Bedouin was reverence paid to ancestors, on whose graves stones were erected and simple sacrifices made, or
to certain heroes from the past who were venerated as founders of tribes
and tribal federations or as bringers of culture. In certain cases, a transition from tribal ancestor to tribal god (*jadd*) may be assumed.

There was also a belief in local *deities*, who may have evolved out of
ancestors or *jinn* or may simply have personified the powers of nature,
like the storm-god Quzaḥ. They may also have been taken over from
settled people in some cases. Later they were called *aṣnām, shurakāʾ*, etc.,
but not much is known about Bedouin religious beliefs about them. Of
astral gods, which were much worshipped in South Arabia, only Venus
had an attested cult among the Bedouin. The sun and the moon may have
been worshipped, but this requires further investigation. A god of the
earth was unknown among the Bedouin. Cults were concentrated at
certain places where cult stones (*anṣāb*) were erected or cult trees grew.
White animals (camels, sheep, and goats) and milk libations were characteristic of Bedouin religion, as well as spring festivals in the month of
Rajab when first-born animals were sacrificed. The consecration without
bloodshed of animals who were living in sacred territory (*ḥimā*) was a
typical Bedouin religious practice. Pilgrimages seem to have developed
late and among the sedentary people, not the Bedouin.

---

[2]   HENNINGER, "La religion bédouine préislamique", pp. 128–9.

The veneration of *Allāh*, whom Henninger holds to be autochthonous in Arabia and of nomadic origin, remained in the background. Allāh was venerated before all else as the sky god and the bestower of rain, but even then he was also seen as the creator of the world. Allāh was venerated in the whole of Arabia, with sacrifices, oaths, and calls on him in times of danger; in South Arabia *Raḥīm* was a similar supreme god. Allāh (*al-ilāhu*, the godhead) corresponds to El throughout the Semitic world.

1.2. Oases and Towns

In the oases and towns the situation was different, and various spiritual beings should be distinguished.

1.2.1. Deities: In the settled areas, one of the most striking shifts away from Bedouin religion was the increase in the number of deities and a movement toward polytheism, which is connected in the Arab tradition with the name of ʿAmr ibn Luḥayy, who is supposed to have lived in the third century C.E. This development may have had to do not only with the natural requirements of life in an agricultural or urban setting, but also with Hellenistic religious influences from the North. This rise and differentiation of the gods must have occurred parallel to the movement of Bedouin to the towns, with their social, economic, and political differentiation.

M. Höfner[3] assigns the deities venerated in Arabia in the centuries before Muhammad's appearance to the following categories: (1) the high god Allāh, together with (2) the three "daughters of Allāh" (Manāt, Allāt, and al-ʿUzza, e.g., S. 53:19,20) venerated all over Arabia (al-ʿUzza especially by the Meccan Quraysh); (3) the five deities of Noah's contemporaries (Wadd, Suwāʿ, Yaghūth, Yaʿūq, Nasr); (4) some thirty-five other deities often called by their surnames or titles (*al-*, *dhū-*), of which Hubal is the best known thanks to the fact that his image in human form stood in the Meccan Kaʿba.

Prominent Meccan families had their own house-gods represented by images at home.

All deities had their own creative power and were more active in the course of earthly events than the distant Allāh. In Mecca itself, Manāt (destiny), Quzaḥ (thunderstorm), and Hubal (chance and luck) were prominent, along with Allāh who must have been the protecting deity of the town, just as other towns had their own tutelary god.[4]

---

[3] HÖFNER, "Die vorislamischen Religionen Arabiens", pp. 361–7.
[4] For the interpretation of Allāh as a high god and as the town god of Mecca, see WATT, "Belief in a 'High God' in pre-Islamic Mecca"; ID., "The Qurʾān and Belief in a 'High God'".

These various deities were not brought together in one hierarchically ordered pantheon, nor were they of a very celestial nature; in fact, there does not seem to have been a very great distance between them and the *jinn* as spirits or semi-deities. E. Zbinden has observed that *jinn* were often venerated at the same place as these deities, which would imply that people felt they belonged together.[5]

1.2.2. *Jinn:* Various etymologies have been given of the word *jinn*, from the Arabic root *janna* ("those who are hidden, mysterious" or specifically "covered" or "covering") through a derivation from the Latin *genius* to a borrowing from an Aramaic word used by Christians to indicate pagan gods degraded to demons. In the latter case, *jinn* would originally have referred to degraded deities.

Various theories have been evolved to interpret or explain the belief in *jinn* among the ancient Arabs.[6] The animistic theory, for instance, of which J. Wellhausen was an exponent, has enjoyed some popularity; this assumes a more or less linear evolution from polydemonism as represented by the belief in *jinn* to polytheism and finally monotheism. The high gods, including Allāh, would thus represent the final stage of a long development starting from the *jinn*. W. R. Smith[7] held that the *jinn* were a survival from an earlier, totemic stage of the Bedouins' development; the various *jinn*-clans would in this case originally have represented animal species, each having a special relationship with a given clan or tribe. J. Henninger rightly takes a critical stand towards such general theories of the origin and development of religion as have been applied to Arabian data.[8]

Jinn in ancient Arabia are spirits, basically nature spirits, and not ghosts. They are immaterial in the sense that they consist of the elements of fire, smoke, and dust, but they can take different forms, notably those of animals. A snake, for instance, can always be a disguised *jinnī*. *Jinn* can also take the form of birds and in special cases they appear as human beings. *Jinn* are supposed to reside mostly in deserted places, near trees or ruins, or on particular pieces of land, which means that they have to be placated before Bedouin pitch their tents there. *Jinn* work against the ordinary course of events, mostly causing people different kinds of mishaps, including madness (*junūn*, literally "possession by a *jinnī*"; *majnūn*,

---

[5]   ZBINDEN, *Die Djinn des Islam und der altorientalische Geisterglaube*, pp. 79–80.
[6]   HENNINGER, "Geisterglaube bei den vorislamischen Arabern", pp. 280–2; ID., "La religion bédouine préislamique", pp. 121–4.
[7]   SMITH, *Lectures on the Religion of the Semites*, pp. 126–39, with notes by Stanley A. COOK on pp. 538–41. A refutation of this theory was given by WESTERMARCK, "The Nature of the Arab Ǧinn", pp. 264–8.
[8]   HENNINGER, "Geisterglaube bei den vorislamischen Arabern", p. 282.

literally "possessed by a *jinnī*", means madman). Consequently, the ancient Arabs developed a whole series of possible measures that could be taken against such evil spirits, including the wearing of amulets and the pronouncing of exorcisms.

It must be assumed that in ancient Arabia both deities and *jinn* were venerated in cults; in the case of the former, the cult must have been open and public, whereas the cult of *jinn* may have been largely a private affair. A few Qur'anic verses testify directly to this ancient cult of *jinn*. S. 72:6 says that certain men repeatedly sought the aid of the *jinn*, and S. 6:100 states in so many words that unbelievers made the *jinn* companions of Allāh. S. 37:158 adds that the unbelievers constructed a kinship (*nasab*) between Allāh and the *jinn*. In S. 34:41, the angels are said to affirm that the unbelievers had worshipped the *jinn* and had put their faith in them, whereas S. 6:28 is sometimes interpreted as referring to the practice of making sacrifices to the *jinn*. Certain ancient deities may have arisen from *jinn*, while some *jinn* may stand for degraded deities of older times; there are insufficient data to warrant either hypothesis.[9]

J. Chelhod speaks of a continuous rise of the *jinn* as chthonic powers from the lower to the higher world, a rise which would have been halted by the coming of Islam.[10] This is connected with Chelhod's theory of a fundamental dualism, which he assumes to have characterized the sphere of the invisible, the "supernatural". On the one hand, according to him, there was the notion of a higher world that was ordered, close to heaven, and inhabited by the celestial powers, and, on the other hand, the lower world, which was chaotic, beneath the earth, and inhabited by the chthonic powers. Since, according to this theory, both the higher and the lower world, as religious realities, share the sacred quality, the pure-impure polarity characteristic of the sacred itself runs parallel to the opposition between higher and lower world, the former being charaterized by purity, the latter by impurity. The high god Allāh (El) represents the hidden energy which is the very source of the sacred sphere. The sun goddess would represent a link between both religious worlds, and the *jinn* are permanently seeking to rise from the lower to the higher world to obtain deity status in a movement of purification. Somewhat imprecisely[11], Chelhod refers to remnants of an ancient myth according to which the *jinn* gave their daughters as wives to Allāh; out of these unions were born the angels (represented by the stars), the children of Allāh and the *jinn*. In this myth, the elements of the higher and the lower world are combined into a unified whole.

---

[9]   Cf. *ibid.*, pp. 315–6.
[10] CHELHOD, *Les structures du sacré chez les Arabes*, pp. 77–80, 93–5.
[11] *Ibid.*, p. 79, n. 1 refers to p. 42 of Vol. 5 of Jawād ʿAlī's *Tārīkh al-ʿarab qabl al-islām* without indicating or discussing Jawād ʿAlī's source.

The upward movement of the *jinn* follows from Chelhod's structural scheme of interpretation. T. Fahd, who does not accept this scheme, remarks[12] on the one hand that it is hard to imagine how spirits without individuality or personality and of a profoundly anonymous nature could ever become deities, which at least to a considerable extent were individualized and personified. On the other hand, Fahd does not exclude the possibility that in certain cases *jinn* represent degraded deities of older times or from elsewhere. The *jinn* can act positively toward humankind and, even though they are not themselves individualized or personified, they can very well stand in a permanent relationship to individuals or groups of people. For that matter, they need not be considered gods; their superiority to human beings is already given with the fact that they have weightless bodies and that they are able to perform actions far beyond human powers.

In some cases, particular *jinn* can acquire a degree of individuality, especially through having access to sources of knowledge inaccessible to humankind. Thus, the inspiration of a diviner (*kāhin* or *'arrāf*) and of a poet (*shā'ir*) was ascribed in ancient times and also in the Qur'ān to a being "covered" by a particular *jinnī*, who communicated to the human being possessed in this way powerful utterances concerning reality and the future. All "supernatural" knowledge, indeed, was ascribed by the ancient Arabs to *jinn*. S. 72:9 mentions that *jinn* could listen at the heavenly gates and learn what divine plans and intentions were elaborated in heaven; then they could report this knowledge to particular human beings. Ernst Zbinden is right when he characterizes *jinn* as "mediators of revelation" ("Offenbarungsvermittler") in Arabian religion before Islam.[13]

1.2.3. Angels: It is certain that, among the ancient Arabs, the Meccans at least believed in angels, whether as *jinn*-like beings without divine qualities or as "daughters of Allāh" and thus nearer to the high god. In the Qur'ān, S. 6:8, 11:12 and 17:95 mention that Muhammad's Meccan opponents asked him to make them acquainted with his "angel" in order to prove his prophethood to them. Consequently, they must have known that angels are sent to certain chosen individuals like prophets. On the other hand, S. 17:40, 43:19 and 53:27 state explicitly that the Meccans had made the angels "female beings", who would then be companions or daughters of Allāh, and S. 53:26 shows that these angels were thought to be able to intercede for human beings before Allāh. Chelhod believes that the concept of "angel" indicates a stage in the rise of *jinn* to the heavenly spheres, and he tries to show that the angels always remain in commu-

---

[12] FAHD, "Anges, démons et djinns en Islam", p. 190.
[13] ZBINDEN, *Die Djinn des Islam und der altorientalische Geisterglaube*, p. 12.

nication with the *jinn* and the lower world. He stresses in this connection the mythical view that the angels are the children of unions between Allāh and daughters of the *jinn*.[14]

1.2.4. Shayṭāns: In ancient Arabia, *shayṭāns* were thought to be serpents and, like *jinn*, they could attach themselves to a human being to inspire him or her. They had no demonic character in the current sense of the word, and their role was negligible compared to that of the *jinn*.

1.2.5. Allāh: Several arguments have been adduced to establish that, already before Muhammad's birth, polytheism was on the wane and there was a movement toward monotheism in and around Mecca. One argument is that the economic expansion of the Quraysh and the Meccan confederation brought with it the need for a broader kind of religion to which any Arab could adhere. Chelhod even speaks of the birth of a "national" religion[15] and sees a broadening and growth in the role of Allāh that would be reflected in his taking over the prerogatives of Qamar, the moon god and old Lord of Heaven.[16] He also observes before the rise of Islam the spread of a common religious terminology throughout Arabia, at the same time that power is centralized in Allāh in the heavenly sphere.

    T. Fahd, in his interpretation of Allāh as *al-Ilāh*, an impersonal character ("the godhead"), holds that before Islam Allāh was "[...] un appellatif applicable à toute divinité supérieure du panthéon arabe"[17]. The Arabs, in his view, always invoked Allāh as "[...] le dénominateur commun entre toutes les divinités du panthéon"[18]. Behind the different symbols, names and attributes of a divine nature that were used, the Arabs were essentially conscious of the working of one unique godhead, *al-Ilāh*. There was a long monotheistic tradition; only those who were called *mushrikūn* substituted for the cult of the godhead that of his names and attributes.

    The foregoing remarks suggest that religion in Central Arabia up to the seventh century of our era was neither the same everywhere, nor fixed in its forms or free from internal conflicts. Different religious traditions existed among the Bedouin and the settled people; there was a great proliferation of gods and goddesses with cults, some of which rose while others fell; deities and *jinn* could move towards or away from each other; finally, there was a tension between the veneration of the high god Allāh

---

[14] CHELHOD, *Les structures du sacré chez les Arabes*, pp. 79–80.
[15] *Ibid.*, p. 104.
[16] *Ibid.*, pp. 96, 104.
[17] FAHD, *Le panthéon de l'Arabie centrale à la veille de l'hégire*, p. 44.
[18] *Ibid.*, p. 253.

on the one hand and that of "his daughters", other deities and *jinn* on the other hand.

Such shifts and changes in the spiritual world must have been directly or indirectly connected with the sedentarization of nomads, new religious needs in the oases and towns in the course of their development, and the rise of Mecca's hegemony in the sixth century C.E. in particular. For such social, economic, and political developments changed the context in which people lived, which in turn had important repercussions for morality and religion. The Arab awareness of having one religious tradition in common notwithstanding the development of local traditions—with common forms of ritual behavior, a common pilgrimage in the month Rajab, and a common veneration of Allāh and his "daughters"—is bound up with common patterns of trade, political allegiances, and the deep awareness of constituting one people, notwithstanding the constant strife and struggle between tribes and clans and notwithstanding the political ambitions of cities like Mecca under the Quraysh.

This is not to speak of influences on the Central Arabian scene from South Arabia and indirectly Ethiopia, the northern fringe of Arabia and indirectly Byzantium and Persia or to take into account the presence of Christian and Jewish communities in Arabia. There is reason to suppose that, by the end of the sixth century C.E., the belief in a multitude of deities was on the decline, but that their worship was retained as a public ritual, at least in Mecca. There is also reason to suppose that the belief both in a distant high god Allāh and in the working of *jinn*—not only as disturbing elements but also as inspirers of divination, poetry, and music—had not diminished. Our contention then is that the transition to Islam should be seen historically as part of an overall internal development process that had been underway for centuries. In the course of this process, Jewish and Christian elements were assimilated to the ideological structure, and there arose a tendency towards universality as opposed to the existing local cults. This tendency assumed an ultimate religious character in the revelatory events that happened to Muhammad. His role in this overall process, with all its religious, ideological, social, economic, and, of course, political aspects was vital. The radical changes introduced by the Qur'ān to the relations between Allāh, on the one hand, and the deities and *jinn* on the other testify that Allāh was now seen as playing a more active role on earth. But we shall first look at some data brought to light north of Arabia proper: in Palmyra.

2. A Sidelight from Palmyra

Since most of the data advanced until now have reached us through Muslim sources that had an interest in playing down the role of the *jinn*, we should see whether sources from elsewhere can throw some light on the classification of spiritual beings in Arabia before Islam and on the *jinn* in particular.[19]

As early as in 1949, J. Starcky wrote that the term GNY' found in inscriptions around Palmyra was derived from Arabic, the Arabic *janā* or *janiy* (to stretch) being related to the verb *ganan*, GN standing in all Semitic languages for "to cover, to protect".[20] Starcky held that the first inscriptions about *jinn* were Safaitic ones in North Arabia and that later inscriptions found in the Syrian desert were a result of Arab invasions during the second half of the first millennium B.C. The Palmyrene inscriptions of Genneas date from the second and third centuries. They speak of a *ginnayā* (plural *ginnayē*); Starcky stressed its tutelary function and saw in it one deity. Starcky also pursued an earlier observation by H. Lammens[21] about an ancient *masjid al-jinn* existing in Mecca and W. Albright's hypothesis[22] that the *jinn* could have been deities from elsewhere that were accepted relatively late by the Arabs. Starcky submitted that, before Islam, the Arabs might very well have considered the *jinn* gods "[...] quoique leur rôle bienfaisant ne soit guère marqué"[23]. Some twenty years later, in 1970–1, D. Schlumberger, while refuting Starcky's idea that *ginnayā* was a proper name, also stressed that the word GNY' (meaning "divinity" in Palmyrene) was of Arabic origin. This term was used in the Arabized Syrian steppe and desert, whereas its equivalent "LH" was used in towns like Palmyra, where Aramaic was the cultural language.[24] Both Starcky and Schlumberger stressed the importance of the Arabic concept of *jinn* in the Palmyrene region and pointed out that the concept referred not to spirits, but to deities.

The discussion about the relationship between monotheism and spiritual beings in the Near East during the Hellenistic period took a new turn with J. Teixidor's investigations into the relevant inscriptions in the North Arabian area. In his study of 1977, the author was able to show trends in popular piety in the last centuries of the first millennium B.C. that were quite distinct from Hellenistic religious patterns more current among the intellectual classes. Teixidor maintains that monotheism has always been latent among the Semites[25], but that the Near Eastern inscriptions from about 500 B.C. on show a clear trend toward a practical

---

[19] We are grateful to Han J.W. Drijvers of the University of Groningen for drawing our attention to North Arabian materials and for providing relevant bibliographical data.

[20] Jean STARCKY, "Gennéas: B. L'inscription", *Syria*, 26 (1949), pp. 248–57, especially p. 255. This is part of a longer article by SEYRIG and STARCKY.

[21] LAMMENS, "Les sanctuaires préislamites dans l'Arabie occidentale", pp. 63 and 69, quoted by STARCKY (see previous note), p. 256.

[22] ALBRIGHT, quoted by Starcky in "Gennéas" (see above n. 20), p. 256.

[23] STARCKY, *ibid.*, p. 256.

[24] SCHLUMBERGER, "Le prétendu dieu Gennéas".

[25] TEIXIDOR, *The Pagan God*, p. 13.

monotheism[26], with a fidelity simultaneously to a supreme god and to more specialized "deputy" gods and angels with specific functions in the world.[27] As a general pattern, the worship of a supreme god simply coexisted with that of other, minor gods, and in North Arabia worship was probably directed towards a unique god who was believed to manifest himself in a plurality of ways.[28] Basically, according to this view, there was no Arabian "pantheon" with an undiscriminated plurality of gods, as commonly represented, but rather the belief in one supreme god with whom other divine beings were associated.[29] This supreme god was indicated by proto-Semitic *il(u)* which developed to *el* in Northwest Semitic, *ilah* in Nabataean[30]—and, we may add, *allāh* in Arabic.

Among Semitic peoples the gods were named after the places where they were worshipped.[31] The cult was directed not only to a particular idol but also to a particular altar.[32] Like the altars, the stones erected for the gods[33] could themselves become objects of worship. As far as the idols were concerned, Teixidor maintains that in North Arabia in an early period they probably consisted of stones of various forms and that only later—under foreign influence—statues were adopted as representations of the gods.[34] This corresponds with the statement in later Arabic sources that before Islam the Arabs had exchanged their original cult of stones for that of statues with the appearance of a person. Teixidor affirms that the image (*ṣalm*) was believed to be the tutelary numen of a given locality, just as the *ginnayē* (equated to *jinn*) were known as supernatural protectors in the Palmyrene region: as tutelary deities of villages, settlements, encampments, tribes, and so on.[35] The ancestral gods stood for the uniqueness or idiosyncrasy of a particular group or tribe.[36] They were not in conflict with the supreme god; one may point here to the religion of the Hebrews with its "household gods".

In the last centuries of the first millennium B.C., when a practical monotheism became manifest and a supreme god—often a weather god to whom heaven belonged—was held to retain all power, myths must have lost their relevance. This corresponds to the fact that hardly any mythology is known to us from the Arabian peninsula, except for the South in an earlier period.

---

[26] *Ibid.*, p. 161.
[27] *Ibid.*, pp. 15–7.
[28] *Ibid.*, pp. 75–6.
[29] *Ibid.*, p. 76.
[30] *Ibid.*, p. 83.
[31] *Ibid.*, p. 91.
[32] Nabataean *mesgida*: *ibid.*, p. 85.
[33] Nabataean *baetils*: *ibid.*, p. 87.
[34] *Ibid.*, p. 73.
[35] *Ibid.*, p. 75.
[36] *Ibid.*, p. 162.

Of particular interest for the problem of the *jinn* is Teixidor's study of Palmyra.[37] After discussing the cult of the supreme god, the sun and the moon, and Allāt (*al-Ilāt*) as the female deity of heaven, whose temple in Palmyra must have been the cultic center of North Arabian tribes in the region[38], the author treats the *ginnayē* (*gny'*), which he sees as Arab gods with the function of tutelary deities.[39] These *ginnayē* were comparable to the Roman *genii*: they were deities who were tutelaries of persons and places, who were believed to manifest themselves as human beings and to take care of human lives and enterprises, and who were frequently invoked in pairs.[40] They protected flocks and caravans and also those who had settled or were in process of sedentarization.[41] Shrines erected for such *ginnayē* are found especially in the semi-nomadic surroundings of Palmyra in places that were centers of settled life and halts for passing caravans. Teixidor holds the *ginnayē* to be "[...] a specific class of divine beings whose function was to be guardians, a task that fully equates them to the Judeo-Christian angels."[42] Their Aramaic equivalent were the *gad*.[43] One might conclude that the *ginnayē* were venerated, but not on the same level as the ancestral gods, let alone the supreme god.

These data from Northern Arabia and in particular the Palmyrene scene shed new light on the problem of the relations between Allāh, the deities, and the *jinn* in Central and especially West Arabia. Even if the conclusion is not warranted that before Muhammad's activities *jinn* were venerated as full *deities* in Mecca—in Palmyra, Teixidor sometimes views them as deities, sometimes as equivalent to angels—they should be seen at least as *angelic beings*, most probably with a tutelary function. In any case, the *jinn* were at the time much closer to Allāh's divine "associates" than later Islamic tradition was willing and able to admit.

Another inference to be drawn from the Palmyrene data is that there may be structural parallels between the rise of a pantheon in northern trade centers like Palmyra on the one hand and in a commercial town like Mecca on the other. All commercial centers attracted Bedouin to settle, and as a consequence the Bedouin's religion would encounter the religion of the townspeople, which could take Hellenistic forms. So *jinn* and deities could come together, since they were both under the authority of the supreme god. In the urban context, the cult of the supreme deity with its associates would proliferate, with tutelary spiritual beings taking care

---

[37] TEIXIDOR, *The Pantheon of Palmyra*.
[38] Cf. DRIJVERS, "Das Heiligtum der arabischen Göttin Allāt im westlichen Stadtteil von Palmyra".
[39] TEIXIDOR, *The Pantheon of Palmyra*, ch. IV.
[40] *Ibid.*, p. 77.
[41] *Ibid.*, p. 78.
[42] *Ibid.*, p. 89.
[43] Cf. the ancient Arabian *jadd* or tribal god mentioned at the beginning of this chapter.

of the daily needs of the people. Under Hellenistic influence, stone idols were transformed into statues.

A third conclusion equally confirms what we said earlier. For more than a thousand years before the rise of Islam, a latent "Semitic" monotheism had asserted itself in the Near East. This monotheism could, however, take various forms in connection with ancestral gods and should not be supposed to exhibit one homogeneous structure at all times and places; its variations and different forms should be studied in detail. All available evidence contests the idea "[...] that monotheism is an exclusive patrimony of the Judeo-Christian tradition"[44], though within this tradition it has been represented apologetically in this way.

This and other parallel developments in the Northern, Central, and also Southern Arabian region in various periods between 1000 B.C. and 1000 C.E. need to be studied in teamwork by historians of religion of the Near East. Finally, for a long time to come, Islam would mark the definite "monotheization" of the Near and Middle East, though some other earlier forms of monotheism were to survive until the present day.

3. A New Ordering of the Spiritual Beings in the Qur'ān

What does the Qur'ān say about classes of spiritual beings and their mutual relations?

3.1. Allāh

The revelations received by Muhammad proclaim Allāh to be the sole and supreme God, omnipotent over his creation, both in its present contingent existence and at the Day of Judgment. Not only the unbelievers but also the deities, *jinn*, and *shayṭāns* will be judged (S. 26:94/5). In terms of the overall process we described in the first sections, Allāh appropriates the attributes of the other deities as his "beautiful names". This not only puts an end to his association with companions, it also stops the presumed rise of chthonic powers to the heavenly spheres, where they might acquire divine knowledge or even become deities themselves. Heaven and earth, as well as the world beneath, are now kept separate from each other, except for initiatives Allāh is thought to take in his communicating directives to humankind through prophets and in his providential steering of the universe, either directly or through his angels. These new views are articulated in the Qur'ān with the help of elements derived mainly from existing Arabian, Jewish, and Christian traditions,

---

[44] *Ibid.*, p. 156.

but which gain fresh significance in light of the new views. Numerous scholars[45] have stressed the essentially "Arabian" character of the deity Allāh proclaimed in the Qur'ān. Some scholars[46] have drawn attention to striking parallels between the Allāh described in the Qur'ān and the Jahwe described in the Old Testament. Allāh is a god of struggle and combat, and he has the qualities of a leader and general. His care for his believers is expressed in terms of the care a patriarch takes of his kin. His power on the one hand and his benevolence on the other are stressed in his maintenance of justice. There are no names and attributes suggesting pluriformity of the divine or "polytheism" (*shirk*), and he is held to be essentially one and unique. He has certain astral features and can manifest himself through natural phenomena. Consequently, Islam as proclaimed by Muhammad is much more in line with nomadic and perhaps general Semitic religious feeling than the religious institutions of the Quraysh in Mecca. J. Chelhod has correctly observed that, when attacking the *mushrikūn*, the Qur'ān attacks less paganism and polytheism as such than what may be called the "deviationism" of the Meccans.[47] In others words, Muhammad's work was largely that of a reformer working in an urban context with references to basic religious notions dating from before the establishment of towns, while discarding or at least reinterpreting all religious notions that had appeared in the meantime. This corresponds with T. Fahd's thesis that Allāh had always remained the common denominator of all deities venerated by the Arabs and that Allāh was an "appellatif", rather than one deity beside the others. It was the deviant believers or *mushrikūn* who had substituted for the cult of the supreme god particular cults of his names and attributes as independent entities, as "daughters of Allāh", or as other deities. In fact, the Arabs' rapid acceptance of the seemingly "new" Islamic religion and its further acceptance—after the Arab conquest—throughout the Middle East, are somewhat easier to understand if we accept not only that those participating in the Islamic venture had common political and economic interests, but also that there was nothing strange or new in calling on a primordial deity who was basically known to all and in whose name Arabs—by becoming Muslims—could unite. Muhammad himself, moreover, was the first to stress the continuity between the original religion (*Urreligion*) of Adam, the revelations of the prophets, and Islam.

---

[45] See the literature mentioned by HENNINGER, "La religion bédouine préislamique", p. 134 and in n. 79 of that study. Cf. CHELHOD, *Les structures du sacré chez les Arabes*, p. 105.
[46] For instance CHELHOD, *Les structures du sacré chez les Arabes*, pp. 105–6.
[47] *Ibid.*, p. 111.

3.2. The Jinn

How, further, are the *jinn* described in the Qur'ān? The word itself occurs only in the Meccan revelations, and here the existence of the *jinn* is unambiguously affirmed. The *jinn* were created by Allāh (S. 15:27, 55:15). Both *jinn* and human beings were created to worship Allāh (S. 51:56); messengers from Allāh had been chosen among both the *jinn* and humankind to convey to their fellow beings Allāh's revelation (S. 6:130), and this happened from generation to generation (S. 7:38, etc.). Like human beings, *jinn* too were converted on hearing *sūras* of the Qur'ān (S. 72:1–3, 46:29–32). In fact, there is a striking parallelism between human beings on the one hand and *jinn* on the other, the two categories of creation together being called *al-thaqalānī*, probably meaning "the two weighty ones" (S. 55:31). Both categories have the same kind of social organization and both consist of "believers" and "unbelievers" in the message of the Qur'ān. Idolatry consists in putting on the same level the great works of Allāh and those of the *jinn* and *shayāṭīn*, who have superhuman powers but whom only unbelievers can consider companions or kin of Allāh. It is clear that Muhammad shares the belief in *jinn* current in his time; S. 72 (of the second Meccan period) is even named for them. Besides the word *jinn*, *jānn* occurs, for instance in S. 15:27 and in S. 55:14,39,56,74; it also occurs in S. 27:10 and 28:31 in connection with Moses' staff in the presence of Pharaoh. S. 27:39 mentions "one of the *jinn*, an *'ifrīt*". According to the Qur'ān, the *jinn* can harm human beings, are uncontrollable, and have seductive powers just like human beings (S. 114:6). They can appear in the form of a snake (the *jānn* of Moses; it has been suggested that Muhammad considered all snakes as potential *jinn*[48]); they possess supernatural powers and capacities. These views of the *jinn* were already in existence, but there are some new elements that cannot have been derived from ancient Arab beliefs and which Muhammad cannot have thought up himself. *Jinn* want to listen at the gate of heaven in order to acquire supernatural knowledge, and the angels expel them, once the Qur'ān has been revealed, with stones or stars (S. 72:8–9; perhaps falling stars?). Some of the *jinn* served Solomon, who had power over them (S. 34:12–4 and 27:38–44). The *jinn* were created from smokeless flame (S. 55:14); some of them are converted, the others will be judged on the Last Day. These particular views must have been derived from Jewish and perhaps also Christian popular demonology. More important, however, than such elements considered in themselves, is the general view of the *jinn* developed in the Qur'ān, or rather the two successive views, in which the *jinn* are first "de-demonized" and

[48] ZBINDEN, *Die Djinn des Islam und der altorientalische Geisterglaube*, p. 93, with a reference to some *ḥadīths* (al-Bukhārī 59:14; Muslim 39:139–41).

later "re-demonized".[49] The earliest preaching of Muhammad affirms
that *jinn* have no power of their own, as had generally been believed.
Muhammad proclaims that *jinn* have been created like human beings and
should serve and worship Allāh; they too have had prophets (S. 6:130)
and the Qur'ān is also meant for them (S. 46:29–32 and 72:1–2).
Muhammad preaches to both human beings and *jinn* (S. 55:33,39), who
together constitute *al-thaqalānī*. *Jinn*, consequently, are a group parallel
to humankind; they can convert, they will be judged on the Last Day as
they were judged in the past (S. 46:18). Most important, perhaps, they no
longer dispose of special supernatural knowledge. Whereas before, they
could listen at the gate of heaven and communicate the special knowledge
they had acquired in this way to *kāhins* and *shā'irs*, they are now expelled
by the angels (S. 72:8–9, etc.). In other words, people can believe in *jinn*
but should not worship them and should not seek aid or special knowledge from them. The *jinn* have been radically "de-demonized" by being
proclaimed creatures of Allāh, but we shall see shortly that they are
subsequently "re-demonized" by being largely identified with the *shayāṭīn*.
First they could move between earth and heaven; then they became a
species parallel to humankind; finally they almost become demons or
shayāṭīn themselves, and the distinction between believing and unbelieving *jinn* disappears. As J. Chelhod nicely formulates it: "[...] ils oscillent
en effet entre les hommes et les démons qui finissent pourtant par les
absorber."[50] In Medina there is no longer mention of *jinn*, only of Iblīs
and his *shayāṭīn*. But to appreciate fully the dimensions of the *jinn* within
the world of spiritual beings as the Qur'ān describes them, we should
consider first the way in which the Qur'ān views the other spiritual
beings: the deities, the angels, and the demons.

3.3. The Deities

The fact that Allāh was proclaimed the sole deity in the revelation to
Muhammad implied that no spiritual companions (*shurakā'*) could be
associated with him, and that the existing concept of God should be
purified. The Qur'ān does not deny the existence of such beings, but
declares them to be angels only, just as it denounces any association of
the *jinn* with Allāh. It is only in later Islam that these deities, including
the "daughters of Allāh", are degraded to *jinn* and *shayāṭīn*. In the
Qur'ān, their divine quality is simply denied and their cult forbidden.

---

[49] *Ibid.*, resp. pp. 85 and 88–9. Cf. CHELHOD, *Les structures du sacré chez les Arabes*, pp.
      83–4.
[50] CHELHOD, *Les structures du sacré chez les Arabes*, p. 85.

3.4. The Angels

Parallel to the downgrading of the deities, there is an upgrading of the
angels, who can now no longer be considered *jinn*-like beings, as they
were before Muhammad. The angels, living by their inherent goodness
according to the will of Allāh and always in his presence, are distinguished from human beings and *jinn*, who can be good or bad, are subject
to moral judgment and, of course, must face the Last Judgment. Among
the angels, only Hārūt and Mārūt (S. 2:102), because of their action in
Babel, are bad; this is an incidental borrowing from Jewish tradition. The
fundamental mistake of the unbelievers is that they consider the angels,
who are only servants of Allāh, as "female beings", i.e., as "daughters of
Allāh" (S. 43:19 and 53:27). It is interesting to see that in the Qur'ān,
angels and *jinn* are radically distinct categories of beings. Nowhere are
angels and *jinn* mentioned together, and *jinn* are nowhere considered
angels. On the contrary, the angels are essentially adversaries of the
shayāṭīn and the evil *jinn*. We can see the occurrence of a fundamental
polarization of the "intermediaries" at this stage in the Qur'ān. In earlier
times, the frontiers were more fluid and there was no radical opposition
between good and bad classes of beings.

The angels, then, were created from light to restore order again (*iṣlāḥ*)
in the works of Allāh and to inhabit his heavens. They have a variety of
tasks. As far as the demons (*shayāṭīn* and evil *jinn*) are concerned, the
angels must suppress their revolts and guard the gates of heaven against
their curiosity and possible attack. As far as humankind is concerned, the
angels are the messengers of Allāh to the prophets (S. 53:1). They appeal
to humankind to obey Allāh's commands and protect believers and
support them in their struggle against Iblīs and the *shayāṭīn*, who want
to deflect them from the straight path. As for the universe, the creation
of Allāh, they supervise and direct its movements. The Qur'ān already
distinguishes among the angels, saying that *al-ḥafaẓa* (S. 6:61) or *al-ḥāfiẓ*
(S. 86:4 and 82:10) keep the record of a person's actions and that *al-
mu'aqqibāt* take care of him or her (S. 13:11). In the early Meccan period,
Iblīs is considered a degraded or fallen angel, not a *jinnī* as in later
revelations.

3.5. The Demons and Iblīs

The existence of demons, like that of *jinn* and angels, is clearly affirmed
in the Qur'ān. Significantly, the word *shayāṭīn* is used synonymously with
jinn in a number of cases, referring for instance to the servants of
Solomon, the listeners at the gate of heaven, the seducers of human
beings. The deities of the unbelievers are sometimes considered to be in
fact *shayāṭīn* (S. 2:14, and 4:76,117,119–20, etc.), just as they are else-

where seen as *jinn* (S. 6:100 and 34:41). The status of the *shayāṭīn* in the Qur'ān is, however, closely connected with the position of Iblīs.

According to S. 15:28–42, Iblīs was the only angel who refused to bow down before Adam in disobedience to Allāh's command, presumably because Adam had been created from lowlier matter (clay) than the angels, who had been created from light. As a result, Iblīs has become humankind's rival and even enemy, because the human being is the privileged creature of Allah. Iblīs, however, cannot oppose Allāh, but acts within his plans. Later texts say that Iblīs was not originally an angel but a *jinnī* (S. 18:50); he was created from fire (S. 7:12). What is important, however, is the fact that Iblīs' disobedience to Allāh's command made him the supreme *shayṭān*, with an enormous following of male and female *shayāṭīn* who are at his service, together with those *jinn* who disobey Allāh's commands and so become *shayāṭīn*, too.

Consequently, the good order of creation is constantly threatened by the actions of Iblīs and his *shayāṭīn*, which are however checked by the angels. The greatest seduction *shayāṭīn* can achieve is to have themselves be worshipped as gods. The unbelievers' deities are called the work of *shayṭān* (S. 4:117,119–20, etc.) or even considered *shayāṭīn* themselves (S. 2:41). There are armies of *shayāṭīn*. *Shayāṭīn* can perform superhuman deeds like the *jinn*. They are intensely ugly. *Shayāṭīn* are at work as seducers both among *jinn* and among humankind (S. 6:112, cf. 41:2). Evil as such is identical to a personified *shayṭān* (S. 34:20–1, 2:34–6, 20:115–20). In the Qur'ān, *Shayṭān* is called *mārid* ("rebellious"); the same is said of the *shayāṭīn* (S. 31:8–9, 15:16–8). Moreover, the latter transmit lies to the poets (S. 26:210,221,223–4; 6:121).

In this connection, the question has been raised as to the difference between evil *jinn* and *shayāṭīn* and why both words occur in the Meccan periods. E. Zbinden takes it that the expression "*jinn*" is an Arabic concept arising out of ancient Arabian religious beliefs, while the word *shayṭān* was introduced and used as a loan word for demon. Muhammad would have identified disobedient, unbelieving, and demonic *jinn* with *shayāṭīn* and vice versa.[51] T. Fahd also thinks that the use of both *shayāṭīn* and *jinn* results from superimposing one demonology on another of different origin, from ancient Arabia and the Jewish-Christian tradition respectively.[52] Once *shayāṭīn* had been accepted as designating evil beings or demons and once Muhammad had started to ascribe all evil actions directed against the cause of Islam to Iblīs and his *shayāṭīn*, he tended to denounce the *shayāṭīn* on all occasions, assuming that, apart from some believing spirits, the *jinn* were evil spirits identical to the *shayāṭīn*. This

---

[51] ZBINDEN, *Die Djinn des Islam und der altorientalische Geisterglaube*, p. 88.
[52] FAHD, "Anges, démons et djinns en Islam", p. 186.

is what we have called the later "re-demonization" of the *jinn* by Muhammad. The absence of the word *jinn* in the Medinan period can probably best be explained by the identification of *jinn* with *shayāṭīn* and the dropping of the first, still ambiguous term in favor of the second, unambiguous one. This thus polarizes spiritual beings, with Allāh and the angels on the good side, Iblīs and his *shayāṭīn* on the bad side. As we have said, however, Iblīs is not the "enemy" of Allāh, as would be the case in a dualistic system; he acts within Allāh's plans.

Whereas a *shayṭān* in earlier times was simply a source of inspiration for *kāhins* and *shāʿirs*, in Islam he became a demon and was made subordinate to Iblīs. After the condemnation of Iblīs, this fallen angel or *jinnī* became the epitome of the evil forces confronting humankind. Both *jinn* and *shayāṭīn* are confounded in a synthesis of the Arabian and the Judeo-Christian concept: whereas Iblīs had been an angel, Muhammad makes a *jinnī* of him. The spiritual beings, probably under Judeo-Christian influences, are now clearly distinguished from one another: the angels, as messengers of heaven, aid humankind, whereas the *jinn* and *shayāṭīn*, messengers of Iblīs, attack humankind.

Even though all divine power comes to be seen as concentrated in Allāh as a result of Muhammad's preaching, two interesting points are to be noted. In the first place, particular actions and in part even the ultimate destiny of a person come to depend on intermediary forces that remain indispensable and even decisive for the affairs of the world. In the second place, it is not between God and Satan but in the world of intermediary beings that a polarization has taken place between the forces of good and evil, of pure and impure, as the two poles of the sacred.

4. Spiritual Beings and the Doctrine of Revelation

The changes in the spiritual beings' classification and rank proclaimed in the prophet's recitations (*qurʾāns*) are related to changes that took place on earth during and in the nature of Muhammad's activity, and they would later have important practical consequences. For instance, his "re-demonization" of the *jinn* and unmasking of the frightful forces of the *shayāṭīn* is connected with his claim to be inspired by an angel who passes on messages from Allāh. This claim is also related to the reproach addressed to Muhammad by his Meccan enemies that he was merely a man, perhaps a poet (*shāʿir*), possessed by a *jinnī* (S. 81:22 and 37:36). In fact, Muhammad's appearance challenged traditional concepts of inspiration then current in Mecca, and his preaching legitimated itself through a new doctrine of inspiration that traced its source not to *jinn*, but to Allāh by way of an angel.

In ancient Arabia the true order of things, including the order of the universe, could be communicated in different ways.[53] It could be communicated by a "héros civilisateur" or an "ancêtre éponyme" in ancient, indeed mythical times. It could also be communicated in the present by a *jinnī* or *shaytān* who served as a messenger from heaven. Or it could be communicated through prophetic revelation to some chosen people. For the ancient Arabs, the lower spiritual beings like *jinn* and *shayātīn* took care of communicating to humankind the rules for the social order and the universe through the medium of poets and *kāhins*, who had extended divinatory activities. Muhammad and subsequently Islam, however, recognized as valid only communication through prophetic revelation and rejected any inspiration by heavenly forces lower than angels. This stand brought about Muhammad's claim of near infallibility both as a prophet and as a statesman, and it degraded all claims of rival pretenders, poets, and *kāhins* as the work of demons, *shayātīn*. Where the *kāhin* was supposed to be inspired by a *jinnī*, Muhammad interpreted this *in malam partem*, equating the *jinnī* with a *shaytān*, just as the Qur'ān says that the poet, too, is inspired by a *shaytān*.

For his part, Muhammad claims to be a prophet who has received his *qur'āns* not from a *jinnī* but from the "Spirit of Holiness" (*rūh al-qudus*, S. 16:10); in contrast to this, S. 26:220–6 gives a pitiless verdict on the demonic origin of poetic inspiration. In short, Muhammad's claim to prophethood at the same time appropriates all "supernatural" knowledge, degrades any other inspiration—religious or otherwise—and presupposes a particular view of spiritual beings in the broadest sense of the word. At the beginning of Muhammad's career, the *jinn* were held to be Allāh's creatures, accepting or rejecting the prophet's message. But when Muhammad's legitimacy is at stake and he is reproached with being inspired by a *jinnī*, the *jinn* are demonized and their works are practically identified with those of the *shayātīn*. T. Fahd correctly observes how rudimentary the angelology and demonology of early Islam were and how anthropomorphic the thinking about spiritual beings was. The doctrine of revelation in Islam carries traces of this: "La conception de l'inspiration et de la révélation s'en est inexorablement ressentie."[54]

We may conclude that more knowledge of the belief in spiritual beings and intermediaries current before and during Muhammad's lifetime and of Muhammad's own views about them and their mutual relations is needed to understand what Muhammad and his contemporaries, adherents, and enemies considered to be "revelation". This is all the more important because in Islam prophecy and revelation are identified with each other, on the basis of the assumptions just mentioned. According to

---

[53] CHELHOD, *Les structures du sacré chez les Arabes*, p. 113.
[54] FAHD, *La divination arabe*, pp. 75–6.

the Qur'ān, the *nabī* and the *kāhin* are diametrically opposed to each other. Whereas the prophet is devoted to the supreme God and represents monotheism, the diviner serves lower deities and evil spirits and represents polytheism, *ishrāk*. T. Fahd adds that the whole *Sunna* literature agrees in giving a negative judgment on the value of messages transmitted by *jinn* and *shayāṭīn*. There is no longer any religious knowledge to be obtained in the ancient way once Muhammad has appeared: *lā kihāna ba'd nubuwwa*. And he observes in conclusion that Muhammad, as a *nabī*, could not cultivate personal relations with the God whom he proclaimed. In his claim to be inspired by an intermediary angel, Gabriel, he adhered to the restrictive concept of revelation existing in Arabia in his lifetime.[55]

The new order imposed on the spiritual beings in the Qur'anic view thus had direct consequences for the historical role of the prophet himself. It had consequences for the history of the early Muslim community as well. Muhammad's experience with his enemies in the late Meccan and early Medinan period must have sharpened his awareness of the workings of *shayāṭīn*. The victory at Badr ascribed to the assistance of angels, the building of the Medinan community and state under the guidance of prophecy, the institutionalization of the new *dīn*, and the *jihād* for the sake of Allāh may all have enhanced the community's awareness of Allāh's support for his prophet and his community. This support was effected by means of heavenly intermediaries, which at the time were thought to mix freely with human beings.

Selected Literature

ALBRIGHT, William Foxwell, "Islam and the Religions of the Ancient Orient", *Journal of the American Oriental Society*, 60 (1940), pp. 283–301.
CHELHOD, Joseph, *Introduction à la sociologie de l'Islam: De l'animisme à l'universalisme* (Islam d'hier et d'aujourd'hui 12), Paris: Maisonneuve et Larose, 1958.
—, *Les structures du sacré chez les Arabes* (Islam d'hier et d'aujourd'hui 13), Paris: Maisonneuve et Larose, 1964 (nouv. éd. 1986).
DRIJVERS, Han J. W., "Das Heiligtum der arabischen Göttin Allāt im westlichen Stadtteil von Palmyra", *Antike Welt*, 7 (1976), pp. 28–38.
EICHLER, Paul Arno, *Die Dschinn, Teufel und Engel im Koran*, Inaugural-Dissertation, Leipzig: Klein, 1928.
EICKELMAN, DALE F., "Musaylima: An Approach to the Social Anthropology of Seventh-Century Arabia", *Journal of the Economic and Social History of the Orient*, 10 (1967), pp. 17–52.

---

[55] *Ibid.*, p. 522: "Ces intermédiaires occupent une place dominante dans la divination arabe […]. La conception de l'inspiration prophétique dans l'Islam primitif en est fortement imprégnée, puisque le Prophète arabe n'a pas réussi à avoir des relations directes et personnelles avec Allāh."

FAHD, Taufiq, *La divination arabe: Etudes religieuses, sociologiques et folkloriques sur le milieu natif de l'Islam*, Leiden: E. J. Brill, 1966.

—, *Le panthéon de l'Arabie centrale à la veille de l'hégire* (Institut Français d'Archéologie de Beyrouth, Bibliothèque archéologique et historique 88), Paris: Geuthner, 1968.

—, "Anges, démons et djinns en Islam", in *Génies, anges et démons: Égypte – Babylone – Israël – Islam – Peuples Altaïques – Inde – Birmanie – Asie du Sud-Est – Tibet – Chine* (Sources orientales VIII), par Dimitri MEEKS et al., Paris: Seuil, 1971, pp. 153–214.

GOLDZIHER, Ignaz, "Die Ğinnen der Dichter", *Zeitschrift der Deutschen Morgenländischen Gesellschaft*, 45 (1891), pp. 685–90.

HENNINGER, Joseph, "La société bédouine ancienne", in *L'antica società beduina: Studi di W. Dostal*, raccolti da Francesco GABRIELI (Studi Semitici 2), Roma: Centro di Studi Semitici, Istituto di Studi Orientali, Università, 1959, pp. 69–93.

—, "La religion bédouine préislamique", *ibid.*, pp. 115–40 (also in the author's *Arabica Sacra* [see below], 1981, pp. 11–33).

—, "Geisterglaube bei den vorislamischen Arabern", in *Festschrift Paul Schebesta zum 75. Geburtstag* ... (Studia Instituti Anthropos 18), Wien/Mödling: St. Gabriel-Verlag, 1963, pp. 279–316 (also in the author's *Arabica Sacra* [see below], 1981, pp. 118–69).

—, *Über Lebensraum und Lebensformen der Frühsemiten* (Arbeitsgemeinschaft für Forschung des Landes Nordrhein-Westfalen, Geisteswissenschaften, Heft 151), Köln/Opladen: Westdeutscher Verlag, 1968.

—, "Zum frühsemitischen Nomadentum", in *Viehwirtschaft und Hirtenkultur: Ethnographische Studien* (Studia Ethnographica 3), ed. by László FÖLDES, Budapest: Akadémiai Kiadó, 1969, pp. 33–68.

—, *Arabica Sacra: Aufsätze zur Religionsgeschichte Arabiens und seiner Randgebiete. Contributions à l'histoire religieuse de l'Arabie et de ses régions limitrophes* (Orbis biblicus et orientalis 40), Freiburg, Switzerland: Universitätsverlag, and Göttingen: Vandenhoeck & Ruprecht, 1981. See in particular, besides "La religion bédouine préislamique", and "Geisterglaube bei den vorislamischen Arabern": "Über religiöse Strukturen nomadischer Gruppen", pp. 34–57, and "Einiges über Ahnenkult bei arabischen Beduinen", pp. 170–88.

HÖFNER, Maria, "Die vorislamischen Religionen Arabiens", in *Die Religionen Altsyriens, Altarabiens und der Mandäer*, von Hartmut GESE, Maria HÖFNER, Kurt RUDOLPH (Religionen der Menschheit 10,2), Stuttgart, etc.: W. Kohlhammer, 1970, pp. 233–402.

LAMMENS, Henri, "Les sanctuaires préislamites dans l'Arabie occidentale", *Mélanges de l'Université Saint-Joseph*, 11 (1926), pp. 39–173.

MACDONALD, D.B., et al., Art. "Djinn", in *The Encyclopaedia of Islam*, new edition, Vol. II, Leiden: E. J. Brill, and London: Luzac, 1965, pp. 546–50.

SCHLUMBERGER, Daniel, "Le prétendu dieu Gennéas", *Mélanges de l'Université Saint-Joseph*, 46 (1970–71), pp. 209–22.

SEYRIG, Henri, and Jean STARCKY, "Gennéas", *Syria*, 26 (1949), pp. 231–57.

SMITH, William Robertson, *Lectures on the Religion of the Semites: The Fundamental Institutions* (first published 1927), third edition, with an introduction and additional notes by Stanley A. COOK. Prolegomenon by J. MUILENBERG (The Library of Biblical Studies), New York: Ktav, 1969.

TEIXIDOR, Javier, *The Pagan God: Popular Religion in the Greco-Roman Near East*, Princeton, N. J.: Princeton University Press, 1977.

—, *The Pantheon of Palmyra* (E.P.R.O.E.R. 79), Leiden: E. J. Brill, 1979.

WATT, William Montgomery, "Belief in a 'High God' in pre-Islamic Mecca", in *Actes du Ve Congrès international d'arabisants et d'islamisants. Bruxelles, 31 août – 6 septembre 1970* (Correspondance d'Orient 11), Brussels: Publications du Centre pour l'étude des problèmes du monde musulman contemporain, 1971, pp. 499–505.

—, "The Qur'ān and Belief in a 'High God'", in *Proceedings of the Ninth Congress of the Union Européenne des Arabisants et Islamisants. Amsterdam, 1st to 7th Sept. 1978* (Publications of the Netherlands Institute of Archaeology and Arabic Studies 4), ed. by Rudolph PETERS, Leiden: E. J. Brill, 1981, pp. 327–33.

WELLHAUSEN, Julius, *Reste Arabischen Heidentums gesammelt und erläutert*, zweite Ausgabe, Berlin: Georg Reimer, 1897.

WENSINCK, Arent J., "The Etymology of the Arabic Djinn (spirits)", *Verslagen en mededeelingen der Koninklijke Akademie, afdeling letterkunde*, 5.IV (1920), pp. 506–14 (also: "Supplementary Notes on the Etymology of the Arabic Djinn [spirits]", *ibid.*, pp. 514a–514c).

WESTERMARCK, Edward, "The Nature of the Arab Ǧinn, Illustrated by the Present Beliefs of the People of Morocco", *The Journal of the Anthropological Institute of Great Britain and Ireland*, 29 (New Series 2) (1899), pp. 252–69.

ZBINDEN, Ernst, *Die Djinn des Islam und der altorientalische Geisterglaube*, Bern & Stuttgart: Paul Haupt, 1953.

Chapter 2

Faith and Reason in the Argumentation of the Qur'ān

The present chapter[1] intends to give a first preliminary answer to the question whether there is a logical connection between the Qur'anic concept of reason, on the one hand, and some specific forms of reasoning, as used in the Qur'anic argumentation, on the other hand.[2] Sections 1 and 2 are devoted to a consideration of the concept of reason and of examples of Qur'anic argumentation respectively, while section 3 raises the question of their logical connection and their relationship to faith. In some final remarks we indicate why this problem is a relevant one.

Our presentation cannot claim to be exhaustive; the choice of Qur'anic texts, for instance in section 2, was made in order to give some striking examples, especially from the Medinan period, in the first Sūras of the Qur'ān, after the *Fātiha*. Furthermore, we are not concerned here with the internal logic, the semantics of the Qur'anic concepts themselves, like paradise – fire, revelation – prophet, sin – punishment. We are only concerned with the logic of the arguments Muhammad used in his appeal to faith, as they were recorded in the Qur'ān. The stories, commandments, and admonitions are not considered here, nor are the miracles of Allāh, even though they are used as arguments in themselves.

---

[1] A first version of this text appeared under the same title in *Perennitas: Studi in onore di Angelo Brelich*, Rome: Edizione dell'Ateneo, 1980, pp. 619–33.

   References to the Qur'ān give the verse number first according to the "Cairo edition" (*al-Muṣḥaf al-sharīf* or *al-Qur'ān al-Karīm*, Cairo 1344/1924) and then according to Gustav FLÜGEL's edition (*Alcorani textus arabicus*, Leipzig 1834). The Arabic text being the starting point, the English translations are based on Arthur J. ARBERRY's *The Koran interpreted*, London: Oxford University Press, 1964 (numerous reprints). Marmaduke PICKTHALL's (*The Glorious Koran: A Bi-lingual Edition with English Translation, Introduction and Notes*, London: Allen & Unwin, 1976 etc.) and George SALE's (*The Koran, trans. into English from the Original Arabic* [1734], London: Warne, 1887) translations were also consulted.

[2] On this subject, cf. NASR, "Revelation, Intellect and Reason in the Quran"; SAIYIDAIN, "Qurān's Invitation to Think"; HAQUE, "The Holy Quran and Rational Thinking".

1. The Qur'anic Concept of Reason

Where the Qur'ān makes an appeal to humankind to believe in God and His revelation (S. 3:193/190, etc.), its "verses" (*āyāt*) are said to make things clear, to clarify things: they are "*āyāt mubbayyināt*" (S. 24:34, and elsewhere). What does the Qur'ān say about the intellectual capacities of human beings, so that they may grasp these verses, understand their appeal, and be able to respond mindfully to it? The following texts are of interest here, because they link a person's intellectual capacities with his or her potential faith or piety.

1.1. A Person's Intellectual Capacities in Connection with Faith

In four places it is stated that Allāh gave humans "hearing, sight, and heart" (S. 16:78/80; 23:78/80; 32:9/8; 67:23), whereby the Arabic word for "heart" (*fu'ād*) implies a person's mental capacities. In S. 32:9/8 it is moreover said that Allāh also breathed into the human being "of his spirit" (*rūḥ*). In all four verses, the mentioning of this gift of "hearing, sight, and heart" is followed by the reproach that the human being is not grateful enough for this gift, or by the expression of hope that he or she will be grateful. Then, in sixteen places, people are addressed as "you who are gifted with hearts" (*yā ūlī 'l-albāb*), which may be translated by "you people of understanding". Like *fu'ād* (pl. *af'ida*), *lubb* (pl. *albāb*) indicates a natural, mental quality of a person; it signifies "heart", "core", as well as "understanding". When *yā ūlī 'l-albāb* is used in the vocative, it implies, besides a way of addressing, also an appeal: to understanding in general and to religious understanding in particular.

So S. 2:179/175: "There is life in retaliation, you people of understanding: perhaps you will be God-fearing". In S. 38:43/42 it is said that Job received from Allāh his family back: out of mercy and as an admonishment (*dhikrā*) for "people of understanding". There is a connection between understanding and accepting admonishment: only the "people of understanding" let themselves be admonished (S. 2:269/272; 3:7/9; 13:19; 39:9/12).

In S. 12:111, it is said that in the report about the earlier prophets there is an "instructive warning" (*'ibra*) for the "people of understanding". In the creation of heaven and earth and in the change of day and night there are "signs for people of understanding" (*la-āyāt li-ūlī 'l-albāb*), people who, by the way, "*yadhkurūna*" and "*yatafakkarūna*" (S. 3:190/187).

As in the first text mentioned (S. 2:179/175), in S. 2:197/193, 5:100 and 65:10 there is also an explicit call to "people of understanding" to fear God: imperative "*fa-'ttaqu'llah*", "*wa-'ttaquni*". And in S. 39:18 mention is made of "those who listen to the Word and who follow the best of it. They are those whom Allah guideth. They are people of understanding (*ūlī 'l-albāb*)".

We may conclude that the people who are "gifted with hearts" (*albāb* or *af'ida*), who have intellectual capacities, are supposed to have religious attention as such.

1.2. The Use a Person Makes of his or her Intellectual Capacities in Connection with Faith

For this use there are several verbs in the Qur'ān, with some interesting nuances.

1.2.1. *Tadabbara* (to ponder) in S. 4:82/84: "Do they [people of the Scriptures] not ponder the Qur'ān (*a-falā yatadabbarūna 'l-qur'ān*)?" This occurs twelve times, but only one time in connection with faith.

1.2.2. *Tafakkara* (to reflect) in S. 2:266/268 after the parable of the smitten vineyard presented as a sign of Allāh: "Maybe you will reflect (*la'allakum tatafakkarūna*)" and in S. 6:50 after the metaphor of the difference between the blind man and the seeing man: "Don't you reflect (*afa-lā tatafakkarūna*)?" In S. 59:21, it is said that Allāh strikes the similitudes (*amthāl*) for people: "Maybe they will reflect (*la'allahum yatafakkarūna*)." And S. 7:184/183: "Or did they not reflect (*awa-lam yatafakkarū*)?"—namely that Muhammad was not a crazy man—followed by "Did they not consider (*lam yanturū*) the reign of God over heaven and earth?" This occurs eighteen times, four of them in connection with faith.

1.2.3. *Faqiha* (to understand). In S. 8:65/66, after mentioning that twenty believers will carry victory over two hundred unbelievers and one hundred faithful over one thousand unfaithful, it is said that this happens because the unbelievers are "people who do not understand": *bi-annahum qawmun lā yafqahūna*. In S. 9:87/88 and 63:3, it is said that people "do not understand, because their hearts have been sealed": *tubi'a 'alā qulūbihim fa-hum lā yafqahūna*. And S. 63:7, after the denunciation of an error made by the hypocrites (*al-munāfiqūna*), states that they just do not understand: *wa-lākinna al-munāfiqīna lā yafqahūna*. Finally, it is said of Allāh in S. 6:65: "Behold, look how we explain the signs [verses? *Āyāt*]: perhaps they [the unbelievers] will understand: *la'allahum yafqahūna*. *Faqiha* occurs nineteen times in the Qur'ān, of which five are in connection with faith, but always in a negative way: those who do not believe, really have no capacity to "*faqiha*". The act of *faqiha* presupposes faith.

1.2.4. *Fahima* (to understand) occurs only once in the Qur'ān, in the *fa''la* form with Allāh as subject: S. 21:79 says about Solomon that Allāh "made him understand" a particular legal case: *fa-fahhamnāhā sulaimāna*.

1.2.5. '*Alima* (to know) indicates "to possess knowledge" (*'ilm*), which may be a revealed knowledge or a knowledge acquired by the senses and by reflection. It occurs many times in the Qur'ān. In connection with our problem, the following texts may be noted, in which, by the way, the human lack of knowledge is stressed.

As is well-known, of course, in S. 96:5 Allāh is said to have taught the human being what he or she did not know earlier: '*allama 'l-insāna mā lam ya'lam*. We note S. 17:85/87, with reference to the *rūḥ* as "*amr rabbī*"; it is said as a contrast to the believers: "You have been given only little knowledge." And S. 5:101 warns human beings against asking about things that would hurt them if they were manifested to them. They should wait until they are properly revealed (by the Qur'ān). So *'ilm* is knowledge that one receives: *ūtū al-'ilma* (S. 34:6) and signifies the acquisition of something special. There is not an active use of a person's intellectual capacities. S. 30:30/29 and 30:6/5 state explicitly that "most people do not know": *wa-lākinna akthara 'l-nāsi lā ya'lamūna*. And the latter text adds that most people only know the externals of this life (*zāhiran min al-ḥayāti al-dunyā*) and are negligent about "the other life" (*al-ākhira*) and asks whether they have not reflected in themselves (*awa-lam yatafakkarū fī anfusihim*)—which apparently is a prerequisite for obtaining knowledge. Does this reflection perhaps serve to make a person aware of his or her lack of knowledge? If someone without knowledge (*bi-ghayr 'ilmin*)—and without guidance and Scripture—disputes about God (*yujādilu fī 'llāhi*, S. 22:8), that is foolishness. The opposite of knowledge is ignorance (*jahl*): the believers should turn away from the ignorant (*al-jāhilīna*, S. 7:199/198). And the religion of Abraham can be rejected only by someone who fools him- or herself: *man safiha nafsahu* (S. 2:130/124).

As background, it is important to remember that the *āyāt* (verses) have been made clear to the people "who know" (*li-qawmin ya'lamūna*, S. 41:3/2 and 6:97), whereas S. 6:98 says the same with regard "to the people who understand" (*li-qawmin yafqahūna*). Similarly, S. 13:3 and 4 state that nature has its signs for people who reflect (*li-qawmin yata-fakkarūna*) and for people who understand or think (*li-qawmin ya'qilūna*).

And here we come to the last verb to be considered, indicating the use of intellectual capacities in connection with faith. This is:

1.2.6. '*Aqala* (to understand, to think, to use one's intelligence). This occurs 49 times, 19 of them in connection with faith. We should remember that the noun *'aql* does not occur in the Qur'ān. The verb indicates the active use of a person's natural intelligence, his or her capacity to draw the right conclusions.

On many occasions it is said, as an exhortation or admonishment: *a-falā ta'qilūna*: Do you not understand, do you not see the evidence—or the absurdity—of it? (S. 2:44/41; 2:76/71; 3:65/68; 6:32; 7:169/168; 12:109; 21:67; 36:60) The unbelievers positively do not understand (S. 2:170/165; 5:57/62; 49:4). Allāh lays abomination (*rijs*) upon those who do not understand (S. 10:100). The commandments and signs are there: "So perhaps [hopefully] you will understand" (*la ʿallakum taʿqilūna*, S. 2:73/68; 2:242/243; 6:151/152; 57:17/16)—or "if you understand" (*in kuntum taʿqilūna*, S. 3:118/114). As has been said earlier, signs in nature are there "for people who understand" (*li-qawmin yaʿqilūna*, S. 45:5/4).

S. 8:22 gives the verdict—or golden rule—: *inna sharra 'l-dawābbi ʿinda 'llāhi al-summu, al-bukum al-ladhīna lā yaʿqilūna*, "surely the worst of beasts in God's sight are those that are deaf and dumb and do not understand".

ʿAqala, consequently, is an innate quality in a person which he or she should develop. It leads people to see the evidence of the "signs". If a person does not "*ʿaqala*", he or she remains blind, and finally an unbeliever.

2. Forms of Argumentation in the Qur'ān

The Qur'anic discourse is full of arguments to convince or to admonish people, to refute errors or to demonstrate truths. For the greater part, these arguments are very accessible to us, and we can understand and appreciate them as such. In the following, we shall try to show something of their inherent rationality, something of the logic of these arguments on different levels, starting from the most fundamental, with illustrations on each level. We leave aside indirect argumentation through parables and metaphors, which is of a more subtle nature: we limit ourselves to rational argumentation.

2.1. First, we can distinguish a kind of "logic of life" itself, which reveals truths inherent in life as such.

1) Having established that man is not able to deal equally with his different wives, however much he may wish to do so, the concluding advice in the Qur'ān is that man, nevertheless, should not turn away from one of them and leave her in suspense (S. 4:129/128). This is a human argument with no visible immediate relationship with religion.

2) After the observation that a nation has passed away, it is said: "Theirs is what they earned, yours shall be what you have earned", after which is added: "Ye shall not be questioned as to that which they have done" (implicit: only as to what you have done) (S. 2:141/135). Here the respective responsibilities are outlined, the one being different from the other, on the basis of a final judgment.

3) "Every soul" must taste of death, "ye" (vocative address) shall surely be paid in full your wages on the day of resurrection. A person who is brought into "Paradise" is happy. But life of "this world" is but a possession of deceit (S. 3:185/182).

By using the argument of an absolute contrast between this life and Paradise, between the fate of deceit and death and the prospect of eternal bless, a negative judgment is implicitly made about the nature of this life. In the argument, the existence of a Hereafter is postulated; this "technique" of making implicit assumptions in the argumentation is found many more times in the Qur'ān.

2.2. In the second place, there is a kind of "logic of revelation", whereby it is assumed, again implicitly, that there is something like "revelation".

1) It is said to the people of the Scriptures: "What is the matter with you? Why do you give such a [probably: wrong] judgment (*kaifa tahkumūna*)?" (S. 68:36) And then there follows as a kind of explanation: "Or do you possess a Scripture into which you could look [and in which you could find what you want]?"

An explanation of the (wrong) judgment is sought in the possible possession of a revelation. Praiseworthy as such a possession may sound, the argument continues with an ironical implication that this revelation may have been used for selfish purposes. This type of "paradox" between divine revelation and the human use of it also occurs elsewhere in Qur'anic argumentation.

2) Given the existence of a revelation from Allāh (without proof), an argument is made against possible rivals as a logical implication of the very fact of "revelation": "Most wrong is someone who claims inspiration or a similar revelation from Allāh, when he or she is not inspired" (S. 6:94). This is severely condemned as a lie about or even against Allāh.

Muhammad's belief that he receives revelations from Allāh makes it necessary, in view of his enemies' doubts, to develop a number of arguments to "safeguard" these revelations, both against suspicion that they might not come from Allāh and against claims that there might be other revelations from Allāh.

2.3. Third, there is a kind of "logic of faith" that is developed as soon as the existence of faith is assumed, established, and defended against internal doubts.

1) Many verses attest that the acceptance of faith has a number of implications and consequences that lead to differences among the believers. An interesting way of expressing this is the argument given in S. 3:135: "Do you think that ye can enter Paradise and Allāh not know those of you who have fought well or those who have endured?"

2) An argument like the following is pertinent in its subtle defense against all possible unbelief among the new believers: "He does not bid you take the angels and the prophets for your lords; shall He bid you misbelieve again when you have once submitted?" (S. 3:74)

3) And in Moses' prayer to God for his community after the affair of the golden calf we find a similar argument that the Lord may let his believers survive even after they have committed sin: "Wilt Thou destroy us because of what the foolish ones among us (*as-sufahā minnā*) have done? It is only a trial on your part (*fitnatuka*), whereby Thou leadest astray whom Thou wilt, and guidest whom Thou wilt" (S. 7:155/154).

As with revelation, a particular argumentation is used to guarantee the survival of faith. Not only does the argument contain implicit assumptions about revelation and faith, it nearly always appeals to Allāh as the final authority.

4) The "logic of faith" has its own practical pressure. For instance, in calling to fight, it is said: "Are you afraid of the unbelievers? Better be afraid of Allāh!" (S. 9:13) And: "The heat of hell is greater [than that of the desert]" (S. 9:81/82).

On the basis of this "logic of revelation" and "logic of faith", together with a fundamental "logic of life", a particularly fruitful field for argumentation can be opened to analysis: the debates and discussions between the Prophet, on the one hand, and the people of the Scriptures plus the unbelievers and hypocrites, on the other hand. Out of many examples we may take some at random:

2.4. With regard to the People of the Scriptures[3]:

1) S. 2:77/72: "Don't they know that Allāh knows what they keep to themselves and what they manifest?" We find here a nice example of what may be called "the argument from the absolute": the human discourse is interrupted by recourse to Allāh's thought and action. In this particular case: Against all human concealment and hypocrisy, the "argument from the absolute" of God's all-knowledge is used: so that lying by the people of Scripture is senseless in advance.

2) "How can you people of the Scriptures not believe in God's signs, while Allāh [Himself] is witness to what you do" (S. 2:98/93), and "How can you people not believe, while unto you are recited the verses of Allāh, and among you is His Prophet" (S. 12:101/96)?

Naive as the argument may appear at first sight, on further consideration it is tellingly addressed to people of the Scriptures, who are supposed to believe in God's presence, His signs, and prophets sent by Him. In fact,

---

[3]   Cf. Waardenburg, "Koranisches Religionsgespräch".

one could hardly imagine a better argument precisely against the non-believing people of the Scriptures.

3) S. 2:91/85: "Believe in what Allāh has revealed." Answer: "We believe in what has been revealed to us." Conclusive argument: "But they disbelieve in all that has come afterwards (*wa-yakfurūna bimā warā'ahu*), although it confirms what they have."

The argument is reasonable indeed: if you believe in God's revelation and in what God has revealed to you, there is no reason not to believe what He revealed to others after His specific revelation to you. It presupposes the recognition that God, being God, is free to reveal Himself to the people and in the way He wants. It also suggests that someone who denies this does not really believe in God.

4) A well-known way of arguing is to take a statement in which the adversary attacks someone and apply it to the attacker instead. So, e.g., S. 5:64/69: "The Jews say: Allāh's hand is fettered. [But] their [own] hands are [or: ought to be] fettered and they are accursed for saying so." And S. 3:69/62 warns the believers that a group of the people of Scripture would feign to be able to lead them astray. The answer is then: "But they only lead themselves astray, and they do not perceive."

In such reversals one recognizes a certain tactic of arguing. This tactic is also used in the debates with the unbelievers.

2.5. *With regard to the* other unbelievers[4]:

1) A nice example of reversal of the argument, turning it back on the original speaker, is S. 2:11/10: "Do not commit evil." Answer: "We do what is right." Conclusion: "But they are indeed the evildoers, without perceiving it!" And Verse 13/12: "Believe as others do." Answer: "We do not believe as fools." Conclusion: "But it is they who are the fools without knowing it!"

2) Since there is a logic of faith with its own assumptions, unbelief becomes so to speak "illogical", insofar as there is something "nonsensical" in it that causes it to lead not to sense but to nonsense. In section 1, I gave some examples of the connection between faith and the use of intelligence: a connection that seems to be essential in the Qur'ān. In the same way, there is a connection between unbelief and stupidity. We need only recall the aforementioned S. 5:103/102: "Those who disbelieve invent a lie against Allāh. Most of them have no sense" (*wa-aktharuhum lā ya'qilūna*: "they do not understand, they do not think, they do not use their intelligence"). Compare the dispute of the evildoers in hell (S. 7:37/35–39/37); the evil people have hearts but cannot understand with them (S. 7:179/178).

---

4   Cf. WAARDENBURG, "Un débat coranique contre les polythéistes".

When unbelief is illogical in itself, the only real victim of such unbelief is the unbeliever him- or herself. So S. 4:111: "Whoso committeth sin committeth it only against him- or herself." Cf. S. 3:176/170: "Those who purchase misbelief with faith do not hurt God at all, and for them is grievous woe." And in the translation of A. J. Arberry: "And thou art not to suppose that they who disbelieve have outstripped me; they cannot frustrate my will" (S. 8:59/61).

3) On the other hand, the interesting observation is made that, for the unbelievers, the prophets and generally the faithful seem fools. Noah was held to be "in manifest error" by the leaders (al-malā') of his people (S. 7:60/58). And in S. 7:66–67/64–65 the council (al-malā') of the people of ʿĀd says to Hūd: "We see thee in folly, and we think that thou art one of the liars." Upon which Hūd answers: "My people, there is no folly in me; but I am a messenger from the Lord of all Being [...]" etc. There are other similar reproaches of foolishness made by unbelievers in the Qur'ān; in the answers there is an appeal to Allāh. So the hypocrites and sick of heart say of the believers: "Their religion has deluded them." The answer: "But whosoever puts his or her trust in God, surely God is almighty, all-wise" (S. 8:49/51).

4) For our purpose of analyzing Qur'anic argumentation in terms of the problem of faith and reason, S. 25:33/35 is most important. Here Allāh's answer to the words of the unbelievers is mentioned. "They do not bring to thee any similitude (mathal) without Us bringing thee the truth (al-haqq), and something better in exposition (ahsana tafsīran)." In other words, the revelation guarantees the faithful a deeper insight into all matters on which the unbelievers pronounce. This spiritual superiority, based on the given revelation, is in the last analysis the force of all the Prophet's arguing against the unbelievers, the people of the Scriptures, and other partners of discussion.

5) An interesting argument may be added, namely the one used to convince the unbelievers in a shrewd tactical way: if they abandon themselves, Allāh will forgive them, but if they remain where they are, they must realize that "the wont (sunnat) of the ancients is already gone" (S. 8:38/39).

2.6. Faith in Allāh as God

The pivot of Qur'anic argumentation, however, is its notion of Allāh as "God": here lies a key to the structure of nearly all arguments based on the logic of revelation and faith and of the debates with people of the Scriptures and unbelievers. We have mentioned already the "recourse to Allāh" and "the argument from the absolute". It is striking indeed to notice the natural, self-evident way in which Allāh is discussed.

1) Most striking in its intellectual appeal is the famous *Lā ilāh illā*
'llāh: "There is no god but Allāh!", often followed by: "He is the mighty,
the wise." A number of interpretations have been given of this formula.
It may be considered, for instance, a logical argument that parts from an
existing belief in several divine forces and reduces them to one force or
entity: as such, it strikes the religious mind and urges it to reflect. But it
can also be considered as an argument that would be the theological
argument *par excellence*: only Allāh can claim to possess all the properties inherent in a real godhead. The assumption is then that everybody
knows what these properties are. A similar effect is in the argument that
contrasts the reality of Allāh with the reality of this world, whereby Allāh
is the best resort against the appetites and vanities of this world (S. 3:14/
12). Compare also Abraham's discovery of his Lord (S. 6:78–80) as
Creator of this world.

2) It is somehow nonsensical not to believe in Allāh, who is at the very
origin of a person's life. "How can one disbelieve in God when He gives
life and resurrects" (S. 2:28/26, and elsewhere)? The prophets wonder
how any doubt at all about God is possible, since He created heaven and
earth (S. 14:10/11). He knows what a person hides in his or her breast
or what he or she shows (S. 3:29). In other words: Allāh even knows of
possible unbelief on a person's part. So why should one not believe?

3) It is illogical that Allāh might have a son. "God is only one God.
Glory be to Him—He is exalted above any claim that He should have a
son!" (S. 4:171/169) "The Creator of the heavens and the earth—how
should He have a son, seeing that He has no consort, and He created all
things, and He has knowledge of everything?" (S. 6:101) What is remarkable is that God is spoken of as being evident for the natural intelligence,
whereas the same natural intelligence rejects with the same evidence any
son of God.

4) An interesting argument to refute any belief in divine forces other
than Allāh is given in S. 6:40: "Say: what do you think? If Allāh's
chastisement comes upon you, or the Hour comes upon you, will you call
upon any other than God if you speak truly?" The very fact of Allāh's
judgment makes the other divinities simply ridiculous. So also S. 6:22–
24: "And on the day when We shall muster them all together, then We
shall say unto those who associate other gods [with Allāh]: Where are
[now] your associates whom you were asserting? Then they will have no
proving (*fitnatuhum*) but to say: 'By God our Lord, we never associated
other gods with Thee.' Behold how they lie against themselves, and how
that which they were forging (*yaftarūna*) has gone astray from them!"

Of course there are many more arguments brought forward against
idolatry as divine forces associated with Allāh, arguments on which we
cannot dwell here (for instance S. 7:191–195/194: Idols do not create or
have power to help, but are created themselves, etc.). And if anyone still

does not believe in the coming judgment, the following pressing argument is presented: "And they say: There is naught save our life in the world, and we shall not be raised [again]. If thou couldst see when they are set before their Lord! He will say: Is this not real? They will say: Yea, verily, by our Lord! He will say: Taste now the retribution for what ye used to disbelieve" (S. 6:29–30).

5) Many times a quick reference to Allāh functions as an argument to restore the proportions of a given problem. So for instance S. 3:154/148 "Have we any chance in the affair?" Say: "The affair is that of Allāh." Or S. 4:49/52: "Hast thou not seen those who praise themselves for purity?" "Nay, Allāh purifieth whom He will [...]." There are many more expressions that show that only with the reminder that all things start with Allāh can the truth of things be made clear.

6) Another example of such a recourse to Allāh is a text against those unbelievers who say that good things come from Allāh and evil things from Muhammad, upon which the definite answer is given: "Say: 'All is from Allāh. What is amiss with these people that they come not nigh to understand a happening?'" (S. 4:78/80)

7) I conclude with another nice piece of argumentation, S. 10:31/32–36/37. On the question of who makes life possible, the people (the unbelievers?) cannot but answer: that is Allāh. Once this truth is no longer regarded, there can be only error, and the word of the Lord is realized against the unbelievers: that they do not believe. On the question whether one of the associated powers can originate creation and bring it back again, there is only one answer: that is Allāh alone. Consequently, Allāh should be followed.

The structure of this argument represents an essential manner of Muslim argumentation as it repeatedly occurs not only in the Qur'ān, but also throughout Muslim religious thought: by jumping to an "absolute absolute" all "relative absolutes" are unmasked and the world becomes relative *per se*. If one looks for a specifically Muslim "logic", there it is: the jump to the "absolute absolute" is performed by means of human intelligence.

3. Connections Between the Qur'anic Concept of Reason and Specific Forms of Reasoning in Qur'anic Argumentation

Our first inquiry—into some key terms used in the Qur'ān for the mental capacities of a human being—has shown that, in the Qur'anic view, a person is a being gifted with mental capacities that he or she has to use like his or her other capacities. People have to reflect (*tafakkara*), they have to think and understand the signs (*'aqala*), they have to acquire knowledge (*'alima*), and with a first faith they have to understand (*faqiha*).

All this will lead them to recognition of and abandonment to Allāh. To arrive at understanding and insight, a person must basically believe; for other ways of thought, no faith is required *a priori*. From the texts, we may conclude that the full employment of a person's mental capacities both implies and leads to faith in Allāh. This does not mean, of course, that the act of faith (*īmān, islām*) is not clearly distinguished from the exercise of a person's mind.

Our second inquiry—into some structures of arguments used in the Qur'ān—has shown that there is a kind of basic rationality or "logic" in the Qur'ān, which we have called the logic of life, of revelation, and of faith; this logic shows up in particular ways of thinking. In its appeal, the Qur'ān continuously uses arguments in order to make those addressed think in the proposed way: this is true of believers as well as people of the Scriptures and pagan unbelievers. In other words, the appeal of the Qur'anic message, if this term may be employed, consists of the full use of rational arguments, implicit assumptions, recourses to the "absolute" absolute, and arguments pressing the acceptance of ultimate realities. This is done so elaborately in the Qur'ān since the people addressed are supposed to possess the necessary rational abilities to be convinced by arguments. Here, reason is not used to formulate abstract doctrines, but is part of a continuous discourse with people who must be convinced. This discourse assumes certain religious *a priori* notions, like Allāh, the Hereafter, Revelation, and so on, the existence of which is not proved in a philosophical, "monological", and abstract way, but which may be accepted once the individual has entered the proposed way of thinking, and this happens finally in the act of "faith". This faith is not held to be something absurd, but rather something reasonable, though leading to paradoxes.

Further investigation shows that an essential part of the discourse concerns the necessity for humankind to recognize the *āyāt*, the "signs" of Allāh. These *āyāt* are demonstrated, on the one hand, in the happenings of nature, the succession of time, and the created nature of the world, including human beings. On the other hand, the language by which the mind is opened to the *āyāt* has a symbolic and even revelationary quality: it is itself built up from *āyāt*, that is to say the Qur'anic verses. Consequently, the "real" things themselves and the "real" language about them are all "signs" referring to Allāh. Thing and name coincide in their reference to God, and a person, by using his or her mind properly, is able to see this reference, to recognize an irresistible logic in it, and to believe.

4. The Study of Reason in Islam and in Other Religions

The connection demonstrated between faith and reason in the Qur'ān explains, first of all, the confidence in rational argumentation that the prophet shows in his discussions with people of the Scriptures and even with pagan unbelievers. The former may have their special revelation, but both they and the polytheists are supposed to have mental capacities enabling them to come to faith. Consequently, discussion is not useless. It brings them to reason and then possibly to faith.

Second, this connection explains why the prophet, in his discourse, does not seem to be able to see what we may call the tension between religious representations and reasoning about them, or between faith and reason in general. Consequently, he is not really able to understand why others can refuse his message.

Third, this connection explains why the Qur'ān proclaims the existence of God, of the Hereafter, and of the Qur'anic revelation itself as being clear proof and evidence. There is nothing miraculous in people's believing these things since both the thing and the name are *āyāt*, which a person by his or her nature is able to perceive.

Fourth, this connection shows the germ of later Muslim theological affirmations—formulated with the help of conceptualizations on Greek models—in the sense that Islam is the reasonable religion and that everything in Islam, including its revelation, is witnessed to by reason.

The interest of the problem seen in a wider perspective is that we have in the Qur'ān, and in the Islamic religion for which it is sacred Scripture, a good example of a coherent "signification system", whose language has had from the beginning a thoroughly religious character. By means of this kind of language, the argumentation that was followed could proclaim itself to be in harmony with self-evident, natural, human reasoning. This assumption has had tremendous consequences for the way in which Muslims have taken cognizance of reality from within the Islamic mental universe inasmuch as it is based upon the Qur'ān and its particular rationality. They held this kind of reasoning to be universally valid.

Scholarly research has not always sufficiently appreciated the inherent rationality of the arguments used in the Qur'ān. This is partly because the terms used in the Qur'ān for thought processes have not yet been analyzed carefully enough. Partly it is simply because Qur'anic statements—and Islamic reasoning in general—are misunderstood if one assumes that there must be a basic conflict between faith and reason. This assumption has been customary in the dominant intellectual traditions of the West and it has been cultivated in particular ways. It leads, however, to serious misunderstandings of religious texts and discourses in other cultures and religions—like Islam—in which "faith" and "reason" do not contradict but complement each other.

The present inquiry is of a preliminary nature; the themes briefly discussed here deserve far more extensive treatment.

Selected Literature

ARKOUN, Mohammed, *Lectures du Coran*, Paris: Maisonneuve et Larose, 1982.

HAQUE, Serajul, "The Holy Quran and Rational Thinking", in *International Islamic Conference (February 1968)*, Vol. I: *English Papers*, ed. by M. A. KHAN, Islamabad: Islamic Research Institute of Pakistan, 1970, pp. 63–7.

IZUTSU, Toshihiko, *God and Man in the Koran: Semantics of the Koranic Weltanschauung* (1964), New York 1980.

NASR, Seyyed Hossein, "Revelation, Intellect and Reason in the Quran", in *International Islamic Conference (February 1968)*, Vol. I: *English Papers*, ed. by M. A. KHAN, Islamabad: Islamic Research Institute of Pakistan, 1970, pp. 59–62 (Repr.: *Journal of the Regional Cultural Institute*, 1:3 [1968], pp. 60–4).

SAIYIDAIN, K. G., "Qurān's Invitation to Think", *Islam and the Modern Age*, 4:2 (1973), pp. 5–27.

WAARDENBURG, Jacques D. J., "Koranisches Religionsgespräch", in *Liber Amicorum: Studies in Honour of Professor Dr. C. J. Bleeker*, Leiden: E. J. Brill, 1969, pp. 208–53.

—, "Un débat coranique contre les polythéistes", in *Ex Orbe Religionum: Studia Geo Widengren*, Pars altera (Studies in the History of Religions 22), Leiden: E. J. Brill, 1972, pp. 143–54.

Section 2

Islam as a Religion

Chapter 3
Islamic Attitudes to Signs[1]

Islam, which even as a term has great symbolic power, is rich in signs that hint at meaningful realities beyond the immediately given. In its various cultural contexts, Islam recognizes symbols that allow people to experience such realities and that represent cores or even structures of meaning. Roughly speaking, if signs in Islam provide an orientation, symbols provide structure, and there are links between them. Both convey religious and other meanings. Qur'anic verses (*āyāt*) can be read both as signs and as symbols.

Before proceeding to further analysis, it is helpful to establish a clear distinction between normative and practiced Islam. Normative Islam develops the truths and norms that are accepted as valid for the whole Muslim community irrespective of place and time. It does this by interpreting and elaborating texts that are considered to have absolute authority. Normative Islam tends to stress the sign character of religious things, that is to say the orientation they give towards objective truths and realities that stand for themselves. This remains so even if the signs may be interpreted differently by different people in different situations.

Practiced Islam can be subdivided into literate and non-literate (usually called "popular") Islam. As lived in different cultures and societies, it is rich in social symbolism that in many respects conveys explicit or implied religious norms and meanings.

Moreover, Islam itself can be seen as a sign and can be symbolically used for many aims and purposes. These can vary from down-to-earth political motivations through morality and legal rulings to higher spiritual intentions. It is precisely when we study Islam in a sense wider than that of a normative system and take into account what it meant and means to different groups of Muslims who practice and interpret it in a large variety of situations and broader contexts, that we can try to grasp how people live with their Islam. The fundamental problem is gaining insight into processes of signification and symbolization where an explicit

---

[1] Revised version of my article in *Encyclopedic Dictionary of Semiotics*, ed. by Thomas A. SEBEOK, Vol. 1, Berlin & New York: Walter de Gruyter, 1987, pp. 392–400.

appeal is made to Islam. Appeals to Islam as a religion are always made from within a given Muslim social and cultural context.

1. The Fundamental Signs: Revelation

According to Muslim understanding, the religious signs *par excellence* are the prophetic *qur'āns* or "recitations" uttered by Muhammad and brought together into what has become known as the Qur'ān. They are supposed to be universally valid. The Arabic term for a verse of the Qur'ān is *āya*, which literally means "sign", and each verse is indeed seen by Muslims as a sign through which divine words are conveyed to humankind and through which people are linked to what theologians call the "Word of God". The Qur'ān itself, significantly, speaks of most *āyāt* as clear in themselves, comprehensible to the faithful when they are attentive during recitation. The ability to understand the signs becomes a means of distinguishing between believers and nonbelievers. Whereas the latter declare them to be false, the believers recognize the *āyāt* to be miracles. In the same way, believers recognize the whole of the "recitation" or *qur'ān* by Muhammad as the Prophet's miracle *par excellence*, revealing truths that otherwise would have remained unknown and that must be considered as of divine origin.

Besides the verses of the Qur'ān themselves, the Qur'ān also mentions other "signs" of divine origin. First, there are the signs of nature that refer back to the Creator. Second, there are the signs of history, in particular the miracles attesting to the veracity of the various prophets and the punishments of nonbelievers that serve as deterrent or warning "signs" for later generations. These three categories of signs—of revelation, nature, and history—are ultimately signs of divine mercy toward creation, which is not only sustained by God's mercy but also equipped with the proper signs and signals as to how it should continue to exist, indicating the rules that provide the order God wants for his creation.

The Qur'ān gives a number of indications about the deity. God is unique in that there is nothing divine outside of him and that He is a unity in himself. This is the essential Oneness or *tawhīd* (literally "holding" God "to be one") of God, which reflects itself in the unity of the creation, including the unity of the human being. When the latter loses sight of this Oneness, it is to his or her own detriment. God reveals His mercy and compassion by sending His signs and by guiding humankind and creation through them.

People's basic response to the signs through which the deity can be recognized must be *islām* (literally "abandoning, surrendering oneself", that is to say, to God). In Arabic, *islām* is a verbal noun (*masdar*), the verbal aspect of which largely dominates in the Qur'ān. However, by the end of Muhammad's activity, the nominal aspect predominates, so that *islām* then becomes the religion (*dīn*), the totality of the life, belief, and value system of the Muslim community and its realization on earth.

Islam is the outward "sign" of conversion to God, implying the rejection of any "divinization" of created beings; as an outward act, it should be followed by or be simultaneous with the inner act of faith (*īmān*). Translated into action, the human response to the given signs should be that of obedience to God's will as contained in the religious laws that the major prophets conveyed to humankind. To give shape to this response, one should join the community of followers of such a prophet. No *a priori* separation should be made between a spiritual or religious and a worldly realm, since the whole of social and individual life should be brought into obedience to God.

This scheme of God-given signs to which one should respond implies that within, besides, or beyond ordinary reality, other realities exist, the supreme one being the deity as the creator of the whole. Once humankind had been created with a certain freedom and corresponding responsibility, God revealed His will through a series of prophets who figure as "transmitters". The various religious communities consisting of the followers of these prophets, consequently, possess not only an ordinary "common sense" knowledge but also a particular "revealed" communal knowledge about the meaning of the fundamental signs. People arrive at right belief and action if they "surrender" themselves to the prophetic message that they received and that was expressed through signs. Fundamentally, it is held that humankind should surrender to the "Signifier", revealing right belief and action through his signs.

2. Signs Recognized Within Normative Islam

The signs falling within this category are characteristic of the Muslim community in particular. They make it possible to distinguish those who are Muslims from the communities of followers of other prophets and from unbelievers. These signs can be divided into primary and secondary ones, the first group deduced directly from the Qur'ān, the second from tradition (*Sunna*).

2.1. Primary Signs

The first and most important "sign" of being a Muslim is the Islamic profession of faith (*shahāda*): "I testify that there is no deity except God and that Muhammad is the prophet of God." Though this text itself does not occur in the Qur'ān, it has been deduced from it. Several doctrines have been derived from this profession of faith, including the unity and

uniqueness of God, Muhammad's prophethood as the last and definitive
one, the primacy of unity over plurality, and the absolute separation
between what is human and what is divine. Islam implies a continuous
testimony of faith, whose highest form is the martyr's testimony to his
faith, the *shahīd*, in particular when he dies in *jihād*.

The *shahāda* is the first of five ritual religious duties that are incumbent upon each Muslim individually, the five *'ibādāt*, considered as
worship. The next two are the *salāt* (ritual prayer, five times a day, the
Friday noon *salāt* to be performed in a prayer hall [mosque] together
with other believers) and the *zakāt* (obligatory contribution to the needy
of the community or to fixed aims of communal interest). The last two
'ibādāt that are obligatory for each Muslim are the *sawm* (abstention,
fasting during the day in the month Ramadān) and the *hajj* (pilgrimage
to Mecca once in one's lifetime in the first ten days of the month Dhū'l-
hijja). In addition to these five individual religious duties, there is the duty
of *jihād* (exertion for the sake of God), which is incumbent upon the
community as a whole. It may take the form of war, but can also take
other forms to promote "the rights of God" (*huqūq Allāh*, e.g., apologetic activity, moral and religious exertion in piety). The *'ibādāt* are the
most important distinctive religious features of each Muslim community.

Other primary signs of Sunnī Islam are the five articles of faith (belief
in God's *tawhīd*, in angels, in revealed scriptures, in the Day of Judgment,
and in divine decree or "predestination"). Important are the main prescriptions (*mu'āmalāt*) for social life, which entail rules of family law
(marriage, divorce, inheritance), prohibitions (theft, adultery, usury, and
the consumption of pork and strong drink), for which particular punishments are ordained, and the so-called forbidden professions (prostitu-
tion, selling alcoholic drinks, etc.) connected with them.

Most of the primary signs of normative Islam are connected with
behavior, in particular ritual action. They constitute the prominent features of the Muslim community.

2.2. Secondary Signs

The secondary signs are not deduced from the Qur'ān directly, but from
the so-called "tradition of the Prophet" (*Sunnat al-nabī*), which became
authoritative later than the Qur'ān and contains reports (*hadīths*) on
particular sayings or actions of Muhammad. The Qur'ān is considered
direct revelation, and the *Sunna* has in fact the status of an indirect
revelation. Certain *hadīths* may be quoted to clarify Qur'anic texts, and
Qur'anic texts can be quoted in support of the secondary signs mentioned
in the *Sunna*. The following secondary signs are to be found all over the
Muslim world: a minimum knowledge of the Qur'ān and the *hadīths*
(prophetical traditions) is required; this demands as a corollary some

knowledge of the Arabic language and in any case the recognition of Arabic as the religious language of Islam.

The prescriptions of normative Islam are considered to be contained in the Islamic religious law or *Sharī'a*. Its validity is recognized at least nominally, though there are many different views about its application. One of the duties of the caliph, as the head of the Islamic nation at least until 1258, was to further the application of the *Sharī'a*. In connection with the patriarchal structure of Muslim societies and the expectations Muslims have of political leadership, Muslim countries concentrate much executive power in the hands of the head of state.

A class distinct from the state authorities (except in present-day Iran) is that of the *'ulamā'*, religious scholars also dealing (as *fuqahā'*) with the interpretation of the *Sharī'a*. They have been responsible for the development of normative Islam in the so-called "sciences of religion" (*'ulūm al-dīn*). Another group of religious leaders is the leaders (*sheykhs*) of the mystical orders (*turuq*). They have considered it their task, first, to care for the religious or other needs of the people, including offering solutions through religious experience. In addition to mosques, further religious institutions to be found all over the Muslim world are religious schools or *madrasas*, devotional centers of mystical orders, and more recently Islamic voluntary associations and Islamic political parties. A typical juridical institution in Islam is that of the *waqf*, a tax-exempt inalienable endowment established for religious purposes. Mention must be made of the Islamic holy places (Mecca, Medina, Jerusalem, and, for the Shī'īs, Karbala and Najaf in Iraq and Mashhad and Qom in Iran). The Islamic calendar started in the year of the *hijra* of Muhammad from Mecca to Medina, 622 A.D., and consists of years with twelve months of twenty-nine or thirty days each. Well-known celebrations are the "Great Feast" of the sacrifice during the *hajj*, and the "Small Feast" at the end of the fast in the month Ramadān.

Four areas in particular have enjoyed a certain sign and symbol value in Islam up to modern times. From the very beginning of Muhammad's prophetic activity, the expectation of the end of time has been part of normative Islam. Eschatological expectations have led to much speculation and in popular Islam and in crisis situations generally these have remained alive until now, when people are sensitive to "the signs of the times".

Particularly in the medieval period, representations of the social order were rich in symbolism. This has also been formally expressed, for instance in the division of the world into a territory under Islamic authority and an area outside it (*dār al-islām* and *dār al-harb*), justice equated with the application of the *Sharī'a*, a clear distinction between the social responsibilities of men and women, and thus the division of society into male and female domains.

There has been a particular symbolization of the order of nature arising from the Qur'ān's attention to the intrinsic harmony and beauty of the creation and the task of the believers—themselves a part of creation—to recognize this beauty and contemplate its Maker. In theory and practice, Islam prescribes that one thinks and lives in harmony with nature, not violating its order.

In spiritually oriented circles, people are conscious of the domain of the inner reality as being a part of creation in addition to the reality outside. Here, too, there is the notion of an intrinsic inner order symbolized by the idea of a person's movement toward God being his or her "deeper" history, for which the mystics have developed an intricate pedagogy. In this way everything—including perceptions of the external world—could acquire dimensions of infinity.

These four areas—eschatology, the social order, the order of nature, and a person's inner reality—have given rise in turn to many forms of cultural expression with typical "Islamic" connotations. Behind them lies the consciousness of a God-given harmony, the absence of any notion of a religious fall, the absence of the feeling of an absolute separation between the natural and the supernatural, and an awareness of the existence of spiritual realities, emanating from God, which take earthly shape. God and His creation, God and humankind remain separate realities, however.

For normative Islam, the sign predominates over the symbol, the sign referring to realities that exist in themselves and that humankind should recognize, even if people cannot directly participate in them. The accent put on "signs" and analogical relationships between the signifying and the signified is connected with the strict separation maintained in normative Islam between the human and the divine. References to the divine order of things can only be made by analogy to realities here on earth; here again the notion of "signs" is important, since it guarantees the objective, separate reality of what is beyond earthly things. But although the signs are supposed to be clear in themselves, referring as they do to an order of creation and a sustaining activity of the Creator, not everyone understands them.

3. Signs and Symbols in Practiced, Living Islam (Popular Islam)

Whereas in Sunnī Islam, which comprises more than 90% of all Muslims, dramatic representation, certainly of religious subjects, is unknown, Shī'ī Islam not only developed mourning rites to commemorate the killing of Muhammad's grandson Husayn near Karbala in 680 A.D. but also the ta'ziyeh, in which the tragic events of Karbala are dramatically reenacted. Mourning rites and ta'ziyeh have a highly symbolic character, expressing an expiation of guilt among the followers of ʿAlī and Husayn and strengthening the will of Shīʿī Muslims to fight injustice for the sake of religion. This symbolic action found a particular application during the demonstrations that took place in Iran at the end of 1978 during the first ten days of the month Muharram, the religious mourning period. Young men clad in white shrouds affronted the regular army in the streets of Teheran, ready to die for the sake of religion. In other respects too, living Shīʿī Islam, whether literate or not, is rich in religious symbolism with sociopolitical overtones.

In Sunnī Islam too, distinctive forms of religious symbolism took shape on a popular level, often linked to local traditions about miracles or about holy men who bestow blessings (*baraka*). As distinct from normative Islam, where the separation between the human and the divine is stressed, in popular Islam the miraculous, the "realities beyond" have come within human reach, largely through the mediation of holy men, often Sūfī *sheykhs*. The latter not only developed their own experience and insight "on the way to God", but also guided that of their more or less initiated followers. Often they even extended their authority to cover what can be called worldly affairs of social and political action. As religious leaders on a popular level, they have sometimes become rivals of the educated religious scholars (*ʿulamāʾ*), who possess authority in matters relating to normative Islam and are more distant from the common people.

Sūfī guidance and practices of popular Islam are largely a response to problems that people have in everyday life. Here it is not signs but symbols, not knowledge but participatory experience that play a major part. As a consequence, a kind of "degradation" of religious signs may take place if, for instance, Qurʾanic verses are used as symbols supposed to convey immediate *baraka* (blessing) or to give a ready solution to problems. A further step down is to reduce the symbol to an effective tool in itself, accompanied by practices that are usually described as "magical".

Behind mystical experience, symbolic participation, and "magical" activities in Islam as it is practiced and lived lies the belief in miracles as an ever-present possibility beyond the ordinary experience of life and the awareness of a certain arbitrariness in the normal order of things. In all Muslim regions there are particular celebrations of the events of nature and the happenings of life. Local religious festivities have a significance besides the "official" feasts of normative Islam. Noteworthy in this connection is the development of the feast of the nativity of Muhammad (*mawlīd*), now celebrated all over the Muslim world without being canonical. All such celebrations and festivities are rich in symbolism connected both with local cultural traditions and particular "signs" of normative Islam.

In brief, in addition to the numerous signs recognized and upheld in or by normative Islam, Muslim societies and cultures have developed and cultivated a great variety of local religious symbolisms and symbols. They arose in part out of the elaboration of particular elements of normative Islam and in part out of local cultural traditions and local history, with its holy men, celebrations, and symbolic actions to which some kind of efficacy is attributed. A characteristic feature in all these cases of symbolism in practiced living Islam is that the "realities beyond", to which the signs of normative Islam refer, have here been more or less "subjectivized" with a view to particular problems and needs for which people seek a solution. As distinct from normative Islam, this living Islam gives priority to symbols over signs. Signs can be made into symbols and symbols can be treated as tools efficient in themselves. As a rule, in living Islam, as in living religion generally, extraordinary things are first perceived as signs of a "beyond" that is somehow capable of intruding into the reality of ordinary life. They may then be viewed and treated as a means to participate in this "beyond". In living Islam and popular religion generally, no clear separation can be made between religious and other aspects of these significations and symbolizations. Practical, worldly aspects are implied together with the religious ones. In the cultural traditions that prevail in the Muslim world, most social and political symbolisms have a religious connotation that is not easy to grasp for the "rationalized" children of modernity.

4. The Symbolic Use of Islamic Elements and of Islam Itself

The fundamental signs of normative Islam contained in the Qur'ān and supplemented by the *Sunna* are almost unlimited. They constitute a reservoir of sometimes self-contradicting texts that are at the disposal of the Muslim community. It is the task of the religious scholars (*'ulamā'*) chiefly to use reason to read the right meanings from these signs. The work of these scholars, which constitutes the body of the Islamic religious sciences, has been recorded in a number of texts that have become religiously significant themselves. It contains more or less authoritative traditions of exegesis and hermeneutics of the fundamental signs and symbols of Islam. Given the richness of the material, it stands to reason that, even if there are generally accepted criteria of establishing the relative weight of the texts, different conclusions can still be reached through different "readings" of a particular text. From the very beginning of Islam, certain texts have always been taken to support specific religious, juridical, political, or other options of the interpreters, who allowed themselves to give more or less scope for the use of reason in their work.

A clue to the symbolic use of Islamic elements and of Islam as such is found in the fact that for the Muslim community "Islam" stands for all that is good. Again, a great number of different opinions can legitimately be held as long as authoritative texts, as "signs", can be adduced in support of them. A scholar, Muslim or otherwise, may seek a solution to a particular problem through a careful unprejudiced study of the available texts, without knowing the answer in advance. In social practice, however, the well-being of the community at large or the interests of those who are in power will largely determine the solution to be reached. For this, the supporting authoritative texts must be brought together. As soon as the solution can be proved to be "Islamic", it is legitimized.

This mechanism can be illustrated by the way in which the adjective *Islamic* has been used in different periods and contexts. We have to seek the motivations and intentions that have determined the use of the word. Throughout history, very different groups, schools, and ideologies within the Muslim community have legitimized themselves by calling themselves "Islamic" while providing a particular interpretation or "reading" of Islam. From the first century of Islam on, the word *Islamic* could be "stamped" on foreign elements to allow them to be assimilated within the Muslim community, e.g., through a fictitious *hadīth*. In the propagation of Islam, *Islamic* has stood for the true norms and ideals as opposed to the lesser ways of life of non-Muslims; and in the Ottoman-Persian wars, the term could be used as a battle cry for the advancement of the Sultan's or the Shah's cause. In the nineteenth century, the word *Islamic* began to imply the intention of uniting Muslims under the banner of Islam and of defending Muslim society and culture against Western aggression and domination. This stress on a distinct Islamic quality of Muslim societies and cultures has led, a hundred years later, to the emergence of Islamic ideologies intent on revitalizing Muslim societies after a period of moral and ideological suffocation combined with economic and political stagnation. In these and many other cases, the terms "Islam" and "Islamic" have been used symbolically, supported by the "signs" of textual evidence, to express particular intentions and mobilize large portions of the Muslim people.

A closer analysis of Muslim societies will probably bring to light that within each society a conflict has been waged over the use of the word *Islam* and the kind of Muslim community desired. This happened for a variety of reasons: to advance personal or group interests, to arrive at a certain equilibrium of opposing interests, to promote a certain interiorization and spiritualization, to legitimate the stability needed for development and progress, or, on the contrary, to bring about far-reaching changes through a puritanical reformism or revolution—all legitimized by the words *Islam* or *Islamic*. Such a symbolic use of *Islam* can have especially unpredictable and far-reaching effects in societies with local traditions that are more or less strongly linked to Islam, where many aspects of social and cultural life have a symbolic value, where social and political changes are accompanied by strong ideological expressions, and where—last but not least—Islam is unquestioningly held to be the highest norm and value to which one can appeal.

The ideological use to which Islam has often been put, in particular at the present time, is one form of the symbolic use of Islamic elements and of Islam itself. The ideologized form is most suited to political aims and purposes, so that there is a clear correlation between the ideologization and the politicization of Islam at the present time. But even admitting that Islam, through the strongly social nature of its signs, is particularly suited to political use, we should keep in mind that such a political use is only one aspect of the much wider symbolic use that can be made of the sign character of Islamic elements and Islam itself.

5. Signification and Symbolization in Islam

At the beginning of this chapter I stressed the preponderant place occupied by "signs" in Muhammad's prophetic activity, both in the words proclaimed and in the actions prescribed. The Qur'ān and *Sunna*, indeed, do not give descriptions, judgments, and prescriptions merely for their own sake, but always with a reference to transcendent realities. This endows them with a more or less clear character as signs pointing to these realities. We have seen that these signs are interpreted, "read", and elaborated in normative Islam, but that they may also find particular applications in the many symbols that can be found in practiced and living Islam. In popular Islam they may even be degraded to the status of mere objects of manipulation. Attention has also been drawn to the symbolic use that can be made of elements of Islam and of Islam itself, with different motivations, aims, and intentions. I argued that there is a correlation between the ideological and the political use of Islam, especially visible at the present time. On the whole, mysticism tends to interpret the signs as symbols for specific states of the soul and the mind. Philosophical theology (*kalām*) tends to maintain the sign character proper but also to use those signs that support particular solutions for theological problems. And just as practical manipulation tends to reify signs in order to apply them as an immediate solution to given problems of life, an ideologization of the signs transforms them into ideas suitable for political action.

These many "readings" and uses made of Islam and its elements point to the immense sign and symbol quality of Islam itself, representing to its adherents as it does both the true religion and the right social order. This is a source of confusion especially for Western observers, but it emphasizes the manifold uses to which Islam can be put. If Islam is used without regard for its transcendent connotations, it may prove an efficient tool in the short run to bring about particular forms of human action. In the long run, however, its intrinsic sign power may work in favor of contrary action; and contrary ideologizations of Islam, too, can be justified by textual support.

The mutual communication and understanding between Muslims in different parts of the world and their sense of the continuity of Islam throughout history may derive in the end from a common faith, but this is hardly accessible to scholarly study. What can be observed and studied, however, is the occurrence of communication and understanding within a social fabric in which signs and symbols, through shared texts and rites, play an important role. They constitute points of contact and of mutual recognition and also elements of certain basic paradigms according to which reality is read and judged on a fundamental level. In social practice, however, there are nearly unlimited variations possible on the levels of cognition, feeling, and intuition.

It is precisely in the sense of the common acceptance of fundamental signs that one can speak of an Islamic commonwealth and one Muslim community transcending space and time. In the Islamic faith, the problems of life and their possible solution are perceived in terms of these signs. Although the signs are read in different ways by different Muslim groups in different situations and with different intentions and interests, the continuity and the communality of Islam itself is given with the signs, which do not change.

Although Islamic studies have achieved good results until now in the study of factual realities in both the past and the present of Islam, its signification and symbolic aspects have received less attention. An exception should be made, on the one hand, for the study of religious symbolism in Islamic mystical literature, and, on the other hand, for the study of symbolisms in anthropological fieldwork. The study of the relationship between the changing symbolic readings of particular Islamic texts or of particular Muslim activities, on the one hand, and, on the other hand, the firm fundamental "signs" of Islam with which such symbols are connected has hardly been undertaken. Apparently, the "signs" of Islam constitute a common "Islamic universe" for the believers.

I plead for a further study of Islam as a universal and relatively open sign system that provides people with the possibility of meaningful orientation and action whatever the circumstances may be. Such an approach is able to throw new light on the tremendous forces that can be mobilized by an appeal to Islam, compared to other major religions and ideologies at present and in the foreseeable future. The study of Islam as an open sign, symbol, and signification system demands, however, a careful study of the signs and symbols as they are actually read and applied in social and personal life.

Selected Literature

SCHIMMEL, Annemarie, *Deciphering the Signs of God: A Phenomenological Approach to Islam*, Edinburgh: Edinburgh University Press, and Albany, N. Y.: SUNY Press, 1994.

WAARDENBURG, Jacques D. J., "Islam Studied as a Symbol and Signification System", *Humaniora Islamica*, 2 (1974), pp. 267–85.

—, "The Language of Religion, and the Study of Religions as Sign Systems", in *Science of Religion: Studies in Methodology*, ed. by Lauri HONKO (Religion and Reason 13), The Hague, etc.: Mouton, 1979, pp. 441–57 and 482–3.

—, "Islamforschung aus religionswissenschaftlicher Sicht", in *Ausgewählte Vorträge, XXI. Deutscher Orientalistentag (Berlin, March 1980)*, ed. by Fritz STEPPAT, Wiesbaden: Franz Steiner, 1982, pp. 197–211 (for the English summary text see below chapter 4 on "Islam Studied in the Perspective of Science of Religion").

Chapter 4

Islam Studied in the Perspective of Science of Religion[1]

1. A Perspective of the Science of Religion

Our starting point is that Islam, both as a religious tradition and as a religious cultural framework of various Muslim communities and socie-ties, is always linked to groups and persons who identify themselves as Muslims, refer to Islam, and have practices that they consider "Islamic". Neither in history nor in social reality is there an Islam that exists in itself. Of course one can abstract and conceive Islam as the sum of meanings and significations for which people appeal to Islam. Such significations can be very diverse, quite concrete or very abstract, more ideologically oriented or more religious, and so on.

Our second starting point is that a certain fact only has a similar religious meaning for given groups or persons when these groups or persons belong to the same religious community or religious culture. Even then, the content of the "subject's" meaning of such a religious fact will differ for the groups or the individuals concerned. In other words, in the broad Islamic community (*umma*) the same data may be recognized as having religious meaning (as normative Islam prescribes it), but in practice different Muslim groups as well as individuals will give to these data different interpretations, often leading to different practices. In these interpretations, not only the intentions and convictions of the people concerned play an important role, but also their own interest and of course the concrete situations and contexts.

One consequence of these two starting points is that, on the level of empirical research, we should avoid premature generalizations and be attentive to the general concepts we are accustomed to use. This is particularly true for the use of terms that received their meaning in the course of the history of Western culture. Examples are concepts such as "religion" or "worldview", "ideology" or "faith". The precise study of

---

[1]   English summary translation of my "Islamforschung aus religionswissenschaftlicher Sicht". The notes of the German text have been omitted here.

the properly religious aspects of Islam starts only when we focus on those data that have a religious meaning or significance not in our view but in the view of a number of Muslims. Such study involves special attention to those interpretations that various Muslim groups or persons gave or give to these data. It comes to an end when one has succeeded not only in understanding, but also in explaining these various interpretations.

How difficult such study is becomes clear in the example of the Qur'ān, which is the only really "absolute" religious phenomenon for all Muslims, since they accept that it has a divine origin. The different ways in which the Qur'ān has been interpreted, applied, and used in the Muslim community are to be the subject of serious research. One may add on a theoretical level that Islamic studies—simply for the structural reason that most Western scholars of Islam are not Muslims themselves— tend to do insufficient justice to the meaning dimension of the Qur'ān as it is experienced by faithful Muslims. I contend that scholarship should recognize the existence—for Muslims—of the "sign" character not only of individual verses (āyāt) of the Qur'ān, but also of the Qur'ān as a whole.[2] A next step would be to try to understand the ways in which various Muslim groups and persons have read and still read these "signs".

For an attentive theoretical observer of a religion like Islam, one thing is evident. As a religion, Islam functions as a certain kind of signification system. On a first level, we find the Qur'anic āyāt and generally known hadīths. On a second level, we find certain religious duties as well as certain theological doctrines. Certain phenomena of nature and certain historical events that have a religious meaning constitute a third level of signs. On top of this, we find further levels of signs that refer to representations, ideas, and practices that existed or exist in various religious Muslim groupings and in various local Muslim communities.

What gives Islam its effective power as a religion seems to be that what outsiders take as simple facts can be viewed and perhaps also experienced by Muslims in many different ways as religious signs. The study of Islam as a religion should therefore also focus on the various ways in which these signs are "read" and on the effects that these various "readings" had and still can have in the life of Muslim groups and communities. Important changes in political, economic, and social conditions have led to new ways of reading these religious signs and to new interpretations of Islam.

In view of these approaches to readings of the Qur'ān, I suggest that Islamic religious phenomena, in terms of their meaning and significance for Muslims, can be most adequately considered a "signification system" or a "network of signs". The interpretations and ways of reading these

---

[2]   Cf. above Chapter 3 on "Islamic Attitudes to Signs".

"signs", including Qur'anic *āyāt*, should be the subject of further research. This corresponds with the reference the Qur'ān makes to "God-
given" signs not only in the Qur'ān itself, but also in life, nature, and
history—which as such are to be seen precisely as "God's signs".

Islam presupposes that these signs are indeed given by God but also
that humankind should draw lessons from them and act accordingly. In
the perspective of the science of religion, it is important to study the ways
in which this understanding has taken place and what conclusions have
been drawn in practical action. I would like to draw at least some
guidelines for the proposed study of Islam as a signification system or a
network of signs. Such a study should of course prove its value through
concrete research results obtained through the proposed approach.

2. Islam as the Interpretation and Application of "Signs"

I want to consider Islam as a religion. Of course, it is not simply a religion
like the others, and in Islam we find a particular conceptualization of
what religion is and should be. There are valid arguments for approaching Islam phenomenologically as a signification system, a network of
signs, or, better, as a network of data to which Muslims attribute a sign
character. This, I contend, will be the starting point of studying Islam's
religious aspects.

First, in this way we avoid the trap of constructing an "Islam made in the
West", that is to say, an interpretation of Islamic materials imposing a
scheme of concepts developed in the West and fundamentally foreign to
Islamic concepts. I plead that we should understand Islamic phenomena
as they are understood in the Muslim world.

Second, this point of departure leads to an approach that runs parallel
to a Muslim interest and claim to interpret the world, humankind, and
society by means of signs given in the Qur'ān and elsewhere. This happens not only in the theory of the Islamic religious sciences (*'ulūm al-dīn*)
but also in Muslim social life, political action, and one's way of life
generally. Such an interpretation of reality and of human life can also be
taken to find or to justify a solution for concrete problems.

Third, the study of the different ways in which Muslims in the course
of time have read certain Qur'anic texts and other "signs" in various
contexts and situations allows us to ask for certain fundamental orientations toward life and the world that have been valid in the Muslim
community since its very beginnings. We can study similar fundamental
orientations that have been valid in the Jewish and the Christian community. In Islam, rules of behavior based on such orientations have been
elaborated into a religious law (*Sharī'a*) in the discipline of jurisprudence
(*fiqh*). I submit that the religious meaning of the prescripts of the *Sharī'a*

is to be found in their character as "signs" concerning the way in which humanity and society should be but are not yet at present.

But in addition to normative *Sharī'a* and normative Islam in general, there are also other orientations, rules, and social structures in Muslim societies, with "signs" belonging to them.

The rise of new Islamic ideologies in the nineteenth and twentieth centuries and their impact in critical and sometimes revolutionary times have revealed an important point. With the help of certain basic "signs" very disparate facts can yet be seen as constituting—symbolically—a significant coherence. There is evidence that the use of particular quotations from the Qur'ān and *hadīths* can serve to place certain experiences of reality in a meaningful overall structure or to move people to a particular way of life and behavior. As far as I know, hardly anyone has studied in depth such ways of giving meaning and significance. Research has shown that a tension exists between discourse and reality and between sign and fact. But this barely touches upon the problem. The true question is rather what happens when words are used to go beyond given realities and when the signs become more powerful than the given factual realities. The notion of "sign" is fundamental to an understanding of Muslim culture and society and probably to an understanding of other societies and cultures as well.

The key to solve the problem why proper thought and behavior in Muslim societies is seen in terms of certain symbolic connections and why the connections Muslims consider meaningful differ from those in other societies, seems to lie in this orientation toward an Islamic signification system. This holds true even if one takes into account the many differences among various Muslim societies with subsidiary social rules and practices. This becomes especially evident when different signs of orientation bind together in "knots of meaning" that not only reveal certain connections in the given reality but that also constitute an autonomous paradigm for action or thought.

I am thinking, for instance, of the function of Muhammad's biography, which offers a model or example of Muslim life, and of the successive political ways of acting in the Iranian manifestations of December 1978, according to the Muharram celebration. A call to Islam, for instance in protest movements against Western influence, should be understood not only as a way of legitimizing a particular political activity or action, but rather in the first place as symbolizing one's own identity, which one wants to give a finally religious foundation. Many data in Muslim history and social life have been studied as facts already. The task is now to see in which ways such data have been interpreted socially by various groups of Muslims, how they are viewed within broader, non-factual connections, and in what way certain meaning structures pervade the life of the individual and the group in given situations, not only in imagining and thinking but also in behaving and acting. We may attribute such structures perhaps to pure fantasy, but they exist and they have to be studied.

There is one final argument for our suggestion that, to understand religious meanings for which Muslims are sensitive, we should study Islam in terms of a signification system or a network of signs: It allows us to arrive at a better understanding of the way in which individual Muslims or Muslim groups communicate with each other. The system of signs that provide orientation is like a language through which people can come into contact and communication with each other. Apart from all other forms of communication, they have these signs—texts, ritual gestures, references to Islam—in common and are open to their potential significances.

3. Islam in the Perspective of Science of Religion

Let me summarize the main lines of this rather simple approach to certain concrete research data. Analogous to the way in which, in anthropology, religions within a concrete cultural context have been described as "symbol systems", Islam, as a widespread religion that comprises numerous cultures, can best be described as a signification system, a network of signs. The many local religious symbol systems of concrete Muslim cultures and societies can be subsumed under this network.

In normative Islam, the Qur'anic *āyāt* (verses) are the only signs that are immediately given in the true sense of the word. But also the *Sunna* (Tradition), the practice of *'ibādāt* (worship) and the fundamental rules of the *Sharī'a* are valid as signs, just as nature and history contain signs to which the Qur'ān draws attention. In daily Muslim life, there are moreover a great number of "signs" in various life situations.

In the course of the history of Muslim communities, many forms of religious experience and spirituality, worldviews and ideologies, modes of social behavior and common ideals developed that in one way or another appealed to Islam and that referred to certain "signs" in the Qur'ān, the *hadīths* or elsewhere. In particular, the notion of a divine law, the idea of a just social order, and the longing for a true community of the faithful have had practical consequences up to the present time for Muslim social and political behavior.

Religious data, then, are to be studied first of all in their concrete historical and social contexts. In a second step, we should ask what these data meant or mean for the people concerned, or rather for different groups of people, including possible religious meanings. It will become clear that such religious meanings arise when these data are viewed and interpreted as "signs". The readings of these signs, the way in which they are interpreted, and the consequences that are drawn from them for human behavior and action deserve special attention in this research approach.

This more or less discrete view of Islam as a network of signs, continuously constructed and interpreted, tries to avoid any "imperialistic" violation from outside that could be attributed to a hegemonic West. It seeks those meanings and significances that have been valid for Muslims, according to their own testimony. This approach may make it possible to view quite a few problems of Islamic studies in a new light. This seems to be the case especially with questions, meanings, and significations that the Muslims concerned consider to be religious.

4. The Application of this Approach in Islamic Studies

I conclude by mentioning some advantages of this approach and, in particular, how it enables us to capture the "religious" aspects of Islamic data and Islam itself in given contexts.

Our approach presupposes philological and literary, historical or anthropological work, both factual research and studying facts in the light of a problem, hypothesis or theory, as is especially current in the social sciences. In all these studies, at a certain point the question arises of the meaning and significance that the data had or have for those who were immediately concerned with them, either as groups or as individuals. This holds particularly true for those data with a "religious" meaning or significance, taking "religious", not according to Western definitions but according to Islamic understandings.

Based on factual research problems of the disciplines mentioned, the question of the "subject's meanings" of given facts is legitimate in scholarly research. I came across this question particularly in the case of Islam—and also of Judaism—especially in contact with adherents, where I tried to grasp what a particular person meant, how he or she interpreted particular data in his or her discourse and even what a particular relevant fact, text, or behavior implicitly meant to him or her. The question of a "subject's meaning" arose in connection with problems of understanding and communication especially in contemporary contexts.

The theory that Islam functions in Muslim societies and communities as a kind of signification system with whose help Muslims take certain given data of life not only as facts but also as "signs"—whose meaning is to be elucidated with the help of Qur'anic passages or *hadīth* texts— throws new light on the problem of a subject's meaning. On the one hand, these texts themselves are "signs" that have to be decoded, understood, and assimilated by the faithful. On the other hand, certain data of human life, events of past or contemporary history, and rules given by the order of nature have a "sign" character, whose meaning can be deciphered with the help of the "signs" given by Islam, which ultimately go back to a metaphysical foundation, a revelation that cannot be questioned. This theory opens a new field of research in Islamic studies: the ways in which groups of Muslims, when they appeal to Islam, derive meaning from elements of Islam to recognize meaning in certain data of life or to assign meaning and significance to such data. Considering Islam as a signification system gives access to what happens when Muslims appeal to Islam. The subject of research is then the various ways in which and means by which Muslims, individually or as a group in a particular situation and context, appealed to Islam and "read" specific religious texts to obtain meaning, that is to say to see connections or to solve given problems. In principle, the theory enables us to reconstruct the hermeneutics with which individual Muslims interpreted or interpret their Islam and lived or live with it.

A valuable advantage of this approach for Islamic studies is that it does justice to the unity of Islamic civilization and the Muslim commonwealth. Our ever-increasing specialization of disciplines and of themes within the disciplines and our steady recognition of the nearly infinite differentiation of the societies and cultures in which Muslims live tend to make us lose sight of the "unity" of these societies and cultures, as predicated by the Islam with which Muslims identify. It is precisely Muslims who assume and from time to time proclaim such a unity among themselves. The notion of Islam as a common signification system maintains such a view of unity, but allows for nearly endless kinds of differentiation in terms of individual or group interpretations and practices of the common signification system.

Precisely by keeping an eye open to specific common "signs" of Muslim societies on a religious level, the possibility is given to compare different interpretations or "readings" as well as practices of Islam in different or similar times and places.

Last but not least, we can now better understand the ways people from the various Muslim regions feel they belong to the same community and somehow in communication with each other. The signs of Islam may be read and interpreted differently in different situations, but all regard the Qur'anic passages as meaningful signs. This is constitutive for Muslim communal awareness and implies a distinction between Muslims and non-Muslims.

The approach I have sketched here originates in the science of religion and in particular in those kinds of research that address problems of meaning and significance. However, research on Islam as a signification system or as a network of signs does not necessarily limit itself to specifically religious elements. Religious, ethical, socio-cultural, esthetic, and other meanings are always linked to each other, and these links are also a subject for inquiry. Moreover, in ordinary life, most things have no specifically religious meaning. In Islamic studies, however, we should be attentive to any appeal that Muslims make to Islam and see what it means to them.

Part of our task as I see it is to investigate the ways in which certain structures of significance or connections of meaning are superimposed on factual realities, so that reality itself becomes meaningful. The impulse to this approach derives from the science of religion, specifically its phenomenological variety. This approach, however, can also be applied in research on aspects of Muslim life that have hardly anything to do with religion. It turns out to be extremely useful in the study of situations that raise the question of the significance certain data have for given individual or groups of Muslims.

It appears that this approach can be applied not only to documents from the past, but also to situations at the present time. The various disciplines and their methods as thus far applied in Islamic studies, however, hardly provide instruments to identify structures of meaning and significance and certainly not in view of the religious aspects of Islam according to Muslim understanding. Current methods do not allow us to identify meaning structures where religious and other meanings are intimately connected. In fact, there is much confusion about the role of the religious aspects of Islam in various movements in Muslim societies, in existing tensions for instance in the Middle East, in relationships between Muslims and non-Muslims, and among Muslims now living in Western Europe or North America.

Rather than first defining what Islam is or should be as a religion and then investigating how it works and what impact it has, we prefer another start. In our scholarly disciplines, we should start studying concrete practices and ways of behaving, representations, concepts, and ideals held by given Muslim groups or individuals. Then we should pose the question what these matters mean and signify to the people concerned. Even if there is nothing religious in them, the result is still important; we are not necessarily looking for "religion".

However, if certain data evidently have a religious significance for the people concerned, we should be attentive. Careful research should then be able to identify particular elements of Islam that function as "signs" for the people concerned, elements that represent meanings and give significance to life. Further research should be able to reconstruct coherent meaning structures that are alive for these people and that they superimpose on reality.

It may turn out that the actual behavior of Muslims is more religious and that Islam as a religion reveals itself as more vital for Muslims than is commonly assumed in the West, including in Western scholarly research. Muslims themselves may underplay religion in their contact with Westerners, including Western scholars.

Religion, it seems to me, is never something definitely given, a "thing"—although it can easily be reified. From a scholarly point of view, we deal less with religions as given entities, however defined, than with different ways in which given data, situations, or problems are viewed and experienced as religiously significant. By "religiously" we mean: in terms of notions of religion as current in the culture or society concerned. In Islam at least, it seems that data are religiously significant for people when they experience them as signs or symbols referring to Islam. They connect them then with religious elements of Islam like Qur'anic passages, *hadīths*, or rituals that have a "sign" character themselves. People then try to appropriate such signs.

Selected Literature

Approaches to Islam in Religious Studies, ed. by Richard C. MARTIN, Tucson, Ariz.: University of Arizona Press, 1985.

BÜRGEL, Johann C., *Allmacht und Mächtigkeit: Religion und Welt im Islam*, Munich: Beck, 1991.

MARTIN, Richard C., *Islamic Studies: A History of Religions Approach*, Upper Saddle River, N. J.: Prentice Hall, 1982, 1996^2.

SCHIMMEL, Annemarie, *Deciphering the Signs of God: A Phenomenological Approach to Islam*, Edinburgh: Edinburgh University Press, and Albany, N. Y.: SUNY Press, 1994.

SCHÖLLER, Marco, *Methode und Wahrheit in der Islamwissenschaft: Prolegomena*, Wiesbaden: Harrassowitz, 2000.

WAARDENBURG, Jacques D. J., "Assumptions and Presuppositions in Islamic Studies", *Rocznik Orientalistyczny*, 43 (1984), pp. 161–70.

—, "Islamforschung aus religionswissenschaftlicher Sicht", in *Ausgewählte Vorträge, XXI. Deutscher Orientalistentag (Berlin, March 1980)*, ed. by Fritz STEPPAT, Wiesbaden: Franz Steiner, 1982, pp. 197–211.

—, "Islamic Studies and the History of Religions: An Evaluation", in *Mapping Islamic Studies: Genealogy, Continuity and Change*, ed. by Azim NANJI (Religion and Reason 38), Berlin and New York: Mouton de Gruyter, 1997, pp. 181–219.

Section 3

Structures and Interpretations of Islam

Chapter 5
Official, Popular, and Normative Religion in Islam[1]

1. A Medieval Muslim View

In his *Kitāb iqtiḍā' aṣ-ṣirāṭ al-mustaqīm mukhālafat aṣḥāb al-jaḥīm* (Book of the Necessity of the Straight Path Against the People of Hell)[2], Ibn Taymīya (1263–1328 C.E.) combats what may be called "popular religion" among Muslims in his time. He treats such popular religion as a kind of *ʿīd* (festival) in the widest sense of the word, at a time, in a place or with a ritual that cannot be considered lawful according to the *Sharīʿa* (religious law). These religious celebrations consequently have no divine sanction and in his view ought to be forbidden and suppressed. Ibn Taymīya is thinking here of *mawlīd al-nabī* (the birthday of Muhammad, a feast unknown in early Islam) and of the participation by Muslims in certain parts of Christian festivities or in festivals celebrating the forces of nature (for instance in springtime with symbols of creativity, rebirth, and new life) as they exist in countries south and east of the Mediterranean. But he is also thinking of saint veneration and the veneration of the dead, where human beings take another human being as a possible intercessor with God and even as a potential granter of wishes. All these forms of popular religion are *bidʿa* (innovation) introduced outside and beyond what true Islam prescribes and allows.

Ibn Taymīya was not the first jurist-theologian who objected to popular religion in Islam, but he was one of the first who wanted to prove methodically that such forms of popular religion are incompatible with the Qur'ān and the *Sunna* (religious tradition of early Islam based on the words and deeds of the Prophet) and contrary to the explicit formulations of the *Sharīʿa* and of *kalām* (theological thinking). The jurists before him and the state authorities had never given official recognition to such

---

[1] This contribution is a revised version of a paper "Official and Popular Religion as a Problem in Islamic Studies", in *Official and Popular Religion: Analysis of a Theme for Religious Studies*, ed. by Pieter Hendrik VRIJHOF and Jacques D. J. WAARDENBURG (Religion and Society 19), The Hague: Mouton Publishers, 1979, pp. 340–86.
   Islam as a religion is here taken in the broadest sense as the religion of people who define themselves as Muslims.

[2] MEMON, *Ibn Taimīya* (see selected literature, section 1.).

manifestations of popular religion, but they had been quite lenient in practice and had looked upon their occurrence with indulgence. However, a puritanical mind like Ibn Taymīya's, with a deep belief in Islam as the religion of *tawhīd* (testifying to the perfect Unity of God), had the ability to draw out the implications of this with the utmost clarity. He judged definitively that such popular religious practices promote idolatry, that they are conductive to *shirk* (associationism, or polytheism in the widest sense of the word), and that they are thus by their very nature antithetical to religious truth as proclaimed in Islam. Popular religion should be suppressed by the state authorities, and Ibn Taymīya demanded that they do so.[3]

Like others before him, Ibn Taymīya explains the occurrence of such popular religion as borrowings from other religions, in particular from paganism as it existed before Islam in Arabia and elsewhere, and from Eastern Christianity with its rituals, feasts, and veneration of saints. He does not deny the existence of the forces that are venerated or feared but he defends the supreme reality of God's might and power which alone deserves to be venerated and served. He is particularly vehement in his attacks on ideas and practices that had developed in Islam in connection with the belief in the intercession of one human being for another. Such a belief shifts a person's faith from the Creator to a creature and tends to do away with the essential disparity between the Creator and the creature. In the first case, it leads generally to *shirk* and in Sūfī mysticism to the doctrine of *walāya* (sainthood, saintship), and in the second case to the Sūfī doctrine of *ittihād* (mystical union of humans with God).[4]

It is important to note that the jurist-theologian Ibn Taymīya thought what he was doing in defending true Islam against human accretions was *mutatis mutandis* the same as what Muhammad had done in defending true *tawhīd* against human distortions and deformations. Just as Ibn Taymīya saw practices of religious festivals and intercession in popular religion as deformations of true *tawhīd*, Muhammad had seen a number of beliefs and practices of Judaism and Christianity as deformations of true *tawhīd*. From a Muslim point of view, Judaism and Christianity, like most religions other than Islam, can be considered "popular" deformations of the one true religion. There is something sacred about the unity and uniqueness of God that should be defended against such human deformations, which in their essence go back to *shirk* and *ittihād*. The problem of normative and popular religion has been formulated in the

---

[3]   This in fact was done by the Wahhābīs, who adhered like Ibn Taymīya to the strict Hanbalī *madhhab* (juridical school). In a way, they applied a certain number of Ibn Taymīya's ideas. See below Chapter 11 on "The Wahhābīs in Eighteenth and Nineteenth Century Arabia".

[4]   On Ibn Taymīya's attitude to speculative and more popular Sūfism, see MEMON, *op. cit.*, pp. 26–46 and 46–85 respectively.

Muslim community in its own terms as a fundamental one, of a juridical and theological nature. The normative and official religion is that of true *tawḥīd*, and although Islam has no "official" organization of its own, throughout Islamic history this *tawḥīd* has been upheld by Muslim religious scholars in opposition to the popular religion with forms of *shirk*. However, what can be said about popular religion in Islam from a scholarly point of view is another question.

2. Popular Religion in Islam

2.1. Popular Forms

When Europeans visited Muslim countries up to the early twentieth century and in some cases up to World War Two, they often reported about Islam and described it as a number of customs and practices, beliefs and loyalties that would now be called "popular Islam". A basic human interest in what is visibly different from one's own society and in the exotic generally, as well as other interests, may have drawn the attention of the visitors especially toward popular forms of Islam[5], but it is fair to say that the latter must have been much more abundant at that time than today. One may speak on the whole of a certain decline of popular Islam since the modernization of Muslim countries started, with more schooling and greater literacy, with a more rationalized way of life, and with the penetration of Western ideas. The political independence of these countries has led to a massive impact of state-supported ideologies, which are by their nature inimical to popular religion and tend to play it down as "folklore". One may think also of new waves of purification of Islam, like the earlier one of Ibn Taymīya, which have arisen through the reformers since the end of the nineteenth century or through more fundamentalistic ideologies that are text-oriented and call for a return to the true Islam of the Qur'ān and *Sunna*.

We can classify the most striking *forms* of popular Islam in the following way:

1. celebrations of *rites de passage*;
2. celebrations of the sequence of the seasons of nature and of the weeks, months, and years;
3. communal celebrations outside the seasons that secure the coherence of the group, such as pilgrimages, tribal elections or celebrations of particular families or classes within the tribe;

---

[5] For the attitude of Western scholars to the opposition between official and popular Islam, and some reasons for it, see the Appendix "A Note on the Contexts of Earlier Research on Official and Popular Islam" (see below under heading 6.).

4. ways in which a particular religious significance has been bestowed on individuals (Sūfī *sheykhs*, *ashrāf* [descendants of Muhammad], *mujtahids* [innovating scholars], and other prominent religious leaders) either during their lifetime or after their death, leading then also to saint veneration and the veneration of the dead;

5. forms of religious behavior that arise in response to unforeseen events and crises, such as natural disasters and catastrophes in the social order or in individual life;

6. specific and not officially recognized religious forms that may occur among Muslim women, in Muslim festivals (musical performances, forms of *dhikr* or "mentioning the name of God", cults with emotional religious expressions), in the institution of new Muslim feasts (like that of *mawlīd al-nabī*), in certain Muslim ways of life (circumcision, the use of protective objects as amulets, forms of "magical" action);

7. ways of life and ideas in explicitly religious groups (*turuq* or mystical brotherhoods, Muslim "brotherhoods" and "societies");

8. religious customs confined to specific Muslim communities, for instance various "sects" (Khārijīs and groups of Shī'īs), or to Muslim communities in specific regions, especially outside the heartlands of Islam.

Although such forms of popular Islam may sometimes constitute a sort of alternative religion, in nearly all cases they have an important cultural and social structural function within the total life pattern of the societies concerned. They frequently provide a sacral structure for communal life, aid in the face of the practical problems of individual and social life, and offer possibilities for more religious natures to express and realize themselves. They are part and parcel of traditional Muslim societies.

2.2. Popular Movements

Things take on a slightly different aspect if one considers popular movements instead of forms. Throughout Islamic history, a number of movements of clearly Islamic inspiration have arisen but have had little to do with the recognized Islamic religious leadership. Although they are only remotely related to the forms of popular Islam just mentioned, they should be taken into consideration as well in any discussion of what is to be understood by popular religion in Islam. Indeed, as Dr. Kenneth Brown suggested in a letter to me, Islam itself can be called a "popular" movement at its inception.

1) First, one thinks of the various more or less popular movements that opposed the Umayyad dynasty (661–750 C.E.) and its governance, inasmuch as these movements were religiously motivated and touched larger sections of the Muslim population. One may think of the participants in

the "great *fitna*" (discord) with Mecca as its center against Damascus (681–92 C.E.), the *mawālī* (newly converted Muslims admitted as client members to Arab tribes) claiming equal rights with the older Arab-born Muslims, and other religious opposition groups, partly sectarian, asking for a greater stress on the role of Islam in state affairs than the Umayyads (with the exception of 'Umar II, 717–20 C.E.) were willing to concede. Such movements finally contributed to the downfall of the Umayyad dynasty in the 'Abbāsid revolution.

2) One can think of other religiously motivated groups in the first centuries of Islam that were able to mobilize significant segments of the population for their religio-political protests and ideals: Khārijīs, Shī'īs of various persuasion with their popular uprisings in Baghdad, Sunnī groups that could be mobilized by their leaders to oppose the Shī'īs, and other dissidents in the streets. Best known among them is the Hanbalī mob, which did not hesitate to march through the streets of the capital to ask for the liberation of Ahmad ibn Hanbal, who was imprisoned in the 840s because he held to his belief in the uncreated nature of the Qur'ān against the official stand of the Caliph, who propounded the createdness of the Qur'ān. In such popular movements, the influence of the ordinary Qur'ān reciters is noticeable, and in later eighth to tenth-century Baghdad, religious issues were very much the concern of the people and may have constituted the core of popular Muslim movements. In this context, one must also mention religious-social protest movements against 'Abbāsid governance, like those of the *Zanj* (ninth century C.E.), African slaves in southern Mesopotamia who had become Muslims, of the Mazdakites (eighth century C.E.), and other opposition movements (like the Khurranites) in Iran, of the Qarmatians (tenth century C.E.) in Northeast Arabia, and others whom, although defending or appealing to Muslim ideas and practices, the ruling dynasty could consider as being close to religious nihilists.

3) One cannot help but think of the Sūfīs and the Sūfī brotherhoods (*turuq*) that absorbed great numbers of people and instructed them religiously. In contrast to the official, normative Islam of the *'ulamā'* (religious scholars, jurist-theologians), the Islam of the mystics can rightly be held to have been a lived, popular, and even "alternative" Islam.[6]

4) There were religiously motivated, more or less violent popular movements of various kinds: (a) militant religious movements proclaiming *jihād*, sometimes with Mahdist claims, for instance the eleventh-century Almohads in Morocco and later in Spain, the activities of the Shehu Usuman Dan Fodio in West Africa at the beginning of the nine-

---

[6]   So for instance Hamilton Alexander Rosskeen Gibb, *Islam: A Historical Survey* (first edition titled: *Mohammedanism*), London, Oxford and New York: Oxford University Press, 1975², ch. 8 "Sufism", pp. 86–99.

teenth century, and the Mahdist movement in the Sudan at the end of that
century; (b) movements of resistance, at least in the beginning stages,
against Western ideological intrusion and political interference in the
nineteenth and the beginning of the twentieth century; (c) Muslim brotherhoods active in a number of countries after World War Two and
opposing too secular a conduct of affairs of state, especially after the
achievement of independence.

5) twentieth-century political movements like that of Pan-Islamism,
the Caliphate Movement in India in the twenties, various independence
movements and broader movements against the West or states like Israel
or India. They refer to Islamic ideals and values, are often of a militant
character, make a broad appeal to the Muslim masses, and have as such
a "popular" character.

6) The peaceful expansion of Islam in South and Southeast Asia, in
Africa South of the Sahara, and in East Africa, mainly through trade and
Sūfī preaching, had an essentially popular character and, certainly in the
beginning, had little connections with the "official" circles of the leading
ʿulamāʾ.

7) The banner of Islam could always serve as a popular symbol against
adherents of other religions, in situations of tension and conflict both
within and outside of Muslim territory.

A number of these popular movements were quite powerful and brought
about political changes. They lacked the static character of the popular
forms of Islam described in the previous section. In its movements,
popular Islam has always been exceedingly dynamic, exerting a strong
emotional appeal liable to bring about changes and to adapt itself to new
circumstances. It has promoted the expansion of Islam and its defense
against potential enemies.

2.3. Some Characteristics of Popular Islam

Both the forms and the movements just described have appealed to
something in the people, which has shown itself to be deeply sensitive and
very much alive. They appealed to a whole set of emotions, values, and
ideals that may have remained under the surface in everyday life but that
could manifest themselves in situations of stress and need, in festive
celebrations, in fundamental religious rituals, and in metaphysical
orientations. Such values and ideals are transmitted in the ordinary
situations of life and constitute a kind of "invisible religion" of a communal nature, which is difficult for the outside observer to grasp but which
can always be invoked in connection with actions and solidarities deemed
to be properly "Islamic".

This popular kind of Islam may be far both from the religious Muslim
scholars (ʿulamāʾ), and the cultural elite in general, and also from the

political, especially the central state authorities. Among the people the feeling often prevails that there is too much injustice in society and state and that a properly Islamic order and way of life are lacking because of negligence on the part of the authorities. The local horizon and the disproportion between Islamic ideals and actual political and social realities may account for a certain aloofness of popular Islam from state affairs, but also for the occasional outburst of religiously motivated movements in times of crisis. This is all intimately connected with the economic situation of the groups concerned; socio-economic and human sufferings determine to a large extent what kinds of protest actions can occur, mostly with an appeal to Islamic religion or an Islamic ideology. In the former colonies, for instance, a Muslim population often tended to gather against the Western administration under the banner of Islam. This is as much a part of popular Islam as is the folklore that strikes the visitor's eye.

Popular Islam seen in this way is less static than it seems at first sight. It is responsive in various ways, mostly difficult to perceive, to external events and changes that occur in society. It contributes to shaping communal moral consciousness among the people with a constant reference to Islam and its religious and moral values. In its political manifestations, it may take violent forms at times and then be suppressed by the authorities. In its daily occurrence, however, it tends to be looked down upon by the more enlightened Muslims, modernists, religious scholars or otherwise, who see it as a kind of folk religion or as evidence of primitiveness. Popular Islam changes considerably with the growing literacy of the population, and many aspects of it seem to disappear; in fact it has been most important in preliterate, traditional Muslim societies. As an expression of a communal and sometimes even collective Islamic consciousness and solidarity, however, it continues to exist in all Muslim communities.

2.4. Popular Islam Within the Framework of Practiced Islam

What has been said earlier about popular Islam can be expanded now within a larger framework. First, until the moment when it is reduced to the level of folklore, popular Islam appears to be an essential part of Muslim societies and can perform various functions in social and individual life. Second, much of what is called "popular" Islam is in fact a concrete (medical, political, social, and so on) use of particular elements of the many symbols and symbolic actions that Muslims of various orientations consider as belonging to Islam. Popular Islam then comes down to a particular kind of "practiced" Islam. Interactions between official and popular Islam can be largely understood as an interaction between the more theoretical considerations of the religious scholars and the more ritual and practical activities in Muslim societies, both justifying themselves by means of Islamic religion. Third, specific psychological motivations, forms, and movements of popular Islam vary widely according to their social function and practical effects among men and women, Bedouin, peasants and townfolk, different classes, and particularly different regions with varying cultural traditions. In many cases, a functional symbiosis can be recognized between a particular kind of practices of popular Islam and the way in which official Islam is represented in a given society.

I shall now give three examples of forms of Islam that are part and parcel of practiced Islam but that cannot be called "popular" Islam as described above.

1) The development of mysticism and the place of Sūfī piety in Islam place the problem of popular Islam in a wider framework. The origin of Sūfism was quite "orthodox"; it started as the consistent application of religious norms contained in the Qur'ān and the early *Sunna*. As it developed, it took its own course, assimilating influences from outside, and even came close to becoming a kind of "alternative" Islam alongside the normative Islam as defined by the scholars. By the end of the twelfth century C.E., however, through the influence of al-Ghazzālī (1058–1111 C.E.), except for extreme mystical positions that explicitly contradicted official doctrine, it was incorporated within the mainstream of Islam, which had to be expanded accordingly. The Sūfīs considered themselves to represent a profounder Islam than the *'ulamā'*, because they paid attention to its inner aspects, spirituality, and religious experience. In practice, Sūfism gave rise to a kind of popular Islam that stresses miracles and the veneration of saints. Parallel to particular groups' acceptance of individual Sūfīs and their doctrines, in the social realm the religious brotherhoods or Sūfī orders (*turuq*) were admitted into the mainstream of Islam and Muslim societies. These brotherhoods became intimately connected with certain geographical areas (including quarters of towns), professions, and social classes, and at certain times and places some of them had so much influence that they could almost be considered part of official Islam.

The existence of Sūfism in Islamic history is also important from another point of view. Sūfī writings and the history of the different *turuq* are the principal sources for our knowledge of personal religious life and experience in Islam. Indeed, Islam as it was actually lived in the past, is difficult to discover. Most texts deal with the norms that should be adhered to and followed; the evidence about what people really believed and did is dispersed through historical, literary, and religious writings. Even if theologians like Ibn Taymīya criticized certain abuses in their time, the precise extent to which such customs were actually practiced cannot be gauged. The influence of Sūfism on everyday religious life in most places seems to have diminished significantly since the nineteenth century, whether because of the movements of return to a pure or purified Islam, the "scriptural" movement of the reformers who restored the authority of Qur'ān and *Sunna* against that of the Sūfī *sheykh* or the traditional *'ālim*, the political use of Islam as an ideology, or the development of modernization through rationalization with its critical tendencies with regard to religion.

2) Just as Sūfism is more than popular Islam, so the Shī'a cannot be simply reduced to a kind of popular Islam. In fact, the Shī'īs explicitly claim to represent true Islam and deny that the Sunnīs do so. From the Shī'ī point of view, represented by nearly ten percent of Muslims, it is the Sunnīs who represent a kind of "popular" Islam in the sense that they do not recognize the proper authorities (*Imāms*) and that they lack deeper knowledge and insight. The Sūfīs have also leveled this last reproach against Sunnī Islam, that is, that it has reduced religion to outward forms and legal distinctions, to the detriment of spirituality.

3) Another element that came to Islam after its early beginnings, but that cannot simply be regarded as popular religion although it bears traces of it, is the *customary law* (*'ādat*) prevailing in particular in areas islamicized later. Elements of Byzantine law that prevailed in the Near East before the Arab conquest found their way into Islamic customary law. In areas that are more on the periphery, like India, Indonesia, and Africa south of the Sahara, great parts of locally valid customary law have been retained and function in a way that is complementary to the *Sharī'a*. In a strict sense, this could be called "popular" religious law, but since it was recognized by the local Muslim judiciary, it became "official" in the same way as parts of Sūfism became "official" when they were recognized as a valid complement to the legal and doctrinal injunctions of Islam.

The acceptance of ancient Arab customs in official Islam presents a special case. On the one hand, the notion of a charismatic leader, as seems to have been alive in South Arabia, has been applied by the Shī'īs to Muhammad, his son-in-law 'Alī, and the latter's descendants. The popular custom of looking at the leader in this way became an essential element of Shī'a Islam. On the other hand, one may think of the way in which Muhammad himself promoted the ancient popular Arabian ritual of the *hajj* to a prescribed ritual duty of Islam.

We can go even further. From the point of view of the history of religions, it can be argued that historical practiced Islam is largely an Arab variant of more general religious notions and practices that were current in the Near East in the sixth and seventh centuries C.E., if not earlier. One can think of the idea that prophethood is needed for law-giving and founding or "restoring" a religion, or that the authority of a scripture rests on revelation. Even the concept of a universal religion and what it meant for the community of its adherents had been in the air centuries before Muhammad started his preaching.

It may be concluded that the typically "popular" forms and movements in Islam can be put within the wider framework of practiced Islam. Moreover, this practiced Islam should be seen in the wider context of practiced religion at given times and places.

3. Official Religion and its Representatives in Islam

Since there is no worldwide organized religious institution in Islam that can establish what is to be considered "official" Islam, the question arises whether we can speak here of official religion at all and, if so, what may be the criteria of calling something "official Islam" with a recognized leadership.

In medieval Islamic thought, the term "official" Islam is applied to what is religiously lawful and what, consequently, enjoys divine sanction. Its contents are held to go back to the Qur'anic text considered "revelation" and ancient *Sunna*. Phrased differently, all that goes back to something that is religiously authoritative like a revelation whose faithful transmission is authoritatively guaranteed, and that is expressed in an authoritative way, enjoys religious authority and can be called official and normative Islam. In Muslim terms, revelation is the true official and normative religion. Whenever a community fails to transmit and apply this revelation faithfully in its social and individual life, ignorance and error prevail.

Juridically speaking, official religion implies that qualified people in certain offices can perform specific activities that are religiously binding and juridically valid. For example, the *'ulamā'* establish the conditions for a *jihād* and the caliph carries it out, the *muftī* gives responses (*fatwās*) to legal questions and the *qādī* administers justice. In other words, to carry out certain activities with a religious bearing, a certain office or status is required and it is through religious law that one can know what "official" status is needed in these cases and which prescriptions apply.

Theologically speaking, opinions on religious subjects, too, are officially valid only under certain conditions. Such opinions need to go back to the Qur'anic text and ancient *Sunna*, thus being connected with revelation, and be supported by the *ijmā'* (consensus) of the faithful or at least of the qualified specialists. The religious opinion of a single individual can only obtain an official, that is, recognized and authoritative character if it is based on data contained within the revelation. If, however, such a person has immediate access to revelation, like a prophet, or is recognized by *ijmā'* as a *muhyī al-dīn* (literally a "reviver of religion") or as a *mujtahid* (independent scholar) in Shī'ī Islam, he is not obliged to prove this separately for each of his opinions although he can be asked to do so.

From this point of view, acts and opinions become official only under specific conditions established by religious law. The early Fātimid rulers in Tunisia in the first half of the tenth century could be seen as adhering to a "popular" Shī'ī religion until the moment that the ruler was proclaimed the only legal caliph. At that moment he took on an official capacity. The Umayyad ruler in Spain obtained this capacity when he proclaimed himself "orthodox" (Sunnī) caliph not long afterwards. In a similar way, customs and opinions became valid, authoritative, and "official" in the sense that they should be adopted within the Muslim community as soon as qualified 'ulamā' considered them to be "Islamic". The process of assimilating data from outside the community and giving them an Islamic label, first in the form of a hadīth and later by a fatwā, is in the first place a legal validation, so that Muslims can practice them. In this way they are "officialized".

In social practice, however, there was another criterion for "official" Islam besides the theological and juridical considerations just mentioned. In fact, official Islam has been held to be that kind of Islam whose representative leaders stood close to the state authorities and supported them with a religious legitimation. This state of affairs has to do with the fact that at least Sunnī Islam does not know a separate "official" spiritual institution. The caliph, for instance, was not a spiritual head of the community; he was only held to create the external conditions under which the Sharī'a could be applied. The 'ulamā' could only formulate the content of the Sharī'a, and not impose it. It was left to the believers individually—as well as to the Muslim community as a whole—to follow its injunctions. Only the Shī'īs expected their Imām—the technical term for caliph also among Sunnīs—to be the spiritual as well as political leader of the community.

The relationships between the jurist-theologians and the political state authorities and their division of tasks have been shaped through history. It was only for a few decades that the caliph, as the political head of the community, also took responsibility for the content of law and religious doctrine. This happened when al-Ma'mūn (813–33), together with Mu'tazilite theologians, proclaimed the doctrine of the createdness of the Qur'ān as "official" and when he instituted a mihna (inquisition) against this doctrine's opponents. A few decades later, the caliph al-Mutawakkil (847–61) and more traditionalist theologians revoked this doctrinal position. Subsequently, the state authority kept aloof from problems of the content of law and religious doctrine, at least in Sunnī Islam. For political reasons, the sultan, on behalf of the caliph, reinforced the Sunnī institutions in the second half of the eleventh century, and, in practice, brought them under state control in those areas where the caliph still ruled.

A century later, in 1171, Salāh al-Dīn (Saladin) imposed Sunnī Islam instead of the Shī'a in Egypt and Greater Syria. At that time, the educational program of the 'ulamā' in the madrasas had become largely standardized by "official" teaching of religious law and doctrine, and those who had finished their religious studies could be assumed to become loyal servants of the caliph or other head of state. Later, in the Ottoman Empire, the relationships between the jurist-theologians and the government officials would be carefully institutionalized and a certain equilibrium established between the sultan and the sheykh al-islām. The state itself was then ruled largely by non-religious qānūn legislation promulgated by the sultan alongside the Sharī'a as the official religious law. As a religion, Islam remained more or less helpless against the interest of the state. This has increased with the creation of national states in the twentieth century.

Since the twelfth century, the predominance of Sunnī Islam has been assured in Muslim states. Exceptions were Iran where Twelver Shī'ī Islam has dominated since the sixteenth century, Yemen that had other kinds of Shī'ī Islam, and Oman with its important Ibādī community. The Sunnī 'ulamā' had to accept their dependence on the state while being aware that this situation left much to be desired for a complete implementation of the Sharī'a. The Shī'īs, in general, have been more demanding toward the state authority than the Sunnīs.

In conclusion, "official" Islam has become ever more conditioned by state interests. It would be unjust to say that in Sunnī Islam the opinions of the leading 'ulamā' were official merely because they were close to the state authorities. The principal reason why their opinion had an "official" character in the Muslim community was their own religious learning, their upholding of the Sharī'a as an absolute norm, and the very fact that their opinions were accepted by ijmā'. That they also had a number of interests in common with the state authorities reinforced, however, their official status and contributed to the recognition of their views and opinions as "official" Islam. The links between the jurist-theologians and the state have been severed to some extent with the rise, especially in the twentieth century, of "Muslim" states that are no longer based exclusively on Sharī'a principles and that have their own power structures. Still, a basic loyalty of the 'ulamā' to the state remains. In the "Islamic" states, that apply Sharī'a prescriptions beyond family law, the weight of the 'ulamā' is of course greater in state affairs.

We have already mentioned that individuals can be recognized as having a personal religious authority. For scholars, this is true if the ijmā' of the community of scholars explicitly or implicitly recognizes them as such because of their learning in religious matters. It was assumed that each century had its muhyī al-dīn whose authority must be recognized. This happened, for example, to al-Ghazzālī. For mystics, on a spiritual level, the procedure was in a way easier. The recognition of a spiritual authority by a great number of followers, in fact the members of his Sūfī *tarīqa*, was sufficient to give his words and deeds an "official" authority within the *tarīqa*. Saintly figures were also recognized by Muslims outside a particular *tarīqa*.

To sum up, religious leaders in Islam derive their authority in religious matters not from a religious organization or an established institution, but from the knowledge they have of the data of revelation, that is to say from their religious learning, or from spiritual insight. The knowledge (*ʿilm*) pertains to Qur'ān and *Sunna*, *fiqh* and *kalām*. The spiritual insight (*maʿrifa*) pertains to one's own experience, especially in Sūfī traditions. Such insight (*maʿrifa*) differs from knowledge (*ʿilm*). The Shīʿa recognizes moreover the spiritual authority of the descendants of the prophet (as *Imāms*) and of certain recognized independent religious scholars (*mujtahids*).

4. The Concept of Normative Islam

After having discussed what is to be considered "official" religion in Islam, I would like to suggest the use of a concept that is more suitable and more applicable to the study of Islam as a religion. Since one of its characteristics is the constant search for clear norms for human life, it is often better to speak of "normative" than of "official" Islam linked to state interests. "Normative Islam" is that form of Islam through which Muslims have access to the ultimate norms that are valid for life, action, and thought. At once the polarity becomes evident between this normative Islam and the Islam that is in fact practiced.

The formal basis of normative Islam for all Muslims is what Muhammad as a prophet and leader of the community is held to have instituted as Islamic religion, especially through the revelation he brought (the Qur'ān) and the example he gave in words and deeds (the ancient *Sunna*). After his death, it was only the religious scholars, and specifically the jurist-theologians, who could establish, mainly on the basis of Qur'ān and *Sunna*, what duties were incumbent on Muslims. In this way, a tradition of normative Islam crystallized in the first centuries. One of the ensuing problems of later times has been to decide how rules that once were formulated as part of this normative Islam can be reinterpreted, changed, or even abrogated in accordance with the particular needs and problems of later times. In classical Muslim terms, normative Islam is the *Sharīʿa*.

Since there is no organizational institution, normative Islam, once formulated, can be enforced only indirectly. We have seen the duties of the *ʿulamāʾ* and of the caliph in this respect. In general, the pressure of ordinary people faithful keeping to tradition, the *ahl al-sunna wa'l-*

jamā'a, has been instrumental in the upholding of normative Islam. Periodically, however, movements have arisen throughout the history of Islam that call for purification and reform, for going back to Qur'ān and *Sunna*. These movements impose strict standards of conduct as well as the elimination of new and "foreign" elements that have insinuated themselves into "original" Islam and corrupted it. Through an appeal to revealed Scripture and tradition, the whole community is then morally and socially placed under the rules of strict normative Islam. No Muslim, however, can be forced to follow the *Sharī'a* completely, although certain religious duties ought to be performed by everyone.

Certain factors work or have worked in favor of an implementation of this normative Islam. One of them was the Islamization of the Middle East at an early date and in an intense form; the further a region is from the heartlands of Islam, the more local customs may survive.

Another factor is the degree to which this normative Islam has been rationalized by the religious scholars and is presented and accepted as a coherent system. A particular kind of rationalization takes place today in the development of new Islamic ideologies and their presentation of Islam as a single coherent view of life and world. Rationalization is typical of Islam as a scriptural religion that lays a heavy accent on knowledge and reason. But the development of a scholastic rational system may also have indirectly favored as a reaction the occurrence of a less rationally-aligned, more "spiritual" or more "popular" Islam that better satisfies non-rational human needs.

A third factor promoting the influence of normative Islam is popular literacy. Throughout Islamic history and certainly in all reform movements, learning to read and write Arabic as the language of the Qur'ān has been stressed and a religious school system teaching Islam has functioned from the very beginning. The importance of education in Islam is again closely connected with its having a scripture containing the basic norms that the faithful should know.

A fourth important factor is political unity. Different ethnic communities and other socio-cultural groups tend to develop their own diverging cultures that also have their own religious forms. Since unity of religion is an important factor in political stability, governments of larger Muslim countries have tried to promote in various ways a certain unity and uniformity of Islam within their countries. As a consequence, the normative Islam advanced by the religious scholars has often received support from the state authorities and became "official". In fact, different kinds of Islam are often connected with different political structures, with their own social, economic, ethnic, geographical, and historical backgrounds. A good example is the enforcement of Twelver Shī'ī Islam by the Safavid dynasty in sixteenth-century Persia, as opposed to the official position of Sunnī Islam in the Ottoman empire, Persia's natural enemy.

A fifth factor is geographical location. In certain cases, isolated areas such as desert regions have favored an implementation of normative Islam, not only in hope of restoring Islam as it was in Arabia at the time of the prophet and the first caliphs, but also because in such regions there were hardly any influences from outside until the mid-twentieth century. Whether the Bedouin individually have always been an example of a *Sharī'a*-oriented life to their fellow-Muslims is another question.

Generally speaking, in order to establish itself, normative Islam needs specific institutions like mosques, religious schools, jurisdiction with Islamic personal law, provisions to keep the ritual laws regarding food, rules of worship and fasting, and so on.

In my view, the concept of "normative" Islam is scholarly better suited to the data and structures of this religion than the concept of "official" Islam that is linked to state recognition. It can be used without prejudice for all Muslim groups that appeal to Islam as their norm for individual and social life. The concept is a formal one, and consequently can be applied to the different kinds of Sunnī and Shī'a Islam as well as to Khārijī, 'Alawī, and Ahmadī Islam, all searching to implement "Islam". Furthermore, all that has been said earlier about the relationship and interaction between popular and official Islam holds even more true for that between practiced and normative Islam. The search for the ultimate norms of normative Islam is incumbent not only on the religious leadership but on Muslims generally including intellectuals. Elements from outside or new elements can become part of normative Islam, but they may pass first through life practice. In Muslim societies, normative and popular practiced Islam appear to fulfill complementary functions, so that they should not be seen as completely separated from each other.

5. Conclusion

Seen in retrospect, Islam has shown a tendency, especially in its first centuries, to increase the volume of what is religiously authoritative. The same holds true for those regions in which Islamization has taken place and where the weight of authoritative Islamic religious tradition has become ever heavier. After the first centuries of Islam, we also find a stabilization of the status and role of the religious scholars.

Not only practiced Islam but also normative Islam as it is perceived by people—what Islam is held to prescribe—is subject to changes. They may arise out of purifications in connection with a return to Qur'ān and *Sunna* or to pure *tawhīd*. They may also arise out of adaptations to new situations, for instance as a consequence of modernization processes that lead to new interpretations of the cultural and religious heritage. Changes in normative Islam could be due to rational thought but they have seldom come about through the direct influence of other religions. Such changes were due only to a limited extent to the influence of popular Islam, since this tended to lead a life apart from the centers of religious learning and from modern society. The increasing modernization of society, however, has influenced both practiced and normative Islam. On issues like the personal status (marriage, repudiation, inheritance, and so on), however, a confrontation of "modernity" with normative Islam could well occur.

It will have become clear that, in the absence of an "official" institutional organization in Islam, the relationships between official and popular, and between practiced and normative religion become more subtle. They are closely related with the political relationships, in particular those between state and society, in each country. In the absence of an organized religious authority, in present-day states different kinds of official as well as popular Islam can be established or grow and different views can be held about what normative Islam prescribes as an absolute norm. This demands a relative tolerance that was not displayed by some Hanbalī reformers like Ibn Taymīya. It also demands a certain understanding that popular Islam must keep within its own sphere of life and not compete with official Islam as far as the general issues of the Muslim community are concerned. On the whole, modern states have increased their social and political control over expressions of popular Islam and have suppressed its extreme forms. In the event of unrest and disorder, the state authorities can intervene.

A further consequence of the fact that Islam has no institutional religious organization is that it has a somewhat amorphous character in its relations with the "outside" world, including religions that happen to have such an organization. Representatives of the latter tend to look to the guardians of official Islam, that is to say the ʿulamāʾ, as representative Muslims. Beyond these circles of specialists, however, the contacts between adherents of Islam and other religions actually have taken place much more in the sphere of social and cultural life and of practiced, even popular Islam.

Our main conclusion is that, until recently and still today in certain regions, Islam has been an agglomeration of very different kinds and sorts of religion. A certain unification, but also a new differentiation of them is taking place now, due among other things to the media and means of communication and especially to present-day social movements and political developments in Muslim countries. As a result of important changes in these countries, Islam can now function in new ways not always easy for Islamicists or political scientists to understand. There is reason to assume that a century ago, official Sunnī Islam was much less known and spread in Muslim societies than today. It was in fact restricted to a limited number of communities; especially outside the towns and the heartlands, many Muslim communities had in practice a kind of popular religion with only a veneer of official Islam. This situation may have been still more prevalent in former centuries. It indirectly suggests the limits of the influence of the religious scholars within the world of Islam, even if they succeeded in having normative Islam accepted as an absolute norm in all Muslim societies.

It was apparently the "fundamentalist" Hanbalī reforms and the reform movements of the nineteenth and twentieth centuries that intensified and rationalized the permanent tension between normative and practiced Islam. They also rationalized the tension between the existing official, state-linked Islam and their own proposals for a reformed Islam, denying some or all of the claims of this official Islam.

Such tensions are inherent to Islam even if we concede that each expression of normative Islam is in fact a particular interpretation and application of Islam as an absolute norm. Whenever the people felt that a Muslim society was moving too far from normative Islam, a reform movement could start that claimed to be going back to the Qur'ān and *Sunna* and to be restoring the true original Islam, possibly with the help of arms. It would seem that the interplay between the more or less "fundamentalist" reform movements with their call "back to true Islam!", often supported by some 'ulamā', on the one hand, and popular religion's recapturing of its lost terrain in due time with its appeal to satisfy specific religious needs, on the other hand, is one of the fundamental structures of this religion. The tension between "modernizing" initiatives adapting religious prescriptions to the demands of the time and traditional structures from the past is typical of modern times.

The tension between the absolute norms of "normative" Islam (however considered) and empirical reality appears to be a third basic structure. Against any given socio-political reality, recourse is always possible to absolute norms—such as justice—for human life and society. Seen in this light, normative Islam will endure, even if only a few Muslims actually would live up to it, because it can always be recognized as an absolute norm that puts reality under judgment.

Throughout its history, Islamic religion has shown great leniency toward the weakness of human beings in the face of both the harshness of reality and the high demands of religion. Perhaps Muslims did not experience the tension between normative and practiced Islam as a failure of their religion or a proof of human sin, but rather as an indication of human weakness. But this tension and the ensuing problems are precisely what will interest an Islamicist concerned with "official" and "popular", "practiced" and "normative" religion in Islam.

6. Appendix: A Note on the Contexts of Earlier Research on Official and Popular Islam

The distinction made in Islamic studies between official and popular Islam can be traced back in European scholarship to at least the middle of the nineteenth century. I think of Edward William Lane's account of the "popular" manners and customs of the "modern Egyptians" (1836). The interest in Islam as a religion expanded then in various ways and its scholarly study increased in scope and improved in quality through more methodical and disciplined approaches. An important factor contributing to this development of Islamic studies was that scholars had gained access to new sources, through the discovery and edition of little-known manuscripts and through more direct contacts with lived, practiced Islam. The question is whether there were reasons, apart from the nature of the available sources, why the distinction between an official and a popular Islam has been stressed so much.

6.1. Most important perhaps was the *situation of scholarly research* at the time. The study of Islam took place in various disciplines. There was the quickly developing textual research opening up an enormous literature, religious and otherwise, written by Muslims over a period of some thirteen centuries. This textual research presupposes a sound knowledge of the major languages of Islam, in the first place Arabic, to which Persian and Turkish and much later Urdu were added. Attention was of course first directed toward those texts considered to be authoritative religious documents from the first centuries of Islam, starting with the Qur'ān. These texts continued to be authoritative during the whole history of Islam, and it could easily be assumed that they represented a kind of official Islam in written form, providing the norms and truths according to which the faithful should live.

Historical research was to correct this impression by showing for instance that doctrines had varied according to schools, times, and places and that not all texts were of the same importance. It was clear that the history of Islam as a religion was much more than just the history of its religious literature. Historical research on Islam is concerned with historical realities and events, including the historical and social setting of the texts, the schools that acknowledged or rejected their authority, the debates on issues held to be relevant, and the different ways in which these texts were used. Historical studies show that different groups in Islamic history had defined "official Islam" in different ways and that it was not foreseeable at the outset what would later come to be "orthodox" and what would be considered sects. Such studies could also investigate the historical developments that caused particular opinions and doctrines to be "officially" recognized as well as the contrast between official Islam as expressed in the religious texts and historical reality.

Another correction to a too literary conception of "official Islam" was made by anthropological and sociological fieldwork in given Muslim communities. Here much stress was placed on the religion as it was actually found and observed, on the norms and ideals that existed and were in fact valid among the people, and on the connections between this lived religion and the societies the people belonged to. Here another unilateral view arose, since social scientists rarely knew the authoritative texts of Islam and the historical development of its law and doctrine. They tended to stress popular Islam as they found it with all its "primitive" elements, at least as they appeared to the eyes of a Western observer, often to the exclusion of the doctrines of the official Islam which clearly were not applied as they ought to be. For anthropologists, popular Islam was then the real Islam of the people, and official Islam was considered to be the religious norms and ideals of some remote theologians and jurists.

There were other reasons, too, that could easily prejudice the proper scholarly study of Islam, including the relationship between official and popular Islam. These reasons have to do with the particular situation in which the observers and scholars stood and that led to certain tendencies of research of which the observers themselves may have been aware only on certain occasions.

6.2. The *political situation* in which scholars had to work at the time implied a strong separation of "theory" (scholarship) from "practice" (application). Scholars in the universities concentrated in their study of Islam mainly on textual and historical research; they rarely went to Muslim countries and then largely to consult manuscripts. On the other hand, scholars working on contemporary Islam and who did research in the field were mostly in direct or indirect government service; they often worked in close contact with the Western colonial administrators on site.

The study of the "practice" of Islam was not a matter of complete indifference to the Western colonizing states. In fact, such studies provided a considerable amount of factual information about the Muslim inhabitants, which could be very useful for the administration concerned, whether in Morocco, Libya, India, or Java. In much of this research there was an implicit assumption that the links between the particular Muslim country and the mother country in Europe should be continued as they existed. Moreover, those developments in the Muslim country should be supported that were profitable or at least not harmful to the interests of the mother country. Consequently, not only the colonial administration but also the scholars connected with it mostly had a negative view of any Muslim movement that opposed the Western mother country, and indeed of all forms of Islam that implied a threat to the colonial power's rule.

So there was a definite interest in establishing an opposition between "medieval" Islam and modern civilization, in accentuating the "primitive" and "exotic" sides of Islam, and in showing the discrepancy between this "real", lived Islam and the "official", normative Islam of the books. Muslim rebellions or the Pan-Islamic movement could create nervousness among administrators and field Islamicists alike, and even Islamic self-confidence could irritate the Westerner. In quite a few descriptions, support was given to the simple people's folk religion as a factor of stability and to mystical Islam as an otherworldly and finally harmless outlook on life and reality; the more challenging demands of official Islam were then considered inapplicable norms stemming from a medieval tradition.

It was true, of course, that only a small part of the *Sharī'a* was applied and that the lived religion differed greatly from what the norms prescribed. Western scholars were rightly struck by these facts. Their mistake, however, was that they nearly always took the given facts and the *status quo* as the point of departure for their interpretations. They did not inquire about the deeper reasons for apparent discrepancies or about whether there were not more complex relationships between official and popular Islam than could be seen on the surface. They did not see Muslims as actors in their own right.

In fact, before World War One, it seems to have been almost impossible to imagine that there might be a living official Islam with its own dynamic and inspiration, that there might be an interaction between this normative Islam and popular, practiced Islam, and that a network of structural relationships might come about between different forms of Islam and deeper social and political aspirations that were alive in Muslim societies. Did scholars at the time not realize that it was to some extent the colonial or half-colonial situation itself that drove Islam into becoming largely an "underground" religion and that Islam's vitality was to a large extent paralyzed by this situation as well as by the rapid secular modernization process? A certain number of Islamicists specialized in Islamic and *'ādat* law, which were of immediate interest for the judiciary; it has been correctly observed that there were more jurists than anthropologists studying living Islam at the time.

Only now, at a relative distance, can we see the ways in which the colonial situation and the interests of colonial administrations conditioned scholarly investigations at the time. The nearly absolute opposition found between the "theory and practice" of Islam, between normative and popular Islam, seems a case in point. Western students of Islam—to the degree that they are not politically involved in other ways— are able to view contemporary developments of Muslim societies more impartially when their governments are less immediately involved in the internal affairs of Muslim countries.

6.3. We must also take into account the *religious situation* in which scholars interested in Islam as a religion had to work up to the mid-twentieth century. This situation was marked by the expansion of Western Christianity through missionary efforts. People connected with the missions tended to separate Islam as a religion and faith from its social reality; otherwise a religious change or conversion from Islam to Christianity could scarcely be envisaged. The fact that in the West religion was often considered a system of norms, ideals, and spirituality existing, so to say, in itself may have contributed to regarding Islam in the same light.

Parallel to the colonial bias, there was thus a certain religious bias in the study of Islam. Moreover, Islam as a religion had a largely negative connotation in Europe at the time. In the study of Islam as a religion there was frequently an implicit rule that those aspects that looked positive from a Christian point of view should be studied attentively; the aspects that looked negative could be used as an argument against Islam and for Christianity. When possible, those religious developments were to be supported that favored missionary work or that at least would not harm Christianity. There could not but be an instinctive antipathy among Christians toward any kind of Islam that openly opposed Christianity and a kind of implicit hatred could arise against violence in the name of Islam and those forms of Islam that threatened the expansion of Christianity. In a number of cases, this meant a certain deprecation of normative Islam, whose norms were shown either of low standard or not to be applied in practice. The miseries of the people were often attributed to Islam and the "primitive" aspects of popular Islam were stressed.

Whereas the colonial situation stressed the contrast between Western culture—in this case the mother country—and Islam, the missionary situation stressed the contrast between Christianity and Islam. Both schemes implied that Islam was in a crisis, lifeless, or even at its end. The "practice" of Islam was shown not to correspond with what the "theory" or doctrine prescribed and this practice was a sad spectacle.

In a way, the failures of scholars interested in Islam as a religion were more tragic than the failures of scholars involved in their own government's interests. The latter could hardly arrive at true knowledge, because of external, mainly political, conditions, whereas the former could hardly perceive correctly what religious Muslims would be willing to tell them about their religion and faith, because of their commitment to their own religion's missionary work. In neither case could justice be done to Islam as a lived religion, and so the problem of official and popular Islam—and of what was really going on in the Muslim communities—could not be handled properly. In various ways, the political and religious situation at the time before independence made disinterested scholarly research of Muslim communities extremely difficult.

6.4. The handicaps scholarly research suffered from because of the existing political and religious situation were all the greater since no correction could be made by *scholars who were Muslims themselves.* There
were at the time very few Muslims in a position to know the approaches
of Western scholarship, to discuss and possibly contradict Western interpretations of Islam, and to be taken seriously on this score by Western
scholars.

Muslim scholars of Islam were working at the time within the normative system of Islam itself. Their protests against Western interpretations were expressed in terms of another discourse than that of Western
scholarship and could easily be treated by the latter as Islamic apologetics.
Those Muslim scholars of Islam who had been trained in Western scholarship nearly always studied Islamic texts and history. They were hardly
interested in popular, more or less "primitive" forms of Islam that were
alien to the modern world and from which they probably wanted to keep
aloof both as Muslims and as educated scholars.

In the situation of the time, with Western attacks on Islam, Muslim
scholars could not but have a tendency to defend Islam as a norm and as
an ideal, which they themselves had a vital interest in separating from
practiced Islam. Because of their "defensive" situation, it was practically
impossible for them to do justice to the problem of the relationship
between official and popular Islam.

These and other factors may explain to some extent why previous studies,
especially before World War Two, bringing together so much factual
information about Islam, could make only a modest contribution to the
understanding of official and popular, practical and normative Islam and
their complex mutual relationships.

Selected Literature

1. General

GOLDZIHER, Ignaz, "Glanures païennes dans l'Islam", in ID., *Gesammelte Schriften*,
    6 Vols., Hildesheim: Georg Olms, Vol. II, 1968, pp. 369–99.
—, "Le culte des saints chez les musulmans", in *ibid.*, Vol. VI, 1973, pp. 62–156.
—, "Le culte des ancêtres et le culte des saints chez les Arabes", in *ibid.*, Vol. VI,
    1973, pp. 157–84.
GRUNEBAUM, Gustave Edmund von, *Muhammadan Festivals*, New York: H.
    Schuman, 1951 (Repr. New York: Olive Branch Press, 1988).
HORTEN, Max, *Die religiöse Gedankenwelt des Volkes im heutigen Islam*, Halle:
    Niemeyer, 1917–18.
KRISS, Rudolf, and Hubert KRISS-HEINRICH, *Volksglaube im Bereich des Islam*, Vol.
    I: *Wallfahrtswesen und Heiligenverehrung*; Vol. II: *Amulette, Zauberformeln
    und Beschwörungen*, Wiesbaden: Otto Harrassowitz, 1960–2.

MEMON, Muhammad Umar, *Ibn Taimīya's Struggle against Popular Religion: With an Annotated Translation of his Kitāb iqtiḍā' aṣ-ṣirāṭ al-mustaqīm mukhālafat aṣḥāb al-jaḥīm* (Religion and Society 1), The Hague and Paris: Mouton, 1976.

MÜLLER, Klaus E., *Kulturhistorische Studien zur Genese pseudo-islamischer Sektengebilde in Vorderasien* (Studien zur Kulturkunde 22), Wiesbaden: Franz Steiner, 1967.

WINKLER, Hans Alexander, *Siegel und Charaktere in der muhammedanischen Zauberei* (Studien zur Geschichte und Kultur des islamischen Orients 7), Berlin: Walter de Gruyter, 1930 (Repr. Munich: Arbeitsgemeinschaft für Religions- u. Weltanschauungsfragen, 1980).

ZWEMER, Samuel Marinus, *Studies in Popular Islam: A Collection of Papers Dealing with the Superstitions and Beliefs of the Common People*, London: Sheldon Press, and New York: Macmillan, 1939.

2. Ottoman Empire, Balkans, Anatolia

BIRGE, John Kingsley, *The Bektashi Order of Dervishes* (Luzac's Oriental Religions Series 7), London: Luzac, 1937 (Repr. 1994).

HASLUCK, Frederick William, *Christianity and Islam under the Sultans*, ed. by Margaret M. HASLUCK, 2 Vols., Oxford: Clarendon Press, 1929.

KISSLING, Hans Joachim, "The Sociological and Educational Role of the Dervish Orders in the Ottoman Empire", *The American Anthropologist*, 56 (1954), pp. 23–35.

—, "Aus dem Derwischwesen Südosteuropas", in *Grazer und Münchener Balkanologische Studien*, Redaktion Walther WÜNSCH, Munich: Trofenik, 1967, pp. 56–70.

3. Egypt

AMMAR, Hamed M., *Growing up in an Egyptian Village: Silwa, Province of Aswan* (International Library of Sociology and Social Reconstruction), London: Routledge and Kegan Paul, 1954.

AYROUT, Henry Habib, *The Egyptian Peasant* (Beacon Books on World Affairs), Boston, Mass.: Beacon Press, 1963 (Revised edition of *The Fellaheen*, Cairo: R. Schindler, [1945?]; trans. from the French: *Moeurs et coutumes des fellahs*, Paris: Payot, 1938).

BERGER, Morroe, *Islam in Egypt Today: Social and Political Aspects of Popular Religion*, Cambridge: Cambridge University Press, 1970.

BLACKMAN, Winifred S., *The Fellāhīn of Upper Egypt: Their Religious, Social and Industrial Life Today*, London: G.G. Harrap & Cie., 1927 (Repr. London: F. Cass, 1968).

GILSENAN, Michael, *Saint and Sufi in Modern Egypt: An Essay in the Sociology of Religion* (Oxford Monographs on Social Anthropology), Oxford: Clarendon Press, 1973.

KAHLE, Paul, *Die Totenklage im heutigen Ägypten: Arabische Texte mit Übersetzung und Erläuterungen*, Göttingen: Vandenhoeck & Ruprecht, 1923 (published originally in *Eucharisterion: Studien zur Religion und Literatur des Alten und Neuen Testaments. Festschrift Hermann Gunkel* [FRLANT 36], ed. by Hans SCHMIDT, Göttingen: Vandenhoeck & Ruprecht, 1923).

LANE, Edward William, *An Account of the Manners and Customs of the Modern Egyptians*, London: C. Knight and Co., 1936 (numerous reprints).
McPHERSON, Joseph Williams, *The Moulids of Egypt (Egyptian Saints-Days)*, Cairo: Nile Mission Press, 1941.
WINKLER, Hans Alexander, *Ägyptische Volkskunde*, Stuttgart: Kohlhammer, 1936.

4. Palestine and Jordan

CANAAN, Taufik, *Mohammedan Saints and Sanctuaries in Palestine* (Luzac's Oriental Religions Series 5), London: Luzac, 1927.
GRANQVIST, Hilma, *Muslim Death and Burial: Arab Customs and Traditions Studied in a Village in Jordan* (Commentationes humanarum litterarum 34,1), Helsinki: Societas Scientiarum Fennica, 1965.

5. Iraq

FERNEA, Robert A., *Shaykh and Effendi: Changing Patterns of Authority among the El Shabana of Southern Iraq* (Harvard Middle Eastern Studies 14), Cambridge, Mass.: Harvard University Press, 1970.

6. Arabia

BUJRA, Abdallah S., *The Politics of Social Stratification: A Study of Political Change in a South Arabian Town*, Oxford: Clarendon Press, 1971.
SNOUCK HURGRONJE, Christiaan, *Mekka in the Latter Part of the 19th Century*, trans. from German, Leiden: E. J. Brill, 1931 (Repr. 1970).

7. North Africa in general

BEL, Alfred, *La religion musulmane en Berbérie: Esquisse d'histoire et de sociologie religieuse. Etablissement et développement de l'Islam en Berbérie du VIIe au XXe siècle*, Paris: Geuthner, 1938.
BOUSQUET, Georges-Henri, *L'Islam maghrébin: Introduction à l'étude générale de l'Islam*, Alger: La Maison des livres, 1941, 1954[4] (revue et fortement augmentée).
DEPONT, Octave, and Xavier COPPOLANI, *Les confréries religieuses musulmanes*, Alger: A. Jourdan, 1897 (Repr. in 2 Vols., Paris: Maisonneuve, etc., 1987).
DERMENGHEM, Emile, *Le culte des Saints dans l'Islam maghrébin*, Paris: Gallimard, 1955.
DOUTTÉ, Edmond, *La société musulmane du Maghrib: Magie et religion dans l'Afrique du Nord*, Alger: Société musulmane du Maghrib, 1909.

8. Morocco

BROWN, Kenneth, *People of Salé: Tradition and Change in a Moroccan City 1830–1930*, Manchester: Manchester University Press, 1976.
CUPERUS, Wybo Sijo, *Al-Fātiha dans la pratique religieuse musulmane du Maroc: À partir du 19ème siècle*, Diss. Univ. of Utrecht: Elinkwijk, 1973.
DRAGUE, Georges, *Esquisse d'histoire religieuse du Maroc: Confréries et Zaouïas* (Cahiers de l'Afrique et de l'Asie 2), Paris: J. Peyronnet, 1951.
EICKELMAN, Dale F., *Moroccan Islam: Tradition and Society in a Pilgrimage Center*, Chicago: University of Chicago Press, 1976.
GELLNER, Ernest, *Saints of the Atlas*, Chicago: University of Chicago Press, and London: Weidenfeld and Nicholson, 1969.

VOINOT, Louis, *Pèlerinages judéo-musulmans du Maroc* (Notes et Documents de l'Institut des Hautes Etudes Marocaines 4), Paris: Larose, 1948.

WESTERMARCK, Edward, *Marriage Ceremonies in Morocco*, London: Macmillan & Co., 1914 (Repr. 1971).

—, *Ritual and Belief in Morocco*, 2 Vols., London: Macmillan & Co., 1926 (Repr. 1971).

9. Algeria, Tunisia, Libya

CERBELLA, Gino, and Mustafa AGELI, *Le Feste Musulmane in Tripoli: Appunti etnografici*, Tripoli: Barbera, 1949.

DARMON, Raoul, *La situation des cultes en Tunisie*, Paris: A. Rousseau, 1928, 1930².

—, *La déformation des cultes en Tunisie*, Tunis: S.A.P.I., 1945.

LINGS, Martin, *A Sufi Saint of the Twentieth Century: Shaikh Ahmad al-Alawi. His Spiritual Heritage and Legacy*, Berkeley, Cal. etc.: University of California Press, 1973 (1st ed. London: Allen and Unwin, 1961).

NARDUCCI, Guglielmo, *Superstizioni libiche* (Contributo agli studi di etnografia libica 1), Tripoli: Minerva, 1938.

PANETTA, Ester, *Pratiche e credenze popolari libiche: Testi in arabo bengasino tradotti e annotati* (Pubblicazioni dell'Istituto per l'Oriente), Rome: Istituto per l'Oriente, 1940.

ZIADEH, Nicola A., *Sanusiyah: A Study of a Revivalist Movement in Islam*, Leiden: E. J. Brill, 1958 (Repr. 1968).

10. Africa South of the Sahara

HISKETT, Mervyn, *The Sword of Truth: The Life and Times of the Shehu Usuman Dan Fodio*, New York, etc.: Oxford University Press, 1973.

Islam in Africa, ed. by James KRITZECK and William H. LEWIS, New York, etc.: Van Nostrand-Reinhold, 1969.

Islam in Tropical Africa: Studies Presented and Discussed at the Fifth International African Seminar, Ahmadu Bello University, Zaria, January 1964, ed. by Ioan M. LEWIS, London: Oxford University Press, 1966.

MARTIN, Bradford G., *Muslim Brotherhoods in Nineteenth-Century Africa* (African Studies Series 18), London, etc.: Cambridge University Press, 1976.

MONTEIL, Vincent, *L'Islam noir*, Paris: Édition du Seuil, 1964, 1971².

11. Iran, Afghanistan, Pakistan, India

BARTH, Fredrik, *Political Leadership among Swat Pathans* (London School of Economics and Political Science: Monographs on Social Anthropology 19), London: Athlone Press, 1959 (Repr. 1980).

DONALDSON, Bess Allen, *The Wild Rue: A Study of Muhammadan Magic and Folklore in Iran*, London: Luzac, 1938.

SUBHAN, John A., *Sufism, its Saints and Shrines: An Introduction to the Study of Sufism with Special Reference to India*, Lucknow: Lucknow Publishing House, 1938 (Revised Edition 1960).

12. Indonesia

BOUSQUET, Georges-Henri, "Introduction à l'étude de l'Islam indonésien", *Revue des Études Islamiques*, Paris: P. Geuthner, 1938, Cahiers II-III, pp. 135–259.

GEERTZ, Clifford, *The Religion of Java*, London: Macmillan, and New York: Free Press of Glencoe, 1960 (etc.).

SNOUCK HURGRONJE, Christiaan, *The Achehnese*, 2 Vols., trans. from Dutch, Leiden: E.J. Brill, 1906 (Repr. New York: AMS Press, 1984).

—, *Verspreide Geschriften*, Vols. IV. 1 and 2, Bonn and Leipzig: Schroeder, 1924.

Chapter 6
Are there Hermeneutic Principles in Islam?

The ways in which Muslims have interpreted their religion and specifically its texts constitute a new field of scholarly research. As Peter Heath stated, in 1989, "[t]he modern study of Islamic hermeneutics is in its infancy. One reason for this is the field's vastness"[1]. I limit myself here to the Qur'ān, not so much dealing with the Qur'ān itself[2] as with ways in which the Qur'ān has been interpreted in the Muslim tradition, the methodology of this interpretation. This is a rather technical and abstract subject, and in dealing with it I shall address certain questions to Islamic *tafsīr* (Qur'ān interpretation) from the point of view of the science of religions (*Religionswissenschaft*).[3] To answer these questions and to find some logic in Muslim Qur'ān interpretations, I shall use materials brought to light by textual research.[4] Finally, I shall propose a way in which we can study the various interpretations that Muslims have given of Qur'ān texts, the Qur'ān itself, and Islam as impartially and objectively as possible.

1. Introduction

Let me formulate some preliminary questions.

1) In what sense can we speak of hermeneutics in Islam, meaning rules of interpretation, especially applied to sacred texts? Do we find any specific

---

[1] HEATH, "Creative Hermeneutics" (see selected literature under section 2.2.). The quotation is right at the beginning of the article (p. 173), which compares the hermeneutic methods of al-Tabarī (838–922), Ibn Sīnā (980–1037), and Ibn al-ʿArabī (1165–1240). For the author of the article, "[i]nterpretation is a dialectically creative process" (p. 210). See also RIPPIN, "The Present State of *Tafsīr* Studies" (see literature under 1.1.).

[2] For a reliable scholarly German translation of the Qur'ān, see Rudi PARET, *Der Koran: Übersetzung*, Stuttgart, etc.: Kohlhammer, 1966 (paperback edition 1979). For a reliable scholarly German commentary of the Qur'ān, see Adel Théodore KHOURY, *Der Koran: Arabisch-Deutsch. Übersetzung und wissenschaftlicher Kommentar*, Gütersloh: Gerd Mohn, 1990 ff.

[3] For an introduction to the subject, see LICHTENSTAEDTER, "Qur'ān and Qur'ān Exegesis" (see literature under 1.2.). See also RIPPIN, "The Present State of *Tafsīr* Studies", and ID., "Tafsīr" (see literature under 1.1. and 1.2.).

[4] A useful anthology of classical *tafsīr* texts in translation is given by GAETJE, *The Qur'ān and its Exegesis* (see literature under 1.4.). For an example of a classical *tafsīr* of Sūra

kind of thinking underlying the exegetical activity called *tafsīr*? And if there is something like hermeneutics in Islam, as a methodology of the search for meaning in texts or otherwise, are we dealing with rules that have been explicitly formulated and consciously applied by Muslim scholars? Or have we to search for rules of interpretation *post factum*, since they were implicitly present in the Muslim interpretations, without having been made explicit by Muslim exegetes at the time? Do we find, for example, in Islam a parallel to the seven ways in which the ancient rabbis read their Scriptures, or to the four levels of interpretation used by the Alexandrian and medieval theologians for Biblical exegesis?

2) To what extent have Muslim interpretations of the contents of the Qur'ān been conditioned by Islamic theological views about the origin, nature, and truth of the Qur'ān as Scripture? Does the interpretation of separate verses (*āyāt*) relate to the overall interpretation of the Scripture as such? More specifically, how does the meaning of individual verses relate to the overall meaning or message of the Scripture itself, and how is this overall meaning understood?[5] Such a connection would imply that, to grasp the hermeneutics of the Qur'ān, we should pay special attention to Islamic theologies existing around and about the meaning of the contents of the Qur'ān.

3) To assess the ways in which a certain exegetical procedure draws a religious meaning from a text, do we not need first a critical and empirical knowledge of the text on a purely philological level? And do we not need an equally critical historical knowledge of the context of a particular text in order to make a reasonable guess at what the verse may have meant to the first hearers, including the Prophet himself?[6]

4) A scholar studying the exegesis of Qur'anic texts may feel attraction or repulsion for certain texts on an emotional level. But inasmuch as scholarship is an attempt to arrive at knowledge that is generally valid, including knowledge about Scriptures and the ways in which they have been read, we should avoid taking an attitude either for or against the contents of the text. Our concern should be the text itself and its meaning, including the meaning people have found in the text and the way they have interpreted it. In other words, we are not concerned with what the text may mean to us, only with what it "means" as a text and what it has

---

12 given in translation, see BEESTON, *Baydāwī's Commentary on Surāh 12 of the Qur'ān* (see literature under 1.3.).

[5]   No theology of the Qur'ān has yet been written parallel to the theologies that have been developed of the Old and New Testament. Generally speaking, the question of the meaning of individual verses has dominated Muslim studies of the Qur'ān.

[6]   Such philological and contextual research was already carried out by the early Muslim commentators with the means at their disposal at the time.

meant and means to others[7] and where such a meaning shows religious features.

5) In trying to assess what the Qur'ān has meant to Muslims, we should inquire about the specific role of the specialists—the *mutakallimūn*, *'ulamā'*, *fuqahā'*. To what extent did they represent the larger community and convey their knowledge to it? In what sense was their interpretation authoritative and what were the limits of their authority? The interpretation of the Qur'ān is, in practice, the work of a much broader circle of people who work together on certain texts, searching for and discussing their meaning. They constitute a community precisely by recognizing themselves as "learners" and stressing the need for "obedience" to the text. The study of Scripture has not been restricted to university professors proposing their individual interpretations, but rather has been the effort of persons who have worked together to make sense of what they read. In this way, they constituted a special sort of community around the text.[8]

In this chapter we shall briefly consider classical *tafsīr* or Qur'ān interpretation, some new twentieth-century developments in this interpretation, and something of present-day discussions about the rules that should govern Muslim exegesis of Qur'ān texts and Muslim understanding of the Qur'ān. The same kind of study can and should be made, of course, about hermeneutics in Christianity and Judaism, not to speak of other religions with a Scripture that plays a vital part in the life of the community concerned.[9]

2. Classical Tafsīr

There has been new scholarly interest in *tafsīr* during the last thirty years or so, after the first survey Goldziher presented of it some eighty years ago.[10] Apart from a number of articles on the subject, several mono-

---

[7] Although the interest in the meaning and significance of a text for someone else implies a sense of the relevance of the text, it is only indirectly connected with the meaning the text could have for the scholar. The question of the "true" meaning and of the "meaning to me" is suspended in order to see the plurality of meanings that a text can have for different people and groups on an empirical level. In fact, the variety of interpretations given of certain texts may be seen as a sign of their richness of meaning.

[8] Reading and trying to understand a fragment of the Qur'ān is not only an individual but also a communal activity. One can often observe the Qur'ān being read in small groups, with mostly one person with recognized authority able to explain the text to the other participants.

[9] Scholarly study can have a positive impact on dialogue efforts, especially when it comes to studying together texts of each other's Scriptures.

[10] GOLDZIHER, *Die Richtungen der islamischen Koranauslegung* (see literature under 1.4.).

graphs have appeared on both classical and twentieth-century Qur'ān exegesis, at least one conference on the history of the interpretation of the Qur'ān has been held, and the term *tafsīr* shows up as a separate item in several encyclopedias.[11] Any understanding of Islam as a religion requires not only a familiarity with the Qur'ān within the limits and possibilities natural for non-Muslim scholars, but also insight into the ways the Qur'ān has been interpreted in the course of time by Muslims who derive meaning from it.

Not only "scholarly" but much more practical reasons gave rise to efforts at interpretation, when Muslims wanted to be sure what a particular verse meant. There are *hadīths* and even Qur'ān verses suggesting that people asked Muhammad himself, for practical purposes, about the meaning of particular verses he had recited. The beginnings and early development of *tafsīr* literature have recently come to light.[12] Some Muslim scholars who are dealing with the question have published their findings in Western languages.[13]

John S. Wansbrough distinguishes five kinds of *tafsīr* literature, two of which seem to be the most important.[14] The first is what he calls narrative *tafsīr*, which creates an edifying story embroidering a particular verse that alludes, for instance, to a historical event and arouses curiosity. The second is legal *tafsīr*, which deduces from particular verses precise prescriptions for human religious, social, and personal behavior. The search for the meaning of Qur'anic verses was often a response to very practical needs when people looked for guidance for their way of life and for making decisions.[15] The Qur'ān was to become the first source for the elaboration of the *Sharī'a*, before the *Sunna*, *ijmā'*, and *qiyās*, and other, minor sources of religious law.

2.1. Some Features of Islamic Tafsīr

A number of features of classical *tafsīr*, some of them derived from Guy Monnot's study[16], will strike scholars used to working in the field of Biblical exegesis as being distinctive of Qur'anic exegesis:

1) It is largely philological in character and requires not only good knowledge of the particular Arabic of the Qur'ān and of what is consid-

[11] E. J. Brill in Leiden is publishing an *Encyclopedia of the Qur'ān* (vol. 1, 2001).
[12] See for instance LEEMHUIS, "Origins and Early Development of the *Tafsīr* Tradition" (see literature under 2.2.).
[13] See for instance AYOUB, *The Qur'ān and Its Interpreters* (see literature under 1.4.), in particular the "Introduction" to Vol. I (pp. 1–40).
[14] WANSBROUGH, *Qur'anic Studies* (see literature under 1.1.).
[15] Muslims put full confidence in the Qur'ān and recognize the authority of any text quoted from the Qur'ān and/or studied by them.
[16] MONNOT, "La démarche classique de l'exégèse musulmane" (see literature under 1.2.).

ered pre-Islamic poetry, but also of Arabic grammar and lexicography as developed in the first centuries of Islam. The meaning of a number of words, moreover, is difficult to establish with absolute certainty.

2) The *tafsīr bi'l-ma'thūr*, which is based on the existing tradition of exegesis of a particular verse, juxtaposes various interpretations of the verse. The reader has to decide for him- or herself which of the proposed interpretations he or she prefers.

3) The first rule of *tafsīr* is that the Qur'ān is to be understood by itself, so that for the understanding of difficult Qur'ān verses, first, other verses whose meaning is clear are adduced. The Qur'ān itself already makes a distinction between what are called "clear" verses (*āyāt muhkamāt*) and "ambiguous" verses (*āyāt mutashābihāt*). Whereas the meaning of the first can be established without much doubt, the explanation of the latter is a delicate matter. It can only be done by referring to clear verses on the subject. The Qur'ān discourages speculation about their meaning, so many exegetes prefer to leave this open.[17] However, it is not always clear why certain verses and not others are adduced to elucidate the meaning of a particular verse. It often seems to be a highly arbitrary choice.

4) The second rule of *tafsīr* is that Muhammad is to be considered as the first exegete or hermeneut of the Qur'ān. Consequently, in case of unclarity, after the Qur'ān itself, the *Sunna* (*Hadīth* literature) should be used as a subsidiary source of information.[18] Preference will go to those *hadīths* that go back to the Prophet; otherwise *hadīths* of the Companions (first generation) will do; and if they are not conclusive, one can resort to *hadīths* of the Followers (second generation). The *Sunna* can also provide information, for instance, about the situation in which Muhammad recited a particular verse (*asbāb al-nuzūl*).

5) The literal meaning of a verse is the true meaning, unless it is in flagrant opposition to reason; then another meaning, for instance an allegorical one, may be sought for.

6) Consensus (*ijmā'*) or at least a large majority of scholarly opinions is an argument that an interpretation is valid.

7) The presence of historical facts on an issue does not outweigh the content of a Qur'anic verse on that issue.

8) The esthetic perfection (*i'jāz*) of the Qur'ān prohibits interpretations that would detract from it.

9) Each *āya* or a small group of *āyāt* belonging together constitutes a unit of revelation in its own right, with its own independent value and immediate truth.

---

[17] This is not only a sign of avowed ignorance, but also of respect for the text.

[18] Speight, "The Function of *hadīth* as Commentary on the Qur'ān, as seen in the Six Authoritative Collections" (see literature under 3.).

10) In practice, many readers and users of the Qur'ān deny categorically that they give an interpretation to the text. On the contrary, they will affirm that they have direct access to the truth expressed by a particular verse. From the beginning of Islam, there has been opposition to the very effort of *tafsīr*, and the need for *tafsīr*, *ta'wīl*, and hermeneutics generally has been denied in these quarters.[19] Revelation, according to this view, is sufficient in itself to manifest the meaning of the verse to human beings in a direct way. Or the Qur'ān is taken as a source of meditation and not an object of intellectual activity.[20] In both cases, hermeneutics is seen as an unnecessary intellectual exercise.

2.2. Scholarly and Practical Tafsīr

In this connection it may be useful to make a distinction between scholarly and practical interpretations of Qur'anic verses.

In scholarly interpretations, only "learned" as opposed to political, pedagogical, strictly personal, or opportunistic arguments count; these interpretations can go squarely against current practices or opinions. Great scholars of *tafsīr*, like al-Tabarī (838–922)[21], al-Zamakhsharī (1075–1144), Fakhr al-Dīn al-Rāzī (1149–1209), and Ibn Kathīr (ca. 1300–73) composed running commentaries on the Qur'ān that were monuments of learning. They could develop critical views of the state of the religious sciences (ʿulūm al-dīn) of Islam in their time, since they had mastered the art of interpreting the Qur'ān, which constitutes so to speak the lynchpin of the Islamic religious sciences. Their effort of interpretation arose to a large extent from the problems of meaning given with the Qur'anic text itself. For instance, a number of texts obviously contradict each other, and there are texts whose literal meaning would undercut basic theological theses, like the unity and uniqueness of God (*tawhīd*), the prophethood (*nubuwwa*) of Muhammad and his predecessors, or the miraculous and inimitable perfection (*iʿjāz*) of the Qur'ān.[22]

Alongside this "scholarly", intellectual *tafsīr*, a practical, "lived" one has existed throughout Islamic history. It could arise in private or communal life without public consequences. It could, however, also be the result of

---

[19] BIRKELAND, *Old Muslim Opposition against Interpretation of the Koran* (see literature under 3.).
[20] Mysticism in Islam developed largely out of meditation on the Qur'ān, as is clear from a number of technical terms that go back to Qur'anic concepts. See about Sūfī *tafsīr* and *ta'wīl* below.
[21] Al-Tabarī's hermeneutics has been the subject of several studies. See for instance GILLIOT, *Exégèse, langue et théologie en Islam* (see literature under 1.3.). See also McAULIFFE, "Qur'anic Hermeneutics" (see literature under 2.2.). Cf. HEATH's article of 1989 quoted above in note 1.
[22] Cf. BOULLATA, "The Rhetorical Interpretation of the Qur'ān" (see literature under 3.).

the search by diverse interests—juridical, theological, political—for support for their cause in the Qur'ān. Sometimes it is difficult to know whether a particular interpretation of a verse is deduced correctly from the text concerned or if it is rather given to support a certain cause that has nothing to do with the obvious literal meaning of the text. So *tafsīr* could serve certain religious causes, to support a particular doctrine or school of *kalām* in its polemics with other schools, sects, or religions, or to support a particular doctrine or school of *fiqh* in its refutation of other legal schools or religious laws. And throughout Islamic history, *tafsīr* has also been used to serve political causes, in support either of those in power or of a faction in opposition to the rulers. The exegesis of the Qur'anic verses on Christians acquired an increasingly polemical character in times of tension between the communities.[23]

2.3. The Qur'ān as Scripture

Let me note a few other characteristics of Muslim *tafsīr* that are related to the concept of Scripture in Islam.[24]

1) For Muslims, the recitation of the Qur'ān[25] evokes sacred reality, supposed to be divinely revealed, containing absolute orientations for thinking and norms for acting. The intensive study of the Qur'ān and its verses (*āyāt*) has led among Muslims in many quarters to the construction of what one may call a "Qur'anic universe" of the mind. Especially those who know the Qur'ān by heart but also many others construct a spiritual world of Qur'anic verses by which to conduct life and to judge reality. The very familiarity with the *āyāt* and the Qur'ān itself makes for a universe of meaning resources, which can be enriched with a number of well-known *hadīths* and which is fundamentally self-sufficient. Critical hermeneutics plays no part here: what happens is that a universe is constructed with the help of Qur'anic verses as building blocks, and this construction is based on the sacredness of the Qur'ān itself. Different spiritual orientations have given rise to different such universes, and vice versa. Each such universe unmistakably has its particular intentions and finality.

2) The fact that each verse is considered to be a literal revelation of a divine truth communicated through these precise words with their various meanings gives any interpretative activity a particular theological

---

[23] On the *tafsīr* of Qur'anic verses on the Christians, see McAuliffe, *Qur'ānic Christians* (see literature under 1.5.).

[24] The Qur'ān is not just text, or even recited text, but Scripture. "Scriptures are not texts!", as Wilfred C. Smith wrote in his *What is Scripture? A Comparative Approach*, London: SCM Press, 1993, p. 223.

[25] On the Qur'ān as "spoken Word", see Graham, *Beyond the Written Word* (see literature under 3.), especially pp. 79–115.

background or dimension. The Qur'ān is a multitude of divine Words as well as the immediate presence of God's Word and the act of God's speaking.[26] There is a specific concept of prophetic Revelation here, a specific concept of Truth contained in very precise wordings, and a specific concept of God's Speech and his Word resulting from it.[27] The sacralization of the Qur'ān as Scripture with a fixed corpus of *āyāt* and, in the Sunnī tradition, fixed limits put on their interpretation narrows the scope of exegetical activity. Although there is no institutional authority to determine the limits of interpretation, *tafsīr* in Sunnī Islam has developed its own scholarly tradition (*sunna*) that is difficult to break through, as recent experiences testify.

3) As with so many movements outside the main Churches in Christianity that practice the free use of the Bible, in Islam, the non-Sunnī Muslim schools and communities have developed their own kind of exegesis, distinct from that current in Sunnī Islam. The various Shī'ī schools, for instance, give special weight and authority to those Qur'ān interpretations that were, and in the case of the Ismā'īlīs still are, given by the Imāms. The views of the fifth Imām, Ja'far al-Sādiq, for instance, and his interpretation of Qur'anic verses enjoy a nearly absolute authority in Twelver Shī'ī Islam.[28] The same holds true for the teachings of the Ismā'īlī Imāms in Sevener Shī'ī Islam.[29] Here, even more than is the case in Twelver Shī'ī Islam, it is not only a "Qur'anic universe" of *āyāt* and *akhbār (hadīths)* that is created, but an entire spiritual universe. We find here visions of life, the world, reality, and God that go far beyond the relatively controlled "Qur'anic universe" of traditional Sunnī signature.[30]

2.4. Tafsīr and Ta'wīl: Sūfī and Shī'ī

In the first centuries of classical Qur'ān interpretation, the term used for it was *ta'wīl*. At a later stage, however, it was called *tafsīr*, the word *ta'wīl* being then reserved for more far-reaching spiritual interpretations.

---

[26] In *kalām* (Islamic scholastic theology), the relationship between God's Words, Word, and Speech (act of speaking) has been a subject of much discussion. This also concerned the status of the Qur'ān. See for instance Johan BOUMAN, *Le conflit autour du Coran et la solution d'al-Bāqillānî*, Diss. Utrecht, 1959 and Johannes R.T.M. PETERS, *God's Created Speech: A Study in the Speculative Theology of 'Abd al-Jabbār*, Leiden: E. J. Brill, 1976.

[27] We urgently need ongoing impartial study of the Islamic concepts of Revelation and revealed Truth, of God's Speech and Word(s), including the discussions in the Muslim community about these and similar concepts in the past as well as in the present.

[28] On Twelver Shī'ī hermeneutics see CORBIN, "Shī'ī Hermeneutics" (see literature under 2.3.).

[29] On Ismā'īlī hermeneutics see NANJI, "Toward a Hermeneutic of Qur'ānic and Other Narratives of Isma'īlī Thought" (see literature under 2.3.).

[30] In descriptions of such spiritual worlds, Qur'ān verses seem largely to serve as reference points for a kind of thinking that has its own logic.

To this day, Sunnī *'ulamā'* practice the discipline of *tafsīr* in the form described above, with much emphasis on philology, as one of the most important "religious sciences" (*'ulūm al-dīn*) of Islam. *Tafsīr* may be called the heart of Islamic religious thinking, and it supports the discipline of scholastic theology (*kalām*). For Sunnī *fuqahā'*, *tafsīr* is a crucial discipline, like the study of tradition (*'ilm al-hadīth*) indispensable for the discipline of *fiqh*, which establishes the right behavior of Muslims as contained in the *Sharī'a*. In the Shī'a, *tafsīr* is equally indispensable, but there is more individual freedom than in the Sunnī tradition.[31] On a spiritual level, the results of *tafsīr* are especially palpable in a person's acquiring knowledge of and insight into the work of God in his Creation, by means of the relevant texts of the Qur'ān, which can lead to further meditation.[32]

Ta'wīl, on the other hand, seems to be much less subject to philological and rational control than *tafsīr*. In Sunnī Islam, it is especially the mystics who practice *ta'wīl*. They give a spiritual interpretation of certain Qur'anic texts that they hold to refer to spiritual realities, for instance experiences of specific stages of the mystic path to divine Reality or God. With the help of the Qur'ān, they are searching for the inner meaning of reality, which opens up in the experience of immediate relationship between God and humans. This is the field of the many Sūfī traditions alive in *turuq* (brotherhoods) all over the Muslim world. Here the Sūfī *sheykhs*, rather than *'ulamā'*, provide guidance, interpreting the Qur'ān primarily through the soul rather than the intellect. One of the best examples of such mystical *ta'wīl* is Ibn al-'Arabī's Qur'ān interpretation.[33] Sūfī *ta'wīl* follows certain rules, and Gerhard Böwering speaks here of a particular hermeneutic, the key of which is the progress on the mystical path.[34] Henry Corbin paid special attention to Sūfī hermeneutics.[35]

Another field in which the Qur'ān is commonly interpreted by *ta'wīl* is that of Shī'a spirituality. From very early on, adherents of the Shī'a reproached the Sunnīs for the fact that the Qur'ān corpus established under Othmān had suppressed certain verses that favor 'Alī and other members of the Prophet's family and their descendants. Alternatively, Shī'a *'ulamā'* gave typical Shī'ī *ta'wīl* interpretations of those Qur'ān

---

[31]   On Twelver Shī'ī *tafsīr*, see AYOUB, "The Speaking Qur'ān and the Silent Qur'ān" (see literature under 2.3.). Cf. note 28.

[32]   Such meditation, however, can also be achieved in a direct way through experience, without "intellectual" *tafsīr*.

[33]   See GOLDZIHER's study mentioned above in note 10, pp. 216–57.

[34]   BÖWERING, *The Mystical Vision of Existence in Classical Islam* (see literature under 2.3.). A nice example of Sūfī *ta'wīl* is given by Bruce ROSS in his "Islamic Hermeneutics and Shihabuddin Suhrawardi's Language of the Ants", *Analecta Husserliana*, 43 (1994), pp. 179–94. For esoteric Sūfī and Shī'ī *ta'wīl*, see LORY, *Les commentaires ésotériques du Coran d'après 'Abd al-Razzāq al-Qāshānī* (see literature under 2.3.).

[35]   CORBIN, "L'intériorisation du sens en herméneutique soufie iranienne" (see literature under 2.3.).

verses regarded as uncertain or ambivalent in meaning (*mutashābih*), claiming that they referred to the Imāms and their teachings.[36] Using *ta'wīl* as a kind of allegorical *tafsīr*, they developed a Shī'ī reading of the Qur'ān, just as the mystics developed their Sūfī reading of it. Within the Shī'ī exegetical traditions, Ismā'īlī *ta'wīl* has again its own place.[37] In all cases the text of the Qur'ān has been the starting point for spiritual growth and insight.[38]

Summarizing, *ta'wīl* stands for those interpretations of Qur'ān verses that differ from *tafsīr* interpretation by bypassing philological and Sunnī historical readings and by eluding the control of reason, as it is exercised in the service of Sunnī traditions and doctrines. Because of their relative freedom, Sūfī and Shī'ī *ta'wīl* could open perspectives in Qur'ān interpretation that remained closed to Sunnī *tafsīr*. Until recently, both Shī'ī and Sūfī *ta'wīl* led to forms of spirituality that seem to have had only limited social implications.[39]

It is perhaps not superfluous to mention the constant quotations of and references to Qur'anic verses encountered in prose and poetry literature as it developed in Islamic civilization, in its many languages and cultural contexts. The language of the Qur'ān has a religious halo; it is considered exemplary, the model of perfect Arabic. In social and cultural life, including politics, Qur'anic verses are readily used or alluded to, and the role of Qur'anic concepts is fundamental in the life of Muslim societies.[40]

Most important perhaps is the fact that, throughout its history, Muslim civilization has established both a tradition of spirituality[41] and a corpus of religious knowledge referring to the Qur'ān. This knowledge is represented by the institutions of Islamic religious learning and their authorities, where tradition has its weight. To change anything in it, new

---

[36] See GOLDZIHER's study mentioned above in note 10, pp. 278–309.

[37] Ismail K. POONAWALA, "Ismā'īlī ta'wīl of the Qur'ān", in *Approaches to the History of the Interpretation of the Qur'an* (see literature under 1.1.), pp. 199–222.

[38] Sometimes Western scholars have had their own personal, theological, or philosophical "hermeneutics" in the study of Muslim spiritual texts. See for instance Charles J. ADAMS, "The Hermeneutics of Henry Corbin", in *Approaches to Islam in Religious Studies*, ed. by Richard C. MARTIN, Tucson, Ariz.: University of Arizona Press, 1985, pp. 129–50.

[39] This is, of course, difficult to judge. What we read as spiritual texts from the past may have implied social and political choices at the time such texts were written. Islamic studies, when concentrating on texts, have not been sufficiently aware of social and political issues existing at the time and in whose light such texts can be read. On the contrary, we are accustomed to have an apolitical reading of the Qur'ān and other religious texts. Muslims may see our "spiritual" or at least intellectual readings as one-sided, idealistic, and naive, though they may be impressed by such spiritual efforts.

[40] One should, of course, be thoroughly familiar with the Qur'ān to recognize quotations of and allusions to Qur'anic *āyāt* in Muslim speeches and writings.

[41] The best presentation of relevant texts in translation is probably that contained in the two volumes *Islamic Spirituality*, ed. by Seyyed Hussein NASR, London: Routledge and Kegan Paul, 1987 and 1991.

approaches to the interpretation of the Qur'ān seem to be needed. Reformists and modernists tried to do this. At present, on the one hand, new "Islamicist" orientations have arisen that claim to have immediate access to the Qur'ān and that develop Islamic ideologies without making interpretation a problem. On the other hand, traditional methods of Qur'ān interpretation have been questioned by certain scholars. Some Muslim scholars have welcomed hermeneutics as an approach that can lead to new orientations and interpretations.

3. Twentieth-century Developments in Qur'ān Interpretation

In the course of the twentieth century, some new trends in Qur'ān interpretation have developed, though without implying a break in the tradition of *tafsīr* literature.[42] They are understandable in the context of the many changes that have occurred in Muslim societies in this period, disrupting numerous social traditions. To cope with the ensuing problems, people for whom Islam represents the highest value and who want to go back to its sources have turned to the Qur'ān for solutions.[43] Consequently, *'ulamā'* of a new generation, leaders of contemporary Islamic movements, and "lay" persons with religious and moral concerns have initiated new efforts in the field of *tafsīr* and *ta'wīl*. We can distinguish four new major trends in their work.

1) If the unique character of the Qur'ān as the definite revelation and miracle of the Arabic language had always been stressed since Muhammad's preaching, this has become more marked in the twentieth century. New efforts have been made to increase the prestige of the Qur'ān, proclaim its profound message, teach the truths of its *āyāt*, and stress its unique and sacred character in various ways. This not only happens in the media, but is also a striking feature of many modern *tafsīrs* written for Muslim readers. They abundantly stress the supernatural, salutary, and miraculous character of the Qur'ān. Moreover, they present Muhammad not only as a prophet sent to bring the Qur'ān, but also as a model for human life. They show that the Qur'ān encourages the use of reason and claims to contain all necessary knowledge. Some commentaries go as

---

[42] BALJON, *Modern Muslim Koran Interpretation*; JANSEN, *The Interpretation of the Koran in Modern Egypt* (for both see literature under 1.4.); JOMIER, *Le commentaire coranique du Manār*; MERAD, *Ibn Bādīs* (for both see literature under 1.3.).

[43] The return to the sources of Islam, the Qur'ān and the authentic *Sunna*, has always been a theme of "puritan" movements in Islam, but particularly so since the mid-nineteenth century. During the last decades, this return to the Qur'ān has been increasingly important in supporting Islamic ideologies.

far as to claim that a number of modern inventions and scientific discoveries are already contained in the Qur'ān.[44]

2) On a practical level, the modernization of society requires a revision of and break with numerous social traditions maintained in traditional societies under the stamp of religion. Reformist and modernist thinkers tried to do away with much existing tradition, which they saw as standing in the way of modernization. Both groups proclaimed the need to return to the basic sources of religion, that is to say the Qur'ān and the authentic *Sunna,* and this entailed a degree of revision of current religious ideas and practices. By means of some new techniques of Qur'ān interpretation (for instance the combination of verses), certain social customs standing in the way of modernization could be stripped of their traditional religious legitimation. Even in the sensitive area of the *Sharī'a, fuqahā'* of a modern reformist orientation could bring about certain changes of interpretation or uphold the application of traditional prescripts by the use of certain juridical devices. But such changes were extremely difficult in the case of explicit and unambiguous Qur'anic prescripts in the fields of personal and criminal law.

3) Nearly all twentieth-century Qur'ān commentaries show the extent to which the Qur'ān stresses the value of reason and reasoning to acquire knowledge. Many reformists and particularly the modernists present Islam as the religion of reason. It is true that the Qur'ān, more than any other Scripture, uses rational arguments and insists on the need to acquire knowledge and insight, but what is meant is primarily "religious" insight. This modern exegesis has encouraged and supported the necessary efforts of education and technical, economic and social development in many Muslim countries and societies.

At a later stage, however, the stress on the use of reason has sometimes led to what may be called a kind of "religious rationalism". Especially the so-called "Islamists" have tended to present Islam itself as a rational structure consisting of well-chosen texts from the Qur'ān. This structure is held to be a model that—just like a technical or scientific model—should be applied squarely to society to arrive at a just, Islamic society. In this way, the recourse to Qur'anic texts has led to a rational "operationalization" of Islam in ideological, social, and political terms, a procedure that has been applied in the projects of the so-called Islamic "revival" of recent years. Very influential have been the Qur'ān commentaries written by Mawdūdī in Pakistan[45] and by Sayyid Qutb in Egypt.[46]

---

[44] See JANSEN's study mentioned above in note 42, pp. 40–54.
[45] See Charles J. ADAMS, "Abū'l-A'lā Mawdūdī's *Tafhīm al-Qur'ān*", in *Approaches to the History of the Interpretation of the Qur'an* (see literature under 1.1.), pp. 307–23.
[46] Sayyid QUTB is the author of *Fī zilāl al-qur'ān* (In the shadow of the Qur'ān). See CARRÉ, *Mystique et politique* (see literature under 1.3.).

4) The most important phenomenon, however, seems to be the way a number of twentieth-century Qur'ān interpretations stress aspects of the Qur'ān other than the legal ones emphasized in the *tafsīrs* of the *fuqahā'*. On the one hand, they reveal broader social values, such as the dignity of human beings, the struggle for social justice, and the building of a new kind of society and state as a sort of middle path between socialism and capitalism. On the other hand, they pay much attention to the moral aspects of life and insist on the essential freedom and responsibility of human beings, their fundamental duties and rights, and their need for moral guidance in order to live according to their destiny. All of this is considered God-given norms.

These four trends are not wholly absent from the classical *tafsīr* tradition, but they are singularly stressed in twentieth-century Qur'ān commentaries, which also depict Islam as the panacea for the evils of the time.

As a result, several new forms of Qur'ān exegesis have appeared in the course of this century, though often with precursors in classical *tafsīr*. The following appear to be the main ones:

1) Strictly *reformist* exegesis is intent on purifying the existing living and especially popular forms of Islam of any innovation (*bid ʿa*) that may have accrued since the time of the Prophet and the four rightly guided caliphs (*al-khulafā' al-rāshidūn*) of Medina. It expresses the ideal of restoring the original Islam (Hanbalī tradition, Saudi Arabia) or of a more or less "puritan" way of life according to the ideas and prescripts of the "Qur'anic universe". It is associated with a literal exegesis of the relevant Qur'anic verses.

2) Political *activist* exegesis is intent on bringing about a "truly Islamic" society and state based on the *Sharīʿa*. It may lead to forming smaller authentic Islamic communities that act "from below", at the grassroots (Muslim Brothers). It may also envisage Islam as a revolutionary force and lead to efforts to seize power and establish an Islamic state "from above" (Khomeinī). It corresponds to a political reading of the Qur'ān that stresses the political character of Scripture.

3) What may be called *modernizing* exegesis takes into account the values of modern culture and science, especially in the West but elsewhere too. It represents a trend to orient the individual and society according to world-wide accepted norms and values that may be in fruitful tension with the specific, more particularistic values of Islam. It subscribes to ideals of fundamental openness to and communication with the whole of humankind and often possesses a philosophical bent inspired by universalistic orientations from the West and other parts of the world. We find here an exegesis that applies reason as an important

criterion of interpretation and tends to rediscover universal values in Scripture.[47]

4) The Islamic *spiritual* exegesis develops a broader religious worldview or universe than that based on Qur'anic texts alone, but remains within the confines of fundamentally Islamic doctrine and practice. The search for spiritual reality may be pursued with the help of Qur'anic *āyāt*, on the basis of mystical experience in which reason certainly plays a role secondary to experience (Sūfī spirituality). It may also be based on a theological metaphysics that takes Qur'anic notions as a point of departure or reference while elevating them through insight (gnostic spirituality).

5) Forms of what may be called a still more *spiritualist* exegesis develop broader spiritual worldviews, referring to Qur'anic texts but giving them spiritual interpretations (*ta'wīl*) that have certain social implications and that the *'ulamā'* think to go beyond Islamic doctrine and practice and in some cases brand heretical. Adherents strive to build new kinds of spiritual and social communities distinct from the established Sunnī and Shī'ī communities. In practice, Muslim opposition to and in some cases persecution of these communities is theologically justified with the argument that peace and order should be maintained. Muslims take very harsh attitudes towards those considered to be heretical apostates. Spiritualist *ta'wīl* of the kind referred to here mostly claims to possess special authority in order to legitimate its interpretation of the Qur'ān.[48]

6) During the last decades of the twentieth century, more *theoretical* enquiries have been pursued with the aim of developing new kinds of interpretation of the Qur'ān and its message. Such interpretations are based on arguments of reason rather than on any special spiritual authority. Methodological orientations are prominent here, often combined with a critical view of established religious institutions and thinking.

4. Present-day Qur'ān Interpretation

4.1. *Western and Muslim studies*

For a long time, *Western* studies of the meaning of Qur'ān texts have been dominated by philological and historical approaches that have

---

[47]   An important variant is the idea that the Qur'anic revelations in Mecca were of a universal nature, addressing the whole of humankind, whereas the Qur'anic revelations in Medina, addressing the Muslim community with its concrete questions, had a more particularistic significance.

[48]   An interesting case is the Qur'ān commentary of the Bāb. See LAWSON, "Interpretation as Revelation" (see literature under 1.3.). For the Qur'ān interpretation by Ghulām Ahmad, the founder of the Ahmadiyya movement, see Yohanan FRIEDMANN, *Prophecy Continuous: Aspects of Ahmadī Religious Thought and its Medieval Background*, Berkeley, Cal. etc.: University of California Press, 1989.

restricted the search of meaning to the study both of the lexicography, etymology and grammar of the text and of its history and the history of the context in which it was written. In the second half of the twentieth century, however, some alternative approaches have been developed that are particularly attentive to the problem of meaning, as is studied in semantics and semiotics.[49] Besides employing techniques of word-counting and analyzing the growth of the lexicon of a text over a certain period of time, they also study the appearance—and, where relevant, disappearance—of particular words and word clusters in a text. Questions have also been raised about the audience a given recited or written text is intended to reach, what kind of message or call for action it implies and, of course, how the public responds.

All of this shows that the problem of the objective meaning and the subjective significance of individual Qur'anic verses and the Qur'ān as a whole has been attracting increasing interest among Western scholars. My guess is that certain polemical attitudes toward the content of the Qur'ān and a certain blindness to the idea of revelation have been replaced by a more adequate explanation and understanding of the text as it presents itself. The same is true for Western studies of the broader interpretations that have been given of the Qur'ān and particular verses in the course of history.

Muslim studies of the Qur'ān will, of course, be primarily concerned with the question of the religious truths conveyed by it and its many *āyāt*. A few Muslim scholars have presented objective descriptions of the contents of the Qur'ān, meant for an interested and not uncritical Western readership.[50] On the other hand, a great number of books written in Arabic, Turkish, Persian, and other "Muslim" languages about the Qur'ān and *tafsīr* aim to convey the Qur'anic truth as a message to Muslim readers. They take a religious point of view and reflect various positions on the problems that confront present-day Muslim societies. In recent years, Muslim scholars like Mohammed Arkoun[51], Hasan Hanafi[52], and Nasr Hamid Abu Zayd[53] have also published innovating studies on methodological and theoretical problems of the hermeneutics of Scripture.

---

[49] See especially Arkoun, *Lectures du Coran* (see literature under 2.1.). Cf. *The Challenge of the Scriptures* (see literature under 4.).

[50] For instance Fazlur Rahman, *Major Themes of the Qur'ān*, Minneapolis and Chicago: Bibliotheca Islamica, 1980; Talbi, "Quelle clé pour lire le Coran?" (see literature under 2.1.).

[51] See Arkoun's study mentioned above in note 49.

[52] Hasan Hanafi, *Les méthodes d'exégèse: Essai sur la science des fondements de la compréhension, "Ilm Usul al-Fiqh"* (PhD. thesis, University of Paris, 1965).

[53] Nasr Hamid Abu Zaid, *Islam und Politik: Kritik des religiösen Diskurses*, Frankfurt a. M.: Dipa Verlag, 1996.

4.2. Qur'anic Universes: Rationality and Presuppositions

In the course of the last hundred years, new subjects have been treated in *tafsīr* and new developments have occurred in the way the rules of *tafsīr* are applied. All of this has been due largely to the fact that the Qur'ān is consulted to provide answers to problems of a practical nature. These problems change with time. What about present-day spiritual "religious universes" elaborated on the basis of Qur'anic texts? In Egypt, for instance, there is a long tradition of constructing vast universes of meaning on the basis of selected texts from the Qur'ān. Such elaborations bear witness to a more or less unbridled religious imaginative power, which is developed, for instance, for the purpose of inculcating morality, preaching a religious life or a just society, elaborating the delights of paradise or the terrors of hell, or just expressing the spiritual enjoyment of the richness of *āyāt*, which are elaborated *ad infinitum*.

To what extent have such "Qur'anic universes" their own *rationality*? Such a rationality may be discovered most easily in the elaborations that spring from straightforward puritan orientations, as can be found in the Qur'ān interpretations of present-day "Islamists", mostly leading to various Islamic ideologies. But it is much more difficult to grasp the assumptions, intentions, and rules according to which the individual or collective imagination constructs more complex "spiritual universes" and to assess the way in which the latter relate to social reality.

This is especially true for those still more open spiritual universes developed on the basis of *ta'wīl*. At first sight they are arbitrary associations of spiritual concepts and experiences. Yet, even in the spiritual field, imagination is not completely arbitrary, and the writings that express them are linked to Muslim traditions of Sūfī and gnostic spirituality, with their own developments and interactions in the course of history. But how are they to be investigated? Several researchers in this field have studied these texts for their own spiritual satisfaction and enrichment, becoming committed to their authors' spiritual causes and sometimes converting to Islam. But good phenomenological studies that maintain a scholarly distance and investigate the implicit and explicit messages, the intentions and underlying rules, in short the inherent rationality of spiritual texts, are rare.

A similar remark should be made about the philosophical and theological *assumptions* of the various "Qur'anic" and broader spiritual universes that have been deduced from the Qur'ān. We are dealing here not only with the *explicit* doctrines that are proper to faith or with explicit prescriptions for correct behavior. These have been well formulated and are quite well-known among both Sunnīs and Shī'īs.

What is much more difficult to grasp are the *implicit* assumptions in the understanding of such forms of spirituality. The fact that very well-intentioned Westerners have thought they could grasp Islamic forms of spirituality with relative ease betrays a certain naiveté. Their efforts have led to a sympathetic attitude to Muslim spirituality, but also to a certain estheticism, a neglect of the commitments involved in spiritual expressions. I believe that, as a rule, the contents of the spirituality of a religion should be presented by adherents of that religion itself; this seems to me a requirement of scholarship. Further reflection is needed on the implicit assumptions of such spirituality, the things that are simply taken for granted, for instance the way thought is expressed in language, especially when a religious value is attributed to this language, which is the case with Arabic and which gives a special weight to Arabic elaborations of Qur'anic texts. There are also social and religious implications in being a Muslim. These are what may be called typically "Islamic" assumptions.

But there are also problems of a more general human nature. They have to do with the *condition humaine*. Such problems—for instance relations between the sexes or violence—are not typical of Muslim societies, but underlie human societies in general, which have to find answers to them. The responses given to them in Muslim societies have resulted in particular social and political structures and features that Westerners tend to call typically "Islamic". The study of such structures, the way they provide answers to universal human problems, and the way these structures function and are interpreted in Muslim societies is helpful to understand the social background of Islamic spirituality.

In Muslim societies' daily life, specific situations are often popularly viewed and judged according to specific Qur'anic verses or *hadīths*. Such texts, which are alive in the collective imagination, provide the matrix for perceiving and judging at least part of reality—the meaningful part. In everyday life, empirical reality does not so much serve to interpret Scripture, but the reverse; the realities of experience are interpreted—and become meaningful—through the Qur'ān.

4.3. The Relevance of Hermeneutics in Islam

I am not sure if we can find in Muslim scholarship itself, outside Sūfī circles, a kind of *explicit* hermeneutics that clearly distinguishes different levels on which a text can be interpreted, such as was developed in the rabbinical and Christian theological traditions. I contend, however, that *tafsīr* and *ta'wīl* are subject to rules and that a certain kind of *implicit* hermeneutics exists in the Muslim tradition and may very well be made explicit and elaborated rationally. In Europe, a hermeneutical tradition based on reason began with Schleiermacher in the wake of Enlightenment.[54] The hermeneutic concerns, based on reason, of Mohammed

---

[54]   Claus von BORMANN, "Hermeneutik: I. Philosophisch-theologisch", in *Theologische Realenzyklopädie*, Vol. 15, Berlin and New York: Walter de Gruyter, 1986, pp. 108–37.

Arkoun, Hasan Hanafi, and Nasr Hamid Abu Zayd at the present time may be considered a similar response to the wave of rational modernization that has been taking hold of Muslim societies. The same holds true for other thinkers in Muslim countries who insist on the value of reason.

Today's hermeneutic and semiotic efforts, although developing on a theoretical level, are not entirely fortuitous. As I see it, they are primarily a response to practical situations, but they imply a search for rationality. They not only have social and, indirectly, political consequences but also direct intellectual implications. They allow greater freedom in the interpretation of Scripture and the application of Scripture to empirical realities, including social and individual life. Their theoretical intention is to open up new kinds of "meaning" in given texts, but this has eminently practical consequences. It is no accident that certainly the religious but also the political establishments in Muslim countries have been more than suspicious of them, as they have always been of intellectuals who display a critical as well as a self-critical sense.

It may be that a profound dilemma is emerging in current efforts to arrive at new ways of interpreting the Qur'ān. One possibility is to take Islamic materials as a starting point, and for the sake of interpretation to adapt typically *Islamic* principles of interpretation as much as possible to cater to needs of the present time. This may go hand in hand with emphasis on the self-sufficiency of Islam. In this case, hermeneutic procedures lead to seeing universal problems in Islamic terms.

Another possibility is to take certain *universal* hermeneutic principles and generally accepted ways of interpreting texts as a starting point and to apply them to Islamic materials. This may be combined with an openness to general problems of humankind and may elucidate the contribution Islamic norms and values could make to a solution of these general problems. The discussion of the interpretation of Islamic texts then forms part of a broader discourse on the explanation and interpretation of Scriptures and other religious texts. In this case, hermeneutic procedures lead to seeing Islamic particularities in universal terms.

5. Toward a New Scholarly View of Qur'ān and Islam

For the further study of Muslim and other interpretations of the Qur'ān and their underlying hermeneutics, it is indispensable to develop an open scholarly view of the Qur'ān.

Unfortunately, hermeneutics in Judaism and Islam are not represented. Cf. Claude GILLIOT, "L'herméneutique en Islam", in *Encyclopédie des Religions*, ed. by Frédéric LENOIR, Paris: Bayard, 1997, pp. 2233–7.

First, the Qur'ān needs to be recognized and respected in scholarly terms as a collection of *āyāt* that have a sign and symbol value for Muslims. With their help, Muslims deal "religiously" with the reality—life, the world, and what is beyond—to which these *āyāt* refer.

Second, through the application of its *āyāt*, the Qur'ān allows people to arrive at particular interpretations of this reality. It leads to a particular kind of "Word-knowledge" of reality and particular forms of moral behavior toward it.

Third, this Qur'anic "Word-knowledge" seems to take precedence over and to impose itself on empirical reality. The Qur'anic "Word-knowledge" apparently functions as a symbolic filter in relation to the experience of reality and the search for meaning in it. Consequently, in practice, the interpretation of the Qur'ān is rarely a mere exercise in understanding the meaning of the *āyāt*. It rather serves to discover meaning in life and reality and to attain insight.

I believe that such an open scholarly view permits us to study Muslim interpretations of the Qur'ān—and Muslim hermeneutics generally—most adequately. In this way, the different readings and interpretations of the Qur'ān can be studied with the necessary scholarly openness, without legal or moral prejudices or spiritual or political biasses, and with a universalist orientation.

I contend that a similar new and open scholarly view should also be developed toward the broader study of Islam. What has been said about the *āyāt* of the Qur'ān is *mutatis mutandis* also valid for the religious elements of Islam. When approached from the angle of the scholarly study of religion (*Religionswissenschaft*), Islam as such can be seen as a system of signs and symbols that can be interpreted and applied in different ways. The Qur'ān with its *āyāt* is itself the main religious "sign and symbol" in Islam, the *āya par excellence*.

Whereas the Qur'ān is a closed corpus of textually fixed signs and symbols, Islam is a rather open system of signs and symbols, including *Sharī'a* prescriptions for ritual, social, and personal behavior. All Muslims share a core of such signs and symbols, including the Qur'ān; outside this core, recognized signs and symbols vary according to religious, cultural, ethnic, or other particularities. In dealing with the realities of life, the world, and what is beyond, Muslims can have recourse to these manifold signs and symbols, familiarize themselves through religious learning with their religious meaning, and arrive at insight. This enables them to lead a meaningful life in society and the world, with an awareness of things beyond empirical reality.

This view of Islam, which I contend is a scholarly one, in principle allows all the different presentations and representations of Islam that have been or are alive in various Muslim social groups to be studied without prejudice. Such presentations can be religious as well as ideological, political as well as spiritual, moral as well as legal; they always have many aspects.

When a Muslim tells us how he or she interprets the Qur'ān and Islam, we should—with some discretion—in principle be able to say what the Qur'ān and Islam means to him or her—scholarly, socially, personally. This, in our perspective, is the fundamental question in studying "life" hermeneutics, whether of the Qur'ān, or of other religious texts, or of Islam itself as applied by Muslims.

6. Conclusion

At the end of this chapter, I cannot but stress the need for further study of the rules underlying Muslim ways of understanding the Qur'ān and Islam. The first reason is the need for better knowledge and understanding of Muslim societies and the significance of Islam for people in them. Without trying to know why Muslims understand things as they do, we cannot grasp the values and norms by which they lived and live.

The second reason is that without such knowledge, any communication between non-Muslims and Muslims on an intellectual level will remain extremely restricted. Such a communication will then remain largely confined to items of practical cooperation. Although that may already be worthwhile, the dialogue of life may lead to exchanges on religious matters, too, and this requires further knowledge.

It should be noticed, however, that, in religion as elsewhere, the meaning of things, including texts and Scriptures, is mostly implicit. Making meanings explicit is often a task assigned to certain specialists. In actual fact, the interpretation of Scripture on a cognitive and intellectually articulate level is the privilege of a few, the khāss, the élite. But the practice of living with the āyāt is open to everyone, the 'āmm, the people at large. In the last resort, the hermeneutics of Scripture is a problem only for the specialists. It takes second place to the profound enjoyment and satisfaction the texts themselves give to those who hear or read and enjoy them. When external authorities, religious or political, impose particular interpretations of the texts, however, things risk to go wrong. Hermeneutics should ensure that the interpretation of texts remains open to discussion.[55]

---

[55]   A German translation of this text was published as "Gibt es im Islam hermeneutische Prinzipien?", in *Hermeneutik in Islam und Christentum: Beiträge zum interreligiösen Dialog*, ed. by Hans-Martin BARTH and Christoph ELSAS, Hamburg: E.-B. Verlag Rissen, 1997, pp. 51–74.

Selected Literature

1. Qur'ān

1.1. Scholarly Research on Tafsīr

Approaches to the Qur'ān, ed. by G. R. HAWTING and Abdul-Kader A. SHAREEF, London and New York: Routledge, 1993.

Approaches to the History of the Interpretation of the Qur'an, ed. by Andrew RIPPIN, Oxford: Clarendon Press, 1988.

RIPPIN, Andrew, "The Present State of *Tafsīr* Studies", *The Muslim World*, 72 (1982), pp. 224–38.

Studies in Qur'ān and Tafsīr. Special issue of the *Journal of the American Academy of Religion*, 47 (1979).

WANSBROUGH, John S., *Qur'anic Studies: Sources and Methods of Scriptural Interpretation*, London: Oxford University Press, 1977.

1.2. Muslim Qur'ān Exegesis (Tafsīr) in general

JULLANDRI, Rashid Ahmad, "Qur'anic Exegesis and Classical Tafsīr", *Islamic Quarterly*, 12 (1968), pp. 71–119.

LICHTENSTAEDTER, Ilse, "Qur'ān and Qur'ān Exegesis", *Humaniora Islamica*, 2 (1974), pp. 3–28.

MIR, Mustansir, "Tafsīr", in *The Oxford Encyclopedia of the Modern Islamic World*, ed. by John L. ESPOSITO, Vol. 4, New York and Oxford: Oxford University Press, 1995, pp. 169–76.

MONNOT, Guy, "La démarche classique de l'exégèse musulmane", in *Les règles de l'interprétation*, ed. by Michel TARDIEU, Paris: Cerf, 1987, pp. 147–61.

RIPPIN, Andrew, "Tafsīr", in *The Encyclopedia of Religion*, ed. by Mircea ELIADE, Vol. 14, New York: Macmillan, and London: Collier Macmillan, 1987, pp. 236–44.

1.3. Tafsīrs of Particular Authors

BEESTON, Alfred Felix Landon, *Baydāwī's Commentary on Sūrah 12 of the Qur'ān*, Oxford: Oxford University Press, 1963.

CARRÉ, Olivier, *Mystique et politique: Lecture révolutionnaire du Coran par Sayyid Qutb, Frère musulman radical*, Paris: Cerf & Presses de la Fondation Nationale des Sciences Politiques, 1984.

GILLIOT, Claude, *Exégèse, langue et théologie en Islam: L'exégèse coranique de Tabarī (m. 311/923)* (Etudes musulmanes 32), Paris: Vrin, 1990.

JOMIER, Jacques, *Le commentaire coranique du Manār: Tendances modernes de l'exégèse coranique en Egypte* (Islam d'hier et d'aujourd'hui 11), Paris: G.-P. Maisonneuve, 1954.

LAWSON, B. Todd, "Interpretation as Revelation: The Qur'ān Commentary of Sayyid 'Alī Muhammad Shīrāzī, the Bāb (1819–1850)", in *Approaches to the History of the Interpretation of the Qur'ān*, ed. by Andrew RIPPIN, Oxford: Clarendon Press, 1988, pp. 223–53.

—, *The Qur'ān Commentary of Sayyid 'Alī Muhammad, the Bāb (1819–1850)* (PhD Diss. McGill University, Montreal 1988).

MERAD, Ali, *Ibn Bādīs, commentateur du Coran*, Paris: Geuthner, 1971.

TABARĪ, Abū Ja'far Muhammad Ibn Jarīr al-, *Commentaire du Coran*. Abrégé, traduit et annoté par Pierre Gode, 5 vols., Paris: Les Heures Claires, 1983–89 (S. 1–7).

1.4. Groups and Types of Tafsīr

AYOUB, Mahmoud M., *The Qur'ān and Its Interpreters*, Albany, N. Y.: Suny Press, 1984ff.

BALJON, Johannes Marinus Simon, *Modern Muslim Koran Interpretation (1880–1960)*, Leiden: E.J. Brill, 1961.

GAETJE, Helmut, *Koran und Koranexegese* (Bibliothek des Morgenlandes), Zurich: Artemis, 1971 (Engl. Trans. *The Qur'ān and its Exegesis: Selected Texts with Classical and Modern Muslim Interpretations*, Berkeley, Cal. etc.: University of California Press, 1976).

GOLDZIHER, Ignaz, *Die Richtungen der islamischen Koranauslegung*, Leiden: E. J. Brill, 1920 (Repr. 1952, 1970).

JANSEN, Johannes J.G., *The Interpretation of the Koran in Modern Egypt*, Leiden: E.J. Brill, 1974.

1.5. Particular Themes in Tafsīr

MCAULIFFE, Jane Dammen, *Qur'ānic Christians: An Analysis of Classical and Modern Exegesis*, New York, etc.: Cambridge University Press, 1991.

SMITH, Jane I., *An Historical and Semantic Study of the Term "Islām" as Seen in a Sequence of Qur'ān Commentaries*, Missoula, Mont.: Scholars Press, 1975.

2. Interpretative Thinking in Islam

2.1. Present-Day Interpretative Thought

ARKOUN, Mohammed, *Lectures du Coran*, Paris: Maisonneuve et Larose, 1982.

TALBI, Mohamed, "Quelle clé pour lire le Coran?", in *Réflexions sur le Coran*, ed. by Mohamed TALBI and Maurice BUCAILLE, Paris: Seghers, 1989, pp. 11–154.

2.2. Interpretative Thought in Tafsīr Literature

HEATH, Peter, "Creative Hermeneutics: A Comparative Analysis of Three Islamic Approaches," *Arabica* 36 (1989), pp. 173–210.

LEEMHUIS, Fred, "Origins and Early Development of the *Tafsīr* Tradition", in *Approaches to the History of the Interpretation of the Qur'an*, ed. by Andrew RIPPIN, Oxford: Clarendon Press, 1988, pp. 1–30.

MCAULIFFE, Jane Dammen, "Qur'anic Hermeneutics: The Views of al-Tabarī and Ibn Kathīr", in *Approaches to the History of the Interpretation of the Qur'an*, ed. by Andrew RIPPIN, Oxford: Clarendon Press, 1988, pp. 46–62.

SĪD, Muhammad 'Atā al-, *The Hermeneutical Problem of the Qur'ān in Islamic History* (PhD. diss., Temple University, Philadelphia, Pa. 1975).

2.3. Sūfī and Shī'ī tafsīr

AYOUB, Mahmoud M., "The Speaking Qur'ān and the Silent Qur'ān: A Study of the Principles and Development of Imāmī *tafsīr*", in *Approaches to the History of the Interpretation of the Qur'ān*, ed. by Andrew RIPPIN, Oxford: Clarendon Press, 1988, pp. 177–98.

BÖWERING, Gerhard, *The Mystical Vision of Existence in Classical Islam: The Quranic Hermeneutics of the Sūfī Sahl At-Tustarī (d. 283/896)*, Berlin and New York: W. de Gruyter, 1980.

CORBIN, Henry, "L'intériorisation du sens en herméneutique soufie iranienne", *Eranos Jahrbuch*, Zurich: Rhein-Verlag, 26 (1958), pp. 57–187.

—, "Shī'ī Hermeneutics", in *Shi'ism: Doctrines, Thought and Spirituality*, ed., annotated, and with an Introduction by Seyyed Hossein NASR, Hamid DABASH, Seyyed Vali Reza NASR, Albany, N.Y.: SUNY Press, 1988, pp. 189–202.

LORY, Pierre, *Les commentaires ésotériques du Coran d'après 'Abd al-Razzāq al-Qāshānī*, Paris: Deux Océans, 1980.

NANJI, Azim, "Toward a Hermeneutic of Qur'ānic and Other Narratives of Ismā'īlī Thought", in *Approaches to Islam in Religious Studies*, ed. by Richard C. MARTIN, Tucson, Ariz.: University of Arizona Press, 1985, pp. 164–73.

POONAWALA, Ismail K., "Ismā'īlī *ta'wīl* of the Qur'ān", in *Approaches to the History of the Interpretation of the Qur'an*, ed. by Andrew RIPPIN, Oxford: Clarendon Press, 1988, pp. 199–222.

3. Special Subjects

BIRKELAND, Harris, *Old Muslim Opposition Against Interpretation of the Koran* (Avhandlinger Utgitt av det Norske Videnskaps-Akademi i Oslo, II. Hist.-Filos. Klasse, 1955/1), Oslo: Norwegian Academy of Science, 1955.

BOULLATA, Issa J., "The Rhetorical Interpretation of the Qur'ān: I'jāz and Related Topics", in *Approaches to the History of the Interpretation of the Qur'an*, ed. by Andrew RIPPIN, Oxford: Clarendon Press, 1988, pp. 139–57.

GRAHAM, William A., "*Qur'ān* as Spoken Word: An Islamic Contribution to the Understanding of Scripture", in *Approaches to Islam in Religious Studies*, ed. by Richard C. MARTIN, Tucson: University of Arizona Press, 1985, pp. 23–40.

SPEIGHT, R. Marston, "The Function of *hadīth* as Commentary on the Qur'ān, as Seen in the Six Authoritative Collections", in *Approaches to the History of the Interpretation of the Qur'ān*, ed. by Andrew RIPPIN, Oxford: Clarendon Press, 1988, pp. 63–81.

4. Qur'ān and Other Scriptures

The Challenge of the Scriptures: The Bible and the Qur'ān, by the Muslim-Christian Research Group, Maryknoll, N.Y.: Orbis Books, 1989 (trans. from the French *Ces Ecritures qui nous questionnent: La Bible et le Coran*, par le Groupe de Recherches Islamo-Chrétien, Paris: Centurion, 1987).

GRAHAM, William A., *Beyond the Written Word: Oral Aspects of Scripture in the History of Religion*, Cambridge, etc.: Cambridge University Press, 1987.

Section 4

Muslim Presentations of Islam and of Human Rights

Chapter 7
Some North African Intellectuals' Presentations of Islam[1]

Although present-day Islam has been studied much in relation to its history and the societies where it occurs, the presentation of Islam by Muslim intellectuals has not yet been researched into in detail. Investigation is needed into the ways in which Islam in recent times has been presented by scholars from different Muslim regions and orientations. It is also timely to examine the ways in which Muslims in North America and Europe, South Africa and Australia, present Islam nowadays to a non-Muslim public.

In this chapter I aim to investigate ways in which some leading North African scholars writing in French articulated their thinking on Islam between about 1960 and 1990. They initiated a Muslim intellectual discourse about Islam with French readers. Under the influence of French language, culture, and intellectual thought, they addressed their problems with logical argumentation and used data resulting from scholarly research to answer more general questions, putting the facts within a more theoretical framework.

To the degree that members of an older generation of the North African intelligentsia were educated according to the French system, they were imbued with French culture and intellectual thought, in addition to the properly Arabic and Islamic education they received. They also have taken up current French ideas about *l'intellectuel*, the thinking person with qualities beyond those of a pragmatic scientist or a person of accumulated erudition, qualities that distinguish *l'intellectuel* also from those who proclaim convictions or preach a faith. Such intellectuals indeed distance themselves from current opinions and judgments, established institutions and loyalties. They are basically free people. They develop their own ideas and positions in relation to what they see as major problems, and they assume their responsibility toward the society

---

[1]   This text is a slightly revised version of a text published under the same title in *Christian-Muslim Encounters*, ed. by Yvonne Yazbeck HADDAD and Wadi HADDAD, Gainesville, Fla. etc.: University Press of Florida, 1995, pp. 358–80.

in which they live and work. And then, typically, they write. This holds true for the six intellectuals I am dealing with here.

Not only French intellectual thinking, therefore, but also the type of the French intellectual has had an impact on the members of a certain French-educated North African elite. This was also the case when they developed their ideas in opposition to ideas of French nationalism and to French depreciatory views of Islam. Whether Islam was approached as a subject of literary and historical inquiry in France itself, of empirical investigations in the field in North Africa, or as part of the globe's many cultures and religions, the general and current view in France has been until recently to consider Islam as fundamentally medieval, a rather old-fashioned religious tradition left behind by the march of history and civilization. Similar ethnocentric views of Islam have been current in other Western countries as well. As far as I can see, there was scarcely a discourse between French and North African intellectuals on an equal footing until after World War Two and particularly the fifties.

It is in North African French language publications that the impact of intellectual thought of French origin is clearest, particularly in the way in which authors reflect on Islam as part of their cultural heritage and their vision of the future. Such publications can shed light on other questions as well. How do the authors explain, interpret, and articulate Islam to a French public that professes various faiths and ideologies, including that of *laïcité* (secular society), but shares a cultural framework of which Islam until now has not been a part. To what extent did these authors, once independence had been achieved, feel the need to identify themselves, their society, and their culture constructively and to accentuate precisely those norms and values, symbolized by Islam, that distinguished them from French culture? They may have taken such Islamic norms and values as subjects of detached study, remnants from a lost past, but they also recognized in them elements of an Islamic ideal structure that still has a normative quality. In any case, by consciously integrating Islam in their newly assumed identity and by speaking about it, North African intellectuals started a new type of discourse with French society and culture. The very fact that their books and articles have been published by French publishers and by journals in France shows that there has been an interest in them in France, at least among a more educated public. One may also assume that these authors, by choosing to write in French, have engaged in a discourse not only with French readers, but also with their own compatriots and others for whom the French language is the privileged vehicle of intellectual discourse.

I am leaving aside here historical and sociological studies about North African society and culture, French literature by authors from the region, and publications by North African authors in Arabic as well as in European languages other than French. Also excluded are texts read in

French by North African participants in international meetings like the seminars on Islam in Algiers, the Muslim-Christian dialogues organized in Tunis, and the many other meetings of Euro-Arab and Muslim-Christian dialogue in which North African speakers have been involved. What follows is not a study of Islam in North Africa nor a study of North African contributions to various dialogue efforts, although some publications on these subjects with contributions by North African authors are mentioned in the notes.

Hence I am restricting this account to six prominent North African intellectuals in the French tradition, nearly all of whom have written a substantial *thèse d'Etat* (dissertation for a state doctorate). Scholarly research by these authors, however, is treated here only insofar as it reveals a particular interpretation of Islam. Since these writings are few and in any case unique, it will be difficult to draw any general conclusion here about North African writings on Islam. The main French-language publications of these authors are mentioned in the notes.

1. Some Common Features

The publications of the authors chosen are distinguished by certain common features. First of all, they do not preach Islam, warn against French culture, or announce a fast judgment of Western civilization. Second, the authors are very much aware of a common history between Islam and Europe, the southern and the northern shores of the Mediterranean, North Africa and France. By concentrating on France, however, they tend to neglect the equally common history of North Africa with Italy, Spain, and Portugal on the one hand and the Ottoman Empire on the other. The relations between North Africa and more distant European countries (Great Britain, the Netherlands, and Germany) as well as the common history of the Balkans and Russia with the Ottoman Empire also fall outside their sights. They hardly mention the Palestine-Israel conflict or the earlier history of the Jews in Europe. A third common characteristic is that these authors envisage a common future with France, Europe, and the world at large, and that they are committed to this future. A fourth common feature is the extent to which these publications comply with the more formal demands of French culture: written in excellent French and mostly provided with copious notes and references, they bear witness to erudition and *esprit*.

The influence of French intellectual thought on these authors reveals itself particularly in their predominantly rational interpretation of Islam. Transrational views of Islam, as were propounded at the time by Louis Massignon and Henry Corbin in Paris, seem not to have found much of an echo among them. The cooler critical reflection, on the contrary, of scholars like Robert Brunschvig and Régis Blachère, Claude Cahen, and Maxime Rodinson has certainly had an impact. The work of Louis Gardet, promoting understanding by the use of reason, sympathetic study, and personal dialogue has also borne fruit. We have difficulty discovering clear traces of French doctrinal positivism, or even of the work of Émile Durkheim, in the work of our six authors. But they seem to have been exposed to Marxian analysis and certain hermeneutical problems when they studied at French universities in the fifties and sixties.

2. The Straightforward Presentation of Islam: Malek Bennabi

Following an earlier work in French on Le phénomène coranique[2], Malek Bennabi (1905–1973, Algerian engineer) published in 1954 his Vocation de l'Islam[3], a straightforward presentation of Islam as a driving force in Algerian society. Written shortly after the Arab-Israeli war of 1948, the book was published in 1954 in the series Frontières ouvertes, through which Seuil publishing house in Paris at the time drew attention to a number of Third World countries in a perspective broader than that of French politics. In the foreword, Bennabi significantly defines his stand toward H. A. R. Gibb's Modern Trends in Islam[4], a French translation of which had appeared in 1949. He thoroughly rejects Gibb's idea that the Arab mind is atomistic and incapable of discerning laws and that the humanism of modern reform movements in Islam is due to the influence of European culture rather than to specific Qur'anic orientations. Bennabi mocks European "humanism", which went out to subdue and colonize the rest of the world. He takes seriously, however, Gibb's description of what Bennabi calls the "quasi-infantile pathology" of the Muslim world, and he stresses that many Muslims can profit and learn from Gibb's diagnosis. Bennabi is willing to listen to orientalists.

Even after some fifty years, Bennabi's book remains prophetic, foreshadowing the terrible Algerian war that would follow. Describing what he calls "post-Almohad" society and its decline compared to the standard of classical Muslim civilization, Bennabi argues that this "post-Almohad"

---

2   Malek BENNABI, Le phénomène coranique: Essai d'une théorie sur le Coran, Alger: Sharikat al-Nahḍa li 'l-ṭibaʿa wa 'l-Nashr, 1946 (Engl. translation The Qur'anic Phenomenon: An Attempt at a Theory of Understanding the Holy Qur'an, trans. Abu bilal KIRKARI, Indianapolis: American Trust Publications, 1983).

3   ID., Vocation de l'Islam, Paris: Seuil, 1954 (Engl. translation Islam in History and Society [Islamic Research Institute Publications 73], trans. Asma RASHID, Chicago: Kazi Publications, 1988 [Repr. 1994]). See also the first part of the autobiography of the author, Mémoires d'un témoin du siècle, Alger: Entreprise Nationale du Livre, 1965.

4   Hamilton Alexander Rosskeen GIBB, Modern Trends in Islam, Chicago: University of Chicago Press, 1947 (French translation by Bernard VERNIER, Les tendances modernes de l'Islam, Paris: G. P. Maisonneuve, 1949).

society made man "colonizable", prone to be colonized, not only because of aggression from outside but particularly because of its inner weakness and pretense to self-sufficiency. The author welcomes the reformist and modernist movements in the second half of the nineteenth and the early twentieth centuries, seeing in them a renaissance expressed in Islamic terms. When describing post-World War One history and the colonial impact of France on North Africa and of the West on the Muslim world at large, Bennabi analyzes critically the internal and external factors of what he calls chaos. Not only the modern Muslim world, but also the modern Western world that enjoys the semblance of power finds itself in a moral chaos, for colonialism "kills the colonized materially and the colonizer morally"[5].

Bennabi calls for a new phase in the Muslim renaissance, in which the complex of *colonisabilité* will be overcome, the social values of Islam observed, and a religious reform starting from the Qur'ān carried out as a prerequisite for social reforms. Perceptively, he observes that the center of the Muslim world is moving eastward in the direction of Pakistan, India, and even Indonesia.

Bennabi's presentation in French already contains the main elements of a prolific *da'wa* literature that was to appear in nearly all Islamic languages during the four following decades, calling for Muslim societies to renew themselves by returning to the sources of Islam and castigating the moral failure of the West. Looking back, one cannot help but be astonished that a book like this has not been read more widely in the West, since in its critical analysis it exemplifies a lucid Muslim reading of the signs of the times, while showing intellectual and moral self-restraint.

3. Description of Arab-Islamic and European Civilization Side by Side: Hichem Djaït

The Tunisian historian Hichem Djaït (born in 1935) published in French scholarly works on the early history of the town Kufa[6] and also on the intricate relationships between religion and politics during the first decades of Islam after Muhammad's death.[7] Of special interest in our context, however, are his work on the Arab-Islamic personality[8] and his book on Europe and Islam.[9]

---

[5]   Cf. BENNABI, *Vocation*, p. 111.
[6]   Hichem DJAÏT, *Al-Kufa: Naissance de la ville islamique*, Paris: Maisonneuve et Larose, 1986.
[7]   ID., *La grande discorde: Religion et politique dans l'Islam des origines*, Paris: Gallimard, 1989.
[8]   ID., *La personnalité et le devenir arabo-islamique*, Paris: Seuil, 1974.
[9]   ID., *L'Europe et l'Islam*, Paris: Seuil, 1978 (Engl. translation *Europe and Islam*, Berkeley, Cal. & London: University of California Press, 1985).

His first book, *La personnalité et le devenir arabo-islamique*, stands in what we may call the more personalist tradition of North African thinkers. In 1964, for instance, the Moroccan author Mohamed Aziz Lahbabi, influenced by French personalist philosophy, published a booklet on Muslim personalism in which he develops the basic notions on human person to be found in Qur'ān and *Sunna*. Ten years later Djaït tried to describe in his book the profile of the Muslim person as it emerged historically within the Arab setting, in both the Mashriq and the Maghreb. The term "Arab-Islamic (or Arab-Muslim) personality" has become current particularly in North African (Tunisian) thinking. It has served to identify the (North African) Arab Muslim, in particular in contrast to Europe, stressing his or her particular history and destiny. This special concern for the human person is continued by authors committed to interreligious dialogue, such as Mohamed Talbi, and by Mohammed Arkoun in his more critical philosophical thinking. Compared to a number of Arab thinkers of the Middle East, North African authors generally distinguish themselves by a certain realism, critical rationalism, and a kind of "personalizing" perception of human relationships and reality. Besides discussing the Arab-Muslim person, Djaït also deals with Arab unity, the organization of society and the state, and, in a separate chapter, "Reform and renewal in religion". Here Djaït calls for a renewed vision of faith, both intellectually and in the heart, and refers to both Muslim and European philosophers (for example, Iqbal and Hegel).

Djaït's book *L'Europe et l'Islam*, as the title indicates, treats Euro-Arab relationships throughout history. The first part deals with the ways Europeans have viewed Islam. After a description of the general medieval and more modern Eurocentric vision of Islam, Djaït concentrates on three special topics: French intellectuals and Islam (Enlightenment thinkers, travelers, present-day intellectuals); European scholarship and Islam (Renan's ideological bias, Islamicist orientalists' achievements, and Eurocentric or Christianocentric biases including modern anthropology, where he discusses in particular Claude Lévi-Strauss' views on Islam and Muslim societies); and finally the relationship between German thought (which most Muslim authors admire) and Islam, focusing in particular on the ideas of Georg Wilhelm Friedrich Hegel and Oswald Spengler. Throughout this part of his book, Djaït shows perspicacity and lucidity in the way he describes particular European views. He is not uncritical of France; he complains about the provincial and closed character of French as compared with American universities[10], and he correctly observes that whereas France has always attracted "liberal" Europeanized

---

[10]   ID., *L'Europe et l'Islam*, p. 47.

intellectuals from Arab and other Muslim countries, it has hardly welcomed Muslim thinkers representing what Djaït calls an "Islamic authenticity"[11]. This is true indeed. Louis Massignon's sympathies for the Arabs and Islam, and the settling of more traditional Muslim thinkers like Muhammad Hamidullah in Paris, were exceptional; in general, both laicist and Catholic France have not been much interested in taking the religious faith, substance, contents, or message of Islam seriously as a possible alternative. Throughout the nineteenth and the twentieth centuries and to this day, Islam has been perceived in France largely according to the parameters of the existing political, laicist, and ecclesiastic Catholic positions in the country.

The second part of Djaït's book deals more explicitly with Islam and Europe as two historical structures. He describes Europe's historical dynamism and Islam's insistence on universal values, and stresses the need to reread and rewrite world history in a less Eurocentric and more universal perspective. He presents the properties of Islam as a civilization, a culture, and a body politic: characteristic features in history, evident breaks in historical continuity with the arrival of the Europeans, and problems of alienation and historical backwardness in a more universal perspective. Interestingly enough, the book closes with a chapter on the specific features not of Islam but of Europe. There is a little menu of everything, seen through thick French pebble glasses; Djaït presents his somewhat gloomy reflections on the future of European culture very much as French journalists at the time wrote about other civilizations. Compared to other Muslim authors, however, Djaït's is a more liberal, universalist spirit.

4. Reaching for Dialogue: Ali Merad and Mohamed Talbi

The Algerian historian Ali Merad (born 1929) is known for his scholarly work on the reformist movement in Algeria between the two world wars[12] and on the religious thought of Ibn Bādīs (1889–1940), who during those years wrote a commentary on the Qur'ān based on reformist principles.[13] His little booklet on contemporary Islam[14] is a rather unproblematic factual presentation, in which the period after 1960 is hardly treated, except for some very general data and a brief description of the ways in which Islam is expanding.

---

[11] Cf. *ibid.*, p. 86.
[12] Ali MERAD, *Le réformisme musulman en Algérie de 1925 à 1940: Essai d'histoire religieuse et sociale*, Paris and The Hague: Mouton, 1967.
[13] ID., *Ibn Bādīs, commentateur du Coran*, Paris: Geuthner, 1971.
[14] ID., *L'Islam contemporain*, Paris: Presses Universitaires de France, 1984, 1995⁵.

As a professor at the University of Lyon III and more recently at Paris IV, Merad has been involved in dialogue efforts between Muslim and (mainly Catholic) Christians in France. He also looks for dialogue on a practical level to improve the often miserable situation of so many North Africans in France in the present time of unemployment, political pressures, and general uncertainty about the future. In 1978, he made available to the French public a modest anthology of religious Islamic texts. His *Charles de Foucauld au regard de l'Islam*[15] describes with appreciation a Christian hermit (d. 1917) who tried to provide a link between France and Christianity on the one hand, and North Africa and Islam on the other.

The Tunisian scholar Mohamed Talbi (born 1920), now a retired professor of history at the University of Tunis, is also committed to promoting dialogue between Muslims and Christians, perhaps more in self-critical ethical and religious terms than the others. His scholarly work led to his extensive *thèse d'Etat* on the Tunisian dynasty of the Aghlabids (800–909)[16] preceding the Shī'ī dynasty of the Fātimids, which former took power in Tunisia in 909 and conquered Egypt in 969.

During the last thirty years, Talbi has participated in a number of official and personal dialogues with Christians in both North Africa and Europe. In an article on Islam and the West, published in 1987, he complains about the current poverty of Muslim initiatives or even responses to Euro-Arab or Islamo-Christian dialogue. In a brochure on the subject, published in 1972, he explicitly declared Islam to be open to dialogue with other faiths and cultures. In 1989, he and the French Orthodox Christian Olivier Clément published together a large book called *Un respect têtu*[17], "A Dogged Respect", in which both authors testify to the search for common truth. For Talbi, the Muslim-Christian dialogue is not just a social event but a significant religious matter, and he has done everything possible to promote such dialogue in Tunisia and elsewhere.[18]

---

[15]   ID., *Charles de Foucauld au regard de l'Islam*, Paris: Chalet, 1975. For Ali Merad's contributions to Muslim-Christian dialogue, see for instance his contributions in Armand ABECASSIS, Ali MERAD, and Daniel PÉZERIL, *N'avons-nous pas le même Père?*, Paris: Chalet, 1972, and in Jean Paul GABUS, Ali MERAD, and Youakim MOUBARAC, *Islam et christianisme en dialogue*, Paris: Cerf, 1982.

[16]   Mohamed TALBI, *L'émirat aghlabide 184–296/800–909: Histoire politique*, Paris: A. Maisonneuve, 1966. He also published *Ibn Khaldūn et l'histoire*, Tunis: Maison tunisienne de l'édition, 1973.

[17]   Mohamed TALBI and Olivier CLÉMENT, *Un respect têtu*, Paris: Nouvelle Cité, 1989. Cf. Mohamed TALBI, *Islam et dialogue: Réflexions sur un thème d'actualité*, Tunis: Maison tunisienne de l'édition, 1972. See also ID., "Islam et Occident: Les possibilités et les conditions d'une meilleure compréhension", *Les Cahiers de Tunisie*, 33 (1987), pp. 5–46.

[18]   See Mohamed TALBI, *Plaidoyer pour un Islam moderne*, Tunis: Cérès, and Paris: Desclé de Brouwer, 1998.

5. Comparative Historical Analysis: Abdallah Laroui

The Moroccan historian Abdallah Laroui (born 1933), professor at the University of Rabat, has published in French two scholarly historical studies. The first is on the history of the Maghreb[19], and the second, his *thèse d'Etat*, on the origins of Moroccan nationalism.[20] He has also made a name for himself outside the circle of specialists by publishing three volumes of essays on contemporary Arab ideology[21], on the crisis of Arab intellectuals[22], and on Islam and modernity[23].

As a historian inspired by Marxian principles, Laroui normally carries out his analysis of Arab Muslim societies, their history, and their ideologies without speaking much about Islam as a religion. One interesting exception is his fierce rebuttal to Gustav E. von Grunebaum's theory and practice of cultural analysis.[24] Laroui establishes the primacy of what he calls "real" history over "cultural" history as von Grunebaum understood it; he also shows that von Grunebaum's assumptions and presuppositions led him to describe and evaluate Islam as a medieval and premodern culture, inherently different from, if not opposed to, the modern West. Subsequently, Laroui tries to put von Grunebaum's model and his many scholarly findings within a broader framework of historical study.

At the end of his criticism, Laroui proposes four domains in the study of Islam that ought to be approached successively: (1) Islam as history, including power with all its local and temporal specificities; (2) Islam as culture (with a process of continuous traditionalization); (3) Islam as morality, with a basic "Muslim personality" and a characteristic lifestyle and behavior; and (4) Islam as a faith. In Laroui's view the domain of faith has hardly been elucidated in Islamic studies until now and does not

---

[19] Abdallah LAROUI, *L'histoire du Maghreb: Essai de synthèse*, Paris: Maspéro, 1970 (Engl. translation *The History of the Maghrib: An Interpretive Essay* [Princeton Studies on the Near East], trans. Ralph MANHEIM, Princeton, N. J.: Princeton University Press, 1977).

[20] ID., *Les origines sociales et culturelles du nationalisme marocain, 1830–1912*, Paris: Maspéro, 1977.

[21] ID., *L'idéologie arabe contemporaine: Essai critique*, Paris: Maspéro, 1967 (rééd. 1977).

[22] ID., *La crise des intellectuels arabes: Traditionalisme ou historicisme?*, Paris: Maspéro, 1974 (Engl. translation *The Crisis of the Arab Intellectual: Traditionalism or Historicism?*, trans. Diarmid CAMMELL, Berkeley, Cal. & London: University of California Press, 1976).

[23] ID., *Islam et modernité*, Paris: La Découverte, 1987. See also his *L'Algérie et le Sahara marocain*, Casablanca: Serar, 1976.

[24] Ch. 3 of *La crise des intellectuels arabes* (see above note 22), "Les Arabes et l'anthropologie culturelle: Remarques sur la méthode de Gustave von Grunebaum" (pp. 59–102 of the French edition). Laroui presents his views on history and historical research in *Islam et histoire: Essai d'épistémologie*, Paris: Flammarion, 1999.

simply coincide with the study of *fiqh*, *kalām*, and *akhlāq* (ethics). Faith has to be studied as the fourth and highest level of society, determined by the three underlying levels of history, culture, and morality. Laroui is apparently thinking, for instance, of an inquiry into the logical foundations of the *Sunna*, a present-day reinterpretation of the various catechisms (*'aqīdas*) written in Islamic history, and an in-depth study of the concept of Islamic faith with its characteristic resistance to all that is not Islamic. In Laroui's scheme, the level of faith cannot influence the first level, that of power; the infrastructural situation precedes faith and conditions any realization and historical articulation of it. For Laroui, Islam evidently is not a static entity; each use of the word *islām* indicates a new reality.

As he argues in *Islam et modernité*, the issue is not so much a "return" of Islam since the middle of the nineteenth century (or earlier or later, depending on the region), but rather the appearance of what he calls a "neo-Islam" with an ideological structure quite different from that of "classical" Islam. The strengthening of this neo-Islam since the 1970s is largely due to political forces, in particular new kinds of relationships between Arab countries. Whereas such countries as Egypt, Syria, and Iraq were formerly centers of Arab culture, in recent decades, countries like Saudi Arabia, the Gulf states, and Libya have become rich and have furthered this "neo-Islam" in order to legitimate their new role of ideological domination, as Laroui interprets it. The masses are sensitive to any appeal to Islam; everywhere in the world there is a resurgence of tradition, and this holds equally true for the Muslim countries. "Neo-Islam", which represents a resurgence of Islamic tradition, poses sociopolitical rather than religious problems, the latter belonging to the domain of religious feeling.[25]

His volume on Islam and modernity contains two essays (chapters 5 and 6) illustrating the kind of comparative historical analysis Laroui wants to make of analogous developments in the history of Europe and Islam. One example is his comparison between Ibn Khaldūn (1332–1406) and Machiavelli (1468–1527)—two thinkers who both discovered, the latter apparently independently of the former, a new field of investigation and knowledge that until then had been largely unexplored: the human being as a political being. Laroui contends that they used the same method because they had the same epistemological postulates. He subsequently analyzes some striking particular differences between the two thinkers by means of the Islamic elements of the world view in which Ibn Khaldūn worked. Both thinkers, however, refused utopian solutions, employed formal logic in analyzing political life, and sought to offer

---

[25]   ID., *Islam et modernité*, pp. 94–5.

conclusive proofs for their arguments. Both accepted a permanent dualism between consciousness (*conscience*) and instinct, and both envisaged the human being as a socio-political animal.

The second example of comparative historical analysis that Laroui offers concerns the rationalism of the European (especially French) Enlightenment and that of the Salafīya reformists. According to Laroui, Voltaire's interpretation of religion on the one hand and Jamāl al-Dīn al-Afghānī's reinterpretation of Islam on the other both refer to a kind of natural, rational religion without need of mediation and accessible to every human being. Again, having postulated this similarity between the two schools of thought, Laroui analyzes some striking differences between them, such as the acceptance or negation of evil as a metaphysical problem. The author proceeds in this line of thought and posits Islam as a "naturalism for human usage"[26].

Subsequently, Laroui proposes other comparisons: between the "marginal" thinkers of Islam and the eighteenth-century Enlightenment philosophers, between gnostic currents in both contexts, especially in regions bordering each other, and between certain attitudes to life found in both cultures. Laroui's interest in such comparisons is in the first place methodological. Such comparisons can also function, however, to facilitate a better understanding between the two civilizations, which since the beginning have been characterized by a nearly perennial structural opposition to each other.

6. The Effort to Think about Commonly Recognized Problems: Mohammed Arkoun

The last of our six North African intellectuals is Mohammed Arkoun, an Algerian of Berber origin (born in 1928). He studied in Paris and since 1961 has been a professor of the history of Islamic thought at the University of Paris III. Arkoun has done a special study of the tenth-century Muslim intellectual Miskawayh (936–1030), whom he characterizes as a true humanist.[27] A number of Arkoun's scholarly essays were collected in volumes on Islamic thought[28], readings of the Qur'ān[29], and

---

[26]   Cf. *ibid.*, p. 145.

[27]   Mohammed ARKOUN, *Deux Epîtres de Miskawayh: Edition critique*, Damascus: Institut Français d'Études Arabes, 1961; ID., *Traité d'éthique: Traduction française annoteé du Tahdhīb al-akhlāq de Miskawayh*, Damascus: Institut Français d'Études Arabes, 1969; ID., *L'humanisme arabe au IVe/Xe siècle: Miskaway philosophe et historien*, Paris: Vrin, 1970, 1982².

[28]   ID., *Essais sur la pensée islamique*, Paris: Maisonneuve et Larose, 1973, 1984³.

[29]   ID., *Lectures du Coran*, Paris: Maisonneuve et Larose, 1982; Tunis: Alif, 1991².

a critique of Islamic reason.[30] Smaller books deal with Arab thought[31] and with ethics and politics in Islam.[32] Arkoun is committed to interreligious dialogue, especially with Christians, and published several books on this subject together with Christian authors (with Louis Gardet[33], with Arosio and Borrmans[34], and with the Islamic-Christian research group[35]). His basic approaches and findings were synthesized in a smaller book, *Ouvertures sur l'Islam*, "Overtures to Islam" (1989)[36], which will be our point of departure here.

If, with the exception of Malik Bennabi, the preceding authors can be qualified as historians, sometimes using a sociological approach as in the case of Laroui, Arkoun is a born philosopher and subsequently an erudite (*adīb*), familiar with the arts in general, the humanities and social sciences in particular, and semiology (semiotics) specifically. In his writings and at conferences, he addresses himself to a Western public, the French in particular, as well as to a younger Muslim student generation, and, if I see it correctly, to the critically thinking faithful of religious traditions in general and of the monotheistic faiths in particular.

To start with the last concern: Arkoun observes and criticizes the existence of a kind of complicity among the faithful of the three monotheistic religions to preserve their respective dogmatic definitions, using the latter to establish themselves and their community continuously as an "orthodoxy" instead of striving for a new space of intelligibility (*OI*, p. 9). For instance, Islam, like Christianity, has entertained a medieval vision, of a theological nature, of other religions and communities. Both in Christianity and in Islam particular theological systems have had an enormous impact on the ways in which people have understood themselves and the world. This framework of perception survives to the present day. Even though scholarly research has to a large extent brought about the secularization of the conditions of intelligibility and understanding, people continue to have a perception of each other that is biased by the divisions originally established by their religions (*OI*, pp. 22–3).

Until recently Islam has been characterized by a religious discourse that Arkoun terms "mythical", that is, constantly drawing on the Qur'ān.

---

[30] ID., *Pour une critique de la raison islamique*, Paris: Maisonneuve et Larose, 1984.
[31] ID., *La pensée arabe*, Paris: Presses Universitaires de France, 1975, 1996[5].
[32] ID., *L'Islam, morale et politique*, Paris: Unesco & Desclée de Brouwer, 1986.
[33] ID. and Louis GARDET, *L'Islam, hier, demain*, Paris: Buchet-Chastel, 1978, 1982[2].
[34] Mohammed ARKOUN, Mario AROSIO, and Maurice BORRMANS, *L'Islam, religion et société*, Paris: Cerf, 1982.
[35] Groupe de Recherches Islamo-Chrétien (G.R.I.C.), *Ces Écritures qui nous questionnent: La Bible et le Coran*, Paris: Centurion, 1987.
[36] Mohammed ARKOUN, *Ouvertures sur l'Islam*, Paris: Grancher, 1989. Hereafter this edition is cited as *OI* with the corresponding page numbers. An English translation appeared in 1994: *Rethinking Islam: Common Questions, Uncommon Answers*, Boulder, Colo. etc.: Westview Press, 1994.

However, with a growing openness to Europe in the course of the nineteenth and twentieth centuries, a new "liberal" trend arose among Muslim intellectuals, which favored imitation of the Western cultural model. This meant the rise of a new discourse as an alternative to the traditional religious one: a Western discourse in which Western values dominated.

From the beginning of the twentieth century on, sometimes earlier and sometimes later, there arose a new, secular nationalist trend that was furthered by a reformist Islamic trend. Both opposed the liberal trend that had been open to the West. From this time on, Islam ceased to be used as a mythical religious discourse drawing on the Qur'ān. Rather it served as a mobilizing ideological discourse manipulating popular and traditional beliefs in order to recommend and impose purely political projects, such as those of the Arab nation, the Arab socialist revolution, or the Islamic state. Here, directed ideology has taken the place of myth (*OI*, pp. 25–6).

Arkoun puts his finger on similar politically directed attempts to ideologize the religious-mythical contents of the Jewish and Christian scriptures and traditions at the present time. As a consequence, each religion defends its own starting points, postulates, and dogmas ever more ideologically.

This degeneration of the faiths, however, in fact began much earlier, and in this connection it is relevant to relate how Arkoun presents the beginnings of Islam. As he sees it, Muhammad basically introduced a new political system in the Arabia of his day, a system that was articulated with the help of a new religious symbolism and that made particular use of the symbolism of the alliance between God and humankind. A new semiological system replaced what came to be called the *jāhilīya*, and a new state surpassing tribal solidarities arose to apply and impose the new political order. But in Islam, as earlier in Judaism, the original creative religious symbolism degenerated into juridical codes, automatic rituals, scholastic doctrines and—last but not least—ideologies of domination (*OI*, pp. 36–8).

Indeed, this development was closely linked to the process of empire-building, which led to a government control (*étatisation*, *Verstaatlichung*) of Islam. With the growth and subsequent centralization of the caliphal empire, not only did a judiciary emerge that needed a common juridical code, but the religious was also subordinated to the political (*OI*, p. 39). Whereas during Muhammad's lifetime there had been a double—symbolic as well as political—expression of leadership (as Arkoun puts it, the Qur'ān is the best witness to Muhammad's creativity in the realm of "symbolic realism"), this ended abruptly once the empire had been established. Not only was this sort of creativity at an end but the symbolic capital conveyed by the Qur'ān was now even used to construct an Islam that was both "official" (with government blessing) and "orthodox" (eliminating rival interpretations from obtaining power). And whereas in the Qur'ān the sacred was purified and concentrated in God, in the Muslim societies of subsequent periods, the sacred, on an empirical level, was again dispersed in a number of objects, as had been the case before Islam. A sacralization of Qur'ān and *Sunna* took place with the consequence that they were defended in apologetic literature at all costs (*OI*, pp. 40–1).

Thus according to Arkoun, Islam arose as a political system with a religious symbolism of its own. During the "imperial" period, this religious symbolism was systematized rationally in the religious sciences that represented official orthodox Islam supported by the state. In the twentieth century, in the course of a new politicization of Islam the religious discourse, with its symbolic and mythical elements, made room for an ideological discourse that used those elements for political purposes. Especially since the sixties, an ideological "Islamic" model has evolved that tends to armor itself against scholarly inquiry; it consists of a universe of the collective imagination, ideologically depicted as "Islamic" (*OI*, p. 27). And what has happened to Islam has also happened to Judaism and Christianity with their own official and orthodox versions of religion, their ideologizations in the course of the twentieth century, and their growing degradation into politics.

Arkoun then discusses a subject hardly envisaged by Muslim scholars until now: the essentially critical role of the science of religion in the study of the three great monotheistic religions and their mutual relations. He observes a continuous—historical and contemporary—rivalry among the three communities of Judaism, Christianity, and Islam. All three want to monopolize the management of what Arkoun calls the "symbolic capital", this monopolization being linked to what these three religious traditions call and claim as "Revelation". Arkoun adds that the theologians of each community are responsible not only for the management of the symbolic capital that represents the community's "goods of salvation", but also for legitimizing in this way each community's natural will to dominate. The construction of a "Judeo-Christian" vision of the history of salvation, which includes Judaism and Christianity but excludes Islam, is a recent product of such activity (*OI*, pp. 16–7). In this way the most sacred values of these traditions have been changed into communal "property", a "symbolic capital" managed by theologians. Each community constitutes and legitimates its own separate identity in distinction from the others by means of this "symbolic capital".

It is to the science of religion that Arkoun assigns the task of a thorough criticism of theological reasoning (*OI*, p. 17). In fact, he wants the humanities and social sciences to address all those matters in dispute that have been bequeathed by the theological constructions of former times.

Historical research, for instance, can show how different groups have drawn from a common stock of signs and symbols to produce their respective exclusive systems of belief and nonbelief (*OI*, p. 20). The science of religion must analyze the dimension of the imaginative (*l'imagi-naire*) as it arose in the three religions and in the many societies that constitute these religions. It should make a special effort to reach the radical dimension these three traditions have in common, as a counter-weight to the many efforts made to show their differences.

At the end of his book, Arkoun is deeply concerned with the nature of the data that the three religious traditions claim to be revelation. He pleads for a modern kind of theology able to discuss the phenomenon of revela-tion as an issue in itself. It should work in the perspective of "comparative theology" going beyond polemics and beyond what Arkoun calls "ex-changes of false tolerance" between the three religious traditions (cf. *OI*, p. 45). I shall come back to these broad tasks Arkoun assigns to the schol-arly study of religion in general, and the three monotheistic traditions in particular, but let me first stress another ongoing concern of his.

Arkoun is very much concerned about the kind of knowledge that not only the Islamic theological disciplines but also the West has acquired of Islam. He questions the objective nature and the validity of this knowl-edge (*OI*, p. 13). Is much of it not simply a construct of the Western collective imagination, especially the ways in which Islam is presented by the media and at schools in the West? In particular during the last thirty years, the Western media have presented to the West a current hard-line construct of Islam made by Muslim "Islamists". It has now simply be-come part of the Western collective imagination, which connects Islam with Khomeinī and political extremism.

As a consequence, instead of better mutual knowledge and under-standing between the two religious traditions, there is nowadays rather a confrontation between two different realms of collective imagination, namely the Muslim and the Western one. Where then does real knowl-edge start? Islamic studies worthy of the name should abandon thinking about Islam as something existing in itself and instead examine and interrogate Islam in the light of the modern humanities and social sciences (*OI*, p. 11).

7. Significance for Islamic Studies and Other Religious Studies

I would like to assess the work of the various aforementioned authors who have expressed themselves within the framework of French intellec-tual thought in terms of Islamic Studies. Indeed, any Christian-Muslim encounter on an intellectual level demands a common effort to under-stand not only the Christian, but also the Islamic faith. An encounter between people who do not seriously investigate their own and each other's religion may result in a dialogue, but not one in intellectual terms.

Descriptive studies of twentieth-century intellectual movements in Islam and the Muslim commonwealth, such as have been carried out by Ali Merad, are indispensable, if only for the wealth of information they offer. Scholars coming from the tradition studied are often better able than outsiders to describe various aspects of such movements, provided they do not bow to current fashions and ideologies. Ali Merad also describes meetings between Muslims and Christians at the present time, both in Muslim countries and in Europe.

Such descriptive studies of twentieth-century developments can be usefully supplemented on the one hand by studies of the history of Islam in earlier times and its impact on the identity of present-day Muslims and, on the other hand, by studies of the history of relations between the Muslim and European worlds, which have left their mark both on present-day Muslim identity and on contemporary relations between Muslims and Europeans. The work of Hichem Djaït offers this kind of cultural history, covering what is common to Europe and Islam and what is specific to the Arab-Muslim and to the European worlds respectively. Whereas nearly all European historians have described Arab and Islamic history as a history that is different, even separate from that of Europe, the awareness of a common, not only Mediterranean but even Euro-Arab history is gradually gaining ground.

History, however, is much more than cultural and religious history. Solid studies of the economic, demographic, ethnic, political, and other determinants of the history of Arab-Muslim regions and their relations with Europe are still very much lacking. The work of Abdallah Laroui is important in various respects. He not only describes North African history and its determinant factors as a development originating in the region itself and twentieth-century Arab ideological movements in terms of similar infrastructural determinants. He also presents an in-depth analysis of the ways in which analogous ideas, orientations, and trends of thought developed in Europe and in the Arab world. Here again we find the awareness of a cultural history held in common, notwithstanding the particular traits of Muslim and European thought that, in times of political and ideological struggle, tended to be absolutized. More than that of the authors mentioned before, Laroui's work has its own coherent epistemology, is critical of ideology, and is inspired but not slavishly determined by Marxian principles of historical research.

None of these scholars, however, focused principally on Islam as a religion. This is the contribution of Malek Bennabi, whose work is unique in the sense that, some fifty years ago, it already presented the Qur'ān and Islam to French readers as a religious and ideological recourse for Muslim societies. His is an honest intellectual search for independence and dignity on a religious as well as political level, but it now has documentary rather than scholarly importance for Islamic studies and the study of religion generally.

The only North African scholar writing in French who has made a concerted original effort in the field of Islamic Studies in our time and who published in French is Mohammed Arkoun. I would like to summarize certain respects in which his work makes an important contribution to Islamic Studies, to the study of religion generally, and to Muslim-Christian encounter on an intellectual level. More than any other Muslim scholar of Islam I know, Arkoun raises questions that are relevant and finally inescapable for the Islamic, Christian, and also Jewish traditions. If the questions raised by Arkoun, difficult as they may be, are not appropriately discussed and treated by younger generations, Muslims and non-Muslims alike, this would be a sad example of intellectual decline.

First, Arkoun wants critical scholarship, real science of religion, to be applied to Islam. Specifically he calls for the application of historical, sociological, and anthropological methods in the study of Muslim societies and Islamic history in general, and of semiotic and linguistic methods in the study of Islamic texts. This includes a consistent effort to lay bare the political interests and implications of expressions that most scholars of Islam until now have tended to study for their cultural and religious significance.

A good example is Arkoun's treatment of what happened to Muhammad's original symbolic word expressions contained in the Qur'ān (OI^{37}, pp. 35, 38, 46). After the creative moment of an open religious discourse as offered in the Qur'ān, the "symbolic capital" contained in Qur'ān and *hadīths* was fought over by different factions in the community who wanted to control its "symbolic charge", which they needed to legitimate their thirst for political power. In a next phase, this symbolic charge was tamed and rationalized in various theological disciplines such as *tafsīr* and *'ilm al-hadīth*, *fiqh* and *kalām*. However, as the price of this rationalization, the texts in question gradually lost much of their symbolic power. Much later, under European influence and with the rise of secular thinking, the symbols that had originally functioned in a religious discourse started to operate as simple signals in an ideological discourse in which religious aims and purposes had largely been lost. Whereas such signals used to indicate whether one belonged to the "old" or the "new" trend of thought, in the last twenty years the meaning has been inverted, with the accent being put on the affirmation of an Islamic identity. The veil, for instance, has changed from a "traditional" into a self-assertive

---

[37] For the abbreviation used hereafter, see above note 36.

symbol, like the short beard and other signals that nowadays mean "properly Islamic", whereas fifty years ago they indicated a traditionalism of bygone times.

In his study of Islam with the tools of the modern humanities and social sciences, Arkoun opens up new subjects of research that should be studied in other traditions as well. What, for instance, are the conditions in which particular politico-religious "imaginatives" (*imaginaires*) arise in a community, such as what Arkoun calls the "Medinan experience" under Muhammad and the *rāshidūn* caliphs? What have been the social and cultural conditions of the development of the rational as well as the imaginative aspects of Islamic life and thought in particular times and places? How should Muslim authors' and historians' rational and imaginative perception of the past be distinguished and evaluated historically?

Second, Arkoun advocates rational enlightenment in his thinking about his own religion and religion in general. He applies modern historical and social scientific critical research to what he calls "Islamic reason/rationality" (*la raison islamique*), that is to say, classical Islamic thought patterns and their ideological effects, which he judges critically. He is an Enlightenment thinker in that he has faith in reason and rational knowledge and sees dogmatism, sacralization, and ideologization as major barriers to thought. This attitude also shows up in his high regard for modern reason, to which he assigns an essentially constructive function— after it has destroyed false kinds of knowledge. Modern reason strives for a kind of knowledge that integrates the rational and the imaginative and seeks what Arkoun calls a "comprehensive intelligibility" (*intelligibilité comprehensive*). A good example is his call for a philosophical criticism of the notions of truth as held in the three monotheistic religions (*OI*, p. 89). The way in which truth has been conceived in these religions has led to mutual exclusion; for any serious communication and dialogue (*réciprocité des consciences*), this concept of truth has simply to be abandoned, which means a serious epistemological rupture. Another example is his consistent criticism of Islamic reason/rationality (*OI*, pp. 71, 105) understood as a theological construct. Instead of this, he wants to introduce what he calls "modern reason" (scientific and philosophical) and in this way to put an end to intellectual stagnation in Islam. It is time to unmask the harmful ideological effects (*OI*, p. 79) of a situation that has been sacralized for more than ten centuries (*OI*, p. 77).

As part of his search for rational enlightenment, Arkoun has opened up some new domains of research in Islamic studies, even though he derived the approaches from elsewhere. First he uses the notion of discourse, and that of religious discourse in particular, as a guiding concept, for instance in Qur'anic studies, even broaching a theory of religious discourse (*OI*, p. 69). He considers the application of semiotic theory and research techniques as a key to studying meaning. He considers Muham-

mad's *islām* for instance as a new semiological system opposed to the old
jāhilīya system. Arkoun has a keen nose for problems of meaning. He
opposes Marcel Gauchet's idea of "the debt of significance" (*la dette de
sens*) as a heuristic key to having access to latent meanings (*OI*, pp. 33–
4), rejecting present-day ideological trends that simply impose a certain
meaning on the subject under study. Arkoun contends that today we have
to do with an impoverishment of meaning and a degeneration of symbolic
universes (*OI*, pp. 35, 47–8, 137). He affirms, for instance, that "one
observes a degeneration of myth to mythologies, a dilapidation of the
symbolic capital left by Islam, a reduction of the sign to a signal" (cf. *OI*,
p. 121). He developed and applied a theory of reading a text (*OI*, p. 71)
in broader philosophical terms and with greater objectivity than is the
case in much of current hermeneutic theory and practice. Arkoun also
opened up the field of the imaginative (*l'imaginaire*) in relation to historical and social reality in Islamic studies. In this respect too, Arkoun must
be recognized as a pioneer, at least on a theoretical level.

Third, Arkoun urges closer cooperation between scholars on the subject
of the three monotheistic religions, Judaism, Christianity, and Islam, and
their mutual relations. Common research should center on what the three
religions call "revelation" (*OI*, pp. 53–61). The science of religion should
study the three religions' orthodox and other teachings on the subject of
their historical and theological origin. It should investigate the ideological
and psychological functions of such teachings and determine their semantic and anthropological limits and even inadequacies. The fact that a text
is held to be revelation should be studied primarily as a linguistic and
cultural given. Theological discourses on revelation, including the ways
in which such discourses have reified "revelations", should be subjected
to scientific inquiry. In all three religions, it was an oral discourse that
was the primary vehicle of revelation, and in all three religions there is
an analogous relationship between the "spoken words" in the plural and
the "heavenly Word" in the singular.

The textual fixation of the religious discourse had far-reaching consequences. It made "revelation" accessible only from within an official closed
corpus of fixed texts; this puts the exegete in a hermeneutic situation. It
also enabled various groups of people to sacralize, transcendentalize, and
absolutize their own behavior and words simply by appealing to particular
scriptural texts. Arkoun wants to consider revelation again as an event of
meaning, a source of living tradition, something that opens to the future.
It is definitively opposed to repetitive behavior and to the formation of
rigidly closed systems of thought. Revelation properly understood provides human beings primarily with mental space and creates a spiritual
ethos. In practice, however, in all three religions it has served to legitimate
domination, which is contrary to its primary function (*OI*, p. 72).

Fourth, the work of Arkoun destroys the idea that Muslims cannot make a critical study of Muhammad (*OI*, ch. 9) and the Qur'ān (*OI*, chs. 6–8); he breaks an existing taboo. He explicitly pleads for a comparative historical study of the three "Book religions" (*OI*, p. 120). He compares, for instance, the relations between religion and state in Islam and Christianity, offering new insight (*OI*, ch. 3). Refreshingly, Arkoun shows no tendency to glorify, magnify, or estheticize Islam, and he certainly has no inclination to enter into polemics or apologetic reasoning.

Throughout the book, one senses how much Arkoun is concerned with the current ideologization of Islam: "the triumph of an area of society's imagination that is qualified as 'Islamic'". He offers his own definition of ideologization: "There is an ideological derivation in Islamic thinking whenever an author [...] establishes a Qur'anic discourse that initially was open as a closed cognitive system"[38]. He also gives an explanation of such an ideologization of Islam as of any religion: when there are attacks from the outside, the Muslim world assembles around an Islam made "ideologically efficient"[39]. In recent times, for instance, the Salafīya and subsequent movements have developed a "mythological" vision of original and classical Islam into something ideologically useful, rooted in a society's imagination (*imaginaire social*, *OI*, pp. 27, 131).

Against the perennial tendency to ideologization, not only in religion but also in scholarship, Arkoun advocates methodological plurality, open problematics, and a philosophical attitude, "in order to go beyond the ravaging ideologies" (cf. *OI*, p. 127). As a committed thinker and scholar, Arkoun makes a sharp distinction between the "theoretical" Islamology of Western universities, of philological inspiration, and an "applied" Islamology that seeks to read and study the past and present of Islam on the basis of present-day expressions and problems of Muslim societies. Applied Islamology should address itself to the largest possible public without incurring the condemnation, haughty rejection, or even indifference of erudite scholars (*OI*, p. 8).

8. Applied Islamology

Arkoun probably coined the expression "applied Islamology"[40] in analogy to the expression "applied anthropology", which the French anthro-

---

[38] "le triomphe d'un imaginaire social qualifié d'islamique"; "il y a dérivé idéologique dans le cadre de la pensée islamique chaque fois qu'un auteur lui-même echo plus ou moins fidèle d'une école, d'une communauté, d'une tradition – érigé en système cognitif clos un discours coranique initialement ouvert" (*OI*, p. 158).

[39] "il a fallu se rassembler autour d'un Islam orthodoxe, dogmatique, rigide, mais idéologiquement efficace" (*OI*, p. 131).

[40] Mohammed ARKOUN, "Pour une islamologie appliquée", first published in 1976 and reproduced in his *Pour une critique de la raison islamique*, 1984, ch. 1 (pp. 43–63).

pologist Roger Bastide introduced.[41] In a way, all Islamology that is not purely academic—that is to say, an exclusively scholarly pursuit—constitutes some kind of "applied" scholarship. Moreover, even pure scholarship plays a role in society and in relations between people from different societies. In the case of the six authors under consideration, for instance, the social relevance of their research is striking.

Of the four historians, Laroui concentrates on Moroccan history and the rise of the national movement, Merad explores the role of reformist Islam in the national movement of Algeria, Talbi works on Tunisian history in earlier times, and Djaït devotes himself to the study of Arab history in the first century and a half with particular attention to the role of Islam. Furthermore, Laroui has paid attention to the Arab intelligentsia facing present-day problems of the Arab world, and Talbi has cherished the cause of dialogue on a personalist basis, beyond the frontiers of denominational systems and communal structures, stimulating Muslims to take part in it. Merad, too, has been open to dialogue, also in a practical sense with a view to improving the situation of North Africans living in France. Djaït has a vivid sense of the rise and decline of cultures and civilizations and has been concerned about inter-Arab, Arab-European, and Arab-Western relations.

Of the two authors concentrating on Islam, Bennabi has been concerned with Islam as a resource for the moral and ideological reconstruction of Algeria, and Arkoun's basic concern has been the study of the humanist tradition in Islamic intellectual history and the role of the human person. Whereas Bennabi has made a concerted effort to mobilize his people in the framework of an Islamic movement, Arkoun has been sensitive to the manipulation of religion by political and other interests, as it has taken place throughout the history of Islamic and other religious traditions. When he subjects the various forms of established religion to a critical analysis, he is inspired not only by rational enlightenment, which employs the human and social sciences, but also by the Qur'ān, which works with religious symbolism. He has developed his views in publications as well as in lectures given in Muslim and Western countries.

As a consequence, all six authors are profoundly aware of the relevance of their work for the future of their societies, their countries, the Arab world, and the wider Muslim world. It would have been strange if this had not been the case, and this distinguishes them quite naturally from Western scholars scarcely ever concerned with the future of Muslim societies for their own sake. So all six authors, besides their scholarly research, are somehow involved in the practical effects of their studies on Muslim societies and have their place in what may be called "applied" Islamology.

---

[41]   Roger BASTIDE, *Anthropologie appliquée*, Paris: Payot, 1971.

For Arkoun, however, applied Islamology has a special meaning; it serves what I would like to call an intellectual renewal of Islam and potentially all three monotheistic religions. Knowing Western Islamology well and recognizing what it has achieved in terms of textual studies, he recognizes its limitations as a purely Western discourse that defines Islam largely by means of its classical texts. In his view, Islamic studies should be subject to epistemological self-criticism, assimilate the many new developments in the human and social sciences, and develop a greater awareness of the problems with which Muslim societies are confronted today.

Applied Islamology as conceived and advocated by Arkoun is meant to overcome a certain distrust that Muslims feel toward Orientalism by promoting active cooperation between Muslim and non-Muslim scholars. Applied Islamology must ultimately create conditions under which intellectual freedom can be restored and developed. Muslim thought needs to be liberated from old taboos, obsolete mythologies, and the weight of political forces and ideologies. More than before, the Muslim intelligentsia should take part actively in the intellectual ventures in which Western thought has been involved for centuries, and this in all freedom. Applied Islamology should take seriously the vital concerns of Muslim thought at the present time and it should respond to them. Accordingly, the Islamologist "applying" his or her knowledge should be not only a scholar but also a promoter of all reflection that aims at renewal and emancipation.

When studying Islam, applied Islamology should introduce comparative research and question Islamic materials in the same way as the present-day humanities and social sciences investigate materials of other religions. As a consequence, it should subject the Islamic theological system to critical inquiry just like that directed at theological systems in other religions. Until now, at least in the three monotheistic religions, theologies have functioned largely as "cultural systems of mutual exclusion". They legitimated opposing interests of the religious communities and their leaderships and they stood in the way of true communication and dialogue.

9. Conclusion

The task set out at the beginning of this chapter was to analyze the ways in which six North African intellectuals have presented Islam in French-language publications during recent decades. The first conclusion must be that none of the authors confines himself to a simple presentation of Islam; each communicates results of his scholarly research and searches for scholarly cooperation. Moreover, some of them formulate broader questions that apply not only to Islam but to Christianity as well, which is an invitation to dialogue on an intellectual level. Arkoun in particular takes a philosophical stand.

A second conclusion is that it is no longer French scholars who study and teach in France Islamic history, thought, and institutions, as was the case in the days when our six authors were students. Many more scholars from North African countries are now carrying out research in this field and this has renewed discussions on the ways in which Islamic studies are to be pursued. Differences in approach depend not only on different theoretical frameworks and methodologies but also on personal backgrounds and different causes to which scholars can be dedicated. Those from Muslim societies are naturally aware of the relevance and possible application of their work for the future of their societies.

Third, I would say that Arkoun's appeal to broaden Islamic studies beyond the study of texts deserves a positive response. Many Western scholars of Islam are basically specialists in textual work and are not always able to situate these texts and their various interpretations and applications in their proper intellectual and religious, historical, and social contexts. The lack of concern of quite a few Western researchers in present-day problems of Muslim societies—which irritates Arkoun and many other Muslim scholars—must be deplored. However, within the context of academic freedom, it is the responsibility of individual researchers to remedy this; measures cannot be dictated from above, though pedagogy can and should be improved. Scholarly cooperation between qualified researchers of different backgrounds, including the societies studied, is not only a sound demand, but also a scholarly necessity.

Finally, I would suggest that similar inquiries be made into the ways in which Islam in recent times has been presented by scholars from other Muslim regions in Africa, the Middle East, and Asia. It is also timely to examine the ways in which Muslims in North America and Europe, South Africa and Australia, present Islam nowadays.

Chapter 8
Human Rights, Human Dignity, and Islam

1. Introduction

There is a whole library on human rights at the United Nations in Geneva, and it would be difficult to find questions that have not already been asked by eminent philosophers, jurists, and diplomats or by people of good will and common sense.[1] All I can do here is to resort to my own discipline, the science of religion, and to discuss some questions that arise from this particular perspective. Strangely enough, although many religious people have been concerned with human rights, until now the science of religion seems to have paid little attention to them. The topic does not appear, for instance, in the *Encyclopedia of Religion*, edited by the late Mircea Eliade and published in 1987. What, then, do human rights mean in religious terms to people of various religions and in particular to Muslims? How do they react to it and how is their reaction to be explained and interpreted?

I propose to treat our subject in five points. First, I shall give a short historical introduction to the Declaration of Human Rights, with a summary of their characteristics, asking what they mean in human terms. Second, I shall briefly look at some religious reactions from the monotheistic religions to human rights and indicate some characteristics of these reactions, in other words asking what human rights mean in religious terms. Third, I shall pay special attention to Muslim reactions and the development of alternative Islamic declarations of human rights, asking what human rights mean to Muslims. Fourth, I am afraid that we shall have to consider for a moment the sad circumstances of so many of our fellow human beings, at present and in the foreseeable future. And finally, I shall try to offer some conclusions about the basic struggle for human dignity, among Muslims and the rest of us, in the face of the dangers threatening it. The basic question is not, as the title may have suggested, whether Islam as such is opposed to human rights and human dignity, but

---

[1]   This chapter is based on my Ganander Lecture delivered to the Finnish Society for the Study of Comparative Religion, Helsinki, 15 November 1990. An earlier version of this text was published in *Temenos*, 27 (1991), pp. 151–82.

in what ways Muslims can participate in the human struggle for dignity and survival, and what, for them, constitutes human dignity.

2. History[2]

One preliminary document of human rights was political—the "Bill of Rights" drawn up in 1689 and imposed by the British Parliament on the new King, the Dutch *stadtholder* William III who had been called to the British throne to succeed James II. The Bill of Rights stipulated the law's superiority to the King, no longer considered as a sovereign ruling by divine right. It enshrines the fundamental rights and freedoms of the people against the king.

The first real document of human rights was again political—the "Declaration of Virginia", drawn up in June 1776 by the British colonies in America who wanted to free themselves from British rule. It led to the War of Independence (1776–81) and the establishment of the United States of America. The declaration enumerated the citizens' basic freedoms, the separation between legislature, executive, and judiciary, and free elections.

On August 26, 1789 the French Constituent Assembly accepted the "Declaration of the rights of man and the citizen", which formed a Preamble to the Constitution of 1791. It formulated the inalienable and sacred natural rights of the human person, denouncing violations of human rights as the only causes of the misfortune of societies and of the corruption of governments. It was followed by two other declarations. One served as a preamble to the new Constitution of June 1793; it stressed freedom, allowing assassination of the tyrant and opposing slavery. The other one, proclaimed in August 1795, formulated the duties as well as the rights of people in society (freedom, security, property) and replaced the statement that people are born free and enjoy equal rights by the formula of people's equality before the law.

These declarations of human rights clearly intend to protect the individual against any arbitrary power, the American one stressing the freedom and independence of the person, the French ones seeking to establish a precise socio-political order, opposing any absolutist power and promoting the common well-being. They proclaim the political rights of people who, as citizens, discover and make democracy.

More recently, the "Charter" of the United Nations, proclaiming the faith of the nations in the fundamental rights of men and women, was adopted by the Constitutive Assembly on June 25, 1945. A United Na-

---

[2] For the relevant historical texts, see *La conquête des droits de l'homme*.

tions Commission on Human Rights, which continues to work, prepared the "Universal Declaration of Human Rights" (with "Preamble"). This was discussed and amended by the General Assembly and adopted on December 10, 1948.[3] The rights enumerated in the French declaration of 1789 were extended to include the right to work and leisure time, to social security, and freedom of movement. The declaration also condemned torture, slavery, and racism. After a short discussion, any reference to a divinity was left out.

Articles 3 to 21 treat individual freedoms, Articles 22 to 27 economic and social rights (including the right to work and to establish unions and children's right to social security and education) and cultural rights (including the freedom of conscience and of religion, which entails the right to change and manifest one's religion).

The last three Articles (28–30) establish the need for a framework within which rights can be realized. The individual not only enjoys rights but also has duties; individuals must submit to some legal restrictions to ensure the acknowledgment of and respect for the rights and freedoms of others. No state has the right to act in violation of the rights and freedoms of a human being. No interpretation of the Declaration by a state or a particular group is possible. Whereas the Declaration itself does not imply precise legal commitments, its application is more or less guaranteed by more than 20 conventions that are binding on the signatory states. The first two, from the year 1966, are most important: the "International Convention on Economic, Social and Cultural Rights" (with Article 1 establishing the right of peoples to self-determination and to enjoy their natural riches and resources) and the "International Convention on Civil and Political Rights". The U.N. Commission on Human Rights reports annually to the U.N. General Assembly. The U.N. has a Centre for Human Rights in Geneva.

In November 1950, the Council of Europe promulgated the "European Convention for the Protection of Human Rights and Fundamental Freedoms"[4] and created a European Commission of Human Rights[5] and a European Court of Justice of Human Rights.

There is now an immense literature on human rights, partly of a technical juridical nature.[6] Following the example of France in 1898 after

---

3   "The Universal Declaration of Human Rights" has become an authoritative text; it has been accepted and signed by nearly all member states of the United Nations.
     The U.N.O. publishes a *Yearbook of the Human Rights Committee*, containing *Annual Reports to the General Assembly*.
4   The European Convention for the Protection of Human Rights and Fundamental Freedoms was accepted in Rome, November 1950; from 1952 until 1985, eight Protocols were added to it.
5   MONCONDUIT, *La Commission européenne des droits de l'homme*.
6   The basic texts on human rights adopted by international organizations are easily accessible in a booklet *Human Rights: A Compilation of International Instruments*. Regular

the Dreyfus affair, committees or associations have been formed in an increasing number of countries to work for the observance of human rights in them.[7]

3. Some Characteristics of the Declarations of Human Rights

Formulated in situations in which people revolted against various forms of political oppression, social deprivation, and deprivation of human dignity, the various declarations of human rights aimed to open up a new era in which those in power would respect the human dignity of their people by safeguarding their human rights. Monarchical tyranny, colonial oppression, fundamental inequalities of traditional society, belligerence, and criminal acts against particular groups of people were to be halted. This was still restricted to the internal domain of the state. Whereas the first declarations were valid within one particular state, after World War Two the various states themselves had to be bound, and we see a movement from the national to the international level. Thus, human rights have started to move into the realm of international law.

Although it is true that, under current circumstances, states cannot be forced to sign the 1948 Universal Declaration of Human Rights, to sign and ratify the following Conventions, to apply the specific items of the Declaration they have signed and the Conventions they have signed and ratified, the last thirty years have shown the moral force of the appeal to human rights (for instance, by people like Israel Shahak [1933–2001] in Israel and Andrej Sakharov [b. 1921] in the USSR) and the impact of world opinion, given the unwillingness of states to be on the blacklist of countries violating human rights.[8] Organizations like Amnesty International[9] or, in our case, the Association for the Defense of the Human

---

publications in this field are *Israel Yearbook on Human Rights*, Tel Aviv, 1971–; *Human Rights Quarterly*, Baltimore, 1979–; *Human Rights Law Journal*, Kehl am Rhein, 1980–; *Harvard Human Rights Journal*, Cambridge, Mass., 1987–.

[7] The "Ligue des droits de l'homme" in France, for instance, is one of about forty national leagues for human rights in the world, constituting together the "International Federation of Human Rights" (Fédération internationale des Droits de l'Homme). There is also the International Commission of Jurists, with its seat in Geneva, and in France an "Association pour le Développement des Libertés Fondamentales".

[8] Official "blacklists" are contained in the *Annual Reports* of the U.N. Human Rights Committee to the U.N. General Assembly, and in the *Country Reports on Human Rights Practices* submitted by the U.S. Department of State to the Committees on Foreign Affairs and on Foreign Relations of the U.S. Congress (annually).

[9] See the *Amnesty International Reports*, and the special *Country Reports* about human rights violations. A French edition of the *Amnesty International Report* is published in Paris by La Découverte publishers.

Rights and Democratic Freedoms in the Arab World[10], are able to provide information to whoever wants it about fundamental violations of human rights in a number of countries, information to which the states concerned are increasingly forced to respond.

Another characteristic of the human rights declarations is that, born of indignation about forms of degradation of human dignity, they have been formulated in terms of the European eighteenth-century Enlightenment and Western twentieth-century humanistic thinking. This is shown in their insistence on the rights of individuals rather than groups, in the idealistic tone of their articulation of human dignity, and in their remoteness from any religious legitimation of human rights and from any religious institution. In fact, several items of the Universal Declaration of Human Rights could be and have been used to criticize particular elements of religious traditions and certain organized religions, for instance the Catholic stand on family planning, not only in the West but also, and especially, in the Third World. In other words, since the articulation of human rights expresses protest against all that curbs human dignity, it is relevant not only to state practices but also to religious practices.

4. Some Religious Reactions

Religious reactions to Human Rights Declarations have varied and research on this falls fully within the scope of the science of religion.

Until Vatican II, the Roman Catholic Church was more than reticent about declarations of human rights, including the U.N.'s. The Church was the great loser in the French Revolution, with its secularist currents, and thereafter it condemned human rights. Only in 1975, in "Justitia et Pax", do we find a recognition of the inalienable rights of any individual; it adds that the Church has to provide the necessary orientation for

---

[10] The "Association de défense des droits de l'Homme et des libertés démocratiques dans le monde arabe" was established in Paris in January 1983. The Association has published annual reports under the title *Les droits de l'Homme dans le monde arabe*, since 1985 through La Découverte publishers.

  Cf. the now annual publication on *Human Rights in the Arab World*, *Ḥuqūq al-insān fī 'l-waṭanī 'l-'arabī* of which Nr. 24 appeared in 1990. Earlier names were *Ḥuqūq al-insān al-'arabī* (Arabs' Human Rights, 1986/17) or simply *Ḥuqūq al-insān* (Human Rights, 1986/18).

  Several Arab countries such as Egypt and Tunisia have national Human Right Committees; in Morocco there were three such Committees by the end of 1990. One should also mention the Union of Arab Lawyers, with its seat in Cairo.

  In Lausanne there has been an "Association en Suisse de défense des droits de l'Homme au Magreb", which published the *Magreb Tribune* (1986).

humankind to achieve these rights, which find their most complete expression in the Gospel.[11]

The Orthodox Church, too, was reticent about human rights. They were considered rationalistic (an old reproach directed at the cultural expressions of Western Europe) and, because of their anthropocentric concern, as a possible expression of human arrogance towards God.

Among Protestants, several opinions were held.[12] On the one hand, there were those who denied that human beings, as creatures of God and moreover as sinners, could claim to have any rights at all. On the other hand, there were those who accepted human rights, upholding the freedom of conscience and expression and rejecting decisive human authorities between God and the human person. They were strongly moved by ethical considerations.

The World Council of Churches moved toward recognizing human rights, reformulating them at a conference held at St. Pölten in 1974 as follows:

1) the right to life as addressed against any unjust system,
2) the right to cultural identity,
3) the right to participate in political decisions,
4) the right to hold differing opinions and conceptions against any totalitarianism,
5) the right to human dignity,
6) the right to freedom of choice in religious matters.

In February 1976, the World Reformed Alliance published a document presenting a theological justification of human rights, trying to base them not upon human nature but upon the right that God has over human beings (divine right) and calling on member Churches to act accordingly.

Jewish reactions have been positive toward the struggle against injustice implied in human rights. Orthodox Jews, however, maintain that the Torah contains all the prescriptions necessary for human rights and duties and that in light of this a Declaration of Human Rights is superfluous.

Muslim reactions will be discussed below; most remarkable here is the attempt to formulate an alternative, Islamic Declaration of Human Rights.

Among the monotheistic reactions, finally, I should mention that of the Bahā'ī community, which has taken a positive stand and made great efforts to have the rights of freedom of conscience and religious freedom accepted by the United Nations on November 25, 1981.

---

[11] See also JOHN PAUL II, "Redemptor Hominis". Cf. Jozef PUNT, *Die Idee der Menschenrechte: Ihre geschichtliche Entwicklung und ihre Rezeption durch die moderne katholische Sozialverkündigung*, Zurich: Schöningh, 1987.
[12] On Protestant theological positions on human rights, see Martin HECKEL, *Die Menschenrechte im Spiegel der reformatorischen Theologie*, Heidelberg: Winter, 1987.

5. Some Characteristics of the Religious Reactions

The reactions just sketched are interesting for several reasons. Just as particular points of human rights can be used to attack elements of religious traditions and organized religions, so also religions can use particular human rights for apologetic purposes. It is significant that religious leaders nearly always originally adopted a critical attitude. Following that, there were several possibilities of accepting human rights in principle, once it had become clear that public opinion was increasingly in favor of them.

One possibility was to say that, fundamentally, they were nothing new and that the religion concerned had a concept of human dignity and law that went further or was more profound than the Human Rights Declaration. Such were the responses of Jews, Catholics, and many Protestants. They claimed that the more human rights are recognized, the more the excellence of these religions becomes evident. These religions claim they already have Human Rights—with capitals—in depth.

Another possibility, among Protestants, is to accept human rights as an ethical norm or code and then to proceed by developing a theological basis for them with an appeal to Scripture, particularly by attributing their origin and that of human dignity less to human nature than to God's grace. While the former position is that there a concept of religious law and nature, to which the human rights can be subordinated, is already present, in the latter, a theological foundation is given independently of any general notion of law or nature.

A very different approach is followed by minority religions such as the Bahā'ī, that have less need to defend established claims and possessions than to win acceptance for themselves. Here human rights are gladly accepted, especially the right to religious freedom, which is stressed. The overall intention here is to seek the protection of human rights and even to broaden their scope, just as oppressed or persecuted people gladly accept human rights, which they hope will alter their sad circumstances.

A very different possibility is to develop an ideology out of human rights and make it into either a kind of humanistic doctrine or a political activism functioning almost as a religion. People then tend to lose the capacity to perceive the discrepancy between the norms contained in human rights and the realities of the human situation in most parts of the world. Or, the other way round, such an ideology of human rights tends to be used to denounce not so much actual violations, for instance in political reality, as to attack entire religions and ideological systems for being *as such* contrary to human rights. Roman Catholicism is attacked because of its hierarchical structure, its stand on women and marriage, and its pretensions to absolute authority, Judaism because of its exclusive concern with the Jewish people, Islam because it links religion with politics, its lower status for women, its corporal punishments, etc. Granted that there are ideological features in any declaration of human rights, it still makes quite a difference whether the text of the Universal Declaration as a whole is ideologized, be it to sketch an ideal utopia or to serve as a weapon of inquisition.

I contend that most religious responses to the Universal Declaration of Human Rights still reflect an ideological use of these human rights for the benefit of the religions concerned, be it apologetically or polemically. Ideological or not, human rights undoubtedly have a spiritual meaning for religious people, just as they have a political meaning in social life.

6. Islam: A Special Case?

6.1. Saudi Arabia

A number of Islamic organizations and 'ulamā' responded in a special manner to the Universal Declaration of Human Rights of 1948. In this, Saudi Arabia played the leading role. Saudi Arabia, like Israel, is not a signatory to the Universal Declaration and its two Conventions, arguing that to maintain human dignity, Saudi Arabia wants to draw on the eternal Sharī'a, based on revelation, and not on legislation inspired by what it calls materialist considerations subject to change. It also states that Islam has different means of assuring respect for human dignity, and it claims to be the Islamic State par excellence.

Saudi Arabia's position is unusual, but it is emulated to a large extent by the Arab Gulf States, Mauretania and a few other countries that have also declined to sign the Declaration and the two main Conventions. On June 15, 1970, the government of Saudi Arabia published a memorandum concerning Human Rights in Islam and their application in the country.[13] Unlike the human rights of the Universal Declaration, the human rights of Islam are not moral formulae but precise prescriptions and commands whose application is guaranteed by legislation.

---

[13]   In answer to a request from the U.N. Human Rights Committee through the League of Arab States, Saudi Arabia submitted a memorandum titled (in the French version): Le Mémorandum du Gouvernement du Royaume d'Arabie Saoudite relatif au Dogme des droits de l'Homme en Islam et à son application dans le Royaume, adressé aux Organisations Internationales intéressées. It is addressed to the General Secretariat of the League of Arab States and probably dates from 1970 or 1971. It reiterates that Saudi Arabia does not adhere to the U.N. Universal Declaration of Human Rights of 1948 and does not sign the Convention on Economic, Social and Cultural Rights. The memorandum was published in 1972 in Riyadh together with the "Colloques de Riyadh" of 1972 by the Saudi Ministry of Information (57 pp.). Cf. below notes 14 and 15.

Three frequently controversial points are specifically explained in the Saudi memorandum:

1) Forbidding the marriage of a Muslim woman and a non-Muslim and of a Muslim with a polytheistic woman (which violates Article 16 of the Declaration) has its rationale in the desire to preserve the family from dissolution.

2) Prohibiting a Muslim from changing his religion (which violates Article 18 of the Declaration) is justified in terms of the desire to counter the machinations of those who want to sow disorder on earth.

3) Forbidding the organization of labor unions (which violates Article 8 of Convention I) has its rationale in the desire to protect workers and other wage-earners from the activities of saboteurs from abroad.

The most interesting aspect of this memorandum is the assured tone in which it conveys that the *Sharī'a* is perfect, that it is well applied in Saudi Arabia, that opposition to certain articles of the Universal Declaration is justified, and that Saudi Arabia has done all it can to ensure the observance of economic, social, and cultural rights, with particular attention to education.

Subsequently, Saudi *'ulamā'* and jurists from Europe took part in a series of meetings held in 1972 and 1974: in Riyadh (1972)[14], in Paris, the Vatican, Geneva, and Strasbourg (1974).[15]

---

[14] The results were published from a Saudi point of view under the title (in the French version): *Colloques de Ryad – entre un groupe de canonistes et de juristes de l'Arabie Saoudite et un groupe de juristes et d'intellectuels venus d'Europe – sur Le dogme musulman et les droits de l'Homme en Islam*. This publication contains also the memorandum mentioned in note 13. Cf. below note 15.

[15] The texts of the meetings were published from a Saudi point of view in a comprehensive publication titled (in the French version): *Colloques de Riyad, de Paris, du Vatican, de Genève et de Strasbourg sur le dogme musulman et les droits de l'homme en Islam entre juristes de l'Arabie Saoudite et éminents juristes et intellectuels européens*, Riyadh, 1974.

The subjects of the meetings were the following:

Paris (October 10, 1974): Aperçu sur le Royaume de l'Arabie Saoudite et son système législatif fondé sur la Loi Coranique.

The Vatican (October 25, 1974): Les droits de l'Homme en Islam: La culture comme moyen d'épanouissement de l'Homme et la contribution des musulmans à la paix et au respect des Droits de l'Homme.

Geneva (October 30, 1974): La conception de l'Homme en Islam et l'aspiration des Hommes vers la paix.

Paris (November 2, 1974): Aperçu sur les droits de l'Homme en Islam et en Arabie Saoudite et la condition de la femme en Islam.

Strasbourg (November 4, 1974): Les droits de l'Homme et l'unité de la famille humaine en Islam.

As the title indicates, this comprehensive publication also contains the *Colloques de Ryad* mentioned in note 14, on pp. 5–37. It also contains the memorandum mentioned in note 13, on pp. 41–75. It was published in Beirut by Dar al-kitab al-lubnani (n.d., 268 pp.).

The European jurists had raised questions about:

1) the way in which necessary changes are introduced in legislation if there is one unchangeable *Sharīʿa*;

2) corporal punishment;

3) the status of women;

4) the prohibition of labor unions;

5) the absence of a constitution in Saudi Arabia though the King had promised it;

6) the creation in certain Muslim countries of special martial courts not provided for in Islamic law.

I will pass over the Saudi answers, which permit little discussion, for instance the observation that the King's power is effectively limited by the *Sharīʿa*, so that the King does not have absolute power.

The 1974 conference dealt successively with Saudi Arabia's legal system and the *Sharīʿa* in general, the problem of cultural rights in Islam, in particular (religious) education, the concept of the human being in Islam and his or her striving for peace, the status of women in Islam (inequality in the law of succession and of testimony, unilateral divorce, polygamy, the veil), the unity of the human family, as well as the problem of the secular state and of secular education. On all these points, the delegation of Saudi *ʿulamāʾ* provides a kind of apodictic answer revealing that they have hardly grasped the point of the question, that there is hardly any self-criticism, and that the level of intellectual discourse is very low indeed.

The position of Saudi Arabia, which obviously wanted to push the matter of human rights during Faisal's rule, a period of modernization, is prominently represented by the international "Organization of Islamic Conference", founded in 1969. One sees traces of its influence in the Conference's project to formulate an Islamic declaration of human rights.[16]

6.2. Kuwait

In December 1980, a Colloquium on Human Rights in Islam was held independently in Kuwait.[17] This was a private initiative.

---

[16] The "Organization of Islamic Conference" held its first three summit meetings in Rabat (1969), Lahore (1974), and Mecca-Taʾif (January 1981). It had appointed a committee to prepare a text on Human Rights in Islam. A first version was published in the periodical *Rābitat al-ʿālam al-islāmī* (The Muslim World League Journal), 18, 1979/1 (December 1979, Muharram 1400), pp. 149–52. For a French translation of this text by Maurice BORRMANS, see *Islamochristiana*, 9 (1983), pp. 92–6.

[17] This Colloquium was held in Kuwait December 9–14, 1980. It was organized by the International Commission of Jurists in Geneva, the Union of Arab Lawyers in Cairo, and the University of Kuwait. It was independent from the "Organization of Islamic Conference" but it gave suggestions for the text on Human Rights in Islam which the Committee

6.3. *"Organization of Islamic Conference"*

Immediately afterward, a Document on Human Rights in Islam was prepared by the Committee on Human Rights of the "Organization of Islamic Conference"[18]. Its Preamble states that present-day humanity is in need of religious support and means of self-restraint to protect its rights, and that rights and freedoms in Islam (read: the Muslim world) are part of the religion revealed through the Qur'ān. This clearly is meant to be read not only by Muslims but especially by non-Muslims.

The document recognizes, among other things, the freedom of opinion, expression, and religious observance according to the divine inspiration received by each individual, which forbids any forcible conversion and any conversion of Muslims to another religion. The human person has the right to benefit from scholarly, literary, and technical advances, as long as they are not opposed to the precepts of the *Sharī'a*. Restricting the freedom of others is forbidden, as is restricting life through torture or any other humiliating treatment; laws of exception that allow recourse to a degrading treatment of human beings may not be promulgated.

In the document's view, the family is the basis of human society, human life, and humanity; anyone has the right to marry and procreate until God decides otherwise. Necessary conditions of marriage are "unity of religion" for the Muslim woman, and "faith in God" for the Muslim man. Abortion is forbidden except for medical reasons; motherhood must be protected; children have the right to education and moral and financial care. The father decides on the child's education in the light of the *Sharī'a*. The state must provide an education system, and education should aim at the individual's fulfillment in this world and the next,

---

mentioned in note 16 would prepare for the summit meeting in Mecca-Ta'if in January 1981.

The Proceedings of the Colloquium of Kuwait were published in 1982 under the title (in the French version): *Les Droits de l'Homme en Islam*. Among its recommendations are the call to all Muslim states to ratify all international Declarations and Conventions on human rights and the call to a summit meeting of the "Organization of Islamic Conference" in Mecca-Ta'if, to be held in January 1981, to establish an Islamic Charter of Human Rights. The official French text to the Conclusions and Recommendations of the Colloquium of Kuwait was reproduced in *Islamochristiana*, 9 (1983), pp. 78–91.

[18] Immediately after the Colloquium of Kuwait, the committee appointed by the "Organization of Islamic Conference" (O.I.C.) to prepare a text on Human Rights in Islam met on December 15 and 16, 1980 and formulated a proposed "Document on Human Rights in Islam" (*Wāthiqa ḥuqūq al-insān fī 'l-islām*). This document was meant to be discussed and accepted by the Mecca-Ta'if summit meeting (January 25–29, 1981), but lack of time prevented this. Since 1981, several Muslim Conferences on Human Rights in Islam have been held by the O.I.C., the fifth one in Teheran (December 1989). Cf. note 23.

For a French translation of the proposed "Document on Human Rights in Islam" by Maurice Borrmans, see *Islamochristiana*, 9 (1983), pp. 96–101.

The French translations of the three texts mentioned in notes 16, 17, and 18 were published as appendices to an extremely useful article by Caspar, "Les déclarations des droits de l'homme en Islam depuis dix ans".

strengthening faith and respect for and defense of the individual's rights and duties.

Interestingly enough, this document does not speak of the illegitimacy of labor unions or of precise marriage restrictions. All rights and freedoms must be measured against the prescriptions of the *Sharī'a*, which is the only valid reference.

The text of this document was meant to be adopted at the summit meeting of the Organization of Islamic Conference in Mecca-Ta'if in January 1981, but this could not be realized. In the "Mecca Declaration", however, the summit pronounced itself in favor of peace and dialogue with the rest of the world.

6.4. Islamic Council of Europe

Parallel to these initiatives by Saudi Arabia, both nationally and in the context of the Organization of Islamic Conference, a similar initiative in Europe was taken by the Islamic Council of Europe, which has its seat in London. On April 12, 1980, the "Universal Islamic Declaration" was made public in London[19], and on September 19, 1981, an International Conference on Human Rights in Islam was held in Paris, where the "Universal Islamic Declaration of Human Rights" was proclaimed on the same day.[20] I shall call this simply the "Islamic Declaration", as distinct from the "Universal Declaration" of 1948. Here again, the Saudi voice carried weight in the preparation. It is meant for a European audience but, since it was formulated by a private Islamic body, it does not commit or even involve governments in Muslim countries. The official text is in

---

[19] *The Universal Islamic Declaration (al-bayān al-islāmī al-'ālami)* of April 12, 1980 (26 Jumada al-ula 1400) consists of seven Articles plus a Manifest and a Commitment (*Manifeste et engagement* in the French version, which has 25 pp.). It is accompanied by a letter signed in London by Salem Azzam, Secretary General of the Islamic Council Europe at the time.

[20] On September 19, 1981 (21 Dhu'l Qada 1401) an International Conference on Human Rights in Islam was held in the Unesco building in Paris, organized by the Islamic Council Europe, which had already organized a similar International Islamic Conference in London in April 1976. The Director of Unesco, Amadou-Mahtar M'Bow, gave an address to the Conference in which he hailed the achievements of Islam in the field of human rights. The same day, the "International Islamic Council", which has the same address as the "Islamic Council of Europe" in London, "proclaimed the *Universal Islamic Declaration of Human Rights* at its international conference held today, 19 September 1981, at Unesco". Muslim participants in the conference put forward seven statements. The Arabic authoritative text as well as the slightly different English and French versions meant for the European public were published in London in 1981. A literal French translation of the Arabic text by Maurice BORRMANS was published in *Islamochristiana*, 9 (1983), pp. 121–40, and a literal English translation of the same text by Penelope JOHNSTONE was published in *Islamochristiana*, 9 (1983), pp. 103–20.

Arabic; the English and French versions, obviously meant for the broader European public, are not translations but adaptations that display an apologetic tendency.

Since this declaration is a response to the declarations of the U.N. (New York 1948), the Council of Europe (Rome 1950), and the European Conference on Security and Cooperation (Helsinki 1975), it deserves our attention. The text is preceded by a preamble.

The preamble states without further ado that human rights were put into words and protected with the arrival of Islam fourteen centuries ago. Muslims must invite all people to adopt Islam as their religion. This is followed by eleven considerations concerning the basis of Islamic faith, defining the Muslim community in its European environment. The preamble concludes by enumerating twelve characteristics of the authentic Islamic society to be realized on the basis of the human rights formulated in the declaration.

This is a society of full equality in rights and duties, in which rulers and ruled are equal before the *Sharī'a* and before the court and in which the family is important. It is a society in which the rulers put the *Sharī'a* into practice, in which all believe in the One God, in which the principle of consultation prevails. Each individual is able to assume responsibilities according to one's capacities, and each individual is the conscience of society and has the right to bring a charge before the court. It is a society that rejects oppression and guarantees security, freedom, justice, and the defense of the rights that the *Sharī'a* has conferred on human beings.

The text itself contains 23 Articles:

Articles 1–3 deal with life and freedom (their sacred character can be restricted only by the *Sharī'a*); all are equal before the *Sharī'a* without any distinction except that arising from their works.

Articles 4–5 deal with justice. For a Muslim, only the *Sharī'a* counts. Nobody can force a Muslim to obey an order contrary to the *Sharī'a*. A Muslim may refuse to obey out of loyalty to truth. A person is presumed innocent before the court until his or her guilt has been proved. No punishment should exceed that fixed by the *Sharī'a*.

Articles 6–10 oppose the misuse of power, torture, infringement of honor and reputation, all persecution, and the abuse of power vis-à-vis minorities.

Articles 11–14 deal with political rights. Each individual has the right to information as far as the social interest permits and has the right and duty to participate in government according to the principle of consultation. Everyone has the right to choose freely who will govern his or her community as well as the right to call officials to account. Thus each individual has the right to set up institutions in order to exercise the right of participation in the life of the religious, cultural, or political community. The right to freedom of thought, belief (no one is allowed to ridicule the beliefs of others), and expression is recognized within the general limits of the *Sharī'a*, as is the duty to fight a government that acts unjustly, since commanding what is beneficial and prohibiting what is reprehensible is a right and a duty. Freedom of expression implies the freedom to practice one's religion according to one's belief.

Articles 15–18 deal with economic rights.

Articles 19–23 deal with the family according to classical standards.

Spouses enjoy rights equivalent to the duties laid down by the *Sharī'a*. The husband is responsible for education. The children have the right to education both in family and school and to preparation for adult life. Consequently, burdening children with tasks that may hinder their physical growth is forbidden. A married woman has the right to live with her husband wherever he wants, etc.

In the French and English versions, however, there are some significant changes as compared with the Arabic original text:

1) There are no quotations from the Qur'ān and *Sunna*.

2) The first part of the Preamble is replaced by an Introduction on the difference between the ideal code of Islam and reality. The hope is expressed that this declaration will give an impetus to Muslim people.

3) The Preamble adds five considerations, for instance the aspiration of humankind for a juster world order, and the waste and unjust distribution of means of subsistence. It then affirms seven beliefs.

4) Instead of mentioning that the father decides on the education of the children, it states that all people have the right to marry and educate their children according to their religion, traditions, and culture.

5) The prayer formulae at the beginning and the end are omitted.

Two years later, in 1983, the Islamic Council of Europe published a model of an Islamic constitution.[21]

6.5. Some Features of this Islamic Approach

What are the main features of this Islamic approach, inspired by Saudi attitudes, to the overall subject of human rights?[22] Three are striking at first sight.

---

[21] *A Model of an Islamic Constitution*, 1983. This is the last document of a triad published by the Islamic Council of Europe between 1980 and 1983. On these documents, see *Islamochristiana*, 9 (1983), and, in German, Martin FORSTNER, "Allgemeine islamische Menschenrechtserklärung", *CIBEDO-Dokumentation*, 15–16 (1982), pp. 1–75.

[22] There is a rich literature dealing with human rights in Islam. The most important collective publications are the following, in chronological order:
1) Special issue of *Majalla rābitati 'l-'ālam al-islāmī*, 18 (1979) (1979/1 = Muharram 1400). See above note 16.

174 Muslim Presentations of Islam and of Human Rights

First, all matters are derived from Islamic sources: Qur'ān and *Sunna* on the one hand, *Sharī'a* or Islamic religious law on the other. Even though the categories and themes of the Universal Declaration of 1948 are used, the actual contents, derived from the *Sharī'a* in rational terms, claim to be based on the Qur'ān and *Sunna*.

Second, these are not a body of rights that humans possess from birth, given with their nature, but a whole set of prescriptions incumbent on them, found in or deduced from the sources, and interpreted as divine commands that constitute human's duties and rights, obligations and privileges. What are called human rights are in fact human duties toward God or God's rights over humans.

Third, the *Sharī'a* is the final and only true criterion for judging human actions. In the legal vocabulary of the authors of the declarations, Saudi *'ulamā'*, no human-made law is credible and nothing outside the *Sharī'a*, whether of an ethical or a more legal nature, is taken into consideration. And the contents of the *Sharī'a* can evidently be formulated only by these *'ulamā'* who, it should be pointed out, represent the puritan Hanbalī way of interpreting the *Sharī'a*, which is applied only in Saudi Arabia and a few Gulf States.

Most interesting and important, however, is the very idea of formulating an Islamic alternative to the Universal Declaration of Human Rights. No other religion or ideology, as far as I know, has taken this initiative, which parallels other Muslim initiatives to create Islamic alternatives to Western institutions. The reasons why this process is taking place are complex.

In certain Muslim writings, there is a tendency to oppose things Islamic to things Western, Islam to the West (rather than to Christianity, and to the USA rather than to Europe). The roots of this aloofness from the West appear to be in part political, as a natural reaction to Western, specifically American political and economic dominance. But they also have to do with deeper processes of searching for orientation and articulating identity. That the West does not like the creation of models alternative to Western ones, which are assumed to be universal, confirms my feeling that the Muslim and Western worlds are moving away from each

---

2) Report on the Colloquium of Kuwait 1980. See above note 17.
3) Special issue *CIBEDO-Dokumentation*, 1982/15–16. See FORSTNER (previous note).
4) Special issue *Islamochristiana*, 9 (1983).
5) The anthology edited by HIRSCH, *Islam et droits de l'homme*.
6) The proceedings of a conference on the subject organized by the University of Tunis: *Droits de l'homme: IIIème Rencontre islamo-chrétienne*.

For a comparison between Islamic and Christian views of human rights, see BOUMA, "Christian and Islamic Valuation of Human Rights". Cf. *La liberté religieuse dans le judaïsme, le christianisme et l'islam* and TRAER, "Human Rights in Islam".

For separate publications on the subject by Muslim authors, see below note 36.

other. So far, Saudi Arabia has tried to take the lead in this moving away from the West in a conservative sense, while Iran has done the same in a revolutionary form. One can only speculate how an Islamic declaration of human rights would look if it were sponsored by Iran rather than by Saudi Arabia, not to speak of versions by other Muslim countries, which might be very different.[23]

7. The Islamic and the Universal Declaration Compared

Let us look now more closely into the differences between the Islamic Declaration of Human Rights (Paris 1981) and the Universal Declaration of Human Rights (New York 1948), analyzing successively three general and two specific items in the declarations.

7.1. General Items

7.1.1. The Notion of Freedom. Whereas freedom appears clearly in Article 3 of the Universal Declaration (where each individual has the right to life, freedom, and personal security), it is not mentioned in the Memorandum of Saudi Arabia (1970). The Declaration of the Organization of Islamic Conference does not speak of freedom as a birthright, but only of a freedom of religion and conscience. Indeed, the notion of free will and thus of freedom has been understood in a much more restricted sense in the history of Islamic thought than in that of Christianity and the West. In Islam, freedom is seen as an active abandonment of the human being to God so that God can act through him or her; the supreme freedom is to surrender it to God. Human rights are in fact "duties" towards God, corollaries of God's rights over human beings.

7.1.2. The Notion of Equality. Whereas the Universal Declaration (Article 2) states that everyone can claim the same rights and freedoms without any distinction whatsoever, the Islamic Declaration (Paris 1981) states that all human beings are equal before the *Sharīʿa* and that all human beings are equal in the human value (*qīma*) they represent. The Memorandum of Saudi Arabia (1970) insists on not discriminating between human beings with regard to their dignity and fundamental rights. The Declaration project of the Organization of Islamic Conference (Article 1) mentions that all people are equal in their human dignity and in

---

[23] Iran organized an international seminar on "Identification of Human Rights and its Principles" in Teheran from September 9–12, 1991. Libya formulated its own Declaration of Human Rights, called in the French version *La grande Charte verte des droits de l'Homme de l'ère jamahiriyenne*, Baida 1988 (17 pp.).

performing duties and responsibilities. In other terms, the Islamic Declarations stress the equality of people before the *Sharī'a*, in human value or dignity and in accomplishing duties.

Indeed, in the history of Islamic thought, much stress has been laid on the contractual relationship or alliance between God the Creator and humankind, His creatures, who all have to fulfill his demands and who will all be judged equally on the degree to which they practice justice, that is to say, God's justice. Equality is a right, and each person has to respect his or her fellow beings. The question remains in what sense equality exists between Muslims and non-Muslims.

7.1.3. The Notion of Community. Article 29 of the Universal Declaration deals with the relation between the rights and freedoms of different people so as to satisfy the demands of a democratic society. The preamble of the Islamic Declaration (Paris 1981) deals extensively with the demands of an authentic Islamic society. In the Memorandum of Saudi Arabia (1970), the definition of human rights includes the appeal for greater mutual understanding for cooperation and mutual help in all domains without consideration of race and religion. The Declaration of the Organization of Islamic Conference explicitly mentions that humankind constitutes one family united by its adoration of the Almighty and its recognition of Adam as the father of all human beings. In the Islamic Declarations, human society occupies a prominent position in its own right, much more so than in the Universal Declaration. From an Islamic point of view, indeed, human rights are not regarded as individual rights but as the rights of a community, the community of the faithful. The individual, as part of this community, shares responsibility for its well-being and purity. And in particular the community's political leaders have to rule permitting it to prosper as God wants it to. In addition to the three religious concepts characteristic of the Islamic approach mentioned above—recourse to Islamic Scripture, God's rights over the human being, the *Sharī'a* as the criterion of legal judgment—there is this fourth socio-religious concept of the religious community taking precedence over the individual, which gives a specific direction to the Islamic declarations of human rights differing from the declaration accepted by the United Nations.

7.2. Specific Items

Let us now look briefly at two specific items in these various declarations: religious freedom and the equality of religious people.

7.2.1. Religious Freedom. Freedom of thought, conscience, and religion, including the freedom to change and publicly proclaim one's religion or conviction, is mentioned in Article 18 of the Universal Declaration.[24] The clause "freedom to change one's religion" has provoked strong reactions from some Muslim countries. The Islamic Declaration stipulates that this freedom is limited by the *Sharī'a*. "No one has the right to propagate errors or abuse anything that may vilify the Islamic community" (Articles 12–13). It also states that each person has the right to participate in the life of his or her natural (religious) community.

The Declaration of the Organization of Islamic Conference forbids the Muslim who has been led to Islam to convert to another religion.

The Qur'ān stipulates a person's freedom to believe or not to believe (S. 18:29). "There is no compulsion in religion" (S. 2:256). Consequently there should be no compulsion to enter Islam. As to those who abandon Islam, they will be punished in the Hereafter; only S. 9:74 refers to a punishment for apostates, but this is not described in precise terms: "[...] God will punish them with a painful punishment in this world and the next one and they will find neither friend nor defender on earth" (S. 9:74). It was the first caliph, Abū Bakr, who declared the death penalty for apostates during the campaigns of the *ridda*, when those abandoning their religion were considered to be betraying the community of the faithful and the weaker members had to be protected. At present, some Muslim scholars consider the death penalty for apostasy from Islam to be a product of the social desire to preserve the homogeneity of one's community, felt especially strongly in ancient times.[25]

In the present-day debate, supporters of the traditional position argue that persons often change their religion under external pressures or for material reasons and that the death penalty must be maintained and the right to change one's religion abolished. In actual practice, in most Muslim countries apostasy arouses the worst emotions and has very serious civil consequences: dissolution of marriage, separation from children, loss of the right of inheritance; in Iran apostates incur the death penalty. Likewise, conversion to Islam is favored in Muslim countries and materially rewarded.

---

[24] On November 25, 1981 the U.N. Assembly accepted the "Declaration on the elimination of all forms of intolerance and of discrimination based on religion or belief". It contains eight articles on the subject that are relevant to the U.N. Commission on Human Rights. See BENITO, *Elimination of all Forms of Intolerance and Discrimination Based on Religion or Belief*.

On the Islamic notion of religious freedom, see TALBI, "Religious Liberty". On the differences between Islamic and Western notions of religious freedom, see for instance *Human Rights and the Conflicts of Culture*. Cf. *La liberté religieuse dans le judaïsme, le christianisme et l'islam.*

[25] The Qur'ān does not prescribe the death penalty for apostasy from Islam; the subject is under discussion.

7.2.2. Equality of Religious People. Difference of religion should not play any part whatsoever in human rights and freedoms, according to the Universal Declaration (Article 2).[26] The Convention on Economic, Social and Cultural Rights states that persons belonging to minorities may not be deprived of the right to practice their own religion together with the other members of their group (Article 27). According to the declaration on the elimination of all forms of intolerance and of discrimination based on religion or belief, no one can be discriminated against on the basis of his or her religion or conviction (Article 2).

The Islamic declaration states that each individual member of the Islamic Community may assume public charges and functions; Muslims together must be united against any foreigner who would wrong the least of those who are under their protection (*ḥadīth*) (Article 11). On the other hand, everyone must respect the religion of others; nobody should ridicule the beliefs of someone else or incite social hostility towards him or her (Article 12).

The Declaration of the Organization of Islamic Conference does not mention religion and simply states that each individual has the right to occupy public positions according to the conditions pertinent to them.

In the classical period of Islam, the non-Muslims living in Muslim territory were distinguished according to four categories[27]:

1) Monotheists living outside Arabia. Muslims could conclude treaties with the People of the Book, who then recognized Muslim political authority, obtained *dhimmī* status and became second-class citizens with a lower status than the Muslims. The difference in status between non-Muslims and Muslims varied according to circumstances.

2) Monotheists living in Arabia, with a few exceptions in Yemen, had to choose between leaving their region or converting to Islam.

3) Polytheists had to choose between a fight to the death or conversion.

4) Apostates were killed unless they returned to Islam, if they were in Muslim-ruled territory.

---

[26] The equality of people of different religious faith and conviction is implied in the Universal Declaration of Human Rights of the U.N. of 1948. It is also part of the "Declaration on the elimination of all forms of intolerance and of discrimination based on religion or belief", accepted by the U.N. Assembly on November 25, 1981. Cf. above note 24.

   The problem of equality of people of different faiths and convictions in Muslim countries is an unsolved issue. On first sight it seems to be largely a socio-political problem of the treatment of minority groups with religions or convictions different than those of the majority. However, old Muslim social traditions of how to treat non-Muslim minorities still prevail and much ideology has been developed on both sides. Non-Muslim minorities in Muslim countries have in fact to fight for their survival.

[27] A classical study on the problem is Antoine FATTAL, *Le statut légal des non-musulmans en pays d'Islam*, Beirut: Imprimerie Catholique, 1958.

The distinction between Muslims and non-Muslims meant inequality. A non-Muslim could not be a judge in a case involving a Muslim; the evidence of a non-Muslim had no legal validity.

Some voices have been raised to abolish the inequality between Muslims and non-Muslims and the *dhimmī* status of the latter, with the argument that the idea of *dhimmīs* is part of a tribal social organization and does not apply to modern states, which are pluralistic.[28] And whereas in former times the religious division coincided largely with a territorial division (*dār al-islām* and *dār al-harb*), this is no longer the case. Along-side the very widespread older conviction of the absolute superiority of the Islamic community and the corresponding contempt for non-Muslims who might be mistrusted as representatives of foreign powers, attitudes of real tolerance are now emerging here and there.

The position of Christian and other religious minorities in Muslim countries, and certainly in the heartlands of Islam, is far from satisfactory when measured against the criteria of the Universal Declaration of Human Rights. We see social and economic pressures for conversion to Islam, the refusal to grant Church facilities in Saudi Arabia notwithstanding the presence of at least 300,000 Christian immigrant workers in 1990, a growing extension of Islamic norms in the judiciary, etc.

With regard to both the item on religious freedom and that on the equality of religious people, the current Islamic outlook as described diverges significantly from that of the Universal Declaration. This is due not only to an inherent belief in religious superiority, based on the conviction that Muslims possess God's latest revelation; similar claims have been made by other religious systems, such as the Roman Catholic Church. It is also due to the widespread feeling among Muslims that they constitute an intrinsic close-knit community, that all non-Muslims are outsiders, and that through the exercise of political power this community can become more truly islamicized and extended.

8. Sad Human Realities

When we read what religious leaders have written about the contribution their religions are able to make to proclaim and defend human rights, we cannot but be impressed by the huge potential that religions, each one in its own way, have to implement the human dignity of men and women.[29] The United Nations and related agencies have a great potential too.[30]

---

[28] The social sciences can contribute to the debate by showing the role of contexts in traditional religious prescripts.

[29] See for instance SWIDLER, *Human Rights in Religious Traditions*.

[30] See *United Nations Action in the Field of Human Rights*.

Regional organizations have been created to implement human rights.[31]
Increasingly, the rights of peoples, and not only individuals, are stressed.[32]

Yet here a scholar working in the field of the science of religions has
something to say. Whatever the religions say is a normative, prescriptive
statement, in a sphere at best spiritual and ideal but at worst otherworldly
and dreamy. It can also become narrowly legalistic and moralistic. And
without appropriate human action, it is elusive, evasive: illusory in the
profound sense of the word. It can even become dangerous.

Few of us have been in a position to realize properly the sad conditions in which the greater part of humanity lives or the forms of humili-
ation and oppression under which most people suffer. When measuring
the actual situation of humankind against the Universal Declaration of
Human Rights, we might conclude either that these human rights are
hardly implemented or that, if these are natural or God-given rights,
there are hardly any human beings left on earth.

Space does not allow me to go deeper into this aspect of the subject.
It was especially after Solzhenitsyn's revelations that the wider public
became aware of a world of human suffering carefully concealed by an
ideology pretending to be scientific. Ideologies and religions often mask
violations of human rights: otherwise we would probably not be able to
stand them. The terrible thing about religious leaders and spokesmen is
that they claim that their religion is right, absolutely right, even when
they are refusing family planning, democratic control of government, or
equal political, social, and juridical treatment of the privileged and non-
privileged, the Chosen and non-Chosen, the rich and the poor, men and
women.

Do I shock the reader when I describe religions as possessing not only
a huge potential for the implementation of human rights but also for
masking violations of the same human rights? Disregarding for a moment

---

[31]   Several regional organizations have been active. For the Americas, there is the "American
Declaration of the Rights and Duties of Man" (1948) and the "American Convention on
Human Rights" (1969). See Karel VASAK, *La commission interaméricaine des droits de
l'homme: La protection internationale des droits de l'homme sur le continent américain*,
Paris: Pichon et Durand-Auzias, 1968.
   For Africa there is the "African Charter on Human and Peoples' Rights", drafted in
Banjul and accepted by the Organization of African Unity in Nairobi, June 1981. There
is an African Commission on Human and Peoples' Rights.
   The League of Arab States established a Permanent Arab Commission on Human
Rights (1968) and made a draft "Arab Charter of Human Rights" (1971) and a draft
"Arab Covenant on Human Rights" (1979), with little implementation however. The
text of this *Mashrū' al-mithāq al-'arabī li-huqūq al-insān* differs from the text of the
Mashrū' mithāq huqūq al-insān wa'l-sha'b fī 'l-watani 'l-'arabī, which was accepted by
a number of Arab jurists in 1986 and 1987.
[32]   See for instance François RIGAUX, *Pour une déclaration universelle des droits des peuples:
Identité nationale et coopération internationale*, Brussels: Vie Ouvrière, 1990.

Christianity, for instance in Northern Ireland, and Judaism, for instance in Israel, about which much could be said, may I just point to some Muslim countries? Reports of Amnesty International and other international bodies speak about the presence and treatment of political prisoners in all Arab countries, Turkey, Iran, Sudan, Pakistan, and Indonesia; about government measures involving flagrant violations of the rights of minority groups including religious minority groups in these countries.[33] I do not even mention the ways in which people in so many countries try to survive far below the minimum standards necessary for nutrition, health care, and child protection.

And here we arrive at the burning question: how can we explain this subsistence of the greater part of humankind in flagrant contradiction to what human rights guarantee? There are two ways of reasoning and they do not exclude each other.

First, most Third World societies find themselves in situations of military, political and economic dependence and are subjected to its corollaries: domination of people and exploitation of their natural resources. Certain institutions in the West, but not only here, have favored modern structures of domination and exploitation that consequently have led to so many violations of human rights in Third World countries.

Second, from any moral point of view, Third World countries bear a considerable responsibility themselves. Much leadership is too much self-interested and keen of sheer power to serve the cause of human rights, lacking the standards for it. Tragically, by not admitting opposition or even serious critical discussion, it has violated fundamentally the human right of dissension and debate. Instead of opening space to human rights by admitting discussion, it has too often blocked the way to put human rights effectively in place.

9. Conclusion

Let me return now to our title: "Human Rights, Human Dignity, and Islam" and summarize what I have said.

Since there are no immediate sanctions, the legal character of human rights is restricted. They proclaim norms that touch on the domain of law

---

[33] On willful violations of certain human rights or willful negligence of violations as they in fact occur in Muslim and other countries, see the *Annual Reports* by the United Nations Committee on Human Rights and by the U.S. Department of State (which now also reports on religious liberty), the *Amnesty International Reports* and *Country Reports*, the annual reports *Les droits de l'Homme dans le monde arabe*, and *Ḥuqūq al-insān fī 'l-waṭanī 'l-'arabī*. Not only individuals or groups but also governments and their security forces are responsible here. See for instance the reports published by *Middle East Watch*.

as well as ethics. I asked what human rights mean to people: how people have reacted to them on the individual human and on the religious level. And my attention was drawn to the fact that, in difference from the Universal Declaration and the Conventions of Human Rights adopted by the United Nations, Muslim organizations have formulated specifically Islamic Declarations of Human Rights, of a denominational nature, introducing a particular religious norm and legitimation.

Any formulation of human rights carries in it a project of the human person and society as they essentially are and as they should be. The Universal Declaration provides a general formula omitting any particular religious reference. This does not exclude the right of particular religious bodies to provide their own supplement to the general formula. Their particular rules, however, cannot substitute rules considered and accepted as generally valid. But they can supplement them for their own members according to the various religious and cultural codes that regulate the way in which human life ought to be oriented and directed in these religious communities, and that are valid in their own contexts. I mentioned how the World Council of Churches, the Vatican, the Reformed World Alliance, and the Jewish and Bahā'ī communities have interpreted and applied the Universal Declaration in their own particular ways.

In many religions a divine order of the forces of nature has been perceived, regulated, and venerated. In other religions the forces of communal life have been perceived, interpreted, and regulated as corresponding to a basic social order, given with the Creation, which humankind is responsible for upholding. Consequently, Muslims not only formulate "Islamic" Declarations of Human Rights, but in so doing refer to the *Sharī'a*, which they believe perfectly guarantees that basic social order.

There are some striking features in these Islamic Declarations.

First, they claim to have "universal" validity, just as the Papal pronouncements do, but the word "universal" here has a different meaning than in the Universal Declaration adopted by the United Nations.

Second, they reveal the same desire for "particularization" that is exemplified in other Islamic institutions created during the last twenty-five years—Islamic political, economic, social, and cultural organizations both on a national level and internationally. This is part of a widespread phenomenon in other religions as well. Once general institutions have been organized, religious denominations tend to create particular Catholic, Protestant, Jewish, etc. institutions of the same kind for their membership.

Third, there is now a distinct tendency to identify as specifically "Western" something originally considered to be of a general or universal nature, though elaborated in the West.

Fourth, they reflect a desire not only to proclaim what is "Islamic" within the Muslim community but also to bear witness to the outside, non-Muslim world.

Finally, there is in the Islamic declarations, prepared by 'ulamā', a dominating concern with the Sharī'a. Whereas the Western Declarations are inspired by philosophical and ethical concerns (rights and duties are properties formulated by persons), the Islamic Declarations continuously refer to a perfect religious law (rights and duties and demands are prescriptions to which one has to submit). Scholars of religion have insufficiently studied the Islamic sense of justice, and especially its religious dimension, in its own right.[34]

In the present world context, in which people are more informed than in the past about the extent to which human rights have been and are being violated on a massive scale, the function of any declaration of human rights becomes less Platonic or even idealist than in former times. Human rights can now function to legitimate protest against intolerable conditions of life. They can lead to action for the sake of human dignity. They can also contribute to the improvement of legal provisions in all domains touching on human rights, developing our sense of justice; in the course of time, ever more values of human existence have manifested themselves, mostly as a result of bitter sufferings. Seen in a historical perspective, the Declarations of Human Rights are in the line of the laws of Hammurabi, the Decalogue, the laws of Manu: they all try to formulate the basic rules to be obeyed so that human life may be bearable and become meaningful and truly human.[35]

And what about Islam?[36] For the trained Islamicist, today's many different movements, interpretations, and applications of Islam testify to the intense struggle taking place over the fundamental values of Muslim life, society, and culture in very different social contexts. The trained scholar of the science of religion recognizes in other religions a similar battle over the fundamental values of life, again in many different social contexts. But in the case of Islam, on a deeper level of analysis, most contemporary movements, too easily depicted in the Western media as examples of religious fanaticism and lust for power, appear to be clamors for human dignity. They give a particular expression to it in the terms of Islamic Scripture and tradition, and they symbolize this by the perfect value of "Islam".

---

[34] An excellent introduction remains KHADDURI, *The Islamic Conception of Justice*.
[35] In their social contexts, religions provide social order.
[36] For books by Muslim authors on human rights and Islam see, for instance, BANI SADR, *Le Coran et les droits de l'homme*; BENNANI, *L'islamisme et les droits de l'homme*; BERRY, *Man's Rights in Islam, L'islam et les droits de l'homme, Ḥuqūq al-insān fī'l-islām*; FERJANI, *Islamisme, laïcité et droits de l'homme*; NADVI, *Human Rights and Obligations in the Light of the Qur'ān and the Hadīth*. Cf. above note 22.

Rather than being efforts to destroy the West, present-day virulent protests in the name of Islam appear to be outcries against what are seen as the fundamental causes of violations of human dignity. These targets are often symbolized by "the West". In the end, the Islamic Declaration of Human Rights is not simply an alternative particularistic version of the Universal Declaration of Human Rights. Interpreted from within the Islamic framework from which it has arisen, it is a call for a transcendent source of justice, when mundane justice has failed and human dignity is violated in so many ways.

Human rights are violated in so many Muslim and other Third World societies, not only by political systems and regimes whose secret services employ terror, but also by other sources of fear: violence, poverty, a hopeless existence. It is not Islam, however interpreted, that is the reason for such degradations of human existence. I would say, on the contrary, that it is thanks to their particular religious faith, their Islam, that so many Muslims are still aware of their human dignity and live accordingly. They formulate human rights the way they do and certainly are keen to communicate with men and women of good will everywhere who also defend universal human rights and strive to uphold human dignity, our humanity.

Selected Literature

1. Documents

AMNESTY INTERNATIONAL, *Annual Reports* and *Country Reports*, London: Amnesty International, 1962–.

La conquête des droits de l'homme: Textes fondamentaux, Paris: Le Cherche Midi, 1988.

SAUDI ARABIA: *Le Mémorandum du Gouvernement du Royaume d'Arabie Saoudite relatif au Dogme des droits de l'Homme en Islam et à son application dans le Royaume, adressé aux Organisations Internationales intéressées*, Riyadh, 1972 (text submitted to the General Secretariat of the League of the Arab States).

Colloques de Riyad, de Paris, du Vatican, de Genève et de Strasbourg sur le dogme musulman et les droits de l'homme en Islam entre juristes de l'Arabie Saoudite et éminents juristes et intellectuels européens, Riyadh, 1974.

ISLAMIC COUNCIL OF EUROPE, *The Universal Islamic Declaration (al-bayān al-islāmī al-'ālami)*, London: Islamic Council of Europe, April 12, 1980.

— and International Islamic Council, *Universal Islamic Declaration of Human Rights* (proclaimed in Paris on September 19, 1981), London: Islamic Council of Europe, 1981.

—, *A Model of an Islamic Constitution (Namūdhaj li-'l-dustūr al-islāmī)*, London: Islamic Council of Europe, 1983.

UNITED NATIONS: *United Nations Action in the Field of Human Rights*, New York: United Nations, 1983 etc.

—, *Human Rights: A Compilation of International Instruments*, New York: United Nations, 1988 etc.

—, *Annual Reports of the Human Rights Committee to the General Assembly*, New York: United Nations, 1983 etc.

2. *Studies*

ALDEEB ABU-SAHLIEH, Sami A., *Les musulmans face aux droits de l'homme: Religion, droit politique. Etude et documents*, Bochum: Dieter Winkler, 1994.
—, *Les mouvements islamistes et les droits de l'homme*, Bochum: D. Winkler, 1998.
BANI SADR, Abol-Hassan, *Le Coran et les droits de l'homme*, Paris: Maisonneuve & Larose, 1989.
BENITO, Elizabeth Odio, *Elimination of all Forms of Intolerance and Discrimination Based on Religion or Belief*, Geneva: Centre for Human Rights, U.N., 1989.
BENNANI, Boubaker Jalal, *L'islamisme et les droits de l'homme*, Lausanne: Editions de l'Aire, 1984.
BERRY, Zakaria al-, *Man's Rights in Islam, L'islam et les droits de l'homme, Ḥuqūq al-insān fī'l-islām*, Heliopolis 1981.
BORRMANS, Maurice, "Convergences et divergences entre la Déclaration universelle des droits de l'homme de 1948 et les récentes Déclarations des droits de l'homme dans l'Islam", *Islamochristiana*, 24 (1999), pp. 1–17.
BOUMA, Cees, "Christian and Islamic Valuation of Human Rights: Consequences for Minorities", *Journal of the Institute of Muslim Minority Affairs*, 11 (1990), pp. 30–49.
CASPAR, Robert, "Les déclarations des droits de l'homme en Islam depuis dix ans", *Islamochristiana*, 9 (1983), pp. 59–102.
Droits de l'homme: IIIème Rencontre islamo-chrétienne, Carthage 24–29 mai 1982, Tunis: CERES, 1985.
FERJANI, Mohamed-Cherif, *Islamisme, laïcité et droits de l'homme: Un siècle de débat sans cesse reporté au sein de la pensée arabe contemporaine*, Paris: L'Harmattan, 1991.
HIRSCH, Emmanuel, *Islam et droits de l'homme* (Bibliothèque des droits de l'homme et des libertés fondamentales B 3), Paris: Librairie des Libertés, 1984.
Human Rights and the Conflicts of Culture: Western and Islamic Perspectives on Religious Liberty, ed. by David LITTLE, John KELSAY, and Abdulaziz SACHEDINA, Columbia, S. C.: University of South Carolina Press, 1988.
KHADDURI, Majid, *The Islamic Conception of Justice*, Baltimore: Johns Hopkins University Press, 1984.
La liberté religieuse dans le judaïsme, le christianisme et l'islam, ed. by Eric BINET and Roselyne CHENU, Paris: Cerf, 1981.
MAYER, Ann E., *Islam and Human Rights,* Boulder, Colo.: Westview Press, 1991, 1999[3].
MONCONDUIT, François, *La Commission européenne des droits de l'homme* (Aspects européens: Collection d'études relatives à intégration européenne. Série E, Droit no. 4), Leyden: A. W. Sijthoff, 1965.
NADVI, Syed Muzaffar-ud-Din, *Human Rights and Obligations in the Light of the Qur'ān and the Hadīth*, Lahore: Star Press, 1980[3].
SWIDLER, Arlene, *Human Rights in Religious Traditions*, New York: Pilgrim, 1982.
TALBI, Mohamed, "Religious Liberty: A Muslim Perspective", *Islamochristiana*, 11 (1985), pp. 99–113.
TRAER, Robert, "Human Rights in Islam", *Islamic Studies*, 28 (1989), pp. 117–31.

Section 5

Social Reality and Islam

Chapter 9
Islamic Religious Tradition and Social Development[1]

1. Preliminary Remarks

The role religion plays and can play in development processes has attracted attention both from those who, on the basis of a particular analysis or worldview, judge religion *a priori* to be an obstacle to the development of society and from those who, of the opposite persuasion, assign religion a positive role in whatever circumstances, be it a particular religion, be it religion in general. One of the weaknesses of both positions is that they investigate different social circumstances with different religions at different times and places by means of one specific value concept of religion. I do not want to give here any general evaluation of religion *a priori* but merely to concentrate on one specific religious tradition, that of Islam.

In fact, a fruitful approach to the problem of the role of religion in development processes is to start with the fact of tradition. Reformulated, the problem is then the role a particular religion plays, and can play, in the tension that exists between tradition-bound societies and their need to develop for their sheer survival. We are here concerned with the social and cultural forms of such societies: the presence of social and cultural traditions on the one hand, and the need for new social and cultural forms and expressions on the other hand. It is precisely through given social and cultural forms that religion plays an important role, and it is largely through changes in these forms that we can assess what kinds of development take place in a society.

I assume here that the combination of a social tradition that is "established", in the sense that it determines all human relations, and cultural forms that are "fixed", in the sense that they hardly change, constitute a closed sphere, and are not able to express new contents, constitutes a major obstacle to development. In that case, changing reality cannot very well be assimilated and elaborated in new terms, intellectually or otherwise. A religion may, but need not necessarily, I think, be instrumental in

---

[1]   Updated version of a paper with the same title in *Current Progress in the Methodology of the Science of Religion*, ed. by Witold TYLOCH, Warsaw: Polish Scientific Publishers, 1984, pp. 271–89.

creating such a stagnant social and cultural situation. In fact, there are at least three alternatives for the role a given religion can play in regard to a given social and cultural tradition:

1) A religion may legitimate a particular tradition and make it "religious". In this case, tradition and religion are closely linked and may even be identified with each other. This is the case in most tribal religions and to a large extent the Hindu and Jewish religious traditions. In Islam this is the position of "orthodox" (Sunnī) Islam inasmuch as it recognizes local traditions (ʿādāt) besides the Sunna with a capital S (authoritative tradition of the Prophet) to have religious value.

2) A religion also may reinterpret a given tradition at a given moment and select certain vital and essential elements from it while leaving others aside. This implies a split in the tradition and a reinterpretation of the elements and principles judged to be relevant and worthy of retention. This is the case, for instance, in Reform Judaism, in the Protestant Reformation, and in reform movements in general that want to go back to the pure origins or message of the religion under consideration. In Islam, this has been the position of the various "reform (islāh) movements", in particular during the last hundred years.

3) A religion may make a resolute break with an existing tradition, setting against it new norms as a result of which a kind of religious revolt takes place. This happened, for instance, with the separation of the Buddhist community from the Vedic religion, that of the Christian community from Judaism, and that of the Bahāʾī community from Islam, where the break went so far that not only sects but new religions arose. Such religious revolts can take place on the basis of an immediate revelation or insight or other profound experiences touching something "absolute" in people that transforms and mobilizes them. Within Islam, the Khārijī movement some decades after Muhammad's death or more recently the Wahhābī movement in Arabia come to mind. Islam itself also represents a religious protest: a separation from polytheism, existing monotheisms, and unbelief.

These three alternative relationships between a given religion and a particular social and cultural tradition imply that we should take religion as an active principle that can act in at least three different ways in relation to tradition. One may also speak of three "ideal types" of religion that are relevant for our theme:

1) Religion as legitimation, leading to the formation of an autonomous religious tradition that grows in the course of time;

2) Religion as reinterpretation, leading to a religious discernment within a given tradition (social, cultural, and then also religious);

3) Religion as protest, leading to a religious judgment of and a crisis within a given tradition.

2. Religious Tradition

When considering more closely the concept of tradition, in particular that of religious tradition, we may start by making a descriptive distinction between various kinds of tradition: great versus little traditions, religious versus non-religious traditions, traditions bound to local or regional areas versus more abstract traditions beyond immediate communication, traditions bound to specific ethnic, professional, or other groups versus traditions that stress individual experience or personalization.

Tradition has an inherent character of process since it consists of a transmission, conscious or unconscious, of social and cultural elements that are part of a particular way of life or a specific organization of it. In this process of transmission, those who are at the receiving end are not simply passive receptacles. In fact, the vitality and very survival of a tradition depends on people assimilating elements of it because of the orientation and style or "taste" they give to life and the appeal of the community that partakes in the tradition. Tradition as transmission is an operation that implies an appeal; certain elements of it have a symbolic value and the tradition itself may even acquire a mythical value. Indeed, the social symbolism in a tradition refers to certain values that are pertinent to the cohesion and survival of the community and which the tradition upholds. This helps to explain why a tradition in a process of rationalization tends to develop into ideology, which, depending on circumstances, may develop beyond the tradition from which it originated. Traditions have their own history, and whereas some may experience an outburst of energy, others may come to a dead end. When circumstances change, a tradition can adopt new expressions, redefine itself, and take a new direction. In trying circumstances it can contribute to strengthen the community by providing shared meanings. It may even go underground, which implies that some elements are concealed.

Needless to stress, a tradition precedes the individual born into it, who appropriates values through it, and who arrives at his own way of life precisely with reference to it. Individuals and groups always stand within traditions, but usually they have a certain freedom of choice to the extent that a tradition allows for variations. In more pluriform societies, it is possible to step over from one to another tradition. There is always an extreme possibility of stepping out of a given tradition without entering into another one. Paradoxically enough, the very originality of religious people, revolutionaries, and artists has sometimes given rise to new kinds of traditions.

3. Traditions in Third World Societies

The presence and force of tradition in Asia, Africa, and Latin America have struck most Western observers: travellers, colonists, administrators as much as traders, development agents, and anthropologists. The idea fostered by some that these traditions might either be manipulated politically from above or eradicated rationally by science has underestimated their inherent vitality. Apart from their value as a cultural expression and even as culture in itself, they perform a vital function in the sense indicated in the section above. This holds true in particular in turbulent times and chaotic situations, when people can fall back on them, finding not only a warm welcome in the community but also protection, direction, identity, and sometimes even a kind of sacralization of life.

In the third world, new situations have arisen with the attainment of independence, new communications with the outside world, the acceptance of new values in addition to those given by local traditions. Various degrees of rationalization of existing traditions occur. There may be, for instance, a differentiation of a given tradition into a mainstream, which public authority often gives official standing, and other branches or sidestreams that continue to exist parallel to the main branch. Or rationalized ideologies may originate traditions by themselves. The modernization process that takes place everywhere does not necessarily destroy all traditions. A number of them survive for particular life events or in protected groups or isolated areas. Other traditions may survive precisely by consciously allowing for change and making it possible, thanks to values that transcend external changes by virtue of certain transcendental references.

Along with possible internal developments of third world traditions, external factors can determine the further course of existing traditions. These include not merely momentary political events, but also broader political developments like the acquisition of political independence, changes of political power, the relations between large powers with their ideologies, or regional conflicts. Technological and economic factors greatly influence the weal and woe of all traditions by determining their material means. One factor that transcends the difference between internal and external is education, at home and at school, since it lies at the very root of any transmission process. Especially in third world countries, education has become a state interest, since no state can afford illiteracy. The various traditions existing within a country are expected to share a common orientation in the national interest, and this should start from the beginning, that is to say in childhood.

4. Tradition in Islam and in Muslim Societies

For the sake of clarity, we should make a clear distinction between the religiously normative tradition or *Sunna* contained in authoritative *hadīths* (reports about Muhammad's sayings and doings during his life), on the one hand, and the many local traditional customs that can be found in all Muslim societies and are known under the name of *'ādāt* (or *'urf*), on the other hand. As in all major religions, in Islam, too, there is an intrinsic tension between the normative great tradition and the local small traditions. And, as in other major religions, a distinction must be made between those adherents who have given the *Sunna* or their local tradition a rigid character, and others who have less reified their religious tradition, *Sunna* or *'urf* (or *'ādāt*), and have kept it more open. Furthermore, the orientations of the state must be borne in mind. No state can afford to adopt a thoroughly secular line of conduct, or even to fail to esteem Islam highly as a religion, when the majority of the population is Muslim. In public, Islam, its Scripture, and its normative tradition or *Sunna* cannot be attacked or eradicated; local customs can be, but even then only within certain limits. Consequently, as a rule, in Muslim societies all development, social or otherwise, has to keep silent on religious matters or to refer to Islam positively. Certain developments can be encouraged by showing that they correspond with the spirit of Islam.

4.1. Two Kinds of Tradition

The normative character of the *Sunna* is based on the fact that it covers thousands of reports or sayings (*hadīths*) that are ascribed to Muhammad or his companions. After the Qur'ān, which is considered revealed, the *Sunna* establishes an authoritative religious example for Muslim life. A pious Muslim tries to live as much as possible according to Qur'ān and *Sunna*. In fact, the total contents of the *Sunna* are known only to the *muhaddithūn*, religious specialists in matters of religious tradition who have developed since the beginnings of Islam a whole religious science of tradition (*'ilm al-hadīth*) in Islam about the validity, weight, meaning, and implications of the different *hadīths*.

As mentioned above, in contrast to this ideal, normative religious concept of *Sunna*, there is the totality of ways of life and thought as local customs (*'urf* or *'ādāt*) that are in fact valid in tradition-bound Muslim societies and that vary from one society to the other. Although they often have hardly anything to do with the contents of the *Sunna*, these local customs have mostly obtained a religious legitimation. Local Muslim communities then consider them to be sanctioned by religion, to have a validity as local *sunna*, and to be "Islamic" in the sense that a good Muslim in that particular community has to live according to them.

Although this idea is often sustained by religious figures such as mystics (*ṣūfīs*) and local religious leaders (*sheykhs, mollahs*), in fact the local customs do not have the status of the normative ancient *Sunna*. On the contrary, they are open to criticism on normative Islamic grounds for this reason. By referring to the *Sunna*, one can judge which part of the local living customs, *'urf* or *'ādāt*, does not stem from *hadīths* and consequently is not strict normative tradition (*Sunna*) for a Muslim; in some cases this can be the majority of the existing *'urf* (*'ādāt*) prescriptions.

4.2. Internal Mechanisms of Change within Tradition

Within the ideal realm of the Islamic science of tradition and of Islamic jurisprudence there is a constant self-critical reflection that can prune, so to speak, the outgrowth of traditions in Muslim societies and in Islam, at least in principle. We have seen that local traditions can always be scrutinized and criticized on the basis of the Qur'ān and normative *Sunna*. Those parts that are not covered by Qur'ān and *Sunna* can be relegated to the category of customs without a link to normative Islam.

Now the question arises whether the normative *Sunna* itself can also be criticized. It certainly can. First of all, the *Sunna* contains elements of varying importance and is not one homogeneous whole. Certain *hadīths* are "stronger" than others, and the contents of some are more important than those of others. There are also differences in the interpretation of important *hadīths*. But a second consideration is still more important: it is not the *Sunna* in itself that prescribes what should be done. This is done by religious law, *Sharī'a*, and for religious law the *Sunna* is only one of the available sources for establishing the legal quality of an action, whether it is prescribed, forbidden, or otherwise. Besides the Qur'ān and the *Sunna*, there are other sources possessing weight and authority, which the religious juridical scholars (*fuqahā'* and *'ulamā'*) can use in given circumstances for the treatment of particular cases. This implies that the *Sunna* itself can in fact be criticized in an indirect way, internally by differentiation and exegesis and externally by the use of other sources, too, leading to juridical statements (*fatwās*). *Muftīs* who give juridical statements and *qādīs* who administer religious law mostly in special (*Sharī'a*) courts have to take into account the needs of contemporary society. They can judge certain elements of the *Sunna* to be more or less relevant in their treatment of a particular case, indirectly if not directly, by implication if not explicitly. The religious sciences of Islam allow in principle (1) the superseding of local customs by Qur'ān and *Sunna*, and (2) the superseding of those parts of the *Sunna* that are contrary to the needs of contemporary society by *fiqh*, the science of jurisprudence, which establishes what the *Sharī'a* prescribes in a given case. Newly formulated rules, indeed, can not only replace local customs and tradi-

tions but also modify in principle a particular application of the normative religious tradition or *Sunna*, without necessarily denying the eternal
truth of the *Sunna* or the *Sharī'a* as such.

Even apart from practical realities, Islamic jurisprudence is complex.
There are four different schools of religious law that differ, among other
things, in the place they give to the *Sunna* as a source of law. Another
complication is that religious law in most Muslim countries nowadays is
applied only in matters of family law, in different ways in different
countries, including the Islamic states based on *Sharī'a*. Infringements
against purely religious injunctions (*'ibādāt*) and what may be called
cases of Islamic "criminal law" (*hudūd* punishments) can be brought to
religious courts only in a small number of Islamic countries basing
themselves on *Sharī'a*. So the actual functioning of Islamic jurisprudence
in Muslim countries is more restricted than for instance a hundred years
ago.

It should be clear that, even on purely Islamic grounds, neither local
customs nor religious tradition are as immobile a mass as has sometimes
been suggested. On closer analysis, there is an inner dialectic within
Islamic religion itself that allows us to assess the relevance of certain
traditions according to the needs of present-day society, with the use of
reason. In fact, however, as we shall see, the most important modifica-
tions of the religious tradition in Muslim countries have not been the
result of new interpretations of the *Sharī'a*, but of direct governmental
measures through secular law.

4.3. Attitudes Taken Toward Tradition

Before coming to some concrete examples, let me briefly review the main
attitudes that have been taken with regard to tradition and customs,
Sunna and *'urf* (*'ādāt*), in the Muslim community itself.

1) The majority point of view, characteristically called that of the "Sunnīs"
(those who follow the *Sunna*), has always been to accept the totality of
the *Sunna* as contained in the recognized collections of *hadīths* and to
assign an authority to it second only to that of the Qur'ān. To reach a
decision, they will always first refer to passages of the Qur'ān and sayings
of the *Sunna*. In general, however, they maintain a lenient attitude toward local traditional customs on condition that the primary authority
of the *Sunna* receives overall recognition. The pious life is held to follow
Qur'ān and *Sunna* as much as possible.

2) Within the Sunnī fold, from time to time movements have arisen that
call for a literal reading of Qur'ān and *Sunna* and that work for their
direct application and implementation to the utmost extent possible. Such
movements tend to identify the *Sharī'a* with the literal text of Qur'ān and

Sunna. As a consequence, they are in general intolerant toward diverging local traditional customs and they do not think highly of juridical and theological schools other than their own, especially if such schools assign high value to the use of reason or if they give priority to urgent human needs or the needs of society.

3) The reformist movements of the nineteenth and twentieth centuries have made an attempt to purify the whole body of the *Sunna* and also the local traditional customs by referring back to certain basic texts in Qur'ān and *Sunna*, which they see as expressing the eternal truths or principles of Islam. In this light, certain parts of the *Sunna* are judged to be not relevant at the present time, and many traditional customs are outrightly rejected. The reformists have tried to use reason to separate the eternal from the temporary truths and principles of Islam, and they often have claimed Islam to be a reasonable religion. They have taken into account the demands of the time and the needs of society. They had little appreciation for local traditional customs which they judged to be irrational and non-Islamic. On the whole, they have paid much attention to the educational problems in Muslim societies and have sought to provide better instruction in the principles of Islam than had been done earlier.

4) Typical "modernists" stress humane and social values of general validity. They have often discovered these values in the West or in the former socialist countries and found testimonies for them in the Qur'ān and the *Sunna*, which they tend to interpret largely according to their own enlightened ideas. They have a certain contempt for local traditional customs, which they see as being far removed from the values they stand for.

5) The particular attitude of personal piety that stretches from medieval Sūfism to present-day personal religion has always respected the *Sunna* but has taken mainly those elements from it that are an incentive to personal edification and spiritual life. On the whole, Sūfīs have given more attention to the religious experience of tradition than to its social dimension. As a consequence, they have been selective in their use and interpretation of the *Sunna* and open-minded toward local traditions whenever they saw religious value in them.

6) At the present time, quite a number of "social" Muslims recognize in principle the value of those parts of the *Sunna* that have a social significance for Muslim societies and the Muslim community as a whole.

In general it may be said that faithful and practicing Muslims know a certain number of edifying and moralizing *hadīths* by heart, and they may read little books containing important *hadīths* of this type. The whole of the *Sunna*, however, is largely beyond them, though it is respected and venerated, somewhat in the way that Christians look upon the Church Fathers of the first centuries and Jews upon the rabbinical Sages. Knowing the *Sunna*—like the Qur'ān—demands a life of study and a certain devotion.

5. Religious Tradition in Muslim Countries

With the exception of a few communist countries like Albania before the 1990s, no government of a country or region with a Muslim majority has dared to turn against Islam as religious tradition both in the public and in the private sphere. If they did, they would attempt to suppress both local traditional religious customs and the implementation of the *Sunna* as a religious norm. It is interesting, in this respect, to see how relatively mild the colonial powers' attitude toward Islamic religion was. Islam was the recognized religion of the "natives", and although imperial ideologies were always promulgated, the colonial powers rarely interfered directly with Islamic religious matters. It did not occur to them to suppress Islam in its *Sunna* and local traditions, although they tried to channel it in the interests of the mother country while avoiding open clashes as far as possible. In the colonial period, not only the *Sunna* but also the local traditional customs of popular Islam were left intact, although they were relegated more and more to the margin in modernizing societies.

Among Muslim governments, only the Turkish republic of Kemal Pasha Atatürk in the 1920s and 1930s carried out a secularist policy in the sense that, for the sake of national modernization and development, Islam was to be restricted to the private sphere. But this experiment, propagated with the force of both words and actions, backfired after World War Two, and at present no political party in Turkey can afford to ban Islam from public life. In this way, Turkey has arrived, in principle, at the same situation as other countries with a Muslim majority, except for the fact that the percentage of the secularized elite is probably greater here. An official breakaway from Islam, however, is nowhere possible and everywhere a *modus vivendi* is sought so that, among other things, needed social reforms are carried out without hurting Muslim feelings too much and thus risking a palpable Muslim opposition. Various kinds of juridical and other expedients are used to bring about significant social changes and developments by making them in one way or another acceptable to the Muslim population.

I think that in a number of cases these government policies come down to a conscious redirection of the people's existing social and cultural traditions, claiming to be in the national interest of development, justice, and public order. The fact that, although the authority of the *Sunna* of the Prophet is recognized, its contents have always been at a certain distance from the people, facilitates attempts to redirect traditional views and ways of life. The lack of power of the religious jurists or *'ulamā'*, the pressure of the government, and the alienation of the *'ulamā'* from modern society and the outside world at large make their opposition to such government policies virtually impossible.

Even when governments use themes like "revolution" and "modernization" to identify their policies in Muslim countries, in actual fact they do not really break with ongoing traditions, but sharply inflect them by developing them further along lines parallel to those developments of society that are deemed necessary. Such a procedure is in the interest of Muslim governments, just as it is in the interest of those Muslim minorities in non-Muslim countries that have to adapt themselves to survive. The overall strategy seems to be not to break with the social and cultural tradition but to continue it in a new direction. If there are religious objections against particular social reforms or developments, the government counters them with a positive legal statement (*fatwā*) that takes into account elements of the Qur'ān and the *Sunna* as well as other sources of law. On the whole, one may even claim that Islam is particularly capable of adapting to at least certain social developments.

6. Examples from the Middle East

Some good bibliographies appeared in the 1970s on Middle Eastern studies that give an idea of the progress of research since World War Two. Although some excellent surveys and sociological studies of the region were written, the lack of studies on the relationship between social and other kinds of development, on the one hand, and the Islamic religious tradition, on the other, is striking. Hardly anything scholarly was written about development in relation to the religious factor in the Middle East, the impact of religion or the role of religious tradition in the region that would enable definite theoretical conclusions to be drawn about its changes. This holds true not only for Islam but also for Christianity and Judaism in the region, including in Israel. The bizarre result is that although everyone knows of the weight of religion in the Middle East, hardly anyone has studied the subject systematically. And if little has been done by Western scholarship, still less scholarly work has been written on the subject by scholars from the region itself. This phenomenon testifies in itself to the impact and weight of religious traditions within the region. There is in fact a bewildering variety of different forms of Islam throughout the Arab world alone, and still more if one includes Turkey, Iran, Pakistan, and Afghanistan within the region of the Middle East. All of these traditions and forms of Islam have their impact on the various societies in the region in the wider context of the political situations.

I shall limit myself here to some examples of concrete encounters between social developments and the Islamic religious tradition in the Arab world.

6.1. Modernization of Law

A subject that has received much attention[2] is that of the status and place of *woman* in Muslim society, that is to say her legal status and social position vis-à-vis her husband as well as her role in society and public affairs at large, including paid work outside the home. Both religious law (*Sharī'a*) and local traditional customs have made her position quite unfavorable compared to the position of women in modern Western societies. The influence of Western concepts with regard to women and of Western models of new state legislation have brought about various changes. An emancipation movement started in Muslim societies and has been carried on by both men and women, and particular texts of the Qur'ān have been interpreted in such a way that current *Sharī'a* rulings and local customs have had to be revised.

The result has been new national, not religiously-inspired, legislation covering three major items in important Arab countries. First, *monogamy*, or better *monogyny*, has become the rule for the law. Notwithstanding the fact that the Qur'ān allows four wives, through a legal device only one wife has been declared to be the rule (to which exceptions may still be made, however); moreover, marriages are required to be registered. Second, private repudiation of the wife by the husband has been largely replaced by a formal *divorce procedure* through the court. Given that the Qur'ān allows repudiation, a number of laws have been introduced with the clause that the woman should agree, which results in a divorce procedure that can also be initiated by the wife. Third, woman's life is *no longer restricted to the home*. Although this has been a tradition in Muslim societies, with the exception of the Bedouin, peasant women, and poorest city women, all Muslim countries have passed legislation giving women some degree of public responsibility and enabling them to take paid jobs. Notwithstanding *Sunna* and local customs, women now have active and passive voting rights, receive salaries, are part of social security schemes, and participate nearly everywhere in the public services.

Although this is a very significant social development that runs counter to the Islamic religious tradition, the problems are still immense. The laws must be applied and everyone must have access to the courts. The

---

[2]   See for instance al-QAZZAZ, *Women in the Middle East and North Africa* (see Selected Literature section 1.). Much has been published on the subject since then. See also under "Women in Muslim Societies" in the *Further Reading* section at the end of the book (p. 412).

attitudes toward the opposite sex that are acquired in early youth and
have existed for centuries change with difficulty, since there is a whole
undercurrent of socio-cultural tradition that has to be redirected. But the
process has definitely started, and although "Islamists" want differently,
at least officially an appeal can no longer be made to Islam for the
maintenance of traditions that block social dynamics.

Another important issue where Islamic religious tradition, both *Sunna*
and local custom, and also Muslim religious feeling have opposed developments necessary for the sheer survival of society in a number of Arab and
other Muslim countries is that of *family planning*.[3] Children have been
seen as a blessing from God, the more so when infant mortality was high
and when the offspring are male. In countries like Egypt, Tunisia, and
Morocco, governments have hinted more or less discretely at the possibility of the planned limitation of the number of children, for the sake of
both human and national interest. Religious legal support can be gained
to a certain extent, since in the *Sunna* the practice of *coitus interruptus*
(*'azl*) is considered permissible in case of necessity. Consequently, semi-
governmental institutions and private organizations have provided information and guidance in these matters. It remains, however, a sensitive
matter in which, besides religious tradition and feelings, many other
factors like the level of education and "Islamist" pressure also enter the
picture.

A third example of the concrete meeting of an issue of social development and the Islamic religious tradition is in the field of the *'ibādāt*, the
purely religious duties. In 1960, the Tunisian president Bourguiba suggested that in the month of *Ramadān*, the Tunisians, instead of fasting in
the daytime, should put all their efforts into increased work productivity
as the kind of "asceticism" appropriate for a country in the process of
rapid development for the sake of survival.[4] He received the support of
two religious scholars, who issued *fatwās* allowing this interpretation of

[3] George F. BROWN, "Moroccan Family Planning Program: Progress and Problems", *De-
mography*, 5:2 (1968), pp. 627–31; Erwin GRÄF, "Die Stellungnahme des islamischen
Rechts zu Geburtenregelung (*Tanzīm Al-Nasl*) und Geburtenbeschränkung (*Taḥdīd Al-
Nasl*)", in *Der Orient in der Forschung: Festschrift für Otto Spies zum 5. April 1966*, ed.
by Wilhelm HOENERBACH, Wiesbaden: Otto Harrassowitz, 1967, pp. 209–32; G. H. A.
JUYNBOLL, "The Ḥadīṭ in the Discussion on Birth-control", in *Actas do IV Congresso de
Estudios Arabes e Islâmicos, Coimbra – Lisboa 1968, 1 a 8 de Setembro de 1968*, Leiden:
E. J. Brill, 1971, pp. 373–9; Jacques VALLIN, "Limitation des naissances en Tunisie: Efforts
et résultats", *Population*, Paris, 26:2 (mars 1971), pp. 181–204; Ahmad AL-SHARABĀṢĪ, *Ad-
dīn wa-tanzīn al-usra*, Cairo: Ministry of Social Affairs, 1966 (Engl. trans. by SayedISMAIL:
Islam and Family Planning, Cairo: Egyptian Family Planning Association, 1969).
[4] Jochen GENTZ, "Tunesische Fatwas über das Fasten im Ramaḍān", *Die Welt des Islams*, 7
(1961), pp. 39–66; Francis HOURS, "A propos du jeûne du mois de Ramadan en Tunisie",
Orient, Paris, 13 (1960), pp. 43–52; Pierre RONDOT, "Jeûne du Ramadan et lutte contre le
sous-développement en Tunisie", *L'Afrique et l'Asie*, 50 (1960), pp. 45–9.

fasting (*sawm*) under the present circumstances, but other *'ulamā'* were very much opposed. Although this new interpretation of the *Ramadān* obligations would have had positive effects on the economic and social development of Tunisia, Bourguiba's initiative has not met with success. Up to now, *Ramadān* fasting in Muslim countries still amounts to much waste of energy and potential productivity, from an economic point of view.

These concrete examples could be extended infinitely, and one could examine, for instance, current discussions on subjects varying from the interest rate on capital loans or production of and trade in alcoholic drinks to the organization and tasks of the state. The examples given suffice, however, to make clear that on concrete issues national governments have been able to go ahead, even in opposition to the Islamic religious tradition. The responses of a number of *'ulamā'*, religious scholars, show that on such issues the religious law (*Sharī'a*) is more capable of reinterpretation and adaptation than had been assumed.[5]

6.2. Modernization and Islam in the Middle East

We now want to give two examples of modernization in social development, not in concrete issues but in two sectors of cultural life that were formerly almost completely under the sway of religious tradition but that have meanwhile emancipated themselves to a considerable extent.

The first sector is the crucial one of *education*. Whereas traditional education has for centuries been a fundamentally religious one, in the nineteenth and twentieth centuries, modern types of educational institutions were founded, partly as a result of the work of foreign missions, where Islam was no longer the focus of the curriculum. After independence, the governments of all Muslim countries made a course of "Introduction to Religion" (Islam) compulsory at the primary and mostly also the secondary level and supervise the textbooks used for it. Consequently, children receive at school a standard common orientation in religious matters, mostly linked to the cultural heritage of the Arab world or of the country concerned. Of particular interest for our theme is the swift rise of national modern schools besides and instead of the older schools of religious learning (*madrasas*), including in higher education[6], which indicates a considerable social development. In a further stage, under the

---

[5]   J. N. D. ANDERSON, "Law as a Social Force in Islamic Culture and History", *Bulletin of the School of African and Oriental Studies*, 20 (1957), pp. 13–40; ID., "The Role of Personal Statutes in Social Development in Islamic Countries", *Comparative Studies in Society and History*, 13:1 (January 1971), pp. 16–31.

[6]   WAARDENBURG, "Some Institutional Aspects of Muslim Higher Education and their Relation to Islam"; ID., *Les universités dans le monde arabe actuel*; ID., *L'enseignement dans le monde arabe* (for all three see Selected Literature section 3. b.).

supervision not of a religious institution but of a public ministry, a basic
introduction to Islam and fundamental Islamic concepts was introduced
into the curriculum. This was less an application of the religious tradition
than a common moral and historical orientation of the pupils and students, on the basis of Islamic values and history. The ideological and
religious content of schoolbooks, in particular with regard to history,
society, and religion[7], has become the subject of various investigations.

The second sector where modernization is striking is what may be
called the development of a *civic sense*. Whereas people were formerly
oriented according to the values of Islam and the Muslim community at
large, since independence governments in all Muslim countries have sought
to inculcate a common civic sense through the communication media, the
school system, agencies of national public guidance, and so on. This has
had considerable success, since people, for the development of their nation,
have become willing to accomplish social services even at the price of
sacrifices. Both nationalism[8] and socialism[9] have been curbed by being kept
within the limits of a transnational and trans-class religion; values like
social justice, independence, and self-respect have been brought nearer to
the people. On first sight, publications pertaining to such civic sense strike
us because of their ideological mumbo-jumbo, but in fact they awaken
people to a consciousness of their responsibilities, rights, and duties as
citizens, and, as in education, an appeal is made to basic Islamic values.

Other sectors than those of education and civic sense could be examined in which modernization has been so sweeping that the religious
tradition has nearly disappeared; the army, business practices, and public
administration are but a few. Islam is redefined here in terms of basic
values considered to be universal.[10]

[7] OBDEIJN, *L'enseignement de l'histoire dans la Tunisie moderne* (see Selected Literature 3.
b.); CARRÉ, "Une tentative d'analyse de contenu de textes scolaires religieux", *Revue
Française de Sociologie*, 12:1 (Jan.–Mars 1971), pp. 93–107; ID., *Enseignement islamique
et idéal socialiste*; ID., *La Légitimation islamique des socialismes arabes* (for both see
Selected Literature section 3. b.).
There has also been a diffident attitude to foreign schools and learning. See André
MIQUEL, "Continuité et changement dans les pays arabes", in *Education, développement
et démocratie*, ed. by Robert CASTEL and Jean-Claude PASSERON, Paris and The Hague:
Mouton, 1967, pp. 191–204.
[8] While for a long time a discussion was carried on about the role of Islam in Arab
nationalism, it concerns at the present time rather the role of Islam in Arabism. See for
instance CEMAM Reports 2/73 (Summer and Autumn 1973), *Controversy, Dialogue
and the New Arab Man*, Beirut: Dar el-Mashreq, 1973.
[9] *Arab Socialism: A Documentary Survey* (see Selected Literature section 3. c.); M. H.
KERR, "Le socialisme révolutionnaire et la tradition islamique", in *Renaissance du monde
arabe* (see Selected Literature section 2.), pp. 427–34; MINTJES, *Social Justice in Islam*.
Cf. the books of CARRÉ mentioned above in note 7.
[10] Ernest C. DAWN, "Arab Islām in the Modern Age", *The Middle East Journal*, 19 (1965),
pp. 435–46; H. SAAB, "Modèles islamiques de modernisation au Moyen-Orient", in
Renaissance du monde arabe (see previous note), pp. 277–91.

6.3. Development of Religious Thought

In the two preceding sections, I tried to show that the Islamic religious tradition in the Middle East could delay but not stop social developments. Here I may indicate briefly that, in this region, Muslim religious thought itself has developed considerably since the 1950s, in connection with developments of and in the societies.

The reformists already took this path by looking for fundamental values and principles of Islam differing from the many time-bound forms and traditions of historical Islam. Later Muslim thinkers have expressed themselves in other ways as well to arrive at a critical view of traditional Islamic thought and to reformulate Islam in terms relevant to the present time and new social developments. New Islamic institutions organize international congresses where experts in religious law and theology meet, like the Muslim World League in Mecca, or the Academy of Islamic Research of al-Azhar in Cairo. The more conservative developments of thought at al-Azhar mirror a typical Islamic religious reaction to present-day social and other developments.[11]

A number of Muslim thinkers show concern with the relevance of Islam to current social and economic problems and try to develop a new kind of Muslim ethics or principles of an Islamic economy.[12] Others have analyzed "from within" how the religious thought of Islam should re-form itself and develop self-critically to assimilate the modern world as a given reality and interpret it in a positive sense.[13] Still others, as individuals and personal thinkers[14], arrived at sometimes startling positions in their thought about the human being, society, and God. Such positions would simply have been considered heretical in the religious Islamic tradition, but they were reached in an attempt to bring together a real concern with the vital social problems of the present time and the fundamentals of Islam as a religion. Exceptionally, a Muslim critic may hold the current state of Islam responsible for the mishaps that befell the Arab world after the two World Wars.[15]

---

[11] Hava LAZARUS-YAFEH, "Contemporary Religious Thought among the 'Ulamā' of al-Azhar", *Asian and African Studies*, 7 (1971), pp. 211–36.

[12] As an example: *The Employer and the Employee*.

[13] Fazlur RAHMAN, "The Impact of Modernity on Islam", *Islamic Studies*, 5:2 (1966), pp. 113–28; ID., "Islamic Modernism: Its Scope, Method and Alternatives", *International Journal for Middle East Studies*, 1:4 (October 1970), pp. 317–33.

[14] Hichem DJAÏT, *La personnalité et le devenir arabo-islamiques*, Paris: Seuil, 1974; H. HANAFI, "Théologie ou anthropologie?", in *Renaissance du monde arabe* (see above note 9), pp. 233–64.

[15] Ṣādiq Jalāl AL-'AẒM, *Naqḍ al-fikr al-dīnī*, Beirut: Dār al-Talī'a, 1969. Cf. Stefan WILD, "Gott und Mensch im Libanon: Die Affäre Sadiq al-'Azm", *Der Islam*, 48:2 (February 1972), pp. 206–53.

6.4. *Concluding Remarks on Middle Eastern Developments and Islam*

Events in the Middle East and the development of Middle Eastern countries have often been seen in terms of the West: not only in terms of
Western interests but also of Western schemes of interpretation and
approaches in general.[16] Since the 1960s, countries of the Middle East
have been increasingly conscious of going their own ways politically and
economically. This consciousness became the stronger where the material
and financial means to realize development plans were present or could
be acquired through support from outside, in particular the USA.[17]

Similar considerations hold true for the relationship between development and religion. There are a few well-known studies in sociology of
religion that deal with this subject[18], but the relationship is still seen too
often with Western eyes and analyzed too much according to Western
models. There is an urgent need for scholarly work coming from researchers of the region itself in order to obtain not only better information but also a more adequate interpretation of the data. And the goals
of development and the role of religion can be set only by the people
concerned, that is to say by those who adhere to religions like Islam or
Christianity, in cooperation with experts and politicians of the region in
matters of development.

---

[16] C.A.O. VAN NIEUWENHUIJZE, *Development: A Challenge to Whom? An Essay on the
Present State and the Next Stage in Development Studies, with Special Reference to
Sociology and with Examples from the Middle East*, The Hague and Paris: Mouton,
1969; ID. (Ed.), *Development: The Western View – La perspective occidentale du
développement*, The Hague and Paris: Mouton, 1972.

[17] It is interesting to give some details about some institutions created in the 1970s for the
development of Muslim countries. The "Islamic Development Bank" was founded in
1974 and began its operations in Jidda in 1975. The authorized capital is 2,000 million
"Islamic Dinars" (1 Dinar = 1 I.M.F. SDR); the subscribed capital was 755 million
Islamic Dinars in 1975; there were 23 members. In Mecca, the "Islamic Panel on
Economic Affairs", composed of representatives of Muslim countries, has been established. It seeks to give advice to pilgrims on how to improve the economy in their country
and to instruct them on Islamic principles of economics. The "International Conference
on Islamic Economics" has a permanent secretariat established at King Abdul Aziz
University, Jidda, which convenes conferences every two years and encourages studies on
the subject; the first conference took place in Jidda in February 1976. In 1972, an
"International Islamic News Agency" was founded in Kuala Lumpur, which started to
publish a news bulletin three times a week. The Islamic Development Bank and the
International Islamic News Agency are activities of the "Organization of Islamic Con-
ference" in Mecca. On the economic situation of the Arab world in the 1970s, see Yusif
A. SAYIGH, *The Economies of the Arab World*, London: Croom Helm, 1978.

[18] I think for instance of the work of scholars like Robert N. BELLAH, Henri DESROCHE,
François HOUTART, François-A. ISAMBERT, and others in the 1960s and 1970s. Cf. the
papers on the subject submitted at the 13th "Conférence Internationale de Sociologie
Religieuse" at Lloret de Mar, 1975, published by the C.I.S.R. at Lille, 1975.

The Middle East remains full of contradictions and paradoxes for the analyst who looks for rationality and rules. In Qadhdhāfī's *Green Book* about the best social order[19], the description of the goals of the perfect social order makes no mention of Islam at all, although the Arabic original for the word "law" in the English translation is *Sharī'a*. The "technocrats" may leave the religious factor out, but the political leaders who address themselves to the people of Muslim nations usually refer to Islamic values. Yet as this example shows, even this is no longer an absolute rule.

In this connection, the role of the intellectuals, besides experts, technicians, and politicians, is a crucial one. They are in a position to reflect on current norms and values, both those of development and those of cultural and social traditions.[20]

7. Conclusion

If it is true that the development of ideas runs parallel to the development of social institutions generally, the first rule seems to be that new ideas, to be acceptable, should not hurt Muslim feelings or undermine the respect for Islam. The second rule would be that they are presented as being, on a deeper level, not in contrast with Islam as a religious faith, whatever the social and cultural traditions existing in Muslim societies. In certain cases, the umbrella of Islam can facilitate the introduction of new developments and reforms for concrete issues. In other cases, Islam itself can be used as a meaningful normative incentive for development. The ideological presentation of Islam to a Muslim population—with the idea of "Islamic" development—has an important function in changing existing passive attitudes into more active ones and in making people aware of their own role and task in bringing about a more just society.

Generally speaking, at least two models present themselves for the use of Islam as an incentive for social development:

1) Specific social changes and cultural innovations take place as part of overall processes. The living social and cultural tradition must then *assimilate* and digest them, giving them sense and meaning in relation to the life of the people. Here an appeal can be made to Islamic values, as contained in the living tradition.

2) Those positive elements and values of a living social and cultural tradition that refer to basic norms of Islam can be used as an incentive or *stimulus* to work actively for the development of a more just society.

---

[19] Muammar al-QADHAFI, *The Green Book*, 2 Parts, London: Martin Brian and O'Keeffe, 1976.

[20] LAROUI, *L'idéologie arabe contemporaine*; ID., *The Crisis of the Arab Intellectual*. See in the last-mentioned book in particular the chapter on "Tradition and traditionalization".

We often tend to look down on the hundreds of pamphlets and minor publications that advertize Islam as the panacea for all kinds of problems, including political, economic, and social ones. Elementary as their level may be, apart from their factual truth or untruth, they nevertheless represent the use of Islamic ideology in view of a better society. That is to say, they mobilize people with the help of Islamic values placed in a social perspective.

If such literature justifies and directs development in terms of Islamic principles, we have a case of our second model. Until now, this model has not been applied systematically on a larger scale, and the current literature is indeed difficult to read because it seems to be so chaotic. But whoever could succeed in making clear to Muslim masses that Islam's notion of a just society prescribes work for development would have access to sources of mental nuclear power. Indeed, Islam has already proved its power to function as an identity carrier against a hostile non-Muslim world in often trying circumstances. It also has proved its value for political mobilization and self-sacrifice. It may very well be used too, with an appeal to both reason and revelation as a powerful mobilizer for people to work for a just and better society. Not only governments but also government-supported institutions and private associations can refer or appeal to Islam in order to further social and other developments.

There is no doubt that the Islamic religious tradition, both normative *Sunna* and local *'urf* (*'ādāt*), has often been an obstacle to development, and demonstrably it still is in many cases. There seems to be, however, no inherent necessity that this must always be the case. Local traditional customs that enjoy religious sanction can be overturned by the practical benefits of modernization and concomitant ideas of more general human values. They can also be played down in the light of the Qur'ān or in favor of the *Sunna* as the normative religious tradition. And if, in their turn, certain elements of the *Sunna* itself turn out to be an obstacle to development, these can be superseded by legal means: *fatwās* or *Sharī'a* consultations. Then, by legal reasoning, taking a particular action can be made plausible even if it conflicts with a *hadīth* of former times. Examples have been given of the introduction of social developments and innovations that would have been unacceptable for religious tradition a hundred or even fifty years ago.

Besides this gradual overcoming of obstacles in the Islamic religious tradition to the introduction of a particular social improvement, we have also seen a more direct and positive way to use Islam to make people ready for development. Certain Qur'ān texts and *hadīths* can in fact be used to develop ideas that are, and can be to a still greater extent, an intellectual incentive and a moral stimulus to social service and serious work for development toward a better society, also in terms of Islam. The crucial point seems to be that Islam here is taken as a *norm* and not as an *empirical reality*. Islam may become an obstacle to development by being identified with empirical tradition, *Sunna* and/or *'urf* (*'ādāt*). However, in principle, it can also function as a critical norm to be applied to any of them, as a dynamic principle of further development out of traditions of the past. *This is possible if Islam as a religion is not held to be identical to a given religious tradition, but rather to be an appeal for a just society to be realized by responsible men and women.*

The idea that Islam as a religion is against development can, it seems to me, be defended only on the wider assumption that religion in general is one of the major obstacles to development, with proper definitions being given both of "development" and of "religion". It seems to me that the West has held the idea of Islam being inimical to development on at least two accounts. First, Islam has been perceived against the background of a basic antagonism between a modern West and a backward Muslim world. Second, an easy equation has been made between Islam as a religion and the tradition-bound Muslim societies for whose often sad conditions Islam was made responsible. Throughout, there has been an amazing underestimation of the vitality of the Islamic faith, of the tensions between norm and reality which are implicit in Islam as a religion and that are given with any religion. The West has also had little idea of the tremendous potential of certain elements of the Islamic religious tradition. People can not only live by that tradition and reinterpret it but they can also appeal to the core of that very Islam as a principle that gives an orientation and activates. And now the question posed at the beginning of this chapter—that of the role religion plays and can play in development processes—can be better formulated: *what kind of Islam, and what kind of religion, is opposed to what kind of development?*

Until now there have only been a limited number of instances in which Muslim leaders have been able to mobilize religious tradition in favor of development or in which Muslim social and cultural traditions have been functional for development. One conclusion could be that social and other developments take place best if Islam is not mentioned at all and is simply left out. This may be possible for development in the West, where religion is no longer in the heart of social and cultural traditions, but it is impossible at least in the Middle East and other Muslim countries where Islam is very much at the heart of living social and cultural traditions.

Another conclusion could be that the living social and cultural tradition with its Islamic elements has not been alive enough. If this is granted, the lack of vitality is most probably due not so much to Islam as a religion, but rather to a lack of economic force on the part of the societies and people concerned. This lack could be explained very well by empirical facts including infrastructures and political interests. When a society has regained its socio-economic vitality, it may very well respond to Islamic incentives for development.

A third conclusion would then impose itself automatically. The conscious political use made of Islam during the last thirty years or so, wanted or unwanted and also imposed from outside, has been a major obstacle to the constructive use of Islam for the social developments Muslim countries bitterly need.

Besides drawing attention to positive contributions that the religious tradition of Islam can make to social development and giving some instances of important social innovations introduced in the Muslim Middle East, I have tried to reformulate the old problem of "Islam and development" in such terms that it can be made the subject of further research. The development of Muslim thinking about society—both in Western and in Muslim countries—and about the role of various kinds of religion in it, should be part of the investigation.[21]

Selected Literature

1. Bibliographies

Arab Culture and Society in Change: A Partially Annotated Bibliography of Books and Articles in English, French, German and Italian, compiled by the staff of CEMAM, Saint Joseph's University, Beirut, Lebanon, Beirut: Dar el-Mashreq, 1973.

Bibliographie de la culture arabe contemporaine (French and English annotations), Paris: Sindbad/Les Presses de l'UNESCO, 1981.

The Contemporary Middle East 1948–1973: A Selective and Annotated Bibliography, compiled by George N. ATIYEH, Boston: G. K. Hall, 1975.

Essai de Bibliographie sélective et annotée sur l'Islam maghrébin contemporain: Maroc, Algérie, Tunisie, Libye (1830–1978), by Pessah SHINAR, Paris: Edition du Centre National de la Recherche Scientifique, 1983.

Women in the Middle East and North Africa: An Annotated Bibliography (Middle East Monographs 2), by Ayad al-QAZZAZ, Austin, Tex.: Center for Middle Eastern Studies at the University of Texas at Austin, 1977.

2. Middle East

The Economics and Politics of the Middle East, by Abraham S. BECKER, Bent HANSEN, and Malcolm H. KERR, New York etc.: American Elsevier Publishing Company, 1975.

LAROUI, Abdallah, *L'idéologie arabe contemporaine: Essai critique*, Paris: François Maspéro, 1967.

---

[21] Further research will also be needed on various forms of popular, practiced Islam and their role in development processes. See above Chapter 5 on "Official, Popular, and Normative Religion in Islam".

—, *The Crisis of the Arab Intellectual: Traditionalism or Historicism?*, trans. Diarmid CAMMELL, Berkeley, Cal. & London: University of California Press, 1976 (French original *La crise des intellectuels arabes: Traditionalisme ou historicisme?*, Paris: François Maspéro, 1974).

NIEUWENHUIJZE, Christoffel Anthonie Olivier van, *Sociology of the Middle East: A Stocktaking and Interpretation*, Leiden: E. J. Brill, 1971.

Religion in the Middle East: Three Religions in Concord und Conflict, ed. by Arthur J. ARBERRY, 2 Vols., Cambridge: Cambridge University Press, 1969.

Renaissance du monde arabe, ed. by Anouar ABDEL-MALEK, Abdel-Aziz BELAL and Hassan HANAFI, Gembloux, Belgium: J. Duculot, 1972.

The Study of the Middle East: Research and Scholarship in the Humanities and Social Sciences, ed. by Leonard BINDER, New York etc.: John Wiley and Sons, 1976.

3. Development, Education, Social Justice

a. Development

Development: The Western View – La perspective occidentale du développement, ed. by Christoffel Anthonie Olivier van NIEUWENHUIJZE, The Hague and Paris: Mouton, 1972.

NIEUWENHUIJZE, Christoffel Anthonie Olivier van, *Development: A Challenge to Whom? An Essay on the Present State and the Next Stage in Development Studies, with Special Reference to Sociology and with Examples from the Middle East*, The Hague and Paris: Mouton, 1969.

WAARDENBURG, Jacques D.J., "Notes on Islam and Development", *Exchange*, Leiden, 4 (March 1974), pp. 3–43.

b. Education

CARRÉ, Olivier, *Enseignement islamique et idéal socialiste: Analyse conceptuelle des manuels d'instruction musulmane en Egypte*, Beirut: Dar el-Machreq, 1974.

—, *La légitimation islamique des socialismes arabes: Analyse conceptuelle combinatoire de manuels scolaires égyptiens, syriens et irakiens*, Paris: Presses de la Fondation Nationale des Sciences Politiques, 1979.

OBDEIJN, Herman L. M., *L'enseignement de l'histoire dans la Tunisie moderne (1881–1970)*, PhD. Dissertation, Tilburg, Netherlands: Moller Instituut, 1975.

WAARDENBURG, Jacques D. J., "Some Institutional Aspects of Muslim Higher Education and their Relation to Islam", *Numen*, 12 (1965), pp. 96–138.

—, *Les universités dans le monde arabe actuel*, 2 Vols., The Hague and Paris: Mouton, 1966.

—, *L'enseignement dans le monde arabe*, Louvain-la-Neuve: Centre d'Études et de Recherches sur le Monde Arabe Contemporain (Cahier 22), 1983.

c. Social Justice

Arab Socialism: A Documentary Survey, ed. by Sami A. HANNA and George H. GARDNER, Leiden: E. J. Brill, 1969.

The Employer and the Employee: Islamic Concept, ed. by Hakim MOHAMMED SAID, Karachi: Dar al-Fikr al-Islami, 1972.

MINTJES, Harry, *Social Justice in Islam*, Amsterdam: Institute for the Study of Religion, Free University, 1977.

Chapter 10
Islam's Function as a Civil Religion[1]

If, during the struggle for political survival, when the independence of
Muslim countries was at stake, people primarily stressed their national
and ethnic identity, in the new kinds of struggle going on nowadays
throughout the Muslim world increasing numbers of people apparently
identify themselves more consciously by means of Islam.[2] New interpretations and applications of the Islamic sign and symbol system are developed, and new articulations of Muslim identity arise not only ideologically but also in behavior and dress and religious activities.[3]

Such developments and attitudes were unexpected in the 1950's. Researchers dealing with the contemporary scene spoke then of Westernization, modernization, and secularization as processes inexorably gov-
erning the destiny of Muslim societies.[4] But the changes and events in
particular during the last thirty years have drawn attention to certain
deeper dimensions in Muslim societies and other resources unrelated to
technological improvement. We, in our turn, wonder how it was possible
for sociologists and political analysts at the time to fail to ask about the
inner workings of Muslim societies. Apparently they were more or less
blind to the appeal that elements of Islamic religion and culture can exert
in Muslim communities if they are propagated by persons nourishing an
ethical and religious indignation against the existing state of affairs. Their
search, stimulated by trying circumstances, could then lead to a discovery

---

[1] This is a reworked and enlarged version of a text that was published under the same title
in *Yād-Nāma: In memoria di Alessandro Bausani*, ed. by Biancamaria Scarcia Amoretti
and Lucia Rostagno, Vol. I: *Islamistica* (Studi orientali 10), Rome: Bardi, 1991, pp. 495–
512.

[2] For centuries, people in Muslim countries, Muslims and non-Muslims, have identified
themselves primarily according to their religion, Muslims being conscious of their
Muslim identity as different from that of Europeans and Americans.

[3] See Jacques D.J. Waardenburg, "Islamforschung aus religionswissenschaftlicher Sicht",
in *Ausgewählte Vorträge: XXI. Deutscher Orientalistentag, 24. bis 29. März 1980 in
Berlin* (Zeitschrift der Deutschen Morgenländischen Gesellschaft. Supplementa 5), Wiesbaden: Steiner, 1983, pp. 197–211. For new articulations of Muslim identity see for
instance below Chapter 14 on "Puritan Patterns in Islamic Revival Movements".

[4] This was also the case with the late Gustave E. von Grunebaum, whose studies concerned
Islamic cultural history. See his *Modern Islam*.

or rediscovery of certain basic values and a kind of rediscovery and reformulation of Islam.[5] As a result, commitment to Islam is no longer determined by tradition only; it is increasingly the result of conscious choices by individuals who have found in their Islam answers to problems that worried them and the groups of which they were part. This is the Islam, as truth and source of values, of which believers speak.

1. Islam

From a historical or social scientific point of view, however, it is impossible to speak of one single entity, "Islam", in any specific sense. What has been considered "Islamic" has varied in the course of history, even if the same basic sources of religious truth have been acknowledged by practically everybody. Variations of Islam have developed as a result not only of different intellectual, spiritual, and religious orientations, but also of social and political conditions. It is to the latter that we address ourselves here when we try to find out in what sense Islam may be said to function as a "civil religion" in Muslim states and societies.

The present-day Muslim world comprises very different kinds of *societies*: nomadic, semi-nomadic, pastoral, agricultural, and urban; industrialized, half-industrialized, or unindustrialized; with or without primary and further education; under or outside the impact of modern technology in its various forms; hamlets, villages, towns, and gigantic cities. Such an immense variety of societies inevitably implies different kinds of Muslim communities and different social forms of Islam. The communal nature of Muslim commitments to Islam encourages a variety of social forms and expressions of Islam according to the different kinds of societies and concomitant cultural traditions to be found throughout the Muslim world. Whereas traditional societies have had their own religious structures, in modernizing—including migrant—societies new religious structures such as voluntary associations and *da 'wa* movements have lately arisen in connection with social development—or lack of development. A concept like social justice has been rediscovered as an Islamic value and the need for its application has been stressed.

In the present-day Muslim world it is in particular the various constellations of power and the corresponding differences in *political organization* that make for distinct forms of Islamic legitimation and different

---

[5]   There has been a tradition of respect for certain religious norms and ideals and for living spirituality in Islam. Lately, the revolt against palpable injustice, political oppression, etc. has contributed to a rediscovery of such Islamic values as social justice. See below Chapter 18 on "Islam as a Vehicle of Protest". See also my "Fondamentalisme et activisme dans l'Islam arabe contemporain".

usages of Islam as a political instrument. Nomadic egalitarianism with leaders chosen for life, tribal chiefs with personal followers, hierarchical social classes with hereditary leaders, central authority with powerful means of imposing itself, military classes asserting power, merchants adapting themselves to different authorities, migrant workers living at the mercy of both Muslim and non-Muslim government policies: all these political constellations influence the structures in which Islam is articulated politically as well as the political demands that appeal to Islam.

2. The State

Among the different political structures to be found in Muslim countries since the attainment of independence, those of the state seem to be the most important ones nowadays.[6] Variations in state organization and government policy affect the institutional setting of Islam and the forms it takes. We can put the existing states on a scale between an officially "Islamic" and an officially "atheistic" state.

First, states proclaiming their Islamic character will tend to impose one interpretation of Islam as the official one, to assign a particular role to Islam in social life, and to exert control over Islamic institutions, trying to curb possible opposition by influential leaders. Saudi Arabia and Iran are examples of this.[7] Second, states wanting to make their policies acceptable to a Muslim majority population will try to promote ideological versions of Islam designed to legitimize these policies, preferably enlisting the cooperation of religious leaders ('ulamā') prepared to support the state policy. Nasser's Egypt was a good example of this. Third, states seeking to check existing Muslim traditions and institutions, for instance because they hamper development or because of the presence of sizable non-Muslim minorities, will tend to distance themselves from Islam in state affairs and stress the separation of religion and state, assuring equal treatment of the majority and minorities. Syria may be cited as an example of this. A fourth and extreme case were the officially atheistic states, which made the disappearance of Islam, as of all religion, a long-term objective, although political compromises could be admitted in the short term. The Soviet Union was a good example.[8] Consequently, different kinds of state involvement with Islam imply different Muslim political structures and different political usages of Islam.

One well-known indicator of the place occupied by a particular state between the extremes of Islamic and atheistic states is the degree to which

---

[6] See for instance JOHANSEN, *Islam und Staat*.
[7] See below Chapter 17 on "The Rise of Islamic States".
[8] See for instance BENNIGSEN and WIMBUSH, *Muslims of the Soviet Empire*.

the *Sharīʿa* is applied in it. On the one hand, there are Islamic states such as Saudi Arabia and Iran that claim to be based on and to apply the *Sharīʿa*, and on the other there were the Muslim regions of the Soviet Union and the Muslim regions of the People's Republic of China where the *Sharīʿa* was or is categorically rejected as valid law. But there are also other indicators of the extent of a state's involvement in Islam, varying from the requirement that the President be a Muslim (in nearly all Muslim majority states) to the claim that the King, by virtue of his office, is the protector of religion (as in Morocco); from the modest assertion that the rules of the *Sharīʿa* shall not be infringed (for instance in Syria) to the proud claim that the new political system is the true realization of the *Sharīʿa* (as in Iran); from the view that Islam is one of the religions corresponding to the basic principles of the state (as in Indonesia) to the conviction that no religion except Islam may maintain places of worship or hold public religious services (as in Saudi Arabia).

The weight of Islam in the policics of Muslim governments in religious matters—and also in their general aims and purposes—is attested to indirectly by the fact that, throughout history, and in particular nowadays, political opposition in Muslim countries has very often appealed to Islam and its sources to reproach the political leadership for its failure to rule according to Islamic norms. One reason for this phenomenon at the present time may be that criticism of government is rarely allowed direct expression, so that it must find an indirect outlet, such as being couched in Islamic terms. Another reason is simple expediency: measuring a government's performance against the precepts of Divine Law will always be politically efficient and appeal to the populace. But other reasons must also be assumed, such as real indignation at cases of appalling injustice and the honest desire for a society built on the basis of eternal norms and values transcending political interests.

The sheer fact of an opposition expressed more or less covertly in Islamic terms by Islamist and activist pressure groups forces the state to respond in the same language. From that moment on, a typically Muslim political discourse develops that does not refer to universal principles or Western values, but uses specifically Islamic terms to debate the relation between government (as a political structure and as policy making) and Islam (as a totality of norms and values and as a way of living). A state's response to challenges by Islamists and Muslim activists—along with the degree to which *Sharīʿa* injunctions are applied—is another indicator of the place it occupies at a particular moment on the scale between an Islamic and an atheistic state.

A warning should, however, be made about all scholarly research on these matters. If it was already difficult to know what was going on in Eastern bloc states during the Cold War, it is even more difficult to know what is really happening in present-day Third World states, including

Muslim and in particular Islamic states where freedom of expression is greatly limited. Most observations merely register what is said and done by different groups and people and compare this to what the representatives of the state say and do publicly. Such representatives may be cabinet ministers or high-ranking administrators, but official statements they make are dependent on decisions made from day to day by some persons at the top, and in some cases one man. As in other Third World countries, the functioning of Muslim states in actual practice is at most analogous to the way in which Western states function with open debate on organization and policies.

Another handicap to understanding what happens in Muslim states is that most students tend to apply Western models, such as those of state-church relationships. As long as scholarship does not free itself from Western schemes born of a specific tradition and experience, we will not have access to what are considered values in other societies, and we will not really be able to grasp what is going on in Muslim countries. On the other hand, once we have discovered certain structures in other states and societies, we may very well inquire whether similar structures cannot be found in Western states and societies, too. This holds particularly true for the phenomena of "civil" religion.

3. Civil Religion

Since Robert N. Bellah's article "Civil religion in America", published in 1967[9], discussions have arisen among sociologists and other scholars of religion about the definition of civil religion and the presence of civil religion in the USA in the past and at the present[10], as well as about the presence of civil religion elsewhere in the world.[11] Here we follow the definition of civil religion given by Liebman and Don-Yehiya in their study of this phenomenon in the state of Israel: "… the ceremonials, myths and creeds which legitimate the social order, unite the population, and mobilize the society's members in pursuit of its dominant political goals."[12] Civil religion endows civil institutions, including state institu-

---

[9]   BELLAH, "Civil Religion in America". Cf. also ID., "American Civil Religion in the 1970's", in *American Civil Religion*, ed. by R. E. RICHEY and D. G. JONES, pp. 255–78; ID., "Religion and the Legitimation of the American Republic", *Society*, 15 (1978), pp. 16–23; *The Broken Covenant*.

[10] See for instance *American Civil Religion* (see previous note); and, among many articles, HAMMOND, "The Sociology of American Civil Religion".

[11] BELLAH and HAMMOND, *Varieties of Civil Religion*. Cf. *Religion des Bürgers: Zivilreligion in Amerika und Europa*, ed. by Heinz KLEGER and Alois MÜLLER, Munich: Kaiser, 1986.

[12] LIEBMAN and DON-YEHIYA, *Civil Religion in Israel*, p. IX. Cf. the definition "… a symbol system that provides sacred legitimation of the social order" (p. 5) and "the system of

tions, with a sacralized aura, lending them a religious glamour. Roman religion, for instance, was largely a civil religion and functioned as such. Whereas *civic* religion has to do with the rules of behavior of individual citizens[13], *civil* religion involves political authority and in particular the state and the attitude of citizens towards the state.[14]

Liebman and Don-Yehiya's study mentioned above gives some characteristics of civil religion, of which the following may be mentioned here[15]:

1. In contrast to traditional religion, a civil religion serves secular purposes and it is secular authorities who bestow authority and guard the religion. It does not necessarily appeal to a belief in revelation and transcendent reality as a source of authority; at its core stands a corporate reality (a society, a state) rather than a transcendent power, and the recognized authority is not so much God as society. It touches the communal rather than the personal identity of the people involved.

2. In contrast to traditional religion, the beliefs prevailing in civil religion are much more sensitive to socio-political change; its mythical cores have a reconciling and even cathartic function with regard to the fundamental problems and dilemmas of society. A civil ritual in particular refers primarily to a given group or society, without encouraging a search for a deeper meaning or making an important impact on other domains of the participants' lives. There is no separate organization, since the state constitutes its institutions and the state leaders themselves make up the elite of the civil religion. In fact, civil religion is "... supported by, and transmitted in part through, the instrumentality of the state ... Indeed, the virtual identity of political and civil religious institutions is an important difference between traditional and civil religion"[16].

3. Civil religion is based on a consensus in the community about the validity of its existence, content, and role in communal life in a given society and state. Protests against it may be raised by religious leaders and their followers who stress transcendent reality and revelation as the basis

---

sacred symbols, that is, the beliefs and practices which integrate the society, legitimate the social order, and mobilize the population in social efforts while transmitting the central values and worldview that dominate the society" (p. 24). "The objective of civil religion is the sanctification of the society in which it functions" (p. 5).

[13] F. E. REYNOLDS, when investigating the subject in Thailand, concluded that *civic*, rather than *civil*, religion was to be found here. See his "Civic Religion and National Community in Thailand".

[14] See also the article "Civil religion" by R. NISBET in the *Encyclopedia of Religion*, Vol. III, pp. 524–7.

[15] For the following we refer to Chapter One of the book by LIEBMAN and DON-YEHIYA mentioned in note 12, "Traditional Religion and Civil Religion: Defining Terms", pp. 1–24.

[16] *Ibid.*, pp. 12 and 10 respectively.

of religion. It may also be opposed by those secularists who want to do away with every religious element in public life.

4. As mentioned above, the contents of a civil religion may change according to circumstances; it may also vary among social groupings of the society, each group having its own preferred variant of the given civil religion. Consequently, several forms of a civil religion may coexist in a society.

5. Civil religion, as determined by civil state authorities, is consequently the opposite of those forms of religion that are determined by religious authorities. The latter seek not only to defend these forms against the state, but also to impose them on the state.

Given these characteristics, there are various ways to affirm and identify the presence of a civil religion in a given society and state:

1. Civil and state authorities use particular elements from a given religious tradition in a representative way for purposes that are not religious themselves, but rather of a socio-political nature.

2. At public meetings of a socio-political nature, certain religious ceremonies take place.

3. Elements of the religious tradition are used to symbolically transcend certain points of conflict between groups in the society concerned.

4. It is, however, difficult to identify all existing aspects of a civil religion and to prove its functioning convincingly. This is due to the fact that civil religion is largely of a symbolic nature. It is rich in allusions and has different meanings for different groups. Moreover, it lacks an organization of its own.

There are several general arguments to support the contention that, just as Judaism functions as a civil religion in the state of Israel, as Liebman and Don-Yehiya have proved, Islam functions in fact largely as a civil religion in Muslim countries in order to sustain the given civil and state institutions[17]:

1. Throughout history, both religious and political leaders have claimed Islam to be *dīn wa-dawla*, thus linking religion with political action.[18] In traditional Muslim societies the community lived under religious law upheld by the religious leaders (*'ulamā'*) in a society and state obeying the authority of the political leaders.

2. Even if Muslims, inadvertently or not, withdraw from the "religious" domain of Islam when neglecting their religious duties, they do not

---

[17] Two studies on Islam functioning as a civil religion in particular circumstances are REGAN, "Islam, Intellectuals and Civil Religion in Malaysia", and BRAWELL, "Civil Religion in Contemporary Iran". The latter article deals with Iran before the revolution of 1979.

[18] The translation of *dīn* as "religion" and of *dawla* as "state" needs to be qualified, since the meanings of the Arabic and English words do not really coincide.

by the same token leave the "communal" domain, but remain "social" Muslims. In other words, within the Muslim community there has always been a strong sense of a "communal" Islam side by side with a more specifically "religious" one.[19] Besides the traditional "religious" Islam of the *Sharī'a* (Law) and *tasawwuf* (mysticism) there is a "communal" Islam that, in the absence of an independent religious organization able to resist, lends itself to subordination by the existing political authority.

3. In present-day Muslim countries after independence, we increasingly find a kind of "officialized" Islam. That is to say, the official media present Islam in such a way that certain elements of the religious tradition are stressed, largely under the influence of the state, which has a vested interest in strengthening national cohesion by stressing common Islamic elements as well as enhancing its own authority by means of it. This "officialized" Islam takes very different forms in countries like Turkey, Saudi Arabia, Libya, Malaysia, and Iran where the state actively propagates it, or Egypt and Pakistan, where the state has made multiple appeals to Islam to legitimate its policies. Traditional forms have survived in Morocco and Jordan, where we find a more classical type of "official" Islam. The rise of an "officialized" Islam goes together with a growing subordination of the religious leadership (*'ulamā'*) to the state.

4. The "officialized" version of Islam favored by the state is opposed particularly by those who, for whatever reasons, oppose the state, which acquires increasingly totalitarian features the more it succeeds in interpreting and defining Islam and using it in its own way. In other words, in this context the political debate about the nature of the state and the government policies to be pursued takes the form of a discourse about the nature of Islam and the correct implementation of the *Sharī'a*. The rise of an "officialized" Islam supported by the state and certain *'ulamā'*, in addition to the traditional religious Islam supported by the *'ulamā'* in general, as well as the emergence of various forms of opposition to this "officialized" Islam—in particular by fundamentalist and activist movements—represent a profound dilemma for the society and state involved. Which one is the true form of Islam? All parties, however, agree that public order and certain basic institutions of the state are to be preserved, although there are differences of opinion about the exact role of Islam. The commonly held assumption that Islam is a basic feature of society and the state implies that Islam can function as a civil religion under the guidance of the state.[20]

---

[19] In this sense, Islam is also a *civic* religion, apart from government policies. Cf. above note 13.

[20] The state will then prosecute those who do not recognize Islam's authority.

218   Social Reality and Islam

4. Civil Religion in Islamic History

If there is reason to speak of a particular function of Islam as a civil
religion in present-day Muslim societies and states, can we also assign this
function to Islam in the past? It is helpful indeed to place present-day
relationships between state and religion and their different uses of Islam
in Muslim states within a wider framework. For this purpose, I propose
three basic models distinguishable, with numerous variations, in Islamic
history and which prevailed in three historical periods.[21] I disregard here
the prophetic period during Muhammad's lifetime. We should take due
notice of the fact that in Mecca (ca. 610–22) Muhammad did not wield
political power, but only religious and moral authority. Only in Medina
(622–32) did he have both religious authority and political power.

4.1. The Medieval Period and the Period of the Muslim Empires

The medieval period is characterized by the Caliphate, first that of the
Rāshidūn and then that of the Sunnī Umayyad and ʿAbbāsid dynasties;
under the latter (750–1258), the classical theory of political authority
and its organization in Islam was developed. Moreover, separate Sunnī
political structures developed in Spain and Morocco and in the eastern
provinces; the Mamlūk state (1260–1517) provided the transition from
the Ayyūbids (1171–1260) to the centuries of Ottoman rule (1517–1917)
in the Near East. Alternative Shīʿī political-religious structures also developed, the most significant being the Fātimid caliphate in Egypt between
969 and 1171.

The medieval period with its dynasties was followed by three Muslim
empires: the Sunnī late thirteenth-century Ottoman Empire around the
Mediterranean and the sixteenth-century Mughal empire in India, and
the sixteenth-century Shīʿī empire in Iran with the Safavid, Zand and
Qājār dynasties. These empires had a more elaborate hierarchical bureaucracy of both political and religious officials. Without entering into the
organizational or other differences between them, I propose to subsume
the political-religious structures of the three empires under the four
coordinates of government, religious leadership, Islamic institutions, and
Islamic theory.

4.1.1. The *government* in all cases was Muslim and the state Islamic,
insofar as the *Sharīʿa* was to a large extent recognized as valid law. Until

---

[21]   The three models have been developed to distinguish three different major usages of
Islam as civil religion and suggest a general characterization of the way Islam has
functioned as a civil religion in different historical periods. Further inquiry on the basis
of historical documents should check and elaborate the proposed characterization.

1258, the head of state was the ʿAbbāsid caliph, but a sultan under the caliph directed political affairs from the second half of the eleventh century on. The chief administrator was the *wazīr*, an office existing since early ʿAbbāsid times.

4.1.2. The *religious leadership* consisted of *ʿulamāʾ*, whose education took on more standardized forms from the end of the eleventh century on through the *madrasa* system. As scholars of the religious law (*Sharīʿa*), in this capacity called *fuqahāʾ*, they had to uphold the norms of Islam. They enjoyed prestige and had considerable social influence in practically all domains but in particular in the judicial and educational fields. Only in the later empires were they organized in a hierarchical structure upheld by the state. The *ʿulamāʾ* generally supported the government, whatever its policies, but they could intervene on the people's behalf in cases of evident oppression and injustice. Sunnī *ʿulamāʾ* distinguished themselves from other Muslims only through their knowledge; they had no priestly or pastoral function but could advise individuals as well as the government, for instance by means of *fatwās* on particular issues. An alternative religious leadership was that of the leading *sheykhs* in the Sūfī *turuq*, who could wield power within their own network and did have a pastoral function. They were closer to the people than the *ʿulamāʾ* but, with some exceptions, had less access to government officials than them.

4.1.3. Islamic *institutions* in this model are the classical ones, including until 1258 the office of the caliphate, which, in the eyes of the *ʿulamāʾ*, was to remain an office prescribed by religion until well into the twentieth century. The empires created new institutions but they were not supposed to hamper the classical ones.

4.1.4. Sunnī Islamic *theory* about political structure was developed under the ʿAbbāsid dynasty. The state was supposed to be based on the *Sharīʿa* and to organize society in such a way that the people could live entirely according to the injunctions of religion, which were developed in the classical works of *fiqh* (jurisprudence). The normative Islam formulated by the *ʿulamāʾ* had a legal character; it tended to leave ethics and the more experiential side of religion to the individual conscience. This normative Islam was the official religion of the state. For the sake of public order, the state imposed sanctions on certain transgressions of religious law in public, while the *qādīs* (judges), who were appointed by the caliph or the government, had their own sphere of jurisdiction.

Shīʿī theory of the state was first developed in Ismāʿīlī circles in Fāṭimid times in Egypt and later in Yemen and India. Twelver (Imāmī) Shīʿī thought on the subject was elaborated in Iran in Safavid and later times. In contrast to their Sunnī and Ismāʿīlī colleagues, Twelver (Imāmī) 'ulamā' had an eye for the provisional character of state authority and the government currently holding power.

In classical Islamic political thought, the state was described normatively, that is to say as it should be. The usual attitude toward the factual state as it was and functioned in reality—in contrast to the ideal—was one of acceptance, on the principle that in any case a bad state was better than none. Overthrowing a government, even a bad one, opened up the possibility of society destroying itself.

Throughout this period, Islam may be said to have functioned as a civil religion, insofar as the state used Islam to legitimate its institutions and policies and was largely supported by the 'ulamā'. They were prepared to become qādī or to function harmoniously within the overall social-political structure in other ways.

4.2. The Period of Orientations toward the West
(first Europe, later also the USA)

The second model, radically different from the first, is that of orientations toward the West: first imposed from outside by Western colonization and then emulated by groups who emancipated themselves by adopting different forms of "Westernization"[22]. In the second half of the nineteenth century, most Muslim lands had come under Western political authority as annexed territories (Algeria), colonies (British India and the Dutch Indies), or protectorates (Tunisia, Egypt), joined somewhat later by the mandates (Fertile Crescent) and recipients of financial subsidies (the Sa'ūdī emirate). Nearly all these countries were later to gain political independence and establish themselves as new nation-states. A few Muslim countries succeeded in keeping their political independence, chief among them Turkey and Iran, which both underwent processes of accelerated modernization imposed by regimes that were in practice secular. In this model, the distinctive mark has been the orientation toward the West. Though its historical beginning largely coincides with Western occupation, it ends not at the moment of political independence but rather when the West loses its fascination as a source of norms and values. This may already have begun before independence, especially when the West showed itself incapable of living up to its own standards. What do the four coordinates of this model look like?

---

[22] It is important to make a distinction between, on the one hand, the rise of various expectations with regard to the West and corresponding orientations toward it, and, on the other hand, the reality of political domination and economic exploitation (colonization) by Western countries.

4.2.1. Government. In colonial days, European states, that is to say non-Muslims, exerted final political authority over most of the Muslim countries and could put strong pressure on the other ones. This authority was then transferred to the nationalist leaders who had led the struggle for independence and tended to have a rather modern, not to say secular outlook. The nationalist governments of the new nation-states were politically free but generally wanted their states to conform to Western models often derived from the European power that had ruled them. Given the fact that nearly all political leaders and higher administrators had received their education and training at Western institutions and sometimes also in Western countries, this orientation toward the West is not surprising. In fact, these leaders had profound reservations about traditional Islamic institutions and leadership, including the *'ulamā'*, as they existed at the eve of independence, and they were prepared to change them in favor of the modernization and development of the country.

4.2.2. Religious leadership. In this period with the corresponding model, the traditional Sunnī and Shī'ī *'ulamā'* saw their power quickly diminishing. New, modern institutions arose and their own activities were restricted to ever more limited domains of society, where they slowly became marginalized. A new intelligentsia considered the *'ulamā'* remnants of a past that must make way for something new. A new group of reformist—and even modernist— *'ulamā'* has arisen, small in number but with a certain openness to the demands of modern times. As for the Sūfī *sheykhs* with their *turuq*, they were in an even worse position than the traditional *'ulamā'*. The new nationalist leadership saw them as even more of an obstacle to modernization and also as wielders of regional influence, an even greater obstacle to an efficient central government.

At this time a new kind of Islamic "lay" leadership arose, the leaders and spokesmen of Islamic associations and movements like the Muslim Brotherhood. They had an organized membership and were intent on an increasing commitment to Islam and on propagating Islamic ethics and an Islamic way of life both among their members and in society at large. They propagated their *da'wa* (call) in word and deed and obtained considerable social as well as religious influence in the country, whether they participated actively in politics or not.

4.2.3. Most Islamic *institutions* in this period came under indirect and sometimes direct government control, often because of their need for government funding. Governments tended to marginalize the existing Islamic institutions when modernizing society as a whole and to finance and support alternative modern institutions that were to play a leading role. Thanks to new private Islamic associations, however, certain new Islamic institutions have arisen, offering mutual assistance and religious instruction. On the other hand, traditional institutions of folk or popular Islam often ceased to interest the younger generation. Sometimes they were consciously destroyed by the state, which wanted to modernize the country regardless of what it considered to be traditional and backward folklore.

4.2.4. Islamic theory. The classical theory of the *Sharī'a* concerning the political structure of society and the state is no longer applied in this model. Political theory acquires a rather ideal, abstract character completely divorced from political realities. In reformist circles, new ideas on Islamic government arose gradually, as in the Salafīya movement and the Muslim Brotherhood in Egypt. Such ideas referred constantly to Qur'ān and *Sunna* and vigorously opposed secular concepts of the state and society as were current in the circles of nationalist leaders. There came about a striking ideologization of Islam, with an apologetic undertone. Altogether, Islamic ideologies were developed in this stage more indirectly, as an alternative to Western ideologies and to the Western secular concept of nationalism, than directly as a consequence of the existing Western rule. In some cases, *da'wa* movements or even theocratic movements like the Darul Islam in Indonesia took violent action to realize the ideal of an Islamic state during or immediately after the struggle for independence. However, among these activists, the theoretical reflection remained weak.

During this period, the traditional Muslim political and religious authorities in most countries were extremely weak. Turkey and Iran had maintained their independence, but under the influence of modernization the *'ulamā'* lost most of their power. The political, institutional, and ideological role of Islam changed greatly from what it had been in the time of the Caliphate and the great Muslim empires. Yet, I suggest that Islam, even apart from its own religious practices, continued to be important as a "civil religion", no longer upholding the established traditional state and religious institutions but as an ideological defense against a powerful West. Since the new Western rulers were not Muslims themselves, Islam served to preserve an elementary separation between the rulers and the ruled, the powerful West and the dominated Muslim world. Islam served, indeed, as a civil religion for secular purposes: as an elementary defense against a possible loss of identity under the spell and domination of the West.

4.3. The Period of Reorientations towards Islam

The third model presupposes this phase of Western orientations as well as the existence of new Muslim nation-states. New orientations toward Islam developed even in those Muslim regions that were not (yet) politically independent, such as Israel's occupied territories and the Muslim regions of the Soviet Union and the People's Republic of China. The coordinates of this model are very different from those of the preceding one.[23]

4.3.1. Government. After fifty years or more of independence and, in most countries, at least one revolution, government is no longer in the hands of the nationalist leaders of the first generation. The new nation-states have acquired a certain history, developing in directions that were hardly foreseeable at the time independence was achieved. During these years, in most countries the initially democratic structures have strongly receded or even been suspended or abolished altogether. The Muslim states, generally speaking, no longer enjoy democratic decision-making and many of them have in fact become totalitarian states, often dominated by a small elite or simply the military.

4.3.2. Religious leadership. In this period and in this model, with the exception of Iran, the *'ulamā'*, both traditional-orthodox and reformist-modernist, have become heavily dependent on the state, both financially and politically. Their income from *waqfs* has sharply decreased and they lack the political power to oppose the state. The Sūfi *sheykhs'* existence and influence has also been sharply reduced; many states are suspicious of the *turuq*. New developments of *turuq* are, however, taking place in regions like West Africa and everywhere in urban settings where, as a source of moral and practical mutual assistance, they help people find meaning in a new communal life.

On the other hand, "lay" leaders of *da'wa* movements and Islamic associations have generally increased in number and influence and are watched by the state authority. Some of the movements are primarily religious, but in most cases there are socio-political objectives as well. The rise of these movements is related to the emancipation of new groups and, continuing into the future, the gradual emergence of new sections of the population such as peasants who moved to the cities. Their attitude toward government policies may be ambivalent or one of clear protest. With the growing power of the state and of the political leadership generally, religious leaders are confronted, perhaps more than ever before, with the dilemma of obedience or opposition. They may keep silent or be declared opponents of the established political structure and the state. Or, as a third possibility, they may concentrate on religious matters for the time being, without making political choices.

---

[23] There is an abundant literature on this period in connection with the revitalization of Islam. Here we merely trace some broad lines immediately relevant to our subject: Islam's functioning as a civil religion.

4.3.3. The situation of the Islamic *institutions* has here become more complex than in the previous two models. Most traditional Islamic institutions have been brought under direct or indirect government control. Through its Ministries of Awqāf (*waqfs*), or of Religious Affairs the state has founded new Islamic institutions and organizations parallel to existing private ones (as in Malaysia). Private Islamic institutions, sometimes connected with *da'wa* movements, can take a public stand at variance with the government only when it is expressed in Islamic terminology. Such new institutions can adopt a straightforward orientation only in purely religious matters.

4.3.4. Islamic *theory* in this third model remains in part the heritage of traditional Islamic thinking on political structures in terms of an ideal system. But besides this, completely new versions of Islamic political theory and its expression in political structures are developed. A reformist, and later "fundamentalist", version tends to refer continuously to Qur'ān and *Sunna*. Elements of this version are taken over by the state when it encourages the elaboration of an officially-approved version of Islam to legitimate and support its policies. Alternative versions express a critical attitude toward such policies in an Islamic guise; they may even take more radical, revolutionary forms. Other versions offer grandiose systems proclaiming the virtues of Islam as a spiritual solution to present-day problems. The latter versions are extremely idealized, projecting Islamic norms and ideals beyond the immediate political situation and sustaining hopes and expectations for a better society and state in the future.

In this third model, Islam as a "civil religion" seems to be taking forms that are very different from the other two models, but again, it is the state that has an interest in using Islam as a civil religion for its secular aims and purposes. More than ever before, the state has become implicated in policies leading to changes in the traditional social and, consequently, religious structures. On the whole, the governments of the new Muslim nation-states have dealt with Islamic matters no colonial government would have cared to become involved in. Concerted efforts have been made to apply a particular "officially" supported version of Islam in social practice, teach it at schools, and spread it through the media. It seems to me that the rise of an "officialized" government-supported Islam is one of the most important developments in Islam in most Muslim countries over the last fifty years. In this way, a kind of official sanction is given to particular forms or interpretations of Islam; certain forms are not recognized; other forms may even, in the context of political problems, be forbidden. Such an "officialized" Islam inevitably evokes various responses among the population, which in turn are also expressed in terms of Islam. If I see things correctly, the ensuing discourse and debate establishes and identifies the contents of Islam as a support for state and society. That is to say, it promotes Islam as a civil religion, distinct from its being a religion for its own sake.[24]

5. Islam's Function as a Civil Religion

If we define a civil religion as that kind of religion that is supportive of existing political institutions and of the state itself, nearly every religion has functioned as a civil religion in particular circumstances. This is certainly true of Islam.

In each of the three periods considered there has been an intrinsic correlation between the four coordinates of government, religious leadership, Islamic institutions, and Islamic theory. There has always been a correspondence between political authorities and their institutions on the one hand and religious authorities and their institutions on the other. In each model, not only do Islamic theory, institutions, and leadership legitimize the existing political leadership, but the political authorities also prove capable of using Islamic theory and institutions for their own purposes, exerting increasing control over Islamic leadership and institutions. Although this is particularly the case in the third model, that is, in the most recent period (in Iran, too, the political 'ulamā' dominate their non-political colleagues), Islam has apparently always played an important role as a civil religion. The ways in which this has happened and continues to happen require further exploration.

Selected Literature

American Civil Religion, ed. by Russell E. RICHEY and Donald G. JONES, New York: Harper & Row, 1974.
BELLAH, Robert N., "Civil Religion in America", *Daedalus*, 96 (1967), pp. 1–21 (Repr. ID., *Beyond Belief: Essays on Religion in a Posttraditional World*, New York: Harper & Row, 1970 = 1991).
— and Phillip E. HAMMOND, *Varieties of Civil Religion*, San Francisco: Harper & Row, 1980.
BENNIGSEN, Alexandre, and S. Enders WIMBUSH, *Muslims of the Soviet Empire: A Guide*, London: Hurst, 1985.
BRAWELL, G. W., "Civil Religion in Contemporary Iran", *Journal of Church and State*, 2 (1979), pp. 233–46.

---

[24] An underlying contention of this chapter is that Islam as a sign and symbol system (see above Chapter 3) allows for a number of "readings", both spiritual (religious) and social (political). Fundamentally speaking, it is the *interpretation* of Islamic data, including the Qur'ān, that makes it a religion, a political system, a law, or a social structure, in the Western sense of these words.

The Broken Covenant: American Civil Religion in Time of Trial, ed. by Robert N. BELLAH, New York: Seabury Press, 1975.

GRUNEBAUM, Gustave E. von, *Modern Islam: The Search for Cultural Identity*, Berkeley & Los Angeles: University of California Press, 1962 (pocket edition New York: Vintage Books, 1964).

HAMMOND, Phillip E., "The Sociology of American Civil Religion: A Bibliographic Essay", *Sociological Analysis*, 37 (1976), pp. 169–82.

JOHANSEN, Baber, *Islam und Staat* (Argument Studienhefte SH 54), Berlin: Argument-Verlag, 1982.

LIEBMAN, Charles S., and Eliezer DON-YEHIYA, *Civil Religion in Israel: Traditional Judaism and Political Culture in the Jewish State*, Berkeley & Los Angeles: University of California Press, 1983.

NISBET, R., Art. "Civil religion", in *Encyclopedia of Religion*, ed. by Mircea ELIADE, New York 1987, Vol. III, pp. 524–7.

REGAN, D., "Islam, Intellectuals and Civil Religion in Malaysia", *Sociological Analysis*, 37 (1976), pp. 95–110.

REYNOLDS, F. E., "Civic Religion and National Community in Thailand", *Journal of Asian Studies*, 36 (1977), pp. 267–82.

WAARDENBURG, Jacques D. J., "Fondamentalisme et activisme dans l'Islam arabe contemporain", in *Pratique et théologie: Volume publié en l'honneur de Claude Bridel*, Geneva: Labor et Fides, 1989, pp. 91–108.

Section 6

The Case of Arabia

Chapter 11
The Wahhābīs in Eighteenth and Nineteenth Century Arabia

This chapter concentrates on the movement that arose in response to the religious call (*da'wa*) of Muhammad ibn 'Abd al-Wahhāb (1703–92), the Wahhābī movement. We concentrate on its history until the twentieth century, leaving out of consideration its influence on regions outside Arabia. The first part provides some biographical details about the founder and sets out the substance of his call, which led to the foundation of the Wahhābīya community in Najd in Central Arabia. Then I explore the way in which the Sa'ūd family exercised leadership of the community and gave a powerful impetus to the movement in the eighteenth and nineteenth centuries and mention political consequences of their actions. Finally, I address the infrastructural factors that, together with the effect of the religious call and astute political leadership, can help to explain the rise and success of the movement.

Secondary material, that is to say studies previously published that are based on doctrinal and historical writings by Wahhābī authors, is the main source for this paper. We have no records left by outsiders who could have observed the Wahhābī movement in Najd itself during the period treated here. This did not become possible until the twentieth century, when 'Abd al-'Azīz II (ca. 1879–1953), the founder of the modern Saudi Arabia, renewed the Wahhābī call.

1. Muhammad ibn 'Abd al-Wahhāb

Muhammad ibn 'Abd al-Wahhāb was born in al-'Uyaina in Najd in 1703 into one of the families of Banu Sinan of the Tamim tribe. He came from a Hanbalī family with a tradition of learning. His grandfather, Sheykh Sulaymān b. Muhammad, had been Mufti of Najd and had had a number of pupils. His father, 'Abd al-Wahhāb ibn Sulaymān, was *qādī* at al-'Uyaina, teaching in the local mosque. Al-'Uyaina at the time had a certain prosperity but no particular intellectual resources. After receiving religious instruction from his father, who had himself written a tract against the veneration of human beings (saints), a practice the Hanbalī

tradition had opposed since its beginnings, Muhammad went as a young
man to Medina to pursue his studies further in this center of religious
learning.

Historians report that two teachers in Medina, Sulaymān al-Kurdī
and Muhammad Hayāt al-Sindī, discovered traces of "heresy" in the
young man's religious ideas. It may be assumed that already at that time
he was strongly opposed to all forms of veneration of human beings,
whether Shīʿī Imāms or Shīʿī or Sunnī holy men or saints, to whom
miracles were often ascribed. This attitude may have been reinforced by
what he saw in Medina of "pious" practices around the tomb of the
prophet Muhammad, who is buried there. In both Mecca and Medina he
must have seen the exploitation of pilgrims by the inhabitants of these
cities, who indulged in an ostentatious and materialistic way of life
painful to anyone who took the religious precepts seriously. It is known
that, already in his youth, Muhammad had also been struck by "primitive" religious practices of the Bedouin related to the veneration of trees
and rocks. Such practices must have been current in Central Arabia at the
time, and it may be asked whether this relatively inaccessible region of the
Peninsula had been islamicized at all since the Prophet's death in 632
C.E., beyond the Bedouin's nominal conversion to the Islamic faith.

As a student in Medina, Muhammad ibn ʿAbd al-Wahhāb was a
faithful pupil of Sheykh ʿAbd Allāh Ibrāhīm al-Najdī (al-Madanī), who
stressed the decadence of Islam in Najd and the need for serious religious
reform there. The Sheykh's teaching was in the Hanbalī tradition and
inspired in particular by the ideas of Ibn Taymīya (1263–1328), the great
"puritan" reformer along Hanbalī lines, and Sheykh ʿAbd al-Bāqī al-
Hanbalī (d. 1661), a great authority on tradition (Sunna). By means of a
diploma, Muhammad ibn ʿAbd al-Wahhāb received permission to continue Sheykh ʿAbd Allāh's teaching, which means that the latter also
considered him a trustworthy transmitter of his ideas. Another important
teacher with whom he studied was the above-mentioned Muhammad
Hayāt al-Sindī, who was well versed in the Sunna and equally keen on
reforming current Islamic practices. He also advocated a re-opening of
ijtihād, i.e., the independent "free" interpretation of the sources of religion, in particular Qur'ān and Sunna.

After his studies in Medina, Muhammad ibn ʿAbd al-Wahhāb studied
for some years in Basra with Sheykh Muhammad al-Majmūʿī, an authority in the fields of the Arabic language and Sunna; he is said to have been
a tutor in the house of the local qādī Husayn. As a port city with a
considerable Shīʿī population, Basra must have increased the young man's
zeal for reforms. According to his Arab biographers, the local ʿulamāʾ
pressed him to leave the town, since the existing order was somewhat
disturbed by his attacks on "idolatry" (shirk) and the veneration of
human beings. They report on journeys the young man is said to have

made to Baghdad, where he married a wealthy woman who subsequently died, and further to Kurdistan, Hamadan, Isfahan, Qom, and even Damascus (where he is supposed to have become a true Hanbalī) and Cairo. Such accounts, however, may have been meant to enhance the image of the founder as a widely traveled scholar rather than to render facts truly. More certain is that he was in al-Ahsā', on the Gulf coast, for studies.

Around 1739, Muhammad ibn ʿAbd al-Wahhāb joined his father in Huraimla, where he must have written his most important book, the *Kitāb al-tawhīd* (Book on the Oneness, i.e., of God). Now that his ideas had crystallized, he started preaching and acquired pupils and adherents. His biographers speak of a certain animosity of his brother Sulaymān toward him; Sulaymān is said to have written a tract attacking Muhammad's ideas while their father warned Muhammad to be more careful in proclaiming them. After his father's death in 1740, Muhammad succeeded him in teaching but seems to have been urged to leave Huraimla shortly afterwards. He went back to his birthplace, al-ʿUyaina, where he spread his ideas for some years. He even succeeded in convincing the local Emir ʿUthmān b. Bishr (of the Banū Muʿammar) to cut down some sacred trees and destroy some domes over graves of "holy men". Through his preaching he became known in the whole region, and his religious zeal gave him much prestige with the population. Biographers mention, however, the animosity of his cousin ʿAbd Allāh b. Husayn. His stay in al-ʿUyaina came to an end because the Emir of the whole region up to the coast requested that Muhammad ibn ʿAbd al-Wahhāb be expelled, since religious feelings of (presumably Shīʿī) people in al-Ahsā' had been hurt. He was able to leave with his family and his property, which must have been considerable at the time.

He was received in 1743 by his pupil Sheykh Muhammad ibn Suwailam, who lived in the town of Darʿīya and who is reported to have had about 70 houses at the time. Here he also met Sheykh ʿĪsā ibn Qāsim, received visitors, and could preach. The oasis was ruled by the Emir Muhammad ibn Saʿūd, of the Bedouin dynasty of the Āl Saʿūd, who were part of the large tribal confederation of the ʿAnāza. Two brothers of the Emir, Mushārī (who was reported to have destroyed some funerary monuments, following the exhortations of the new call) and Tanayān, as well as Muhammad's wife, arranged the Sheykh's introduction to the Emir, who accepted his call and doctrine and took upon himself its defense and further propagation, as well as the protection of the Sheykh himself. A simple mosque was built, and instruction in the new doctrine as elaborated on the basis of the Sheykh's *Kitāb al-tawhīd* became obligatory for everyone. It is told that all the inhabitants accepted the new doctrine except four, who left the place. Darʿīya thus became the first stronghold of the Wahhābī movement spiritually, politically, and even militarily, its inhabitants receiving training in the use of firearms.

Historians speak of a formal "pact" of allegiance concluded between the Emir Muhammad ibn Saʿūd and the Sheykh Muhammad ibn ʿAbd al-Wahhāb in 1744 C.E. (1157 AH). Such an allegiance (*bayʿa*) had existed in former times, when the representatives of the community recognized a new Caliph as its worldly leader. Through this pact, the Bedouin principality became an Islamic "nomocracy" (a political entity based on the authority of Islamic religious law), the political sovereignty exercised by the ruler being distinct from the authority of the scholars of religion (*ʿulamāʾ*). This construction has remained the foundation of the Wahhābī state up to the present day. On a personal level, the destiny of Muhammad ibn ʿAbd al-Wahhāb and his family (Āl al-Sheykh) and that of Muhammad ibn Saʿūd and his family (Āl Saʿūd) were to be and have remained linked to each other, the continuity both of the political leadership and of the Wahhābī character of the state being guaranteed accordingly.

When the Sheykh died at the age of 89 years in 1792, he had seen the successful expansion of the new state and increasing acceptance of the call he had proclaimed since about the age of 35. He is reported to have died poor, not having sought wealth for himself, and to have been buried anonymously in Darʿīya as prescribed by his own doctrine. He appears never to have had ambitions for temporal power or desire for a particular spiritual status; he kept the simple title of *Sheykh*. It seems to have been the Sheykh who insisted that the ruler of the Wahhābī state should be not only *Amīr* but also *Imām*, head of the new Islamic state, or even *Imām al-Muslimīn*, the leader of the true Muslim community (which had been the classical title of the Caliph). In fact, the Sheykh was the real power behind the throne. After his death, however, the Emir ʿAbd al-ʿAzīz I (1766–1803) and his successors would be considered both the spiritual and temporal chief of the Wahhābīs. There were to be intermarriages, however, between the Āl al-Sheykh and the Āl Saʿūd, and the descendants of the Sheykh would continue to play an active role in the state, maintaining and propagating the doctrine, occupying important functions requiring knowledge of religion and seeking to remain the conscience of the community and the nation-state.[1]

2. Doctrines

2.1. The Doctrine of Tawhīd

From the beginning, Wahhābīs called themselves *ahl al-tawhīd*, that is, those who profess the Oneness of God. They called their movement the call from Najd, or the call for Oneness of God, or simply the Call (*al-*

---

[1]   LAOUST, *Essai sur les doctrines sociales et politiques de Takī-Dīn Ahmad b. Taimīya*, pp. 506–10; PHILBY, *Arabia*, pp. 8–13, 54–6.

da'wa). They considered themselves to be within the confines of "ortho-dox" Sunnī doctrine. The doctrine and moral practice of *tawhīd* (One-ness) has been central to the movement from its beginning. God is absolute and cannot be compared to anything else. His most important attribute or quality is his oneness. He is absolutely one in the sense that there is no division within Him, and there is nothing divine outside Him, as the profession of faith (*lā ilāha illā'llāh* ...) expresses, i.e., He is also absolutely unique. As a logical consequence, the movement has always been fervently opposed to anything infringing on the oneness of God, whether it be idolatry or the veneration of "holy men", or states of mind in which anything other than God acquires an absolute character. All of this is considered the sin of *shirk*, associating anything with God. This in itself is good Sunnī doctrine, but Muhammad ibn 'Abd al-Wahhāb rigor-ously advanced it to the extreme as the absolute norm for any Muslim; it was the very essence of his call. This led to a strengthening of the moral and religious fiber, so that people would refrain from anything that might infringe *tawhīd*. Sometimes it led to violent religious and political action.

2.2. Theology

In points of theological doctrine, the movement wanted to keep to Qur'ān and *Sunna* as the only valid sources of religious knowledge, very much as Ahmad ibn Hanbal (780–855) had proclaimed some nine centuries earlier. From his teaching developed the so-called Hanbalī *madhhab* (legal "school"), within which Muhammad ibn 'Abd al-Wahhāb should be situated. Muhammad (d. 632) is of course recognized as the Prophet, but the Wahhābīs do not declare him to be infallible. His precepts are to be obeyed and his example followed, but any veneration or cult of him is strictly forbidden. Consequently, Muslims should not make pilgrim-ages to the tomb of Muhammad in Medina, though they are free to visit it. Muhammad can have an interceding role, but only with the authori-zation and agreement of God himself. The "Companions" of Muhammad should be respected but they can be criticized for certain of their actions.

Among the founders of the four Sunnī *madhhabs* or legal "schools" Ahmad ibn Hanbal followed the *Sunna* most scrupulously. Unlike Ibn Taymīya, Muhammad ibn 'Abd al-Wahhāb did not say that all Muslims should go back only to the doctrine of the *Salaf*, the pious contemporaries of the Prophet. He considered that after these contemporaries, the first three generations of Muslims (up to ca. 810 C.E.) provided the model for right thinking and behavior. He vigorously combated all non-Sunnī schools of thought and rejected philosophical theology (*kalām*) in what-ever form. Muslims were to adhere strictly to Qur'ān and *Sunna*. Only in later times was the movement to accept analogical reasoning (*qiyās*) as a way of interpreting these two sources of religion permitted alongside

the consensus (*ijmā*) that prevailed in the third century of the Hijra
(ninth century C.E.). Qur'anic exegesis along Wahhābī lines is literalist
and rejects innovations after the classical Qur'ān commentaries, as well
as innovations in other religious domains, at least as they have occurred
since the third century of Islam. The Wahhābī attitude to mysticism has
been less clear-cut: the *turuq* (brotherhoods), the *zāwiyas* (schools or
"convents" with a communal life), forms of asceticism, and liturgies were
forbidden to the degree that they were contrary to the *Sunna*. But the
mystical intention of "interiorizing" acts of worship and of devoting
oneself totally to God has been accepted and applied as the basis of the
religious and moral life of the community.

2.3. Community

The ideas about communal life largely follow from the tenets just mentioned. For Muhammad ibn 'Abd al-Wahhāb, the Muslim community's
aim is to apply the *sharī'a* (sacred law), prescribing what is religiously
good and proscribing what is religiously bad. He stresses even more than
Ibn Taymīya the equality of all Muslims. No special respect should be
paid to descendants of the Prophet; marriages between members of the
community should be exempt from the conditions of social equality
current in Muslim societies. On the other hand, he is more inclined to
excommunicate people from the Muslim community than any of his
predecessors of the Hanbalī school. As soon as someone infringes the
tawhīd and does not respond to the subsequent appeal to repent, he or
she can be excommunicated. In fact, according to strict standards, the
majority of Muslims are not true Muslims at all, but have lapsed into
forms of *shirk*, and this legitimates conducting *jihād* against them. In
doctrinal treatises, different kinds of *shirk* and different kinds of unbelief
are distinguished.

The Wahhābī territory was called "land of the Muslims" and there was
a marked tendency to consider all outside territory (of Bedouin who had
not submitted, the Ottoman Sultan, and Arab rulers other than the Sa'ūdis)
as the domain of *kufr*, that is the land of war, against which *jihād* could be
waged and in fact was waged when circumstances permitted. Muhammad
ibn 'Abd al-Wahhāb and the Wahhābīs after him regarded themselves as
the one and only rightly-guided Islamic community. The *umma* (Muslim
community) takes precedence over any other social ties, in particular tribal
particularism, but also over individual rights and privileges. There ought
to be complete solidarity among members of the movement, and any trace
of secession or civil disturbance has to be eliminated for the sake of the
community. All the (male) members share equal rights and responsibilities,
and unity and equality are stressed again and again. Only within the community can Islam be practiced as it ought to be. One of the consequences

drawn from this is that Muslims should migrate from any country or region in which *shirk* and *kufr* are manifest and where Islam cannot be professed properly. They should settle in Islamic territory (*dār al-islām*), which then acquires the name of *dār al-hijra*.

The Wahhābīs, however, interpret this *hijra* ("migration") also on a moral level. Later, in the 1910s and 1920s, ʿAbd al-ʿAzīz II was to use the doctrine of *hijrat al-uhramāt*, the "abandoning of all that is forbidden [by God and the Prophet Muhammad]", as an incentive to settle the Bedouin in new agricultural communities. This is nothing less than a complete "conversion", both personal and social, the Islamic community being of another kind than the natural ties of family, clan and tribe.

2.4. Leadership

In the community, leadership belongs to the *Imām*, who should be strictly obeyed as long as he does not order disobedience to God. Muhammad ibn ʿAbd al-Wahhāb describes the function of the *Imām* in the same terms as Ibn Taymīya did in the fourteenth century. His duties include ensuring that the principles and practices of religion are well enacted. The imamate and emirate of the Wahhābī state were created "in order to force the people, in their own interest, to obey God and his Prophet"[2]. Thus the Imām can regulate the behavior of his subjects down to the smallest details, and he is obliged "to consecrate to God in the *jihād* the persons and property of the Muslims"[3]. Perhaps even more than that of Ibn Taymīya, Wahhābī doctrine has strengthened the position and power of the *Imām* as the more or less absolute leader of the community. Cooperation between the *ʿulamāʾ*, those who know the precepts of religion, and the *Imām*, as the leader of the community, is thereby presupposed. The state is not absolute in itself. It is only a temporal rule organizing things to give the *Sharīʿa* the most effective sanctions and coercive power. Interestingly enough, Muhammad ibn ʿAbd al-Wahhāb does not speak at all of the caliphate, which, during his lifetime, was assumed to be embodied in the Ottoman Sultan. The Wahhābīs' feeling was that one could accept the rule of anyone who followed the *Sharīʿa* like the Wahhābī *Imām*, and they probably saw the Ottomans as usurpers of the caliphate, but they never preached open rebellion against the Ottoman rulers.

2.5. Jihād

More than any other Sunnī thinker, including Ibn Taymīya, Muhammad ibn ʿAbd al-Wahhāb elevated the *jihād* to one of the principal activities

---

[2]   LAOUST, *Essai* (see above note 1), p. 527.
[3]   *Ibid.*, p. 528.

in Islam. He directed it not only against non-Muslims but also against all
Muslims who had forsaken the cause of Islam. Three kinds of *jihād* are
distinguished: against apostates who leave Islam altogether, against dis-
senters who still recognize the authority of the *Imām*, and against seces-
sionists who sow disorder or desert from the Islamic community. "Any
Muslim who, for whatever reason, fell into conflict with their [i.e, the
Wahhābīs'] interpretation of Islam or challenged their authority was
generally considered to be an apostate unbeliever, and was liable to the
severest sanctions, although these were not clearly defined."[4] *Jihād* was
to be waged against all those who had committed *shirk*, violated one of
the cultic or moral prescriptions of Islam, or indulged in the cult of "holy
men"[5]. But for the Wahhābī Muslim, *jihād* is more than an incidental
armed struggle; it represents a continuous endeavor:

> As a member of the Islamic community, he struggles for an internal
> spiritual reform in the path of God against the profane aspects of his
> human existence while at the same time waging an external struggle
> against those who oppose his goal or the well-being of his religion.[6]

Other Muslims believe this as well, but the Wahhābīs have taken the
command very seriously. When *jihād* slackens, Islam will degenerate. The
Wahhābīs wage *jihād* against dissension in the community, which they
consider a basic evil and ascribe to the introduction of "innovation" in
religion after the models that existed in the third century after the Hijra
(ninth century C.E.).

The aim of *jihād* is to bring about the rule of the Word of God, and
it can take many forms besides that of armed conflict. Every Muslim in
the Wahhābī community has the obligation to practice "good counsel",
that is, to correct his brothers (and sisters) fraternally if they have
committed an infraction against religion, and to do his utmost to improve
and strengthen the community. Among the tasks the *Imām* must perform
in the name of *jihād* are also the development of education, the issuing
of decrees concerning communal life, the prevention of reprehensible
actions and damage to people's property or honor.

This conception of *jihād* implied that superstitions and the cult of
"holy men" were to be abolished with radical, violent methods appropriate to the rooting out of evil. Superstitions in Arabia covered in particular
cultic practices related to trees, stones, and caves. In the seventh century,
Muhammad had already called for all remnants of the *jāhilīya*, the pagan
time of ignorance before him, to be destroyed. Muhammad ibn ʿAbd al-

---

[4]   HELMS, *The Cohesion of Saudi Arabia*, p. 99.
[5]   LAOUST, *Essai* (see above note 1), p. 529.
[6]   HELMS, *Cohesion* (see above note 4), p. 96.

Wahhāb did the same, and his followers, too, speak of the "time of ignorance" before his reforms in the eighteenth century. The cult of "holy men" was considered to be *shirk*, "associationism", as a cult of idols instead of God. Included in the category of "holy men" whose cult was to be abolished fell not only those whom people considered saints and to whose tombs they went to implore blessings, but also Sheykhs of mystical brotherhoods (*turuq*) claiming to have charismatic powers, the *Imāms* of the Shī'īs, and other descendants of the Prophet, as the case might be. Ridding the graves in cemeteries of all ornaments, domes, or even inscriptions, and eradicating all forms of cult except the worship of God were practices that spread the fame of the Wahhābīs, along with their regular warfare, which did not always spare women and children. Thus they became known and feared for the violence they committed with religious zeal.

The *Imām* has to ensure that the Qur'anic punishments are applied and that the religious rituals and obligations like worship, fasting, and religious taxation (*zakāt*) are well performed. Muhammad ibn 'Abd al-Wahhāb is unique in prescribing to all Muslims obligatory attendance at public prayer and payment of *zakāt* even on windfall profits, as in trade.

2.6. Religious Devotion

Of particular interest for the purity-orientedness of the movement is the moral aspect of the doctrines of Muhammad ibn 'Abd al-Wahhāb. When preaching *tawhīd* (Oneness, i.e., of God) he had two things in mind. First, the "objective" recognition of the oneness and the unique almighty character of God, or the acknowledgment that oneness in the proper sense belongs only to God. Second, the subjective "appropriation" of this objective oneness: as a oneness of adoration. In this the believer subjectively accepts nothing and no one else but God as his master, thus achieving both devotion to God alone and a unified moral consciousness proper to a person who takes the utmost care only to serve God in his actions. This devotion of oneself to God and the demand for such a devotion of life from the community as a whole led to an intransigent moral rigorism as the dominant tone in Wahhābī society.[7]

There is an extremely rigid element in this religious devotion. Whereas certain Sūfīs had considered *tawhīd* to be the continuous endeavor to realize mystical union, Muhammad ibn 'Abd al-Wahhāb taught in the "puritanical" Hanbalī tradition that Oneness should be understood subjectively as "oneness of adoration": a complete abandonment to, worship of, and glorification of God alone. For this reason, Henri Laoust stresses

---

[7]   LAOUST, *Essai* (see above note 1), pp. 531–2.

the importance of the notion of *ʿibāda* (worship) in the call of Muhammad ibn ʿAbd al-Wahhāb, which indicates total obedience to God, a free and methodical serving of God. God has created human beings to serve Him; they, consequently, should continuously render a disciplined service to God alone, following the precepts which God himself has ordained and revealed through his Prophet. This service of God implies resignation of oneself to the sovereign will and decision of God, devotion through appropriate words and actions to the community, and avoidance of major sins. Above all, human beings should guard against any possible "infiltration" of the heart by a hidden "associationism" in which something would gain an importance that is due only to God. Life becomes a continuous training, as part of *jihād*, in sincere and total devotion to God, combined with a meticulous observance of the prescriptions of the sacred Law.[8]

With these doctrines, Muhammad ibn ʿAbd al-Wahhāb stands in the line of a range of reformist thinkers along Hanbalī lines. Apart from Muhammad himself, I just mention the names of Ibn Taymīya (1263–1328) and his pupil Ibn Qayyim al-Jawzīya (d. 1350), of Abū Yaʿlā al-Farrāʾ (d. 1066), Ibn Tūmart (d. 1130), Ibn ʿAqīl (d. 1120), and the legal works of al-Hujāwī (d. 968/1560–1) and al-Mardāwī (d. 885/1480–1). Wahhābī doctrine has been severely criticized by a number of Sunnī and Shīʿī authors.[9] In the twentieth century, Muhammad Rashīd Ridā came to its defense.[10]

3. Eighteenth and Nineteenth Century History

3.1. First Expansion

The first decades of the Wahhābī state of Darʿīya were a period of endless struggle to bring Bedouin tribes under Saʿūdi and Wahhābī authority. In 1755, the Emir and Imām ʿAbd al-ʿAzīz I (ruled 1766–1803), who is considered to have been the real founder of the first Wahhābī empire, occupied Riyadh and made it his capital. After each conquest, a garrison was installed consisting of well-paid leaders who showed religious zeal for the Wahhābī cause, while teachers and preachers were appointed to instruct the new subjects in the call. In larger places a *qādī* and Mufti would be installed, in smaller places only a *qādī*. In 1786, Najd was under Wahhābī control and the Emir could think of building a larger Arab Sunnī state where Islam would be restored in its original purity, in

---

[8] *Ibid.*, pp. 514–33.
[9] KAROUT, *Anti-Wahhābītische Polemik im XIX. Jahrhundert.*
[10] RIDĀ, *Al-Wahhābīya waʾl-Hijāz.*

contrast to the existing Ottoman and Persian empires. The state expanded eastward with the submission of the Banū Khālid in al-Ahsā' on the Gulf, southward with the conquest of Najrān, and northward with incursions into Iraq, often as reprisals against unsuccessful punitive expeditions sent from Basra and Baghdad at the order of the Ottoman authorities in Istanbul. On April 21, 1802, the Wahhābīs took Karbela during a Shī'ī religious holiday, profaning and pillaging the shrine of Imām Husayn and carrying out a massacre among the inhabitants.

3.2. The Hejaz

Relations were complex with the Sherifs of Mecca, who had been masters of this important part of Arabia since the Turkish evacuation of the Hejaz at the beginning of the eighteenth century. Muhammad ibn 'Abd al-Wahhāb had sent a deputation to Mecca to discuss his doctrine with the Meccan scholars of religion, claiming that his call was not a heresy, that the destruction of domes over graves was an expression of piety, and that intercession by saints (denied by the Wahhābīs) was not Sunnī "orthodox" doctrine. As a result of this discussion, the Wahhābī doctrine was recognized as in accord with the school of Ibn Hanbal and consequently had to be tolerated. Yet sometimes the Holy Places were forbidden to Wahhābīs or, at the time when the Wahhābīs were still declared to be enemies of true religion, even to pilgrims who had traveled through Wahhābī territory. In 1798, however, the Sherif of Mecca, Ghālib, was obliged to drop his ban simply because no pilgrims could reach Mecca overland anymore except through Wahhābī territory. Alois Musil has aptly described the situation and way of life of the inhabitants of Mecca and Medina at the time:

> The profit derived from the numerous pilgrims and from the rich gifts they brought enabled the inhabitants of Mecca and al-Medina to live in luxury. These townsfolk had become accustomed to beautiful dress, many ornaments, and gay entertainments and could afford to smoke tobacco and drink not only coffee but intoxicating liquors. The Wahhābites intended to purge the holy cities of such dissipation and to train their inhabitants in modesty and simplicity. By accepting Wahhābite guidance the inhabitants of Mecca and al-Medina would have lost not merely their income and comforts but the respect with which they were regarded by the pilgrims. Loath to consent to such humiliation, they were, naturally enough, ready for war to protect their earthly well-being.[11]

It should be remembered that, living in a province where agriculture was possible and where an urban culture existed in and around the Holy

---

[11] Musil, *Northern Nejd*, p. 65.

Cities considered to be the center of the Islamic world, the Hejazīs tended to look down on the Bedouin of Najd. They considered them little better than barbarians, lacking proper culture and adhering to a form of Islam that was either riddled with paganism or so rigidly puritanical as to frighten off anyone who enjoyed a more comfortable lifestyle and a higher level of education. Muslims living in towns, villages, and oases could not but fear the prowess and lust for riches and power of Bedouin, Wahhābīs or not.

The subsequent events can be mentioned here in a few words. In 1803, ʿAbd al-ʿAzīz took Mecca, which had been evacuated by Ghālib. Idolatrous practices were rooted out and persons suspected of being associated with them were killed. The garrison ʿAbd al-ʿAzīz had left in the town was then in its turn largely massacred by the inhabitants who had returned. The new Emir, Saʿūd (1803–14), took Medina by the end of 1804 and retook Mecca in February 1806 after a siege. Mecca was now pillaged, and Medina, which had tried to revolt, underwent the same fate.

Under the new rule in the Hejaz, the practices of the Wahhābīs were forced on both the inhabitants and the pilgrims. The holy sepulchres were destroyed or locked up, pilgrimages to them stopped, gold, silver, and silk ornaments forbidden, music silenced, and both coffee and tobacco proscribed. The beautiful *mahmal* processions, which had arrived every year for the *hajj* from Egypt and Syria accompanied by musicians, were denied admittance on the grounds that they incited the pilgrims to idolatry and reminded the inhabitants of the nominal rule of the Sultan in Istanbul.[12]

3.3. Ottoman Reaction

The fact that the Ottoman government no longer exercised actual authority over the Holy Places, that Wahhābī doctrines were now officially recognized in the Hejaz, that the Friday sermon here was no longer said in the name of the Sultan-Caliph in Istanbul, and that pilgrim caravans organized by the Ottoman authorities were forbidden to enter Mecca demanded a reaction. The new state was growing dangerously. In April 1806, an attack on another Shīʿī holy city, Najaf, could just be thwarted, but in July 1810 the Wahhābī army stood at the gates of Damascus. In the same year it took the region of Asir south of the Hejaz. The energetic Sultan Mahmūd II, who had come to power in Istanbul in July 1808, coordinated his action with Muhammad ʿAlī, the strong man in Egypt since 1811. Two major expeditions from Egypt to the Hejaz and from there to Najd, in 1811–15 and 1816–18 respectively, crushed the Wahhābī state. On September 9, 1818, after a siege of more than five months,

---

[12] *Ibid.*, pp. 266–7.

Dar'īya was taken and completely destroyed, as were other towns and villages of the Wahhābīs, with their natural resources of palm trees. Many people were killed and all the members of the Sa'ūd and the Sheykh families were brought to Egypt as prisoners; only a single person succeeded in escaping. The Wahhābī Imām 'Abd Allāh ibn Sa'ūd and some close collaborators were beheaded in public in Istanbul on December 17, 1818.

4. Infrastructural Foundations of the Wahhābī State

The history of the Wahhābī movement in Arabia is not only that of Muhammad ibn 'Abd al-Wahhāb's doctrines and their impact but also that of the Āl (family of) Sa'ūd. In the foregoing, we paid much attention to Wahhābī ideology and its expansion. It is time now to consider the power base and the expansion of the Sa'ūd family in alliance with Wahhābī ideology. We follow here in broad lines the analysis David A. McMurray offered.[13]

His first hypothesis is that, for centuries, there had been long-distance trade between the Gulf coast and the Hejaz through the Arabian desert, as a result of which a settled population had built up in Najd. But in the sixteenth and seventeenth centuries, when the Europeans started to transport goods from the East, either by the sea route or overland via Basra and Baghdad to Aleppo, this trans-Arabian trade declined rapidly. A shortage of money brought about a decline of the oasis towns and the trade possibilities of the nomadic tribes, in response to which Najd fell back on the elementary sources of production. These were oasis-agriculture and pastoralism (with a certain interdependence), along with the well-known Bedouin raiding of each other and the oases. This raiding probably increased to the extent that trade decreased. Najd was divided into a number of petty emirates based in the various towns, which were ruled by powerful families. There was no central authority, and the power of the emirs was no longer based on tribal connections but on the settled population and on control over the region's trade and agriculture. These emirs gradually increased their military force in order to maintain control over their regions.

His second hypothesis is that the Āl Sa'ūd succeeded in establishing a state capable of using force to extract the available sources of income from agricultural and pastoral surplus, through tributes and by direct appropriation through raiding. Military power was at the basis of the Wahhābī state, and conversion to Wahhābism meant in fact economic and political subservience to the state of Dar'īya.

---

[13] McMurray, "The Rise of the Wahhābī and Sanūsī Movements".

Dar'īya expanded its authority in three ways: first by open warfare; these expeditions were financed through the confiscation of all booty. Second, the oasis dwellers were terrorized. If they submitted and gave their allegiance to Dar'īya, they only had to pay taxes; but if they resisted, their date groves were cut down and they were deprived of their livelihood. And third, propaganda was disseminated among the nomadic tribes. They had to be convinced of the advantages of submitting and paying tribute but then also joining in the division of spoils after raids which had become a state enterprise.

5. Consolidation of the State

The Āl Sa'ūd succeeded in building up and centralizing state power, thus consolidating the state, at the price of disrupting tribal structures. They managed to do this in various ways:

1) There was no standing army that might have become an opposing power. After each campaign, the army was disbanded and only at the outset of a new campaign were soldiers conscripted, both from the oases and all the tribes. Additionally, the Sa'ūd family established a private militia of volunteers from the tribes at its disposal.

2) Local forms of power and control were broken up. Sheykhs who resisted were simply sent to Dar'īya and replaced by an appointed kinsman; the military leaders had to reside in Dar'īya; local qādīs were replaced by trained appointees paid solely from state funds; local treasuries were placed under the administration of clerks from Dar'īya. Dependency on Dar'īya was enhanced by the fact that the tax collectors were all sent out from Dar'īya and that the appointed qādīs unified the dispensation of justice.

3) The fact that leadership remained in the Āl Sa'ūd through hereditary succession guaranteed continuity of leadership and accumulation of power. It also meant a break with traditional tribal practice, in which a new Sheykh was chosen only after the death of the last one, so that continuity could not be anticipated.

4) All the territory under Wahhābī control was pacified by means of measures like collective punishment, fines imposed on all parties involved in a conflict, and the substitution of the payment of blood money for revenge as far as possible. Such measures were consistently applied.

5) The state assured internal security with rigorous means, maintaining law and order. This created an almost unheard-of situation of peace, which may have been an impetus for the conversion of groups who would now be able to live without fear of raiding or attack.

6) The state established dependable sources of revenue. Treasures were brought in as booty; zakāt was collected everywhere; taxation was

levied in the conquered territories. Areas on the periphery of Wahhābī control paid tribute to be left in peace; dues were levied on commercial traffic and even on pirating in the Gulf. Commerce was encouraged in several ways, except that trading with non-Wahhābīs was prohibited. But above all, the state was economically based largely on the expropriation of agricultural land. All territories that revolted were confiscated by the state, and there was an immense expansion of state lands in the oases, which were agricultural. This must have provided the main source of income of the Wahhābī state.

The state did not only take, it also gave. There was a sophisticated system of revenue collection from herdsmen as well as settled agriculturalists, but also a system of redistribution, not only for the tasks of the state but also to relieve the hardship of the poor, to compensate losses suffered by soldiers, and so on. Even if Najd did not reach a very high level of development, there was a huge improvement in living conditions compared to fifty years earlier. The British envoy Capt. Sadleir, who crossed the desert at the time of Ibrāhīm's pitiless devastations (ca. 1819), describes how much cultivated land—not only date palms—there had been and how the ruins bore witness to extensive buildings in the towns. The state of the Āl Saʿūd had an economic basis that was self-sufficient and lent force to the spread of Wahhābī ideology.

McMurray concludes by saying that the Wahhābī movement arose in reaction to the decline of international trade routes through Najd. It developed its social structure in opposition to the tribal system current in Arabia: tribal loyalty was replaced by loyalty to the state and to the Wahhābī creed. There was mass conscription and the Saʿūds' private guard was not kin-based. State law was enforced over tribal law and state collection of tribute was enforced over local tribute arrangements. Finally, thanks to the rule of inheritance, leadership within the Saʿūd family was institutionalized. As a result, the new state was able to dominate both oases and tribes.

6. Survival of the Āl Saʿūd

From 1818 to 1821, there was nothing left of Wahhābī rule or religious authority. But in 1821, Turkī, a cousin of the late ʿAbd Allāh ibn Saʿūd, succeeded in restoring the Wahhābī state around the new capital, Riyadh, which had not been destroyed by the Egyptians. Turkī was assassinated in 1834. His successor, Faisal ibn Saʿūd, managed during his second period of rule (1843–65) to reconquer the major part of Najd and to establish his authority over the greater part of the Gulf. As in former times, this meant acknowledgment of Wahhābī rule and payment of an annual tribute. Faisal ibn Saʿūd gave ʿAbd Allāh b. Rashīd (ruled 1834–47) the governorship of Hail, where he established another Wahhābī state, the Shammār confederation.

A longstanding rivalry between the Banū Rashīd in Hail and the Banū Saʿūd in Darʿīya ended when the former took Riyadh in 1884 and when the last members of the Saʿūd dynasty sought refuge with Sheykh Mubārak of Kuwait after an unsuccessful insurrection in 1891. The Banū Rashīd applied the Wahhābī precepts less rigorously and more selectively than the Saʿūds had done. They exercised tolerance in particular toward the almost independent Bedouin tribes of the desert.[14]

It was only under the leadership of ʿAbd al-ʿAzīz II, commonly called Ibn Saʿūd (1879–1953), that Wahhābī doctrines and practices were revitalized and that the Wahhābī state was restored in a new form, uniting the larger part of Arabia. As a result, the Kingdom of Saudi Arabia was established in 1932.

Selected Literature

CASKEL, Werner, "Altes und neues Wahhābītentum", *Ephemerides Orientales*, L, Nr. 38 (April 1929), Leipzig: Otto Harrassowitz, pp. 1–10.

DIFFELEN, Roeloef Willem van, *De leer der Wahhabieten*, Leiden: E. J. Brill, 1927.

HARTMANN, R., "Die Wahhābīten", *Zeitschrift der Deutschen Morgenländischen Gesellschaft*, N.F. 3 (1924), pp. 176–213.

HELMS, Christine Moss, *The Cohesion of Saudi Arabia: Evolution of Political Identity*, London: Croom Helm, 1981.

KAROUT, Zeinab I., *Anti-Wahhābītische Polemik im XIX. Jahrhundert*, Diss. Bonn, 1978.

LAOUST, Henri, *Essai sur les doctrines sociales et politiques de Takī-Dīn Ahmad b. Taimīya: Canoniste hanbalite né à Harran en 661/1262, mort à Damas en 728/1328*, Cairo: Imprimerie de l'Institut Français d'Archéologie Orientale, 1939.

—, *Les schismes dans l'Islam: Introduction à une étude de la religion musulmane*, Paris: Payot, 1965.

McMURRAY, David A., "The Rise of the Wahhābī and Sanūsī Movements" (Paper prepared at the Department of Anthropology, University of Texas at Austin, Spring 1983).

MARGOLIOUTH, David Samuel, "Wahhābīya", in *Shorter Encyclopaedia of Islam*, ed. by Hamilton A.R. GIBB and J.H. KRAMERS, Leiden: E.J. Brill, 1953, 1991³, pp. 618–21.

MUSIL, Alois, *Northern Nejd: A Topographical Itinerary*, New York: The American Society, 1928.

PHILBY, Harry St. John Bridger, *Arabia*, New York: Charles Scribner's Sons, 1930.

---

[14] PHILBY's *Arabia*.

Puin, Gerd-Rüdiger, "Aspekte der Wahhābītischen Reform, auf der Grundlage von Ibn Gennāms 'Raudḥat al-afkār'", in *Studien zum Minderheitenproblem im Islam* (Bonner Orientalistische Studien, N.S. 27/1), Wiesbaden: Harrassowitz, 1973, pp. 45–99.

Rāshīd Ridā, Muhammad, *Al-Wahhābīya wa'l-Hijāz*, Cairo, 1344.

Rentz, George Snavley, *Muhammad ibn ʿAbd al-Wahhāb (1703/04–1792) and the Beginning of the Unitarian Empire in Arabia* (unpublished Ph.D. dissertation), University of California, Berkeley, Cal. 1948.

Schacht, J., "Zur Wahhābītischen Literatur", *Zeitschrift für Semitistik und verwandte Gebiete*, 6 (1928), pp. 200–13.

Winder, Richard Bayly, *Saudi Arabia in the Nineteenth Century*, New York: St. Martin's Press, 1965 (Repr. 1980).

Chapter 12
Saudi Arabia: The King and the Consul

This chapter concerns the life of the founder of Saudi Arabia, ʿAbd al-ʿAzīz's (1876?–1953), with special attention to the views a Dutch consul posted at Jidda held of the king since their first meeting in 1926. I shall first present the main historical events leading up to the founding of the Kingdom of Saudi Arabia in 1932 (1351). Second, I shall address the views of Daniel van der Meulen (1894–1989; 1311/2–1409/10), Dutch Consul and later Minister Plenipotentiary of the Netherlands in Jidda (1926–31 [1344–50] and 1941–45 [1360–64]) on these events and the rise of Saudi Arabia in general. I shall compare some of his views with those held by Harry St. John Bridger Philby (1885–1960 [1302/3–79/80]). Third, I shall report on some of Van der Meulen's publications and private notes relating to King ʿAbd al-ʿAzīz; Van der Meulen was able to meet the King on several occasions and developed an evident admiration for him. In conclusion, I shall show that the writings of competent and more critical or sympathetic observers like Van der Meulen can constitute an important source for the understanding of history in addition to the official documents. This is especially the case if these writings throw some new light on the personalities who made or were directly involved in making history.

1. Some Historical Facts

ʿAbd al-ʿAzīz ibn ʿAbd al-Rahman Āl Saʿūd was born in Riyadh, capital of the Saʿūds in 1876 (1293)[1] as the eldest son of ʿAbd al-Rahman ibn Faisal Āl Saʿūd (d. 1927 [1346]) and Sarah bint Sudairi. In January 1891

---

[1]   The date is not certain. In the article "Abd al-Aziz", the new edition of the *Encyclopaedia of Islam* gives his birth date as ca. 1880 / ca. 1291 (Supplement, Fascicules 1–2, Leiden: E. J. Brill, 1980, p. 3), but these years do not correspond. VAN DER MEULEN writes that "it must have been about the 20th of Dhul Hijja 1297 A.H. corresponding to 26th of November A.D. 1880" (*The Wells of Ibn Saʿud*, p. 37). In his historical accounts, Van der Meulen most probably relied on data provided by PHILBY in his *Arabian Jubilee*.
   The Islamic dates were added for a presentation of this text to a Muslim audience in January 1999.

(Jumada II, 1308), the family left Riyadh to escape the domination of the
Āl Rashīd of Hā'il, who had captured it in 1885 (1302/3) and who had
occupied the whole of Najd in 1891 (1308/9). ʿAbd al-ʿAzīz was then a
boy and seems to have been suffering from rheumatic fever.[2] He spent
some time with his mother and other relatives in Bahrain, a virtual British
protectorate. He then joined ʿAbd al-Rahman to live with the Banū
Murra where he gained experience of Bedouin life. Next he accompanied
his father to Kuwait, on the invitation of Muhammad Āl Sabāh and at the
instigation of the Ottoman government, which paid them a small pension;
apparently they lived there in very modest circumstances. Mubārak Āl
Sabāh, a half-brother of Muhammad, came to power after murdering his
half-brother in May 1896 (1313).

Mubārak took an interest in the young ʿAbd al-ʿAzīz and initiated him
into international politics, whose influence was felt in the city. The Turks
were allied with the Germans, while Russia and especially Britain resisted
German and Ottoman influence around the Gulf. Whereas the Turks
supported the Āl Rashīd, the British backed the Āl Sabāh.

ʿAbd al-ʿAzīz distinguished himself by retaking Riyadh from the Banū
Rashīd by surprise with a small group of followers on January 15, 1901
(5 Shawwal 1319). By 1904 (1321/2), he had made himself master of the
territory his grandfather Faisal ibn Turkī (d. 1865) had ruled in Najd half
a century earlier. He succeeded in conquering al-Hasa' in 1913 and
established his authority up to the Gulf. These conquests were made
possible through the creation of the Ikhwān, "Brethren", who devoted
their lives to the cause of Islam and were completely loyal to the state. As
soldiers, the Ikhwān seem to have been almost invincible, resulting in the
military successes of ʿAbd al-ʿAzīz, whom they had to obey blindly.

The organization of the Ikhwān after 1912 (1330) was part of a
broader scheme of disciplining the Bedouin, whose continuous conflicts
made any central authority and state formation difficult. Since 1909,
(1327) great numbers of Bedouin had been settled in *hijar* (singular *hijra*,
"agricultural settlement"), moving from the desert to cultivated land. At
the same time they had to give up their old ways of life—considered
jāhilīya (ignorance), *kufr* (unbelief), and *shirk* (polytheism, idolatry)—
and received fresh training in the properly Wahhābī doctrine and way of
life.

The *hijar* were large agricultural colonies around natural springs or
wells that made the exploitation of oases possible. In these colonies, the

---

[2]   This detail is given by VAN DER MEULEN: "The boy, then ill with rheumatic fever ..." (*The
Wells of Ibn Saʿud*, p. 39). When leaving Riyadh, ʿAbd al-Rahman sent his wife and the
children to Bahrain. "Abd ar-Rahman decided not to expose the women and children to
further desert hardships. Abd al Aziz was still suffering from his rheumatic fever and was
too weak to follow his father" (*ibid.*, p. 40). Van der Meulen suggests that the boy was
cured in Bahrain (p. 41).

old tribal bonds were replaced by religious fraternity and no particu-
larisms were allowed. Each *hijra* had its own *mutawwi'ūn* (literally
"those who subdue"), the religious personnel employed in teaching the
people; they might be called "missionaries" of the Wahhābī cause and, if
necessary, they could carry out punishments. The thus "converted"
Bedouin became Ikhwān, aroused by the *mutawwi'ūn* to religious zeal
and unconditional obedience to the Imām, the father of 'Abd al-'Azīz.
The way they were disciplined and Wahhābī ideology was inculcated in
them left them no other choice. As a result of this indoctrination, the
Ikhwān are reported to have been extremely distrustful of anything
coming from abroad. They considered the world beyond Najd simply
balad al-kuffār (the Land of the Infidels), the infidels being in this case
non-Wahhābī Muslims. Consequently, the Ikhwān tended to see life
simply in terms of Holy War in the literal sense of the word.

In the towns, as distinct from the desert and the sparse agricultural
land, the Wahhābī institutions and way of life had a longer history, and
here the new state had more immediate control than in the desert regions.
Tribal *sheykhs*, for instance, were brought to Riyadh for further training,
but also so that they could be held responsible for possible disturbances
in their tribes. All tribes were treated equally and the old distinction
between the "leading" tribes and the "dependent" ones that had to pay
them tribute, was abandoned; they all had the same duty to pay *zakāt*.
All state authorities had a religious basis, the *Imām* himself ('Abd al-
Rahman, the father of 'Abd al-'Azīz), the *'ulamā'* (in particular the Āl al-
Sheykh), and the *mutawwi'ūn* ("missionaries" but also "religious police"). This situation gave 'Abd al-'Azīz immense power as an absolute
leader. "State" decisions were in fact the decisions of 'Abd al-'Azīz, who
was in personal contact not only with the leaders but also with broad
groups of the population, whom he received at his public audiences.
Paying *zakāt* was a sign of obedience.

With the outbreak of World War One, the Arabian Peninsula acquired
strategic importance. The Ottoman Turks were the official rulers of the
larger part of it, but their authority was largely restricted to the Hejaz
and the border areas. Behind the Turks, German interests were involved,
and the plan to let the Sultan-Caliph of Istanbul proclaim a *jihād* of all
Muslims against their non-Muslim rulers had been worked out in Germany. The British interest, in turn, was to subvert the Ottoman empire
by arousing the Arabs against the Turks.

It was in this sense that the British government's Arab Bureau in Cairo
incited Husayn ibn Alī, Sherif of Mecca, to proclaim an "Arab Revolt"
against Ottoman Turkish rule. He did so in Mecca in June 1916 (Sha'ban
1334), upon which the British sent him arms and money with T.E.
Lawrence, their representative and an expert on Arab affairs. On the
other hand, the India Office in London, which was responsible for

waging war in Iraq, had already despatched William Shakespear from Kuwait with a military and political mission to ʿAbd al-ʿAzīz in October 1914 (Dhuʾl Hijja 1332). He was instructed to persuade the latter to join the British cause against the Turks, who, for their part, were busy encouraging Arab tribes to support them. Britain in return would recognize ʿAbd al-ʿAzīz's independent rule in Najd and al-Hasaʾ, guarantee his independence and protect him against possible Turkish attacks. This was agreed at a new meeting between Captain Shakespear and ʿAbd al-ʿAzīz in January 1915 (1 Rabiʿ 1, 1333). As a result of the British efforts ʿAbd al-ʿAzīz signed a treaty with Sir Percy Cox at Qatif in December 1915 (Safar 1334) that ratified his earlier agreement with Shakespear. Britain would supply him with arms and money for the duration of hostilities in return for his joining the war on the British side. The two men met again at Ujair in November 1916 (Muharram 1335). There, ʿAbd al-ʿAzīz inquired about promises the British had meanwhile made to Husayn ibn Alī of Mecca, who had now become King of the Hejaz.[3] ʿAbd al-ʿAzīz spent the years 1916 and 1917 (1334–5) largely in warfare against Arab tribes supported by the Turks, especially the Banū Rashīd, and at the end of 1917 (1335) he had Central Arabia under his control.[4] By that time, on November 30, 1917 (15 Safar 1336), St. John Philby, coming from the Gulf, arrived at Riyadh, negotiated with ʿAbd al-ʿAzīz on behalf of the British, and continued his journey to the Hejaz, where he met Husayn ibn Alī in January 1918 (Rabiʿ 1, 1336). The latter refused to let him go back to Najd by land, so Philby returned to ʿAbd al-ʿAzīz via Egypt, Bombay, and Basra. He then stayed in Riyadh as head of the British Political Mission to Central Arabia. Just as the Arab Bureau had put Lawrence at Husayn ibn Alī's disposal, the India Office put Philby at ʿAbd al-ʿAzīz's disposal; apparently there was no coordination between the two offices.

After World War One, ʿAbd al-ʿAzīz's son Faisal was invited to visit Britain; accompanied by Philby, he arrived in London at the end of October 1919 (Safar 1338). In the meantime, ʿAbd al-ʿAzīz annexed Asir in 1919 (1338) and ended the power of his archenemy the Āl Rashīd by taking Hāʾil, the capital of the Banū Rashīd, on November 2, 1921 (1 Rabiʿ 1, 1340). The dependent territories of Najd, which already included al-Hasaʾ, were extended considerably in this way. ʿAbd al-ʿAzīz was now absolute ruler of Central Arabia, which was subject to Wahhābī doctrine and practice.

The relations between ʿAbd al-ʿAzīz and Husayn ibn Alī had never been friendly and led to war in the so-called al-Khurma-Turaba dispute of 1918 (1337), with a battle in which Husayn was the aggressor. The British still

---

3 On the relations between ʿAbd al-ʿAzīz and the British during World War One, see VAN DER MEULEN, *The Wells of Ibn Saʿud*, pp. 70–4.
4 In the meantime, on March 11, 1917 (28 Jumada 1, 1336), the British had captured Baghdad reducing Turkish pressure in the region.

supported Husayn, who was now King of the Hejaz; this was the policy line of Lawrence, who favored Husayn and in particular his son Faisal ibn Husayn ibn Alī (1885–1933). The latter, after his misadventure as King of Syria, became King of Iraq, bordering Najd, in August 1921 (Dhu'l-hijja 1340). The policy suggested by Philby, who favored ʿAbd al-ʿAzīz, was not followed. The latter was well aware of the fact that he could not act as long as the British did not allow him to do so. The British succeeded in containing the Wahhābī state, whose Ikhwān were repulsed from Iraq and Transjordan or simply annihilated. In the autumn of 1922 (1341), ʿAbd al-ʿAzīz signed a treaty, again with Percy Cox in Ujair, concerning the borders between his territories and Iraq. In the same year he conquered al-Jauf and a confrontation between Najd and the Hejaz threatened.

In the meantime, King Husayn ibn Alī's misrule, his extortion of money even from *hajjis*, and the general state of corruption in the Hejaz made the British reconsider their support for him. He became ever more pretentious, taking the title of Caliph on March 7, 1924, shortly after the Turkish Grand Assembly in Ankara had abrogated the caliphate on March 3, 1924 (26 Rajab 1342). This evoked opposition in the Muslim world and ʿAbd al-ʿAzīz's anger. A conference for reconciliation held under British auspices in Kuwait failed and was dissolved on April 12, 1924 (7 Ramadān 1342). Confrontation between the Wahhābī Saudi Sultanate of Najd and the Hashimi Kingdom of the Hejaz was now unavoidable.

The Ikhwān took Ta'if on their own in 1924 (1343), murdering and plundering and throwing the Hejaz into panic. King Husayn abdicated in favor of his son Alī and sought refuge in Aqaba. The Hejazīs hated the Najdīs, whom they considered uncouth, and feared a repetition of the events of 1803. Muslims all over the world were in anguish about what might happen to the Holy Places. Not only the Muslim world but the West as well was shocked by the potential impact of a new independent Islamic state founded in the twentieth century and moreover of an extreme if not sectarian orientation. ʿAbd al-ʿAzīz, however, called the dreaded Ikhwān to order. On October 16, 1924 (17 Rabiʿ 1, 1343) they entered Mecca in the state of *ihrām* and performed the *ʿumra*, avoiding bloodshed; ʿAbd al-ʿAzīz followed later, equally in the state of *ihrām*. Medina fell after a siege on December 5, 1925 (19 Jumada 1, 1344), and Jidda was taken after a siege of one year on December 23, 1925 (7 Jumada 2, 1344), after Alī ibn Husayn had abdicated and left for Iraq.

To the relief of Muslims all over the world, it was announced that the Holy Places, now under the Āl Saʿūd's protection, would remain open to Muslims of any school and conviction. All places were purified according to the Wahhābī prescriptions but without violence; as the only exception, the dome above Muhammad's grave in the mosque of Medina was allowed to be maintained, but praying there was forbidden.

On January 8, 1926 (23 Jumada 2, 1344), 'Abd al-'Azīz was pro-claimed King of the Hejaz. The new state was immediately recognized by Britain, France, and the Netherlands, and a British cruiser called at the port of Jidda on March 1, 1926 (16 Sha'ban 1344) on a friendship visit. 'Abd al-'Azīz had come to Jidda for the occasion and a few days later he received the newly accredited Dutch consul, Daniel van der Meulen, together with his predecessor, C. O. van der Plas, at the house of Muhammad Nasif Effendi.

Developments in Arabia had been closely followed by colonial countries with large Muslim populations, and the Netherlands were no exception. The mastermind here was Christiaan Snouck Hurgronje, who as a young man had spent several months in Mecca in 1884–5 (1301/2) and had been kept informed of developments there during the following forty years. The Dutch consulate in Jidda was in charge of the *hajjis* coming from Indonesia, who were more numerous than those of other countries. Jidda was thus an important post for information about what was going on among Indonesian Muslims. When Snouck chose Van der Meulen as the new consul, he undoubtedly hoped that his former student would carry out the policies he himself had defended during his active life. After World War One, however, more conservative forces had started to dominate Dutch colonial policy, whatever the promises made to the Indonesians in wartime. All of this was much to Snouck Hurgronje's dismay. Van der Meulen succeeded Van der Plas, a brilliant linguist and fluent in Arabic, as Van der Meulen would also become. But before going into this subject we should present some more historical facts.

One of the first measures 'Abd al-'Azīz took after conquering Mecca and Medina was to provide better conditions for the *hajjis*. Sanitary provi-sions were improved, security was guaranteed, and the customary extor-tion of money from pilgrims—even by public authorities—were ended and corruption was fought.[5] On the other hand, the *hajj* taxes were raised in compensation for the better services rendered to the pilgrims. Until the

---

[5]   VAN DER MEULEN reports on the hardship of the *hajj* in general and of financial extortions and abuses of pilgrims under King Husayn (*The Wells of Ibn Sa'ud*, pp. 18–9, 90, 114, 116). He describes the improvements in the treatment of the pilgrims introduced by 'Abd al-'Azīz (*ibid.*, pp. 100, 103, 115, 119, 126). According to Van der Meulen, Western colonial governments had already pleaded for such improvements for a long time. They also maintained that foreign nationals (chiefly from India and Indonesia) should not be subjected to the *hudūd* punishments as the Hejazīs now were. They put pressure on 'Abd al-'Azīz that Medina should not be put under artillery fire during the siege of 1925 (*ibid.*, p. 97). 'Abd al-'Azīz's policies brought about confidence on the part of colonial govern-ments that had Muslim subjects who wanted to perform the *hajj* (*ibid.*, p. 108). See Chapter 9, "The Pilgrimage", in *The Wells of Ibn Sa'ud*, pp. 114–26. On the regular duties of the Dutch Consul in Jidda regarding Indonesian pilgrims at the time, see VAN DER MEULEN, *Don't You Hear the Thunder*, pp. 84–90.

1940s, these taxes were still the state's main source of income. Regarding
the international character of the *hajj* and the worries existing for instance among Indian Muslims, two international Muslim Congresses
were organized in Mecca in the summers of 1926 and 1927 (1344 and
1346). ʿAbd al-ʿAzīz there affirmed his full personal responsibility for the
Holy Places, the *hajj* itself, and the *hajjis*. He rejected any form of
international Muslim jurisdiction or even supervision, as well as any form
of pan-Islamic or pan-Arab policy.

In his policies and ideology, ʿAbd al-ʿAzīz kept aloof from the surrounding Arab countries, restricting himself to the territories under his
rule in Arabia proper. This corresponded with the containment policy
Britain applied to the Wahhābī state practically since World War One, if
not earlier. As a result, the role of the Ikhwān as a military force shifted
from conquest to policing. The Ikhwān, disciplined and drilled in the
spirit of *jihād*, saw this abandonment of forceful action to convert the
whole Muslim community to Wahhābī doctrine and practice as a soften-
ing, if not a betrayal, of the old ideals. By implication, the Wahhābī
character of the state was reduced. Shortly before, in 1927 (12/12/1346),
ʿAbd al-ʿAzīz's father ʿAbd al-Rahman, who was an *ʿālim* and had the
title of *Imām* of the Wahhābī state, had died.

As a first step to unification, on January 29, 1927 (25 Rajab 1345)
ʿAbd al-ʿAzīz was proclaimed King of Hejaz, Najd, and Najd's Dependen-
cies. A revolt led by Hamad ibn Rifadah broke out in the Hejaz against
this policy in 1932 (1350/1) but was put down quickly. The political
process was crowned with the unification of the whole territory as the
Kingdom of Saudi Arabia consisting of Najd, al-Hasa', Hejaz, and Asir.
ʿAbd al-ʿAzīz was proclaimed King of Saudi Arabia on September 26,
1932 (21 Jumada 1, 1351).

In 1934 (1352) there was a short war with Yemen, which turned to
Saudi Arabia's advantage. An attempt on ʿAbd al-ʿAzīz's life by Yemenis
in the Great Mosque at Mecca failed. The only other independent state
on the peninsula besides Yemen was Oman, which, interestingly enough,
also has a puritan community, the Khārijīs, in the interior of the country.
Aden was a British colony and Hadramaut and the smaller emirates along
the Gulf were British protectorates. Saudi Arabia was to be an Islamic
state where Wahhābī Hanbalism was to remain the official *madhhab*,
though other Muslims could follow their own *madhāhib*. The person of
ʿAbd al-ʿAzīz would stand as the model for the Wahhābī lifestyle. Ultimately, Wahhābī Hanbalism did not stand in the way of certain measures
of modernization that were initiated by ʿAbd al-ʿAzīz himself. His son
Faisal (r. 1964–1975) would carry out an active policy of modernizing
the country and of founding international Islamic organizations in which
Saudi Arabia would play a pivotal role.

Several initiatives that ʿAbd al-ʿAzīz took in subsequent years deserve mention. First, in the 1930s, oil was discovered in Arabia, and the King, who had been plagued by financial problems during the recession of 1929 (1348) and the following years, when *hajj* revenues diminished, gladly accepted American oil companies, in particular Aramco, which offered favorable contracts. The extraction of oil was seen at the time as a purely economic matter; the oil companies were not to interfere in the internal affairs of the country, and this led to the creation of two separate worlds.[6]

Second, in regard to the Palestine question, ʿAbd al-ʿAzīz took initiatives to cooperate with some other Arab countries during the 1930s. He had serious discussions on the question with Roosevelt and Churchill in Egypt in February 1945 (Rabiʿ 1, 1365).[7] Together with King Farouk of Egypt, he gave a public warning about the consequences of Zionist immigration into Palestine.

Third, during World War Two, ʿAbd al-ʿAzīz, who was one of the few rulers of an Arab country which had not known European colonialism, opted for the Allied side from the beginning. This contrasted with the stand taken by a number of Arab politicians, including some prominent officials in his immediate circle, who either wavered or sided with the Axis.

Following the increasing international interest in ʿAbd al-ʿAzīz, in particular after he took the Hejaz in 1924–5 (1342–4), several books about him were published in the West. First and foremost are two books by St. John Philby, *The Heart of Arabia* (1922) and *Arabia of the Wahhabis* (1928); Philby is also the author of a number of other books on Arabia, including a scholarly biography of the King titled *Arabian Jubilee* (1952). The Arab American Amin al-Rihani published a book on

---

6   On the one hand there was the world of Saʿūdī society, on the other that of American technology. Van der Meulen repeatedly draws attention to the fact that there should have been an Arab spiritual foundation to respond to technology; apparently this was lacking. His reproach to the Americans that they should have insisted on their religion's right to conduct public worship in Saudi Arabia must be seen in this connection. VAN DER MEULEN thinks that ʿAbd al-ʿAzīz would have granted this right if the Americans had been more pressing. See his book *Ontwakend Arabië* (see below n. 14), pp. 140–1.

7   The meeting between ʿAbd al-ʿAzīz and Franklin D. Roosevelt took place aboard the USS Quincy on the Great Bitter Lake (Egypt) on Sunday, February 14, 1945 (1 Rabiʿ 1, 1364) and lasted several hours. Later—one week before his death—Roosevelt confirmed in writing certain promises that he had made during the meeting. Apparently, ʿAbd al-ʿAzīz thought that through Roosevelt he had convinced the USA to support the Palestinian cause. He met Churchill a few days later at Wadi Fayyum near Cairo; the latter did not make any promise. ʿAbd al-ʿAzīz told Van der Meulen about the two meetings after his return to Saudi Arabia, where people celebrated the apparent success of his effort. History would teach otherwise. On these meetings with Roosevelt and Churchill, see HOWARTH, *The Desert King*, pp. 199–209. Cf. VAN DER MEULEN, *The Wells of Ibn Saʿud*, pp. 164–6.

several Arab kings, first in Arabic, and then published the section on ʿAbd al-ʿAzīz in English translation with the title *Ibn Saud of Arabia: His People and his Land* (1928). In 1933 appeared Kenneth Williams's *Ibn Saud*, followed a year later by H. C. Armstrong's *Lord of Arabia*.[8] A certain Western public has felt a fascination for ʿAbd al-ʿAzīz, and in this connection we should note Van der Meulen's views on the rise of Saudi Arabia and the figure of ʿAbd al-ʿAzīz.

2. Daniel van der Meulen on Islam and the Rise of Saudi Arabia

Since the life and work of Van der Meulen is not widely known, some background information on his views about the rise of Saudi Arabia and ʿAbd al-ʿAzīz is appropriate here.[9]

Van der Meulen was born in Laren (Gld.) in the Netherlands in 1894 (1311/2). His father was a schoolteacher and belonged to the Reformed Church (*Gereformeerde Kerk*), one of the Dutch branches of Calvinism. Daniel himself was a convinced and practicing Protestant Christian throughout his lifetime. After primary and secondary school, he enrolled in 1912 (1330) at the University of Leiden in the department where future members of the civil service in the former Dutch Indies received their training. This was a three years' course at the time, so that he entered the civil service on Sumatra during World War One (in which the Netherlands were neutral) in the autumn of 1915 (1333) and stayed there for eight years, returning to Holland in 1923 (1341).

Here he was chosen to become the future Dutch Consul in Jidda, which meant that he had to carry out intensive studies of Arabic and Islam, again at the University of Leiden, under the direct guidance of Christiaan Snouck Hurgronje during the years 1923–25 (1342–44). He left Holland on January 2, 1926 (17 Jumada 2, 1344), arriving by ship in Jidda a month later on February 6 (23 Rajab) after a short stay in Egypt. He arrived, then, a few weeks after Jidda had been captured by ʿAbd al-ʿAzīz.

His posting at the Jidda Consulate was for six years, until 1931.[10] He did not stay in the post all year, but only for that part of the year when

---

8 The imaginative interest in Arabia was further stimulated in the West by two books by Thomas Edward LAWRENCE, *The Seven Pillars of Wisdom* (London: J. Cape, 1935) and *Revolt in the Desert* (London: J. Cape, 1927). These do not, however, deal with ʿAbd al-ʿAzīz.

9 See his autobiography, *Don't You Hear the Thunder*. Cf. in Dutch his *Hoort gij de donder niet? Begin van het einde der Nederlandse gezagsvoering in Indië. Een persoonlijke terugblik* (Don't You Hear the Thunder? The Beginning of the End of Netherlands' Rule in the Indies. A Personal Account Looking Back), Franeker: T. Wever, 1977.

Indonesian *hajjis* (*djawa*) arrived for the *hajj*, performed it, and left again to return to Indonesia. They had Dutch pilgrim passports; the Dutch government had to see to their arrival, accommodation, and departure from the Hejaz and to intervene in case of difficulties. Van der Meulen was also an enthusiastic traveler, both privately and on duty. He went to Yemen from February 25 until April 22, 1931 (7 Shawwal – 4 Hija 1349), and when he had to be on duty in Hadramaut, he took the opportunity to explore an unknown part of the country in the summer of 1931 (beginning of 1350), together with the German geographer Hermann von Wissmann. They published the results together in *Hadhramaut: Some of its Mysteries Unveiled* (1932). This book gave him an international reputation.

From 1931 until 1939 (1350–58), Van der Meulen returned to a civil service posting in Sumatra. In March 1939 (Muharram/Safar 1358), he was in Aden again, where he and von Wissmann planned to continue the exploration they had started in 1931 (1349). This happened in the spring of 1939 (1358). After the war, he published their results in the book *Aden to the Hadhramaut: A Journey in South Arabia* (1947).

Van der Meulen then took up a civil service post in Makassar, South Celebes (Sulawesi), where he arrived in mid-1939 (Jumada 1 or 2, 1358), just before the outbreak of World War Two. Over a year later, the now London-based Dutch government requested him to take up the post in Jidda again, which had meanwhile been upgraded into a legation. Van der Meulen had left the Indies just before the Japanese conquest and arrived in Jidda by ship on April 2, 1941 (5 Rabiʿ 2, 1360). He would stay there until the summer of 1945 (1364).[11] On arrival, he had to immediately repatriate a number of Indonesian pilgrims, but during the war, of course, hardly any Indonesian *hajjis* arrived. He had, however, to send a number of Indonesians to India and carried out other duties.

During the war, Van der Meulen had to accomplish missions to Yemen and famine-stricken Hadramaut, to Egypt and Transjordan, and to Palestine, where he worked on a report for the Dutch government, at the time in exile in London, on the situation of Arabs, Jews, and British, with ideas about a possible solution.[12] All of these were diplomatic tasks of a certain importance. At the end of 1944 (Muharram 1364), he had an audience with ʿAbd al-ʿAzīz in Marat under unexpected conditions, when the latter was on his way to Egypt to meet Roosevelt and Churchill, precisely about Palestine.

From the end of November 1945 (Dhu'l-Hijja 1364) on, Van der Meulen was again in the civil service in the Dutch Indies, a few years

---

[10] See *Don't You Hear the Thunder*, Ch. III, "The unexpected turn-off to Arabia" (pp. 69–98).
[11] *Ibid.*, Ch. VI, "For a second time to Jedda" (pp. 111–49).

before sovereignty was transferred to Indonesia, a development he had regarded as necessary for some time. He worked here for nearly three years for the Dutch government Information Agency. In July 1948 (Ramadān 1367), he returned to the Netherlands, where he was to spend the rest of his life.

From 1949 until 1951 (1368–70), he was organizer and Director of the Netherlands Broadcasting in Arabic, in Hilversum, and he retired in 1951 (1370) at the age of 57. In 1952, he made his last journey to Hadramaut and also paid a last visit to ʿAbd al-ʿAzīz. During the last 28 years of his life, he wrote books and articles, gave addresses and lectured about Saudi, Middle Eastern, and Indonesian developments. And of course he continued traveling, also in Saudi Arabia. Van der Meulen passed away in 1989 (1409/10) at the respectable age of 95.

Apart from his publications, the legacy of Van der Meulen contains a great number of photographs taken in Arabia, the Indies, and elsewhere, various kinds of documents, and, perhaps most important, a number of diaries that he meticulously kept during his years in Arabia and the Dutch East Indies. They contain the material from which he wrote his memoirs, published in English under the title *Don't you Hear the Thunder: A Dutchman's Life Story* (1981).[13]

Even more important for our subject is his book *The Wells of Ibn Saʿud* (1957).[14] It reads like an epic history and sometimes even like a boy's adventure book; the Dutch texts in particular are extremely well written. It is full of personal observations and experiences and evokes a number of more or less well-known people and a human world intensely lived and experienced but now belonging to the past. These pages make it clear how much ʿAbd al-ʿAzīz's life and work had meant to the attentive observer from the Netherlands and how attached he felt to the Arabs and Arabia.

Beyond these published memoirs there are a number of diaries, parts of which have been typed out. They open a window onto the past and give a glimpse of how Van der Meulen witnessed and judged two major

---

[12]   On this subject, see *ibid.*, pp. 121–2 and 123–33.

[13]   This is an elaboration of an earlier memoir previously published in Dutch under the title *Ik stond er bij: Het einde van ons koloniale rijk* (I Was a Witness: The End of Our Colonial Empire), Baarn: Bosch en Keuning, no year (ca. 1965). This memoir was then elaborated into the book *Hoort gij de donder niet?* (see above n. 9). The book *Don't You Hear the Thunder* is a revised version and translation, adapted to a British readership, of this Dutch book of 1977.

[14]   Much of the material, but not everything, arranged differently and expressed more freely, is to be found in a paperback that appeared in Dutch under the title *Ontwakend Arabië: Koning Ibn Saʿud, de laatste Bedoeïnenvorst van Arabië* (Arabia Awakening: King Ibn Saʿud, the Last Bedouin Ruler of Arabia), Amsterdam: H. Meulenhof, 1953, 1958.

events of his time, the rise of Saudi Arabia and the end of the Dutch East Indies. It may be hoped that one day all these archival materials will be brought together and made accessible to the interested public.[15]

Before going into Van der Meulen's experiences of Saudi Arabia and ʿAbd al-ʿAzīz, a few words are in place about his views on Islam. As a pupil of Snouck Hurgronje, Van der Meulen saw Islam in the first place as a legal and doctrinal system that had been constructed during its first centuries and handed down to the present time. But whereas Snouck Hurgronje considered that a future for Muslims would be possible only if they jumped into the modern world and outside the system, possibly keeping the Islamic religion as a personal matter, Van der Meulen looked for a future within the possibilities offered by a reform of the system itself.

According to Van der Meulen, Islam, in the traditional forms of its system, finds itself in a crisis in the modern world, since the traditional forms do not respond to the needs and problems of this world. So, like many Protestant missionaries at the time, he used to speak of the "crisis" of Islam.[16] He was searching for forces and orientations in the contemporary Muslim world that would establish a connection between the Islamic faith and the problems of the modern world. This would require effective reforms of the system and a revision of traditional rules of life.

Van der Meulen respected the religious faith of Islam, steady in a transient modern world. Standing as he did in the Calvinist tradition, which had experienced similar problems that had led to intense internal discussions in Protestant Holland in the last decades of the nineteenth century, Van der Meulen was sensitive to the situation of contemporary Islam. His hope was apparently that, by returning to the sources of the religions, Islam as well as Christianity would be able to respond to the problems of the modern world.

There is reason to assume that he saw ʿAbd al-ʿAzīz's radical religious reforms in Arabia as a potential answer to the challenge of modernity, very much akin to the way in which a new, open-minded faith orientation in his own Church proclaimed a responsibility of believers for the well-being of the world. We must leave aside here the question of the common ground between Van der Meulen's own faith and the faith of the Muslims he met. With such an attitude toward Islam, he entered into communication with the Arabs he met in a quite natural way. His own communicative abilities were a great help in this.

---

[15] D. van der Meulen's widow, Dr. Helene van der Meulen-Duhm, was kind enough to allow me to consult the typed texts as well as other documents. I would like to express my heartfelt thanks to her.

[16] VAN DER MEULEN, "Crisis in the World of Islam".

Snouck Hurgronje, too, was strongly interested in the movement initiated by 'Abd al-'Azīz. He published articles on the subject in the Dutch newspaper *De Telegraaf* in 1924, 1927, 1928, and 1932 (1342–51) and received regular first-hand information from Van der Meulen in Jidda. Since Van der Meulen arrived some six weeks after Jidda had fallen into 'Abd al-'Azīz's hands, he not only heard about the scandals of the preceding regime but also witnessed the beginning of a new era in which puritan religion and morality as well as justice were to govern.

His expectations of the new ruler, known for his exalted religious and moral standards and for his demands for an Islamic society without compromise, were high. In several places, Van der Meulen expresses the hope that 'Abd al-'Azīz will bring about a true reformation, a spiritual rebirth of Islam not only in Arabia but in the Muslim world in general, thanks to a reinterpretation of the sources of Islam. In the following years, however, he had to recognize that 'Abd al-'Azīz's reforms remained limited to the Saudi state and that the latter had no specific message to the Muslim world at large. Van der Meulen concluded that the reforms carried out by 'Abd al-'Azīz were such that they could be applied only within Arabia and not outside it.[17]

Van der Meulen saw 'Abd al-'Azīz as a political realist and a statesman, but an honest one who kept his word. Becoming King rather than Imām of Saudi Arabia gave him political but hardly religious leadership. His approach to the modern world was pragmatic rather than moved by a vision of universal claims. This pragmatic attitude would also explain his openness to American rather than British or Dutch propositions to overcome the financial difficulties of the years after 1928 (1346/7), when the income from the *hajj* tax decreased with the decrease of the number of pilgrims who could afford to pay the *hajj*. His trust in American offers in connection with gold mining and oil exploration and exploitation in fact provided a solution to his financial problems.

But Van der Meulen was quick to observe that the spiritual problems involved were not recognized by the Americans and not met adequately by the Saudis. In Van der Meulen's view, it was the arrival of the dollars that swept away the religious inspiration of the Wahhābī puritan reform. He was not, however, enough of a scholar to inquire into the dynamics and limits of the Wahhābī doctrine and way of life. What would happen to it in a society that extended from a Bedouin to an agricultural and also urban structure, and in a state that was moving away from personal and religious loyalties to the more impersonal structures of modernity?

---

[17]   See *The Wells of Ibn Sa'ud*, Ch. 8, "First Wahhabi Impacts" (pp. 102–13). With modernization, the influence of Wahhābism diminishes. See for instance *Ontwakend Arabië* (see above n. 14), Ch. 7 (pp. 97–110). The real challenge for Wahhābism, according to VAN DER MEULEN, was the arrival of the petro-dollars.

Van der Meulen was keen to observe and describe the acts in which ʿAbd al-ʿAzīz consciously moved beyond the borders of his own kingdom. I already mentioned the King's loyalty to the Allied cause in World War Two, nicely expressed in a telegram he apparently sent to Churchill immediately after the retreat from Dunkirk, when the chances of Allied victory looked bleak.

I also mentioned ʿAbd al-ʿAzīz's mid-1930s initiative for cooperation between Arab states regarding the Palestine problem. Notwithstanding his tension with the Hashemites who ruled in Iraq and Transjordan and his criticisms of Egyptian politics, the common danger of Zionism required cooperation between all Arabs. The Arab League, however, then moved beyond his own, personal plans.[18]

The third act of reaching out beyond the Saudi borders was when he defended the case of the Palestinians at his meetings with Roosevelt and Churchill in February 1945 (Rabīʿ 1, 1364). In fact, ʿAbd al-ʿAzīz was a profound anti-Zionist, and we need a study of his attitude especially in and after the 1948 (1367) war. On this subject, Van der Meulen took a more internationally-oriented position, but he defended the Arab and in particular the Palestinian side.[19]

Van der Meulen does not give any information about Wahhābī influence in other Muslim countries, except a reference to Muhammad Rashīd Ridā's visit to ʿAbd al-ʿAzīz in 1926 in search of cooperation. The visit seems to have remained without much result.[20] From the perspective of Wahhābī Najd, to be Islamic, other countries had simply to follow the example of the Wahhābī state, but there was no call for a more general "Islamic revolution".

It is interesting to compare Van der Meulen's views with those of Philby, both men having a nearly unconditional attachment to the person of ʿAbd al-ʿAzīz and an admiration for the man's achievements. Philby started as a man of the British Empire and then switched to becoming a man of the Saudi state. In the end he may be called a rebel against the system from which he came. Van der Meulen, on the other hand, was a man who continued to work within the framework of a small country's colonial and diplomatic apparatus and remained rooted in a Dutch way of life. He was a critical realist within the system; he may be called a dissident at most in regard to colonial policies and customary ways of considering and judging Islam. Van der Meulen had the greatest respect for Philby as a scholar, celebrating his important geographical explorations through-

---

[18] See *The Wells of Ibn Saʿud*, Ch. 12, "The Arab League" (pp. 167–73).
[19] See *ibid.*, Ch. 11, "The Palestine Problem" (pp. 149–66) and *Don't You Hear the Thunder*, pp. 120–2 and 123–33.
[20] *The Wells of Ibn Saʿud*, p. 21.

out Arabia and especially in the Empty Quarter and drawing attention to
Philby's extensive writings, designed and collected and still waiting for
publication and further elaboration.[21] He considered the latter's *Arabian
Jubilee* of 1952 (1371), which provides a biography of ʿAbd al-ʿAzīz on
the occasion of his 50 years of rule, as a historical masterpiece. But he
found Philby's suggestion that they should both convert to Islam strange[22];
it showed that Philby had little feel for Van der Meulen's Calvinist
backbone. Van der Meulen judged Philby's conversion to Islam[23] nega-
tively, for whatever reasons, remarking: "If Philby had only been a
believer, he would not have needed to become a Muslim …"[24]. Philby, of
course, was a giant and there were never any other Westerners as close
to ʿAbd al-ʿAzīz. Yet Van der Meulen's characterization of him is worth
quoting.[25] Philby certainly was no easy character for either the Westerners or the Arabs to deal with.[26]

3. Daniel van der Meulen and King ʿAbd al-ʿAzīz

According to his publications, Van der Meulen met ʿAbd al-ʿAzīz on
several occasions. The first was a few weeks after his arrival at the
beginning of March 1926 (mid-Shaʿban 1344) in Jidda, where he and his
predecessor at the Jidda consulate, C. O. van der Plas, had a private
conversation with the king in Arabic, without interpreters. A year later,
in 1927 (1345), he again had a private conversation with him. The third
time, as I have noted, was mid-December 1944, in a gathering attended

---

[21] See in Dutch VAN DER MEULEN's memorial "Harry St John Bridger Philby, overleden te
      Beiroet op 30 September 1960 in de ouderdom van 75 jaar", *Tijdschrift van het
      Koninklijk Nederlands Aardrijkskundig Genootschap*, 78:2 (1961), pp. 167–71.
[22] *Don't You Hear the Thunder*, p. 95.
[23] The conversion took place in Mecca in the evening of August 7, 1930.
[24] *Ontwakend Arabië* (see above n. 14), p. 85.
[25] *The Wells of Ibn Saʿud*, pp. 83–5; *Ontwakend Arabië* (see above n. 14), pp. 77–8, 85.
      See the following note.
[26] VAN DER MEULEN contrasts Philby and ʿAbd al-ʿAzīz, suggesting Philby's limits: "… Once
      in the heart of the country he [i.e., Philby] met a man who was great because he dared
      to be himself, to stand alone and to struggle towards his goal believing in his vocation
      and in divine guidance. Philby was different, he did not go to Arabia because of a
      vocation and as he did not believe in God how could he believe in His guidance? …
          Philby is the greatest explorer Arabia has yet seen. Exploration was his real work,
      perhaps his original goal, and the work that will probably fill his life to his dying day.
      The human heart of Arabia and the profundities of her creed do not seem to have been
      disclosed to him. His hero was outspoken about that which mattered most for him, his
      faith. Even Philby must have seen that there was a reality, a source of strength and a
      means of guidance. But his books about Arabia do not reach beyond what is visible, what
      is measurable with instruments. He did not speak about that hidden treasure of Arabia,
      its spiritual wealth …" (*The Wells of Ibn Saʿud*, pp. 83–5; cf. *Ontwakend Arabië* [see
      above n. 14], pp. 77–8).

by his soldiers in the royal audience tent in Marat along the road from Riyadh to Jidda. The King then gave an emotional anti-Jewish speech on his way to meet Roosevelt and Churchill in Egypt, to plead with them for the Palestinian people against Zionist immigration and potential state formation.[27] The next meeting was after ʿAbd al-ʿAzīz's return from Egypt, where he had seen Roosevelt and Churchill, when his "success" was celebrated by the people, probably March 1945 (Rabiʿ 1 or 2, 1364). ʿAbd al-ʿAzīz told Van der Meulen what had happened. And the last time was on March 4, 1952 (17 Jumada II, 1372), in the King's palace in Riyadh at a reception for some prominent leaders of Aramco.[28] ʿAbd al-ʿAzīz passed away a year later, at the age of 73, if his birth date was 1880 as Van der Meulen assumed. In Van der Meulen's books and writings there are suggestions of other meetings and conversations with ʿAbd al-ʿAzīz, but I have not been able to locate them with precision.

On the other hand, there was a personal relation between the King's son Faisal and Van der Meulen. This goes back to a visit Prince Faisal paid to the Netherlands in October 1926 (Rabiʿ 1 or 2, 1345) to express his father's thanks for the country's recognition of his rule in the Hejaz after the taking of Jidda. Van der Meulen accompanied Faisal during these days and met him again later. Faisal visited the Netherlands again on official visits in 1927 (1346), May 1932 (Muharram 1351), and in 1935 (1354). Among Van der Meulen's papers are copies of two moving letters he wrote to the then King Faisal (r. 1964–75), dated September 21, 1966 (5 Jumada 2, 1386) and January 11, 1968 (10 Shawwal 1387). There is also the copy of a letter he wrote to King Fahd on October 5, 1982 (16 Dhu'l Hijja 1402).

In his personal notes about ʿAbd al-ʿAzīz, Van der Meulen makes some psychological observations that are worth mentioning. The King's father, ʿAbd al-Rahman Āl Saʿūd, who was an ʿālim and the Wahhābī Imām, had known many disappointments in life and put his faith in God alone. He educated his son in this sense, and this bore fruit.

ʿAbd al-ʿAzīz entertained friendly relations with Bahrain. As a boy he probably was attended by a Christian physician for his rheumatical fever. Later he kept confidence in the staff of the new American Christian hospital and kept in contact with these Christians.[29]

---

[27] *Ontwakend Arabië* (see above n. 14), pp. 113–22; *The Wells of Ibn Saʿud*, pp. 152–64; *Don't You Hear the Thunder*, p. 123.

[28] See *The Wells of Ibn Saʿud*, Ch. 16, "The Last Audience" (pp. 220–30).

[29] "There came a day when ʿAbd al-ʿAziz, the King Saʿud, was in urgent need of treatment for an affection of the throat. His private doctor, a young Syrian, realized that an operation was necessary but not being a surgeon did not dare to undertake the operation. It was then that the King thought of the medical mission that had been established in Bahrain by the Dutch Reformed Church of America and an urgent request for help was sent to the American doctors in Bahrain. Dr. Paul Harrison, who later told me the

On several occasions, Van der Meulen remarks that ʿAbd al-ʿAzīz felt himself to be an instrument of God's work, to be thrown aside when no longer of use. He had grown up in his religion and faith so that he lived with it, and when a given situation was against him, he would turn in faith against that situation and trust that it would be reversed.

Van der Meulen draws attention to other psychological features as well. Whereas nearly all Bedouin youth were caught up in internal tribal rivalries that imprisoned them in their little worlds, ʿAbd al-ʿAzīz had been with Mubārak Āl Sabāh in Kuwait when he was growing up. He had learned about the world outside Arabia and the way in which its forces were conditioning Arabian life. Few people were initiated as well into the intricate game of international politics.

He was a master in his dealings with the Bedouin, whom he knew well and whom he considered victims of their tribal divisions. Through his personal example and his eloquent speeches, he was able to mobilize these rather stubborn people. Once having mobilized them, he succeeded in submitting them to an extraordinary discipline nurtured by both ideology and religion and reinforced by his physical authority.

In his personal contacts, with his particular voice and a certain smile, ʿAbd al-ʿAzīz could easily win people for himself. This gift was noticed by several Westerners who happened to meet him. In turn, the King himself remarked that, notwithstanding the harsh way the British imposed their interests, in his dealings with them he had met some eminent individuals who had become his personal friends. Friendship was something of immense importance to him. Van der Meulen signals his utter straightforwardness, honesty, and trustworthiness—exceptional in Bedouin dealings with each other—and also a self-restraint and a patience rare in Bedouin life.

We have a striking description of the way in which ʿAbd al-ʿAzīz conducted his first conversation with Van der Meulen and Van der Plas in Jidda in March 1926. After the initial greetings, he started by saying that the West must have the impression that he was a brute; he wanted, however to impose security, tranquility, and justice in his realm. He did this with severe means and heavy punishments, but in the end this was better and certainly more effective among the Bedouin than the light punishments to which the West subjected its prisoners. The death penalty can be less cruel than long prison sentences. As far as the so-called

---

story, was soon on his way to the mainland. Having seen the King he, too, came to the conclusion that an immediate operation was necessary. 'I knew it,' the King said, 'and you may do it. But first say your prayer in your Christian way as I am told is your custom.' The relationship developed and Dr. Storm and Dr. Dame could, thanks to the King's initiative, make the first survey of health conditions in the outer provinces of the country, giving special attention to the incidence of leprosy" (*The Wells of Ibn Saʿud*, p. 41).

fanaticism of the Wahhābīs was concerned, ʿAbd al-ʿAzīz spoke about what he believed his task to be:

"You have doubtless also heard many stories about the fanaticism of the Wahhabis. It is good that you should know the truth about our creed and that of our brothers. We believe that Allah the Exalted One uses us as His instrument. As long as we serve Him we will succeed, no power can check us and no enemy will be able to kill us. Should we become a useless weapon in His hands then He will throw us aside, *wa sanahmiduhu*—and we shall praise Him."

His long sentences, full of ideas, were periodically broken off with "*Naʿam?*"—Yes?—meaning 'Do you follow me?' He spoke as a man of great conviction and concluded in a credo of short, terse remarks each of which was preceded by the words "We believe."

Ibn Saud impressed on us that whatever he was and whatever he did could be reduced to what he believed. His confession of faith was that of the Wahhabi. He seemed a quite different person from that of the fantastic tales that had come to us in Jedda from Najd. His creed was that of a Wahhabi who looked beyond the frontiers of his desert land, who had now come into contact with international Islam and who understood that he could only rule the Holy Land of Islam as the trustee of the world-embracing community of Muhammad.

He thought himself competent to do this and he felt the urge to formulate his task for himself and for others because by doing so his ideas became crystallized. I had to admit to being most impressed. Ibn Saud was the first Muslim who gave me a feeling of closeness to my own innermost convictions. Perhaps that was caused by his simple respect of and belief in divine guidance in his life, perhaps it was his inner urge to spare what was deepest of himself. He had the courage to lay bare before strangers the very foundation of his life. He was proud of his uncomplicated creed, sure that he held the truth and convinced that his hearers would at least respect him for it. And that we did.

This meeting was more than an official audience. For me it was like being admitted into another's sanctum sanctorum. My heart warmed to Ibn Saud and I could not help being moved. I knew that I had met a man who aroused expectations in me. This man would be a blessing to his land and to its tens of thousands of yearly visitors. I even cherished the hope that this would be the man to find for Islam the solution to its growing spiritual crisis. Whoever could have expected that from a Wahhabi from Najd![30]

---

[30] *The Wells of Ibn Saʿud*, pp. 100–1. See also *Don't You Hear the Thunder*, pp. 81–2. Cf. in Dutch *Ontwakend Arabië* (see above n. 14), pp. 95–6. VAN DER MEULEN concludes here by saying that it did him good to meet someone who could speak about his faith openly (p. 96).

Another striking discussion concerned the question whether Van der
Meulen could claim to be a real Christian and if he could visit Mecca. In
this connection, ʿAbd al-ʿAzīz made the significant remark that he had
rarely met a Westerner doing his best to live according to his religion.

> I remember that about a year after my arrival I had a private conversation
> with Ibn Saʿud and asked him his opinion on the question of the exclusion
> of Christians from Mecca and Medina. The King said to me: "Real
> Christians were allowed by the Prophet to be in Mecca."
>
> I was very astonished to hear so moderate a statement from the Wahhabi
> leader. Seizing my chance I said: "So Your Majesty would allow me to go
> to Mecca?"
>
> "I said real Christians. You don't pretend that you are one?"
>
> "I do try to be one."
>
> "Do you mean that you are doing what is written in your Book?"
>
> "I earnestly try to."
>
> "But you drink whisky, you play at cards, you dance with the wives of
> your colleagues?"
>
> "No, Your Majesty. I have no taste for those things."
>
> "Then I would have to allow you to come to Mecca."
>
> "That is what I hoped you would do."
>
> "But I am not going to give you my permission. If your colleagues heard
> that you had gone, they would insist on being given equal rights, and I
> would never want to have them in Mecca. Besides, my bedouin followers
> are unlearned fanatics. You would get into trouble with them and before
> I could help you, you might be killed."
>
> No Muslim, and certainly no Muslim leader, had ever before spoken
> to me like that.[31]

A third conversation is also worth reporting. ʿAbd al-ʿAzīz testified to his
faith sincerely and persuasively. When he finally stopped, Van der Meulen
looked at him, took a deep breath and said to him: "Your Majesty, I
respect your faith, which is strong. Do you also respect the faith which
I have? Do you allow me to speak to you about it?"[32] The text says the
following:

> When I, as the new Dutch Consul, had my first personal interview with
> Ibn Saud, who by then had assumed the title of King, I said that I wanted
> to tell him how much he had impressed me by his deep convictions. He
> seemed surprised. Then I asked him if he also respected my belief. He
> thought there was little difference between the two, both shared the same
> Prophets. I said that there was also a real difference. Did that mean that
> I believed in the Christian Holy Book? I said I did. But you don't live

---

[31] *The Wells of Ibn Saʿud*, p. 15.
[32] Oral communication from Dr. Helene van der Meulen-Duhm, May 9, 1998.

according to its rules? I said that I earnestly tried to follow its precepts. He then said that I was the first diplomat from the West to tell him that he believed and obeyed his Book.

My colleagues did not agree with this approach, but I think that the course of my future dealings with Ibn Saud proved me to be right. Ibn Saud trusted me ... .[33]

Such reports indicate that ʿAbd al-ʿAzīz himself was engaging with a Christian in a conversation that in the end became an interfaith dialogue that he obviously enjoyed. Unlike so many descriptions of Wahhābī doctrine and way of life, this was not a presentation or defense of a closed system by specialists but was subject to open interrogation and questioning. And if the ruler himself was able to engage in dialogue with people of another faith, what about his subjects?

On the other hand, the King could put up a stubborn defense of the Qurʾān. A debate was reported between Philby and ʿAbd al-ʿAzīz about the shape of the earth. And whereas the first presented scientific arguments that the earth is a ball, the second stubbornly maintained that the earth is flat, because the Qurʾān says so.[34]

His admiration for ʿAbd al-ʿAzīz notwithstanding, Van der Meulen was also aware of the King's limitations. At the end of *The Wells of Ibn Saʿud*, when referring to his last visit to the King, who died the following year, he expresses regrets that, in the final years of his rule, he had not better prepared for what would come after him.[35] In fact, he could have abdicated in time and been able to train and advise his successor, so as to ensure continuity in the way the country was ruled. Or, since he had unlimited power, he could have taken measures to reform the state institutions and guarantee an administration less dependent on the King. Actually, he was the only one in a position to impose limits on the existing family privileges and to separate family affairs from the institutions and the interests of the state. But he did not do so. Van der Meulen also holds that ʿAbd al-ʿAzīz lacked what he calls the prophetic courage to see and face the real problems of the world of Islam of his time. Instead, he focused on his own country while opening the road to modernization, without any broader "prophetic" vision of the world of Islam as a whole.

---

[33] *Don't You Hear the Thunder*, p. 83.

[34] *The Wells of Ibn Saʿud*, p. 112.

[35] See *The Wells of Ibn Saʿud*, Ch. 19, "Ibn Saʿud's Inheritance" (pp. 247–58). Cf. Ch. 14, "The Americans in Arabia" (pp. 185–202), and Ch. 15, "Agriculture and Water" (pp. 203–19). Cf. in Dutch *Ontwakend Arabië* (see above n. 14), the Introduction (pp. 9–18) and Chs. 11 and 12 (pp. 143–72). Shortly before his death, ʿAbd al-ʿAzīz established on paper the institution of a Council of Ministers in October 1953 (Safar 1373). Probably he was convinced that it was only through his personal absolute power that the Bedouin tribes had been brought and held together and that the unity of Saudi Arabia had been possible.

In the last analysis, ʿAbd al-ʿAzīz, as Van der Meulen sees it, was the last representative of a by-gone era. What brought essential changes to the country was not his puritan Islam, but simply the arrival of oil money and the country's entry into the capitalist system.

Van der Meulen hails ʿAbd al-ʿAzīz as a great statesman, on the pattern of a Bedouin ruler, but not as a spiritual leader. However, Van der Meulen thinks that, for the sake of the country, he should have been both at the same time. At given points and for specific problems, ʿAbd al-ʿAzīz could go beyond existing traditions and advocate the acceptance of modern solutions. However, the *fuqahāʾ* and the *Sharīʿa* as tradition interpreted it weighed heavily on his rule.

In sum, given the conditions in Arabia at the time, Van der Meulen estimates that ʿAbd al-ʿAzīz was a born leader as well as a staunch believer in the tasks God had put upon him. Historically speaking, with ʿAbd al-ʿAzīz, Arabia had the last chances to reform religion before oil modernity entered the country.[36]

4. Conclusion

As in the history of other countries and societies, so also in that of Saudi Arabia, the writings of competent observers can be extremely useful as a complement to the official documentary sources. This is particularly the case for those great historical movements, struggles, and revolutions including entire populations and witnessed by only a few visitors from outside. In using their reports, one should know, of course, as in all history writing, where their particular sympathies lay, what they were able to see, and what they ignored. One should also know more about their overall personality, including the loyalties, values, and causes they personally adhered to.

In the case of the rise of Saudi Arabia as established in 1932 (1351), and of the role of ʿAbd al-ʿAzīz from 1901 (1318) on, the number of such visitors from outside was very small. Until World War One, there were no Westerners in his company, apart from some American medical friends from Bahrain, who visited him in Riyadh. And from World War One on, those Westerners who arrived on the Arabian scene were nearly always in the service of foreign governments. They fulfilled their political or diplomatic tasks but nearly always lacked any elementary knowledge of the people, the culture, and the religion of the country. During World War One there were two exceptions. T. E. Lawrence was sent to the Hejaz, identified with the Arab cause, and supported the Hashemites, in particular Faisal, the future King of Iraq, in British policy-making. He

---

[36]   *Ontwakend Arabië* (see above n. 14), p. 18.

finally failed. St. John Philby was sent to Najd, was taken up as a personal friend by ʿAbd al-ʿAzīz, and supported the Saʿūdī cause in British policy-making. He finally won.

The case of Philby as an observer of the rise of Saudi Arabia is extremely interesting in that his sympathies even led him to shift his support from the British Empire to ʿAbd al-ʿAzīz and his state, to change his religion accordingly, and to embrace Islam in its Wahhābī form. Philby identified with the Saʿūdī cause as he saw it. His life, including his participation in the Saʿūdī venture and his relations with ʿAbd al-ʿAzīz, have been analyzed by Elisabeth Monroe in her book *Philby of Arabia* (1973) and need not detain us here.

If Lawrence and Philby were British, represented a world empire, and appeared on the scene in wartime, the Dutchman Van der Meulen, of a following generation, arrived some ten years later to take care of Indo-nesian Muslims in the port of Jidda. Unlike his British predecessors, he did not represent a powerful country, he was not a scholar, and his studies in Leiden had been practically oriented. He arrived at a moment when the game was over in Arabia. The wars belonged to the past. Unlike the two others, Van der Meulen was a conscious Christian who did not hide that fact from his Muslim counterparts, whom he approached as people who had their faith as he had his. Remaining rooted in his Dutch values and way of life and in his Protestant religion, he did not identify with either the Saʿūdī or the Islamic cause. But being a person of faith himself, he could see ʿAbd al-ʿAzīz also as a person of faith, though a slightly different one, and between the two a kind of dialogue could arise on this basis. This was apparently exceptional among Westerners who met ʿAbd al-ʿAzīz.

Van der Meulen's accounts of Saudi Arabia and its ruler at the time are valuable not only because of the accuracy and precision of his observations, including his photographs, but also because he put his perceptions within a broader framework. This was the framework of Islam as he had learned about it in his own studies, from Christian friends, and through his experience as a civil servant in Muslim countries. Exceptionally in his time, he valued Islam positively as a faith but hoped for reorientations in its rules so that it would open up to the problems of the modern world. Again as an exception, he was open to practical cooperation and dialogue with Indonesians, Arabs, and others who crossed his path.[37]

---

[37] This could also lead to unexpected situations, such as that singular meeting with a Muslim boy who wanted to see him become a Muslim. See *Don't You Hear the Thunder*, pp. 87–8. Van der Meulen participated in several meetings between Christians and Muslims, such as in Bhamdoun in Lebanon (1954 and 1956) and in Toumliline in Morocco in the late 1950s and early 1960s.

Van der Meulen was neither an anthropologist nor a historian. He had a good deal of common sense and could narrate past or contemporary history as an experienced witness. What he told or wrote had gone through the filter of his own experience and thus taken on a personal character. Certain things, for whatever reason, struck him more than others, and he told about them with sympathy. He was inclined to leave out unpleasant things and he was remarkably careful in his reporting of situations in which he had not been present himself. In a way, his diaries were a way not only of fixing but also of retelling and reflecting what had happened and in this way digesting it. He looked up to men endowed with qualities of leadership, and they sometimes had a nearly absolute authority for him. This was certainly the case with his attitude toward Snouck Hurgronje and probably also to ʿAbd al-ʿAzīz; both of them he admired greatly. In his conversations he could take up a clear position, but he let other people talk and listened to them. He had a remarkable ability to narrate and he could fascinate others by reporting about his experiences in far-away countries. One may call him a man of experience, convictions, human communication, and a profound humanity.

On the one hand, there is reason to take Van der Meulen's observations seriously. He not only had a critical sense of reality and an openness to people, but also a quite independent and even critical mind while working in the Foreign Service when he was in Arabia and in the colonial Civil Service when he was in Indonesia. In Arabic and knowledge of Arab life, he had a rare expertise that was strengthened by personal experience. He was extremely careful in his judgment about things Arabic.

On the other hand, in his accounts of the Saudi state, Van der Meulen also had his limitations. He had no sociological training and was not well able to analyze the processes going on in Arabian society at the time, the internal mechanisms of the state, or the concentration of privileges in the hands of the few. He nowhere speaks with any precision about the relations between ʿAbd al-ʿAzīz and the religious leaders or institutions or about institutional developments in the country. There is no indication that he wanted to see another type of state; in his view, a prophetic religion should quite naturally put its imprint on social and political life. His own kind of Christian faith gave him openness to the Islamic faith. He then saw things Islamic within the parameters of his own religious views and of his particular view of Islam as a religion. But is that avoidable?

On balance, however, Van der Meulen's observations and experiences as expressed in his personal and published writings are worthwhile. They can help us to understand better certain less-known aspects of King ʿAbd al-ʿAzīz, the rise of Saudi Arabia, and its first confrontations with modernity.

Selected Literature

Almana, Mohammed, *Arabia Unified: A Portrait of Ibn Saud*, London: Hutchinson Beham, 1980.

Armstrong, Harold Courtenay, *Lord of Arabia, Ibn Saud*, London: A. Barker, 1934.

Goldrup, Lawrence Paul, *Saudi Arabia: 1902–1932. The Development of a Wahhabi Society*, Ph.D. Dissertation, UCLA, 1971.

Habib, John S., *Ibn Saud's Warriors of Islam: The Ikhwān of Najd in the Creation of the Saudi Kingdom, 1910–1930*, Leiden: E. J. Brill, 1978.

Howarth, David Armine, *The Desert King: A Life of Ibn Saud*, London: Collins, 1964.

Meulen, Daniel van der, "Hadramaut", *National Geographic Magazine*, October 1932.

—, "Crisis in the World of Islam", *The Moslem World*, 26 (1936), pp. 337–57.

—, "The Mecca Pilgrimage", *The Moslem World*, 28 (1939), pp. 210–1.

—, *Aden to the Hadhramaut: A Journey in South Arabia*, London: John Murray, 1947.

—, *The Wells of Ibn Saʿud*, London: John Murray, 1957.

—, *Faces in Shem*, London: John Murray, 1961.

—, *Don't You Hear the Thunder? A Dutchman's Life Story*, Leiden: E. J. Brill, 1981.

—, and Hermann von Wissmann, *Hadramaut: Some of its Mysteries Unveiled*, Leiden: E. J. Brill, 1932 (Repr. 1964).

Monroe, Elizabeth, *Philby of Arabia*, London: Faber and Faber, 1973.

Pfullmann, Uwe, *Thronfolge in Saudi-Arabien: Wahhabitische Familienpolitik von 1744 bis 1953* (Zentrum Moderner Orient, Arbeitshefte Nr. 13), Berlin: Das Arabische Buch, 1997.

Philby, Harry St. John Bridger, *Report on Najd Mission 1917–1918*, Baghdad: Gvt Press, 1918.

—, *Southern Najd: Journey to Kharj, Aflaj, etc. 1918*, Cairo: Gvt Press, 1919.

—, *Arabia of the Wahhabis*, London: Constable, 1928.

—, *Arabia*, London: Benn, 1930.

—, *A Pilgrim in Arabia*, limited ed. 1943, London: Hale, 1946.

—, *Arabian Days*, London: Hale, 1948.

—, *Arabian Jubilee*, London: Hale, 1952.

—, *Saudi Arabia*, London: Benn, 1955.

—, *Forty Years in the Wilderness*, London: Hale, 1957.

Rihani, Ameen, *Ibn Saʿoud of Arabia: His People and his Land*, London: Constable, 1928 (Repr. Delmar, N.Y.: Caravan Books, 1938). This book appeared in the USA under the title *Maker of Modern Arabia*, Boston: Houghton Miflin, 1928.

Schacht, Joseph, "Zur Wahhābītischen Literatur", *Zeitschrift für Semitistik und verwandte Gebiete*, 6 (1928), pp. 200–12.

Wahba, Shaikh Hafiz, "Wahhabism in Arabia: Past and present", *Journal of the Royal Central Asian Society*, 16 (1929), pp. 458–67.

—, *Arabian Days*, London: Barker, 1964.

Williams, Kenneth, *Ibn Saud: The Puritan King of Arabia*, London: J. Cape, 1933.

Section 7

Islamic Reform and Intellectual Reflection

Chapter 13
Tsarist Russia and the Dutch East Indies[1]

Muslim reform movements have been the subject of scholarly research for some time. Studies have been devoted to the stricter reform movements like those of the Wahhābīs[2], Shehu Usuman Dan Fodio, and the Sanūsīs, and many more to the modern reform movements in countries like India and Egypt, North Africa, Iran, and of course Ottoman and Republican Turkey.[3] Less attention has been paid, however, to movements that have occurred on the periphery of the Muslim world, partly because direct sources for some of these regions are or have been relatively inaccessible. The aim of this chapter is to demonstrate that there were important reform movements in Tsarist Russia from the middle of the nineteenth century on and in the Dutch East Indies from the beginning of the twentieth century on and that these movements can be usefully compared.

Future historians, when dealing with Islamic studies as they developed during the twentieth century, will probably be keen to show how much these studies have been influenced by ideological bias at the time. Not only twentieth-century Muslims have ideologized Islam: Western researchers, too, have been liable to take positions that could not be justified by scholarly research alone. Since George Antonius[4] and others, we tend to connect the awakening of Muslim societies primarily with rising political resistance to the West, and since H. A. R. Gibb we are inclined to interpret the awakening of Muslim minds primarily in terms of new interpretations of Islam.

As a result, we run the risk of reading back into what took place before World War One and even World War Two much of the ideological movements of nationalism and Islamism that have established their

---

[1] Revised text of a paper published under the title "Muslim Enlightenment and Revitalization: Movements of Modernization and Reform in Tsarist Russia (ca. 1850–1971) and the Dutch East Indies (ca. 1900–1942)", *Die Welt des Islam*, New Series 28 (1988), pp. 569–84.

[2] Cf. above Chapter 11 on "The Wahhābīs in Eighteenth and Nineteenth Century Arabia".

[3] Cf. above Chapter 5 on "Official, Popular, and Normative Religion in Islam".

[4] *The Arab Awakening: The Story of the Arab National Movement*, Beirut: Khayats, 1938 (Repr. London: Hamilton, 1945; 7th imprint New York: Capricorn Books, 1965).

grasp on both Muslim and Western minds during the last fifty years. Present-day ideological concerns can very well prevent us, first, from accurately observing the facts of what really went on earlier, and, second, from offering adequate interpretations of these facts and explaining what took place in Muslim societies at the time.

Islamicists concentrate professionally on Islam; on closer consideration, however, the Muslim awakening before World War One did not concentrate primarily on what Islam was like. It rather seems to have been a growing awareness of the sad condition in which Muslims and Muslim societies found themselves, especially when compared to the West, and of the obvious fact that this poor condition was not up to the norms and ideals of Islam. It was only in part with the help of the notion of Islam and the values and norms they derived from it that Muslim thinkers became aware of this condition and looked for ways to improve it. In this case they referred explicitly to Islam when formulating a new world view and life orientation or when suggesting new ways of action.

If some Islamicists tended to be fascinated by Islam (whatever the ways they perceived it), historical research on the nineteenth- and early twentieth-century Muslim awakening must avoid fascinations. Such research must be cleared as much as possible of ideological biases, and certainly of any ideologization of Islam, whether in the form of taking it as an entity in itself or, on the contrary, of explaining away Islamic qualities by the working of infrastructural factors and overlooking human responses to the latter.

The following data are taken from some peripheral Muslim societies that we do not tend to identify with "Islam" as much as we do the heartlands of Islam, in particular in general studies of Islamic religion and civilization. Studying Muslim societies in Tsarist Russia and the Dutch East Indies and paying attention to modern reform movements may shed some light on how we should study phenomena of Muslim reawakening and enlightenment at all without preconceived negative or positive ideological frameworks. It may also make us aware of the immensity of the task of dealing with the modern and contemporary history of a world religion like Islam. And it may make us aware of our limitations in going beyond the external facts of history to the intentions of the people who made or underwent it and responded to it.

Apart from such methodological concerns, we may also find some features common to modern reform movements in regions that, as far as I know, had no historical contact with each other. There may be resemblances between the visionary leaders who tried to emancipate so many Muslims from seemingly fixed patterns and traditions. Even some common problems of policy toward Islam may show up among Russian and Dutch policy makers and administrators. And perhaps our inquiry may be able to conclude something about certain preconditions for the liberal reform movements described here.

1. The Scene

In each region, Muslims were and are dispersed over very different areas and belong to different ethnic groups. Communications existed overland within Russia and by sea between the Indonesian islands, but in both cases the distances were huge and in practice prevented Muslims from constituting one coherent entity. In each region, one imperial power acquired political authority, be it sometimes after considerable military efforts. Once established, however, other imperial powers did not challenge this authority.

In the case of Russia, we are dealing with centuries of *reconquista* and then *conquista*, eastward against Turkic peoples who had occupied Russian territories in medieval times and southward beyond the Caucasus mountains. Here the conquest was, beyond taking power, also a kind of ideological response to the Tatars and other Turkic peoples who happened to be Muslims. Attempts, mostly unsuccessful, were made to suppress Islamic institutions among the Tatars up to the middle of the eighteenth century.

The Netherlands' imperial drive seems to have been less historically and ideologically determined. Infinitely smaller than Russia and situated on the other side of the globe, she embarked on expansion primarily for economic reasons. Muslims had never occupied Holland, and when the Dutch arrived in Indonesia in the sixteenth century, the peoples there were just in the process of being islamicized. Local Muslim sultans, however, were often seen as political rivals. When the islands were subjected to Dutch power in the nineteenth century, there were rebellions and resistance under the banner of Islam. The Dutch subsequently tended to identify "Islam" as a political force opposed to Dutch authority and thus undermining the *Pax Neerlandica*. The Dutch colonialists had a characteristic fear of uprisings under the banner of Islam, Islamic influences from abroad brought by returning *hajjis*, and what was called the danger of pan-Islam.

1.1. The Colonial Presence

The Muslim regions of Tsarist Russia were in part simply Russian territory; this is clearly the case with the regions inhabited by the Crimean and Volga Tatars. Regions further away were treated as colonies, like Kazakhstan, Azerbaijan, and later Turkestan. The Russians carried out an immense colonization policy, Russian and Ukrainian farmers swarming out to settle in the newly conquered areas and to appropriate the soil.

The Muslim regions of the Dutch East Indies, on the other hand, were simply colonies, mostly under indirect rule. Apart from the owners and administrators of plantations for tobacco, coffee, sugar, tea, and other tropical products, there were not many Dutchmen who actually settled in the country. Most of the Dutchmen came to trade and supervise the local labor force working on the plantations; they never engaged in that bitter struggle for land that has characterized so many Western intrusions into the Third World.

In both cases, economic penetration advanced with the years, and the local economy became more and more tuned toward producing raw materials for Russian and Dutch industry and becoming a market for industrial products of the imperial countries. Whereas industrialization in Indonesia was relatively rare and connected with oil or specific minerals like tin, heavy industry already developed around Baku from the 1870s on and the Tatars played an important role in trade and also in the establishment of industry in their own regions and beyond. Within the Russian empire, the Tatars were middlemen between Russians and the other Muslim peoples, and they attained great financial and economic influence. In Indonesia, the Chinese played this role of middlemen, especially in trade, but since they were not Muslims, they had hardly any impact on Muslim movements except insofar as Indonesian Muslims were sometimes forced to organize themselves to withstand Chinese economic power.

Influences from abroad came from different kinds of foreign Muslims in the two cases. For the Russian Turkic peoples and the Tatars in particular, the Ottoman empire was extremely important. In the series of Russo-Turkish wars, the Muslims in Russia stood behind the government, but there were continuous contacts between Crimean and Volga Tatars on the one hand and Turkish circles in Istanbul on the other. Turkey represented both a cultural and a religious support for the causes the Tatars defended, and if needed Muslims from Russia could always find refuge in Ottoman Turkey with their ethnic and religious brethren. They also had contacts in Egypt.

Compared to this, Indonesian Muslims were in a perilous state. Great ethnic heterogeneity prevailed, with different cultures existing even on one and the same island, and without a powerful Muslim nation nearby to which appeals for protection could be addressed. For moral support, the Indonesian Muslims had to go to Mecca, and this they did; the *hajjis* probably played a more important role in maintaining links with international Islam than did the Ottoman Turkish consul in Batavia. Besides contact with the Holy Places of Islam, Indonesians were also in touch with al-Azhar and the reformist movement in Cairo, with its publication *al-Manār*, and, through the Hadramauti immigrants, with the southern part of the Arabian peninsula. The number of Indonesians studying in Istanbul or going to India appears to have been very small.

In social intercourse, the Russian scene before World War One had some positive features. Tatars could live and find employment in Russian cities, and those who had studied at Russian schools and universities or who had influential economic positions seem really to have been part of Russian society. The same was apparently the case with the Azeris.

In Indonesia, the distance between the Dutch and the local population, including the nobility and the younger intelligentsia, appears to have been great. Children of mixed marriages or liaisons were more or less *déclassés*, with much depending on the father's attitude. Christiaan Snouck Hurgronje[5] had to keep his private life and religious allegiance secret to move freely in higher Dutch circles in the Indies and later the Netherlands.

Both Russia and the Netherlands had cultural policies based on the superiority of Western culture, which was accessible only to a small non-Western elite that had received extensive Russian or Dutch schooling and training. Adaptations were made to accommodate Islam as the religion of the governed people, but local Muslim culture automatically fell back to second place with the arrival of the economic and political system of the West.

Russian and Dutch policy makers and the governed populations themselves tended to equate the polarity between colonizers and colonized with that between Christians—or at least "cultural" Christians—on the one hand and Muslims on the other. In both cases, it should be stressed, the local population, Muslim or otherwise, was poorly represented and in fact could not exercise any real political power, Indonesian regents and nominal sultans often having chosen to support the established rule. In democratic terms, the representation of Muslims in the various *Dumas* after 1905 and in the *Volksraad* after 1919 was ridiculous, the imperial governments doing everything possible to prevent parliamentary representation at all or to nullify its effect.

1.2. Muslim Responses

And what was the Islamic scene like? Both regions, of course, had very traditional forms of Islam. In Russia, these were combined with features of Turkic culture, for instance shamanistic forms of religious expression and customs of Turkic family life from nomadic times. In Indonesia, they were combined with forms of local non-literate religions, often of an animistic type, but also with continuing traditions of Hindu and Buddhist culture. The latter existed especially in the court cultures of Java and Bali. Various *turuq* were active in both regions.

In Russia, we find an elaborate organizational network and even a certain centralization of the Muslim institutions set up by the Russians

---

5   Cf. above Chapter 12 on "Saudi Arabia: The King and the Consul".

after 1788. The muftiat of Orenburg, later Ufa, to which other muftiats were later added, was hierarchically organized and enabled the imperial power to be informed about *madrasas*[6], Koran schools, *Sharī'a* courts[7], *mollahs*, and the financial affairs of its Muslim subjects, and also to influence these Muslim institutions, if only on the level of the appointments of higher Muslim officials. But the Russian government seldom interfered directly with the local Muslim institutions and communities.

The Dutch East Indies had no such centralized system of administrative organization. Local religious leaders, *sheykhs*, *'ulamā'* and their institutions enjoyed a certain autonomy. But the Dutch government distrusted things Islamic and increasingly gathered information about Muslim institutions and activities. This happened through the Office for Native Affairs established at the beginning of the twentieth century in Batavia and known among Indonesians as *Kantor Agama* or "Religious Affairs Bureau". Numerous measures were introduced relating to teachers and educational programs at Muslim schools as well as to the trustworthiness of Muslim leaders. In practice, this meant that the government directly interfered with Muslim affairs at the grass-roots level.

It was in these two very different settings of Russia and the Dutch Indies, ruled by a Tsar and a Queen, that intellectual movements of modernization and reform among Muslims arose in the last quarter of the nineteenth century and the beginning of the twentieth century respectively. We shall look here first at the differences and then at the common features in the development of these movements among Muslims under Russian and Dutch rule.

2. Russia and Indonesia: Differences

Apart from the organizational network supporting traditional Muslim learning, Russia distinguished itself from Indonesia through the existence of Islamic centers of religious learning, the best-known of which was Kazan. Here a sound knowledge of the religious sciences of Islam could be acquired, and *madrasas* outside such centers guaranteed the spread and knowledge of what may be called normative Islam, inculcating a good knowledge of Arabic. Those who wanted to pursue Islamic studies on a still higher level would go to Bukhara, the capital of the independent Emirate of Bukhara in present-day Uzbekistan, which was known not only for its level of learning and Sunnī orthodoxy, but also for its political despotism, even after it had become a protectorate of Russia in 1868.

---

6   M. Mobin Shorish, "Traditional Islamic Education in Central Asia Prior to 1917", in *Passé Turco-Tatar, Présent soviétique*, pp. 317–43.

7   D. S. M. Williams, "Native Courts in Tsarist Central Asia", *Central Asian Review*, 14 (1966), pp. 6–19.

The intellectual "new method" (*Jadīd*) movement of modernization and reform among the Muslims of Russia, in particular the Tatars, arose to a great extent as a protest against the traditional teaching methods and programs current in these centers. For this reason, and as a response to the influence of secular thought current among the nineteenth-century Russian intelligentsia (which itself is a Russian word), the modernization and reform movement among Muslims in Russia had a clearly intellectual character. The great number of journals and other periodicals through which modern ideas were expressed, again principally by Tatar modernists and reformists, bear witness to this.

A second feature of these movements in Russia was the continuous discussions and debates about the language to be used in the modern Muslim schools of the *Jadīd* type. Some wanted it to be the written Tatar language, which had been adapted to modern intellectual expression. Others preferred Ottoman Turkish, which was cultivated in the Ottoman Empire and had a considerable literature. Others again pleaded for other solutions in which other Turkic languages—like Azeri and Kazakh— would also take part.

A third feature was the growing openness of Tatar intellectuals to Russian thought and culture, which however did not lead them to deny the properly Muslim and Turkic values of their own heritage. They studied at Russian schools and universities and were in close contact with groups of contemporary Russian intellectuals who had an interest in the various cultures existing within the empire.

In Indonesia the situation was different. The widespread schooling system was that of the *pesantrens* which taught not so much normative Islam as an Islam impregnated with Ibn al-ʿArabī's mysticism and illumination, incorporating elements of monistic contemplation. In Indonesia there were no strongholds of Sunnī Islamic learning: for these, Indonesian students had to go to Mecca or Cairo. The Indonesian Muslim leaders probably knew Arabic less well than the Tatars, partly because Indonesia was even more on the periphery of Islam than the Tatar regions and Central Asia, which had, after all, been a center of Islamic culture and learning for centuries. For Indonesian Muslims, Malay was the evident Muslim language; this dated back to the time when conversion to Islam implied openness to Malay trade and acceptance of the Malay language. The inspiration of the Indonesian modernization and reform movements, then, was less intellectual and more educational and social. These movements arose in various places, sometimes continuing movements that already existed in the nineteenth century.[8] They presented an Islam more

---

[8]   For nineteenth-century movements in Indonesian Islam, see Karel A. STEENBRINK, *Beberapa aspek tentang Islam di Indonesia abad ke-19*, Jakarta: Bulan Bintang, 1984.

based on Qur'ān and *Sunna* and proposed reforms in the way of life to serve the well-being of the people. In these movements we also find interest in improving the situation of women.

The Muslim movements in Indonesia all took the form of organized associations conforming to the demands of Dutch law; these associations had to be recognized by the government in order to pursue their activities legally. Predominantly cultural and predominantly political associations—and later parties—arose side by side, although cultural associations generally appeared first. Contact with Dutch intellectual life was rare. This was in part because many more Protestant and Catholic missionaries than "intellectuals" came from the Netherlands to the Indies. Only a relatively small number of Indonesian students found their way to the Netherlands, where critical intellectual life was different from what could be found in Russia at the time, anyway.

Islam on Java contained not only remnants of older animistic religion but also spiritual orientations of Hindu and Buddhist origin, together with Islamic mystical doctrines in the line of Ibn al-'Arabī. This gave Indonesian Islam as a whole a spiritual dimension that was different from Russian Islamic spirituality, which was nourished in particular by the Naqshbandī *tarīqa*. Thus while there were more strict reformers going back to Qur'ān and *Sunna*, there were also spiritual reformers who combined the tenets of Islam with a monistic inspiration that had its own intellectual and spiritual variants.

3. Russia and Indonesia: Common Features

Notwithstanding the differences indicated, the histories of the movements of modernization and reform in Russia and in Indonesia basically show the same pattern. The first stage was to focus on educational matters as a requirement for change and development and as an expression of concerns of the mind. The existing Qur'ān schools, *madrasas*, and *pesantrens* were viewed as failing to impart a knowledge conforming to the demands of the time, and this was a suffocating experience: several Muslim reformers mentioned this explicitly. Consequently, they set out either to reform existing schools or to create schools of a new, modern type that would convey the norms and values of Islam to contemporary and future generations, while offering modern programs. Ismail Bey Gasprinskii (1851–1914) is representative of this type, giving an impulse to the *Jadīd* movement. In Indonesia one merely has to think of the Minangkabau and Javanese school reformers. Kijahi Hadji Ahmad Dahlan (Muhammad Darwis, 1868–1923), the founder of the *Muhammadīya* Movement in 1912, moved by religious ritual and practical concerns, also had an open eye for educational problems. In both regions, the desire for better education was, of course, stimulated by the presence of Russians and Dutch whose very domination proved the adage that knowledge is power.

In a second stage, political issues attracted more attention. Sometimes this evolved naturally from cultural concerns, sometimes it identified itself explicitly as a reaction to them. Here the leaders no longer acquiesced in foreign rule but sought an independence beyond cultural and educational autonomy. But one cannot yet characterize the *Sarekat Islam*, founded on Java in 1911, as a fully-fledged national independence movement. Islam remained here the common bond among those who arose to oppose foreign rule. Only later did a clear separation between "religiously neutral" and "Muslim" nationalists appear, as in the rivalry between Sukarno's *Partai Nasional Indonesia*, founded in 1927, and the *Partai Sarekat Islam* just mentioned. In this second stage, leftist politically-oriented Muslim movements, which often practically renounced Islam separated from those that committed themselves to social justice within an Islamic framework. The split between Indonesian communists and the *Sarekat Islam* in 1922 is an example of such a conflict; the year 1917 saw similar problems in Petrograd, which had their follow-up in the following years in the USSR. The question of collaboration with non-Muslims and of working together within a neutral political framework was an urgent one.

In a third stage, the various cultural and political movements of modernization and reform felt a kind of ecumenical urge and necessity to come together. Muslim congresses were held in Russia in 1905, 1906, and 1917. In Indonesia we find the *Al-Islam* congresses of the 1920s, the formation of the *Madjlis Islam A'laa Indonesia* in 1937, and its *Al-Islam* congresses of 1938, 1939, and 1941. In the 1930s, a kind of consensus arose expressing a common critical attitude to the Dutch government and demanding more political autonomy, if not independence.

In the two cases studied, this third stage came to an abrupt end: in Russia, with the revolution of October 1917; in Indonesia, with the Japanese occupation of February 1942. The final results were opposite: the establishment of an atheist state, in the one case, and that of a state based on the religious principles of the *Pancasila*, in the other.

Besides this similarity in the movements' course of development, there is also a marked similarity among those who played a part in this process. The leaders emerging at the beginning of the modernizing reforms in the Muslim regions of Russia and in Indonesia are cultural heroes, as it were, precisely because they did not yet possess that lust for power that characterized later politicians who became fighters. These persons were learned leaders, inspired by a paternal attitude to their often uneducated people, and themselves respecting the established order; perhaps this allowed them to concentrate on educational and cultural issues. They did not lack contact with Russian and Dutch intellectual figures who, although not Muslims themselves, may even have inspired and supported them.

The political personalities of the second stage also had their Western counterparts, but these—if they held official positions—now formed a common front against them. Yet even then negotiation was possible, except where political relations had broken down, as in the *Hijra* policy of the *Partai Sarekat Islam* from 1922 on. In the third stage, the Muslim leaders discussed among themselves and presented the resulting demands to the ruling authorities.

It would be important to trace both the negative and positive aspects of Western rule in the rise and development of Muslim movements of modernization and reform in Russia and Indonesia and elsewhere. The role that certain Western personalities, including scholars and teachers, administrators and missionaries, intellectuals and artists, played in the process deserves further attention.

4. The Study of Movements of Modernization and Reform

Our comparison and contrasting of movements of modernization and reform in Tsarist Russia and the Dutch East Indies suggests some general conclusions.

First, it is difficult and sometimes impossible to establish exactly the historical beginnings of such movements. Most accounts concentrate on some prominent personalities who took decisive initiatives at a certain moment. But the sources tell us little about the upbringing, the intellectual education and the spiritual growth of these persons. Yet the social milieu in which they grew up must have contained both the infrastructural conditions and particular seeds of tradition that could lead to an awakening and a view of the future.

A number of such movements arose in conditions of oppression. Protests against moral decay and the slackening of the truths of religion nearly always hold the current political, economic, and religious leadership responsible for this state of affairs. It is not so much that they had much power, but rather that they did not use it in the right ways that provoked reprobation. Many of these movements arose either under Muslim political authorities who perpetrated manifest forms of injustice or under domination or rule or the threat of such domination or rule by a non-Muslim political authority.

The movements of modernization and reform distinguished themselves from other movements at the time: armed revolts, militant activism, and movements of nostalgic restoration or mystical interiorization. They had a rational outlook and moral concern, combined with a thirst for further schooling and the development of intellectual capacities in view of the future. All of these movements gave high priority to educational reforms and education generally, and they can be seen as movements of enlightenment and emancipation.

Such movements of social and intellectual, cultural and educational modernization and reform, however, seem able to develop only under a benevolent, enlightened political authority, local or foreign, that is willing to support and promote their objectives directly or indirectly. To focus on cultural and religious, intellectual and educational issues, they also need a certain freedom from excessive economic pressures. Several of these movements defended common Muslim economic interests as a *sine qua non* for political independence.

Until now, most scholars have stressed the importance of Western influences on the rise and development of movements of modernization and reform. Of course, without the existing challenges and examples from the West, it is hard to imagine that such movements could have developed as they did. But the inspiration and the very intention of these movements, as far as they considered themselves as Islamic, cannot be explained by sheer imitation. Whenever a real imitation and emulation of the Western example occurred, the Islamic quality of the movement receded into the background. The result was practically an assimilation of Western standards by its members and a dissolution of the movement.

I suggest that, in the properly Muslim movements, Western influences were rather of an indirect nature. We have to do here with an original take-off of movements that had a Muslim identity, whatever their aims and the strategies they adopted to achieve them. It is my guess that certain Western liberal attitudes toward Islam as a religion and culture—which implied confidence in the potential of Muslims to help and develop themselves—indirectly had a beneficial effect on the development of movements of modernization and reform. Oppressive and contemptuous Western attitudes, by contrast, led to resistance and strife. Enlightenment movements presuppose communication and the use of reason.

The movements of modernization and reform primarily addressed the traditional ways of life and structures that, immobilized through sacralizations and fixed rules, stood in the way of change and development, not to mention emancipation. The leaders of these movements saw the *'ulamā'* and *sheykhs* as their spiritual opponents, and most of the latter, representing the established order, vehemently opposed such movements. The spokesmen of modernization and reform took action primarily against fixed tradition and those who upheld it, using essentially peaceful means and concentrating on the realm of the mind. In the second place, these movements offered a clear Muslim alternative to the imperial powers' attempts at the religious and cultural assimilation of Muslims. Such attempts, worked out by authoritative thinkers such as Nikolai Il'minski in Russia and Christiaan Snouck Hurgronje in the Netherlands, were bound to fail.

To justify their vision and legitimate their action against existing traditions, the leaders of the movements of modernization and reform also used arguments from the very sources—Qur'ān and Hadīth—on which the religious traditions claimed to be based. These movements and their underlying orientations distinguished themselves from straightforward reformist movements, however, by their use of the sources. They did not claim to derive their whole world view, their view of society, and their models of action from these sources. They sought rather to interpret the sources with the help of reason, in the light of present-day problems that had to be solved, and with a growing awareness of the historical and social conditions under which these sources had taken shape.

5. Muslim Awakening and Revitalization

In the above I sketched our starting points in the study of Muslim movements of modernization and reform, as they occurred in Russia, Indonesia, and in other Muslim regions and countries. We try to grasp the event of the "awakening" of individuals and groups in Muslim societies, which implied a certain rediscovery of Islam through enlightenment. Movements of modernization and reform apparently were born out of what I call "awakening" and, once institutionalized, had their own history.

The same approach, I contend, is suitable when we seek to identify and study further stages of revitalization of Muslim groups and societies as produced by such movements. Western observers still tend to identify a revitalization of a Muslim society with a revival or resurgence of "Islam" as a kind of force in itself. But in fact, in the stage of revitalization as in the stage of awakening, we have to do with societies and in particular with groups and their leaders who make certain choices and decisions of their own.

Muslim revitalization is not primarily the exercising of authority and power—in some cases violence—in the name of Islam. Throughout Muslim history, people have always called upon Islam to justify their deeds. What seems to be important in a revitalization is the ability of the people concerned to handle their often depressing situations themselves and by their own acts, and not only to survive these situations but also to change and improve them. It is their own initiative, moral sense and "faith" that bring this about, not some metaphysical entity called "Islam".

When studying an "awakening" and the movements arising out of it, we should look for the intentions of the Muslims concerned, who begin to measure their situation against Islamic norms and values. Equally, in the study of "revitalization" we should look first of all for the intentions of those Muslims who want to change and improve their situation. From the middle of the nineteenth century on, if not earlier, an *enlightenment* took place throughout the Muslim world, expressed in various movements. From the middle of the twentieth century, a *revitalization* has apparently been taking place by means of various movements. It would be worthwhile to pay special attention to those elements of the Islamic cultural and religious tradition to which these movements appeal when they mobilize people to assume responsibilities and engage in broader social action. This was the aim the modern reformers and their followers envisaged a century ago and for which they made great efforts.

Selected Literature

1. Islam in Russia

BENNIGSEN, Alexandre, and Chantal LEMERCIER-QUELQUEJAY, *La presse et le mouvement national chez les musulmans de Russie avant 1920*, Paris & The Hague: Mouton, 1960.

CARRÈRE D'ENCAUSSE, Hélène, *Réforme et révolution chez les musulmans de l'empire russe: Bukhara 1867–1924*, Paris: Armand Colin, 1966.

KUTTNER, Thomas, "Russian Jadīdism and the Islamic World: Ismail Gasprinskii in Cairo – 1908. A Call to the Arabs for the Rejuvenation of the Islamic World", *Cahiers du Monde russe et soviétique*, XVI (July–December 1975), fasc. 3–4, pp. 383–424.

LAZZERINI, Edward James, *Ismail Bey Gasprinskii and Muslim Modernism in Russia, 1878–1914*, Ph.D. Dissertation, University of Washington, 1973.

—, "Ğadidism at the Turn of the Twentieth Century: A View from Within", *Cahiers du Monde russe et soviétique*, XVI (July–December 1975), fasc. 2, pp. 245–77.

—, "The Revival of Islamic Culture in Pre-revolutionary Russia: Or, why a Prosopography of the Tatar *ulema?*", in *Passé Turco-Tatar, Présent soviétique* (see below), pp. 367–72.

Passé Turco-Tatar, Présent soviétique: Études offertes à Alexandre Bennigsen, publiées par Chantal LEMERCIER-QUELQUEJAY, Gilles VEINSTEIN, et S. Enders WIMBUSH, Louvain et Paris: Peeters, 1986.

ZENKOVSKY, Serge A., *Pan-Turkism and Islam in Russia*, Cambridge, Mass.: Harvard University Press, 1967.

2. Islam in the Dutch East Indies

ALFIAN, *Islamic Modernism in Indonesian Politics: The Muhammadijah Movement during the Dutch Colonial Period (1912–1942)*, Ph.D. Dissertation, University of Wisconsin, 1969.

BOLAND, Bernard Johan, and I. FARJON, *Islam in Indonesia: A Bibliographical Survey 1600–1942, with post-1945 Addenda* (Koninklijk Instituut voor Taal-, Land- en Volkenkunde, Bibliographical Series 14), Dordrecht, etc.: Foris Publications, 1983.

FEDERSPIEL, Howard M., *The Persatuan Islam*, Ph.D. Dissertation, McGill University, 1966.

JAYLANI, A. Timur, *The Sarekat Islam Movement: Its Contribution to Indonesian Nationalism*, M.A. Thesis, McGill University, 1958.

MEHDEN, Fred Robert von der, *Islam and the Rise of Nationalism in Indonesia*, Ph.D. Dissertation, University of California at Berkeley, 1957.

NAKAMURA, Mitsuo, *The Crescent Arises over the Banyan Tree: A Study of the Muhammadiyah Movement in a Central Javanese Town*, Yogyakarta: Gadjah Mada University Press, 1983.

NIEL, Robert van, *The Emergence of the Modern Indonesian Elite*, The Hague & Bandung: W. van Hoeve, and Chicago: Quadrangle Books, 1960, 1970² (Repr. Dordrecht, etc.: Foris Publications, 1984).

NOER, Deliar, *The Modernist Muslim Movement in Indonesia 1900–1942*, Kuala Lumpur, etc.: Oxford University Press, 1973.

SNOUCK HURGRONJE, Christiaan, *Verspreide Geschriften*, Vols. 4/1 and 4/2, Bonn & Leipzig: Schroeder, 1924.

Chapter 14
Puritan Patterns in Islamic Revival Movements[1]

1. Introduction

Present-day developments in Muslim regions call for a reappraisal of existing methods of research on contemporary Islam. In the 1950s, European scholars of Islam grew up in the aftermath of a period of lethargy in Muslim societies. Naturally, in their study of Islam they were inclined to employ methods and theories stressing the latter's immobility or at least its permanent features. In order to offer a more adequate interpretation of what may be called the dynamics of Islam, however, a reassessment of approaches has to be made. This applies in particular to the study of current Islamic revitalization.

Attention should be directed less to interpreting Islamic data in the light of their implications for the West than to studying them in the context of what is happening in Islamic societies themselves. As a consequence, a number of studies dealing with regional developments and the situations of particular countries have appeared. Equally, the various forms and functions of elements of Islam and the political uses made of them are receiving attention. Both historical continuity and change have come into focus in this way.

Given the abundance of studies dealing with particular situations and developments in which Islam plays a role, the question arises whether anything can be said on a more general level about Islam in Muslim societies. Here we need to consider data arrived at by social scientific and historical research, as well as parallel developments in different Muslim cultural areas including cultural areas where other religions and ideologies are dominant.

2. Islamic Revival Movements and Revitalization of Islam

One way to study current forms of revitalization of Islam, taking into account its particular dynamics, is to delineate different kinds of move-

[1]   Revised text of "The Puritan Pattern in Islamic Revival Movements", *Schweizerische Zeitschrift für Soziologie / Revue suisse de sociologie*, 9 (1983), Nr. 3, pp. 687–701.

ments that have manifested themselves in the last two centuries and to distinguish them according to their basic intentions and the ways in which they have articulated Islam. In this way, at least three kinds of movements can be broadly distinguished: movements of *islāh* (reform) directly appealing to the Qur'ān and *Sunna*; movements of *tajdīd* (modernization) blending universal values with values derived from Scripture; and movements of *tasawwuf* (mysticism) stressing the inner path of the soul toward God, mostly within the framework of a brotherhood (*tarīqa*). Movements that do not appeal directly to Islam, like secular nationalism or socialism, are disregarded here.

Of these three types of movement, those of *islāh* or reform are now preponderant, although the modernization movements obtained considerable force during the period of Western political domination. In fact, the modernization movements tend to stress values common to Islam and the rest of humankind, including the West, whereas most reform movements tend to take a stand against the West. These latter movements, considered here together as Islamic movements of revival of religion (*ihyā' al-dīn*) or "Islamic revival movements", are the substance of what follows.

It is these movements that have played an important political role in forging Muslim solidarity, in encouraging the struggle for independence, and lately in urging greater Islamization of society, stricter application of the *Sharī'a*, and the establishment of Islamic states. It should be kept in mind that the aforementioned movements have arisen in a world in which the majority of Muslims, *ahl al-sunna wa'l-jamā'a*, adhere to the norms of what may be called traditional Sunnī Islam, represented on an intellectual level by the *'ulamā'* who uphold the ideals of the *Sharī'a*. On a popular level, however, this traditional Islam has often been mixed with beliefs and practices that the *'ulamā'* scorn as "superstitions" and to which the revival movements are strongly opposed.

All Islamic revival movements take recourse to Scripture, bypassing to a great extent the scholastic development of Muslim religious thought after the fixation of the text of the Qur'ān, the canonization of the recognized collections of traditions, and the handbooks of the founders of the four great legal schools (*madhāhib*). But we must distinguish among these revival movements according to whether greater stress is placed on thought and education or on practice and action. This is, of course, not an absolute difference, since thought and action are always intertwined, but rather a matter of emphasis.

1) The revival movements stressing thought and education include the reform movements that were started by Muhammad 'Abduh (ca. 1849–1905) in Egypt and Sayyid Ahmad Khān (1817–98) in India at the beginning of the period of foreign rule. They provide a more or less

coherent rational construct of reality as well as of the predicament and task of humankind in the light of Qur'anic revelation. The reform movements opened the door to *ijtihād* (direct study of Scripture) and wanted to purify Islam from all those elements that could not legitimately be deduced from Qur'ān and *Sunna*. They paid much attention to a renewal of Islamic education and the development of society in accordance with what they viewed as the basic principles of Islam.

2) A good example of revival movements that put much stress on practice and action is the Muslim Brotherhood. It was founded by Hasan al-Bannā' (1906–49) in 1928 and developed at the end of the period of foreign rule in Egypt. It aims at a more or less direct implementation of the injunctions of the *Sharīʿa*, often through the immediate application of Qur'anic prescriptions. Islamic education and especially the study of the Qur'ān are pursued with a view to the further Islamization of society and the establishment of an Islamic state in the near or distant future. This type of revival movement naturally becomes involved in political activities and tends to generate Islamist pressure groups and activists.

Revival movements of both types, stressing either thought or action, have occurred throughout the history of Islam and as such are not a new phenomenon. From the very beginning there have been movements that sought inspiration from Qur'ān and *Sunna* as the only sources of religion and immediate insight. They were wary of interpretations and systematizations that increased the remoteness of the sources and that tended to close the door to fresh interpretation.

Moreover, movements of *islāḥ* often combined thought with action, an intellectual with a practical bent. An outstanding example is the movement of the Hanbalī reformer Ibn Taymīya (1263–1328), which later gave rise to the Wahhābī movement in Arabia in the eighteenth century and again in the twentieth century. In connection with revival movements that stress thought, one may think of the impact of al-Ghazzālī (1058–1111), in which mysticism plays a role. Examples from earlier times of revival movements stressing action include the Khārijīs since the early period of Islam, movements inspired by the Mahdi ideal, and popular movements—sometimes inspired by *ʿulamā*'—calling for implementation of the *Sharīʿa*, for instance against prevailing injustice or sometimes against non-Muslim minorities.

The present time furnishes numerous examples of revival movements stressing either thought or action. Those stressing thought include the reform movements of ʿAbduh and Ahmad Khān which have resulted in organizations like the Muhammadīya in Indonesia, the Salafīya in Egypt and similar "Sunnīya" movements in Morocco and other Arab countries nowadays; and the movement around Sharīʿati (1933–77) in Pahlevi Iran.

Revival movements that place the accent on action include the Wahhābī movement, out of which the state of Saudi Arabia emerged[2]; political activism inspired by Jamāl al-Dīn al-Afghānī (1838–97); the Muslim Brotherhood and its offshoots in Egypt, Syria, Jordan, and other Arab countries; *Jamāʿat-i Islāmī* and similar activist groups in Pakistan; and of course Khomeinism in Iran.

3. Common Features of Islamic Revival Movements

Several features are common to the various revival movements; they fall into the following groups:

3.1. There is an explicit call to go back to the Qur'ān and *Sunna* as a source of truth offering guidance for a person's personal and social life. Interpretation of the Qur'ān can employ *ijtihād*, original effort, within certain limits. By implication, the results of medieval scholastic scholarship in the Islamic sciences of religion fall into abeyance and a critical attitude to what happened to Islam in the course of history is adopted. Religious legitimation is clearly restricted to Scripture and ancient *Sunna*, "innovations" (*bidʿa*) being criticized either as survivals from the older pagan traditions or as borrowings from outside. Consequently, war is waged on various forms of popular religion and mysticism and a critical stand is adopted toward the penetration of elements from Western culture and religion to the extent that such elements are out of harmony with the sources and norms of Islamic religion. Only what can be deduced directly or indirectly from the Qur'ān and *Sunna* has authority for Muslim thought and action.

3.2. This critical stand in Islamic revival movements toward existing views and forms of behavior shows up among younger people, for instance, in the personal life style of individuals where dress (veil) and hairstyle indicate Islamic allegiance and where human activities are screened for conformity with Islam. The Islamic orientation also makes a number of social claims: individual and group have a great sense of responsibility toward society at large. This implies, first, bidding farewell to a too-egocentric concentration on the Hereafter and instead concerning oneself with this world, though not without reference to the other world. It also implies an interest in society as it really is and views society as open to reform and management by humans. The traditional authorities tend to be criticized and a more egalitarian mutual encouragement

---

2   Cf. above Chapter 11 on "The Wahhābīs in Eighteenth and Nineteenth Century Arabia" and Chapter 12 on "Saudi Arabia: The King and the Consul".

and also mutual control develop. To bring about an Islamic social order, an appeal is often made for the application of literal details of the *Sharīʿa* or to basic principles contained in the Qur'ān. Just as Qur'ān and *Sunna* are used as sources of religious legitimation, so the *Sharīʿa* is appealed to as a source of religious guidelines.

3.3. Islamic revival movements consist of groupings that are distinct from the older traditional adherents of the *ahl al-sunna wa'l-jamāʿa* and also different from the modernists. This implies an emancipation of groups that were hardly visible until now. They can articulate Islam and themselves in new ways, develop their own leadership, and may develop their own power structures. These new groups are held together, however, not by formal organizational patterns but by what may perhaps be called a new Islamic ethos. This includes features like a conscious departure from the past with criticism of the current state of religion and society, an active commitment to shaping the future, and willingness to work and to offer a remarkable discipline of both individual and group in striving for their goals.

3.4. Revival movements distinguish themselves by their awareness that they are fulfilling a divinely ordered task under supreme guidance from on high. Although their activities may be of a practical, social, and political nature, the religious intentions and motivations behind them are strong. There is an intensive study of the Qur'ān and an awareness of eschatological realities. The ultimate aim is to bring about the social order prefigured in the Qur'ān. The religious longing for a new social order may lead to a relativization and rejection of the existing one and eventually to revolutionary action.

3.5. The element of protest in Islamic revival movements is directed not only against the existing social order or outside non-Islamic influences. In fact these movements may also imply an inner revolt within religion in the name of a newly discovered transcendence, a new Absolute. In general, these movements show a willingness to engage in debate with those traditionalists, mystics, syncretists, modernists, and secularists who draw less rigorous conclusions from their study of Scripture and law.

3.6. Behind the Islamic revival movements lies a vindication of the integrity of Islam against foreign domination, which is sensed almost as a pollution. The urge to purify Islam as it exists from the accretions and corruptions that account for its present state can lead to a passionate religious search for the pristine faith and practice of pure and true Islam.

4. The Puritan Pattern

This review has established some striking surface features that most Islamic revival movements share. Our understanding of these common features will be deepened by the recognition that these features constitute a coherent pattern based on a particular ethos. This pattern is much more than the sum of individual features. It is a configuration of behavior, it has a structure of thought with its own presuppositions and logic, and it has marked religious intentions.

I suggest that we speak here of a *puritan* pattern, since the ethos behind it shows great concern for a radical purification of self and society. The right sort of personal conduct and the right social order are achieved by means of an extreme criticism of existing beliefs, views, and practices. I submit that puritan patterns can be discerned with certain variations in a number of religions and ideologies including Islam.

4.1. Ideological und Practical Aspects

In Islam the puritan pattern appears to comprise the following elements:

1) Ideological Aspects (Thought):

a) Direct recourse by the faithful to *Scripture* (Qur'ān with ancient *Sunna*) as a unique authoritative source of guidance (scripturalism);

b) *purification* of existing religious traditions measured against Scripture; also purification of self and society with a strong sense of human weakness, decay, and pollution, through self-control and self-criticism according to criteria derived from Scripture;

c) stress on the Islamic *ethos* as a way of life, including a strong sense of duty. Life is seen as a call and mission to follow the commands of God and to realize true Islam with a strongly communal concern.

d) Claims of *exclusiveness* are developed about the truth and efficiency of one's own form of Islam with its particular way of approaching transcendence and about the capacity of Islam to realize the ideal society and state.

e) There is a certain *eschatological* dimension in preparing for the Day of Judgment.

2) Practical Aspects (Action):

a) Stress on the *community* as a self-contained and privileged entity open to new members but practically closed for those who want to quit: a relatively closed entity;

b) a professed *egalitarianism* among the members of the community, be it with a strong leadership, male domination, and great social control;

c) efforts to use efficient *organizational tools* to mobilize members in organizations, parties, schools, and groups in the neighborhood or at work;

d) efforts to increase social and political *power* and to arrive at an Islamization of society and eventually an Islamic state;

e) great concern about *social action*, which always has both a religious and a political side.

4.2. The Puritan Pattern as Ideal Type

From a sociological perspective, the puritan pattern corresponds to Max Weber's view of the Puritans but without its Christian articulation. It brings about a rationalization of conduct in this world under the stimulus of something beyond it. It implies a rationalization of life that is stripped of unnecessary structures in view of the desired goal. It stimulates an ascetic attitude within the everyday world, purging it of anything unconductive to the goal which has been set. What the Protestant Ethic was for the Puritans was a special case of the more general *puritan ethos* within any puritan pattern. The Puritans' rationalization of meaning and action corresponds to that of the Muslim revivalists.

The puritan *pattern* may be called an ideal type. It does not occur in its pure form anywhere, even among the Puritans, but it furthers understanding of a number of human attitudes and social realities in religions and ideologies. Equally, the puritan *ethos* is an ideal type of a particular orientation to life, often with strongly religious aspects that stress transcendence. J. Peacock, in his description of what he calls the "reformist configuration", observes that the reformists in Islam have a kind of "Protestant ethos" and concludes his study, to which we owe much, by linking Reformism to Puritanism.[3] I would like to start where Peacock finishes. The puritan pattern supposes continuous reform in thought and action, and it distinguishes itself from reform in the broader sense of the word through its striving for reform in terms of purity and with a characteristic tendency toward purification. The puritan pattern implies a particular lifestyle of members and adherents. In Islam, for instance, there have been Muslims with a traditionalist "purist" lifestyle since the beginning. The reform movements have allowed a more activist variety of this purist lifestyle to be developed, but there is no fundamental conflict between this variety and the traditionalist purist lifestyles. The puritan ethos may be called the code of this purist lifestyle.

In each occurrence, the puritan pattern has many aspects: social, psychological, ideological, political. It often tends to take shape through disaffection with regard to the established order, putting distance between itself and authorities, a conscious recourse to fundamental norms and values, and the further development of a lifestyle in accordance with

---

[3]   PEACOCK, *Muslim Puritans*, pp. 199, 204, 205.

these fundamentals. It may lead to a reversal of the existing order in a "puritan revolt" that seeks to realize the puritan pattern fully, which may result in a still more oppressive "puritan order". The contents and articulation of a puritan pattern vary with the religious and ideological tradition and the context in which it occurs.

5. The Interest of the Puritan Pattern for Islamic Studies

The puritan pattern as described above is a recognizable structure in a number of Muslim societies and groups, including Islamic revival movements, and it shows up in what may be called "puritan" articulations of Islam. There are particular "puritan" ways of reading the Qur'ān and of selecting, interpreting, and practicing particular elements of the sign and symbol system of Islam. It is distinctive of societies in which great emphasis is placed on the adoration of God, keeping God's commands, preserving one's purity in a world fraught with ambivalence, and avoiding sins and faults. It can be discerned in movements and organizations that strive actively toward implementing *Sharī'a* precepts and rules and toward realizing an Islamic society and state. It develops distinctive ideologies in which the demand for general access to the Qur'ān and for purification of life and society are prominent features. It is true that such traits can also be found in other, not specifically puritan Muslim societies, like the mystical brotherhoods and the *Shī'a*. But here these demands are associated with charismatic personalities possessing a spiritual authority that falls outside the puritan pattern and that is typically lacking in puritan societies.

Islamic revival movements not only show a puritan pattern and ethos, but also what I would like to call a puritan *impulse*. This impulse has a particularly marked religious quality and is highly critical toward any form of idolatry and anything religious that finds no legitimation in Scripture. In its earliest stage, it can have a destructive effect on existing religious, cultural, and social structures. But later it tends to evolve a less revolutionary attitude, to stabilize and protect itself against attacks from outside, and even to develop a more or less closed intellectual system.

It would be rewarding to study the contexts in which variations of the puritan impulse, ethos, and pattern have arisen in Islam. Are there particular conditions of life that favor puritan attitudes and the awakening of puritan Islam? Under which conditions can a puritan ethos be imposed on a society? What consequences does it have? In what ways does the puritan impulse lose its initial revolutionary force and lead to a more continuous ethos and lifestyle? Countries like Saudi Arabia, Iran, Pakistan, Sudan, and Afghanistan offer plenty of material.[4]

---

4   Cf. below Chapter 17 on "The Rise of Islamic States".

The concept of a puritan pattern, however, seems to be valid for more than Islam and Islamic studies alone. I already mentioned the English Puritans. In fact there were and still are typically "puritan" structures and movements, including revival movements, in Christianity and in Judaism as well, with important social and political implications. It seems indeed that at the present time a puritan impulse can be found in most religions and ideologies under stress that want to preserve or go back to their particular truth.

Paradoxically, Max Weber himself seems to have regarded Islam as the polar opposite of Puritanism.[5] This may be due to the relative absence of Islamic revival movements during his lifetime, which fell in the colonial period. In contrast to this, I contend that the puritan impulse, ethos, and pattern have a much wider validity and application than seems to have been recognized until now. These concepts indeed may throw new light on present-day movements of revitalization of religions and ideologies. Often an appeal is made to elements of a given religious-cultural tradition, and these elements are then restructured according to puritan patterns.

The puritan pattern, however, has a particularly strong potential in Muslim societies. In Europe, perhaps more than America, the puritan impulse is associated with memories of iconoclasm, cultural barbarism, and destruction of the earth in the name of heaven. Within the Muslim world, violence resulting from the puritan impulse also caused fright and horror, as is shown by Muslim reactions to Wahhābī behavior in the Shī'ite shrines in Iraq and in the graveyards of Mecca and Medina at the beginning of the nineteenth century. But Islam itself has been a reform movement from its very beginning, exhibiting unmistakably puritan features when it faced Meccan paganism, Judaism, and Christianity in Muhammad's lifetime. And throughout Islamic history, the puritan impulse against idolatry and violations of God's unity and universality has remained alive, leading to a number of reform movements displaying the characteristic puritan pattern. Reform according to a puritan pattern seems to be part of Islam itself.

Islamic revival movements carry within them a puritan impulse, ethos, and pattern that have a powerful social and political appeal. This becomes particularly evident in present-day Muslim thought about the Islamic state. The concept of the Islamic state, linking the critical concept of islāh (reform) with the longing for a just society, has striking puritan features. Where an Islamic state has been declared, a puritan way of life imposes itself. It is as if in such a state the puritan pattern could be fully realized.

---

[5]   Bryan S. TURNER, *Weber and Islam: A Critical Study*, London and Boston: Routledge and Kegan Paul, 1974 (Repr. 1998), p. 12.

6. The Islamic State and the Puritan Pattern

Since the Islamic revolution in Iran in 1979, current ideals of the Islamic state have become the subject of scholarly research. The Islamic state had been studied more as an ideal from classical times than in its political, religious, and other aspects. One complicating factor is that the Muslim concept of the "state" (*dawla*) itself, in Muslim tradition and in the living reality of Muslim societies, differs considerably from Western concepts and models of the state.

From the very inception of Islam in Mecca and its first political realization in Medina, and subsequently throughout history, underlying trends have existed that seek to establish the ideal Islamic social order as worked out by the *ʿulamā'* largely on the basis of directives contained in the Qur'ān and ancient *Sunna*. Some rules indeed can be found in the Qur'ān, and Muhammad established a state of a unique kind, which, however, could not remain the same after the prophet's death.

Apart from its political development, the concept of an autonomous *umma* (community) living according to God's will and commands can be traced all the way back to the Meccan period. It underlies later developments of thought on social order in Islam, mostly as an ideal contrasting with current realities. It seems that the ideal of a truly Islamic society developed largely among groups opposed to the existing political leadership and realities. The idealized image of the early community, which included equality among the companions of the prophet, has strikingly "puritan" features. In the circles of the political leaders, however, the idea of an Islamic society has always largely served to legitimize the existing order or to shore up policies dictated by practical necessities.

This dual use of the concept of an Islamic order, both for protest and for legitimation, has always existed. In the course of history, the *ʿulamā'* have intellectually sustained the ideal of an Islamic order of society and developed the *Sharīʿa* in this direction. It has also been alive in mystical brotherhoods, as manifested in the community of faithful brethren obeying a religious leader and following a life in common along the religious path. Interestingly enough, among the Muslim masses adhering to tradition and strongly imbued with a communal sense, the idea that society should be based on Qur'ān and *Sunna* has always remained alive. This idea itself has puritan features; any appeal to it has always found a ready response, as expressed at times in street demonstrations.

In practice, this ideal Islamic society has not taken shape; attempts to realize it have not endured the test of time. Many have viewed this as a basic fault and frustration, and it has led to very different reactions: in *islāh* movements, but also in sectarian activities, Mahdist movements, alternative solutions offered in the mystical brotherhoods, and ever repeated criticism by the *'ulamā'* of the existing state of affairs in society and state. The general idea has been that a society living according to the *Sharī'a* would be the ideal, just, Islamic society.

It seems that although the idea of an Islamic social order and society has always been alive, the problem of an Islamic state has only become urgent when sectarian leadership has managed to obtain political power. Within the orthodox Sunnī community itself, the problem of the state has rather been the problem of the right leader, especially in the medieval period.

The concept of an Islamic state (*dawla*) took a new form in later times when a central authority developed and when the idea of the state became distinct from the idea of society or particular political leaders. A feature of the Ottoman, Safavid, and Moghul empires for instance, is their legitimation as Islamic "states", although they were rather empires under powerful Muslim rulers.

There are several reasons for the development of new thought on the ideal of an Islamic state in modern times. It seems to have started at the time when the great empires just mentioned were suffering visible decline and when the true Islamic state was projected as the right alternative to sad realities. It developed further during the period of resistance to Western domination over Muslim territories, when Western states imposed a political order of a clearly non-Islamic nature. The most forceful incentive to reformulate the old ideal of an Islamic order and society in terms of a more modern Islamic state, however, must have come from the reformers' and their pupils' explicit reintroduction of the notion of *islāh* through a return to Qur'ān and *Sunna*. This *islāh* was intended to lead to a purification of all Muslim societies through the application of true Islam. Interestingly enough, when the nationalist movements developed and largely succeeded in establishing states on Western models, the idea of establishing an "Islamic" state was hardly mentioned by the nationalist leaders and it had influence only among a minority of the people. I suggest that the problem of an Islamic state presented itself explicitly in a new, unprecedented form only after politically independent national states with a Muslim majority had been established.

It was only after independence that the idea of an Islamic society and an Islamic state on a puritan pattern could function as a critical norm by which to judge the existing state of affairs, since the responsibility for it was now borne no longer by foreigners but by Muslims. The idea increased in ideological and political importance when opposition groups could express their protest, resistance, and even revolutionary tendencies against the nationalist leadership more or less freely in terms of Islam and in particular in terms of the idea of an Islamic—as opposed to secular— state. This polemical context explains in part why the idea of the Islamic state has remained so vague but also so attractive to Muslims. In part, the vagueness of this concept is also due to the fact that it is essentially a "religious" notion and reflects a longing with religious aspects. The notion of an Islamic state implies a reference to a kind of absolute Reality formulated in religious law that the Muslim community is somehow expected to realize on earth. A shortcoming in most studies of the Islamic state that have been carried out until now is that no real attention has been paid to the religious and even eschatological dimension of an Islamic state. Its puritan features have not been seriously considered either.

The notion of the "Islamic state" is very much a "puritan" one. It may be said to function as a religious sign referring to an ideal state of affairs: communal life according to God's will, the realization on earth of a divinely prescribed social order and a society of justice according to divine law. I may recall that the notion of the Islamic state is always associated with other ideal notions of a religious nature, mostly with reference to the Qur'ān. What various Muslim religious and political leaders have said in recent times about the Islamic state should be noted. But it should never be identified with actual realities, even if it is claimed that the Islamic state has been realized in a particular case. The desire to realize such a state is typically part of the puritan pattern I described. The nostalgia, longing, and active striving for an alternative social order, a state of affairs different from that given here and now, are the essence of the intention in all discussions about the Islamic state as an ideal and a norm. For Muslims, it seems to me, the Islamic state is essentially a moral and religious phenomenon with eschatological dimensions, but it leads, of course, to political considerations and action.

Most of the current Muslim writings on the Islamic state can be seen as a stage in the long line of calls for the *islāh* of Islam. From Ibn Taymīya to the Wahhābīs and then to the Muslim Brotherhood and other societies with militant attitudes toward the existing social order is not too big a step. And from *islāh* thinking to *islāh* action is not a big step either.

My contention is that in the present circumstances it is precisely the combination of the religious idea of the Islamic state and the trend of *islāh* thinking and acting within Islam that gives the ideal of the Islamic state its strikingly puritan shape. Even in Shī'ī Iran, where charismatic leadership of a different kind prevails, puritan features can be observed. Many expressions and discourses of the current Islamic revival movements have not only clear religious aspects, but also a characteristically puritan flavor.

This revival itself, of course, is much more than a political reaction to the West. It has its own dynamics and religious aspects. It should be noted, moreover, that although the puritan pattern is the most important form that Islamic revival is taking, it is not the only form. There are also pietistic and mystical forms, as well as interesting blendings with other cultures and cultural elements, both "modern" and "traditional". Beyond politics, among the signs of present-day Islamic revival, the variety of puritan forms and patterns predominate, certainly in the organized Islamic revival movements. One reason may be that it offers the most efficient rationalization of action within the Islamic framework. Besides the individual, it is the socio-political order that needs to be purified as a necessary stage on the way to the perfect society in which true law will be applied. This calls for further study by Islamicists, sociologists, and scholars of religion.

Selected Literature

ABOU ZEID, Nasr, *Critique du discours religieux*, Paris: Sindbad-Actes Sud, 1999.

ABU RABI', Ibrahim M., *Intellectual Origins of Islamic Resurgence in the Modern Arab World*, Albany, N. Y.: State University of New York Press, 1996.

ARKOUN, Mohammed, *Pour une critique de la raison islamique*, Paris: Maisonneuve et Larose, 1984.

AZM, Sādiq Ğalāl al-, *Naqd al-fikr ad-dīnī* (Criticism of Religious Thought), Beirut: Dār at Tali'a, 1969.

HADDAD, Yvonne Yazbeck, *Contemporary Islam and the Challenge of History*, Albany, N. Y.: State University of New York Press, 1982.

HUSSAIN, Asaf, *Islamic Movements in Egypt, Pakistan and Iran: An Annotated Bibliography*, London: Mansell, 1983.

Islam and Development: Religion and Socio-Political Change, ed. by John L. ESPOSITO, Syracuse, N. Y.: Syracuse University Press, 1980.

Islam in Transition: Muslim Perspectives, ed. by John J. DONOHUE and John L. ESPOSITO, New York and Oxford: Oxford University Press, 1982.

The Islamic Impact, ed. by Yvonne Yazbeck HADDAD, Byron HAINES and Ellison FINDLY, Syracuse, N. Y.: Syracuse University Press, 1984.

Islamic Resurgence in the Arab World, ed. by Ali E. Hillal DESSOUKI, New York, N. Y.: Praeger, 1982.

Issues in the Islamic Movement, ed. by Kalim SIDDIQUI, London: The Open Press, 1981.

PEACOCK, James L., *Muslim Puritans: Reformist Psychology in Southeast Asian Islam*, Berkeley, Cal., etc.: University of California Press, 1978.

Voices of Resurgent Islam, ed. by John L. ESPOSITO, New York and Oxford: Oxford University Press, 1983.

VOLL, John O., *Islam: Continuity and Change in the Modern World*, Boulder, Colo.: Westview Press, and Harlow: Longman, 1982.

WILD, Stefan, "Gott und Mensch im Libanon: Die Affäre Sādiq al-'Azm", *Der Islam*, 48 (1972), pp. 206–53.

Section 8

Islamic Ideology

Chapter 15
The Call (*Da'wa*) of Islamic Movements[1]

This chapter seeks to show that most if not all Islamic movements have been social answers to a specific *da'wa* (call, appeal). Hence, a study of such movements must inquire about their original *da'wa*. Taking into consideration this origin and the basic call-response structure of Islamic movements can lead to a better understanding not only of these movements but also of some aspects of the present-day revitalization of Islam.[2]

The number of movements that identify themselves as "Islamic" has sharply increased since the Islamic revolution in Iran in 1979.[3] Today's so-called "Islamic movement"[4] is not a single movement that can be attributed to a general cause. It consists in fact of many small movements that all have their own special history, their specific causes and aims and their own internal dynamics. The force of these dynamics seems to be given with a specific *da'wa* and the particular response to it in given situations and contexts.

The act of *da'wa* is a special kind of communication. The speaker addresses a particular person or audience to mobilize him, her, or them to make specific commitments toward Islam. For this purpose, he or she uses Qur'anic texts, *hadīths*, logical arguments, admonitions, warnings, and, of course, his or her own eloquence. In many cases, such a *da'wa* has

---

[1]   Revised version of a text "The Da'wa of Islamic Movements" published in *Actas XVI Congreso Union Européenne d'Arabisants et d'Islamisants (UEAI)*, ed. by Maria de la Concepción VÁZQUEZ DE BENITO and Miguel Ángel MANZANO RODRÍGUEZ, Salamanca: Agencia Española de Cooperación Internacional, Consejo superior de Investigaciones Científicas, 1995, pp. 539–49.

[2]   The so-called "resurgence" of Islam is more than just a political phenomenon (in discourse or action) or a form of social and personal behavior. Though it can largely be explained as a response to given economic, political, and social conditions, the kind of meaning it conveys to the people concerned in various situations and contexts has hardly been studied in a systematic way. One reason may be that, for most Europeans and North Americans, any "resurgence" of Islam apparently has mostly negative connotations.

[3]   See for instance HUSSAIN, *Islamic Movements in Egypt, Pakistan and Iran*. Further bibliographical surveys are needed.

[4]   SIDDIQUI, *Issues in the Islamic Movement*.

a ritual character, but it can also be of a more personal nature and express a religious, social, or political commitment.

The ideological content of the *da'wa*, important as it may be, is only one aspect and in most cases insufficient to explain the force of the appeal and its effects. To give such an explanation, the total context within which a particular *da'wa* is proclaimed must be taken into consideration. There have been *da'was* accompanied by violent action and others that later led to violence.[5] Many *da'was*, however, have led to peaceful conversions. Whenever a *da'wa* refers to Islam, it will have its impact on a Muslim audience to which Islam represents the highest norm and value.

1. The Concept of Da'wa

E. W. Lane[6] gives the basic meaning of *da'wa* as invitation, for instance the invitation to eat and drink or to celebrate an event. Derived meanings include the religious terms for prayer or curse, the call to prayer, and especially the call to accept Islam (*da'watu'l-islām*). In the Qur'ān, *da'wa* has two specific meanings: a call or invitation from God to a human being (S. 30:24), or an appeal by a human being to God in the form of a prayer or a vow (S. 2:123; S. 38:34).

In the course of time, the meaning of *da'wa* developed both in a religious and in a socio-political sense. In the religious sense, in Qur'anic usage *da'wa* is already the call, addressed to people by a prophet in God's name, to adhere to the one true religion (S. 14:46). Each prophet has had his own specific *da'wa* to proclaim; the believers had to accept and repeat the *da'wa* of their prophet. It was Muhammad's particular *da'wa* to repeat the *da'was* of the preceding prophets and summarize them in the final *da'wat al-islām*. At a later stage, *da'wa* came to mean religion, religious law, and authoritative tradition and then became virtually synonymous with *dīn*, *Sharī'a*, and *sunna*: this shows the importance of the concept. Ultimately it was extended to refer to those who have heard and accepted the call, and it came to designate the Islamic community itself (*umma*), considered as a united body precisely because it responded positively to this particular call.

The socio-political sense developed parallel to the religious one. Already at an early stage, *da'wa* signified the invitation or appeal to adopt the cause of a particular individual or family, that is to say, his, her or its claim to leadership (*imāma*) over Muslims. To accept such a *da'wa*

---

5   This has been the case, for instance, with the recent *jihād* movements in Lebanon and Egypt.
6   Edward William LANE, *An Arabic-English Lexicon*, London & Edinburgh: Williams and Norgate, 1867, pp. 883–5 (under "*Da'wa*", Book I, Part 3).

implied recognizing the individual's or family's authority as legitimate and consequently the legitimacy of the society or state founded by that individual or family. Later the meaning of *da'wa* broadened to include adherence to the structure and organization set up by or for this person or family. In the end, seen from a socio-political angle, *da'wa*, as an "invitation to join" could function as a slogan to launch a movement for an Islamic cause, for instance to establish a political entity under the authority and leadership of a particular Muslim.

Consequently, the history of the meaning of *da'ua* supports our contention that at the beginning of most Islamic movements with both spiritual and socio-political aspects stands a *da'wa* that is, so to speak, the motor of such movements.

Thus the concept of *da'wa* is extremely dynamic, covering as it does both the proclamation of an Islamic call to various groups of people and the resulting socio-political movement to promote an Islamic way of life. Religiously, *da'wa* implies the fundamental dependence of persons and society on divine assistance and indicates the call, made on behalf of divine authority, to accept the religion and law revealed and proclaimed to assist humanity. Politically, *da'wa* implies the recognition of a particular socio-political authority and leadership that enjoys a transcendent legitimacy and can therefore make laws held to be of divine origin.

Da'wa was directed in the first place to Muslims, to induce them to live according to Islamic rules, but it then became a missionary appeal to non-Muslims too, to persuade them to accept Islam. In both cases, *da'wa* activates. If I interpret it correctly, the purpose of *da'wa* is to awaken human beings who find themselves in a problematical situation and urge them to live according to Islam. Once someone has heard the call, he or she is supposed to respond positively, that is, to adhere to and promote the movement concerned.

The act of *da'wa* has an important cognitive dimension. It is largely achieved through preaching and thus the communication of fundamental teachings that are to be accepted as true. On a deeper level, the Great Call is, so to speak, incarnated in the Qur'ān, it *is* the Qur'ān.[7] The first thing to be done to grasp this Call from beyond, consequently, is to study the Qur'ān. The next step is to live and act accordingly, which also means to discover the permanent order to things, the eternal norms and rules applicable to human beings, and to abide by them. The third step is to bear witness to Islam's claim to surpass other religions and ideologies, to defend it against attacks, and to strengthen the Muslim community against dangers from outside and inside. In short, the knowledge ac-

---

[7] Consequently, the Qur'ān is both an eminent document of *da'wa* to Muhammad and the main source for all kinds of *da'wa* in the course of Islamic history.

quired through studying the content of the *da'wa*—given with the Qur'ān—should make the individual a believer. It should enlighten his or her consciousness, awaken his or her moral conscience and guide his or her behavior—including passing on the *da'wa* to others.

2. Da'wa Movements in History

There have been innumerable *da'wa* movements throughout Islamic history; the following are the most widely known and may serve as examples.[8] Other such movements often followed these models.

2.1. The prophetical *da'wa* of Muhammad himself was considered the last of a series of *da'was* proclaimed by prophets since early times. Starting after Muhammad's own calling around 610 C.E., the movement was not very successful in Mecca, where it met with considerable opposition. However, once Muhammad had established himself in Medina, his *da'wa* was crowned with success, not only in Medina itself but also among the Bedouin and later in Mecca and other towns in Arabia.

The *da'wa muhammadīya* was the model *par excellence* for all later Islamic *da'was*. It should be noted that there were also other prophetic movements in Arabia at the time that may be considered rival *da'was*, for instance the movement of Musaylima.[9]

2.2. The 'Abbāsid *da'wa*, proclaimed by Abū 'l-'Abbās and Abū Ja'far al-Mansūr in Kufa in 749, led to the reversal of the Umayyads and the inauguration of the 'Abbāsid caliphate, which pursued a more Islamic policy than hitherto. As in other revolutionary movements and *da'wa* movements in general, many forces worked together in the 'Abbāsid revolution, but it may be identified as an Islamic *da'wa* movement.

2.3. The Ismā'īlī *da'wa* took different forms, such as the movement of the Carmathians (end of the ninth century), the Fātimid movement, which established itself in Tunisia in 909 and in 969 moved to Egypt, from where it sent *dā'īs* into Sunnī territory (leading to the Bātiniyya in Mesopotamia in the eleventh century), and the Assassin movement of Nizārī Ismā'īlīs, established by Hasan al-Sabbāh (d. 1124). With the Ismā'īlīs, the *da'wa* became an institution with missionary *dā'īs* spreading the new doctrine.

---

[8]   Art. "*Da'wa*" by M. CANARD in *Encyclopedia of Islam*, Vol. 2, pp. 168–70.
[9]   Dale F. EICKELMAN, "Musaylima: An Approach to the Social Anthropology of Seventh-century Arabia", *Journal of the Economic and Social History of the Orient*, 10 (1967), pp. 17–52.

2.4. In the Islamic West, classic examples of *da'wa* movements leading to the establishment of new dynasties and states are those of the Almoravids (*al-Murābitūn*) under Yūsuf ibn Tāshfīn, who founded Marrākush in 1062, and of the Almohads (*al-Muwahhidūn*) under Muhammad ibn Tūmart (d. 1128), who was for some time considered the expected *mahdī*. The eschatologically oriented Mahdi movements represent a particular category of *da'wa* movements.

2.5. In Arabia, the well-known Wahhābī *da'wa* was proclaimed by Muhammad ibn ʿAbd al-Wahhāb[10] (1703–92) in close collaboration with Muhammad ibn Saʿūd (d. 1765), *amīr* of al-Dirʿīya. The resulting movement, which was successful in Central Arabia and the Hejaz, was crushed by an Egyptian army in 1818. It was revived, however, in 1902 by ʿAbd al-ʿAzīz ibn Saʿūd (d. 1953), who restored the Wahhābī *da'wa* movement. In 1932, he was able to establish present-day Saudi Arabia as a kingdom where the puritan Wahhābī interpretation of Islam has been the official doctrine.[11]

All the *da'wa* movements mentioned above had important political implications. There were other movements, too, in which a *da'wa* played an important role, for instance a great number of Sūfī movements (*turuq*), movements of reform (*islāh*) and renewal (*tajdīd*), Mahdist movements, movements to subject non-Muslims to Muslim rule, and, of course, movements to preach Islam to non-Muslims in and beyond the Middle East. The present listing is confined to the Arab World; examples elsewhere include the Bābī and Bahāʾī movements in Iran and the Ahmadiyya movement in Northwest India and Pakistan.

3. Daʿwa Movements in Recent History

I mention here some representative Islamic movements that arose in the course of the twentieth century with a particular call (*da'wa*) to apply the teachings of Islam in the social and often also the political realm. The number of twentieth-century Islamic movements is nearly endless, and the following examples are taken from the Arab world only; nearly all these Arab Islamic movements have had their equivalents in other regions of the Muslim world.

3.1. The institutionalization of Islamic mission (also called *da'wa*) to non-Muslims in various places during the twentieth century is an innovation.

---

[10]   Cf. above Chapter 11 on "The Wahhābīs in Eighteenth and Nineteenth Century Arabia".
[11]   Cf. above Chapter 12 on "Saudi Arabia: The King and the Consul".

The first institution of this kind was the *Dār al-da'wa wa'l-irshād*, which
was established by Muhammad Rashīd Ridā in Alexandria in 1912 but
had to stop its activities at the outbreak of World War One. Some large-
scale *da'wa* organizations have been established especially since the 1970s,
for instance in Riyadh and Tripoli (Libya), to educate preachers and
missionaries to be sent to non-Muslim areas, for instance in Africa.
Similar institutions exist in Egypt, Pakistan, Malaysia, Indonesia, and
elsewhere. During the twentieth century, the Ahmadiyya movement has
been sending missionaries to Europe, where several Ahmadiyya mosques
have been built after World War Two as part of a missionary effort.
Sunnī *da'was* to Europeans and North Americans can be observed at the
present time.[12]

3.2. In the second half of the nineteenth century, reformers like Muhammad 'Abduh (ca. 1849–1905) in Egypt and the still more remarkable
Sayyid Ahmad Khān (1817–98) in India and their followers inaugurated
a reform (*islāh*) movement that again took the Qur'ān as its starting point
but underlined the supreme value of reason. *Tafsīr* (Qur'anic exegesis)
was to be carried out with the help of reason, broadly conceived, to find
Qur'ān-based solutions to the many problems that beset Muslim societies
during their increasing modernization. In practice, the search was for
rational solutions to such problems that could be justified with the help
of Qur'anic texts and *hadīths*.

3.3. At the beginning of the twentieth century, the Salafīya movement
developed in Egypt under the leadership of Sayyid Muhammad Rashīd
Ridā (1865–1936), the editor of the well-known periodical *Al-Manār*,
which exerted a great influence throughout the Muslim world between
1898 and 1936. Although Ridā recognizes reason as necessary in order
to put Islamic teachings into practice in modern times, Qur'ān and *Sunna*
remain the foundation for any elaboration of Islam. The Salafīya movement can be characterized as neo-orthodox, and it will come as no
surprise that Rashīd Ridā sympathized with the Wahhābī movement
mentioned above, which took power in Western Arabia in the 1920s.

3.4. A new type of Islamic movement is represented by the *Jam'īyat
ikhwān al-muslimīn* (Association of Muslim Brethren)[13] founded in 1928
by Hasan al-Bannā' (1906–49) and some friends. Similar movements
have appeared in other Muslim countries and in Europe throughout the

[12] POSTON, *Islamic Da'wah in the West*.
[13] The Association of Muslim Brethren in Egypt is one of the better-known *da'wa* move-
     ments, due to the study by MITCHELL, *The Society of the Muslim Brothers*. A number of
     other studies have been devoted to the subject.

twentieth century. All these movements have addressed a *da'wa* to Muslims to live according to Islam. They originated as voluntary associations, advocating mutual help and social services among Muslims; but they have also taken part in political activities and in some cases have developed into regular political parties. Consequently, the Muslim Brethren have been forbidden and persecuted in some countries, including Egypt under Gamāl 'Abd al-Nāsir (r. 1954–70) and Syria since the late seventies. The Muslim Brethren were the first to develop current ideas about the Islamization of society and the state. In Egypt they have mostly refrained from violent action since the Nāsir period. Their journal here was titled *al-Da'wa* (until 1982).

3.5. An explicitly apolitical *da'wa* movement is the *Jamā'at al-Tablīgh* founded by Muhammad Ilyās (1885–1944).[14] Originating in Northern India, it has quickly spread to some Arab countries and Europe, where it addresses in particular those "social" Muslims who hardly practice their religion. It can be considered a revival movement, calling for Islamic practice in personal and social life but abstaining from political involvement.

3.6. During the 1970s, the number of *da'wa* groups in Muslim countries increased. Governments of countries like Egypt, Tunisia, and Morocco allowed Islamic organizations to take shape as an alternative to existing leftist movements. Since the successful Islamic revolution in Iran in 1979, the number of Islamic movements everywhere has increased sharply, receiving support from Saudi Arabia and Iran. These movements exert pressure on various states to "islamicize" society, in particular by applying the *Sharī'a* as valid law, as has happened in Bangladesh, Pakistan, and Sudan. Often Islam was elaborated ideologically as being the perfect *Weltanschauung* and the ideal social system, and the spread of such ideological versions of Islam through *da'wa* was advocated.

3.7. In extreme cases, a few newly-founded Islamic organizations have resorted to violence to realize their political projects. This happened during the wars in Lebanon in the 1970s and 1980s and in the territories occupied by Israel. It also happened in Egypt, where the organization *Jamā'at al-takfīr wa'l-hijra* opposed the state and society, which it considered to be living in a state of unbelief and ignorance (*jāhilīya*) and where the extremist organization *al-Jihād* carried out the duty, as it saw it, of assassinating Anwar Sadat.[15] It should be noted, however, that

---

14 See for instance DASSETTO, "The Tabligh Organization in Belgium".
15 KEPEL, *The Prophet & Pharaoh*; JANSEN, *The Neglected Duty*. Both books are one-sided in that they tend to suggest that Islam as such is linked to violence.

practically all Islamic movements declare that they pursue their aims by
peaceful means and a great number of them are not politically organized.
Whenever Islamic organizations are publicly allowed, they increase in
number.[16] In many Arab countries, however, they are proscribed or
strictly supervised.

4. The Increase in Da'wa Movements

Since the late 1960s, and even earlier in some countries, new kinds of
da'wa have found a profound echo among Muslims.

Islamic movements that arose in the twentieth century show the call-
response structure I noted at the beginning of this chapter. Their da'wa
has occurred directly through preaching, exhortation, and persuasion
strengthened by the media and in a more indirect way through social
pressures of various kinds. What are the reasons for this increase in
da'wa movements in recent history? This is a complex problem, the clue
to which seems to be found rather in the recent social history of Muslim
countries than in the religious features of Islam as such.[17]

The past century and a half have witnessed the breakdown of a
number of traditional Muslim societies and consequently a loosening of
traditional values and traditional morality, especially in Middle Eastern
regions plagued by violence and war. This same period has seen the rise
of various Islamic ideologies offering new collective orientations and
commitments, often ending in more populist movements in which self-
criticism is rare. Such ideologies and movements apparently respond to
problems that arise from modernization, industrialization, and urbaniza-
tion and that are directly or indirectly the result of Western influence.
The need to articulate one's identity and for a purpose in life beyond
urgent material needs—not to mention more spiritual needs and orientations—has made many groups of people sensitive to ideological answers. Hence, various ideologies presenting in various ways a da'wa for
Islam as *the* answer have developed and found adherence.

The development of ideologies is facilitated by the rise of centralized
states. These stress the need for national cohesion and can use modern

---

[16] In Algeria, for instance, a great number of Islamic movements arose in the late 1980s
      when this became legally possible. Most of them were politically active until the suppres-
      sion of the *Front Islamique de Salut* in January 1992, and many are still in existence. For
      a study of the more radical movements, see ETIENNE, *L'islamisme radical*. Chapter Five
      treats the *da'wa* as a political discourse. Cf. *Le radicalisme islamique au Sud du Sahara*.
[17] Various responses have been given to the sad social, economic, and political situation of
      the majority of the population in most Muslim countries. One of these responses has
      been the rise of *da'wa* movements, each providing a kind of meaning in thought and
      action that is linked to Islam as a religion.

media to mobilize and guide people for causes of general interest. When the appeal of the national state ideologies had lost its attraction or even led to disillusions, the way for an alternative appeal, that of Islam, was open.

Another reason for the increase in *da'wa* movements and the positive response they receive is an ever-continuing negative reaction to Western power, models, and values. Criticism of the West is often accompanied by a search for viable alternatives, one of them being the affirmation of Islamic norms and values, especially on a more popular level. Islam is also presented as an alternative source of norms and values in the face of the oppression exercised by so many regimes; this perception is at the root of the more politically oriented "Islamist" and activist movements. Finally, the fact of the grave economic and social conditions prevailing for the great majority of the population in nearly all Muslim countries also plays an important role in current positive responses to *da'wa* movements.

5. New Social Meanings of Islam

What sort of Islam is proposed by recent *da'was* and what is the exact nature of their call in recent times? In the new situations that have arisen all over the Muslim world, the idea of Islam itself has indeed started to convey new meanings, at least in the social domain. We are primarily concerned here with the *da'wa* that is followed by a social movement, rather than the *da'wa* leading to a (re)conversion of the individual, even if the two are interrelated. In addition to its fundamental religious and moral meanings, which enjoy general acceptance, the idea of Islam has indeed begun to convey a basically new *social* significance to Muslims, in particular since the middle of the twentieth century.[18]

On the basis of personal communication and reading I submit that Islam, especially in the 1980s and 1990s, has acquired the following additional meanings:

1) There seems to be an increasing sense of demarcation from secularism and purely secular ideologies as well as from other faiths and ideologies. This demarcation is linked to a renewed emphasis on Islamic identity.

2) Moral values relevant at the present time appear to be receiving new stress. Islam is considered to stand not only for the moral behavior of individuals and societies, as was always the case, but also for justice

---

[18] This is most evident for Iran since 1979, but it also holds true for other Muslim countries including Iraq. See for instance WILEY, *The Islamic Movement of Iraqi Shi'as*.

in general, social justice in particular, and an Islamic interpretation of human rights.[19]

3) There is a palpable striving for Islam to be recognized, by non-Muslims too, as a positive value after the experience of enduring generally oppressive foreign domination that looked down upon Islam. The need for Muslims to be authentic and free from alienation is increasingly stressed. It is desired that non-Muslim governments recognize Islam as a valid religion for their own Muslim minorities. All of this leads to movements of resistance, protest, and emancipation under the banner of Islam.

4) In contrast to the secular tendency to consider philosophy and morality, research and education, economics and politics as more or less autonomous domains of activity and thought, there is a tendency both to synthesize and to "islamicize" such domains. Calls are made to further an Islamic orientation of scholarship and Islamic education[20], Islamic economic and Islamic politics, all of this within the framework of an Islamic *Weltanschauung* and an Islamic morality. Mutual consultations of Muslim experts are organized on these and other subjects.[21]

5) New emphasis has been placed on the role of Islam in bringing about a just society, establishing social justice, and guaranteeing fundamental human rights. This is a strong argument for Muslim human rights groups, who constitute a critical opposition to inadequate governments or oppressive regimes. In such cases, a call for a just society may take the form of a special kind of *da'wa*. Such a call may be made in a general sense, advocating an Islamization of society, but it may also be made in a specific sense, as the project of an Islamic state rigorously based on the *Sharī'a*. As long as these calls for an Islamic state are made as a pure ideal, they will remain, like many other calls, utopian. But when political movements arise and actively promote the establishment of such a state, *da'wa* includes the intention to really change the government, the regime, and the state. Such oppositional calls for an Islamic state should be clearly

---

[19] Ann Elizabeth MAYER, *Islam and Human Rights: Tradition and Politics*, Boulder, Colo.: Westview Press, 1991, 1999³. Cf. above Chapter 8 on "Human Rights, Human Dignity, and Islam".

[20] Isma'il al FARUQI, *Islamization of Knowledge: General Principles and Workplan*, Washington, D. C.: International Institute of Islamic Thought, 1982. Cf. "Islamic Education Series", with Syed Ali ASHRAF as general editor and published by Hodder and Stoughton (London) and King Abdulaziz University (Jidda).

[21] Available resources are inventorized. In 1984, the first edition of the *International Directory of Islamic Cultural Institutions* appeared, prepared by TANLAK and LAJIMI at the Research Centre for Islamic History, Art and Culture, of the international "Organization of Islamic Conference" (Istanbul, 1405–1984). In 1991, the first edition of *Qualified Manpower: Specialists in Islamic Studies in the World* was published by ISESCO. Such publications are also valuable for scholarly cooperation.

distinguished from calls to Islam made by rulers in power, who seek to legitimate the status quo. Evidently, appeals to Islam made by those in power are quite different from ones made by those seeking to take power.

The call to Islam expressed in Islamic movements in the twentieth century goes back to a deeper need for justice and order. People seek in the *Sharī'a* as religious law and in Islam as a religion the protection they need. Thus each call for the *Sharī'a* to be applied acquires moral as well as emotional overtones.

The Islam to which the call is made has often been absolutized. The tendency to make Islam something absolute in society has taken various forms, each of them reinforcing the *da'wa* in a particular way.

First, Islam may become an absolute but blind ideal, in the same way that any other religion or worldview can be made blindly absolute and close people's minds.

Second, Islam may be presented as a system of ideas, as an ideology. Just as all religions can be ideologized and all ideologies absolutized, Islam can be presented as an absolute ideology.

Third, Islam may serve as the foundation and symbol of an alternative "utopian" social and political order that people hope to see realized. The basis of such a utopian social order is expressed in mythical terms or by means of certain absolute principles. Islam can indeed be put forward as the absolute foundation of a new utopian social order, with a mixture of "mythical" data (mostly derived from the Qur'ān as "Revelation") and "absolute principles" (like justice and reason).

As a result of such absolutizations, the concept of Islam in twentieth-century Muslim societies has been able to convey an ever-growing number of new meanings in addition to those known throughout Islamic history.

We may now summarize our findings concerning new social meanings of Islam acquired by the Islamic *da'wa* in recent history.

Any Islamic *da'wa* makes Muslims aware of their Islamic identity and strengthens it also in moral and emotional ways. Such a call aims to lead Muslims to an awareness of life, society, and reality at large, not just in a naive, immediate way, but in a normative Islamic light, via Islamic orientations and ways of acting.

Any *da'wa* addressed to non-Muslims is meant to bear witness to a possible new orientation, transformation, and conversion on their part. As a missionary effort, it is carried out on a large scale among non-literate peoples to rescue them from their religious ignorance (*jāhilīya*). It is carried out on a small scale among de-Christianized Westerners to bring them back to a pure monotheism.

In former times, Islamic missions took two major forms. On a practical level, a shared Muslim identity was quite often a prerequisite for Muslims when they embarked on close relationships in marriage, in business, and in social life in certain circles. On a religious level, preachers, teachers, or holy men (*Sūfīs*) who had themselves experienced a "calling" to live and preach among non-Muslims carried out a *da'wa*. In modern times, new forms of *da'wa* to non-Muslims seem to have developed on both a practical and a religious level.[22]

6. Islamic Movements Studied as Da'wa Movements

If it is true that an Islamic *da'wa* constitutes the core of most if not all Islamic movements, the study of such movements should take into consideration their particular *da'wa* character. I thus suggest that particular attention be paid to the following aspects.

1) Any call to Muslims to practice their Islam more diligently and to become better Muslims and any call to non-Muslims to accept Islam as the true religion have meaning primarily within an Islamic framework. For Muslims to be called to a better practice of their religion, they must already be convinced of the excellence of Islam and accept the Qur'ān as unconditional truth. For only on this condition will they be prepared and willing to listen to the Qur'anic *āyāt*. In the same way, a non-Muslim, before being able to accept the *da'wa* addressed to him or her, should be able and willing to discern the message conveyed by the *āyāt*.

2) Any *da'wa* consequently presupposes the unconditional validity of the Qur'anic and Islamic "sign system" as such. But the particular kind of Islam that is preached, its specific forms and contents, remain open to discussion. Past and recent Islamic movements illustrate many kinds of *da'wa* that call to various forms of Islam. In the study of a particular Islamic movement, both its *da'wa* and its specific articulation of Islam should be identified.

3) Not only every *da'wa* preaching but also every *da'wa* movement has its particular aims, and to understand an Islamic movement, these aims should be identified and analyzed in given contexts. I speak here of "intentions", and submit that the inner dynamics of *da'wa* preaching and *da'wa* movements are largely given with their intentions. Insofar as these intentions have an absolute aim, they tend to become absolute themselves too. Forms of belief as well as representations, ideas as well as forms of religious practice, can be made absolute. It would seem that each Islamic *da'wa* contains an unconditional, absolute core. In the study of a *da'wa* movement, due attention must be paid to what is held to be absolute both in the preaching and in the practice of the movement.

---

[22] See for instance KERIMOV, a specialist from the former USSR, "The Socio-political Aspects of the Modern Islamic Mission".

4) If a *da'wa* has resulted in a particular movement and community, it also leads to particular forms of religious and moral behavior in its members. Certain Qur'anic texts are regularly quoted; certain ways of behaving are particularly prescribed; certain interpretations of Islam are held to be authoritative. Like the *turuq*, *da'wa* movements should be seen as just so many variations within the *umma* and so many variations of Islam itself. Each movement has developed its own particular symbolism, its own ways of behaving, and its own interpretation and application of Islam. It has accepted a specific leadership as legitimate, but this leadership may very well pursue various strategies to reach its aim, depending on circumstances.

Looking at developments during the twentieth century, one cannot but be struck by the ever-increasing differentiation of forms and expressions of Islam. Not only within official and practiced Islam and in mystical and popular Islam, but also among the Islamic *da'wa* movements, there are ever more differences and variations—also due to ethnic, social, and political factors—that struggle to realize their particular interpretation of Islam. Within the overall sign and symbol system of Islam, each *da'wa* movement has constituted its own subsystem.

5) For analytical purposes, it is helpful to distinguish within each Islamic movement the ideological and spiritual level from the level of action and daily practice. Some movements are markedly action-oriented whereas others concentrate very much on ideas and spiritual life.[23] Not all social and political movements that bear the label "Islamic" are *da'wa* movements. To deserve this title, a movement must go back to a specific *da'wa*, have an Islamic ideological content, and result in social action by Muslims with visible fruits. Its historical fate will inform us both about the nature of the movement itself, including its *da'wa*, and about the wider context and the specific situation within which it arose and worked by proclaiming its *da'wa*.

Selected Literature

ALTALIB, Hisham, *Training Guide for Islamic Workers*, Herndon, VI: The International Federation of Student Organizations and the International Institute of Islamic Thought, 1991/1411.

CANARD, M., Art. "*Da'wa*", in *Encyclopedia of Islam*, new edition, Vol. 2, Leiden: E. J. Brill, 1965, pp. 168–70.

DASSETTO, Felice, "The Tabligh Organization in Belgium", in *The New Islamic Presence in Western Europe*, ed. by Tomas GERHOLM and Yngve Georg LITHMAN, London: Mansell, 1988, pp. 159–73.

---

[23] Cf. below Chapter 17 on "The Rise of Islamic States", and my "Fundamentalismus und Aktivismus in der islamisch-arabischen Welt der Gegenwart".

ENNAIFER, H'mida, *Les commentaires coraniques contemporains: Analyse de leur méthodologie* (Series "Studi arabo-islamici del PISAI" Nr. 10), Rome: Pontificio Istituto di Studi Arabi e d'Islamistica, 1998.

ETIENNE, Bruno, *L'islamisme radical*, Paris: Hachette, 1987.

FAROOQI, Lutfur Rahman, *Da'wah Directory*, 2 Parts, Islamabad: Resource Centre, Da'wah Academy, International Islamic University, 1992.

Les Frères musulmans: Egypte et Syrie (1928–1982), ed. by Olivier CARRÉ and Gérard MICHAUD, Paris: Gallimard/Julliard, 1983.

HUSSAIN, Asaf, *Islamic Movements in Egypt, Pakistan and Iran: An Annotated Bibliography*, London: Mansell, 1983.

Islam: State and Society (Scandinavian Institute of Asian Studies, Studies on Asian Topics 12), ed. by Klaus FERDINAND and Mehdi MOZAFFARI, London: Curzon Press, and Riverdale, Md.: Riverdale Company, 1988.

KEPEL, Gilles, *The Prophet & Pharaoh: Muslim Extremism in Egypt*, trans. from the French (1984), London: Al Saqi Books, 1985.

JANSEN, Johannes J. G., *The Neglected Duty: The Creed of Sadat's Assassins and Islamic Resurgence in the Middle East*, New York, etc.: Macmillan, 1986.

KERIMOV, Gasym Mamed Ogly, "The Socio-political Aspects of the Modern Islamic Mission", in *Islam: State and Society* (see above), pp. 39–50.

MITCHELL, Richard P., *The Society of the Muslim Brothers*, London: Oxford University Press, 1969.

NADWI, Syed Abul Hasan Ali, *Da'wah in the West: The Qur'ānic Paradigm*, Markfield: The Islamic Foundation, 1992/1413 (20 pp.).

POSTON, Carry, *Islamic Da'wah in the West: Muslim Missionary Activity and the Dynamics of Conversion to Islam*, New York & Oxford: Oxford University Press, 1992.

Qualified Manpower: Specialists in Islamic Studies in the World, Rabat: ISESCO, 1991.

Le radicalisme islamique au Sud du Sahara: Da'wa, arabisation et critique de l'Occident, ed. by René OTAYEK, Paris: Karthala, and Talence: M.S.H.A., 1993.

RAMADAN, Tariq, *Aux sources du renouveau musulman: D'al-Afghani à Hassan al-Banna, un siècle de réformisme islamique*, Paris: Bayard/Centurion, 1998.

REISSNER, Johannes, *Ideologie und Politik der Muslimbrüder Syriens, 1947–1952* (Islamkundliche Untersuchungen 55), Freiburg: Schwarz Verlag, 1980.

SIDDIQUI, Kalim, *Issues in the Islamic Movement*, London: The Open Press, 1981, etc.

SUFI, 'Abd al-Qadir as-, *Jihad: A Groundplan*, Norwich: Diwan Press, 1978.

TANLAK, Acar, and Ahmed LAJIMI, *International Directory of Islamic Cultural Institutions*, Istanbul: Research Centre for Islamic History, Art and Culture of the international "Organization of Islamic Conference", 1984/1405.

WAARDENBURG, Jacques D. J., "Fundamentalismus und Aktivismus in der islamisch-arabischen Welt der Gegenwart", *Orient* (Hamburg), 30 (1989), pp. 39–51.

WILEY, Joyce N., *The Islamic Movement of Iraqi Shi'as*, Boulder and London: Lynne Rienner, 1992.

YAKAN, Fathi, *Problems faced by the da'wah and the dā'iyah*, Kuwait: International Islamic Federation of Student Organizations, 1994/1414.

Chapter 16
Ideologization in Present-Day Islam: An Exploration

1. Introduction

In the course of the nineteenth century, new currents of thought about Islam started to develop in Egypt, Tunisia, the Ottoman Empire, and Iran and among Muslims in India, Russia, and elsewhere that differed from existing ways of thinking on the subject among Muslim scholars at the time. It also was different from the ways in which Sūfīs and mystical brotherhoods practiced Islam in thought and meditation. The new currents of thought took Islam as a subject of reflection in relation to social experience and more generally the conditions of life in Muslim societies. One outcome was the rise of a number of movements of renewal and reform in the Muslim world in the second half of the nineteenth and the first half of the twentieth century.

Seen from a distance, perhaps the most remarkable fact was that these people started to speak and write about Islam in terms of more general ideas. Islamic norms, rules, and prescripts were transformed into ideas that represented general values. Sometimes, such ideas were seen in a vacuum and the human reality of Islam—as well as other religions—was practically neglected. Religion was then represented as an ideal, a spiritual reality, so that we can speak in that case of an idealization of religion. Sometimes, however, people represented religions as systems of ideas aimed at changing the world and society in a particular direction, with a particular vision of the future. In such cases, religion was transformed into ideas that had social consequences, so that we can speak of an ideologization of religion.

This movement of transforming Islam into a system of ideas increased strongly in the course of the twentieth century. Especially since the 1960s, a great number of Muslim voices can be heard that present Islam in new ideas including post-modernist concepts that gained acceptance in the West in the 1980s. Compared with the mid-nineteenth century, the end of the twentieth century testifies to an astonishing variety of Muslim ideas about Islam. The variety of presentations hints at a differentiation of Muslim experience and thinking that could be the subject of a phenomenological study from the perspective of the science of religion.

In this context, I would like to make some exploratory remarks in view of future studies dealing with the development of ideological, intellectual, and spiritual trends in twentieth-century Islam. Here, however, I am only concerned with present-day ideological thinking about Islam and the corresponding ideological movements, in brief the current ideologization of Islam.

Among Muslim thinkers, spiritual, intellectual, and social concerns are interrelated and cannot be rigidly separated from each other. But in present-day ideological movements social concerns are at the center. Broadly speaking, they are at the root of the new ways of thinking about Islam to which I alluded at the beginning and they have naturally led to political thought and action in Muslim countries.

The Western public is not well-informed about the background of such ideological movements in Muslim countries; it is mostly startled by its political expressions as portrayed in the media. My aim here is simply to present a first exploration of ideological currents in present-day Islam, not to take a stand on them. I want to explore their historical and social background, to ask about their aims and objectives, to assess the means used to reach these aims, and finally to grasp at least something of the deeper intentions, forces, and interests moving this ideological thinking. It may very well be that these ideological currents in present-day Islam express social and religious concerns that are not so alien to us as they may initially seem.

2. Ideologizing a Religion

Applications of religions imply the presence of ideological elements. A critical science of religion is able to lay bare the elements that are part of the articulation of a religion for practical purposes and that have consequences for practical life. Its very representation as a system of ideas makes it possible to direct the religion towards certain aims and will give it a particular impact in social life. Whereas a strictly ritual or mythical religion may have a limited number of practical applications, a religion that is transposed into ideas is much more malleable and can be directed in very different ways.

This is of course the case with any ideological system, but if a religion is ideologized, the ideological potential is particularly great. One reason is that, in any religion, certain things are legitimately absolutized and cannot or can hardly be questioned. Another reason is that a religion can offer a cover for various interests, not only those of religious institutions whose continued existence has to be assured but also practical economic and social interests that are served by the very existence of a religion. Those in power will favor a more conservative role and interpretation of the given religion; those not in power may favor a more challenging or even critical interpretation of that religion so as to oppose the established power or authority. As a consequence, any religious ideology has to be analyzed in its relationship to given powers and authorities.

It is, however, not only empirical phenomena or religious systems that can be ideologized. Ideologization can also take place in what may be called spiritual elans. If, for instance, the longing for purity is an elan that pervades many religions, the desire for personal or communal purity can be reduced to an ideological puritanism that imposes itself and can become fundamentally intolerant. The natural elan of hope that we find in so many religions can be reduced to utopian ideologies that are imposed upon people and that can turn out to be tyrannical. And the very search for origins and principles that is an important element in many religions can be reduced to a low-key ideological fundamentalism that refuses any alternative interpretation of the religion's founding rituals, texts, or principles. And last but not least, the natural respect for existing rituals, myths, symbols, or scriptures that consider the religions transmitters of meaning and truth can always be reduced to legalistic forms of behavior, speaking, and thinking that simply repeat themselves. Even the spiritual elan itself can be ideologized when the religion concerned is absolutized as a religion and in fact becomes an object of idolatry. Moreover, a striking feature of ideologies is their rationalizing character. By presenting a system of ideas in a rational way, one tries to convince oneself and others of the truth of the system, leaving aside the question of the presuppositions and axioms that undergird the whole system and its truth claim.

Ideologizing a religion can take place in at least two different ways. On the one hand, one can make a religion more convincing and promote it by bringing its "essence" into words, specifically a rational system of ideas. In this case we have to do with a kind of ideological "essentialization" of the religion one wants to promote. On the other hand, one can present a particular ideological version of a religion in order to promote a general noble cause to which one is committed and that need not be religious itself: human rights, justice, or peace, for instance. In this case we have to do with a kind of ideological "adaptation" of the religion to serve a general cause to be pursued.

Ideologizing a religion, that is to say making a system of ideas out of it with practical aims in mind, is a human activity that takes place in a particular situation. The aims and purposes are not always fully clear to the people concerned. Such an ideological reading in a given situation may offer a kind of solution to perceived problems. But in new situations and with other problems, people may read their religion in a new way and even make a new ideological version of it.

3. The Case of Islam

What happens in our time when Islam is ideologized? One might expect that people would seek the one particular ideology that would be proper to Islam and that could be directly deduced from the Qur'ān. In fact, however, there is no one such an ideology. There have always been a whole range of interpretations of Islam, each one presenting itself as expressing the truth and the essential message of Islam. Many elaborations of Islam in fact go back to this kind of "essential" perception; they are not necessarily ideological in nature, but can be also spiritually or intellectually oriented. Our concern here, however, is ideological elaborations with clear social concerns.

As mentioned above, besides "essentialist" ideologizations of Islam there are also "adapted" ideologizations. In response to Marxist socialism, for instance, these latter claim to offer an "Islamic" socialism respecting the basic norms and values of Islam. It is not always clear, however, whether such adaptations seek primarily to serve the cause of socialism and adapt Islam to it, or if their basic concern is Islam, enriched with socialist values.

This is a general problem in the study of present-day Islamic ideologies. They rose when older liberal, nationalistic, and socialist ideologies declined in most Muslim countries at the beginning of the 1970s. Sometimes Muslim governments favored them. For a new generation they represented new promises. The Islamic ideologies were less demanding intellectually. They lent themselves to practical adaptations, except for "Islamists" who ideologized what they saw as the essence of Islam. Most important they appealed to the imagination. Although they present themselves in a rational way, their religious message and symbolic expression, rather than rational argumentation, gives them a particular appeal to people.

What happens when Islam undergoes this process of ideologization, especially among people with a more modern education who are concerned about religion and society?

First, the idea of Islam that is elaborated here distinguishes itself from the scholarly constructs worked by the traditional specialists of Islam, the 'ulamā' who followed the rules of text interpretation and logical reasoning. It also differs from the more popular Islam of the people, with its manifold varieties, which is primarily directed not toward ideas but toward behavior and action. It is closest to Islam as presented by preachers.

Second, these ideas of Islam are concerned with society; they offer a blueprint of the ideal Muslim community and wider society. The idea of Islam presented here is meant to be a moral and social regulator that imposes certain rules and structures on society. From the outset, the political independence and economic potential of a number of Muslim countries gave a new relevance to the idea of Islam and its role in society. This has been the case again since the 1970s. Muslim groups discuss it; various standpoints and positions are taken; numerous interests are involved. Certain countries have been centers of such ideological discussion, such as Pakistan right after its creation in 1947 (with preceding discussions in British India), Egypt since the 1920s, Turkey since the 1950s, and Iran since the 1960s. Debates about special issues such as the status of women or the organization of the state must be seen against the background of these broader ideological discussions about the nature of the Islam to be realized, that is to say the right idea of Islam.

Third, it is important to note that, whatever the discussions, it was finally the state that decided what kind of Islam and Islamic ideology would be officially supported in the countries concerned and that defined what would be ideologically admissible. It was the state that imposed a particular social order and legitimated it by declaring a particular ideological version of Islam the official one, calling it "Islam". Sometimes this was in continuity with existing traditions and structures, as in Jordan or Morocco. Sometimes this submitted the Islamic structure to practical state interests, as in Turkey. Sometimes it put Islam within a wider framework created by the state in which various religious communities had to cooperate, as in Indonesia. Sometimes the state imposed a very particular version of Islam and Islamic ideology, leaving little place for deviant forms, as in Saudi Arabia or in Khomeinī's Iran. Sometimes the state itself was torn apart between proponents of different Islamic ideologies that tried to impose themselves on the state where the military decided, as in Pakistan. And sometimes a relatively small Muslim majority tried to impose a rigid Islamic ideology and structure not only on the Muslims but also on the country's non-Muslim minorities, which were not or hardly tolerated, as in Sudan. We still leave aside the complex internal political situations of countries like Algeria or Iraq, and countries where both Muslim and non-Muslim minorities play an important role, as in Syria or Lebanon, and the republics that resulted from the disintegration of the former USSR and stressed their Muslim identity. Nearly all these states present and legitimate themselves to their populations with an Islamic ideology.

Fourth, as a logical consequence, any opposition in these countries that claims to act on Islamic principles will try to undermine the Islamic ideological claims of the state. It may do so by presenting its own idea of Islam, saying that the state as it is does not represent true Islam—often referring to existing corruption, injustice, and decreasing morality. Or it may do so by presenting a broader, not specifically Islamic idea of society—often referring to human rights, social justice, or civil society.

Opposition movements can be nourished by "Islamist" ideas on the one hand and by "secularist" ideas on the other hand, all of them developing their own ideology. Inasmuch as such an ideology has not been constructed for political purposes only, there is a particular vision of social reality—and perhaps even more than that—behind it. But in order to win adherents for its particular message, an ideology—whether Islamic or otherwise—must not only find an audience for that message and the rational argumentation supporting it. It should also respond to political and economic interests and find élites willing to support the group in question. These may be the military in Pakistan or Turkey, royal and other privileged families on the Arabian Peninsula, clergy in Iran, businesspeople in Lebanon and Syria. Or they may simply have the trust and confidence of that hidden absolute majority in all the countries concerned: the poorer people.

4. The Internal Context of Islamic Ideologies

The reconsideration of Islam in terms of ideas that developed since the mid-nineteenth century is closely connected with the social history of the Muslim countries. In other words, ideological currents in Islam during this period should be seen in their social context. It is this context that explains to a large extent the ideologization of Islam that has taken place. We shall first concentrate on the context within the Muslim countries themselves.

A fundamental given is the dislocation of traditional societies and the weakening of the established cultural and religious traditions. This can be called modernization, but the term neglects important changes in norms and values that were considered self-evident and that were related to Islam as conceived at the time. After World War Two and independence, high expectations were raised for economic and social development within the framework of a new international economic order. Similar expectations existed for new democratic institutions and justice. With a few exceptions, these expectations were not realized and although the standard of life improved for the new middle classes, the poor remained or became very poor. Again with a few exceptions, existing Islamic institutions could not respond adequately to the new social situations and maintained their traditional religious discourse.

In nearly all countries, these social changes took place in growing political instability; in many cases revolutions brought a new leadership to power. Its first task was to impose order, by force, on often more or less chaotic situations. Practically without exception, the Muslim countries were ruled by authoritarian regimes, some of which became even more oppressive than the colonial powers had been. Many Islamic ideologies are in fact ideological responses to situations of economic exhaustion and political suppression under which the people suffer. To complicate matters, many of the movements promoting these ideologies were fighting to establish themselves and to enlarge their influence. What seems to be a struggle between various ideologies and may be called a "battle for Islam" in fact reflects a struggle for survival between various Muslim groups and interests, that is to say to keep and extend their power. The rise, flourishing, and decline of a great variety of forms of Islam in Muslim countries is linked to the need and greed for various kinds of power to deal with largely chaotic situations.

By the end of the nineteenth and the first half of the twentieth century, the fundamental choice was between the old and the new, *al-qadīm* and *al-jadīd*, those adhering to tradition and those promoting modernity. This implied a discussion about what should and what should not be liable to change, the latter being considered "Islam", of permanent value and validity. The accelerated development in countries that followed the Western development model increased the tension between those who benefited from modernity and those who were its victims or at least warned against too great a confidence in it. There is reason to assume that the "Islamists" working with Islamic ideologies have in fact taken the place of the "traditionalists" of a century ago. Resistance against over-development no longer comes solely from more or less passive traditionalists, but also from the much more active "Islamists", who are replacing Islamic tradition by Islamic ideology.

The presence of authoritarian regimes has given a political incentive to the rise of Islamic ideologies meant to change society. In the 1970s, regimes in Egypt and North Africa tried to use Islamic movements as an alternative to leftist movements that represented an important opposition. The political use of Islam, however, in turn unleashed oppositional movements that bore Islam rather than Karl Marx in their banner. The consequences of political authoritarianism went against norms and values that could be defended in the name of Islam. Much of the "Islamist" ideological literature is in fact a polemic against abuses of power by authoritarian regimes.

The same Islamic ideologies and the accompanying media and literature, by concentrating exclusively on the Islamic issue, tend to exaggerate particularist feelings and awareness in the Muslim world. By immersing themselves so completely in their own religious ideology, the Muslims concerned risk to losing themselves in a continuous absolutization of Islam and their own world, which leads to distorted views of other cultures and religions. By construing an ideological universe above reality as it is—or seems to be in daily experience—the ordinary communication with that reality and people living in that reality may remain hampered until reality itself corrects ideological schemes imposed on it.

5. External Contexts: Relations with the West

The rise of Islamic ideologies, however, should also be viewed in the broader framework of the relationships between Muslim countries and the West, that is to say Western Europe and North America. On a certain level of analysis, these ideologies are to be read as protests against Western dominance and a self-defense against Western encroachments on Islamic identity. The movements of political independence were only one attempt to restore a balance and develop more equal relationships between the Muslims and the rest of the world, including the West.

The encounter with the West, read at first as an encounter with Christianity, quickly turned out to be an encounter with a Western form of secularity and its ideological expression as "secularism". Whereas at the beginning the ideologization of Islam may have been largely a response to Christianity, in the second half of the twentieth century it rather became a response to secularism as found in and ascribed to the West. The confrontation with secularism forced Muslims to formulate anew what is essential in Islam as a religion and to present this in a concentrated form to the Muslim community—and to Westerners, if needed.

The modern West indeed had and has a double face. Science and technology, freedom of conscience and expression, democratic institutions and a system of justice are mostly recognized as its positive values. Its colonial policies, prolonged by interference in countries like Iran, Algeria, Palestine (through Israel), Afghanistan, Bosnia, and the now independent USSR. Muslim republics are seen as its negative sides. Muslim as well as other countries suffered the effects of Western hegemony in the armament race and military conflicts, in direct or indirect political control, and in the free market system, which disintegrates existing social structures with broader economic policies leading to increased indebtedness and to increased misery for large parts of the population. Various militant ideologies of Muslim struggle have arisen from this situation.

If secularism was bad and economic exploitation worse, worst of all—in the views of Islamic ideologies—was Western criticism of Islam. Here, the accusation is that the West wanted and still wants to destroy Islam. The work of Western media, Christian missionaries, and scholarly Orientalists is read as a concerted struggle against Islam. Here again, the ideological response has been prompt: Islam being the highest value in Muslim societies, it should be defended at any cost; the influence of Western criticism of Islam should be rigorously limited, especially as far as younger Muslims are concerned. Indeed, if there is any subject that Islamic ideologies have continuously defended, then it is that of the value of Islam and the dignity of Muslims.

The extent to which Western currents of thought have actually waged war against Islam would be a good subject of inquiry. It would be exaggerated to give general judgments about all missionaries and Orientalists, but there certainly is a point in saying that certain progressive, conservative, and religious ideologies in Europe and the USA have been extremely critical toward social practices current in Muslim societies, toward certain claims of Islamic religion, or simply toward any religion that wanted to take a stand different from Christianity. And self-criticism is a discipline to be learned.

Realities, however, are more complex than our schemes. There are indications that, during the Cold War, Islam received unusual sympathy in the West and that Western interests contributed to the revitalization of Islam, which was seen as a religious bastion against the USSR and China. Were not the Talibān in Afghanistan fanaticized for Islam during the war against the Soviet invaders?

Tensions and conflicts at the borders of the Muslim world certainly have encouraged the crystallization of Islamic ideologies focused on perceived enemies of Islam and Muslims. In this respect, too, unbalanced relationships between Muslim and Western societies have created ideological attacks and self-defenses that make adjustments and compromises still more difficult. The mere presence of Israel first, and then its handling of the occupied territories and their populations have led to a kind of conflictual illness in the region, not only ideological but real and with a heavy price to be paid on both sides.

Given the experience of relations between the Muslim and the European world, it seems to me that at least a considerable number of Islamic ideologies were developed as an ideological resistance and protest against foreign domination, interference, and influence that was felt to be dangerous. Certainly, there have been ideologies in favor of opening up to Europe or to the West in general. But looking back, there have been many more ideologies defending Islam against real or perceived attacks from the West. The existing anti-American, anti-communist, and anti-Zionist publications are simply depressing in their political simplicity and lack of self-criticism; the same holds true for the writings against missionaries, Orientalists and other evil-doers to Islam. Similar ideological accusations have been made against internal enemies: Bahā'īs, Ahmadīs, secularists. Islamic ideologies seem to be a kind of natural or inborn reflex against threats, not so much leading to creative words or action than to refutation by means of ideas.

6. Ideologies Leading to Action

One result of Islamic ideologies has been the establishment of a particular Islamic order in countries like Iran, Pakistan, and Afghanistan.[1] Of course,

---

[1]   On these countries, cf. below Chapter 17 on "The Rise of Islamic States".

a number of reasons can be given for the revolutionary developments that took place in the first two countries in the 1970s and in the latter case between 1995 and 2001, but it cannot be denied that the ground was prepared by Islamic ideologies during the preceding years. "Islamization" and "Re-Islamization" were the terms the leaders themselves used to indicate their aims. The case of Sudan falls within the same category; the Islamic order was enforced upon the South, which, however, refused it. At an earlier stage, with the unification of the main parts of Arabia, an Islamic order was imposed on the conquered territories. Here, it is not the differences between Twelver Shīʿī, Hanafī, Talibān, Brotherhood, and Wahhābī forms of Islamic order that are important, but rather that an Islamic order was imposed at all.

In other Muslim countries there are Islamist pressure groups that have been working for some time to apply *Sharīʿa* law and to establish an Islamic order. Egypt, Nigeria, and Malaysia are examples. Again, it is the fact that pressures have been exerted in this direction and not the differences between them that demand attention.

In all Muslim countries, one can find groups of "Islamist" ideologists and activists promoting Islamization and working for the establishment of more Islamic states based on the *Sharīʿa*. They present an ideological version of Islam, claiming that this will put the country in a state of order. The idea of an Islamic order is especially attractive in disorderly situations, as they exist in many places in the Muslim world.

The underlying idea of all Islamic ideologies used to realize an Islamic order as a social and political reality is that Islam is something beneficial for and to be imposed on society. In traditional Muslim societies, this was commonly accepted, and Islam as articulated at the time was an integral part of the social order, with its religious institutions and social bodies, its scholars and preachers. The existing authority structures were instrumental in inculcating Islam in its accepted forms in the social fabric.

The changes in Muslim societies have brought about the rise of a new approach to Islam as an idea. The discussions of this idea have led to an ideologization of Islam that has crystallized in a number of variant Islamic ideologies in various national, social, and cultural contexts. A few examples illustrate this.

6.1. In *Indonesia*, discussion about Islam has been pursued within the older Muslim groups and parties. It has also been encouraged by the government, which placed it within the ideological framework of the Five Principles of the country, the so-called *Pancasila*. Topics like the following were discussed all over the country since the 1970s in the Suharto period: the contribution of Islam to nation-building, social and economic development; the dialogue between religions in Indonesia in the framework of a basic harmony between religions; Islam's contribution to peace, a just society, and a happy family life, always within the broader framework of the *Pancasila* as a kind of civil religion of the state.

Those in favor of an Islamic state or at least a predominant role for Islam in the country carried out a clear opposition to the government's approach. Once Indonesia had become an independent country, they claimed that it should be organized according to the order prescribed by the majority religion, Islam. Their major concerns since 1945 have been how to islamize Indonesia, how to give the *Sharī'a* its due place in the country, and finally how to establish an Islamic state. As a result, there have been continuous debates about sensitive subjects like the Constitution and its Preamble, the meaning of the *Pancasila*, the marriage law of 1973, Western support given to Indonesian Christians, constitutional reform, and of course the elections after the fall of Suharto, who had practically eliminated Islamic political parties.

6.2. In *Iran, Pakistan* and lately also *Afghanistan*, the debate much more directly concerned the ideology of an Islamic order and its establishment when revolutionary "Islamist" regimes came to power in the 1970s and in Afghanistan in the 1990s. Here the governments have been involved in the politics of Islamization. Starting with the question what Islam requires Muslims to do, the next questions evolved logically: What are the elements of an Islamic order and what are to be the stages of Islamization (also called re-Islamization) as a revolutionary struggle to realize such an Islamic order? What are the requirements of an Islamic state based on the *Sharī'a* and how should an Islamic state be established? What laws are to be enacted in an Islamic state and how? How should justice be administered and what kind of democracy should be applied? What does the *Sharī'a* say about specific subjects and how should these demands be carried out in daily practice? On a practical level, this broaches questions like what are men's responsibilities, how should women behave in public and in private, how should children be educated in the family and at school, and how should secondary and higher education be organized? How should the media present general information to the public, and how should censorship be organized? Although seemingly practical questions, they touch upon essential ideological questions: How should society be guided in an Islamic sense? How should people be made more Islam-conscious and induced to think in an Islamic framework? How can knowledge be "islamicized", in contrast to forms of knowledge that claim to be neutral and objective or that serve aims and purposes that go against fundamental Islamic norms and values?

Although all three countries have their "Islamist" hardliners, the Talibān in Afghanistan went furthest in applying a particularly harsh "Islamic order" in flagrant contrast to the universal declaration of human rights of the United Nations (1948), specifically in points concerning the status of Muslim women and of non-Muslims. Whereas in Pakistan and Iran an existing order was islamized by the "revolutionary" government from above, in Afghanistan at the end of the twentieth century—as in Arabia at its beginning—a completely new order was imposed by force, without even the appearance of a consent of the people concerned.

6.3. Another pattern is found in a number of Muslim countries, especially around the Mediterranean, where the government keeps a clear distance to Islamic currents and movements that strive for a greater Islamization of society. *Turkey* has its own official Islamic institutions supervised by the *Diyanet*. Given the close association between Turkish nationalism and official Islam in Turkey, the state, through its guardian—the army— puts heavy political and ideological pressure on all Islamic organizations outside the *Diyanet* that have Islamic ideologies.

In North Africa, the situation varies in the different countries. *Morocco* has an official institutional setting of Islam headed by the King. Although there are "Islamist" pressure groups of various kinds that advocate a more rigid Islamization of the country, the government does not accede to them. With Muhammad VI, the government takes more liberal attitudes than in his father's (Hasan II) time. *Algeria* has had a turbulent history during the last half-century and lately also in relation to "Islamist" ideologies and politics. After the decades of a secular socialist FLN (*Front de Libération Nationale*) regime, the free elections of 1991 brought to light not only the rise of Islamic parties but also great popular expectations for greater Islamization of the country, such as envisaged by the ideology of the *Front Islamique de Salut* (FIS). After suspension of further elections, civil war developed, with the GIA (*Groupe Islamique Armé*), the military wing of the FIS, and the government making a front against any "Islamist" claims and policies. *Tunisia*, frightened by the developments in Algeria, started to persecute movements and currents in favor of Islamic ideologies and policies.

Egypt during the twentieth century and earlier has been the scene of ideological debates about Islam. After Nasser's repression of "Islamist" opposition, his successor Sadat (r. 1970–81) gave free way to the Muslim Brotherhood and other Islamic organizations in order to counter the leftist opposition against his "open market" policy. After his assassination because of what was called his betrayal of Islam, militant Islamist groups were again forbidden and persecuted. Yet, their continuous pressure has led to an increasing Islamization of the country, with the government zigzaging between pro-Islamic and secular policies.

In the countries mentioned, the anti-Islamist stand of the governments is supported by European and North American countries. Yet, their suppressive policies often lead to a stronger ideological use of Islam by opponents of authoritarianism and corruption, who reproach governments for being un-Islamic, to which the governments concerned answer with their own ideological use of Islam to defend the status quo.

6.4. Muslim countries like Syria and Iraq that advocate secular policies and a separation between state and religion have responded with severity to any attempts at political opposition, whether in the name of Islam or not. Islamic ideologies here are seen as subversive.

Paradoxically, this is also the case in Saudi Arabia and some Gulf Emirates, where the official established versions of Islam, such as the Wahhābī interpretation of the Sharīʿa and other Wahhābī doctrines, are supportive of the government and status quo. Other Islamic ideologies are seen as subversive here, as well.

7. The International Spread of Islamic Ideologies

Certain Muslim countries play an important role in what may be called the internationalization of specific Islamic ideologies. On a small, national scale, this happens with the diffusion of particular Islamic ideologies by Turkish and Moroccan official and private Islamic agencies and organizations among their national émigrés in Europe. Access to national co-citizens through imāms, mosque supervision, and Islamic materials also allows a certain control of the nationals in the "diaspora".

Needless to say, certain totalitarian Muslim regimes promulgating their own "official" versions of Islam awaken alternative versions and Islamic ideologies inside and outside their borders. With further politization of Islam, there is also the increasing danger that Islam will become compromised not only in the eyes of non-Muslims reacting for instance to events in Afghanistan, but also in the opinion of ordinary Muslim people in countries like Pakistan, Iran, or Turkey who have enough of the Islam imposed on them and to which they are continuously exposed.

Countries like Saudi Arabia and Iran and to some extent also Libya and Pakistan are known for their da ʿwa activities (further Islamization of Muslims and missionary Islamization of non-Muslims) in African and European countries and elsewhere. Saudi Arabia and its protégé Pakistan tend to export a strongly conservative reading of Islam meant to support an Islamic order in which Saudi Arabia plays a leading ideological, financial, and political role. Rumors have it that this country supports "Islamist" groups and interests everywhere. Iran and Libya also have da ʿwa activities, but in a much more Islamic-revolutionary sense.

Egypt, itself supported by Saudi funding, plays an important role through its al-Azhar institutions. Not only do Muslim students from Muslim countries come to Egypt to study Islam, but also a considerable number of Egyptian teachers are sent out to teach Islam elsewhere.

International Islamic universities that were established in Islamabad, Kuala Lumpur, and Khartoum in the 1980s carry out through their teaching a similar function of spreading a certain type of Islamic ideologies among intellectually interested groups in Asia and Africa.

International Islamic organizations, often stationed in Saudi Arabia like the Muslim World League, of course play a key role in formulating and spreading particular kinds of Islamic ideologies throughout the Muslim world. From other perspectives, this also happens through the worldwide networks of Islamic organizations like the Muslim Brotherhood, Sūfī *tarīqa* networks, and Islamic media, including satellite TV and Internet, with a variety of interpretations and ideologizations of Islam.

Paradoxically, non-Muslim countries also indirectly play an important role in the spread of Islamic ideologies. A country like Israel, with its policies since the June war of 1967, has contributed immensely to the ideologization and politicization of Islam, which in my view works against its long-term interests. Some major Western countries, including the USA, have instituted short-term policies that worked against the interests of Palestinians, Bosnians, or Muslim immigrants and generally imply a rather negative judgment of Islam as such. This has not only encouraged the growth of problems in Muslim-Western relations, but also the outgrowth of an immense "Islamist" anti-Western rhetoric. It is striking how politicians whose strategies have spurred the growth of militant "Islamist" ideologies have been and are so little aware that what they describe as the danger of Islam, the awakening of a defensive or aggressive Islamic consciousness, has been largely the result of their own queer policies.

Apart from political channels and interests, Islamic ideological stands have spread among common Muslim people in very unofficial ways such as marriage and family links, tribal and ethnic loyalties, professional and especially trade relations, economic and technical assistance programs within the Muslim commonwealth itself, and transnational religious groups like *turuq* that have hardly anything to do with politics. But I should also mention common Muslim protests with growing solidarities against sufferings imposed on Muslims by certain groups of non-Muslims. The natural tendency of Muslims and others is to distance themselves from Western hegemonic behavior and to constitute a common front against it, if not in fact, then in ideas.

8. Some Special Features of Islamic Ideologies

Many kinds of ideologies are operative in human societies and when they call to action, they have, as such, a political character. Compared with most other political ideologies, Islamic ones distinguish themselves by their religious references and background. It gives them a "total", encompassing character. They refer to something held to be absolute and to truths, norms, and meanings that are believed to be given and not humanly constructed. Even if the elaboration of these ideologies quite evidently has been and is a human affair, the causes that they defend claim to have a normative character for human affairs.

From the perspective of the science of religions, any ideologization of Islam carries risks. Surrender to God risks becoming a surrender to Islam, or in fact an ideological version of Islam. A religious ideology, like an absolutized religion, risks becoming an idol for its adherents.

I suggest that ideologies of Islam and Islamic ideologies cannot present Islam itself, but only certain aspects of it, even if they claim to summarize the truth of Islam. In fact, however, wanting to present to Muslims and/ or others what Islamic is and means, they can only present what it is and means to them, at a particular place and time, and in a particular situation and context. By making absolute claims, they merely absolutize one aspect of Islam.

This holds true for the "essentialist" ideologies of Islam. Rather than defining once and for all what Islam is, they bring people together for the cause of Islam. They may lead to better reflection and deeper experience in given situations.

This certainly holds true for the "applied" ideologies in view of particular concrete social and other problems. Once the problem has been present and identified, Islam is defined and identified in such a way that an answer becomes possible. Such applications are tied to particular situations.

The development of Islamic ideologies during the last century and a half, and certainly in the Muslim states in the course of the last half a century, clearly shows that different situations lead to different kinds of ideologization of Islam. There turns out to be an immense variety of ideological forms and articulations of Islam. Any statements about future ideological forms of Islam simplifies reality and may turn out to be utterly wrong. One should always recall that there is not one unifying authority, institution, and thus ideology in Islam. Islam as such has a common sign and signification system, but no common ideology. This fundamental diversity may seem to be a handicap for common action, but for ideological expressions it is an advantage, on the condition that the signs are recognized in their own right.

An important feature of Islamic ideologies, it seems to me, is that, by concentrating on Islam as the highest norm and value, they tend to further a more or less clear separation between those people who are Muslims and those who are not. It is the cause of Islam that divides people, and by making an ideology of it, one inevitably stresses the

division in social life and practice, as well. In human society, where not
only Muslims are active, it is mandatory to have, in addition to the
difference in religion, attention to common purposes and interests on a
broader human level. For certain activities it is correct to stress the
special contribution of Islam; for other activities, the good will of all
people should rather be stressed. In many respects, Islam offers a kind of
specification of something that is universally valid and not an exclusive
and exclusively valid domain.

Much of the ideological versions of Islam since the mid-nineteenth century has something to do with the West and with Europe in particular,
given the impact of the colonial period. From a Western perspective, this
becomes clear rather soon; from a Muslim perspective, the West may be
attacked, but its realities cannot be denied. My provisional hypothesis is
that much of the development of Islamic ideologies—not only those that
refer directly to the West themselves—becomes clearer if viewed within
a broader framework of positive and negative interactions between the
Western and the Muslim world.

   I started by stressing the developments and factors inside Muslim
societies that explain why Islam came to be seen more and more as an
idea and was "ideologized" as such in its application, while its permanent
norms and values were idealized. I went on to show that the relations
between Muslim and Western societies have been rather imbalanced and
that this has been a major factor in the anti-Western ideologization of
Islam. On the one hand, there was Western domination. On the other
hand, however, there was a certain Islamic self-sufficiency. On the part
of the Muslims, except for some eminent minds, little attention was given
to other ways of life, other concepts of the world, and other religions.
And there was an evident lack of knowledge and considered judgment
about cultures and religions outside Islam, for their own sake. Precisely
as an ideology, Islam blocked the view of non-Islamic realities in their
own light. They were seen, precisely, in the light of Islam. That is what
I call "ideology".

9. Further Study of Islamic Ideologies and Ideologization

The study of the ideologizations made of any religion—whether in
Churches, Zionism, or Islamic movements—is disconcerting. We are
constantly faced with the question what people actually did with their
religion, what they made of it, how they used and abused it, or how they
grew through it. Empirical studies should trace the situations, interests,
intentions, and motivations that have led people to construct, spiritualize,
ideologize, and instrumentalize religions in specific situations or in more

general contexts. Further inquiry should be made into the deeper forces at work in and behind the ideologization of religions. Here, however, we are concerned only with ideologizations of Islam, and I suggest some demands to be made on such study, beyond the demands of a technical nature that are in the domain of specialists in the area. I formulate such more general demands coming from the study of religions.

First, I would like to stress the need to study Islamic ideologies and particular ideologizations of Islam without imposing one's own ideas or convictions on the materials studied. Until now, most studies of the subject seem to have been carried out with specific objectives in mind, such as analyzing Islamic fundamentalism, getting Islam under control, bringing Islam into a particular direction, stressing differences between Islam and other religions, or interpreting Islam in terms of a particular form of dialogue. I am convinced that research on a sensitive subject like this one should be carried out with respect for the data studied and without any "ideologization" of the materials—conscious or unconscious—by the scholar himself or herself. If there is one lesson to be learned from the past, it is that foreign interference with Islam leads to ideological resistance.

Second, I would like to take as a postulate in the study of Islamic ideologies—specifically with regard to non-Muslims—that relations between Muslims and non-Muslims need not be conflictual. The idea of unavoidable conflict has been alive on both sides for a long time and there has been a range of Muslim-Western conflicts. There is no proof, however, that this wrong idea will persist when populations mingle, and when there is increasing interdependence between peoples and cooperation between scholars. Of course, there are always problems in relationships, but they need not be insoluble in the long run. Domination and fear of each other, of course, close any parties off from each other. But there is no reason to suppose that domination and fear cannot be overcome.

Third, I see a possible future force leading to a new kind of ideologization of Islam in relation to the West. It would be born out of the growing contrast between an increasingly rich West and a number of impoverished Muslim societies. Western economic and other relationships with these societies and countries need to become more balanced, fed by the need for adequacy and justice in relationships. The Muslim countries concerned need to develop knowledge, education, study, and research. If their atmosphere—with or without Islam—becomes too ideologized and politicized, the future of these countries—including their thinking about Islam—looks grim, like that of other religions that have been excessively ideologized.

Selected Literature

BANNĀ', Ḥasan al-, *Five Tracts of Ḥasan Al-Bannā' (1906–1949): A Selection from the Majmu'at Rasā'il al-Imām al-Shāhid Ḥasan al-Bānna'*, trans. and annotated by Charles WENDELL (University of California Publications, Near Eastern Studies 20), Berkeley and Los Angeles: University of California Press, 1978.

CARRÉ, Olivier, *Mystique et politique: Lecture révolutionnaire du Coran par Sayyid Qutb, Frère musulman radical*, Paris: Cerf & Presses de la Fondation Nationale des Sciences Politiques, 1984.

—, *L'utopie islamique dans l'Orient arabe*, Paris: Presses de la Fondation Nationale des Sciences Politiques, 1991.

Islamic Fundamentalism: Myths and Realities, ed. by Ahmed S. MOUSSALLI, Reading: Ithaca Press, 1997.

KEDDIE, Nikkie R., *An Islamic Response to Imperialism: Political and Religious Writings of Sayyid Jamāl ad-Dīn "al-Afghānī"*, Berkeley, Cal.: University of California Press, 1968.

—, *Sayyid Jamāl ad-Dīn "al-Afghānī": A Political Biography*, Berkeley and Los Angeles: University of California Press, 1972.

MAUDUDI, Seyyed Abul Ala, *West Versus Islam*, New Delhi: International Islamic Publishers, 1992.

NASR, Seyyed Vali Reza, *Mawdudi and the Making of Islamic Revivalism*, New York and Oxford: Oxford University Press, 1996.

NIEUWENHUIJZE, Christoffel Anthonie Olivier van, "Islamism: A Defiant Utopism", *Die Welt des Islam*, 35 (1995), pp. 1–36.

QUTB, Sayyid, *Milestones*, Karachi: International Islamic Publishers, 1988[2].

—, *Islam, the Religion of the Future*, Kuwait: International Islamic Federation of Student Organizations, 1992.

RAHNEMA, Ali, *An Islamic Utopian: A Political Biography of Ali Shari'ati*, London and New York: I. B. Tauris, 2000.

SHARI'ATI, 'Ali, *On the Sociology of Islam: Lectures*, trans. from the Persian by Hamid ALGAR, Berkeley, Cal.: Mizan Press, 1979.

—, *Marxism and Other Western Fallacies: An Islamic Critique*, trans. from the Persian by R. CAMPBELL, Berkeley, Cal.: Mizan Press, 1980.

—, "Intizār, the Religion of Protest", in *Islam in Transition: Muslim Perspectives*, ed. by John J. DONOHUE and John L. ESPOSITO, New York and Oxford: Oxford University Press, 1982, pp. 297–304.

ZEGHAL, Malika, *Gardiens de l'Islam: Les oulémas d'Al Azhar dans l'Egypte contemporaine*, Paris: Presses de la Fondation Nationale des Sciences Politiques, 1996.

Section 9

The International Scene and Islam

Chapter 17

The Rise of Islamic States[1]

This chapter deals with the rise among many "Muslim" states with a Muslim majority, of particular, formally established "Islamic" states that claim to be based on religious law (*Sharī'a*) and that pursue active policies of Islamization. The distinction between Muslim and Islamic states was clearly formulated by E. I. J. Rosenthal in 1965.[2]

After providing historical and contextual perspectives on the call for an Islamic order and Islamic states in recent decades, I ask how the rise of contemporary Islamic states can be related to current processes of religious and social change. Next, a short survey of twentieth-century Muslim thinking on the role of religion in society shows that a number of Muslim authors of very different positions have given thought to the problem of the Islamic state in the course of the last fifty years. The substance of the chapter then concerns four Islamic states: Saudi Arabia, Iran, Pakistan, and Libya. These states are compared in regard to specific themes, reference being made to the cases of Sudan and Afghanistan, too. Finally, attention is paid to the "religious" aspects of contemporary calls for an Islamic order and Islamic states. I show some connections between the call for and rise of Islamic states today and broader processes of change that have both social and religious aspects.

1. The Ideal of an Islamic Order

The recent rise of new Islamic states has contradicted a number of expectations widely held in Western, socialist, and some "Eastern" countries about the essentially secular nature of nationalism and the new nation-states that resulted from it. Pakistan's and Iran's change from more or less secularizing states to Islamic states has been claimed to be "religious" in the Islamic sense of the word. This contrasted with what had been predicted in the West as the gradual "secularization" of Muslim

---

[1]   Revised text of "The Rise of Islamic States Today", *Orient* (Hamburg), 28 (1987), pp. 194–215.
[2]   ROSENTHAL, *Islam in the Modern National State*, p. 26.

countries, at least in political matters, and for which the secularist development in Turkey from the 1920s until the 1950s was widely considered
paradigmatic. My focus here is on this unexpected religious mutation in
the development of nation-states, insofar as it has led to important
constitutional changes putting them on an Islamic basis.

1.1. Historical Perspective

Historically speaking, the idea of an Islamic order as a pattern of just
social organization prescribed by Islam is a goal particular Muslim groups
and communities have been trying to realize since the very beginning of
Islam. Both the Qur'ān and the *Sunna* contain elements for ordering
society, and it is fair to say that the first Islamic state existed in Medina
during the last ten years of Muhammad's life (622–32). The new community (*umma*) distinguished itself from earlier communities in Arabia in
being based on prophetic leadership with particular revelations and in
being supra-tribal and not connected with a particular social class. After
Muhammad's death, that is during the period of the four "rightly-
guided" Caliphs (*al-khulafā' al-rāshidūn*, 632–61), this "Islamic state",
with its immense territorial acquisitions, took new forms, in particular
thanks to the organizing genius of the second Caliph, the pious 'Umar ibn
al-Khattāb (634–44). This Medinan period, during which Islam became
linked to political power over a large empire, served as a paradigm for
most later attempts to bring about the desired "Islamic" order of society.

Under the Umayyad (661–750) and 'Abbāsid (750–1258) dynasties,
when political realities were not entirely consistent with the religious
norms contained in Qur'ān and *Sunna* and elaborated in *fiqh* (jurisprudence), the ideal of a true "Islamic order" arose and was developed
in pious Muslim circles in different directions. It implied an indirect
protest against the saddening political divisions. As an ideal, it was
worked out in various ways: (1) by alternative socio-religious movements
like the Khārijīs and Shī'īs, who sometimes succeeded in creating alternative "Islamic" states; (2) by religious scholars ('ulamā') in their elaboration of religious law (*Sharī'a*); and (3) by charismatic leaders who
developed further rules of religious life and later established mystical
brotherhoods (*turuq*) as social organizations enabling Muslims to live
according to such rules. The very idea of an Islamic order and an Islamic
state with particular institutions was also used, however, by the political
leadership to legitimize the existing Caliphate, the policies pursued by the
Caliphs, and the further administration of the empire.

The just society has always been considered one in which the prescripts
of Islam, based on revelation, would be followed. Throughout Islamic
history, various groups have appealed in various ways to Islam, claiming
to realize such a society. This claim was also made by the Ottoman as well

as the Safavid and Moghul empires that developed in the fifteenth and sixteenth centuries respectively and that substantially changed a number of existing medieval political and religious institutions held to be character- istic of the Islamic state. Throughout Islamic history, however, religious critics and political opponents have always been inclined to reproach the existing political leadership for not really applying the *Sharī'a* and thus not being consistent with the norms of Islam. In classical Muslim thought, the social "Islamic order" was to be deduced from the *Sharī'a*, the political application of which leads to the "Islamic state".

Only in the nineteenth century and under increasing pressure from the West did new ways of reflecting upon the idea of an Islamic state emerge. When the existing Muslim empires began to disintegrate during the eighteenth century, possible reasons for this phenomenon were already sought, and religious circles mostly held departure from the prescripts of Islam responsible. When in the nineteenth and twentieth centuries Mus- lim territory was even occupied by "unbelievers", the question of how to formulate and realize a proper Islamic order and perhaps even to estab- lish a truly Islamic state acquired a new relevance.

From the end of the nineteenth century on, movements of social and religious reform brought about a new way of thinking about the problem of an Islamic order and an Islamic state. The demand for reform of both individual and social thought and action was made with a direct appeal to the Qur'ān and the *Sunna* as the true sources of religion, largely bypassing the medieval scholastic tradition. Nineteenth-century reform- ers like Sayyid Ahmad Khān (1817–98) in India, Muhammad 'Abduh (1849–1905) in Egypt, and their pupils ensured that the problem of a "modern" Islamic order had already become an issue before the Muslim countries became independent. It was, however, the generations of "Is- lamists" (who made an ideology of Islam) and "activists" (who applied this ideology politically) following on the earlier reformers who devel- oped further the idea of a truly Islamic state to be realized in the future, after independence.

Although no Muslim country on gaining independence after World War Two opted to establish an Islamic state based on the *Sharī'a*, in each new nation-state there were Muslim groups actively advocating this idea in word or deed. Thus, the ancient ideal of an Islamic order of society, which had lain dormant during colonial times, became an urgent problem as soon as independence was obtained.

1.2. Contextual Perspective

In addition to the historical perspective, there is a regional, contextual one underlying the recent rise of Islamic states. These states are all situated in or on the edge of the Middle East, which is a turbulent area for many reasons including the existence of conflicting ethnic, religious, national, and international interests, poverty and illiteracy in many circles, military leadership of states, and factions. Then, of course, there is the presence of the state of Israel, which is felt to be a "foreign body" in the area and whose impact on developments in the region as a whole still tends to be underestimated in most Western media and studies. The rise of Islamic states in this region has something to do with it.

Although the region is Muslim, not everything in it is Islam. First of all, there are Christians, Jews, Zoroastrians, and other believers. Many social and cultural elements and structures of Middle Eastern societies go back to pre-Islamic times and have little to do historically with Islam or religion in general. New structures have developed in the region during the last century and a half because of technological development independently of Islam and largely under the impact of the West.

Yet Islam in the Middle East, as elsewhere, in addition to being a faith and a way of life, is also a particular social pattern imposed in various ways on the societies of the region. It is articulated in different ways by different ethnic groups and social classes in different countries. In the area as a whole, Islam is a recognized norm, and an appeal can always be made to the Islamic faith and identity of individuals and groups, the more so since their social and economic conditions are often intolerable.

The formal Islamic states that have arisen in the area represent an attempt to bring about an Islamic order through political power exercised from above. These states—Saudi Arabia and Iran, Pakistan and Libya— play a significant role, both symbolic and real, in the Middle East and the Muslim world. They serve largely as sources of a vital reaction to what is perceived as the demoralization if not disintegration of the Muslim community (*umma*) as a whole. Islamists and activists attribute this disintegration not only to negative influences from outside but also to a moral betrayal of Islam within Muslim societies. Along with establishing Islamic states, there are also attempts to implement an "Islamic order" in ways other than power politics: from below by people seeking to maintain what they consider sound tradition based on Qur'ān and *Sunna*, and in all classes by people looking for a moral, even puritan renewal.

Contemporary Islamic states are not simply medieval remnants. They are rather the result of changes not only in the material sectors of technology, economy, and labor that were brought about for instance by the presence of oil, but also in the sectors of social and cultural life that are vital in Middle Eastern societies. Once established and legitimized as "Islamic", these states bring about changes in other vital sectors as well, including political and social institutions and the distribution and exercise of power.

Many changes that have led to the rise of Islamic states can hardly be related to influences from the West or from the socialist countries. They are due primarily to tensions within the societies themselves, within the overall Middle Eastern context. Yet the leaders and people concerned tend to attribute such tensions mostly to bad influences from outside, and the result is that all states in question distance themselves from the West except when looking for technology and military aid. What then is the Muslim perspective on the rise of Islamic states? To answer this question, we must direct our attention toward twentieth-century Muslim political thinking.

2. Muslim Perspectives on the Role of Religion in Society

2.1. Some General Considerations

The views developed by twentieth-century Muslim thinkers on the role of religion (Islam) in society can be located between two polar positions. At one extreme are the religious modernists advocating the modernization (*tajdīd*) of society. They tend to restrict the application of religion—which they see as a largely moral and spiritual force—to the private sphere of life, and they tend to separate state and religion. Such views are mostly represented by lay thinkers, including administrators, technicians, and scientists, although some technicians practice excessive scripturalism and some *'ulamā'* adopt modernist positions toward traditional thought. Politically speaking, these people are mostly liberals or socialists. This trend of thinking is found in modern Turkey and Syria and was current, for instance, among the founders of Pakistan and the westernized Iranian elite of the Pahlevi period.

At the other extreme are those thinkers who advocate the application of the norms of religion as contained in religious law (*Sharī'a*) to all aspects of life, in particular social and public life. This view is taken by the religious Sunnī or Shī'ī traditionalists and applied in particular by Islamists and activists working in Islamic movements founded for the purpose. Politically, these people are generally conservative. They want to base their political action on norms contained in the *Sharī'a* with direct reference to the Qur'ān and the *Sunna*.

In most countries, this polarity entails a fundamental tension between the "modernist" and more traditional "orthodox" approaches. Many "left-wing" modernists have developed into nationalists with a secular outlook, whereas many "right-wing" traditionalists have developed into Islamic activists. Hence the Muslim Brotherhood and similar organizations arose, which, in various countries, propagate the ideal of an "Islamic order" first within the national states but usually aim at establishing an "Islamic state" at a later stage.

Between the modernists and the traditionalists arose the reformists. They distinguished themselves from the modernists because they did not

accept unconditionally external values (e.g., from the West) but wanted
to measure such values against Qur'ān and *Sunna*. They thus bypassed
much of the medieval scholastic tradition and set themselves apart from
the "traditionalists" who accepted that tradition. This trend of reform
(*islāh*), with its return to the sources of religion (Qur'ān and *Sunna*), has
always been present throughout Islamic history, but it acquired a new
impetus since the 1860s. These reformists diverged from Islamists and
Islamic activists by stressing the role of reason; thus they can be called
Muslim intellectuals, imbued with a strong sense of social responsibility,
for instance in the field of education.

The influence of these groups varies according to country and period:
e.g., in Saudi Arabia until the 1970s there were hardly any traces of
"modernist" Muslim thinking, which goes against the country's official
religious doctrine, whereas modernists predominated in Iran and Pakistan in the 1950s and 1960s. In Libya, the modernists and the traditionalists may have been equally influential in the 1950s and 1960s, while
mystical attitudes such as those of the Sanūsīya exerted a noticeable
influence. In Pakistan, religious impulses have emanated from Islamists
and *'ulamā'* but also from brotherhoods (*turuq*), which have a strong
position there. Iran has its own Shī'ī traditions and theological and
juridical doctrines. In the eighteenth century, among the Shī'ī *'ulamā'*,
independent reasoning (*ijtihād*) by the leading scholars (*mujtahids*) was
recognized; this has no equivalent in Sunnī Islam.

The differences between the various groups are marked in their thinking on the state, that is to say the ideal Islamic state. Since all serious
thinking on the subject implies interpreting the *Sharī'a*, involving certain
techniques of deducing prescriptions and rules from what are called the
"sources" of religion, different concepts of the Islamic state finally depend on different interpretations of the demands of the *Sharī'a*.

There is another aspect of twentieth-century Muslim thinking that is
important for this subject, namely its marked ideologization. A number
of thinkers have elaborated Islam into a more or less complete *Weltanschauung* (worldview) with rules to be followed. Numerous ideologized versions of Islam and of the "Islamic order" have been developed, and
they are used not only as an abstract "Islamic system" but also as a
critical norm to judge factual reality. In this way, a negative judgment can
be pronounced "in the light of Islam" on nearly every given state of
affairs. Often Islamists and activists use such an ideologized version of
Islam to express protest, resistance, or even open opposition to the
political leadership.

In contemporary Muslim societies, the concept of *Islam* is used politically in different ways by different groups with or without power: government leaders and officials, *'ulamā'*, social reformers, Islamists and
activists, Sūfī *sheykhs*, but also victims of the prevailing poverty and

injustice. The same holds true for the concept of the *Islamic state*, and research should be carried out on the ways in which this concept functions as an ideal on the one hand and on the ways in which it is manipulated on the other hand. At present, in Muslim countries the notion of the "Islamic state" always occurs in an ideologically charged context. For the people, it has a strong symbolic value suggesting a reorientation within Muslim societies in contrast to apparent injustice and political and moral weakness. It suggests a defense against real or imagined enemies or an effort toward accelerating the arrival of a reign of justice at the end of times. For Muslims, the notion of the Islamic state always has religious overtones and, among those responsive to it, evokes a longing for something held to be absolute, such as a desire for justice or an aspiration to realize eschatological realities here and now.

Further research on Muslim thinking on the Islamic state requires that complex Islamic concepts with a long history usually going back to the Qur'ān and a variety of meanings be translated and explained as adequately as possible into Western concepts that have of course a different history and meaning. Khomeinī's writings, for instance, are couched in the terminology of medieval Islamic scholasticism, and for anyone not familiar with Qur'anic concepts and Islamic thinking, they are difficult to understand. Yet these writings of twentieth-century Muslim thinkers should be studied carefully. They should be examined for their logical coherence and the intentions directing a particular argumentation. The reader should also learn to see how such concepts are meant to be applied in practice and what various thinkers have said and written about their application.

The basic problem in such research is: how do Muslim thinkers perceive the world through the prisms of norms and ideals associated with the notion of the "Islamic state", and how are actual social realities and experiences interpreted in the light of this notion? Muslim thinking about an "Islamic state" as about other socio-religious topics, is not primarily determined by what is usually called a rational analysis of facts. It is, rather, conditioned by particular views and concepts presupposing Islam as the only faith and worldview worth the name. Other religious traditions developed other views and concepts that guide their thinking about society and the state.

2.2. Some Thinkers and Groups

In his *Modern Islamic Political Thought* (ch. 3), H. Enayat presents a lucid survey of twentieth-century interpretations of the Islamic state. By definition, in the Islamic state both civil and criminal law should be based on the *Sharī'a*. This *Sharī'a*, however, is not a fixed entity, and there are considerable differences between the legal systems and in the legal practice of the new Islamic states, even apart from the choice of different legal schools (madhāhib). Saudi Arabia, for instance, provides an example of the rigid nature of the ruling Wahhābī doctrine; Iran evidences the wide scope of individual judgment permitted to the religious leaders in the Shīʿa, but since 1980, the predominance of Khomeinī's interpretation; in Pakistan, military regimes seeking legitimacy have pursued a policy of re-Islamization; in Libya, a certain synthesis of Islam and socialism is proposed in which direct appeal is made to the Qurʾān only; here al-Qadhdhāfī's ideas predominate. Consequently, even in these formally established Islamic states there is no direct correlation between the commitment to Islam and Sharīʿa and the particular nature of the state organization with its politico-religious legal system. It all depends on what leaders perceive to be genuinely "Islamic" in a given historical context and social situation and what they are striving for.

The contemporary discussion about the Islamic state began after World War One, when the Ottoman Caliphate was first reduced to a spiritual office in 1922 and then abolished by the Turkish General Assembly in 1924. The idea of the Islamic state then became an alternative to that of the Caliphate, which proved to be unworkable in practice. The idea was developed in a reactionary sense in the Wahhābī state doctrine in Saudi Arabia[3] and in a conservative sense in the Salafīya movement as formulated by Muhammad Rashīd Ridā[4] (1865–1935), in Egypt. It was subsequently developed in an Islamist, activist, and later even revolutionary sense in the Muslim Brotherhood since 1928: first in Egypt, then the Near East, and later also in parallel organizations in Pakistan and further east as far as Malaysia and Indonesia. In the Muslim Brotherhood and its parallel Islamist organizations, the ideology of the Islamic state has had an increasing impact. The Islamic states that have been established provide models for further thought and action.

2.2.1. The Salafīya

Muhammad Rashīd Ridā, in his treatise Al-khilāfa aw al-imāma al-ʿuzmā[5], first sketches the foundations of classical Islamic political theory about the state, the responsibility of the Caliph being balanced by that of the "people who loose and bind" (ahl al-hall waʾl-ʿaqd). The latter group comprises representatives of the Muslim community and in particular the ʿulamāʾ. There should be mutual consultation (shūrā) between the Caliph

---

[3] See above Chapter 12 on "Saudi Arabia: The King and the Consul" and below Chapter 18 on "Islam as a Vehicle of Protest".
[4] See above Chapter 14 on "Puritan Patterns in Islamic Revival Movements".
[5] "The Caliphate or the Supreme Leadership", Cairo 1922/3.

and this group of representatives, but it is the Caliph who decides. One of the special tasks of the *'ulamā'* is to resist injustice on the part of the ruler by referring to the *Sharī'a*; according to some jurists, Muslims have a legitimate right to revolt against unjust rulers. In the course of history, however, there have been frequent disparities between the theory and the political practice of the Caliphate.

In the situation of his time (1922), Rashīd Ridā advocates transforming the classical Caliphate into a more spiritual office. Its holder, a man of high moral and scholarly qualities worthy to be head of state and possessing the capacity to exercise *ijtihād*, should be able to give independent legal judgments (*ijtihād*). This spiritual office is to be a symbol of the unity of all Muslims; its particular tasks are to settle disputes and ensure that Muslims adhere to the rules of Islam. This new Islamic state embodies the principle of mutual consultation (*shūrā*), rather than that of popular sovereignty in which parliament makes decisions, as in Western democracies. It exercises the functions of propagating (*da'wa*) Islam— both for the continuous Islamization of Muslim society and for Islamic mission among non-Muslims—and of providing proper Islamic legislation.

Such an Islamic state, indeed, should never adopt foreign laws without adapting them to Islamic norms. It should revive and apply religious law (*Sharī'a*), but it is also allowed to develop new legislation (*ishtirā'*) for matters of civil government (*hukūma madanīya*). In such new legislation, the state should deduce (*istinbāt*) law from the *Sharī'a* in all matters pertaining to religion (Islam), but it remains free to promulgate its own laws (*qānūn*) in non-religious matters that have nothing to do with Islam. The head of state, in Rashīd Ridā's view, should be the moving spirit of the legislative process. Alongside this spiritual Caliphate, but separate from it, there should be a temporal authority: the government. So Rashīd Ridā envisages the parallel existence of a religious and a political authority. His ideas found a receptive ear in Salafīya circles, but never took an organized form.

2.2.2. The Muslim Brothers

After Rashīd Ridā, however, the Muslim Brothers' solid organization forged a much closer link between religion and political action. In the course of time, they even tended to subordinate religion to politics, with a polarization between members and non-members of their organization and an authoritarian militancy in favor of what they considered "pure Islam". In the first decades, they lacked a coherent system of ideas and held different views in different countries, depending on the political scene. So they could pronounce themselves in favor of disparate aims, such as political independence, democracy, opposing a Muslim regime judged to be "un-Islamic", fighting Zionism, etc. In countries like Egypt, Syria, and Pahlevi Iran, the Muslim Brothers faced strong competition from secular ideologies that were supported by the regime, which opposed the Brothers. Their parallel group in Pakistan articulated thought and action in a continuous debate on Islamic issues, building on the fact that Islam was the very reason for Pakistan's creation and existence.

Egypt. The founder of the Muslim Brothers Society in Egypt, Hasan al-Bannā' (1906–49), started around 1928 with a moral and didactic response to what he saw as the critical situation of Egyptian society at that time. In Enayat's view, it was only in 1939 that al-Bannā' turned the Society into a political organization. He then presented Islam as an all-embracing ideology emanating from Qur'ān and *Sunna*. Muslims had a duty to struggle for the liberation of the whole Islamic "homeland" from foreign occupation and to institute free Islamic government. The successive phases of the Palestinian-Zionist confrontation and the Arab-Israeli conflict influenced the gradual politicization of the Muslim Brothers in Egypt. Consequently, the movement developed toward increasing ideological militancy and even violence.

The concept of the Islamic state that the Society of Muslim Brothers in Egypt developed differs in several respects from that of Rashīd Ridā. In their view, religion should lead directly to political action, should develop political ideas in a dualistic and eschatological framework and should present itself as a militant movement to bring about the desired change in society. Muhammad al-Ghazālī, for instance, in his *Min hunā na'lam* ("From Here We Learn", written after the Arab defeat of 1948), does not allow for any human legislation in non-religious matters, as Rashīd Ridā did. He hardly takes into account the variety of human experience, but develops, rather, the idea of one uniform religious law for one monolithic world. Most importantly, he speaks of the indivisibility of religion and politics in the Islamic system and sees both integrated in the *Sharī'a.* Less idealistically-oriented than Rashīd Ridā, he demands that the prevailing bad political and economic conditions be changed first, putting an end to despotism and economic exploitation, before Islam can really be applied in society. He strongly denounces Western imperialism as well as Muslim detractors of Islam, whom he regards under Western influence. In Egypt, it was the radical thinker Sayyid Qutb, a member of the Muslim Brothers who was executed in 1966, who developed the most complete ideological system of how Islam should be thought and applied at the present time. He elaborated, for instance, "Islamic" socialism as an alternative to the "Arab" socialism proclaimed by 'Abd al-Nāsir in Egypt or by the Ba'th in Syria.

Since the 1970s, the Brotherhood has been permitted more freedom of expression.

Other countries. Muslim Brothers have been active in Palestine since the 1930s, after 1945 in Jordan and Syria, and later in less politicized forms in Kuwait.

Iran. A parallel organization of the Muslim Brothers in Iran was that of the radical *Fidā'īyān-i islām* (The Devotees of Islam), founded by Sayyid Mujtabā Navvāb Safavī, who was executed in 1956. Unlike in Egypt, they did not represent a mass movement and they had no intellectual leadership. They were rather renowned for their underground political activity, and some assassinations carried out between 1945 and 1963 were laid at their door. They considered the Pahlevi state to be pagan and sought to destroy it. Their radical concept of Islamic justice found its way into the practice of the Iranian revolutionary courts of 1979 and later. With their particular interpretation of S. 5:33,34, they called for capital punishment for any social and political offense that could be considered as "causing corruption on earth"[6]. They insisted on rigid adherence to the ritual prescriptions of Islam and to Islamic norms of behavior.

Pakistan. In the Pakistani equivalent organization, the *Jamā'at-i Islāmī*, founded by Abu'l-A'lā al-Mawdūdī (1903–79), we find the most articulated version of the Islamic state formulated in the spirit of the Muslim Brotherhood. As with the Egyptian Brothers, whose rise and activities were influenced by the British occupation and the Palestine/Israel conflict, the *Jamā'at's* rise and political development were related to Pakistan's wars with India and the civil war that led to the independence of Bangladesh (1971).

Mawdūdī's own activities dated from the 1920s, when he worked as a journalist in British India. In 1932, he founded the monthly review *Tarjumān al-Qur'ān* (Exegesis of the Qur'ān), which sought to go back to Scripture. He then also started to play a political role. Notwithstanding his insistence on the necessity of independent legal judgment (*ijtihād*), on which issue he differed from nearly all *'ulamā'*, he remained closely associated with certain groups of *'ulamā'*, first in British India and then in Pakistan. Most important for our purposes, however, is that Mawdūdī developed a coherent theory of the Islamic state and the Islamic revolution. In his theory, Mawdūdī treated the issue of the "Islamic state" as the political realization of what he called the "Islamic order" (*nizām-i islām*), a worldview and ethics he explicated in thousands of pages. He insisted on the interdependence of Islamic morality, law, and political theory. He described the realization on earth of the "Islamic order" as a continuous process leading to the "Islamic revolution". This is the gradual transformation of society through Islam's increasing "permeation" of the

---

[6]   ENAYAT, *Modern Islamic Political Thought*, p. 98.

social and moral consciousness. It takes place through the work of sincerely dedicated individuals who set the right example by a life devoted to Islam. Mawdūdī believed that, once the social and moral prerequisites were fulfilled in this way, the Islamic state could be realized as a political reality.

The Islamic state, according to Mawdūdī, has a total, all-encompassing character. It sustains a monolithic culture in which nothing is to be exempt from what Mawdūdī called the "Islamic order" and which he identified with the *Sharīʿa*. He based his theory of the Islamic state on S. 17:23,26–39, deducing from these verses the twelve principles that, according to him, should govern the institutions of the Islamic state and society. Mawdūdī here displayed a certain conservative tendency that is not representative of all Muslim Brothers. He did not want to touch the traditional family structure or private ownership, he rejected class struggle and was opposed to any egalitarian doctrines. In contrast to the Western concept of democracy, he pleaded for an elitist and authoritarian Islamic political order. He defended a very traditional Islamic stance on the status of women in society and the enactment of the *hudūd*, the severe corporal punishments the Qurʾān prescribes for certain crimes.

3. Four Islamic States Compared

Four Islamic states that have arisen in the Middle East in the twentieth century can now be studied in more detail: Saudi Arabia, Iran, Pakistan, and Libya. They seek to realize, in different ways, the ancient ideal of an "Islamic order". But they distinguish themselves from their medieval counterparts through the absence of a Caliph and from the earlier Muslim empires through the acceptance of the concept of the nation-state. As Islamic states, they react against the model of Western secular nation-states, but without being able to break the fetters of nationalism that also characterize Islamic states. Nationalism, by the way, was judged by *ʿulamāʾ* of older generations to be the great enemy of Islam, since it placed insurmountable obstacles in the way of unity among Muslims.

All four states claim to be based on and to apply the *Sharīʿa*. But they do this in very different ways, just as their realization of the ideal of an "Islamic order" takes widely varying forms.

3.1. The Four States

3.1.1. *Saudi Arabia* arose in Najd on the Arabian peninsula, first as an emirate in the eighteenth century and then, reconstituted, in the twentieth century. Only later was the Hejaz, a more agricultural and traditional region of religious culture with Islam's two holy cities of Mecca and

Medina, permanently occupied and added to the state, which became a
unified kingdom in 1932. Thanks to its alliance with the Wahhābī doctrinal school, the state exhibited from the beginning a strong puritan
reformist (islāh) impulse. The Bedouin were to be subordinated to the
ruler and to Islam in its puritan Wahhābī form, and the Hejaz was to be
purified of those religious expressions that could not be derived from the
Qur'ān and that violated Islam's purity. The state emerged in a region
that—apart from the annual hajj—had been isolated from outside influences and had kept its ancient social and political institutions. Throughout its history of the last seventy years, the monarchy has maintained
certain traits of a traditional Arab emirate, even while becoming a dynasty and claiming to be the guardian of religion. Only recently have the
monarchy and the 'ulamā' begun to share some power with the technocrats and bureaucrats of the new middle class. The Wahhābī legal and
doctrinal system, as the official version of Islam in the state, hardly seems
to allow room for other views and doctrines, at least in public life with
its Wahhābī Islamic order.

3.1.2. *Iran* has been an official Shī'ī empire since the beginning of the
sixteenth century and kept its religious tradition closely linked to Iranian
political and cultural identity. It has also had its own holy cities, including
Najaf and Karbela in present-day Iraq. The period from the middle of the
nineteenth century to the late 1970s brought modernization and considerable changes in Iranian society. These changes were mostly imposed
from above and mostly went against the interests of the Shī'ī religious
leaders, traditional guardians of the religious institutions. This was particularly true under the autocratic dynasty of the Pahlevis (1925–79)
which pushed for economic development according to Western and especially American models. This period was radically terminated by a popular revolution, controlled absolutely by Khomeinī. Subsequently, the Shī'ī
'ulamā' took over political power and a particular version of Shī'ī Islam,
developed by Khomeinī, became the official doctrine. Other views and
doctrines were less and less tolerated. The revolution was declared an
"Islamic" revolution, with the Islamic Republican Party assuming power.
Iran had to endure a bloody war against Iraq (1980–8). After Khomeinī's
death (1989), voices have arisen for a liberalization of the strict Shī'ī
Islamic order that had been imposed on Iranian society. Although the
current President, Khatemi, is known to be reform-minded, most representatives of the present-day established religious order support the supreme religious leader, Khamenei, who defends this order which was put
in place after the revolution of 1979.

3.1.3. *Pakistan*, too, goes back to an old Islamic empire, that of the
Moghuls, which was established in Northern India in 1526. The British

succeeded in subduing it after the middle of the eighteenth century and finally eliminated it in 1857. During the colonial period, "communalism" among both Hindus and Muslims in India was strengthened, with the result that conflicts between the Hindu and Muslim communities increased. In 1940, the Muslim League demanded a separate state for the Muslims of British India upon the latter's independence. So Pakistan— East and West—was established in 1947, absorbing the majority of the Muslims of the subcontinent. After an initial period that witnessed the foundation of the state on a modern Western model and an official modernist interpretation of Islam, Islamist pressures from inside succeeded in imposing an increasingly Islamist character on the new state. These pressures were reinforced by various wars with India, apparent political and economic failures, and in particular the civil war of 1971, which resulted in the secession of Bangladesh. Under Zulfikar Bhutto (r. 1971–7), this Islamization was implemented through the existing democratic institutions, but under Zia ul-Haqq (1977–88), Islamization— called Re-Islamization—was enforced from above. This happened especially after the successful Islamic revolution in Iran in 1979, which, together with the war that started with the Soviet invasion in Afghanistan in the same year, precipitated developments in Pakistan. In 1979, the Sharī'a was declared state law. The ideological basis for the transformation of Pakistan into an Islamic state was Mawdūdī's ideas about the "Islamic system" and its political realization. Resistance to the military regime was officially interpreted as an infringement of Islam. After Zia ul-Haqq's death, the provisions of the Islamic state remained enforced. In 1999, Pakistan was suspended from the British Commonwealth.

3.1.4. In *Libya*, Ottoman rule existed along the coast until 1911; from the middle of the nineteenth century on, the Sanūsī brotherhood was dominant in the country. The period of Italian colonization (1911–43) was a brutal experience for the Libyans, and so were the military campaigns during World War Two. Until the early 1960s, when oil exploitation started, Libya was one of the world's poorest countries. During the period of the monarchy (1951–69) which followed years of Libya's status as a trusteeship of the United Nations, the king was at the same time head of state and head of the Sanūsī brotherhood. The revolution of 1969, led by some young Free Officers under Muʿammar al-Qadhdhāfī, abolished the monarchy and sought to hasten the country's development by nationalizing the oil industry. In 1971, Libya was declared an Islamic state. It proclaimed a radical revolution, abolished the Sanūsī structure, and eliminated the existing bourgeoisie. From 1973 on, Islam has been interpreted in terms of continuous social revolution. Revolutionary changes have also taken place within the Islamic institutions themselves. The Qur'ān was declared the sole source of truth and authority, bypassing not only the medieval scholastic tradition but also the *Sunna*. The *Sharī'a* Faculties were abolished. The state has been directed along increasingly revolutionary lines, with a system of direct representation through Committees, without political parties, and with the rejection of private property beyond a minimum and the strict supervision of all social and cultural expressions according to the norms of the *Green Book*. Al-Qadhdhāfī claims to defend the cause of the oppressed peoples in the world. After the end of the sanctions (1992–9) imposed by the UNO on Libya in connection with the Lockerbie plane catastrophe, communications with the outside world have improved.

In two cases, the establishment of an Islamic state based on the *Sharī'a* has given an Islamic religious legitimation to violence against Muslim and non-Muslim civilians and entire groups of people.

The declaration of an Islamic state in Sudan in 1983 and again in 1991 gave a religious legitimation to the military regimes of al-Numairī and al-Bashīr. It was used to justify the continuous war against non-Muslim tribes in the southern part of the country.

The *talibān* regime in Afghanistan (1999–2001) imposed excessively harsh measures on the population, in particular Muslim women and Hindus. These measures were legitimated by an appeal to Islam interpreted in an excessively reactionary way.

3.2. Themes of Comparison

3.2.1. Establishment of the States. Comparing the establishment of these four Islamic states, only in the case of *Iran* can we speak of a real revolution in the sense that it was carried out, not by the armed forces, but by the people in the streets, particularly in the capital Teheran. This revolution, the result of an economic and political crisis, was guided by a charismatic leader, Khomeinī, who returned to Iran on February 1, 1979. The Islamic Republic was proclaimed after a referendum was held in March. Although the aim to establish an Islamic state may have been clear to the religious leaders from the beginning, this seems not to have been the case with the population, so that we should speak of two revolutions succeeding each other. After the first one, which toppled the Shah, a second revolution was unleashed, which transformed the country into a Shī'ī Islamic state and established a power elite of *'ulamā'*.

In contrast to Iran, development of the *Saudi Emirate* in Najd in the mid-eighteenth-century and its revival at the beginning of the twentieth century has been much more continuous. This has been an Islamic state since its inception, and it has been led continuously by one family. Yet the military aspect is not absent here either, since it was by force that 'Abd al-'Azīz II ibn Sa'ūd with his *ikhwān* established his authority over the Bedouin and the Kingdom of the Hejaz in the 1920s, the *ikhwān* being as dedicated to the Islamic new order in Arabia as the *pasdārān* were to be several decades later in Iran. Establishing the Islamic state in Arabia did not entail the transformation of an existing more or less "modern" state apparatus along Islamic lines, but the organization of a state from scratch. Subsequently, a deliberate attempt has been made to modernize the country without infringing upon the essentials of the *Sharī'a*, thus maintaining its character as an Islamic state. Opposition to the regime has come here mostly not from liberal circles but precisely from those who want Islamic norms—according to the Wahhābī interpretation—to be more strictly imposed by the state and who distrust modernization as such. In the process of development, the Wahhābī *'ulamā'* have played an important though not determining role, since they had to accept forces for technological and economic development and consequently for some social development as well.

The transition of *Pakistan* and Libya from Muslim states in a general sense into formal Islamic states was linked to military takeovers, and it is not possible to speak here of an "Islamic" revolution as in Iran. When Islam was declared the state religion in the Pakistani Constitutions of 1956, 1962, and 1973, the possibility of Pakistan being a "modern" Muslim state in which the *Sharī'a* would be only one of the sources of law was consciously left open. Here, it was the pressure of groups such as the *Jamā'at-i Islāmī* and the need of military regimes for legitimation that brought about an increasing Islamization of the country. Authoritarian, somewhat arbitrary measures taken by the military authorities since 1977 have led to an accumulation of power of the regime. In this process, the Iranian revolution and the Soviet invasion in Afghanistan played a catalyzing role. A similar arbitrariness of authoritarian measures should be noted in Iran, but here it benefits the religious and not the military leaders.

During the monarchy, *Libya* was a traditional state, the king being at the same time head of the Sanūsīya, the leading Sūfī brotherhood. Before the 1960s, Libya lived largely on the income generated by foreign military bases. When the exploitation of oil began, chiefly benefiting foreign companies while the population remained as poor as ever, protests began. The military coup of 1969 was inspired by the example of the Egyptian revolution of 1952. When the new Constitution of 1969, implemented in 1971, designated Libya an Islamic state, this did not mean any increase in the power of *'ulamā'* as in the other three states. Al-Qadhdhāfī's interpretation of Islam is that of a continuous revolutionary force to realize the new society, as formulated later in the *Green Book*. Libya is an Islamic state as al-Qadhdhāfī interprets it. It distinguishes itself from the other three Islamic states by its politically radical character, directly opposed to the established conservative character of Saudi Arabia under its monarchy and the institutionalized religious character of Iran's regime, where the *'ulamā'* wield power.

3.2.2. The Rulers. All four states came into existence primarily because of the activities of new rulers who seized or accepted power, often after the demise of powerful predecessors, and imposed an Islamization of society and the state. Originally these rulers were a traditional *amīr* (political chief), a traditional *'ālim* (religious scholar), or army officers. In all four cases, the rulers govern a population with firmly rooted Islamic cultural and religious traditions. Except in Libya, they are supported by groups of *'ulamā'*. In each case, the particular form of Islam that was current among the population started to function in new ways when particular elements of it were stressed and received an ideological interpretation in view of realizing an Islamic state. This is true for Libya at least for the early years of the revolution. The rulers may argue in public that the ideal Islamic society to which people have always aspired is being realized, but often Islam is used politically to impose themselves and legitimize their policies in the eyes of the Muslim populations.

3.2.3. National Cohesion. Besides Islam and Islamic ideologies, other powerful loyalties also strengthen the bond between different groups in each country. In *Saudi Arabia*, these include vested interests and loyalties within the large and influential Sa'ūd family as well as tribal loyalties with the required allegiance of the tribal chiefs to the monarch, together with the perceived threat of revolution, Islamic or otherwise, and foreign intervention. In *Iran*, the revolution of 1979 is still in people's memories and is hammered home by the media and in the schools. The protracted war against Iraq, perceived as the enemy of religion, and hatred of Israel, the United States, and Western imperialism in general, have also brought people closer together. Iranian national feeling has always been dominated by memories of a great past civilization. In *Pakistan*, there are powerful regional, ethnic, and religious loyalties, but in addition to the government's centralizing policies, the extremism of the Talibān in *Afghanistan* supported Pakistani unity just as the threat from India, long perceived as the main enemy, has done. *Libyan* loyalties, finally, have always been regional, focused primarily on Tripolitania and Cyrenaica, but al-Qadhdhāfi seems to have succeeded in transcending them. Important here, besides the figure of the leader, is the *Green Book* and the way its teachings are supposed to govern the revolutionary process in which the country has been involved since 1969. The perception of the United States and the state of Israel as major enemies and the declared solidarity with oppressed peoples all over the world provide a common orientation.

In all four countries, loyalties conflicting with the state, its rules, and its ideology are forbidden or strictly controlled; security services make any political opposition practically impossible; fieldwork by Western scholars is not easy. In each of the Islamic states, national solidarity against the enemies of the state and of Islam is propagated and, if need be, enforced.

3.2.4. Realizing an Islamic Order. In each of the four states, the ideal of an Islamic order is the basis of the official ideology, but it has assumed different forms. In *Saudi Arabia*, the ideal has been formulated and imposed along classical Hanbalite lines in a Wahhābī interpretation. In *Pakistan*, it was cherished by various groups, but Mawdūdī and his *Jamā'at-i Islāmī* elaborated it in terms of a comprehensive Islamic system that the government should realize. In *Libya*, the ideal of an Islamic order has been formulated as that of a Qur'ān-oriented state in continuous revolution. In contrast to these Sunnī versions of the Islamic order, Khomeinī developed a Shī'ī version that was implemented in *Iran*. This resulted in the unique phenomenon of Shī'ī *'ulamā'* acting as guarantors of Islamic public order by holding political power, waging war, conducting economic policies, and applying an austere concept of Islamic justice. In Pakistan and Iran, political debates have started.

3.2.5. Economic Resources. In a way, it is thanks to oil that at least three of the four states mentioned can more or less go their own way and as it were "experiment" with being an Islamic state. Though Pakistan lacks oil resources, it receives aid from Saudi Arabia and the United States, especially since the troubles in Afghanistan started. In Iran and Libya, there was a long struggle to nationalize the oil industry and to end covert foreign domination. Partly as a result, both countries have proclaimed themselves champions of the struggle against Western imperialism and capitalism. Saudi Arabia and the United States share an interest in keeping the status quo.

3.2.6. Historical Relations with the West. The four countries' historical relations with one or more Western powers all have a component of disillusionment. In Arabia, the British did not keep their promises to Sherif Husayn ibn Alī in 1915, and they conducted a containment policy toward Saudi Arabia; Iran underwent British influence and American interference in internal affairs, together with a profoundly experienced clash between Iranian culture and Western-type modernization. Indian Muslims' fears of Hindu dominance were aggravated by British "communalist" policies in colonial India. Libya experienced Italian rule and colonization, was a battleground of Western powers in World War Two, and had to comply with British and American interests after the war in order to survive. In all four cases, there were historical reasons for taking a certain distance to the West.

3.2.7. Relations with other Muslim Countries. The relations of each of the four Islamic states with other Muslim countries are of a special nature. *Saudi Arabia* receives the pilgrims for the *hajj* in and around Mecca every year, which makes it a meeting place for Muslims and a focus of religiously inspired hopes, plans, and expectations. It plays an important role in the international Islamic organizations it largely inspired and that were founded in the 1960s and 1970s. Though its Wahhābī doctrines are considered sectarian by a great number of Muslims, Saudi Arabia sees itself as exemplifying a pure ("puritan") Islamic state. It gives financial aid to a number of Muslim countries, as well as substantial subsidies for the building of mosques and religious schools in nearly all parts of the world. *Iran* may be called an antagonist of Saudi Arabia, not only because of its revolution, the fall of the Shah, and its perceived threat in the Gulf, but also because of its claim that the Iranian revolution is the prototype of a true Islamic revolution that should be followed by other Muslim nations, too. Iran made headlines as a Shīʿī state that takes draconian measures against its dissidents and that repulsed the serious Iraqi attack of 1980. But its example hardly seems to attract other Muslim countries, who rather judge that Islam has somehow been compromised by the "clerical" state of Iran. Islamist groups in the surrounding countries, however, sympathize with Iran, which has an influence among Shīʿīs in Lebanon. *Pakistan* started out wanting to present an example of how Islam could be harmonized with the demands of a modern state. This model function to the outside world, however, has been gradually lost since the country underwent a series of crises, in particular the secession of Bangladesh in 1971, and became practically a military state. *Libya*, finally, is entangled in complex relations with most other Muslim countries. Various attempts at unions with other countries have been made but failed. As a revolutionary state, it is the direct opposite of Saudi Arabia, and there is a clear antagonism between the policies of these two states. Libya also offers subsidies to mosques and religious schools in a number of countries. Like Iran, it is fervently opposed to the United States and the state of Israel.

4. The Religious Dimension

We have seen above that, after independence, the idea of an Islamic society and an Islamic state acquired a new relevance. Even if it was not directly applied in any of the new states, it could be used both as a possible ideal and as a possible norm by which to judge the existing state of affairs. Responsibility for the country no longer devolved upon foreigners but upon the new national leaders who were Muslims themselves. Some groups tried to establish a kind of Islamic state (*dār al-islām*) in isolated areas, but were then subdued by their own governments.

The political importance of the idea grew when opposition groups could more or less freely express their protest against the nationalist leadership in terms of Islam, stressing in particular the idea of an Islamic as opposed to a secular state. The polemical and political connotation of the call for an Islamic state explains, in part, why the idea has remained so vague but also so attractive to Muslims. A more important reason for this vagueness, however, seems to be that the concept of the Islamic state has religious overtones: in the end it is a religious notion and for Muslims reflects religious aspirations and longing. This longing refers to a just society as an aim of religious law. The Muslim community is expected to work toward the realization of such a society. A serious shortcoming in most studies of the Islamic state in my view, is that little or no attention has been paid to this religious and even eschatological dimension of the idea of an Islamic state.

The notion of the "Islamic state" may be said to function for the Muslim community as a sign referring to an ideal state of social and individual affairs. It hints at communal and personal life lived according to God's will, the application of a divinely prescribed and guaranteed social order, and the realization of true justice. To appreciate this deeper significance of the notion of the Islamic state, we should see it in connection with other notions referring to ultimate norms contained in the Qur'ān and the *Sunna*. Only on this level can the full meaning of the notion of the Islamic state be grasped and its fascination for those who suffer injustice be understood.

This consideration implies a symbolic "surplus value". What particular Muslim thinkers and leaders have said in recent times about the Islamic state should in fact never be identified with the actual situation, even if certain circles may claim that the Islamic state has already been realized. Nostalgia, an intense longing and active striving for an alternative social order and political structure, a search for a state of affairs that is fundamentally different from the existing one are the essence of all discussions about the Islamic state within the Muslim community. They are statements not of fact but of intention. For Muslims, the Islamic state is at the same time a political and a religious phenomenon with eschatological dimensions. The hope for its realization, not only in the Hereafter but here on earth, generates special kinds of social and political action, for instance when a leader is recognized as the *mahdī* expected to appear at the end of times.

The religious meaning of present-day calls for an Islamic state can be studied more closely by seeing them in the long line of calls for reform (*islāh*) that have been made throughout Islamic history.[7] This trend is characterized by its continuous exhortation to return to the prescriptions of Qur'ān and *Sunna*, to think independently (*ijtihād*), and to reject all religious forms and customs that are not explicitly mentioned in the

---

[7]   Cf. above Chapter 15 on "The Call (*Da'wa*) of Islamic Movements".

Qur'ān. In the ninth century, it was Ibn Hanbal (780–855) in Baghdad who opposed the theological innovations of his time by holding fast to Scripture and tradition. At the beginning of the eleventh century, Ibn Hazm (994–1064) in Spain wanted to keep strictly to the "clear meaning" (*zāhir*) of Scripture and take this as the measure of all doctrine. Somewhat later, Ibn Taymīya (1263–1328) in Damascus and Cairo called for a radical *islāh*, seeking to abolish all religious innovations that had accrued since Muhammad's days. There were many more thinkers and activists of this *islāh* tradition, a number of whom were attacked or imprisoned for disturbing the existing social order. As we saw above, a powerful impulse to reformulate the old ideal of an Islamic order in modern terms has come from liberal reformers like Sayyid Ahmad Khān in India and Muhammad 'Abduh in Egypt, with his more conservative pupil Muhammad Rashīd Ridā. It was believed that, as a result of reform, *islāh*, religion would be purified and strengthened; through the application of this true Islam, Muslim societies would be revitalized.

We arrive here at a third aspect of the religious dimension of contemporary calls for an Islamic state: it is specific religious organizations that aim to realize the ideal. It is not in fact a very big step from Ibn Taymīya to the eighteenth and twentieth century Wahhābīs who explicitly invoke him as their spiritual forefather in the Hanbalī *madhhab*. Nor is it such a great step from Rashīd Ridā, the intellectual leader of the Salafīya, to Hasan al-Bannā', the political leader of the Society of Muslim Brothers. Both worked in Egypt and their activities overlapped for a period of some seven years. In the organizations that make *islāh* their goal, not only a puritanical doctrine but also a puritanical way of life prevail, combined with a militant attitude to life and a readiness to undertake political and even military action if need be. It is precisely the combination of the idea of an Islamic order and an Islamic state with the trend of *islāh* thinking—a combination strengthened by will and emotion—that leads to puritan lifestyles and more efficient forms of organization than activists had in former times. This now gives the ideal of the Islamic state a certain puritanical character.

The current revitalization of Islam has specific religious aspects. I have stressed here reform (*islāh*) aimed at a new social order—an Islamic order and finally an Islamic state—because it seems to me to be the most important religious form that this revitalization of Islam is taking, but there are other forms too. There are also political and ideological, pietistic and mystical expressions, as well as interesting blends with other cultures and cultural elements, both modern and traditional. The attraction of the ideal of a pure Islamic order and state, however, is great and presently tends to exhibit certain puritan features. Besides the individual, it is always the socio-political order that needs to be disciplined and morally purified. This purification is seen as a necessary stage on the road toward the perfect society in which Divine Law will be applied. As such, this puritan revitalization of Islam is fundamentally different from the social ideals not only of secular nationalists and socialists, but also of traditional piety and of religious brotherhoods.

5. Islamic States and Contemporary History

For Muslim societies and Islam, the colonial period was a critical one. Changes in Islamic patterns and ideals and the rise of new Islamic movements and states should be studied primarily within the context of the societies concerned. However, one has to take into account the impact of the political and economic power of the West on these societies and the responses, often with a direct or indirect appeal to Islam, that this impact from outside evoked.

The rise of new Islamic states should be seen as a stage in a broader historical process, following on the pan-Islamic movement, the national movements, the restructuring of Muslim societies after independence, and the establishment of international Islamic organizations. The first stage of this process was the arousing of feelings of Muslim solidarity by leaders such as Jamāl al-Dīn al-Afghānī (1838–97) and to a certain extent also by the Ottoman Sultan Abdül Hamid II (r. 1876–1909): thus the Muslim peoples could become aware of their fundamental unity through Islam.[8] Discussions about the Caliphate as an institution for all Muslims were particularly relevant in the light of this search for unity. In a second stage, in particular in regions and countries under foreign rule, movements arose to obtain political independence from the encroaching West. This independence, however, could be reached only on the basis of nation-states. In a third stage, once independence had been achieved, the search for a proper order of society in the new nation-state became a central issue, both on an ideological and on a practical political level. In a fourth stage, international cooperation between Muslim nation-states and Muslims generally was needed, and this led to the establishment of international Islamic organizations. In these various stages, particular elements or aspects of Islam were appealed to, and various groups articulated and propagated their particular interpretation of Islam according to their intentions and interests.

The ideals and efforts made by members of Islamist and activist movements to further islamicize societies and if possible to found Islamic states, should be seen as part of the broader process sketched above. These efforts continued the line of earlier "Islamic" support for the

---

[8]   See below Chapter 18 on "Islam as a Vehicle of Protest".

national movements and for revolutionary movements seeking to restruc-
ture society once independence was reached. There had been, of course,
large groups of Muslims who did not participate in national or revolutionary movements on the basis of any Islamic exclusivism. They must
have constituted the large majority, trying to articulate their aspiration
for a just order of society in ways other than those of the ideological
Islamists and political activists. In any case, the phenomena of the new
Islamic states and the groups striving for them and supporting them are
part of historical processes within the Muslim part of the world that need
further study.

The rise of Islamic states should also be seen in the broader context of
the formation of new types of states in the twentieth century generally: not
only in the Muslim part of the world or the Third World, but also elsewhere. The aspiration toward a communist state, the existence of socialist
states or people's republics, the establishment of a National Socialist and
of Fascist states in Europe, the foundation of a Zionist state, and the role
of civil religion in all kinds of states are examples that come to mind. The
apparently instinctive tendency of states and societies facing situations of
danger or crisis to appeal to the resources of a religion or to manipulate
their religion for the sake of survival is highly relevant here. The increased
role of religion in public life in countries as different as Egypt, Israel,
Turkey, India, and the United States are cases in point. It is not only in the
personal and social domain but also in that of state authority and legitimation that religions can offer tremendous resources in societies' struggle for
survival, but also for exacerbating political conflicts as in Northern Ireland, ex-Yugoslavia, Lebanon, Israel, and the Middle East in general. The
situation varies, however, from country to country, and generalizations
often become banalities. What is under consideration here is the general
tendency in the twentieth century for religions, in particular Islam, to
become ideologized from different sides and to be made the instruments of
various political forces and finally state authorities.

6. Conclusion

In the course of this inquiry, it has become evident that things called
"Islamic" have religious as well as social and political aspects. Any
revitalization of Islam will therefore have religious, social, and political
effects. The idea of an Islamic state in modern times could only develop
after the model of the modern nation-state had appeared during the
colonial period and after the Ottoman Caliphate had been abolished.
Once independent nation-states with a Muslim majority had been established, a debate started about the way in which the new state should be
organized. Initially, only a small minority of people supported the project

of an Islamic state based on the *Sharī'a*, but their number increased. With the failure of the secular policies of the first national leaders, however, especially in the field of economic and social development, opposition groups can use the ideal of an Islamic state as a critical norm by which to judge the current state of affairs and as a possible option. Some reasons have been suggested why *puritan* forms of Islamic revitalization in particular can lend force to present-day calls for an Islamic state. On the other hand, there are strong forces that for various reasons are actively opposed to the establishment of an Islamic state or a thoroughly islamicized society in which the *Sharī'a* is consistently applied. The present Islamic states, in fact, are not always considered examples for other Muslim societies and states and are a source of much disillusionment to many Muslims. This is certainly the case if they have remained aware of the fact that the Islamic state is not a democratic one and is in the end a religious rather than a political ideal.

I may finish this chapter by formulating ten main conclusions:

1) The rise of Islamic states in the twentieth century is in part a response to painful problems confronting Muslim societies and countries, in particular in the Middle East including Pakistan. The religious, social, and political aspects of this response are inseparable but can be distinguished. Trying experiences and situations leading to intense suffering have brought to light old hopes and have encouraged or given support to efforts to establish an Islamic order by political means from above, through establishing a new kind of state—the Islamic state.

2) The doctrines adhered to and the political organization realized in the four states examined differ considerably. Various ideological formulations of Islam have served both as a driving force and as a legitimation of a new state of affairs claimed to be based on the *Sharī'a*.

3) The present-day Islamic states should not be considered as solely juridical and political entities. They also claim to represent and guide a moral community and to have a religious character. This involves a number of factors, including the striving for an order that foreshadows the truly Islamic society of complete justice.

4) Islamic states have been proclaimed not only because living according to the *Sharī'a* is a religious obligation but also to halt a certain disintegration of the "Islamic" nature of Muslim societies, which is felt to have occurred especially under foreign influence and rule. The remedy is seen in bringing about an "Islamic" order by making as many of its elements as possible mandatory in public life. Once this order has been secured in a given state, further changes and developments can take place as long as they do not violate the norms claimed and represented by the order. The way of life under this Islamic order in these states is characterized by a particular puritan ethos that also expresses itself in public life, education, and culture.

5) The wish to preserve the fundamental Islamic identity of a society does not exclude other loyalties of a communal nature (e.g., the national identity), provided the latter do not conflict with the Islamic identity.

6) The changes brought about by the establishment of Islamic states are difficult to study, as is the case with all countries passing through revolutionary developments. Once established, these states have a more or less totalitarian claim and character, which is prohibitive of critical research on the spot and obfuscates precise knowledge about what is really happening to the people. On the level of facts, striking changes take place in political organization (great authority devolving on the head of state), in socio-political organization (political parties, status of women, situation of minorities), in economics (banking system), and of course in the field of religion in the usual sense of the word. On the level of norms and values, still greater changes are to be noted when strict Islamic behavior and morality are prescribed and when strict Islamic rules derived from the *Sharīʿa* are officially imposed.

7) Islamic states, as well as those Islamist and activist movements striving for the realization of an Islamic order, are closely linked with the broader phenomenon of Islamic revitalization. The study of such states and movements can provide further insight into the nature of current Islamic revitalization, which should be a subject of research by non-Muslim and Muslim scholars alike.

8) The contexts within which Islamic states have been established and function should always be taken into account. Old social equilibria have collapsed, in particular in the Middle East; tensions have increased in Muslim countries; nearly all these countries face serious economic problems with long-term social consequences. What effects have the new geopolitical context since the end of the Cold War and current world economic policies had on the Muslim part of the world?

9) In Islamic states, the search is hardly for new values but for a reactivation of old ones felt to be authentic and adequate to cope with problems of today.

10) The existence of Islamic states may very well lead, as a reaction, to alternative attempts to realize an Islamic order, not through political power from above but through other forms of social organization and new mentalities with alternative interpretations of Islam.

Selected Literature

1. General: Islamic States

ENAYAT, Hamid, *Modern Islamic Political Thought: The Response of the Shīʿī and Sunnī Muslims to the Twentieth Century*, London and Basingstoke: Macmillan, and Austin, Tex.: University of Texas Press, 1982.

L'Islam et l'Etat dans le monde d'aujourd'hui, ed. by Olivier CARRÉ, Paris: Presses Universitaires de France, 1982.

Radicalismes islamiques, ed. by Olivier CARRÉ and Paul DUMONT, 2 vols., Paris: L'Harmattan, 1985.

ROSENTHAL, Erwin I.J., *Islam in the Modern National State*, London: Cambridge University Press, 1965.

SIVAN, Emmanuel, *Radical Islam: Medieval Theology and Modern Politics*, New Haven: Yale University Press, 1985.

Voices of Resurgent Islam, ed. by John L. ESPOSITO, New York and Oxford: Oxford University Press, 1983.

2. Iran

AKHAVI, Sharough, *Religion and Politics in Contemporary Iran: Clergy-State Relations in the Pahlavi Period*, Albany, N. Y.: State University of New York Press, 1980.

ANEER, Gudmar, *Imām Rūḥullāh Khumainī, Šāh Muḥammad Riẓā Pahlavī and the Religious Traditions of Iran*, Stockholm: Almquist and Wiksell, 1985.

BAKHASH, Shaul, *The Reign of the Ayatollahs: Iran and the Islamic Revolution*, London: Tauris, 1985.

Constitution of the Islamic Republic of Iran, trans. from the Persian by Hamid ALGAR, Berkeley, Cal.: Mizan Press, 1980.

FÜRTIG, Henner, *Islamische Weltauffassung und außenpolitische Konzeptionen der iranischen Staatsführung seit dem Tod Ajatollah Khomeinis* (Zentrum Moderner Orient, Studien 8), Berlin: Das Arabische Buch, 1998.

GÖBEL, Karl-Heinrich, *Moderne schiitische Politik und Staatsidee nach Taufīq al-Fukaikī, Muḥammad Ǧawād Mugnīya, Rūḥullāh Ḫumainī (Khomeyni)*, Opladen: Leske und Budrich, 1984.

HUSSAIN, Asaf, *Islamic Iran: Revolution and Counter Revolution*, New York: St. Martin's Press, 1985.

IRFANI, Suroosh, *Revolutionary Islam in Iran: Popular Liberation or Religious Dictatorship?*, London: Zed Books, 1983.

KEDDIE, Nikki R., and Yann RICHARD, *Roots of Revolution: An Interpretative History of Modern Iran*, New Haven and London: Yale University Press, 1981.

KERMANI, Navid, *Iran: Die Revolution der Kinder*, Munich: C. H. Beck, 2001.

KHOMEINI, Imam, *Islam and Revolution: Writings and Declarations*, Berkeley, Cal.: Mizan Press, 1981.

MOTTAHEDEH, Roy, *The Mantle of the Prophet: Learning and Power in Modern Iran*, New York: Simon & Schuster, and London: Chato & Windus, 1986.

RAJAEE, Farhang, *Islamic Values and World View: Khomeyni on Man, the State and International Politics*, Lanham, New York and London: University Press of America, 1983.

Religion and Politics in Iran: Shi'ism from Quietism to Revolution, ed. by Nikki R. KEDDIE, New Haven and London: Yale University Press, 1983.

3. Libya

ANSELL, Meredith O., and Ibrahim Massaud al-ARIF, *The Libyan Revolution: A Sourcebook of Legal and Historical Documents*, New York: Oleander Press, 1972.

BADRY, Roswitha, *Die Entwicklung der dritten Universaltheorie (DUT) Mu'ammar al-Qaddāfī's in Theorie und Praxis, aus ideengeschichtlicher und historischer Sicht*, Frankfurt, etc.: Peter Lang, 1986.

FATALY, Omar I. el-, and Monte PALMER, *Political Development and Social Change in Libya*, Lexington: Lexington Books, 1980.

The Green Book: Practice and Commentary, ed. by Charles BEZZINA, Valetta: Edam Publishers, 1979.

HAGER, Eva, *Volksmacht und Islam: Eine terminologie- und ideologie-analytische Untersuchung zum Politik- und Religionsverständnis bei Mu'ammar al-Qaddāfī*, Berlin: Klaus Schwarz, 1985.

QADHAFI, Muammar al-, *The Green Book*, 3 vols., London: Martin Brian and O'Keeffe, 1975–9.

VANDEWALLE, Dirk, *Libya since Independence: Oil and State-Building*, London and New York: I. B. Tauris, 1998.

4. Pakistan

AHMAD, Sayed Riaz, *Maulana Maududi and the Islamic State*, Lahore: People's Publishing House, 1976.

AHMED, Ishtiaq, *The Concept of an Islamic State: An Analysis of the Ideological Controversy in Pakistan*, PhD. Dissertation University of Stockholm, Department of Political Science, 1985.

BURKI, Shahid Javid, *Pakistan under Bhutto*, London: Macmillan, 1980.

MAHMOOD, Safdar, *Constitutional Foundations of Pakistan*, Lahore: Progressive Books, 1978.

NASR, Seyyed Vali Reza, *The Vanguard of the Islamic Revolution: The Jamā'at-i Islāmī of Pakistan*, Berkeley and Los Angeles: University of California Press, 1994.

RAHMAN, Fazlur, "Some Islamic Issues in the Ayyūb Khān Era", in *Essays on Islamic Civilization Presented to Niyazi Berkes*, ed. by Donald P. LITTLE, Leiden: E. J. Brill, 1976, pp. 284–302.

SAYEED, Khalid Bin, *Politics in Pakistan*, New York: Praeger, 1980.

5. Saudi Arabia

ABURISH, Saïd K., *The Rise, Corruption and Coming Fall of the House of Saud*, New York: St. Martin's Griffin, 1995, 1996[2].

KHOURY, Adel-Theodor, *Un modèle d'Etat islamique: l'Arabie Saoudite*, Munich: Kaiser, and Mainz: Grünewald, 1983.

MADANI, Nizar Obaid, *The Islamic Content of the Foreign Policy of Saudi Arabia: King Faisal's Call for Islamic Solidarity 1965–1975*, PhD. Dissertation, The American University, Beirut, 1977.

ÖNDER, Zehra, *Saudi-Arabien: Zwischen islamischer Ideologie und westlicher Ökonomie*, Stuttgart: Klett-Cotta, 1980.

PFULLMANN, Uwe, *Thronfolge in Saudi-Arabien: Wahhabitische Familienpolitik von 1744 bis 1953* (Zentrum Moderner Orient, Arbeitshefte Nr. 13), Berlin: Das Arabische Buch, 1997.

PISCATORI, James Paul, *Islam and the International Legal Order: The Case of Saudi Arabia*, PhD. Dissertation, University of Virginia, 1976.

YASSINI, Ayman al-, *Religion and State in the Kingdom of Saudi Arabia*, Boulder and London: Westview Press, 1985.

Chapter 18
Islam as a Vehicle of Protest[1]

A great number of studies have addressed Islam as a religious system or as a social structure or pattern in Muslim societies, and in particular the way Islam can be used politically to legitimize a given regime or a given socio-political order. Since the 1970s, a certain revitalization of Islam has attracted attention to present-day Islamic movements of revival and reform, their social basis, and their political connections. It is legitimate to ask in what ways Islam can be instrumental in bringing about changes in a given situation or even in overthrowing a given socio-political order, that is, to ask about the possible critical use or function of Islam in social and political affairs.

In this connection, it is rewarding to examine the different ways an appeal to Islam has been made to protest against a given situation or against given policies—within or outside Muslim societies—victimizing Muslims. Such a protest implies first a critical judgment and then an unambiguous rejection. This may lead to direct militant action, including resistance against a powerful enemy. It may also lead to a protracted struggle. Such a struggle may express itself in literature and art or on an intellectual level. It may take ideological forms and lead to intense de-bates. But it can also take on social, political, and even military dimensions, depending on the kind of danger perceived, the mobilization of the people, and the resources available for defense and counterattack. In colonial times and afterward too, the West usually played down any legitimate protest function of Islam, calling the latter in given situations simply subversive or disturbing. This is an easy way of responding for those who are used to speaking of Islam from a position of power.

For analytical purposes, however, the potential protest function of Islam, like that of other religions and ideologies, is a valid theme of research. The case of Islam is all the more interesting since more than Judaism and Christianity, its very foundation as a historical religion had

---

[1]   Revised version of a paper "Islam as a Vehicle of Protest", in: *Islamic Dilemmas: Reformers, Nationalists and Industrialization. The Southern Shore of the Mediterranean* (Religion and Society 25), ed. by Ernest GELLNER, Berlin, etc.: Mouton Publishers, 1985, pp. 22–48.

a marked reform and protest character.[2] Elements of protest persisted throughout history and make up a number of currents in present-day Islam. Even conversions to Islam may contain aspects of protest, for instance against certain religious practices, against certain Western or other ways of life, or against the way in which Christianity or any other religion has been used to legitimize doubtful or even immoral acts. Other protests based on an appeal to Islam can be expressed symbolically in ways of dressing, by ritual behavior, or by public demonstrations. Perhaps Islam, more than other religions, is felt to have a militant potential and to lend itself to express protest.

The following inquiry is preliminary and surveys some currents in recent history, in particular in the Arab world, in which Islam has often clearly served as a vehicle of protest. In principle, protests based on specific norms and values to which Islam as a religion refers and that are held to be absolute should be distinguished from protests made on other grounds, in which Islam has primarily an auxiliary ideological role. In practice, however, these two kinds of protest that both appeal to Islam are frequently so closely interwoven that they can hardly be separated. Any appeal to Islam can serve as an argument for protest within the Muslim community and should then be read in this light, even if appeals that Muslims make to Islam can hardly be conclusive to outsiders. In the multiple misunderstandings that result, the simple rule holds that what is seen from outside mostly as "mere protest" and measured in terms of power is seen from the inside mostly in terms of truth, morality, or justice.

In recent times, during the colonial period and that of independence, various kinds of protest, against non-Muslims as well as Muslims and on different levels, have been expressed with an appeal to Islam. I shall first distinguish among levels of protests. Next, I shall give examples of religious movements in Islam in which a clear protest character prevails. These examples suggest the interest and usefulness of the notion of "protest" for further analysis of a number of movements launched in recent times in the name of Islam. Many Muslim protest movements of different kinds have articulated their protests in Islamic terms and thus were able to mobilize the people. Finally, I shall devote some thought to the ways Islam in particular can function as a vehicle of protest. The symbolic value of Islam in Muslim societies, the defensive attitudes that these societies have had to take to survive, and the awareness of basic unconditional norms and values that should not be betrayed are keys to understanding the ways in which many Muslim societies nowadays express protest against what befalls them.

---

[2]   WAARDENBURG, "Towards a Periodization of Earliest Islam according to its Relations with Other Religions".

1. Levels of Protest

We can distinguish different levels on which a protest in the name of a religion such as Islam can be expressed. For practical purposes, I distinguish three main levels: first, a level of protest where Islam plays a "functional" role; second, a level of what may be called "religious culture", where religious movements or groupings that express protest according to specific Islamic norms and values can develop; finally, what I would like to call the "religious dimension" of protest in Islam, insofar as it touches the core of this particular religion.

On the second level, that of religious culture, two subsidiary levels can be distinguished. Religious protest can here be expressed directly, through specific trends and movements intent on it and mentioning it by name. But it can also be expressed indirectly, for instance through the development of specific forms of spirituality such as religious moral and legal thought or the mystical path, rather than engaging in direct fighting.

1.1. Like other religions, Islam can be used to mobilize believers for aims that are not derived from religion alone and that sometimes have nothing to do with it. Islam and the loyalty that Muslims feel toward it can be used functionally for many purposes, among them to express protest. This can serve, for instance, as a defense against intrusion from outside (protests against imperialism) or as a protection against injustice in society (protests against violations of human rights). In the first case, the protest can lead to a call to defend the Muslim community, as in the call to *jihād*. In the second case, within the Muslim community, it can lead to denunciating a tyrannical regime. The aim here, self-defense or self-protection, is of a general nature and is then qualified by an appeal to Islam. In other words, Islam here is a function of vital needs and aims.

1.2. Within Islam as a religious culture, there have always been appeals and movements directly protesting against religious beliefs and social customs judged to be wrong, that is to say contrary to true religion. This kind of protest is most noticeable in what the Qur'ān says about unbelief, various false beliefs, and forms of behavior judged to be against God's will. Preaching in this sense, both to non-believers and to believers, has continued throughout the history of Islam. It implies not only various kinds of missionary activity but also the rise of movements rejecting what they judge to be corruptions of Islam and seeking to restore what they consider to be true Islam. These movements and their ideologies share a vibrant protest against what they view as corrupt forms of Islam and a desire to realize a society in which what they consider to be true Islam reigns.

1.3. Within Islam as a religious culture, there have also been from the beginning what may be called indirect forms of protest against the existing social and religious situation of the Muslim community. Direct ways of expressing protest, not to mention of changing the situation, often were hardly possible. Such an indirect protest could take a spiritual garment and then led to the development of specific "religious" sectors in Islam.

On the one hand, a sacred law was developed, the *Sharī'a*, the totality of rules for behavior both individual and social, both ethical and legal. This was the work of the *'ulamā'* and *fuqahā'*, scholars able to deduce what may be called *normative* Islam from the Qur'ān, the *Sunna* (early tradition), and other sources. On the other hand, after an initial stage of withdrawal from the world that displayed ascetic features, various forms of the mystical path, the *tarīqa*, were developed, that is to say a person's inner life as he or she is held to move throughout life toward God. Elaborating this path was the work of the Sūfīs, mystics able to experience and describe the stages through which the relationship between the soul and God develops. Here it was not external behavior but inner life that was stressed.

'Ulamā' and Sūfīs both insisted on the need to realize a religious way of life communally and individually, rather than submit life to external conditions. Both the law and the mystical path that developed as a result implied a critical attitude and, as I see it, a religious protest against the worldly trends in Muslim society. Taking recourse to *Sharī'a* and *tarīqa*, '*ulamā*' and Sūfīs protested against what they saw as moral and religious decline.

1.4. Finally, the Islamic faith itself apparently contains elements of protest. This may be termed the religious dimension of protest in Islam. It is directed against any divinization or absolutization of elements of creation and against any imprisonment of the human being within the immanent world. The created nature of the world and its immanence are contrasted with God's creating activity and his transcendence.

There seems to be a dialectic in the Islamic faith between the constant protest against the human tendency to *shirk* or idolatry (including absolutizing created things) and the constant stress on *islām* or abandonment of oneself (including carrying out God's will). This dialectic between protest against idolatry and abandonment to God appears to me to be a basic feature of the Islamic faith.

Although the search for harmony is present in Islam as in all religions, there are noticeable elements of protest that arise from a deeper, religious dimension and have given Islam a certain militancy. On this level, Muslims have always been able to say a radical "no" and protest against religious and ideological forms that conflict with the core of their faith. In extreme cases, this has led to rejecting anything non-Islamic.[3]

---

[3]   WAARDENBURG, "World Religions as Seen in the Light of Islam".

2. Three Kinds of Religious Movements with a "Protest" Character

The foregoing analysis of various levels on which Islam can serve as a vehicle of protest not only makes a theoretical point that is more or less valuable in itself. It can also serve as a starting point to improve our understanding of a number of movements in Islamic history and the present time, in particular in the Arab world. Such movements are to be studied in their socio-political and economic setting, and internal as well as external causes and influences should be taken into account. However, attention is also to be paid to the dynamics of the social and cultural traditions in which religious norms and values play an important role, not only the local small tradition but also the "great tradition" of Islam with constant references to Qur'ān and *Sunna* as its basis. Even if many scholars tend to ascribe the real causes of Islamic movements to social and economic factors and their political consequences, the problem of meaning cannot be ignored. After all, it is precisely Islam that is used as an instrument and symbol to express and articulate protest, resistance, and struggle.

A number of Islamic movements during the last hundred and fifty years or so have been both an expression of defense and resistance against Western domination and a protest against moral decline and disintegration within Muslim societies. Notwithstanding the fact that, in the course of the nineteenth and twentieth centuries, it has become ever more difficult to realize Islamic norms and ideals in their entirety and that many elements of Muslim culture have lost their traditional meaning, nevertheless Islam itself retained its symbolic power. In an earlier age, it had functioned as a symbol of glory and harmony; in the nineteenth century it succeeded in becoming a symbol of self-esteem and of protest against injustice.

Earlier times already saw a number of "counter movements" in the Muslim world that had an explicit or implicit character of protest using religious arguments rather than social or political ones. I plead for more serious consideration of these religious arguments in our analysis of Islamic movements. A complete study of protest movements in Muslim countries should of course also consider those that appeal to other values than Islam. These, however, are left out of consideration here.

2.1. Self-Defense Against Outside Domination and Interference

In the course of the often conflictual history between European countries and various parts of the Muslim world, the former increasingly dominated the latter. The West has become sensitive to the many Muslim protest and resistance movements that appeal to Islam to oppose Western influence, interference and domination. This may be the main reason why the West has so often considered Islam its enemy and perceived it as an eminently political and fundamentally anti-Western religion and ideology. There has been little awareness of the fact that sheer power evokes reactions among those who are the victims of it.

The most important variants of these natural protest and resistance movements that appeal to Islam are the following:

2.1.1. Local resistance in Muslim regions to government by non-Muslims: In the nineteenth and early twentieth centuries, a number of local defense and resistance movements rose against increasing Western penetration and occupation, often appealing to Islam and sometimes proclaiming *jihād*.[4] Such movements used religious arguments in their resistance to foreign domination by Western Christians, Hindus, and Jews. First Christianity and then Zionism functioned indeed as ideologies of colonizers of Muslim territory. Until today Zionism is seen as a form of Western imperialism that uses elements of Judaism for political purposes.[5] This has led to an extensive Muslim and also Christian Arab polemical literature vehemently denouncing the religious roots of Zionism, their fictitious character, and their political abuse in the state of Israel.

2.1.2. More coordinated calls for resistance to Western domination: Here the different forms of the so-called pan-Islamic movement, initiated by Jamāl al-Dīn al-Afghānī (1838–97) and exploited by Sultan Abdül Hamid II, are a case in point.[6] Even if most of these forms were in fact more verbal than politically organized, the movement itself gave moral support to increasing Muslim resistance to Western military, political, and economic domination as well as Western religious and cultural influence as enemy number one. This form of "Islamic protest" has had a direct and lasting effect in the spheres of culture and religion.

2.1.3. Defensive attitudes against foreign influences in Muslim countries: The defensive attitudes and action against English, French, Russian, Dutch, and later also American influence in Muslim countries arose primarily from what was sensed as a threat to the Muslim way of life and to Islamic culture. To the extent that Islam is experienced as the integrating factor in that way of life and culture and that outside influence is felt to be threatening, a distance and even a potential conflict is perceived as existing between the foreign culture and Islam. It is only a small step to

---

[4]   PETERS, *Islam and Colonialism.*
[5]   JOHNSON, *Islam and the Politics of Meaning in Palestinian Nationalism.*
[6]   KEDDIE, *An Islamic Response to Imperialism*; ID., *Sayyid Jamāl ad-Dīn "al-Afghānī".*

then use Islam as a basis for protest and symbol of resistance against the foreign culture felt to represent a threat.

The many movements that have been launched in Muslim societies against Western influence have often been interpreted in the West as a kind of xenophobia inherent in Islam. In fact, what is involved here is a defense mechanism against those outside influences that threaten truths, norms, and values considered to be essential.

2.1.4. Protests against Zionism, Christian missions, and Western Orientalism: A well-known example of the ideological use of Islam against political and economic domination of land, and against a threatening ideology that enjoys Western support is the resistance shown by the Muslim world to the Zionist movement and the policies of the state of Israel. The treatment meted out to the Palestinians in Israel and especially in the occupied territories infringes on Islamic and universal norms of human dignity. Strong feelings of solidarity among Muslims play a part in this resistance, aside from more general humane, social, and political considerations.

Another example of a movement of protest and resistance that explicitly appeals to Islam as a religion is the reaction of Muslims to Christian missions. Any attempt at conversion to another religion calls forth a fervent reaction, but in the case of Muslims particularly, this reaction is strong and the number of converts from Islam to Christianity is small. Apologetic literature against Christian missions is abundant but has been little studied.[7] Especially when such missions are felt as a direct attack on Islam or when they are viewed in connection with Western political interests, resistance to religious evangelization is at least as strong as to political Zionism.

Anything felt to be an attack on or denigration of Islam calls forth fierce protest in the name of Islam. This applies also to those Western studies whose critical questions and analytical procedures are considered to undermine the value and truth of Islam. A scholarly analysis by non-Muslims of religious data pertaining to Islam is then perceived as intentionally destructive. Many Muslims link such research to deeper religious, ideological, and political intentions inimical to and aggressive toward Islam. Scholarly research on possible influences from elsewhere on Qur'anic passages, or on the construction of certain *hadīths* after Muhammad's death but attributed to him is then seen as a perfidious attack on the truth and integrity of Islam. Western Orientalism has been subject to protest, and not only from Muslim authors.[8] Islamic studies

---

[7]   DORMAN, *Toward Understanding Islam*. Further research on present-day Islamic apologetic literature is needed.

[8]   SAID, *Orientalism*.

evidently demand solid information, education in depth, and a willingness to learn and to exchange views on both sides.

2.1.5. Islam and development: Another kind of Muslim protest has to do with development. It concerns the often-heard Western reproach that Islam as a religion has largely contributed to the stagnation of development in Muslim as compared to Western countries.[9] In particular, the accusation that Islam is a backward religion—even obstructing modern social and economic development—has called forth sharp protest and vehemently defensive positions. Islam as a religion is held here to be essentially valid for all stages of social and economic development. Those forms of Islam that impede development are judged to be accidental, a result of particular historical situations, and not representative of true Islam. Muslim countries are not bound to follow Western economic development models.

Muslim intellectuals acknowledge that empirical, practiced Islam undergoes a historical development apart from the eternal truths contained in the Qur'ān and that socio-political changes in Muslim societies are to be studied in this light.[10] Certain movements want to elaborate a specific Islamic notion of development as an alternative to Western social and economic development models. "Islamic" economics, for example, expresses a protest against the weaknesses of other kinds of economics, just as an "Islamic" socialism, an "Islamic" nationalism, or an "Islamic" revolution ought to be free from the defects of any other kind of socialism, nationalism, or revolution.

2.2. Religious Protest against Decline: The Reform Movements

Throughout Islamic history there have been movements characterized by religious protest against the state of affairs in society and the course of history. Such "counter movements" identify this course as a decline caused by moral and religious laxity. The arguments they use are primarily religious, mostly derived from Qur'ān and *Sunna*, and they favor the consequent application of the most important prescriptions contained in them. It is useful to distinguish between movements of direct protest and those of indirect protest leading to a certain idealization. The first group shows the following main variants.[11]

2.2.1. Sunnī traditionalists and revivalists: Ever since the first generation after Muhammad's death, there have been faithful believers observing

---

9   WAARDENBURG, "Notes on Islam and Development".
10 *Islam and Development*, ed. by J. L. ESPOSITO.
11 GIBB, *Modern Trends in Islam*; SMITH, *Islam in Modern History*.

Qur'ān and *Sunna* prescriptions. Many of them protested on religious grounds against the political development of the community actually occurring under the caliphs: the Rāshidūn caliphs in Medina, the Umayyads in Damascus, and the Abbāsids in Baghdad. They referred to Qur'ān and *Sunna* to show that government was not being conducted according to God's will, and sermons were a suitable instrument to make this known. Sometimes this led to armed insurrections, especially if such ideas served the interests of a political opposition. Mostly, however, these groups condemned the current government practice as un-Islamic but maintained their obedience on pragmatic grounds, though without much inner loyalty to the government.

Up to the nineteenth century, two main types of such movements in Sunnī Islam, which follow the ancient tradition (*Sunna*) of the prophet, can be distinguished: the *traditionalists*, who appealed in a broad sense to Qur'ān and *Sunna*; and the *revivalists*, who sought and took action to achieve a literal and unconditional application of the religious prescriptions they contained. An example of the first are the Hanbalīs who supported Ahmad ibn Hanbal's defense of Qur'ān and *Sunna* against Mu'tazilite philosophical theology (*kalām*) in ninth-century Baghdad. Examples of the second are the Almohads, with their strict puritan rule in eleventh and twelfth-century North Africa and Spain; the Wahhābī movement in eigthteenth and twentieth-century Arabia[12]; and strict "Islamists" at the present time inspired by Ibn Taymīya.

2.2.2. Non-Sunnī movements: Since Muhammad's death, there have been non-Sunnī religious protest movements, too. They criticized current government practice and the course of history on the basis of interpretations of Islam that the Sunnīs judged to be heretical. Historically, the most important of these groups have been various kinds of Shī'ī movements, especially the Ismā'īlīs or "Seveners" with their countercaliphate of the Fātimids in Cairo (969–1171) and the Imāmīs or "Twelvers", who have had a separate history as a state religion in Iran since the sixteenth century. Exceptional in Islam, the religious leaders or *'ulamā'* have been in power in Iran since 1979, but they had already been politically active earlier.[13]

2.2.3. Mahdist movements: The various Mahdist movements, which proclaim the end of time and the arrival of a reign of justice and peace under a *mahdī*, seen as an eschatological figure, also always denounced the existing state of unbelief and immorality in religious terms and proposed a radical political solution for it. They have always been short-lived but,

---

[12]   Cf. above Chapter 11 on "The Wahhābīs in Eighteenth and Nineteenth Century Arabia".
[13]   KEDDIE, *Religion and Rebellion in Iran.*

exhibiting a "messianic" character, are in fact the most striking religious protest movements in Islam. Particularly well-known is the late nineteenth-century Mahdist state in Sudan.[14]

2.2.4. The Reformist movement: Striking for intellectual Western observers was the reformist movement. Founded in Egypt by Muhammad ʿAbduh (ca. 1849–1905), it was one of the movements of enlightened protest against the state of Islam that occurred after the mid-nineteenth century.[15] Faced with the innumerable religious ideas and practices that considered themselves "Islamic" at the time, sometimes without much foundation, the reformists pleaded for reform (*islāh*). They went back to Qurʾān and ancient *Sunna*, using them as a yardstick to judge existing ideas and practices and as the main source for a truly Islamic way of life and society.

The movement attached great importance to the use of reason, both in general and especially in the interpretation of religious texts, in the renewal of Islamic thought, and in modern science. Maintaining the highest respect for the Qurʾān as well as for reason, the reformists stressed a point made earlier in Islam, namely that there can be no conflict between reason and religion and that Islam is the reasonable, "natural" religion of humankind. Because of their stress on the use of reason and their puritanical attitude, reminiscent of that of the Sunnī traditionalists and revivalists, the reformists were able to exert considerable influence. They attracted intellectuals who no longer felt at home either in the scholastic formulas of religious law and doctrine or in the more emotional expressions of religious experience found in some mystical orders. Starting out from the assumption of an originally pure and reasonable Islam, they leveled a sharp protest against rigidified traditions and against following doctrines on the basis of external authority. Their idea of a pure Islam of revelation and reason, not dependent on time and place, contrasted with local traditions and superstitions that could not be justified through Qurʾān or *Sunna*. The movement returned to the sources to achieve *islāh*, reform. This implied scripturalism, a spread of literacy among the people, and a continuous effort to improve education.[16]

2.2.5. The Muslim Brotherhood: The idea of *islāh* is also found in a number of movements that make a more limited use of reason as a critical and self-critical instrument when addressing specific Qurʾān and *Sunna* texts. They exhibit a stronger character of protest leading to more social and political action than is the case with the reformist movements that

---

[14]   HOLT, *The Mahdist State in the Sudan 1881–1898.*
[15]   ADAMS, *Islam and Modernism in Egypt.*
[16]   GEERTZ, *Islam Observed.*

work more on an intellectual level. They too address themselves to a purification of Islam on the basis of the Qur'ān and the ancient *Sunna*, but they are more politically involved and better organized to take social action than the reformists. The case of the Salafīya movement in Egypt provides an example of a development of reformism into a kind of neo-orthodoxy. The *Ikhwān al-muslimīn*, the Muslim Brotherhood, which started in Egypt, and the *Jamā'at-i Islāmī*, which started in British India, are most representative of this kind of *islāh* of social action.[17] They wage an ideological struggle not only against what they consider a decaying Islam of laxity, scholastic rigidity, and superstition, but also against the secularizing ideas and practices that are part of the process of modernization most nationalist leaders and governments after independence strove for.

2.2.6. Revolutionary movements: A third, more radical variant of *islāh* movements may be distinguished, namely those that seek to replace Western-type nation-states with secular institutions by Islamic states based on the *Sharī'a*, religious law. These movements undertake concerted action to bring about an Islamization process in society. Such Islamist and activist movements represent the most vital protest against the status quo and Western-type government policies in present-day Muslim states.

The first leaders of these states emerged in the nationalist struggle and tended to have a pragmatic, rather secular view of the way their countries would be able to attain at least the necessary minimum of technical, socio-economic, and political development. In most cases, however, development did not go as smoothly as hoped and demanded considerable sacrifices from the population. Political oppression and processes of uprooting connected with modernization provided an audience for those opposition groups that protest on principle against the course of current secular policies. They call for the establishment of a radically different "Islamic" kind of state they envision as the panacea for all existing problems.

Just as secular nation-states were established in protest against colonial foreign domination, so an appeal to establish Islamic states has arisen in protest against the practice of these secular states. In countries like Iran, and in a sense also Pakistan, "Islamic" revolutions have been successfully carried out, toppling earlier regimes. The proclamation of an Islamic state in Sudan, first in 1983 and then again in 1991 left little hope of an end to the civil war between the North and the South of the country. The *talibāns'* seizure of power in Afghanistan led to an Islamist

---

[17] MITCHELL, *The Society of the Muslim Brothers*; al-BANNĀ', *Five Tracts*.

regime imposing draconian measures on the population that could not be justified by classical Islamic law and doctrine. Both Sudan and Afghanistan have suffered decades of war and violence with ominous results. Even if the decisive action is often carried out by military men, the ideologies of such revolutionary movements mostly develop out of revivalist Islamist and activist movements as described above.

Their ideological appeal cannot be explained without reference to the profound hopes and ideals that have continued to exist among the more tradition-oriented faithful who constitute the majority of Muslims everywhere. Though the majority of these people have not been organized or mobilized in Islamic movements themselves, they nourish Islamic hopes and ideals that acquire a utopian force in adverse situations. If such situations become unbearable the way to extremism opens up.

2.3. Indirect Forms of Protest within Islam: Law and the Mystical Path

The movements brought together under this heading also embody a religious protest against current forms of practicing religion, the course of Islamic history, and government policy in Muslim countries. But here the protest is indirect and it is questionable whether the people concerned are themselves always conscious of the protest character of their particular movement. They all project, however, an ideal model in contrast to the state of affairs they experience.

2.3.1. The Law: The study and elaboration of religious law (*Sharīʿa*) by religious scholars in the discipline of religious jurisprudence (*fiqh*) was not a pragmatic legal enterprise. It rather worked out a coherent normative pattern for the individual and communal way of life that in many respects contradicted existing patterns of behavior in society. The *Sharīʿa* had an ideal character that was strengthened by the reasoning of its methodology, the "roots of jurisprudence" (*ʿusūl al-fiqh*). Since the *Sharīʿa* was held to be absolutely normative for all aspects of life, even if only parts of it were in fact applied, we can see the attention given to its elaboration as an implicit but clear protest by religious scholars against given social realities and existing government policies. To the extent that reality deviated from what the norms prescribed, the elaboration of these norms and the declaration of their absolute validity implied a condemnation of and protest against reality.

2.3.2. The Mystical Path: The efforts of the mystics, philosophers, and gnostic thinkers in the course of Islamic history to posit inner experience and spiritual insight as the highest aim in life at least for the individual Muslim, also imply an indirect protest against existing realities. Mysticism, philosophy, and gnosis expressed a double protest. On the one hand, they distanced themselves from the worldly course of events and practices against which the religious scholars, too, protested in their own way. On the other hand, this was also a protest against the external and sometimes formalistic character of the official religion as formulated by the ʿulamāʾ. The mystics could count on the support of traditionalist believers who equally, but more instinctively, rejected the scholars' "rationalization" of religion. Various critical movements of islāh (reform) flourished in the ground prepared by the Sūfīs. Their "puritan" effort, however, was directed toward the social application of Qurʾān and Sunna rather than toward interiorization.

2.4 Muslim Religious Modernism

A singular kind of indirect protest on intellectual or moral grounds against existing ideas and practices legitimized by Islam is the emergence of various kinds of religio-cultural "modernist" movements. They are prepared to honor and accept values and norms from outside Qurʾān and Sunna and also from other, non-Muslim cultures. Movements in the eighth and ninth centuries that strove to assimilate Greek philosophy and science or Persian government practices and scholarship were the "modernists" of that time. The nineteenth and twentieth centuries have seen the emergence of similar movements that view more or less generally accepted human norms and values as being either compatible with or even expressive of the true values of Islam. Sometimes the claim has been made that these values finally originate or at least are best represented in Islam. Here the "catholic" character of Islam is claimed.

Twentieth-century Muslim modernists proclaimed for instance that tolerance and humanism are proper to Islam. Or that socialism is best realized in Islam as a divine command of social justice that makes class struggle superfluous.[18] In a similar way, universal values such as human rights and the dignity of woman have been claimed to be inherent in Islam. In fact it is nearly always possible to appropriate values derived from elsewhere within the context of Islam by appealing to particular passages of Qurʾān or Sunna.

Through their call for reason and their protest against traditionalism and ignorance, modernists have been able to mobilize traditional Muslim societies toward economic, technical, social and other forms of development. Their efforts can also have an apologetic function when they defend Islam against reproaches from outside that it is not tolerant, liberal, social-minded, and so on, if measured against "non-Islamic", say Christian or secular Western norms and values. Modernist thinking can

---

[18] MINTJES, Social Justice in Islam.

also be used by Muslim governments against existing religious prejudices concerning employment and public office for women or family planning.

Modernist attempts to renew Muslim societies temper their "protest" origin and blur views of possible antagonism between Muslims and non-Muslims. The more pragmatic such modernist thinkers are, the more difficult it becomes to distinguish them from intellectual reformists who want to deduce the same values from Qur'ān and early *Sunna*.

2.5. Is Religious Protest a Structural Feature of Islam?

Muhammad's preaching and public activity and the prophetic movement resulting from it included an unmistakable dimension of protest. As Qur'anic passages show, from its beginnings Islam was a movement and a counter-movement at the same time. The germs of Islam as a movement pursuing its own ends and resulting in a religion, culture, and civilization of its own have been studied at great length. As a counter-movement, Islam protested against many things. It protested against *jāhilīya* (pre-Islamic "ignorance") practices and existing forms of injustice; against particularistic concepts of revelation and salvation subscribed to by Jews and Christians; and against what were felt to be misconceptions about the relationship between God and the human being and their essential difference. A radical protest was made against those ideas and practices that conflicted with the axiom of the unity and uniqueness of God and his commands to his creation to carry out his will. Islam as a prophetic religion never completely lost this protest dimension even in its later development. This is largely because the Qur'ān, which preserved the prophetic "protesting" in the most literal way, has remained the core of Islamic religion.

Consequently, Islamic history has seen a number of movements that measure given sad realities against particular texts from Qur'ān and *Sunna* and that customarily base their direct or indirect protest against such realities on their interpretation of these texts. The fact that any absolutization of things perceived or any imprisonment of humankind within the immanent world is bound to evoke protest from Muslims gives a hint of the religious appeal of so many Muslim protest movements in the course of history. Even if such movements rarely succeeded in seizing power in the more densely settled areas and regions, they still fomented unrest and a hope for better times, especially among the less privileged who abandoned themselves to God. Absolute claims and absolutizations coming from outside Islam have in general been more or less radically rejected. Most Islamic ideologies and movements of the nineteenth and twentieth centuries expressed protest not only against mistaken interpretations of Islam but also against the many forms of political oppression, social injustice, and economic exploitation that existed. They also protested against the claims of other ideologies and religions to offer definite solutions for the woes of the time instead of what Islam could offer.

Protest in Muslim societies can apparently have a transcendent direction. In an Islamic framework, it leads to the longing for a religious harmony and ordering of things precisely as a protest against empirical realities and experiences of chaos. This to me seems to be at the root of the Muslim quest for an Islamic society and an Islamic state. Any government choosing a secular ordering of affairs will always meet an opposition that articulates inevitable protests in the direction of Islamic norms and values, toward the ideal of a just society and the dream of an Islamic state.

3. Protest and Islam in the Arab Countries in Particular

There is great variety in the political role and function of Islam in the Arab countries and the Middle East in general.[19] What role then has Islam played in Arab movements of protest and what use did such movements make of Islam to express and legitimize their protest?

The great movements of protest in Arab countries since World War One have been directed against foreign domination (colonialism, imperialism, cultural hegemony), Zionism and the state of Israel (interpreted in part as a form of Western imperialism or in the service of it), and feudal regimes (implying tyranny, corruption, and social injustice). These movements, however, with the exception of the Muslim Brotherhood and related groupings, have not given their protest an explicitly Islamic label, so that in general one cannot speak here of specifically "Islamic" protest movements in the sense described above. Most appeals were made to the Arab nation and Arab culture, of which Islam constitutes an intrinsic part in the consciousness of the people, including a number of Christian Arabs. Calls were also made to defend certain basic values underlying Arab culture and society. These values are often linked to Islam, if not with reference to Qur'anic vocabulary then at least with strong emotional appeal to Muslim Arabs. Although this needs further investigation, I submit that in the great Arab protest movements since World War One, Islam has been closely associated in the mind of the people with particular human values defended. As the supreme value, Islam lends force to that very defense itself. An attack on Arab values is felt by Arab Muslims as an attack on Islam, too, since it forms part of their identity and Islam seems to be the supreme value to be defended.

---

[19]   *Islamic Perspectives*, ed. by K. AHMAD and Z. I. ANSARI; *Islam in Transition*, ed. by J. J. DONOHUE and J. L. ESPOSITO; HUSSAIN, *Islamic Movements in Egypt, Pakistan and Iran*.

Within Arab countries, on a more limited scale, there are other kinds of protest movements that make a more immediate appeal to Islam. They are directed against ideologies from outside (liberal, capitalist, or communist ideologies that contradict certain basic teachings of Islam and must be "islamicized" before being acceptable), against the decline of morality and the decrease of traditional faith (often ascribed to negative influences from the West like secularization) and, of course, against the dissolution of local Muslim traditions or even minor changes in the laws on personal status. Such movements include in Egypt the *Ikhwān al-muslimīn*, the *Jamā'at al-takfīr wa'l-hijra, al-Jamā'a al-islamīya, al-Jihād, Shabāb Muhammad, Hizb al-tahrīr al-islāmī, Jund Allāh*. In Pakistan the *Jamā'at-i islāmī* should be mentioned. Such movements call for the strict application of all Islamic prescriptions. Islam seems to be used here, basically, to formulate an absolute demand and it then becomes easily an absolute ideal.

Whether the appeal to Islam is direct or indirect, these protest movements involve condemnation and rejection. On a local or national scale, certain movements often appeal openly and directly to Islam, whereas movements that extend to the Arab world as a whole imply that it is the Arab culture, nation, and identity that are to be defended, whereby Islam and Islamic values are involved in a more indirect way. The very fact that the protest is couched primarily in words suggests that power is lacking at the moment but it may build up through protest and resistance. For protests are always expressed on the basis of particular norms, values or truths. To the extent that these are accepted by the participants and a growing audience, the protest will develop further and may ultimately constitute a basis for resistance and struggle. It should be noted that, in many cases in the Arab world and elsewhere, open protest is not possible. However, a close analysis of cultural expressions in literature for instance will reveal an indirect, even "symbolic" character of protest that may contain great moral strength and may bear palpable fruits in the future.

The articulation of protests in the Arab world that contain an appeal to Islam deserves further study in terms of media used, of literary genres and social data. Messages conveyed by movements of protest should be taken seriously. They should be placed in their precise contexts, and their appeal to particular groups should be investigated.

I distinguish among basic types of protest. In the Arab world, for instance, a protest that contains an appeal to Islam can be articulated in at least four different ways:

1) it can acquire a militant political character involving intense activity, e.g., in the struggle for independence or for the establishment of an Islamic state;

2) it can have a marked ideological character, including resistance to discrimination and injustice, with an appeal to Qur'anic norms of justice and a perfect but utopian Islamic society[20];

3) it can have a predominantly cultural character when it addresses itself to resisting the influence of another culture, e.g., American, and when it serves to promote indigenous cultural values and guarantee the continuity of the indigenous cultural tradition[21];

4) it also can have a more unconditional religious character, e.g., in rejecting atheism, foreign ideologies, and religions or in striving to overturn the existing situation in favor of an Islamic revolution, or just to strengthen and expand Islam as a religious faith, ideology, or normative pattern.

Further research is needed on the role of particular religious leaders as *'ulamā'*, *sheykhs*, local preachers, and media stars, in nourishing and articulating protests in Islamic terms and also on the function of organized religious groups as *ikhwān* and *turuq* and voluntary associations in this respect. An important factor is the attitude taken by the political and religious authorities, who can admit and support but also suppress and persecute such protest movements. But even if they are suppressed, protest movements that appeal to Islam can in the long run exert considerable influence on Muslims, who recognize the absolute validity of the norms to which the appeal is made. Hence some authors have drawn attention to revolutionary tendencies in Islam and their preconditions[22] or, during the Cold War, to the subversive potentials of Islam in the former USSR[23] or to the psychological basis of the resurgence of Islam.

Before touching the issue of the use of Islam itself as a symbolic form of protest, I should mention the slower but continuous process of positively constructing and building up Muslim societies, personality, and intellectual vigor. Deep-seated moral codes and forces in Muslim societies lend them their power to survive adversities and to face reality.[24]

4. The Use of Islam as a Symbol of Protest

On all four levels I have distinguished in the course of this chapter, expressions of protest that appeal to Islam have a real as well as a symbolic character. The protest is made against a given, real state of affairs and as a refusal, it is a particular, negative response to reality. It is often ex-

---

[20]   UTRECHT, "Religion and Social Protest in Indonesia".
[21]   See above Chapter 5 on "Official, Popular, and Normative Religion in Islam".
[22]   HODGKIN, "The Revolutionary Tradition in Islam"; JOHNSON, *Islam and the Politics of Meaning in Palestinian Nationalism*.
[23]   BENNIGSEN and BROXUP, *The Islamic Threat to the Soviet State*.
[24]   GEERTZ, *Islam Observed*.

pressed, however, in religious terms and refers then to norms and values judged to have an absolute and universal validity. The expression of the protest, consequently, is highly symbolic. This double nature, both real and symbolic, of any protest in the name of Islam is perhaps its fundamental force. People are encouraged to adopt attitudes of resistance and struggle, not for visible material gains only, but within the framework of a wider spiritual struggle whose consequences extend beyond the grave.

In expressions of protest as considered above, Islam's symbolic function is especially activated in the community at the moment that essential aspects of life are felt to be threatened. These include fundamental norms of religious behavior, family relationships and relations between human persons in general, social organization and political autonomy, and of course the truth of the Islamic faith and the dignity of Islam and the Muslims. In Muslim societies as elsewhere, the readiness to defend one's identity against threatening forces by appealing to one's religion is almost instinctive. The fact that, in recent history, Islam has been used to express protests indicates the profound level on which Muslim societies are struggling. Something sacred is threatened; thus a militant appeal to religion is made.

To arrive at a valid approach to the meanings of protests made in the name of Islam, some basic rules should be adopted. It must be admitted, for instance, that a protest that appeals to Islam has some kind of religious meaning for Muslims, whatever other meanings it may have. It should be admitted, too, that many protest movements that have arisen in Muslim societies have evident natural or social causes (for instance oppression, rivalries, violence) but are articulated in Islamic terms. They would have been articulated in other cultural contexts according to the religious or ideological framework valid there. Many protests, of course, have been enunciated in Muslim societies without any direct reference to Islam and we do not deal with them here. But when an appeal has been made to Islam, this deserves attention.

Allowance must be made for the somewhat fluid character of Islam and the corresponding polyvalence of its elements. This, together with the absence of formal organization and representation, gives Islam a certain indefinable character and enables it to be used in many different ways, in particular when it is appealed to. On closer consideration we may say that each protest movement can use Islam in its own way to express refusal. But it is still Islam that is used to articulate the protest and move the people in a given situation. Even simply performing the rituals can imply protest and may be felt accordingly by the participants.

Some pertinent distinctions must then be made in the use of the concept of Islam. The scholarly use of the term indicates a particular culture, system, or religion as an object of investigation. The traditional use of the

382   The International Scene and Islam

word by Muslims indicates what they consider to be their norms and their religion, which probably represents something absolute or sacred to most of them. Muslims generally use the word "Islam" not to indicate an object but to refer to what is held to be right and true, that is to say a moral resource or normative reality they perceive and interpret with certain feelings and intentions. Again, the scholarly study of the social function of particular elements of Islam within a given society is quite different from what Muslims traditionally consider the function of Islam, namely to indicate an unconditional normative pattern that ought to be realized on earth. Unless such distinctions are made, any study of the use of Islam as a symbol of protest is doomed to misinterpret from the very beginning the ways in which "Islam"—in scholarly terms: certain elements of Islam—is used to articulate a protest.

The question should be raised, finally, whether Islam as a religion and ideology might be in a privileged position to express protest and to say "No!". This is to be seen not only in the context of the protest of "Third World" ideologies in general against Western imperialism, but also compared to other religions and ideologies. As mentioned above, Muhammad's preaching and the Qur'ān in particular contain a severe criticism of any absolutization of earthly things and of any imprisonment of human beings within the world. This implies a continuous protest against all forms of *shirk* (attributing "associates" to God) and of atheism. This line has been pursued throughout Islamic history. Although recognizing revelations said to have been given to Moses and Jesus in a written and then largely lost form, Muslims have generally taken a critical attitude to non-Islamic religious and ideological systems, convinced as they are of the absolute character and superiority of Islam and Islamic norms.

I hinted above at an underlying nostalgia and longing among Muslims for a truly Islamic society and state based on the *Sharī'a* and the divine ordinances contained in it. This nostalgic longing nourished by the Qur'ān gives a religious dimension to most social and other protest movements in Muslim societies insofar as they appeal to Islam. It also sharpens the critical sense toward any "man-made" social order. As soon as a social order, though claiming to be Islamic, is felt by Muslims to be oppressive, protests may arise—unless the nature of the oppression constrains any protest to be silent or symbolic. Either the social order is not really Islamic, or it is Islamic but misused for personal purposes.

Islam also lends itself to use as a symbol of protest by evoking grandeur: from the Arab conquests of the first centuries to its great empires—Ottoman, Safavid and Moghul—at the beginning of modern times. It survived colonization and problems of all kinds. At present, it is the second-largest world religion and a world civilization recognized though wrongly interpreted by political scientists like Samuel Huntington.

5. Conclusion

If over the last hundred years Islam has often been used to express militant protest leading to resistance and struggle, this was certainly connected with a position of powerlessness—political, economic, and technological, but also social and cultural—*vis-à-vis* the dominating West. Islamic revitalization has been interpreted in the context of "third-worldism" as providing a common discourse and identity in a time in which traditional societies are dissolved or dissolving.

Protest movements in Muslim societies exhibit defensive features symptomatic of a struggle for survival. Once survival is guaranteed, more creative attitudes may be expected to develop among the Muslim leadership, whether Muslims are a majority or a minority.

Whether or not these protest movements involve a kind of spiritual *jihād*[25], in a broader or in a deeper sense, as a protest against present-day forms of idolatry, moral decline, and religious laxity is an open question. But we can speak of an overall process of the ideologization of Islam since the late nineteenth and especially since the mid-twentieth century. Although we can distinguish a number of interpretations, they all affirm Islam's absolute superiority over other religions and ideologies and contain clear protests against what are considered to be mistakes and errors in Muslim thinking and social life or the false claims of non-Islamic systems, ideologies, and religions.

A subject that needs to be investigated is whether, in this ideological struggle, an appeal to Islam is made as to a system considered to be perfect in itself or rather as representing norms and values that are universal but that appear in Islam in a particular light and perspective. It is quite possible that critical Muslims may develop religious protest against any absolutization of Islam itself as a closed religious system, denouncing it as a form of idolatry.[26]

In conclusion, I would like to stress the urgent need for further study of expressions of moral or religious protest that appeal to Islam. The same holds true for the further study of protest movements in Islam, not only movements against political oppression and social injustice but also and in particular those against what is held to be "wrong" Islam or a wrong application or use of Islam.[27] Any transition from Muslim expressions of protest to more creative attitudes is important, and we need to be able to discern it.

---

[25] Cf. as-Sufi, *Jihad*.
[26] al-ʿAzm, *Naqd al-fikr ad-dīnī* (cf. Id., *Unbehagen in der Moderne: Aufklärung im Islam*, Frankfurt a.M.: Fischer Taschenbuch, 1993); Wild, "Gott und Mensch im Libanon".
[27] Sharīʿatī, *Marxism and Other Western Fallacies*; Id., "Intizar, the Religion of Protest".

Selected Literature

ADAMS, Charles C., *Islam and Modernism in Egypt: A Study of the Modern Reform Movement Inaugurated by Muhammad ʿAbduh* (The American University at Cairo: Oriental Studies), London: Oxford University Press, 1933 (Repr. London, etc.: Routledge, 2000).

ʿAZM, Sādiq Ğalāl al-, *Naqd al-fikr ad-dīnī* (Criticism of Religious Thought), Beirut: Dar at-Tali'a, 1969.

BANNĀ', Hasan al-, *Five Tracts of Hasan Al-Bannā': A Selection from the Majmūʿ at Rasā'il al-Imām al-Shahīd Hasan al-Bannā'*, trans. from the Arabic and annotated by Charles WENDELL (University of California Publications. Near Eastern Studies 20), Berkeley & Los Angeles: University of California Press, 1978.

BENNIGSEN, Alexandre, and Marie BROXUP, *The Islamic Threat to the Soviet State* (Croom Helm Series on the Arab World), London & Canberra: Croom Helm, 1983.

DABASHI, Hamid, *Theology of Discontent: The Ideological Foundation of the Islamic Revolution in Iran*, New York and London: New York University Press, 1993.

DORMAN Jr., Harry Gaylord, *Toward Understanding Islam: Contemporary Apologetic of Islam and Missionary Policy*, New York: Teachers College, Columbia University, 1948.

From Nationalism to Revolutionary Islam, ed. by Said Amir ARJOMAND, London and Basingstoke: Macmillan, 1984.

GEERTZ, Clifford, *Islam Observed: Religious Development in Morocco and Indonesia*, New Haven & London: Yale University Press, 1968.

GIBB, Hamilton Alexander Rosskeen, *Modern Trends in Islam*, Chicago: University of Chicago Press, 1947 (Repr. New York: Octagon Books, 1972).

GREEN, Arnold H., *The Tunisian ʿUlamā' 1873–1915: Social Structure and Response to Ideological Currents* (Social, Economic and Political Studies of the Middle East 22), Leiden: E. J. Brill, 1978.

HADDAD, Yvonne Yazbeck, "The Qur'anic Justification for an Islamic Revolution: The View of Sayyid Qutb", *The Middle East Journal*, 37 (1983), pp. 14–29.

HODGKIN, Thomas, "The Revolutionary Tradition in Islam", *Race and Class*, 21:3 (1980), pp. 221–37.

HOLT, Peter Malcolm, *The Mahdist State in the Sudan 1881–1898: A Study of its Origins, Development and Overthrow*, Oxford: Clarendon Press, 1958, 1977[2].

HUSSAIN, Asaf, *Islamic Movements in Egypt, Pakistan and Iran: An Annotated Bibliography*, London: Mansell, 1983.

Islam and Development: Religion and Sociopolitical Change, ed. by John L. ESPOSITO (Contemporary Issues in the Middle East), Syracuse, N.Y.: Syracuse University Press, 1980.

Islam in Transition: Muslim Perspectives, ed. by John J. DONOHUE and John L. ESPOSITO, New York & Oxford: Oxford University Press, 1982.

Islamic Perspectives: Studies in Honour of Mawlānā Sayyid Abul Aʿlā Mawdūdī, ed. by Khurshid AHMAD and Zafar Ishaq ANSARI, Leicester: The Islamic Foundation, and Jeddah: Saudi Publishing House, 1979/1399H.

JOHANSEN, Baber, "Islam und Staat im 20. Jahrhundert: Soziale und ökonomische Voraussetzungen einer religiösen Protestbewegung", in *Islam und Abendland*, ed. by Ary A. ROEST CROLLIUS, Düsseldorf: Patmos, 1982, pp. 48–115.

JOHNSON, Nels, *Islam and the Politics of Meaning in Palestinian Nationalism*, London, etc.: Kegan Paul, 1982.

KEDDIE, Nikki R., *An Islamic Response to Imperialism: Political and Religious Writings of Sayyid Jamāl ad-Dīn "al-Afghānī"*, Berkeley & Los Angeles: University of California Press, 1968.

—, *Religion and Rebellion in Iran: The Tobacco Protest of 1891–1892*, London: Frank Cass, 1971.

—, *Sayyid Jamāl ad-Dīn "al-Afghānī": A Political Biography*, Berkeley & Los Angeles: University of California Press, 1972.

KHOMEINI, Imam, *Islam and Revolution: Writings and Declarations*, Berkeley, Cal.: Mizan Press, 1981.

KRÄMER, Gudrun, *Gottes Staat als Republik: Reflexionen zeitgenössischer Muslime zu Islam, Menschenrechten und Demokratie* (Studien zu Ethnizität, Religion und Demokratie 1), Baden-Baden: Nomos, 1999.

LAMCHICHI, Abderrahim, *Géopolitique de l'Islamisme*, Paris: L'Harmattan, 2001.

MINTJES, Harry, *Social Justice in Islam*, Amsterdam: Institute for the Study of Religion, Free University, 1977.

MITCHELL, Richard P., *The Society of the Muslim Brothers*, London: Oxford University Press, 1969.

PETERS, Rudolph, *Islam and Colonialism: The Doctrine of jihād in Modern History* (Religion and Society 20), The Hague, etc.: Mouton, 1979.

Religion and Politics in Iran: Shi'ism from Quietism to Revolution, ed. by Nikki R. KEDDIE, New Haven and London: Yale University Press, 1983.

SAID, Edward W., *Orientalism*, New York: Pantheon Books, 1978.

SHARĪ'ATĪ, 'Alī, *Marxism and Other Western Fallacies: An Islamic Critique*, trans. from the Persian by R. CAMPBELL, Berkeley, Cal.: Mizan Press, 1980.

—, "*Intizar*, the Religion of Protest", reprinted in *Islam in Transition* (see above), pp. 297–304.

Shi'ism and Social Protest, ed. by Juan R. I. COLE and Nikki R. KEDDIE, New Haven and London: Yale University Press, 1986.

SMITH, Wilfred Cantwell, *Islam in Modern History*, Princeton: Princeton University Press, 1957 (Mentor pocket 1959).

Spokesmen for the Despised: Fundamentalist Leaders of the Middle East, ed. by R. Scott APPLEBY, Chicago and London: The University of Chicago Press, 1997.

SUFI, 'Abd al-Quādir as-, *Jihad: A Groundplan*, Norwich: Diwan Press, 1978.

UTRECHT, Ernst, "Religion and Social Protest in Indonesia", in *Islam and Society* (Special issue of *Social Compass: International Review of Socio-Religious Studies*, Centre de Recherches Socio-Religieuses, Université Catholique Louvain, 25:3–4 [1978]), pp. 395–418.

WAARDENBURG, Jacques D.J., "Notes on Islam and Development", *Exchange* (Leiden), 4 (March 1974), pp. 3–43.

—, "World Religions as Seen in the Light of Islam", in *Islam: Past Influence and Present Challenge*, ed. by Alford T. WELCH and Pierre CACHIA, Edinburgh: Edinburgh University Press, 1979, pp. 245–75.

—, "Towards a Periodization of Earliest Islam according to its Relations with Other Religions", in *Proceedings of the Ninth Congress of the Union Européenne des Arabisants et Islamisants. Amsterdam, 1st to 7th Sept. 1978* (Publications of the Netherlands Institute of Archaeology and Arabic Studies 4), ed. by Rudolph PETERS, Leiden: E. J. Brill, 1981, pp. 304–26.

WILD, Stefan, "Gott und Mensch im Libanon: Die Affäre Sādiq al-ʿAzm", *Der Islam*, 48 (1972), pp. 206–53.

ZEGHAL, Malika, *Gardiens de l'Islam: Les oulémas d'Al Azhar dans l'Egypte contemporaine*, Paris: Presses de la Fondation Nationale des Sciences Politiques, 1996.

Chapter 19
Islam in Present-Day Muslim States

1. Religious and Political Authorities

Throughout the history of Islam, there has been a certain accommodation between the political leaders and at least an important part of the religious leadership, the *'ulamā'*. Given the conflictual uses that can be made of Islam, we can appreciate that in a given country the state will try to manipulate Islam with the help of certain *'ulamā'*. Part of the compromise is a formula presenting a version of Islam supporting the state and sustaining public order. As a result, Islam functions in public life as a civil religion.

This leads to at least two questions for the contemporary scene. First, who exactly are the religious and political authorities in present-day "Muslim" states with a majority of Muslim inhabitants and in "Islamic" states basing themselves on the *Sharī'a*? Second, how do private and state initiatives use Islam in these states and how do they communicate with each other?

1.1. Religious Authorities

1.1.1. The *'ulamā'* (religious scholars) have traditionally figured as the authorities of religion. The basis of this authority is their knowledge of the *Sharī'a* gained through the study of *fiqh*, the discipline of deducing rules for correct behavior from Qur'ān, *Sunna*, and other sources. The *fuqahā'* are specialists in religious law. They have to be thoroughly familiar with the textual contents of Qur'ān and *hadīths*. Another part of the task of religious scholars is to articulate the properly theological teachings of Islam by means of Scripture and rational arguments and to defend Islam and religion generally by means of reason.

In former times, after studies that could last ten years or more, the *'ulamā'* obtained posts in domains as different as the judiciary (especially what became the *Sharī'a* courts), educational institutions in general and institutions of Islamic learning in particular, and of course as *imāms* of Friday mosques and respected preachers. In the past, their sources of income were *waqfs* (pious foundations) and their own economic pursuits. This gave them considerable independence. In the Ottoman Empire,

The International Scene and Islam

however, they often were paid by the state. In fact, high-class *'ulamā'* could accumulate considerable wealth through marriage alliances, investments in land, trade, or otherwise. Throughout the *dār al-islām* (Muslim world), the *'ulamā'* enjoyed prestige—religious and social—among the people whom they could counsel on the norms of Islam. Pastoral care, however, did not belong to their duties.

All of this is gone now, and except in the properly Islamic states like Iran or if attached to widely respected institutes of learning, the *'ulamā'* have largely become marginal in modern Muslim societies. Although they may enjoy religious and moral authority in broad circles, their influence is decreasing. Historically, with some notable exceptions such as some Hanbalī reformist *'ulamā'* like Ibn Taymīya (1263–1328) and certain Shī'ī religious scholars, *'ulamā'* have rarely squarely opposed the government or public institutions as such. On the contrary, from time to time the government or state officials requested a *fatwā* from the *muftī* (with an official appointment), prescribing how Muslims should act in a particular case. Such a *fatwā* would then furnish a legitimation of the government's policy on this particular point. A *fatwā* often has a conservative tendency, but it can also justify innovations.

The dependence of the *'ulamā'* on the state became much greater in modern times, when they could no longer derive sufficient income from *waqfs*, payments by individuals, or other traditional institutions and rules. As soon as they were paid by the state, the latter would assign them a role in its modernization, socialization, and other policies. Politically, they were expected to align themselves with the state, although they can individually join an Islamic party or association critical of governmental policies. Among themselves, they have nothing like a Church organization, but in certain countries such as Pakistan and Indonesia a number of them have constituted their own party or association. In this way, they can exert a certain pressure on the government to favor Islam in general, to give a wider application to the *Sharī'a*, or to follow a particular interpretation or application of Islam. To the extent that the institutions where future *'ulamā'* are educated have come under government control, their *alumni* tend to acquiesce in government policies.

1.1.2. In former times, leaders of Sūfī *turuq* (dervish orders) and their branches as well as individual holy men could exert authority in Muslim societies, extending also to the social and political domain. In the countryside, this continued far into the twentieth century. Present-day policies of national governments, however, have nearly everywhere not only reduced the number of individual and *tarīqa* Sūfīs, but also often subjected them to government control. With the exception of some African countries like Senegal and some Asian countries like Iran, they are now apparently deprived of real political power.

This means that after a sort of compromise that lasted for centuries, Sūfī Islam has become separate again—as in the first centuries of Islam—from the "official" Islam of the *'ulamā'* and the "officialized" Islam supported by the state.[1] Sūfī Islam now seems to be outside the official circuit. It is the terrain of an apolitical socio-religious Islam that, together with popular Islam, responds to the deeper needs of the people. The example of the former Soviet Union, however, shows that a crypto-political opposition to the state may develop in *tarīqa* circles.

1.1.3. Since the beginnings of Islam, a third kind of religious leadership close to the people has been that of the popular *preachers*, often connected with a mosque as *imāms*. Perhaps more so than in the past, a distinction has now arisen between those preachers who are supported by the government, on the one hand, and what may be called "free" preachers, on the other hand. The first often come from official training courses and have access to the media; they tend to support the government. The latter are outside the official circuit and show a more critical attitude. All preachers know their Qur'ān and *hadīths*, but they are not primarily learned people. They have in any case a very real influence on their audiences that—at the present time of cassettes, video tapes, and internet—extends far beyond the people who attend their sermons in person in the mosque. Their importance has increased.

1.1.4. The fourth and last category of authorities in the field of religion are the leaders of "private" Islamic organizations, *da'wa* movements, and voluntary (often charitable) associations. We think here, for instance, of the leaders of branches of the Muslim Brotherhood. These leaders are often outspoken in their religious and social objectives, having become more cautious, however, in declaring themselves against the current political regime. By definition, these organizations tend to articulate Islam in a way different from the official normative Islam of the *'ulamā'* or the "officialized" version of Islam presented by the government. They may also give a particular socio-political application to Islam. There are also Islamic movements founded at the instigation of governments to counteract alternative *da'wa* movements that pose a threat to them. This fourth kind of religious leaders has become increasingly important in present-day Muslim societies.

1.1.5. Besides these four groups with recognized religious authority, there are also leading personalities who can exert authority in newly founded Islamic institutions, for instance:

---

[1]   For the differentiation between "official" and "officialized" Islam, cf. above Chapter 10 on "Islam's Function as a Civil Religion"; cf. also above Chapter 5 on "Official, Popular, and Normative Religion in Islam".

1) politicians and higher administrators at Ministries of *Awqāf* (*waqfs*) and Religious Affairs;

2) officials in the newly established international Islamic organizations and Islamic universities;

3) scholars who have studied Islam at academic institutions in the West and who can take a stand on certain Islamic matters.[2]

Since religion in Islam is not organized along the lines of Churches, the religious leaders' authority, a few scholars of reputation and a few *Sheykhs al-islām* excepted, has mostly been confined to a particular community. Especially nowadays, the *de facto* recognized religious authorities are many. Consequently, the authority of those who speak in religion's name has become somewhat more elusive than before. But whoever may have religious authority—in the sense of authority to speak on religious matters—, one should always make a distinction between those who are clearly aligned with state interests and those who find themselves outside the official circuit. Independent scholars may sometimes be consulted by the government.

1.2. Political Authorities

Differences between modern and older times, after and before the rise of modern nation-states, are apparently greater here than among religious authorities. The following levels of political authority can be distinguished schematically.

1.2.1. At the top is a small circle of political leaders who make the fundamental government decisions, mostly with one top leader (*za'īm*) appearing as such to the public and carrying responsibility. This in-group constitutes the *dawla*, the rulers in the precise sense of the word. At the beginning of the nation-state, they were mostly nationalist leaders who had been in the forefront of independence movements. Nowadays we have to do with specific in-groups, mostly military leaders who like to wield complete if not absolute power. The remaining monarchs, notwithstanding important differences, can be considered as *za'īms* in their way.

1.2.2. Under this small top is the large body of administrators and civil servants who are the executors of the political decisions made at the top. They may sometimes influence top decisions, but their own competence remains limited. By and large, they function as channels leading from top to bottom through the centralized network of the state bureaucracy.

---

[2]   Cf. above Chapter 7 on "Some North African Intellectuals' Presentations of Islam".

1.2.3. The third category may be characterized as technocrats, experts in key domains such as finance, economics, or the application of modern technology in various fields. They draw up development plans; they organize police, defense, and intelligence; they know what is feasible and what is not. In short, they provide the technical know-how for government decisions and the implementation thereof. To a growing extent, they can be appointed to cabinet ministries.

1.2.4. A fourth category consists of those officials who convey government decisions to the public and to the outside world. Here we are dealing not only with those responsible for information and media, but also with diplomatic representatives in other countries or in international organizations. They may, of course, be sensitive to responses coming from below and from outside and will have to report this to decision-makers.

Modern majority "Muslim" or *Sharī'a*-based "Islamic" states may contain the remnants of earlier political institutions, for instance of consultation (*shūrā*), but they have developed new centers and instruments of power. As in former times, they have to take Islam into consideration, certainly if there is a majority Muslim population. Attention will be given to two issues in particular, the protection of Islamic institutions and the fostering of Islam while promoting certain attitudes among the people toward Islam, in other words, the promotion of Islam—in whatever forms—as a civil religion.

1.2.5. The protection of Islamic institutions involves issues as diverse as the building and upkeep of at least a number of mosques, the appointment of *imāms* in the larger Friday mosques, the provision of the Qur'ān and other important religious texts, the registration of *waqf*-properties, and the salaries of official religious personnel. To this should be added, of course, matters related to the *Sharī'a*, such as its at least partial application in current legislation (personal status law, sometimes penal law), its judiciary organization, rulings on religious minorities, etc. The state has an interest in the organization of faculties of *Sharī'a* at universities, indirect control of *turuq* and *da'wa* organizations and not to speak of practical activities associated with the *hajj*, the rules during the month of fasting (*Ramadān*), the teaching of Islam at schools, and the wider distribution of literature on Islam. The symbolic and ceremonial aspect of the Islamic institutions also has to be organized, from the celebration of religious feasts to the honoring of religious dignitaries at official receptions.

1.2.6. As part of a broader orientation program, the state also promotes certain attitudes among the population toward Islam. Orientations given to the citizens through the media and in school education have an ideological component to the extent that the state wants to promulgate particular views of society and humankind in general. In addition to offering a particular ideology, the state can further Islam in many ways, like founding new mosques with public funds, extending the teaching of Islam and Islamic history in schools, creating training centers, and in some cases giving active support to the spread of Islam abroad.

Special attention, however, is owed to the fact that a Muslim and certainly an Islamic state tends to present a semi-official or "officialized" version of Islam. One need think only of the Islam propagated by Iran or Saudi Arabia. Moreover, political leaders can privilege certain 'ulamā' and preachers above others in exchange for not expressing themselves too critically towards the state. Certain Qur'ān texts and hadīths can be stressed in public life to underscore a particular aspect of Islam that the political leadership wants to promote. In response to "Islamist" activities, such an "officialized" use of Islam has increased in recent times. Each country should be studied as a case in itself, but Islam is always presented as serving the moral force of the country, the unity of the country, and social and economic development. "Islamists", on the other hand, will stress that Islam assures justice, including social justice, and that it condemns all forms of corruption and moral laxity, as well as violations of human rights. In contrast to the "official" version of Islam held by the 'ulamā' and the "officialized" version held by the state, there is consequently a third, "protesting" version of Islam, which condemns existing evil.

As a consequence of this state of affairs, state and religion are not always clearly distinguishable—and not only for the people concerned, many of whom want to stress the "unity" of religion and politics (dīn wa-dunya) anyway. For Western analysts, this presents a problem. The reason I suggest for what may be called an "opacity" to the analysis of what really happens is that Islam is not merely a veil that hides reality. This is a current but superficial opinion. In fact, Islam in the modern Muslim—and certainly the Islamic—nation-state has obtained the positive function of bridging political and religious authorities, ideologies, and institutions. Instead of having a "cover" function, I think that Islam, perhaps more than ever before, is now functioning as a civil religion. Let us look now at the nature of the political problem to which Islam, as a civil religion, gives an original solution.

2. Private and State Initiatives in the Use of Islam

From a political science point of view, in most Muslim and Islamic countries, Islam is used nowadays in the continuing struggle between those who are in power and their opponents. Muslim governments may claim that, at the very least, existing laws and decrees are not in conflict with the Qur'ān and basic rules of the *Sharī'a*. Islamic governments may claim that the entire legislation is based on Qur'ān and *Sharī'a*. Opponents of such regimes, inasmuch as they want to appeal to Islam to give force to their struggle, may argue that the government does not promote Islam sufficiently and that Islam is the true remedy to the country's problems. Even in an Islamic state, the opponents of the government—to the extent that they can express their opinion freely—can argue that the government does not apply the *Sharī'a* rigorously enough. In this scenario, Islam is used either on the initiative of "private" movements and groups, or on the initiative of policy-makers and other state officials.

2.1. Private Initiatives

Many initiatives by private individuals, groups, and movements have called for a greater observation of Islam in Muslim societies. Egypt is paradigmatic in this respect. It has known the reformist Salafīya movement, the activist Muslim Brotherhood, various attempts insisting on properly Islamic ethical and ritual behavior, and last not least some militant activist movements prepared to use violence for the cause of Islam. The response of the government has varied from containment in the case of the Brotherhood, to repression in the case of the militant activists. Similar *da'wa* movements in which Muslims appeal to each other to become better Muslims have arisen in other Muslim countries as well.[3]

It is in particular educated laymen and not *'ulamā'* or Sūfīs who have played an important part in the *da'wa* movements that appeared on the public scene. They focused on themes that had escaped the interest and attention of *'ulamā'* and Sūfī *sheykhs*, like independent thinking and authenticity, social justice and the emancipation of the underprivileged, and of course liberation from foreign domination in its various forms. These educated lay people have discovered the potential of Islam as a source of social ideas and action toward a better society. At the end of the colonial period and in the first decades of independence, such private initiatives often pleaded for a secular society, appealed to Marxism, and rejected any influence of Islam in public life. At present, most private initiatives that make themselves heard speak out in favor of Islam. Often they have a strong moral undertone and a religious commitment with a rather puritan attitude toward the world.

---

[3]   Cf. above Chapter 15 on "The Call (*Da'wa*) of Islamic Movements".

2.2. State Initiatives

In a number of Muslim countries, public authorities keep an eye on the ways in which Islam is observed in public life. Once independence had been reached, most Muslim states had changes in political regimes, and these tended to be more Islam-oriented. From its formal foundation in 1932, Saudi Arabia has known an alliance between the political and the religious authorities. In Iran, the modernizing and secularizing state was taken over by the religious leadership in 1979. After the military takeover of Pakistan by Zia ul-Haqq in 1977, the new political leadership proclaimed an overall Islamization policy. In Libya, the military takeover of 1969 was followed by a social revolution legitimized by the interpretation of Islam as a revolutionary message and process.[4] In all these cases, more or less revolutionary regimes proclaimed that they would establish an ideal Islamic order that would distinguish itself clearly from the Western and Eastern bloc models.

The presence of Islamic states that claim to be based on the *Sharī'a* already has an important symbolic value in itself for the self-awareness of the Muslim world. It also has a real influence in at least two respects. Islamic oil states have developed aid and assistance programs to other Muslim countries, based on the common religion. Such oil states can also exert pressure on other Muslim countries or on specific groups in these countries to ensure more observance of Islam in public life. They evidently hope that such Muslim countries will eventually transform themselves into Islamic states, too.

At present, there seem to be three types of argument that Muslims can voice if they want to oppose the state of affairs prevailing in an Islamic state like Saudi Arabia or Iran. They can say: (a) that Islamization has not been carried far enough; (b) that other means ought to be used to bring about the ideal Islamic order; or (c) that people should develop a new lifestyle based on their own decision, with forms of Islam imbued by the experience of life on a more popular level.

Most state initiatives, however, have not favored the establishment of an "Islamic" state based on the *Sharī'a*. They have sought instead to counteract the uncontrolled *da'wa* movements that arose from private initiatives. Muslim governments are aware of certain dangers such movements pose for rational planning, development policies, national unity, and of course themselves. In the same vein, these governments have been opposed to traditionalism in general, sanctioned by religion, and to a number of customs and structures that, under the cover of religion,

---

4   On Saudi Arabia, Iran, Pakistan, and Libya cf. above Chapter 17 on "The Rise of Islamic States".

constitute a hindrance to those forms of modernization and development that the governments think necessary.

In Muslim states, there have been several forms of opposition to the state that appealed to Islamic values. Five typical Muslim state initiatives to overcome such religious opposition deserve mention:

1) The state could develop the doctrine of *secularism*, as in republican Turkey. The religious response to this initiative was twofold: a new interest in the study of the Qur'ān as Scripture and a new proliferation of folk Islam. As a matter of fact, there were no longer sufficient people able to distinguish what part of Islam as practiced was legitimate and what part was contrary to normative Islam.

2) The state could proclaim and impose an official *atheism*, as happened in the USSR, China, and Albania. In this case, an open response was not possible, but people continued to adhere to certain ritual and moral aspects of Islam linked to communal and family life.

3) The state could further a *nationalist* ideology, as developed in the struggle for independence, but now in view of constructing a modern state. Such an ideology was developed more or less in the image of Western nations, in particular France, Britain, and the USA. It tried to relegate Islam to the private sphere or in any case to exclude the public expression of Islam from the developing sector of society.

4) The state could also favor a *socialist* ideology, for instance of the Nasserist, Ba'th, or Bhutto variety. Such an ideology cherishes the ideal of a just society to which people of different faiths can contribute. The religious response to this state initiative, to the extent that it could express itself, has varied considerably. Religious protests by the Muslim Brotherhood against the Nasser and Ba'th regimes had no chance and were suppressed; protests by the *Jamā'at-i Islāmī* and other religious parties against the "socialist" Bhutto regime succeeded with Bhutto's fall.

5) The state could proclaim a more *general religious basis* for the state, in which the major existing religions could cooperate. This happened in Indonesia with the *Pancasila* formula. By assigning Islam a place within a set of broader religious and humanistic principles, the Indonesian state since its beginnings in 1945 succeeded in countering Muslim activists' demands for an Islamization of the state or even an Islamic state based on the *Sharī'a*. The state developed a kind of enlightened version of Islam, which was taught at schools and spread through the media. The religious Muslim response to this state policy has been complex, and after Suharto's fall the proclaimed religious tolerance was sometimes belied by Muslim activist violence.

3. Tensions Between Private and State Initiatives in the Use of Islam

I suggest that there is a sliding scale between the ideal secular Muslim state, that is to say a secular state with a Muslim majority, and the ideal religious Islamic state, that is to say a state based completely on the *Sharīʿa*. Islam's position in society determines a country's place on the scale. This has to do with the struggle between the various existing private and state initiatives intent either on reinforcing the position of Islam in public life in society or on counteracting any such reinforcement. The character and influence of Islam in a modern nation-state cannot be established, however, merely by measuring the degree of application of the *Sharīʿa* in the state.

In most Muslim countries, there is an intricate debate about what Islam is and how it should be implemented. On closer consideration, there is a struggle between what the state authority supported by leading *ʿulamāʾ* wants, on the one hand, and what "non-state" or private groups and movements want, on the other hand. Among the latter, there is a fundamental debate whether and how Islam should be implemented in public life, extreme secularists wanting to reduce Islam to the private sphere and extreme "Islamists" wanting to subject the public sphere to an ideal Islamic order. The latter are in favor of an Islamization of society and want to establish an Islamic state based on the *Sharīʿa*.

On the "private" side, those pleading for increased Islamization reproach the modern state for not applying the moral and legal norms of Islam. They hold this to be the main cause of the miserable condition in which the majority of Muslims live nowadays, a condition contrary to the norms of human rights and social justice. Apart from sheer political motivations, their appeal is basically ethical and religious, but it is indignant and can take a political and even violent turn.

It is difficult for the state to respond directly to such an appeal, since it cannot deny the validity of the Islamic norms that are invoked. When its opponents disturb the public order, this can be used as an argument to take them to court; in totalitarian states, opponents are eliminated in other ways.

Most Muslim states lack democratic procedures. A centralized power does everything to affirm and assert itself. There often is an *ad hoc* policy toward Islam. Most states tend to promote the elaboration of and instruction in a particular "officialized" version of Islam, but they may remain ambiguous in committing themselves to making Islam the state religion. If the attitude taken toward Islam is sympathetic and positive, the difference between state and religion will not be stressed. But if the state's attitude to Islam is more distant and secular, this difference will be stressed. Any state is a complex body, and in Muslim states attitudes to Islamic claims may shift, depending on pressures from inside or from outside society, including those coming from other Muslim or from Western countries. At a certain point, people may be tired of the way the state is run anyway, whatever it says about Islam. Many people feel their state is oppressive.

Looking attentively, at present the general movement on the scale between the more secular Muslim majority state and the religious Islamic state seems to be toward the latter, since we are witnessing a progressive Islamization of Muslim societies, at least outwardly. However, even among those private and public initiatives that want to increase the public role of Islam, there are considerable differences. Except for extremist positions, there is discussion. The debates are of a relative rather than an absolute nature, because most of them use an Islamic discourse and recognize a plurality of standpoints. I submit that this has to do with the fact that Islam functions as a civil religion. It is common to all and admits different interpretations and applications. In fact it constitutes the fiber of the societies and the basic legitimization of the states in question.

4. Articulations of Islam as a Civil Religion

Since independence, the nation-state has been something new for people in Muslim societies. It is legitimate to ask what Islam means to them in relation to what the state has come to mean for them. When Muslims deny a fundamental separation between religion and state (*dīn wa-dunya*), this implies that they see a particular relationship between them. This relationship is the main argument for my contention that, in Muslim societies, the role of Islam should be studied as that of a civil religion.

In former times, for the mass of people, the presence of political authority and power largely meant the obligation to pay taxes and to render certain services from time to time. In exchange, the political authority guaranteed a certain order; if it was strong enough, it could impose rules that had to be obeyed. The political power of the state and its sanctions, however, were at a great distance from most people, certainly from those outside the towns. It was also very far from the natural communities to which people owed loyalty and in which they participated more or less actively: family, clan and tribe, the ethnic group, and of course the religious community.

A new situation arose for the people when they became involved in the struggle for national independence. The only real alternative to being colonized was to have one's own national state on a modern footing more or less according to the model of Western states. The nationalist leaders had the highest expectations for this new state of their own, which would liberate the people, guarantee freedom from foreign domination, protect them against injustice, offer educational facilities, and improve their mostly poor conditions of life. A whole structure of symbolic values was attached to what had become "our" state and "our" nation.

These values were projected onto the leader who personalized the state and was admired, loved, and served. However, in opposition circles the leader could also arouse negative feelings, distrust, and even emotional disgust. In nearly all cases, people did not think they could influence the leader, since they had hardly ever been able to influence government. In fact, they soon became aware of their distance also to the new power structure of the state enforcing itself on the people.

4.1. The Nation-State

It seems to me that the relationship of the people to the state and its authority, as well as subsequent developments of this relationship among various groups of the population, are key factors in understanding the recent cases of transfer of loyalties from an idealized state to an idealized Islam. Another key factor seems to be the people's instinctive negative response toward the sheer presence of and certainly any intervention in internal affairs by a foreign power. It leads people to stress what distinguishes them from the foreign power, that is to say their own nation and their own religion and way of life.

The existence of nation-states has had far-reaching consequences. For one thing, thanks to modern technology, the power invested in the state grew and expanded to all sectors of society. It became palpable and visible when the old social order started to be transformed into a new one and when old elites had to make more and more room for new rising classes, like the military.

Another feature of the new nation-state was that it was able to impose particular forms of modernization on the country and its society. The state proclaimed the necessity for modernization and carried it out mostly with the help of capital and advisers from abroad. The state also started to use its powers to guide the people and give them an orientation that would facilitate the attainment of the government's objectives. It projected ideologies onto the nation, and the people were supposed to follow. Inasmuch as the nation-state did not meet a fundamental challenge to its exertion of power, it tended to become totalitarian. This had its own consequences.

In the course of the fifty odd years of independence that most Muslim nation-states have enjoyed, the populations must have increasingly experienced their state as something imposing itself on them against their will. It could no longer be seen as the generous "patriarchal" institution that would improve the conditions of life in society. Measured against the high expectations of the beginnings, the reality of the state must have led to disillusionment. The disappointment, however, was softened by the continuing state ideology in each country, which adapted itself to circumstances and to which people had no choice except to adhere. This holds true for all Third World countries.

4.2. Islam as a Limit to the State

In Muslim countries, however, Islam is held as a common value offering in principle the norms according to which life should be conducted. Differences in interpretation and application are thereby accepted. One of the factors inextricably linking society to Islam is the struggle between competing interests to use Islam as a political tool, which may even have enhanced the sense of the value of Islam. During the past two or three decades, this has led to a rediscovery of and reorientation toward Islam by numerous different groups in Muslim societies. It is no longer nationalism or socialism, but Islam—however interpreted—that is the yardstick according to which the state of affairs is morally measured. The nation-state as it is experienced can no longer meet that measure. The idea of another kind of state and society is defined and developed in Islamic terms with religious overtones. In countries with strong Muslim traditions, it would be surprising if this were otherwise. This has consequences for the articulation of Islam.

Throughout Muslim history, the main tasks of political regimes were those of upholding order and justice in society and of establishing institutions and rules that would enable people to live a decent life as Muslims. In older times, a limit was placed on the powers of the political regime in that it was not supposed to create new rules, but merely to apply those already given in the *Sharī'a*. In other words, religion in general and Islam in particular functioned in part to domesticate the state, and the leading *'ulamā'* were and probably still are well aware of this.

I may note in parenthesis that, in the Western tradition, too, the political structure has been altered. In older times, religion, represented by the Churches, imposed limits on the state's natural accretion of power. In the nineteenth century, the West placed additional checks on the state: the democratic process to make political decisions, the people considered as holders of sovereignty, and the separation of the most important functions of the state. In the West, too, the need is felt to control the increase of state power and to use the state as an instrument to reach certain aims, such as a just society.

Modern states everywhere, whether within or outside of the Muslim world, are complex and difficult to grasp. They show many variations and have great means of power with a large bureaucratic apparatus.

They impose rules with sanctions that are often outside the legislative process and mostly insufficiently controlled. Their decisions in social, economic, and foreign-policy making may have immense consequences for human life in the societies concerned. One cannot be blind to the intricate mechanisms of control that a state can now exert over its residents or to the fact that judiciary functions are not always independent from executive political interests. It is not easy, for instance, to obtain solid facts about the way in which certain Muslim states really function today; even parliaments and scholarly bodies often have difficulty obtaining the information they need or want.

4.3. Civil Society and Civil Religion

In this situation, it is in the interest of state and society to maintain a common discourse and to create bridges of communication. One way is that of a civil society, in which the participants in the public sphere accept each other, whether Muslim or not. Another way in which Muslim governments can communicate with a Muslim population is to emphasize Islam, which rulers and ruled have in common. I do not mean here a particular Islamic ideology, but Islam as something culturally given, a universe of discourse, a means of communication. States, whether they are progressive, conservative, or reactionary, increasingly use Islam ideologically and politically and present themselves more in Islamic terms. The state appeals to Islam, legitimates itself through it, and encourages an "officialized" version of it. No wonder a Muslim government asks support from religious leaders to maintain recognized norms and values. But this is exactly what we call civil religion, maintaining the social order through a kind of religion that is accepted by all and makes them better citizens. I do not judge whether this is right or wrong; I merely note that Islam functions here as a civil religion.

Political leadership, the ʿulamāʾ, and certain groups within society have always had common interests. In the modern nation-state, however, these interests have taken on new forms. This implies that political and religious leaders find each other on common ground: Islam. On this basis, a negotiating process may take place in which the religious authorities of one country may align themselves with those of another country, just as there can be political alliances and economic exchanges.

Most important in terms of civil religion is the fact that, after an era in which the paradigm of secularism prevailed, a bargaining process seems to have started, not only between the state and the ʿulamāʾ, but also with "private" groups and movements. The discourse takes place in Islamic terms, with the parties concerned putting their demands on the table. The result, evidently, will be a working compromise and not a definite solution, Islam being treated as a civil religion that the participants want to uphold. Whether or not representatives of a liberal or Sūfī Islam and those insisting on a secular public space will participate remains an open question. If they do not participate, it is a sign that we are observing a denominational, rather than a civil kind of religion.

It seems to me that one of the main differences from former times in which Islam also functioned as a civil religion is that nowadays—except in Iran—the professional 'ulamā' have lost much of their authority. They endure the competition of "private" groups and movements, and they are faced with a powerful state that asks them to make it acceptable to the people. The question remains whether the growing gulf between an authoritarian state and people living under miserable conditions can be bridged in this way. The people may very well choose a more militant form of Islam that demands social justice and that protests against the regime in power and its self-legitimization by means of Islam.

Finally it should be observed that Islam can function as a civil religion, not only in national contexts but in a broader Muslim context as well. This happens, for instance, in international Islamic organizations and conferences. Islam increasingly functions as a trans-national civil religion in the commonwealth of Muslim nations. It is too simple to say that Islam is used here or elsewhere simply as a cover for purely power-political purposes. Rather, Islam as a symbol and signification system provides a kind of symbolism to which political interests have to adjust. That is precisely how civil religion functions.

Selected Literature

1. Regional Studies
A. South Asia

AHMAD, Aziz, and Gustav Edmund von GRUNEBAUM, *Muslim Self-Statement in India and Pakistan 1857–1968*, Wiesbaden: Harrassowitz, 1970.
SATYAPRAKASH, *Muslims in India: A Bibliography of their Religious, Socio-Economic and Political Literature*, Haryana: Indian Documentation Service, 1985.
SCHIMMEL, Annemarie, *Islam in India and Pakistan*, Leiden: E. J. Brill, 1982.
SMITH, Wilfred Cantwell, *Modern Islam in India: A Social Analysis*, Lahore: Minerva Bookshop, 1943. Revised edition London: Victor Gollancz, 1946 (Repr. Lahore: Ashraf, 1963). Second revised edition New Delhi: Usha, 1979.
VEER, Peter T. van der, *Religious Nationalism: Hindus and Muslims in India*, Berkeley, Cal. etc.: University of California Press, 1994.

B. Southeast Asia

BOLAND, B. J., *The Struggle of Islam in Modern Indonesia*, The Hague: Nijhoff, 1971, 1982².
Islam in South-East Asia, ed. by M. B. HOOKER, Leiden: E. J. Brill, 1983.

MULDER, Niels, *Inside Southeast Asia: Religion, Everyday Life, Cultural Change*, Amsterdam and Kuala Lumpur: The Pepin Press, 1996.

Readings on Islam in Southeast Asia, compiled by Ahmad IBRAHIM, Shavon SIDDIQUE, Yasmin HUSSAIN, Singapore: Institute of Southeast Asian Studies, 1985.

C. Central Asia

RASHID, Ahmed, *The Resurgence of Central Asia: Islam or Nationalism?*, London: Zed Books, 1994.

Russia's Muslim Frontiers: New Directions in Cross-Cultural Analysis, ed. by Dale F. EICKELMAN, Bloomington, Ind.: Indiana University Press, 1993.

State, Religion and Society in Central Asia: A Post-Soviet Critique, ed. by Vitaly NAUMKIN, Reading: Ithaca Press, 1993.

D. Africa

African Encounters between Sufis and Islamists, ed. by Eva Evers ROSANDER and David WESTERLUND, London: Hurst, and Athens, Oh.: Ohio University Press, 1997.

COULON, Christian, *Les musulmans et le pouvoir en Afrique noire*, Paris: Karthala, 1983.

CUOQ, Joseph, *Les musulmans en Afrique*, Paris: G.-P. Maisonneuve et Larose, 1975.

Muslim Identity and Social Change in Sub-Saharan Africa, ed. by Louis BRENNER, London: Hurst, 1993.

TRIMINGHAM, J. Spencer, *The Influence of Islam upon Africa* (Arab Background Series), London: Longmans, Green & Co., and Beirut: Librairie du Liban, 1968.

2. Some Country Studies (see also the bibliographies of Chapters 5, 7, and 17)

A. Turkey

BERKES, Niyazi, *The Development of Secularism in Turkey*, Montreal: McGill University Press, 1964 (Repr. London: Hurst, 1998).

Civil Society in the Grip of Nationalism: Studies on Political Culture in Contemporary Turkey, ed. by Stefanos YERASIMOS, Günter SEUFERT, Karin VORHOFF, Istanbul and Würzburg: Ergon, 2000.

OEZDEMIR, Adil, and Kenneth FRANK, *Visible Islam in Modern Turkey*, Houndsville: Macmillan, and New York: St. Martin's Press, 2000.

ZUERCHER, E.-J., *Turkey: A Modern History*, London: I. B. Tauris, 1993.

B. Egypt and Sudan

ABDO, Geneviève, *No God but God: Egypt and the Triumph of Islam*, New York: Oxford University Press, 2000.

LESCH, Ann Mosely, *The Sudan: Contested National Identities*, Bloomington and Indianapolis: Indiana University Press, and Oxford: James Currey, 1998.

C. Iraq and Kuwait

FAROUK-SLUGLETT, Marion, and Peter SLUGLETT, *Iraq since 1958: From Revolution to Dictatorship*, London and New York: I. B. Tauris, 1987, 2001².

KOCH, Christian, *Politische Entwicklung in einem arabischen Golfstaat: Die Rolle von Interessengruppen im Emirat Kuwait*, Berlin: Klaus Schwarz, 2000.

3. World-wide Islam

BRUNNER, Rainer, *Annäherung und Distanz: Schi'a, Azhar und die islamische Ökumene im 20. Jahrhundert* (Islamkundliche Untersuchungen 204), Berlin: Klaus Schwarz, 1996.

Lieux d'islam: Cultes et cultures de l'Afrique à Java, ed. by Mohammad Ali AMIR-MOEZZI, Paris: Ed. Autrement, 1996.

Madrasa: La transmission du savoir dans le monde musulman, ed. by Nicole GRANDIN and Marc GABORIEAU, Paris: Ed. Arguments, 1997.

SCHÖNE, Ellinor, *Islamische Solidarität: Geschichte, Politik, Ideologie der Organisation der Islamischen Konferenz (OIC) 1969–1981* (Islamkundliche Untersuchungen 214), Berlin: Klaus Schwarz, 1997.

SCHULZE, Reinhard, *Islamischer Internationalismus im 20. Jahrhundert: Untersuchungen zur Geschichte der Islamischen Weltliga (Rābitat al-'Ālam al-Islāmī)* (Social, Economic, and Political Studies of the Middle East 4), Leiden and New York: E. J. Brill, 1990.

Further Reading

INTRODUCTION

1. Islamic Studies

Approaches to Islam in Religious Studies, ed. by Richard C. MARTIN, Tucson, Ariz.: University of Arizona Press, 1985.

Islamic Studies: A Tradition and Its Problems, *ed. by Malcolm H. KERR, Malibu, Cal.: Undena Publications, 1980.*

Mapping Islamic Studies: Genealogy, Continuity and Change , ed. by Azim NANJI (Religion and Reason 38), Berlin etc.: Mouton de Gruyter, 1997.

MARTIN, Richard C., *Islamic Studies: A History of Religions Approach*, Upper Saddle River, N. J.: Prentice Hall, 1982, 1996².

RODINSON, Maxime, *Europe and the Mystique of Islam*, Seattle: University of Washington Press, 1991.

SAID, Edward W., *Orientalism*, New York: Pantheon Books, 1978 etc. (Revised ed. Penguin Books, 1995).

WAARDENBURG, Jacques D. J., Art. "Mustashrikūn" ("Orientalists"), in *The Encyclopaedia of Islam*, new ed., Leiden: E. J. Brill, 1993, vol. 7, pp. 735–53.

—, Art. "Islamic Studies", in *The Encyclopedia of Religion*, ed. by Mircea ELIADE, New York: Macmillan, and London: Collier Macmillan, 1987, vol. 7, pp. 457–64.

2. Reference Works

DONZEL, Emeri J. van, *Islamic Desk Reference: Compiled from the Encyclopaedia of Islam*, Leiden: E. J. Brill, 1994.

The Encyclopaedia of Islam, new ed., ed. by Clifford Edmund BOSWORTH, Leiden: E. J. Brill, 1960– .

Index Islamicus, On CD Rom. See: <www.lexisnexis.com/academic>.

The Middle East and North Africa (Yearbook), London: Europa Publications, 1950– .

The Muslim Almanac: A Reference Work on the History, Faith, Culture and Peoples of Islam, ed. by Azim A. NANJI, Detroit: Gale Research, 1996.

The Oxford Encyclopedia of the Modern Islamic World, ed. by John L. ESPOSITO, 4 vols., New York and Oxford: Oxford University Press, 1995.

ROBINSON, Francis, *Atlas of the Islamic World since 1500*, New York: Facts on File, and Oxford: Phaidon, 1982.

3. Islam: History, Culture, Civilization

EICKELMAN, Dale F., *The Middle East: An Anthropological Approach*, Englewood Cliffs, N. J.: Prentice Hall, 1981, revised 4th ed. 2001.

GRUNEBAUM, Gustave Edmund von, *Islam: Essays in the Nature and Growth of a Cultural Tradition*, Menasha, Wis.: American Anthropological Association, 1955; London: Routledge & Kegan Paul, 1961[2].

HODGSON, Marshall G.S., *The Venture of Islam: Conscience and History in a World Civilization*, 3 vols., Chicago and London: University of Chicago Press, 1974 (paperback ed. 1977).

Intellectual Traditions in Islam, ed. by Farhad DAFTARY, London and New York: I. B. Tauris, 2000.

LAPIDUS, Ira M., *A History of Islamic Societies*, Cambridge and Sydney: Cambridge University Press, 1988 (paperback edition 1990).

The World of Islam: Faith, People, Culture, ed. by Bernard LEWIS, London: Thames and Hudson, 1976 (paperback edition 1997).

4. Works in English referred to in the Introduction

CHITTICK, William C., *The Self-Disclosure of God: Principles of Ibn al-'Arabi's Cosmology*, Albany, N. Y.: SUNY Press, 1998.

CRONE, Patricia, and Michael COOK, *Hagarism: The Making of the Islamic World*, Cambridge: Cambridge University Press, 1977.

— and Martin HINDS, *God's Caliph: Religious Authority in the First Centuries of Islam*, Cambridge: Cambridge University Press, 1986.

GEERTZ, Clifford, *The Religion of Java*, London and Glencoe, Ill.: The Free Press, 1960.

—, *Islam observed: Religious Development in Morocco and Indonesia*, New Haven: Yale University Press, 1968.

—, *The Interpretation of Cultures: Selected Essays*, New York: Basic Books, 1973.

GIBB, Hamilton Alexander Rosskeen, *Mohammedanism: An* (2nd ed.: A) *Historical Survey*, London, etc.: Oxford University Press, 1949, 1975[2].

—, *Studies on the Civilization of Islam*, ed. by Stanford J. SHAW and William POLK, Boston: Beacon Press, 1962.

GRAHAM, William A., *Divine Word and Prophetic Word in Early Islam: A Reconsideration of the Sources with Special Reference to the Divine Saying or Hadīth Qudsī*, The Hague: Mouton, 1977.

GRUNEBAUM, Gustave Edmund von, *Modern Islam: The Search for Cultural Identity*, Berkeley, Cal.: University of California Press, 1962 (pocket edition New York: Vintage Books, 1964).

JEFFERY, Arthur, *Materials for the History of the Text of the Qur'ān*, Leiden: E. J. Brill, 1937.

—, *The Foreign Vocabulary of the Qur'ān*, Baroda: Oriental Institute, 1938.

MADELUNG, Wilferd, *The Succession to Muhammad: A Study of the Early Caliphate*, Cambridge: Cambridge University Press, 1997.

NEUWIRTH, Angelika, *Studien zur Komposition der mekkanischen Suren* (Studien zur Sprache, Geschichte und Kultur des islamischen Orients. Neue Folge 10), Berlin/New York: Walter de Gruyter, 1981.

SCHIMMEL, Annemarie, *Mystical Dimensions of Islam*, Chapel Hill, N. C.: University of North Carolina Press, 1975.

WANSBROUGH, John S., *Quranic Studies: Sources and Methods of Scriptural Interpretation*, London: Oxford University Press, 1975.

—, *The Sectarian Milieu: Content and Composition of Islamic Salvific History*, London: Oxford University Press, 1978.

THE BEGINNINGS

See also the Bibliography of Chapter 1.

1. Qur'ān

ABDUL-RAOF, Hussein, *Qur'an Translation: Discourse, Texture and Exegesis*, Richmond, Surrey: Curzon, 2001.

Approaches to the History of the Interpretation of the Qur'an, ed. by Andrew RIPPIN, Oxford: Clarendon Press, 1988.

Approaches to the Qur'ān, ed. by Gerald R. HAWTING and Abdul-Kader SHAREEF, New York and London: Routledge, 1993.

IZUTSU, Toshihiko, *God and Man in the Koran: Semantics of the Koranic Weltanschauung*, Tokyo: Keio Institute of Cultural and Linguistic Studies, 1964 (Repr. Salem: Ayer, 1987).

The Qur'ān as Text, ed. by Stefan WILD (Islamic Philosophy & Theology & Science. Texts and Studies 27), Leiden: E. J. Brill, 1996.

RAHMAN, Fazlur, *Major Themes of the Qur'ān*, Minneapolis: Bibliotheca Islamica, 1980, 1989[2].

RIPPIN, Andrew, *The Qur'ān and Its Interpretive Tradition* (Variorum Collected Studies Series), Burlington, Vt.: Ashgate, 2001.

WELCH, Alford T., Art. "al-Ḳur'ān", in *The Encyclopaedia of Islam*, new ed., vol. 5, Leiden: E. J. Brill, 1986, pp. 400–29.

2. Hadīth

BERG, Herbert, *The Development of Exegesis in Early Islam: The Authenticity of Muslim Literature from the Formation Period* (Curzon Studies in the Qur'ān), London: Curzon, 2000.

BURTON, John, *An Introduction to the Hadīth*, Edinburgh: Edinburgh University Press, 1994.

JUYNBOLL, Gautier H.A., *Studies on the Origins and Uses of Islamic Hadīth*, Aldershot: Variorum, 1996.

3. Muhammad

RODINSON, Maxime, *Muhammad*, New York: Pantheon Books, 1980.

RUBIN, Uri, *The Eye of the Beholder: The Life of Muhammad as viewed by the Early Muslims: A Textual Analysis* (Studies in Late Antiquity and Early Islam 5), Princeton, N. J.: Darwin Press, 1995.

Watt, William Montgomery, *Muhammad at Mecca*, Oxford: Clarendon Press, 1953, 2000³ (also Albany, N. Y.: SUNY Press, 1988).
—, *Muhammad at Medina*, Oxford: Clarendon Press, 1956, 1998⁴ (also Albany, N. Y.: SUNY Press, 1989).

4. Earliest History of Islam

Hawting, Gerald R., *The Idea of Idolatry and the Emergence of Islam: From Polemic to History* (Cambridge Studies in Islamic Civilization), Cambridge: Cambridge University Press, 1999.
Hoyland, Robert G., *Seeing Islam as Others saw It: A Survey and Evaluation of Christian, Jewish and Zoroastrian Writings on Early Islam* (Studies in Late Antiquity and Early Islam 13), Princeton, N. J.: Darwin Press, 1997.
Madelung, Wilferd, *The Succession to Muhammad: A Study of the Early Caliphate*, Cambridge: Cambridge University Press, 1997.
Schick, Robert, *The Christian Communities of Palestine from Byzantine to Islamic Rule: A Historical and Archaeological Study* (Studies in Late Antiquity and Early Islam 2), Princeton, N. J.: Darwin Press, 1995.

Islam As a Religion

1. General Presentations

Ahmed, Akbar S., *Islam Today: A Short Introduction to the Muslim World*, London and New York: I. B. Tauris, 1999 (Repr. 2001).
Arkoun, Mohammed, *Rethinking Islam: Common Questions, Uncommon Answers*, Boulder, Colo.: Westview Press, 1994.
Hofmann, Murad, *Islam: The Alternative*, trans. from German (Munich 1992), Reading, Mass.: Garnet Publishing, 1993.
Nasr, Seyyed Hossein, *A Young Muslim's Guide to the Modern World*, Cambridge: Islamic Texts Society, 1993.
Rahman, Fazlur, *Islam*, New York: Holt, Rinehart and Winston, 1966; 2ⁿᵈ ed. Chicago: University of Chicago Press, 1979.
Smith, Wilfred Cantwell, *On Understanding Islam: Selected Studies* (Religion and Reason 19), The Hague, etc.: Mouton, 1981.
Studies on Islam, trans., ed. by Merlin L. Swartz, New York and Oxford: University of Oxford Press, 1981.

2. Piety, Spirituality, Mysticism

Chittick, William C., *The Self-Disclosure of God: Principles of Ibn al-'Arabī's Cosmology*, Albany, N. Y.: SUNY Press, 1998.
Padwick, Constance E., *Muslim Devotions: A Study of Prayer-Manuals in Common Use*, London: S.P.C.K., 1961 (Repr. Oxford: Oneworld, 1996).
Schimmel, Annemarie, *Mystical Dimensions of Islam*, Chapel Hill, N. C.: University of North Carolina Press, 1975.

3. Islamic Religious Sciences

AYOUB, Mahmoud M., *The Qur'ān and Its Interpreters*, 2 vols., Albany, N. Y.: SUNY Press, 1984–92.

KAMALI, Mohammed Hashim, *Principles of Islamic Jurisprudence*, Cambridge: Islamic Texts Society, 1991.

SIDDIQI, Muhammad Z., *Hadith Literature: Its Origin, Development and Special Features*, ed. and revised by Abdal Hakim MURAD, Cambridge: The Islamic Texts Society, 1993.

WATT, William Montgomery, *Islamic Philosophy and Theology: An Extended Survey*, 2nd ed. (Islamic Surveys 12), Edinburgh: Edinburgh University Press, 1984.

WENSINCK, Arent J., *The Muslim Creed: Its Genesis and Historical Development* (1932), London: Frank Cass, 1965; New Delhi: Oriental Books, 1979.

4. Religious Institutions

JONG, Frederick de, *Ṭuruq and Ṭuruq-Linked Institutions in Nineteenth Century Egypt: A Historical Study in Organizational Dimensions of Islamic Mysticism*, Leiden: E. J. Brill, 1978.

Scholars, Saints, and Sufis: Muslim Religious Institutions in the Middle East since 1500, ed. by Nikki R. KEDDIE, Berkeley, Cal. etc.: University of California Press, 1972.

TRIMINGHAM, J. Spencer, *The Sufi Orders in Islam*, London: Oxford University Press, 1971; Oxford: Oxford University Press, 1998.

The 'Ulamā' in Modern History: Studies in Memory of Professor Uriel Heyd, ed. by Gabriel BAER (special issue *Asian and African Studies* 7 [1971]).

5. Views of Other Religions

GODDARD, Hugh, *Muslim Perceptions of Christianity*, London: Grey Seal, 1996.

Islamic Interpretations of Christianity, ed. by Lloyd RIDGEON, Richmond, Surrey: Curzon, 2001.

Muslim Perceptions of Other Religions: A Historical Survey, ed. by Jacques WAARDENBURG, New York and Oxford: Oxford University Press, 1999.

6. Anthologies

CRAGG, Kenneth, and R. Marston SPEIGHT, *Islam From Within: Anthology of a Religion*, Belmont, Cal.: Wadsworth, 1980.

NASR, Seyyed Hossein, *Islamic Spirituality: Foundations* (World Spirituality 19), London: Routledge & Kegan Paul, 1987; New York: Crossroad, 1991 (paperback edition 1997).

—, *Islamic Spirituality: Manifestations* (World Spirituality 20), New York: Crossroad, 1991 (paperback edition 1997).

Structures And Interpretations Of Islam

1. General Structures

Geertz, Clifford, *The Interpretation of Cultures: Selected Essays*, New York: Basic Books, 1973.

Gellner, Ernest, *Muslim Society* (Cambridge Studies in Social Anthropology 32), Cambridge: Cambridge University Press, 1981, etc.

Gibb, Hamilton Alexander Rosskeen, "The Structure of Religious Thought in Islam", *The Muslim World*, 38 (1948), pp. 17–28, 113–23, 185–97, 280–91.

Gilsenan, Michael, *Recognizing Islam: Religion and Society in the Modern Middle East*, revised ed., London and New York: I. B. Tauris, 2000.

Grunebaum, Gustave Edmund von, "An Analysis of Islamic Civilization and Cultural Anthropology", in *Colloque sur la sociologie musulmane: Actes, 11–14 septembre 1961* (Correspondance d'Orient 5), Bruxelles: Centre pour l'Étude des problèmes du monde musulman contemporain, 1962, pp. 21–73 (repr. in Id., *Modern Islam: The Search for Cultural Identity*, Berkeley, Cal.: University of California Press, 1962 [pocket edition New York: Vintage Books, 1964], pp. 40–97).

Nieuwenhuijze, Christoffel Anthonie Olivier van, *The Lifestyles of Islam: Recourse to Classicism, Need of Realism*, Leiden: E. J. Brill, 1985.

Schimmel, Annemarie, *Deciphering the Signs of God: A Phenomenological Approach to Islam*, Edinburgh: Edinburgh University Press, and Albany, N. Y.: SUNY Press, 1994.

2. Some New Interpretations

See also the Bibliography of Chapter 6.

Brown, Daniel, *Rethinking Tradition in Modern Islamic Thought*, Cambridge: Cambridge University Press, 1996.

Cragg, Kenneth, *The Pen and the Faith: Eight Modern Muslim Writers and the Qur'ān*, London: George Allen & Unwin, 1985.

Grunebaum, Gustave Edmund von, "Attempts of Self-Interpretation in Contemporary Islam" (1947), in Id., *Modern Islam: The Search for Cultural Identity*, Berkeley, Cal.: University of California Press, 1962 (pocket edition New York: Vintage Books, 1964).

Peters, Rudolph, *Jihād in Classical and Modern Islam: A Reader*, Princeton: Markus Wiener, 1996.

3. Non-Sunnī-Interpretations

Friedmann, Yohanan, *Prophecy Continuous: Aspects of Ahmadi Religious Thought and Its Medieval Background*, Berkeley, Los Angeles and London: University of California Press, 1989.

Halm, Heinz, *Shiism*, Edinburgh: Edinburgh University Press, 1991.

Smith, Wilfred Cantwell, Art. "Ahmadiyya", in *The Encyclopaedia of Islam*, new ed., Leiden: E. J. Brill, vol. 1, 1960, pp. 301–3.

THE DEBATE ON HUMAN RIGHTS, CIVIL SOCIETY, DEMOCRACY, AND ISLAM

Democracy without Democrats?, ed. by Ghassan SALAMÉ, London and New York: I. B. Tauris, 1994.

DWYER, Kevin, *Arab Voices: The Human Rights Debate in the Middle East*, London: Routledge, 1991.

ESPOSITO, John L., and John O. VOLL, *Islam and Democracy*, New York: Oxford University Press, 1996.

HEFNER, Robert W., *Civil Islam: Muslims and Democratization in Indonesia*, Princeton, N. J.: Princeton University Press, 2000.

Human Rights and Religious Values: An Uneasy Relationship?, ed. by Abdullahi Ahmed An-NA'IM, Jerald D. GORT, Henry JANSEN, Hendrik M. VROOM (Currents of Encounter 8), Amsterdam: Rodopi, and Grand Rapids, Mich.: Eerdmans, 1995.

Human Rights in Africa: Cross-Cultural Perspectives, ed. by Abdullahi Ahmed An-NA'IM and Francis M. DENG, Washington, D. C.: The Brookings Institution, 1990.

Human Rights in Cross-Cultural Perspectives: A Quest for Consensus, ed. by Abdullahi Ahmed an-NA'IM, Philadelphia, Pa.: University of Pennsylvania Press, 1992.

MAYER, Ann Elizabeth, *Islam and Human Rights: Tradition and Politics*, Boulder, Colo., and San Francisco: Westview Press, 1991, 1995², 1999³ (also London: Pinter).

NA'IM, Abdullahi Ahmed an-, "Qur'ān, Sharī'a and Human Rights: Foundations, Deficiencies and Prospects", in *The Ethics of World Religions and Human Rights*, ed. by Hans KÜNG and Jürgen MOLTMANN, London: SCM Press, 1990, pp. 61–9.

—, "Human Rights in the Muslim World: Socio-Political Conditions and Scriptural Imperatives", *Harvard Human Rights Journal*, 3 (1990), pp. 13–53.

PRICE, Daniel E., *Islamic Political Culture, Democracy, and Human Rights: A Comparative Study*, Westport, Conn.: Praeger, 1999.

Religion and Human Rights: A Christian-Muslim Discussion, ed. by Tarek MITRI, Geneva: World Council of Churches, Office on Interreligious Relations, 1996.

Religious Freedom in the World: A Global Report on Freedom and Persecution, ed. by Paul MARSHALL, Nashville, Tenn.: Broadman & Holman, 2000.

Religious Liberty and Human Rights in Nations and in Religions, ed. by Leonard SWIDLER, Philadelphia, Pa.: Ecumenical Press, and New York: Hippocrene Books, 1986.

SOCIAL REALITY AND ISLAM

1. General Works

EICKELMAN, Dale F., *The Middle East: An Anthropological Approach*, Upper Saddle River, N. J.: Prentice Hall, 1981, 2001⁴.

GEERTZ, Clifford, *Islam Observed: Religious Development in Morocco and Indonesia*, New Haven, Conn., and London: Yale University Press, 1968; Chicago and London: University of Chicago Press, 1971.

LAWRENCE, Bruce B., *Shattering the Myth: Islam Beyond Violence* (Princeton Studies in Muslim Politics), Princeton, N. J.: Princeton University Press, 1998.
NIEUWENHUIJZE, Christoffel Anthonie Olivier van, *Paradise Lost: Reflections on the Struggle for Authenticity in the Middle East*, Leiden: E. J. Brill, 1997.
Religion and Societies: Asia and the Middle East, ed. by Carlo CALDAROLA (Religion and Society 22), Berlin, New York and Amsterdam: Mouton, 1982.
WEEKES, Richard V., *Muslim Peoples: A World Ethnographic Survey*, Westport, Conn., and London: Greenwood Press, 1978; 2nd ed., revised and expanded, in 2 vols., London: Aldwych Press, 1984.

2. Women in Muslim Societies

AFSHAR, Haleh, *Islam and Feminisms: An Iranian Case-Study* (Women's Studies at York Series), New York: St. Martin's Press, and Houndmills: Macmillan Press, 1998.
AHMED, Leila, *Women and Gender in Islam: Historical Roots of a Modern Debate*, New Haven, Conn., and London: Yale University Press, 1992.
FERNEA, Elizabeth Warnock, *In Search of Islamic Feminism: One Woman's Global Journey*, New York etc.: Anchor Books Doubleday, 1998.
HIJAB, Nadia, *Womanpower: The Arab Debate on Women at Work*, Cambridge and New York: Cambridge University Press, 1988.
Islam, Gender, and Social Change, ed. by Yvonne Yazbeck HADDAD and John L. ESPOSITO, New York and Oxford: Oxford University Press, 1998.
KHAN, Nighat Said (ed.), *Voices Within: Dialogues with Women on Islam*, Lahore, Pakistan: ASR Publications, 1992, 1993[3].
MERNISSI, Fatima, *The Veil and the Male Elite: A Feminist Interpretation of Women's Rights in Islam*, Reading, Mass.: Addison-Wesley, 1991.
MILANI, Farzaneh, *Veils and Words: The Emerging Voices of Iranian Women Writers*, London and New York: I. B. Tauris, 1992.
MIR-HOSSEINI, Ziba, *Islam and Gender: The Religious Debate in Contemporary Iran* (Princeton Studies in Muslim Politics), Princeton, N. J.: Princeton University Press, and London: I. B. Tauris, 1999.
MOGHISSI, Haideh, *Feminism and Islamic Fundamentalism: The Limits of Postmodern Analysis*, London and New York: Zed Books, 1999.
POYA, Maryam, *Women, Work and Islamism: Ideology and Resistance in Iran*, London and New York: Zed Books, 1999.
ROALD, Anne Sofie, *Women in Islam: The Western Experience*, London and New York: I. B. Tauris, 2001.
STOWASSER, Barbara Freyer, *Women in the Qur'an: Traditions and Interpretation*, New York and Oxford: Oxford University Press, 1994.
WALTHER, Wiebke, *Women in Islam: From Medieval to Modern Times*, Princeton, N. J.: Markus Wiener, 1993, 1995[2].
Women and Development in the Middle East and North Africa, ed. by Joseph G. and Nancy W. JABBRA, Leiden: E. J. Brill, 1992.

Saudi Arabia

See also the Bibliographies of Chapters 11, 12 and 17.

Alangari, Haifa, *The Struggle for Power in Arabia: Ibn Saud, Hussein and Great Britain, 1914–1924*, Reading, Mass.: Ithaca Press, 1997.

Fandy, Mamoun, *Saudi Arabia and the Politics of Dissent*, Houndmills: Macmillan, 1999.

Jerichow, Anders, *The Saudi File: People, Power, Politics*, Richmond, Surrey: Curzon, 1998.

Khoury, Adel Théodore, *Un modèle d'Etat islamique: L'Arabie Saoudite* (Tendances et courants de l'islam arabe contemporain 2), Munich: Kaiser, and Mainz: Matthias Grünewald, 1983.

Monroe, Elizabeth, *Britain's Moment in the Middle East, 1914–1956*, London: Chatto & Windus, 1963.

Oender, Zehra, *Saudi-Arabien: Zwischen islamischer Ideologie und westlicher Ökonomie*, Stuttgart: Klett-Cotta, 1980.

Vassiliev, Alexei, *The History of Saudi Arabia*, London: Saqi Books, 1998 (paperback edition 2000).

Yassini, Ayman al-, *Religion and State in the Kingdom of Saudi Arabia*, Boulder, Colo., and London: Westview Press, 1985.

Islamic Reform and Intellectual Reflection

See also the Bibliographies of Chapters 14, 17 and 18.

1. Reformists and Modernists

Adams, Charles C., *Islam and Modernism in Egypt: A Study of the Modern Reform Movement Inaugurated by Muhammad 'Abduh*, Cairo: American University in Cairo, 1933 (Repr. London: Routledge, 2000).

Ahmad, Aziz, *Islamic Modernism in India and Pakistan 1857–1964*, London: Oxford University Press, 1967.

Fyzee, Asaf A. A., *A Modern Approach to Islam*, Bombay, London and New York: Asia Publishing House, 1963 (Delhi, Oxford and New York: Oxford University Press, 1981).

Gibb, Hamilton Alexander Rosskeen, *Modern Trends in Islam*, Chicago: University of Chicago Press, 1947 (Repr. New York: Octagon Books, 1972).

Hourani, Albert, *Arabic Thought in the Liberal Age*, London and Oxford: Oxford University Press, 1962, 1970; Cambridge: Cambridge University Press, 1983.

Iqbal, Mohammed, *Six Lectures on the Reconstruction of Religious Thought in Islam*, Lahore: Printed at the Kapur Art Printing Works, 1930.

Merad, Ali, and Algar Hamid, Niyazi Berkes, Aziz Ahmad, Art. "Iṣlāḥ", in *The Encyclopaedia of Islam*, new ed., ed. by Clifford Edmund Bosworth, vol. 4, Leiden: E. J. Brill, 1978, pp. 141–71.

Troll, Christian W., *Sayyid Ahmad Khan: A Reinterpretation of Muslim Theology*, New Delhi: Vikas, 1978.

Zebiri, Kate, *Maḥmūd Shaltūt and Islamic Modernism*, Oxford: Clarendon Press, 1993.

2. Present-day Intellectual Reflection about Islam

ABU ZAID, Nasr Hamid, *Islam und Politik: Kritik des religiösen Diskurses*, Frankfurt a.M.: Dipa-Verlag, 1996.

AHMED, Akbar S., *Postmodernism and Islam: Predicament and Promise*, London and New York: Routledge, 1992.

ARKOUN, Mohammed, *Rethinking Islam: Common Questions, Uncommon Answers*, Boulder, Colo.: Westview Press, 1994.

AZMEH, Aziz al-, *Islams and Modernities*, London and New York: Verso, 1993, 1996².

BOROUJERDI, Mehrzad, *Iranian Intellectuals and the West: The tormented Triumph of Nativism*, Syracuse, N. Y.: Syracuse University Press, 1996.

BOULLATA, Issa J., *Trends and Issues in Contemporary Arab Thought*, Albany, N. Y.: SUNY Press, 1990.

CARRÉ, Olivier, *Islam laïque ou le retour à la Grande Tradition*, Paris: Armand Colin, 1993.

Contemporary Debates in Islam: An Anthology of Modernist and Fundamentalist Thought, ed. by Mansoor MOADDEL and Kamran TALATTOF, Basingstoke, etc.: Macmillan, 2000.

CRAGG, Kenneth, *Counsels in Contemporary Islam* (Islamic Surveys 3), Edinburgh: Edinburgh University Press, 1965.

ENAYAT, Hamid, *Modern Islamic Political Thought: The Response of the Shīʾī and Sunnī Muslims to the Twentieth Century*, Austin, Tex.: University of Texas Press, and London/Basingstoke: Macmillan, 1982.

ESACK, Farid, *Qurʾān, Liberation and Pluralism: An Islamic Perspective of Interreligious Solidarity against Oppression*, Oxford: Oneworld, 1997.

GHEISSARI, Ali, *Iranian Intellectuals in the 20ᵗʰ Century*, Austin, Tex.: University of Texas Press, 1998.

Islam, Globalization and Postmodernity, ed. by Akbar S. AHMAD and Hastings DONNAN, London and New York: Routledge, 1994.

Islam, Modernism and the West: Cultural and Political Relations at the End of the Millennium, ed. by Gema Martin MUÑOZ, London: I. B. Tauris, 1998.

Islam and Modernity: Muslim Intellectuals respond, ed. by John COOPER, Ronald L. NETTLER and Mohamed MAHMOUD, London and New York: I. B. Tauris, 1998.

KAMALI, Mohammed Hashim, *Freedom of Expression in Islam*, Cambridge: Islamic Texts Society, 1997.

Liberal Islam: A Sourcebook, ed. by Charles KURZMAN, New York and Oxford: Oxford University Press, 1998.

Makers of Contemporary Islam, ed. by John L. ESPOSITO and John O. VOLL, New York and Oxford: Oxford University Press, 2001.

NASR, Seyyed Hossein, *Islam and the Plight of Modern Man*, London and New York: Longmans, 1975.

RAHMAN, Fazlur, *Islam and Modernity: Transformation of an Intellectual Tradition*, Chicago and London: University of Chicago Press, 1982, 1984².

SARDAR, Ziauddin, *Islamic Futures: The Shape of Ideas to come*, London and New York: Mansell, 1985.

SOROUSH, ʿAbdolkarim, *Reason, Freedom, and Democracy in Islam: Essential Writings*, trans., ed., and with a critical introduction by Mahmoud SADRI and Ahmad SADRI, New York: Oxford University Press, 2000.

Taha, Mahmoud Mohammed, *The Second Message of Islam*, Syracuse, N. Y.: Syracuse University Press, 1987.
Talbi, Mohamed, *Plaidoyer pour un islam moderne*, Tunis: C.E.R.E.S., and Paris: Desclee de Brouwer, 1998.
Zakaria, Rafiq, *The Struggle within Islam: The Conflict between Religion and Politics*, Delhi: Viking, 1988; Harmondsworth: Penguin, 1989.

Islamic Ideology

See also the Bibliographies of Chapters 14 and 17.

1. Challenges

Grunebaum, Gustave Edmund von, *Modern Islam: The Search for Cultural Identity*, Berkeley, Cal.: University of California Press, 1962 (pocket edition New York: Vintage Books, 1964).
Haddad, Yvonne Yazbeck, *Contemporary Islam and the Challenge of History*, Albany, N. Y.: SUNY Press, 1982.
Islam and the Challenge of Modernity, ed. by Sharifah Shifa al-Attas, Kuala Lumpur: ISTAC, 1996.
Islamic Dilemmas: Reformers, Nationalism, and Industrialization, ed. by Ernest Gellner (Religion and Society 25), The Hague and Berlin: Mouton, 1985.
Kedourie, Elie, *Islam in the Modern World, and Other Studies*, London: Mansell, 1980.
Salvatore, Armando, *Islam and the Political Discourse of Modernity*, Reading, Mass.: Ithaca Press, 1997.

2. Ideologization

Abu Rabi', Ibrahim M., *Intellectual Origins of Islamic Resurgence in the Modern Arab World*, Albany, N. Y.: SUNY Press, 1996.
Attas, Seyyed M.N. al-, *Islam, Secularism and the Philosophy of the Future*, London and New York: Mansell, 1985 (revised ed. *Islam and Secularism*, Kuala Lumpur: ISTAC, 1993).
Azmeh, Aziz al-, *Islams and Modernities*, London: Verso, 1993, 1996².
Dabashi, Hamid, *Theology of Discontent: The Ideological Foundations of the Islamic Revolution in Iran*, New York: New York University Press, 1993.
Intellectuels et militants de l'Islam contemporain, ed. by Gilles Kepel and Yann Richard, Paris: Seuil, 1990.
Islam and the Challenge of Modernity: Historical and Contemporary Contexts. Proceedings of the Inaugural Symposium on Islam and the Challenge of Modernity, Kuala Lumpur, August 1–5, 1994, ed. by Sharifah Shifa al-Attas, Kuala Lumpur: ISTAC, 1996.
Islamic Perspectives: Studies in Honour of Mawlana Sayyid Abul A'la Mawdudi, ed. by Khurshid Ahmad and Zafar Ishaq Ansari, Leicester: Islamic Foundation, and Jeddah: Saudi Publishing House, 1979.
Johnson, Nels, *Islam and the Politics of Meaning in Palestinian Nationalism*, London: Kegan Paul, 1982.

Kʜᴏᴍᴇɪɴɪ, Ruhallah Musawi, *Islam and Revolution: Writings and Declarations of Imām Khomeini*, trans. and annotated by Hamid Aʟɢᴀʀ, Berkeley, Cal.: Mizan Press, 1981; London: Routledge & Kegan Paul, 1985.

Mɪᴛᴄʜᴇʟʟ, Richard P., *The Society of Muslim Brothers*, London: Oxford University Press, 1969.

Mᴏᴜssᴀʟʟɪ, A.S., *Radical Islamic Fundamentalism: The Ideological and Political Discourse of Sayyid Qutb*, Beirut: American University of Beirut, 1992.

—, *Moderate and Radical Islamic Fundamentalism: The Quest for Modernity, Legitimacy, and the Islamic State*, Gainesville, Fla.: University Press of Florida, 1999.

Nᴀsʀ, Seyyed Vali Reza, *The Vanguard of the Islamic Revolution: The Jama'at-i Islami of Pakistan* (Comparative Studies on Muslim Societies 19), Berkeley and Los Angeles: University of California Press, and London: I. B. Tauris, 1994.

Nɪᴇᴜᴡᴇɴʜᴜɪᴊᴢᴇ, Christoffel Anthonie Olivier van, "Islamism: A Defiant Utopism", in *Die Welt des Islam*, 35 (1995), pp. 1–36.

Pioneers of Islamic Revival, ed. by Ali Rᴀʜɴᴇᴍᴀ, London, etc.: Zed Books, 1994.

Sᴀʀᴅᴀʀ, Ziauddin, *The Future of Muslim Civilization*, London: Croom Helm, 1979.

Sʜᴀʀɪ'ᴀᴛɪ, Ali, *On the Sociology of Islam: Lectures*, trans. from the Persian by Hamid Aʟɢᴀʀ, Berkeley, Cal.: Mizan Press, 1979.

—, *Marxism and Other Western Fallacies: An Islamic Critique*, trans. from the Persian by R. Cᴀᴍᴘʙᴇʟʟ, Berkeley, Cal.: Mizan Press, 1980.

Sɪᴠᴀɴ, Emmanuel, *Radical Islam: Medieval Theology and Modern Politics*, New Haven, Conn., and London: Yale University Press, 1985.

3. Islamization of Knowledge

Aʙᴜ Sᴜʟᴀʏᴍᴀɴ, 'Abdul Hamid, *General Principles and Workplan* (Islamization of Knowledge 1), 2ⁿᵈ, revised and expanded ed., Herndon, Va.: International Institute of Islamic Thought, 1989, 1995³.

Fᴀʀᴜqɪ, Isma'il R. al-, *Toward Islamic English* (Islamization of Knowledge 3), Herndon, Va.: International Institute of Islamic Thought, 1986.

Sᴛᴇɴʙᴇʀɢ, Leif, *The Islamization of Science: Four Muslim Positions Developing an Islamic Modernity*, Ph.D. Dissertation, Lund, 1996.

Tʜᴇ Iɴᴛᴇʀɴᴀᴛɪᴏɴᴀʟ Sᴄᴇɴᴇ ᴀɴᴅ Isʟᴀᴍ

See also the Bibliographies of Chapters 17 and 18.

1. Islāmic Movements

Hᴜssᴀɪɴ, Asaf, *Islamic Movements in Egypt, Pakistan and Iran: An Annotated Bibliography*, London: Mansell, 1983.

The Islamic Impulse, ed. by Barbara F. Sᴛᴏᴡᴀssᴇʀ, Washington, D. C.: Georgetown University, Center for Contemporary Arab Studies, 1987.

Issues in the Islamic Movement, ed. by Kalim Sɪᴅᴅɪqᴜɪ, 4 vols., London: The Open Press, 1982–5.

LAPIDUS, Ira M., *Contemporary Islamic Movements in Historical Perspective* (Policy Papers in International Affairs 18), Berkeley, Cal.: University of California, Institute of International Studies, 1983.

2. Supranational Islam

AHSAN, ʿAbdullah al-, *The Organization of the Islamic Conference: An Introduction to an Islamic Political Institution* (Islamization of Knowledge 7), Herndon, Va.: International Institute of Islamic Thought, 1988.

BRUNNER, Rainer, *Annäherung und Distanz: Schiʿa, Azhar und die islamische Ökumene im 20. Jahrhundert* (Islamkundliche Untersuchungen 204), Berlin: Klaus Schwarz, 1996.

KRAMER, Martin S., *Islam Assembled: The Advent of the Muslim Congresses*, New York: Columbia University Press, 1986.

LANDAU, Jacob M., *The Politics of Pan-Islam: Ideology and Organization*, Oxford: Clarendon Press, 1994.

SCHÖNE, Ellinor, *Islamische Solidarität: Geschichte, Politik, Ideologie der Organisation der Islamischen Konferenz (OIC) 1969–1981* (Islamkundliche Untersuchungen 214), Berlin: Klaus Schwarz, 1997.

SCHULZE, Reinhard, *Islamischer Internationalismus im 20. Jahrhundert: Untersuchungen zur Geschichte der Islamischen Weltliga (Rābitat al-ʿĀlam al-Islāmī)* (Social, Economic, and Political Studies of the Middle East 4), Leiden and New York: E. J. Brill, 1990.

3. Geopolitics

EICKELMAN, Dale F., and James PISCATORI, *Muslim Politics* (Princeton Studies in Muslim Politics), Princeton, N. J.: Princeton University Press, 1996.

ESPOSITO, John L., *The Islamic Threat: Myth or Reality?*, New York and Oxford: Oxford University Press, 1992.

KARIM, Karim H., *Islamic Peril: Media and Global Violence*, Montréal, New York and London: Black Rose Books, 2000.

PINTO, Maria do Cén, *Political Islam and the United States: A Study of U.S. Policy Towards Islamist Movements in the Middle East*, Reading, Mass.: Ithaca Press, 1999.

TIBI, Bassam, *The Challenge of Fundamentalism: Political Islam and the New World Disorder*, Berkeley, Cal., etc.: University of California Press, 1998.

—, *Die Verantwortung des Westens: Westliche Dominanz und islamischer Fundamentalismus*, Berlin: Propyläen, 1999.

1. Index of Arabic and Persian Terms

2. Index of Persons

'Abd al-'Azīz I Āl Sa'ūd (r. 1766–1803) 232, 238, 240
'Abd al-'Azīz II ("Ibn Sa'ūd") 229, 244, 246–268, 307, 351–2
'Abd al-Bāqī al-Hanbalī (d. 1661) 230
'Abd al-Rahman ibn Faisal Āl Sa'ūd 246–8, 252, 261
'Abd Allāh Ibrāhīm al-Najdī (al-Madanī) 230
'Abduh, Muhammad 17, 288, 308, 339, 357, 373
Abdül Hamid II 358, 369
Abū Bakr (caliph) 177
Abū 'l-'Abbās (8th c.) 306
Abū Ya'lā al-Farrā' (d. 1066) 238
Abu Zayd, Nasr Hāmid 125, 128
Adam 1, 35, 39, 176
Afghānī, Jamāl al-Dīn al- 147, 290, 358, 369
Ahmad, Ghulām 124
Ahmad Khān, Sayyid 17, 288–9, 308, 339, 357
Āl Sabāh, Mubārak (Sheykh of Kuwait, r. 1896–1915) 244, 247, 262
'Alī 67, 93, 119
'Amr ibn Luhayy 25
Arkoun, Mohammed 58, 125, 128, 132, 142, 147–51, 153–9, 299
Atatürk 197
Azzam, Salem 171

Bāb = Sayyid 'Alī Shīrāzī (ca. 1819–50) 124
Bannā', Hasan al- 289, 308, 346, 357, 374, 384
Bashir, al- (Sudan) 351
Bellah, Robert N. 204n, 214
Bennabi, Malek 140–1, 148, 152–3, 157
Berque, Jacques 4, 15

Bhutto, Zulfikar 350, 363, 395
Bourguiba, Habib (r. 1956–87) 200–1

Churchill, Winston 253, 255, 259, 261
Corbin, Henry 3, 119, 139
Cox, Percy 249–50

Dahlan, Ahmad 280
Dan Fodio, Usuman 89, 109, 273
Darwis, Muhammad 280
Djaït, Hichem 141–3, 152, 157
Don-Yehiya, Eliezer 214–6

Eickelman, Dale F. 11, 306n
Enayat, Hamid 343, 346, 347n

Fahd (Saudi Arabia) 261
Fahd, Toufic 28–9, 35, 39, 41–3
Faisal ibn 'Abd al-'Azīz (r. 1964–75) 249, 252, 261
Faisal ibn Husayn ibn Alī (r. 1921–33) 250, 266
Farouk 253, 402
Faruqi, Ismā'īl Rāji al- 9

Gardet, Louis 15, 140, 148
Gasprinskii, Ismail Bey 280, 285
Ghazālī, Muhammad al- (Egypt) 346
Ghazzālī, Muhammad al- (1058–1111) 92, 96, 289
Gibb, Hamilton Alexander Rosskeen 13, 89n, 140, 273, 371n
Goldziher, Ignaz 113, 119n, 120n
Grunebaum, Gustave E. von 5, 145, 210n

Hamad ibn Rifadah 252
Hanafi, Hasan 125, 128, 203, 209
Hasan II (r. 1962–99) 328
Hasan al-Sabbāh (d. 1124) 306

3. Geographical Names

4. Index of Subjects

5. Index of Concepts

Collective imagination (*l'imaginaire*) 154, 156
~ as a field of research 155
~ in the monotheistic religions 151

Da'wa (call to Islam), see also Index of Arabian and Persian terms
a socio-religious message and its symbolic expression 320
~ as Islamic mission to non-Muslims 307
call to Islam and to live accordingly as a member of the Islamic community 305
making ~ as a kind of communication 303
~ movements in history and at present 306–11
nowadays ~ also used as a call for a just society 312

Dialogue
Euro-Arab ~ 144
interreligious ~ 142, 144
Islamo-Christian ~ 7, 144
~ on a personalist basis 157
~ between 'Abd al-'Azīz II and Van der Meulen 260–5, 268

Discourse, from religious to ideological 148–50

Hermeneutics (rules of interpretation) 117, 121, 130
Islamic ~ 68, 79, 111, 129
Islamic and universal principles of ~ 128

Human rights, see also Index of Subjects

Islamic concepts of ~ 170–9, 182–4
Islamic Council of Europe and ~ 171–3
Islamic Declarations of ~ 182–4
Muslim ~ groups 312
Organization of Islamic Conference (OIC) and ~ 170–1
violations of ~ 366

Ideologies/Ideology in general
concept of ~ 76, 150, 206, 310, 322–4, 330–2
~ and myth 149
ideologizing a religion 318–9

Ideologies, Islamic
~ and relations with the West 324
~ as responses to economic exhaustion and political suppression 323
defense of the value of Islam and the dignity of Muslims in ~ 324
features of ~ 330–2
~ in social context 322–3
internationalization of ~ 329
~ of domination 149
presenting an "Islamic" model 150
rise of ~ 76, 310
state-supported and Islamist ~ 87

Interpretation, ~ of data as a religion, social order, political system, law (in the Western sense of these words) 225 n24; see also under Hermeneutics

Islam
absolutized ~ 313
appealed to ~ 62, 80, 207, 313, 364, 379, 381
changing tradition in ~ 194–5

common sign and signification system but no common ideology 331

concept of ~ 381–2

conceptual forms of ~
neo-Islam 146
normative ~ 61, 89, 97–100, 367, 399
official ~ 94, 96, 99, 102, 376, 389, 392
"officialized" ~ 217, 224, 389, 392, 396, 400
pan-Islam 90, 104, 252, 275, 358, 369
personal ~ 92, 196
popular ~ 85, 87–94, 100
practiced ~ 61, 91–4
pure ~ 93, 99, 291, 373
puritan ~ 121 n43, 266
"religious" ~ 367

construct of ~ 151

degradation of ~ into politics 150

differentiation of ~ 315, 331

empirical and "ultimate" ~ 383

~ identified as
a civil religion 216–25, 387, 392, 397, 400
a community or commonwealth 79
a critical norm and value 340, 342, 399
a culture and civilization 5, 120, 140, 157
a cumulative religious tradition 4, 207
a faith 4, 145–6, 207, 340, 367, 382
a God-given appeal and signs to which one should respond 63, 75–7
an identity 153, 210, 313, 340, 361
a lived religion 105
a moral and social regulator 320, 337, 339
a norm and an empirical reality 207
a political system with a religious symbolism 150
a rational structure 122
the religion of reason 122
a religion in the broadest sense 85 n1

a religious system 364
a sign and symbol itself 61
a social pattern or structure in Muslim societies 340, 364
a source of norms and values 311
a symbol and signification system 57, 74–7, 314–5, 401
a system of signs and symbols variously interpreted and applied 129
a trans-national religion 401

ideologization of ~ 70, 156, 310, 318, 320–3, 331

~ "in itself" out of reach of scholarly study 14

~ in its contexts 317–33, 391–2, 399

integrity of ~ 291

movements in 19th and 20th century (with different concepts of ~); see also under "Islamic: movement(s)"
movements of islāḥ (reform) often considered as Islamic revival movements 98, 101, 143, 196, 203, 273–4, 284, 288–90, 293, 295, 297, 341–2, 371–5
movements of tajdīd (modernization) 196, 279, 282–4, 288, 307, 317, 339, 341–2, 376–7
movements of tasawwuf (mysticism) 288

Muslim understandings of ~ as a subject of research 80

new social meanings of ~ 311–4

political use and politization of ~ 70, 150, 208, 329, 342–3, 364, 392–3

promotion of ~ 389, 393–7

puritan pattern in ~ 292–4

redefinition of ~ 13, 202, 311–4

revelation (concept of) in ~ 125, 151

revitalization of ~ 287–8, 357, 359–61, 364, 372

Scripture (concept of) in ~ 117

secularism and ~ 400

signs and symbols in ~ 61, 63–8, 70–1, 81, their function 61–71, 75–7

social and economic development in ~ 191, 193, 197–202, 205–8, 371

structures of ~ 13, 101

symbolic function and use of ~ 61, 69–70, 365, 368, 381

~ as Call (*da'wa*) 305
~ as Scripture 112, 118
~ as sign and signification system 57, 117–8, 123, 126, 129, 314
hermeneutics of the ~ 112
meaning of the ~ as experienced by the faithful 74, 127
~ pointing to transcendent realities 70
reason and reasoning in the ~ 122
return to the ~ 121n43
~ studies 11–2
universe of the ~ 117–8, 123, 126
word-knowledge of the ~ 129

Religion
articulation of a ~ for practical purposes 318
~ as identity marker 398
~ as sign, symbol and signification system 77
discovery of a new Absolute in ~ 29
essentialization of ~ 319
ideological potential of a ~ 318–9
ideologized ~ in the 20th century 332, 359
idolization of ~ 331
invisible ~ 90
manipulation of ~ 157
normative and practiced ~ in Islam 376
official and popular ~ in Islam 100
personal ~ in Islam 196
puritan impulse in ~ 292, 295
puritan patterns in ~ 292
rationalization of a ~ 376
reification and objectification of ~ 81
return to the sources of a ~ 342
revolt within a ~ as discovery of a new Absolute 291
study of ~ 73, 75, 77–81, 129, 150, 153, 180
universal ~ 93

Revelation
~ as an event of meaning 155
authority of a Scripture rests on ~ 93
concept of prophetic ~ 118
concept of ~ also used to legitimate domination 155
concepts of ~ in the monotheistic religions 155

Signification
processes of ~ and symbolization in religion 61, 68
religious ~ system studied as a network of signs 74–5

Signs 61–71
function of ~ 61, 67, 75–7
Islam as a system of ~ and symbols variously interpreted and applied 61, 63–8, 129
knots of meaning of various signposts constitute paradigms for action and thought 76

Symbolism 65–8, 149–50, 157
real and symbolic character of "Islamic" action 380–1
symbolic use of Islam and its elements 61, 69–70

Symbolization 61, 66
~ and signification in Islam 70–1

Theological
research on comparative theology 151
research on ~ reasoning 150, 154–5
research on ~ systems 148, 158

Tradition
~ as a process of transmission 191
concepts of ~ in Islam 191, 193
small ~ as local traditional customs ('*ādāt*, '*urf*) 193
great ~ as the accepted normative tradition (*Sunna*) of Islam 193

Traditionalists
concept of religious ~ in Islam 341–2

Western
~ criticism of Islam 324
~ domination 368
~ hegemonic behavior 78, 330, 368, 383
~ influence in Muslim societies 370
interaction between the ~ and Muslim worlds 324, 332, 341, 354
~ perceptions of Islam 371
~ policies and Muslim protests 364
~ researchers of Islam 159
~ secularity and Christianity 324
Westernization 210, 220